RACE, EVOLUTION, and BEHAVIOR

a life history perspective

J.
Philippe
Rushton

Transaction Publishers
New Brunswick (USA) and London (UK)

RACE,
EVOLUTION,
and BEHAVIOR

GN
281.4
.R87
1995
Feb.1997

Third printing, 1995.

Library of Congress Catalog Number: 93-21282
ISBN: 1-56000-146-1
Printed in the United States of America

Library of Congress Cataloging-in-Publication Data

Rushton, J. Philippe.
    Race, evolution, and behavior : a life history perspective / J. Philippe Rushton.
        p. cm.
    Includes bibliographical references and index.
    ISBN 1-56000-146-1
    1. Human evolution. 2. Race. 3. Human behavior. 4. Heredity, Human.
I. Title.
GN281.4.R87   1994
573.2—dc20   93-21282
                                                                          CIP

General impressions are never to be trusted. Unfortunately when they are of long standing they become fixed rules of life, and assume a prescriptive right not to be questioned. Consequently, those who are not accustomed to original inquiry entertain a hatred and a horror of statistics. They cannot endure the idea of submitting their sacred impressions to cold-blooded verification. But it is the triumph of scientific men to rise superior to such superstitions, to devise tests by which the value of beliefs may be ascertained, and to feel sufficiently masters of themselves to discard contemptuously whatever may be found untrue.

—Sir Francis Galton

Contents

List of Tables

List of Figures

Preface

Over the last several years I have reviewed the international literature on race differences, gathered novel data and found a distinct pattern. On more than 60 variables, people of east Asian ancestry (Mongoloids, Orientals) and people of African ancestry (Negroids, blacks) define opposite ends of the spectrum, with people of European ancestry (Caucasoids, whites) falling intermediately, and with much variability within each broad grouping (see Glossary regarding terminology). This racial matrix emerges with measures of brain size, intelligence, reproductive behavior, sex hormones, twinning rate, speed of physical maturation, personality, family stability, law-abidingness, and social organization.

To account for the pattern, I proposed a gene-based evolutionary theory familiar to biologists as the r-K scale of reproductive strategy. At one end of this scale are r-strategies, which emphasize high reproductive rates, and, at the other, K-strategies, which emphasize high levels of parental investment. This scale is generally used to compare the life histories of widely disparate species but I used it to describe the immensely smaller variations within the human species. To emphasize that all human beings are K-selected relative to other animals this proposal was referred to as "differential K theory" (Rushton, 1984, 1985a). I hypothesized that Mongoloid people are more K-selected than Caucasoids, who in turn are more K-selected than Negroids.

I also mapped the r-K scale onto human evolution. Molecular genetic evidence indicates that modern humans evolved in Africa sometime after 200,000 years ago, with an African/non-African split occurring about 110,000 years ago and a Mongoloid/Caucasoid split about 41,000 years ago. Evolutionary selection pressures are far different in the hot African savanna where Negroids evolved, than in the cold Arctic environment, where Mongoloids evolved. Hence, it was predictable that these geographic races would show genetic differences in numerous traits. African populations, the earliest to emerge, are least K-selected, and Mongoloids, emerging latest, are most K-selected, with Caucasoids falling intermediately. Such an ordering explains how and why the variables clustered.

It is provocative, to say the least, to treat each of these vast races as a separate human subspecies whose multifarious patterns of behavior are reduced to an average position on a gene-based scale of reproductive strategy. But the question I asked myself repeatedly was: Did the facts fit the theory? Unfortunately not many others wanted to look very closely. My thesis, touching as it did on delicate issues, was denounced as "monstrous." I had engendered one of the most disreputable theories of human evolution in the last 60 years.

I did not always believe that race differences existed in deep structure. Fifteen years ago, as an established social learning theorist, I would have said that any differences that existed would have been primarily environmental in origin (Rushton, 1980). However, I have been persuaded, by data, and findings from numerous sources, that the races do differ, genetically, in the mechanisms underlying their behavior.

A major controversy occurred in Canada after my views became publicly known. Following a 1989 presentation of the theory at the American Association for the Advancement of Science, there was a call for my dismissal by the premier of Ontario, a criminal investigation by the Ontario Provincial Police, a media campaign of opposition, disruptions at the university, and an as yet unresolved investigation by the Ontario Human Rights Commission.

The fire storm of outrage led to countless challenges and rejoinders, so much so that at times the affair took over my life. Work on other topics seemed shallow by comparison. I learned to appreciate the cornerstone implications generated by the issue of race. By its impact on diverse areas of behavioral science, it was possible to imagine research on the topic completing the Darwinian revolution.

The prevailing social science paradigms are fast giving way to gene-culture coevolutionary perspectives. Although genetic, developmental, and psychobiological data are being amassed at an ever-increasing rate, there are few encompassing theories. The gene-based evolutionary models put forward here to explain ethnocentrism and racial group differences may provide a catalyst for understanding individual differences and human nature.

It is a truism in differential psychology that variations within groups are larger than those between them and there is enormous overlap in the racial distributions. This can be illustrated with some unpublished data of mine on the age that young men report having their first sexual intercourse. Relative to whites, Orientals report a disproportionately later date and blacks a disproportionately earlier date. Clearly, this does not mean that all Orientals have a later age of first sexual intercourse than all blacks.

Age of First Sexual Intercourse
(in %)

Race	Under 17	Over 17
Orientals	24	76
Whites	37	63
Blacks	64	36

On any single dimension to be discussed the racial differences are not large. Typically they range from 4 to 34 percentile points. Although often modest, the mean differences do exist, and they do so in a stubborn and consistent pattern. Obviously, however, it is problematic to generalize from a proportionate difference or group average to any particular individual. At the level of the individual, it must be recognized that almost all will have a mixture of r and K characteristics.

It is also necessary to emphasize the indisputable fact that much more research is needed. Objective hypothesis testing about racial differences in behavior has been much neglected over the past 60 years and knowledge is not as advanced as it ought to be. Many of the data sets and theoretical accounts provided here need much improvement. Rough-hewn though some of the evidence may be, it is clear that substantial racial differences do exist and that their pattern cannot be explained adequately except from an evolutionary perspective.

Although the thesis of this book is that genetic variation contributes importantly to the differences between human groups, it is obvious that environmental factors do so too. I would hold, on the currently available evidence, that the genetic and environmental contributions are about equal. Note that genetic effects, like environmental effects, are necessarily mediated by neuroendocrine and psychosocial mechanisms. These offer numerous ways for intervention and the alleviation of suffering.

Acknowledgments

This work belongs in the "London School" tradition founded by Sir Francis Galton. It has had a long gestation. Although I was educated at the University of London, earning a B.Sc. (1970) in psychology from Birkbeck College and a Ph.D. (1973) in social psychology from the London School of Economics and Political Science, I was not aware at the time how much my thinking was influenced by this unique amalgam of evolutionary biology, behavioral genetics, psychometrics, and neuroscience. Until 1980 I pursued my primary research trajectory in social learning theory. However, the discussion about the genetics of intelligence and the biological basis of behavior that occurred there stimulated vital thoughts that might not have happened elsewhere.

The work's specific origin was a book chapter written during an academic term (1981) as the guest of Paul Mussen at the Institute of Human Development of the University of California at Berkeley. In this chapter I broadened my social learning paradigm to encompass sociobiology (Rushton, 1984). Effort continued during a sabbatical (1982–1983) with Hans Eysenck at the University of London's Institute of Psychiatry.

The awarding of a Faculty of Social Science Research Professorship from the University of Western Ontario allowed me a year's relief from teaching duties (1987–1988). So did a fellowship in the John Simon Guggenheim Memorial Foundation (1988–1989), and then another sabbatical from the University of Western Ontario (1989–1990).

My research was initially supported by the Social Sciences and Humanities Research Council of Canada. During 1988–1989 it was assisted by a fellowship from the John Simon Guggenheim Foundation. For the last several years it has been sustained by The Pioneer Fund (U.S.A.). I am deeply grateful to Harry Weyher, president of the Pioneer Fund, for his unwavering support.

Two colleagues at Western provided magnificent help over many years. Douglas Jackson in psychology expanded my knowledge of psychometrics and Davison Ankney in zoology enlightened my thinking on evolution. Their wisdom, however, extends greatly beyond these central areas of expertise.

Excellent long-distance encouragement was provided by Arthur Jensen at the University of California at Berkeley and Richard Lynn at the University of Ulster. Both brought a stream of important items to my attention and regularly consulted on difficult issues. Their research discoveries form important parts of this book.

I am much beholden to those who provided specific advice on earlier drafts of the book: Davison Ankney, Hans Eysenck, Desmond ffolliett, Jeffrey Gray, Barry Gross, Richard Herrnstein, Douglas Jackson, Arthur Jensen, Sandi Johnson, Michael Levin, Richard Lynn, Edward Miller, Travis Osborne, and Harry Weyher. Others prefer to remain anonymous. Because my advisers and benefactors may not approve of all that I have written, they cannot be held accountable for any of the book's failings. I alone am responsible for these.

Finally, I am more indebted to my family than I can possibly express. Without their encouragement, the book might never have been completed.

1

Revamping Social Science

Favoritism for one's own ethnic group may have arisen as an extension of enhancing family and social cohesiveness (chap. 4). Because people give preferential treatment to those who genetically resemble themselves in order to help propagate their genes more effectively, xenophobia may represent a dark side of human altruism.

The propensity to defend one's own group, to see it as special, and not to be susceptible to the laws of evolutionary biology makes the scientific study of ethnicity and race differences problematic. Theories and facts generated in race research may be used by ethnic nationalists to propagate political positions. Antiracists may also engage in rhetoric to deny differences and suppress discoveries. Findings based on the study of race can be threatening. Ideological mine fields abound in ways that do not pertain to other areas of inquiry.

For scientific progress to be made it is necessary to rise above both "racist" and "antiracist" ideology. Suppose that a team of extraterrestrial scientists arrived on earth to study humans. Obviously they would quickly observe that, like many other species, humans showed considerable geographical variation in morphology. Three major geographical populations or "races" would be identified immediately and investigation mounted into how many others existed. Questions about the origin of the body types would be asked and also whether they covaried with life history variables including reproductive tactics in particular. If these scientists had a solid understanding of evolutionary biology, they would also investigate if these populations differed behaviorally, for example with respect to parental investment and social organization, and, if they did, how the differences might have evolved. Such an approach has proved very fruitful for population biologists studying other animals, particularly since E. O. Wilson's (1975) synthesis of sociobiology. If we are as interested in gaining knowledge as would be these "extraterrestrials", then we should apply similar procedures to our study of *Homo sapiens*.

For some, it would have been better if Mother Nature had made people, genetically, all the same. Cooperation would be easier and we could design just one type of society that would fit everybody. However, we are not all the same. Even children within the same family substantially differ from each other both genetically and behaviorally (Plomin & Daniels, 1987). If we ex-

1

amine how wide the differences can be between brothers and sisters who share the same food, watch the same TV, go to the same schools, and have the same parents, how much more different from each other must we expect other humans to be, especially those living in regions far apart that are normally classified as "races"?

The Nature-Nurture Debate

One of the great worldviews of social science has been that economic and other environmental forces are preeminent in the causation of individual behavior. Modern social scientists have also been egalitarian, promoting the idea that all babies are born with essentially equal endowments. It follows that subsequent inequalities in wealth and poverty, success and failure, happiness and misery, and sickness and health are the product of social forces.

John B. Watson (1878–1958), the founder of behaviorism articulated what was to become the social science orthodoxy (1924: 104):

> Give me a dozen healthy infants, well formed, and my own specified world to bring them up in and I'll guarantee to take any one at random and train him to become any type of specialist I might select—doctor, lawyer, artist, merchant-chief and, yes, even beggar-man and thief, regardless of his talents, penchants, tendencies, abilities, vocations, and race of his ancestors. I am going beyond my facts and I admit it, but so have the advocates of the contrary and they have been doing it for many thousands of years. Please note that when this experiment is made I am to be allowed to specify the way the children are to be brought up and the type of world they have to live in.

Benevolent environmentalism generated a plethora of strategies for intervention in the home, the workplace, the mass media, and the criminal justice system. Psychotherapies and self-help systems flourished as people attempted to rectify blemishes and achieve self-fulfillment. Social workers battled the harmful effects of poverty, unemployment, and other factors.

Environmentalism dovetailed with political philosophies striving to generate sweeping changes in human affairs. From capitalist democracies to totalitarian collectivities, social engineering began in earnest. Marxists took the argument furthest, preaching that public ownership of the economic base of society was a necessary precondition for social harmony.

Especially following World War II (1939–1945) and the revulsion to Hitler's racial policies, egalitarianism led to the virtual elimination of Darwinian thinking among Western social scientists (Degler, 1991). The doctrine of biological equality was taken to an extreme among Communists in the Soviet Union and elsewhere (Clark, 1984). Throughout the world, leftists took up the cry "Not in Our Genes" and vociferously asserted that social inequalities were due entirely to repressive environments (Lewontin, Rose, & Kamin, 1984; Lewontin, 1991).

The nature-nurture debate is fought between those who, in effect, advocate an extreme 100 percent environmentalist position and those who advocate a moderate, even 50-50, position. No behavioral geneticist believes in a 100 percent genetic determinism because it is obvious that physical growth and mental development require good nutrition, fresh air, and exercise and that children and neophytes learn best with access to experienced role models. Genetic influence (not determinism) is the key phrase, for genetic effects are necessarily mediated by neuroendocrine and psychosocial systems that have independent influence on phenotypic behavior.

The burning question is how substantial is the genetic contribution to human nature and the differences therein? While lip service has been paid to the view that people are a product of both genes and culture, until recently, many social scientists and philosophers acted as though the human mind was a blank slate and each person exclusively a product of his or her history and economic arrangement.

During the 1980s there was an increased acceptance of behavioral genetics and evolutionary theorizing. Even the most rigid opponents acquiesced as scientific breakthroughs made headlines. Major reviews of the twin and adoption literature appeared in *Science* and other prestigious journals, leading to the widely accepted conclusion that "genetic factors exert a pronounced and pervasive influence on behavioral variability" (Bouchard, Lykken, McGue, Segal, & Tellegen, 1990: 223).

Discoveries in medical genetics heralded what was to come with gene therapy a possibility for a variety of classic psychological disorders including anxiety, depression, and schizophrenia. The project to sequence the entire human genome got underway, a multibillion dollar international undertaking. Although hard-core naysayers such as *Science for the People* remained implacably opposed to developments (Lewontin, 1991), clearly, the climate was changing.

A renewal of interest in human racial origins also characterized the 1980s with Africa identified as the Garden of Eden. In the 1970s dramatic fossil discoveries in East Africa of *Homo habilis* and *Homo erectus,* along with the 3.7 million-year-old footprints and bones of "Lucy" and her fellow australopithecenes captured the public imagination. By the 1980s, through genetic analyses of existing human populations, "Eve" was thought to be a long-armed, thick-boned, well-muscled, dark-skinned woman who lived some 200,000 years ago on the East African savanna. She appeared on the front cover of *Newsweek* (January 11, 1988) and helped center a debate on the evolution of human origins.

Race differences in behavior, although a necessary concomitant of these revisionist viewpoints, were not included in these studies, and constituted an embarrassment for scholars who omitted them. On the topic of race, a righteous conformity had come to prevail. A sign of the times was Sandra Scarr's presidential address to the Behavior Genetics Association in 1986. She observed, in a talk entitled "Three Cheers for Behavioral Genetics," that "the war is largely over.... The mainstream of psychology has joined our tributary, and we are in danger of being swallowed up in a flood of acceptance" (Scarr, 1987: 228). While accepting that genetics underlay social class differences in IQ, she rejected a genetic explanation for racial differences because racial barriers were less permeable. Scarr (1987) interpreted her own work as showing an environmental causation for racial variation.

In this book, new truths about racial group differences are advanced. The stepwise function of racial characteristics made explicit in Table 1.1 is the starting point for discussion. Mongoloids and Caucasoids have the largest brains, whether indexed by weight at autopsy, external head size, or intracranial volume, but have the slowest rate of dental development, indexed by onset of permanent molar teeth, and produce the fewest gametes, indexed by frequency of twin birthing and size of the testes. For example, blacks produce more than 16 two-egg twins per 1,000 live births whereas the figure for whites is 8 and for Orientals it is less than 4.

Most psychological work on race has focused on differentials between blacks and whites in the United States where whites achieve disproportionately higher than blacks. Ever since Arthur Jensen's (1969) classic monograph, a controversy has raged over whether the causes of this disparity involved genetic as well as environmental factors (Eysenck & Kamin, 1981; Loehlin, Lindzey, & Spuhler, 1975). Extensive surveys now show that a plurality of experts believe that Jensen was correct in attributing a portion of the racial variance to genetic differences (Snyderman & Rothman, 1987, 1988).

The intelligence debate was broadened by Richard Lynn (1982, 1991c) who gathered global data showing that Orientals had higher test scores than whites. Others described physiological, maturational, and other behavioral differences among the races (Eysenck, 1971; Jensen, 1973; R. Lynn, 1987). The scientific discussion was also expanded with data on activity level and temperament (Freedman, 1979), crime (J.Q. Wilson & Herrnstein, 1985), personality (P.E. Vernon, 1982), family structure (Moynihan, 1965), and health and longevity (Polednak, 1989).

The present book explores these and other variables in detail. It includes extensive evidence from (a) Mongoloid samples (one-third of the world's population), (b) Negroid samples from other than the United States (most black people live in postcolonial Africa), and (c) multifarious characteristics in addition to mental ability. I conclude that the racial group differences in intelligence are observed worldwide, in Africa and Asia, as well as in Europe and North America, and that they are paralleled by differences in brain size, speed of dental maturation, reproductive physiology, and numerous other variables.

The central theoretical question is: Why should Caucasian populations average so consistently *between* Negroid and Mongoloid populations on so many

TABLE 1.1
Relative Ranking of Races on Diverse Variables

Variable	Orientals	Whites	Blacks
Brain size			
Autopsy data (cm³ equivalents)	1,351	1,356	1,223
Endocranial volume (cm³)	1,415	1,362	1,268
External head measures (cm³)	1,356	1,329	1,294
Cortical neurons (billions)	13.767	13.665	13.185
Intelligence			
IQ test scores	106	100	85
Decision times	Faster	Intermediate	Slower
Cultural achievements	Higher	Higher	Lower
Maturation rate			
Gestation time	?	Intermediate	Earlier
Skeletal development	Later	Intermediate	Earlier
Motor development	Later	Intermediate	Earlier
Dental development	Later	Intermediate	Earlier
Age of first intercourse	Later	Intermediate	Earlier
Age of first pregnancy	Later	Intermediate	Earlier
Life span	Longer	Intermediate	Shorter
Personality			
Activity level	Lower	Intermediate	Higher
Aggressiveness	Lower	Intermediate	Higher
Cautiousness	Higher	Intermediate	Lower
Dominance	Lower	Intermediate	Higher
Impulsivity	Lower	Intermediate	Higher
Self-concept	Lower	Intermediate	Higher
Sociability	Lower	Intermediate	Higher
Social organization			
Marital stability	Higher	Intermediate	Lower
Law abidingness	Higher	Intermediate	Lower
Mental health	Higher	Intermediate	Lower
Administrative capacity	Higher	Higher	Lower
Reproductive effort			
Two-egg twinning (per 1,000 births)	4	8	16
Hormone levels	Lower	Intermediate	Higher
Size of genitalia	Smaller	Intermediate	Larger
Secondary sex characteristics	Smaller	Intermediate	Larger
Intercourse frequencies	Lower	Intermediate	Higher
Permissive attitudes	Lower	Intermediate	Higher
Sexually transmitted diseases	Lower	Intermediate	Higher

traits? It is not simply IQ scores that require explanation. A network of evidence such as that shown in Table 1.1 allows more chance of finding powerful theories than do single dimensions drawn from the set. No environmental factor is known to produce the inverse relation between brain size, maturational speed, and reproductive potency nor to cause so many diverse variables to correlate in so comprehensive a fashion. There is, however, a genetic factor: evolution.

The explanation proposed for the racial pattern originates in life-history theory. A life history is a genetically organized suite of characters that have evolved so as to allocate energy to survival, growth, and reproduction. For example, across 21 primate species, age of eruption of first molar correlates 0.89, 0.85, 0.93, 0.82, 0.86, and 0.85 with body weight, length of gestation, age of weaning, birth interval, sexual maturity, and life span. The highest correlation is 0.98 with brain size (B. H. Smith, 1989).

Theories concerning large brains and long life in primates take on particular importance because humans are the most encephalized and the longest lived of primates. Humans can be viewed as the most extreme on an evolutionary scale trading parental care and social organization for egg production and reproductive potency. This tradeoff may be conceptualized along a continuum of r-K reproductive strategies (E. O. Wilson, 1975).

At one extreme the great apes exemplify the K-strategy, producing one infant every five or six years and providing much parental care. At the other extreme, oysters exemplify the r-strategy, producing 500 million eggs a year but providing no parental care. A female mouse lemur, an r-strategist among primates, produces her first offspring at 9 months of age and has a life expectancy of 15 years. A mouse lemur may mature, have offspring, and die before a K-strategist gorilla has her first offspring.

This cross-species scale may be applied to the immensely smaller variation among human groups. Although all human beings are at the K-selected end of the continuum, some may be more so than others, a proposal introduced as "differential K theory" (Rushton, 1984, 1985a, 1988b). Black women, compared to white women, average a shorter period of ovulation and produce more eggs per ovulation in addition to all the other characteristics in Table 1.1. As mentioned, the rate of dizygotic twinning, a direct index of egg production, is less than 4 per 1,000 births among Mongoloids, 8 per 1,000 among Caucasoids, and 16 or greater per 1,000 among Negroids. Conversely, Mongoloid populations average the largest brains, the highest IQ scores, and the most complex social organizations.

Archaic versions of the three major races appear to differ in antiquity, with Mongoloids being the most recently evolved and Negroids the earliest. As I mentioned in the Preface, Africans emerged from the ancestral *Homo* line about 200,000 years ago, with an African/non-African split occurring about 110,000 years ago, and a Caucasoid/Mongoloid split about 41,000 years ago

(Stringer & Andrews, 1988). Because Bonner (1980) had shown that, in general, animals that emerged later in earth history had larger brains and greater culture than those that had emerged earlier, I extrapolated to the human succession (Rushton, 1992b). Because groups migrating out of Africa into the colder climate of Eurasia encountered more challenging environments, including the last ice age, which ended just 12,000 years ago, they were more stringently selected for intelligence, forward planning, sexual and personal restraint, and a *K*-parenting strategy. The Siberian cold experienced by Oriental populations was the most severe and exerted the greatest selection.

Few social scientists, however, were willing to examine the evidence or to engage in scientific debate. Charles Leslie, an advisory editor of *Social Science and Medicine* exemplified the opposition. Outraged that the journal had published my work on how racial variation in sexuality contributed to the global epidemiology of AIDS, Leslie (1990: 896) used his opening address at the Eleventh International Conference on the Social Sciences and Medicine to condemn the editorial decision to publish me. The justification for his denouncement is illuminating of the state of much social science research.

> [M]ost of the influential work in the social sciences is ideological, and most of our criticisms of each other are ideologically grounded. Non social scientists generally recognize the fact that the social sciences are mostly ideological, and that they have produced in this century a very small amount of scientific knowledge compared to the great bulk of their publications. Our claim to being scientific is one of the main intellectual scandals of the academic world, though most of us live comfortably with our shame.... By and large, we believe in, and our social science is meant to promote, pluralism and democracy.

This view of social science was also exemplified by Caporael and Brewer (1991:1) who edited a special volume of the *Journal of Social Issues,* a publication of the American Psychological Association, to "recapture" evolutionary theory from people like me for those more "socially responsible." Asserted the editors, "Biological explanations of human social behavior tend to be ideologically and politically reactive". One contributor (Fairchild, 1991: 112) went further:

> If ideology is inextricably tied to the generation of knowledge, then all social science writings—including this one—involve certain ideological biases or political agendas.... These biases are typically unstated. The author's ideological biases are as follows: (a) The idea of inherited "racial" differences is false; instead, "race" is a proxy for a host of longstanding historical and environmental variables. (b) Social science has the mandate of applying its theories and methods to alleviate human suffering and inequality.

The evolutionary psychology of race differences has become the most politically incorrect topic in the world today. On no other issue are the outmoded paradigms and obsolete models of the social science orthodoxy so clearly revealed. And on no other topic does the intellectual battle fuse with the political and so much distort basic scientific values. Although nobody denies that some ethnic groups are disproportionately represented in wealth, education, health, and crime, alternative explanations for the differences constitute ideological warfare. Ultimately, the battle is over nothing less than how to conceptualize human nature.

The Revolution Ahead

In the next 10 years, scientists worldwide will devote billions of dollars to the Human Genome Project. In the process, they will decipher all 100,000 human genes, cure certain inherited diseases, (like cystic fibrosis in northern Europeans, Tay Sachs in European Jews, beta thalassemia in eastern Mediterraneans, and sickle-cell in those of West African descent), and inform us more about ourselves than many of us are prepared to know. This knowledge will include why ethnic and racial groups are disproportionately represented in various spheres of activity.

Just as women doctors have advocated that to conceptualize women as being the same as men leads to a neglect of women's problems and their treatment (e.g., premenstrual symptoms and menopause and hormone replacement therapy), so black doctors have become concerned that treating blacks the same as whites is to neglect black problems. For example, 30 percent of the people who have kidney failure and undergo dialysis are black, but estimates are that fewer than 10 percent of organ donors are black. Blacks fare better with organs donated from blacks.

Another example is that genetics contributes to black hypertension. Black men experience a faster heart rate when performing moderate exercise, although the pulse rates of the black and white men while resting showed no significant differences. Black men have higher rates of cancer of the prostate than white men who in turn have higher rates than Oriental men, one determinant of which is testosterone (Polednak, 1989).

Racial differences exist in risk for AIDS with blacks being most at risk and Asians least so (chap. 8). In the United States, blacks, who make up 12 percent of the population, represent 30 percent of those with AIDS. Among women, 53 percent of those with AIDS are black. Fifty-five percent of children with AIDS are black.

Race is also a critical factor in the success of many medicines. For example, Asians are more sensitive to the drugs used to treat anxiety, depression, and schizophrenia, requiring lower dosages; they are also more likely to have side effects with lower dosages (Levy, 1993). Another widely cited example is that Asians are more sensitive to the adverse effects of alcohol, especially to marked facial flushing, palpitation, and tachycardia. Levy (1993: 143) argues that ethnicity should be taken into account in formulary selection and prescribing decisions for individual patients.

Ethnically related disparities exist in every field of endeavor. Continuing with Asians and blacks in the United States, the clear and publicly acknowledged fact is that one has a disproportionately high number who qualify for college educations and the other has a disproportionately high number who qualify for successful careers in professional athletics. In numerous other important outcomes, such as economic standing, crime, illiteracy, poverty, and unemployment, one group or another is disproportionately represented. These disproportionate representations are stubborn, and in America, Britain, and Canada they have resisted strenuous efforts to eliminate them.

With respect to IQ differences in the United States, their possible causes were the subject of a survey of 661 scientists in relevant disciplines (Snyderman & Rothman, 1987, 1988). Of the respondents, 94 percent regarded differences within the white population to have a significant genetic component, the average estimate of the amount being 60 percent. A majority (52 percent) of those responding to the question believed that part of the black-white difference was genetic, compared to only 17 percent of those answering the question who believed it was entirely environmental. The case for genetic determination is even more strongly felt for socioeconomic status differences.

The origin of modern humans is one of the largest unsolved problems in evolution. Explaining race differences may give clues to what happened during early human evolutionary history. It may also provide a universal model of human action. Groups are but aggregates of individuals and ultimately it is at the level of the individual that an account must be sought. Gene-based reproductive strategies provide a better explanation of behavior than sociological forces alone.

It is the thesis of this book that the principles of evolution and sociobiology should be applied to the study of racial group differences among *Homo sapiens*. Lumsden and Wilson (1983: 171) set the stage:

> A guiding principle has nevertheless reemerged from the combined efforts that once inspired Comte, Spencer, and other nineteenth-century visionaries before dying from premature birth and Social Darwinism: that all of the natural science and social sciences form a seamless whole, so that chemistry can be unified with physics, biology with chemistry, psychology with biology, and sociology with psychology—all the way across the domain of inquiry by means of an unbroken web of theory and verification. In the early years the dream was bright.... The bridge between biology and psychology is still something of an article of faith, in the process of being redeemed by neurobiology and the brain sciences. Connections beyond, to the social sciences, are being resisted as resolutely as ever. The newest villain of the piece, the embattled spearhead of the natural-science advance, is sociobiology.

Sir Francis Galton

The work to be presented in this book is part of a historical tradition sometimes known as the "Galton School" and sometimes as the "London School" of Psychology. Started by Sir Francis Galton (1822–1911), the cousin of Charles

Darwin (1809-1882), the tradition has been continued by Karl Pearson, Charles Spearman, Cyril Burt, Hans Eysenck, Richard Lynn, and Arthur Jensen, among others. This historical tradition is too often unacknowledged in contemporary research.

Galton is the originator of scientific research on individual differences. His 1865 article "Hereditary Talents and Character" was published 14 years before Wundt "founded" psychology, at a time when Freud was only 9 years old. A forerunner to *Hereditary Genius* (1869), the article was concerned with the heritability, distribution, and measurement of individual differences in "zeal and industry," as well as intelligence, and appeared 6 years after *The Origin of Species* (Darwin, 1859), and 6 years before *The Descent of Man* (Darwin, 1871). Providing early evidence that individual differences in intelligence were heritable, this article was the first to advocate using twins for proof.

It was Galton who made the first attempt to place the racial question into psychological and statistical terms. Galton's (1853) anthropological work, exploring the tribes of southwest Africa, had stimulated his interest in human differences. To Galton, mathematics did not exist among the Africans, with fingers being used to help count (chap. 5). Galton said it would "sorely puzzle" the Ovaherero to realize that if one sheep cost two sticks of tobacco, two sheep would cost four. Galton (1869: 337) also contrasted an easily stirred impulsive temperament in Africans with a complacency in Chinese. Following the publication of Darwin's (1859) *Origin of Species,* Galton applied Quetelet's (1796-1874) statistical advances regarding deviations from an average and the normal distribution to explain natural selection.

It occurred to Galton (1869) that intellectual ability might be normally distributed. He examined marks from various examinations and found that middle scores were consistently more frequent than very high or very low scores. He applied fourteen grades to human intellect, seven on each side of the mean, using capital and lowercase letters (Figure 1.1). He concluded that 1 person in about 79,000 would fall in the highest grade, *G*, and necessarily the same number in the lower grade of imbeciles, *g;* 1 in 4,300 in grade *F* and in *f,* but 1 in only 4 in each of the average grades, *A* and *a.* To allow for a few persons of such outstanding intellect that they were too few for statistical treatment he designated a grade as *X,* and to its opposite, *x.*

Galton postulated that the distribution of intellect would be the same in all ethnic taxa, but that the mean would differ. Figure 1.1 shows that in his opinion Africans averaged lower than Europeans, but with a large overlap. Galton's estimates turn out to be remarkably similar to those obtained from normative samples of black and white Americans 100 years later (Jensen, 1973: 212-13; see also Figures 2.5 and 6.3).

Galton also judged the range of intellect available in other populations, including dogs and other intelligent animals, and postulated overlap. Thus,

Figure 1.1: Galton's (1869) Classification of English and African Mental Ability

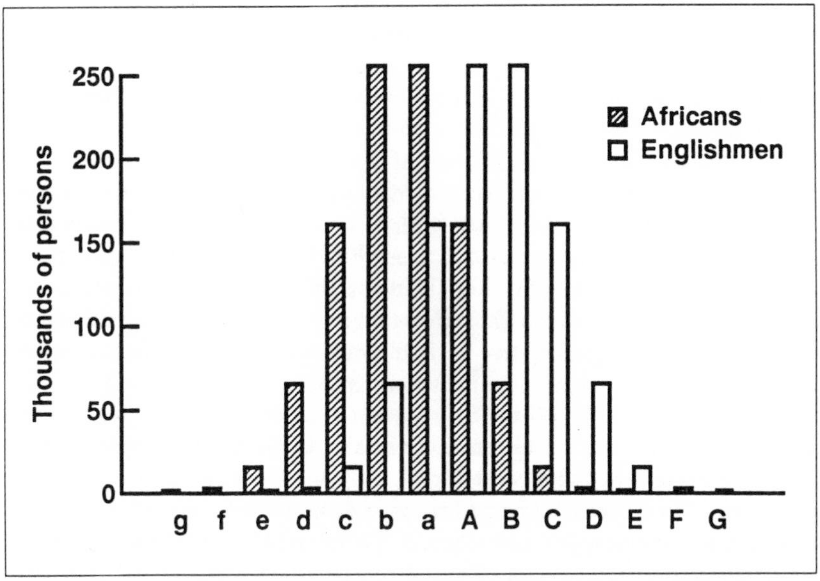

The letters below the baseline are Galton's grades of intelligence from *A* and *a,* above and below average, to *G* and *g,* eminent and imbecile. The left-hand columns represent the number of Africans, while those to the right represent the number of Englishmen. Based on estimates given by Galton (1869, p. 30, 327–328).

the class of *G* of such animals in respect to memory and powers of reason is viewed as superior to the *g* of humankind. Galton was struck by the number of eminent people in the Greek population of Attica in the century beginning 530 B.C. (Pericles, Thucydides, Socrates, Xenophon, Plato, and Euripides among others). He believed the proportion of persons in the highest grades was much greater than in the England of his time.

Galton was not only the first to advocate the use of twins to help disentangle the effects of heredity and environment, he also carried out breeding experiments with plants and animals, anticipating later work in behavioral genetics. Galton (1883, 1889) also studied temperament, as in his article "Good and Bad Temper in English Families" and he pioneered work on assortative mating among spouses, and the interrelationships of intelligence, temperament, and physique. He suggested that socially desirable traits went together because of mate preferences (chap. 4).

Galton was not exclusively hereditarian. He carried out surveys to assess other influences making for eminence, and reported that devoted, high-minded mothers and first-born ordinal position were important predictors (Galton, 1874). Less well known is that Galton (1879, 1883) was interested in mental imagery and invented the word association test, creating stimulus words and gathering statistical information on their unconscious associations. These were published in *Brain* (1879), and Freud can almost certainly be included among the readers of this issue, although he never referred to Galton's paper nor credited Galton with priority in suggesting the existence of unconscious mental processes (Forrest, 1974).

The longest-standing contributions of Galton are statistical. He was among the first to apply the normal distribution, deviation scores, and percentiles to psychological characteristics (1869). He invented the concepts of regression and correlation (1888a, 1889). He was influential in founding the journal *Biometrika* (1901), which, by promulgating statistical techniques for the study of biological variation, including psychological characteristics, helped begin the psychometric tradition. In his anthropometric laboratory, Galton (1883, 1889) pioneered many measurement techniques including those of head size. During the 1880s and 1890s more than 17,000 individuals of all ages from diverse walks of life were tested. For a small fee visitors could have various measurements taken and recorded.

Galton (1888b) was the first to report a quantitative relationship between cranial capacity and mental ability in humans. Galton's subjects were 1,095 Cambridge undergraduates divided into those who had achieved first class honors degrees and those who had not. Galton computed head volume by multiplying head length by breadth by height and plotting the results against age (19 to 25 years) and class of degree (A, B, C). He reported that (1) cranial capacity continued to grow after the age of 19, and (2) men who obtained high honors degrees had a brain size from 2 to 5 percent greater than those who did not.

Years later, when Galton's data were reworked using correlation coefficients, the relation between head size and college grades was found to lie between 0.06 and 0.11 (Pearson, 1906). Pearson (1924: 94) reported Galton's response: "He was very unhappy about the low correlations I found between intelligence and head size, and would cite against me those 'front benches' [the people on the front benches at Royal Society meetings who Galton perceived as having large heads]; it was one of the few instances I noticed when impressions seemed to have more weight with him than measurements." As reviewed in chapter 2, volumetric measures of brain size from magnetic resonance imaging give the substantially higher correlations Galton had predicted.

When Galton died in 1911, his will endowed Karl Pearson with a Chair of Eugenics (later Genetics) at the University of London. Pearson, later Galton's biographer (1914-1930), invented the product-moment correlation and the chi-square goodness-of-fit statistic, and helped inaugurate the great biometric trajectory that included R. A. Fisher (inventor of the analysis of variance) and Sewall Wright (inventor of path analysis), both of whom are best known, along with J. B. S. Haldane, for the "Modern Synthesis" of Darwinian evolution with Mendelian genetics. Few social scientists are aware that the statistics they use were originated for the purpose of estimating the transmission of genetic variance.

A rival to Pearson's Department of Eugenics was the University of London's Psychology Department headed by another Galtonian, Charles Spearman. Spearman invented rank order correlations, factor analysis, discovered the g factor in tests of intelligence, and investigated the interaction of personality and intelligence, finding, like Galton before him, that socially desirable traits such as honesty and intelligence often went together (Spearman, 1927). Spearman's successor was Sir Cyril Burt, and two of Burt's most famous students, Raymond Cattell (1982) and Hans Eysenck (1981) have promulgated this unique amalgam of evolutionary biology, behavioral genetics, psychometrics, and neuroscience to the present day.

Arthur Jensen (1969) also wears the Galton mantle. It is not well known that Jensen's early research was concerned with personality factors in educational attainment. After receiving his doctoral degree at Columbia University, he moved to London to carry out postdoctoral research with Eysenck, learned about the g factor in tests of intelligence, and subsequently pursued the implications. So many psychologists have been influenced by the evolutionary thinking arising out of sociobiology that the Galtonian identity may be lost in what is hopefully an emerging paradigm (Buss, 1984; Rushton, 1984).

Counterrevolution

It may be important to consider why the Galtonian tradition is not better appreciated. Many of the earliest psychologists including Freud, Dewey, James, McDougall, and Thorndike embraced Darwinism with enthusiasm, as did other social thinkers including Karl Marx and Herbert Spencer. At this time, the eugenics movement too was widely supported, as much by socialist reformers as by right-wing traditionalists (Clark, 1984; Kevles, 1985). The mix of political ideology with human biology, however, eventually led to Galton's unpopularity.

By the mid-1930s the political right had gained the ascendancy in claiming evolutionary theory to support their arguments while the political left had come to believe that the concept of "survival of the fittest" was incompatible with the notion of equality. Powerful ideologues, such as the anthropologist Franz Boas (1912, 1940) and his student Margaret Mead, fought against the idea of biological universals. Boas (1912) reported that the head shapes of thousands of immigrants to New York City changed with the amount of time spent in the United States. In *Coming of Age in Samoa* (Mead, 1928) purported to discover a "negative instance" of adolescence being a time of emotional stresses, and its conclusion added significantly to the increasingly antibiological orthodoxy (Caton, 1990; Degler, 1991; Freeman, 1984).

Opposition to the Nazis played a significant role in blunting Galton's impact. From the 1930s onward, scarcely anyone outside Germany and its Axis allies dared to suggest that groups of individuals might be in any genetic respect different to any other lest it should appear that the author was supporting or excusing the Nazi cause. Those who believed in the biological equality of people were free to write what they liked, without fear of contradiction. They made full use of their opportunity in the decades that followed. Politically fueled also by European decolonization and by the U.S. civil rights movement, the idea of a genetically based core of human nature on which individuals and social groups might differ was consistently derogated.

Among the refugees who fled Nazi persecution and entered Britain and the United States in the 1930s and 1940s there were many who exerted a powerful influence on the Zeitgeist of the social sciences, helping to create an orthodoxy of egalitarianism and environmentalism (Degler, 1991). As Degler reminds us, however, from the longer historical perspective it is the decoupling of biology and human behavior that requires explanation. Evolutionary studies of human nature are inherently mainstream. Radical environmentalism and cultural determinism are the anomalous conditions in need of justification.

The Distal-Proximal Continuum

In 1975, E. O. Wilson published *Sociobiology: The New Synthesis.* This was a monumental founding document, an epic treatment of animal behavior and evolutionary theory. In it, Wilson defined the new science as "the systematic study of the biological basis of all social behavior" (p. 4) and named altruism the "central theoretical problem of sociobiology" (p. 3). How could altruism, which by definition reduced personal fitness, possibly evolve by natural selection?

At the roots of the new synthesis was a modernization of Samuel Butler's famous aphorism that a chicken is only an egg's way of making another egg, that is, "the organism is only DNA's way of making more DNA" (E. O. Wilson, 1975: 3). This represented a conceptual advance over Darwin's idea of the survival of the "fittest" individual, for it is now DNA, not the individual, that is "fit." According to this view, an individual organism is only a vehicle, part of an elaborate device that ensures the survival and reproduction of genes with the least possible biochemical alteration. Thus, an appropriate unit of analysis for understanding natural selection and a variety of behavior patterns is the gene. Any means by which a pool of genes, in a group of individuals, can be transmitted more effectively to the next generation will be adopted (Hamilton, 1964). Here, it is suggested, are the origins of maternal behavior, sterility in castes of worker ants, aggression, cooperation, and self-sacrificial altruism. All these phenomena are strategies by which genes can be more readily transmitted. Richard Dawkins (1976) captured this idea perfectly in the title of his book: *The Selfish Gene.*

Although several issues are involved in the controversy over sociobiology, many are the result of a confusion between ultimate and proximate levels of explanation. The diagram shown in Figure 1.2 may be informative. Disagreement and uncertainty occur when explanations move from proximal to more distal levels. Thus, some phenomenologists, situationists, and cognitivists, who focus attention on processes just prior to the behavior, mistrust the view that these processes themselves are partly determined by previous learning. Learning theorists, in turn, often do not readily accept the view that a person's previous learning history is partly a function of inherited traits. Often even behavioral geneticists ignore the broader context of the evolutionary history of the animal from which they are attempting to breed selected traits.

Controversy is less likely to ensue when explanations move from distal to proximal. Evolutionary biologists typically do not find the heritability of traits problematic, and most trait theorists accept that behavioral dispositions are modified by later learning. In addition, learning theorists believe that the products of early experience interact with subsequent situations to produce emotional arousal and cognitive processing, which in turn give rise to the person's phenomenology just prior to his or her behavior.

Proximal wariness of distal explanation may be due in part to concern about extreme reductionism, for example, that phenomenology is entirely reducible to learning, or that learning is only secondary to genetics. Unfortunately, an-

Figure 1.2: The Distal-Proximal Dimension and Levels of Explanation in Social Behavior

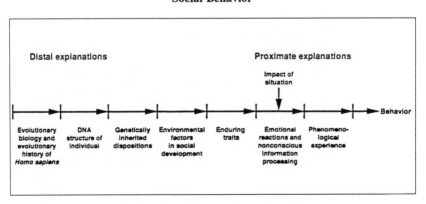

When explanations move from distal to proximal, controversy does not ensue, whereas the converse is not always true. Adapted from Rushton (1984, p. 3, Figure 1). Copyright 1984 by Plenum Press. Reprinted with permission.

other reason for dispute arises from lack of knowledge. Most researchers seem devoted to an exclusive orientation. It is rare for cognitive social learning theorists to know much about evolution or genetics; or for humanistic phenomenologists to understand psychometrics, or for trait theorists to pursue behaviorism. The psychoanalytic and radical behaviorist schisms even create their own journals and professional schools.

2

Character Traits

The belief in a core of human nature around which individuals and groups consistently differed was widely derogated during the 1960s and 1970s. Three main explanations have been advanced for why this occurred. First, the predictive power of trait theories was judged to be weak. Second, the interventionist power of social learning theory was affirmed to be strong. Third, the socially committed emphasized malleability to change an unjust society.

The main empirical reason given for rejecting the trait concept is that different indices of the same trait only correlate, on the average, 0.20 to 0.30, too low a figure to make the trait concept very useful. Major reviews of the literature by trait psychologist Philip E. Vernon (1964) and by social learning theorist Walter Mischel (1968) concluded that 0.30 was the representative correlation of consistency across situations. As Eysenck (1970) and many others have shown, this conclusion is incorrect.

The Altruistic Personality

The most important and largest study of the problem of generality versus specificity in behavior concerned altruism. This is the classic "Character Education Enquiry" carried out by Hartshorne and May in the 1920s and published in three books (Hartshorne & May, 1928; Hartshorne, May, & Maller, 1929; Hartshorne, May, & Shuttleworth, 1930). These investigators gave 11,000 elementary and high school students some 33 different behavioral tests of altruism (referred to as the "service" tests), self-control, and honesty in home, classroom, church, play, and athletic contexts. Concurrently, ratings of the children's reputations with teachers and classmates were obtained. Altogether, more than 170,000 observations were collected. Scores on the various tests were correlated to discover whether behavior is specific to situations or consistent across them.

This study is still regarded as a landmark that has not been surpassed by later work. It will be discussed in some detail because it is the largest examination of the question ever undertaken, it raises most of the major points of interest, and it has been seriously misinterpreted by many investigators. The various tests administered to the children are summarized in Table 2.1.

TABLE 2.1
Some of the Measures Used in the "Studies in the Nature of Character" Investigation

Tests	Nature and scoring of the task
Service tests	
Self-or-class test	Whether the student chose to enter a competition to benefit himself or herself or the class.
Money voting test	Whether the student voted to spend class money on himself or herself or charity.
Learning exercises	Whether the student learned material when performance increments led to money going to the Red Cross.
School-kit test	Number of items donated to charity from a pencil case given to a child.
Envelopes test	Number of jokes, pictures, etc., collected for sick children in an envelope provided.
Honesty tests	
Copying technique	Whether student cheated on a test by copying answers from the person next to him or her.
Duplicating technique	Whether student cheated on a test by altering answers after his or her paper had been duplicated without his or her knowledge.
Improbable achievement	Whether student cheated as indicated by an improbably high level of performance on a task.
Double testing technique	Whether students' scores on an unsupervised test (e.g., number of push-ups) decreased when a retest was supervised.
Stealing	Whether students stole money from a puzzle box.
Lying	Whether students admitted to having cheated on any of the tasks.
Self-control tests	
Story resistance tests	Time students persisted in trying to read the climax of an exciting story when words ran into each other.
Puzzle memory tests	Time spent persisting at difficult puzzles.
Candy test	The number of pieces of candy not eaten in a "resisting temptation" paradigm.
Tickle test	The ability to keep a "wooden face" while being tickled by a feather.
Bad odor test	The ability to keep a "wooden face" while having a bad odor placed under the nose.
Bad taste test	The ability to keep a "wooden face" while testing unrefined cod liver oil.
Knowledge of moral rules	
Cause-effect test	Agreement with items such as "Good marks are chiefly a matter of luck."
Recognition test	Agreement with items such as "Copying composition out of a book but changing some of the words" constituted cheating.
Social-ethical vocabulary	Picking the best definition of words denoting moral virtue (e.g., bravery, malice).
Foresight test	Students wrote out consequences for transgressions such as "John accidentally broke a street lamp with a snowball".
Probability test	Students ranked the probability of various outcomes for such behaviors as "John started across the street without looking both ways."
Reputational ratings	
Recording of helpful acts	For 6 months, teachers recorded helpful acts performed by students.
The "guess who" test	Children wrote names of classmates who fitted very short descriptions (e.g., Here is someone who is kind to younger children . . .).
Check list	Teachers rated each child on adjectives such as kind, considerate, and stingy.

Note. From Rushton, Brainerd & Pressley (1983, p. 22, Table 1). Copyright 1983 by the American Psychological Association. Reprinted with permission.

First, the results based on the measures of altruism showed that any one behavioral test of altruism correlated, on the average, only 0.20 with any other test. But when the five behavioral measures were aggregated into a battery, they correlated a much higher 0.61 with the measures of the child's altruistic reputation among his or her teachers and classmates. Furthermore, the teachers' and peers' perceptions of the students' altruism were in close agreement (r = 0.80). These latter results indicate a considerable degree of consistency in altruistic behavior. In this regard, Hartshorne et al. (1929:107) wrote:

> The correlation between the total service score and the total reputation scores is .61 ... Although this seems low, it should be borne in mind that the correlations between test scores and ratings for intelligence seldom run higher than .50.

Similar results were obtained for the measures of honesty and self-control. Any one behavioral test correlated, on average, only 0.20 with any other test. If, however, the measures were aggregated into batteries, then much higher relationships were found either with other combined behavioral measures, with teachers' ratings of the children, or with the children's moral knowledge scores. Often, these correlations were on the order of 0.50 to 0.60. For example, the battery of tests measuring cheating by copying correlated 0.52 with another battery of tests measuring other types of classroom cheating. Thus, depending on whether the focus is on the relationship between individual measures or on the relationship between averaged groups of behaviors, the notions of situational specificity and situational consistency are both supported. Which of these two conclusions is more accurate?

Hartshorne and colleagues focused on the small correlations of 0.20 and 0.30. Consequently, they argued (1928: 411) for a doctrine of specificity:

> Neither deceit nor its opposite, "honesty" are unified character traits, but rather specific functions of life situations. Most children will deceive in certain situations and not in others. Lying, cheating, and stealing as measured by the test situations used in these studies are only very loosely related.

Their conclusions and data have often been cited in the subsequent literature as supporting situational specificity. For example, Mischel's (1968) influential review argued for specificity on the ground that contexts are important and that people have different methods of dealing with different situations.

Unfortunately Hartshorne and May (1928–30), P. E. Vernon (1964), Mischel (1968), and many others, including me (Rushton, 1976), had seriously overinterpreted the results as implying that there was not enough cross-situational consistency to make the concept of traits very useful. This, however, turned out to be wrong. By focusing on correlations of 0.20 and 0.30 between any two measures, a misleading impression is created. A more accurate picture is obtained by examining the predictability achieved from a number of measures. This is because the randomness in any one measure (error and specificity variance) is averaged out over several measures, leaving a clearer view of what a person's true behavior is like. Correlations of 0.50 and 0.60 based on aggregated measures support the view that there is cross-situational consistency in altruistic and honest behavior.

Further evidence for this conclusion is found in Hartshorne and May's data. Examination of the relationships between the battery of altruism tests and batteries concerned with honesty, self-control, persistence, and moral knowledge suggested a factor of general moral character (see, e.g., Hartshorne et al., 1930: 230, Table 32). Maller (1934) was one of the first to note this. Using Spearman's tetrad difference technique, Maller isolated a common factor in the intercorrelations of the character tests of honesty, altruism, self-control, and persistence. Subsequently, Burton (1963) reanalyzed the Hartshorne and May data and found a general factor that accounted for 35-40 percent of common variance.

As Eysenck (1970), among others, has repeatedly pointed out, failures to take account of the necessity to average across a number of exemplars in order to see consistency led to the widespread and erroneous view that moral behavior is almost completely situation specific. This, in turn, led students of moral development to neglect research aimed at discovering the origins of general moral "traits". The fact that, judging from the aggregated correlational data, moral traits do exist, and, moreover, appear to develop early in life, poses a considerable challenge to developmental research.

The Principle of Aggregation

The argument presented for the existence of moral traits applies, of course, to other personality traits and the ways of assessing them. Focusing on correlations between just two items or situations can lead to major errors of interpretation. The more accurate assessment is to use a *principle of aggregation* and average across a number of measures. As mentioned, this is because the randomness in any one measure (error and specificity variance) is averaged out over several measures, leaving a clearer view of underlying relationships.

Perhaps the most familiar illustration of the effect of aggregation is the rule in educational and personality testing that the reliability of an instrument increases as the number of items increases. For example, single items on the Stanford-Binet IQ test only correlate about 0.15; subtests based on four or five items correlate around 0.30 or 0.40, but the aggregated battery of items that make up the performance subscale correlates around 0.80 with the battery of items that make up the verbal subscale.

One of the earliest illustrations of the principle of aggregation is the so-called "personal equation" in astronomy. In 1795, Maskelyne, the head of the Greenwich observatory, discharged an otherwise capable assistant because he recorded transits of stars across a vertical hairline in the telescope about half a second "too late." Maskelyne estimated the error of his assistant's measurements by comparing them to his own observations, which he naturally assumed to be correct. An account of these facts in a Greenwich observatory report was noted by a German astronomer, Bessel, some decades later, and led him to test astronomers against each other, with the result that no two agreed precisely on the time of a transit. Clearly, the only sensible estimate of a star's transit across the hairline was some average of many observations, not one.

Researchers in the psychometric tradition had long made the argument for aggregation. An early paper by Spearman (1910:273-74) on the proper use of correlation coefficients contains the following observations:

> It is the superposed accident (measurement error) that the present paper attempts to eliminate, herein following the custom of all sciences, one that appears to be an indispensable preliminary to getting at nature's laws. This elimination of the accidents is quite analogous to, and serves just the same purpose as, the ordinary process of "taking means" or "smoothing curves."

> The method is as follows. Let each individual be measured several times with regard to any characteristic to be compared with another.

The principle of aggregation is applied in Figure 2.1 to an aggression questionnaire where correlations of stability increase as a function of the number

Figure 2.1: Relation Between Number of Aggressive Items and Predictability of Other Aggressive Occasions

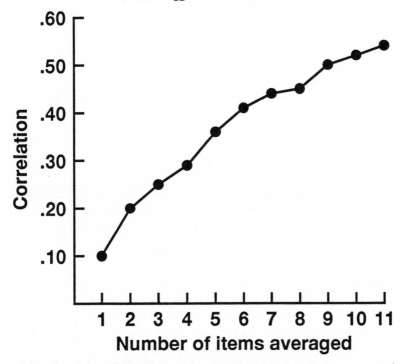

As the number of items being correlated increases from 1 to 7 to 11, the corresponding predictabilities increase from 0.10 to 0.44 to 0.54. From Rushton & Erdle (1987, p. 88, Figure 1). Copyright 1987 by the British Psychological Society. Reprinted with permission.

of items involved. Clearly, if the goal is to predict aggressiveness, aggregated estimates provide increased utility. Similar results occur with group differences. The percentage of variance accounted for by sex differences in the aggression data increase from 1 to 3 to 8 percent as the number of questionnaire items increase from 1 to 5 to 23. Parallel results occur when age and socioeconomic status differences are examined. When age, sex, and SES are combined, the Multiple R increases from an average of 0.18 for single items to 0.39 for the 23 items.

Behavioral Consistency

Unfortunately, Spearman's advice has rarely been taken in some areas of psychology. Psychologists interested in behavioral development have often assessed constructs using only a single measure. It is not surprising, therefore, that relationships involving these constructs have been weak. When multiple measures of each construct are used, relationships become more substantial.

In a series of studies that helped return personality research from a social learning to a trait perspective, Epstein (1977, 1979, 1980) had students complete daily check lists of their feelings and the situations they found themselves in. He found that across several kinds of data the stability coefficients increased from an average of 0.27 for day to day consistency to an average of 0.73 for week to week consistency. Figure 2.2 shows how the stability coefficients increase over time in the aggregated categories.

Thus, daily fluctuations of happy or unhappy moods cohered into typical mood dispositions when measured over longer time periods. Similarly for social contacts, recorded heart rates, and reported somatic and psychosomatic symptoms, the aggregated correlations were over 0.90 for a 14-day aggregate. Also, the increased stability of "situations" with time suggests that the circumstances people find themselves in reflect the choices they have made as a function of their personality.

The decades-long debate over the consistency of personality and the existence of character traits has now been settled. Perhaps the debate should never have occurred. But hindsight is nearly always perfect and many notable researchers had been sufficiently misled by the low correlations across single items of behavior to doubt the value of the trait construct (Rushton, Brainerd, & Pressley, 1983; Epstein & O'Brien, 1985).

Judges' Ratings

One traditionally important source of data has been the judgments and ratings of people made by their teachers and peers. In recent years, judges' ratings have been much maligned on the ground that they are little more than "erroneous constructions of the perceiver." This pervasive view had led to a disenchantment with the use of ratings. The main empirical reason that is cited

Figure 2.2: Stability of Individual Differences as a Function of Number of Days of Measurement

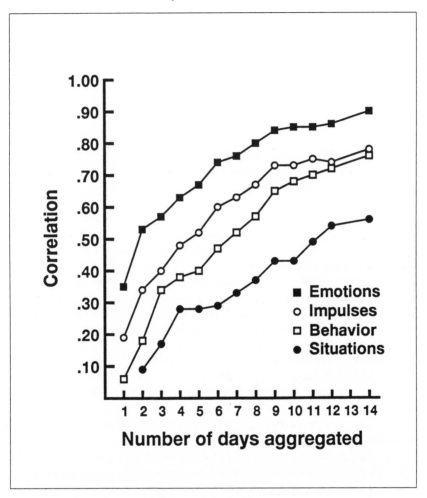

As more measurement days are aggregated people become more predictable. Adapted from Epstein (1977, p. 88, Figure 1).

for rejecting rating methods is that judges' ratings only correlate, on the average, 0.20 to 0.30. However, it is questionable that correlations between two judges' ratings are stable and representative. The validity of judgments increases as the number of judges becomes larger.

Galton (1908) provided an early demonstration from a cattle exhibition where 800 visitors judged the weight of an ox. He found that the individual estimates were distributed in such a way that 50 percent fell between plus or minus three percent of the middlemost value that was itself within one percent of the real value. Galton likened the results to the votes given in a democracy where, with the reservation that the voters be versed in the issues, the *vox populi* was correct. Shortly thereafter, K. Gordon (1924) had subjects order a series of objects by weight. When the number of subjects making the judgment increased from 1 to 5 to 50, the corresponding validities increased from 0.41 to 0.68 to 0.94.

In everyday life, similar averaging techniques are used in subjective decision-making situations. For example, the reliability of decisions about to whom prizes should be awarded for cooking, handicrafts, wine making, physical beauty, and so on is enhanced by averaging the decisions of several judges. This procedure is also routine in forms of athletic competition where performance criteria are partially subjective (e.g., diving, gymnastics). When gradation in qualities to be discriminated are fine, the only fair procedure is to obtain many judgments.

Longitudinal Stability

The question of cross-situational consistency becomes a question about longitudinal consistency when the time dimension is introduced. To what extent, over both time and situation, do a person's behaviors stem from enduring traits of character? When studies measure individual differences by aggregating over many different assessments, longitudinal stability is usually found. But when single measurements or other less reliable techniques are used, longitudinal stability is less marked.

Intelligence is the trait with the strongest stability over time. The ordering of an individual relative to his or her age cohort over the teenage and adult years shows typical correlations of 0.62 to 0.94 over 7 to 40 years (Brody, 1992). The trend is for the correlations to decline as the period of time between administrations of the test increases. But the correlations can be increased by further aggregation. For example, the combined score from tests administered at ages 10, 11, and 12 correlate 0.96 with a combined score from tests administered at ages 17 and 18 (Pinneau, 1961). This latter finding suggests that there was initially no change at all in an individual's score relative to his or her cohorts over the high school years.

Intelligence in infancy, however, is either slightly less stable or somewhat less easy to measure. The correlations between a composite of tests taken from 12 to 24 months predicts the composite at ages 17 and 18 around 0.50 (Pinneau, 1961). Newer techniques based on infant habituation and recognition memory (the infant's response to a novel or familiar stimulus) made in the first year of life predict later IQ assessed between 1 and 8 years of age with a weighted (for sample size) average of between 0.36 and 0.45 (McCall & Carriger, 1993).

The stability of personality has been demonstrated over several 30-year longitudinal studies. To summarize these, Costa and McCrae (1994:21) quote William James (1890/1981), saying that once adulthood has been reached, personality is "set like plaster." At younger ages, personality stability was demonstrated by Jack Block (1971, 1981) in work where the principle of aggregation was strictly adhered to. For about 170 individuals data were first obtained in the 1930s when the subjects were in their early teens. Further data were gathered when the subjects were in their late teens, in their mid-30s, and in their mid-40s. The archival data so generated were enormously wide-ranging and often not in a form permitting of direct quantification. Block systematized the data by employing clinical psychologists to study individual dossiers and to rate the subject's personality using the Q-sort procedure—a set of descriptive statements such as "is anxious," which can be sorted into piles that indicate how representative the statement is of the subject. To ensure independence, the materials for each subject were carefully segregated by age level, and no psychologist rated the materials for the same subject at more than one time period. The assessments by the different raters (usually three for each dossier) were found to agree with one another to a significant degree, and they were averaged to form an overall description of the subject at that age.

Block (1971, 1981) found personality stability across the ages tested. Even the simple correlations between Q-sort items over the 30 years between adolescence and the mid-40s provided evidence for stability. Correlations indicating stability were, for example, for the male sample: "genuinely values intellectual and cognitive matters," 0.58; "is self-defeating," 0.46; and "has fluctuating moods," 0.40; for the female sample, "is an interesting, arresting person," 0.44; "aesthetically reactive," 0.41; and "is cheerful," 0.36. When the whole range of variables for each individual was correlated over 30 years, the mean correlation was 0.31. When typologies were created, the relationships became even more substantial.

Using self-reports instead of judgments made by others, Conley (1984) analyzed test-retest data from 10 to 40 years for major dimensions of personality such as extraversion, neuroticism, and impulsivity. The correlations in different studies ranged from 0.26 to 0.84 for periods extending from 10 to 40 years, with an average of about 0.45 for the 40-year period. Overall the personality traits were only slightly less consistent over time than were measures of intelligence (0.67, in this study).

Longitudinal stability has been cross-validated using different procedures. Thus, one method is used to assess personality at Time 1 (e.g., ratings made by others) and a quite different method at Time 2 (e.g., behavioral observations). Olweus (1979), for example, reported correlations of 0.81 over a 1-year time period between teacher ratings of the aggressive behavior of children and frequency count observations of the actual aggressive behavior. Conley

(1985) reported correlations of about 0.35 between ratings made by a person's acquaintances as they were about to get married and self-reports made some 20 years later.

In a 22-year study of the development of aggression, Eron (1987) found that children rated as aggressive by their peers when they were 8 years old were rated as aggressive by a different set of peers 10 years later and were 3 times more likely to have been entered on police record by the time they were 19 than those not so rated. By age 30, these children were more likely to have engaged in a syndrome of antisocial behavior including criminal convictions, traffic violations, child and spouse abuse, and physical aggressiveness outside the family. Moreover, the stability of aggression was found to exist across three generations, from grandparents to children to grandchildren. The 22-year stability of aggressive behavior is 0.50 for men and 0.35 for women.

Also in the 22-year data, early ratings of prosocial behavior were positively related to later prosocial behavior and negatively related to later antisocial behavior. Children rated as concerned about interpersonal relations at age 8 had higher occupational and educational attainment as well as low aggression, social success, and good mental health, whereas aggression at age 8 predicted social failure, psychopathology, aggression, and low educational and occupational success. In all of these analyses, social class was held constant. Eron's (1987) data suggested that aggression and prosocial behavior are at two ends of a continuum (see Figure 2.3).

The general conclusion is that once people reach the age of 30 there is little change in the major dimensions of personality. McCrae and Costa (1990; Costa & McCrae, 1992) reviewed six longitudinal studies published between 1978 and 1992, including two of their own. The six had quite different samples and rationales but came to the same conclusions. Basic tendencies typically stabilized somewhere between 21 and 30. Retest measures for both self-reports and ratings made by others are typically about 0.70. Moreover, anything these dimensions affect stabilizes as well, such as self-concept, skills, interests, and coping strategies.

Predicting Behavior

Although a great deal of effort has gone into refining paper and pencil and other techniques for measuring attitudes, personality, and intelligence, relatively little attention has been given to the adequacy of measurements on the behavioral end of the relationship. Whereas the person end of the person-behavior relationship has often been measured by multi-item scales, the behavior to be predicted has often comprised a single act.

Fishbein and Ajzen (1974) proposed that multiple-act criteria be used on the behavioral side. Using a variety of attitude scales to measure religious attitudes and a multiple-item religious behavior scale, they found that atti-

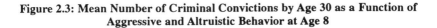

Figure 2.3: Mean Number of Criminal Convictions by Age 30 as a Function of
Aggressive and Altruistic Behavior at Age 8

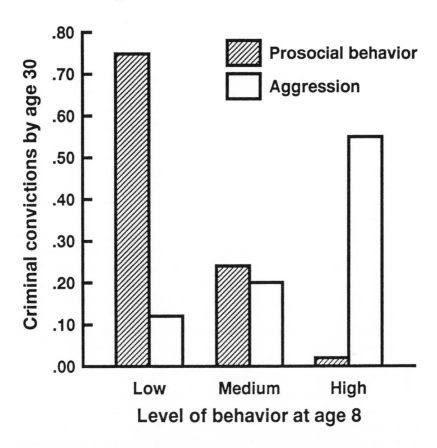

Both boys and girls rated as aggressive by their peers at 8 years old are three times more likely to
have a police record by age 30 than those not so rated. Alternatively, those rated as high in prosocial
behavior at age 8 grow up to be less criminal than those rated as low in prosocial behavior. From
Eron (1987, p. 440, Figure 2). Copyright 1987 by the American Psychological Association.
Reprinted with permission.

tudes were related to multiple-act criteria but had no consistent relationship to
single-act criteria. Whereas the various attitude scales had a mean correlation
with single behaviors ranging from 0.14 to 0.19, their correlations with aggregated behavioral measures ranged from 0.70 to 0.90.

In a similar paper to Fishbein and Ajzen's, Jaccard (1974) carried out an
investigation to determine whether the dominance scales of the California
Psychological Inventory and the Personality Research Form would predict

self-reported dominance behaviors better in the aggregate than they would at the single-item level. The results were in accord with the aggregation expectations. Whereas both personality scales had a mean correlation of 0.20 with individual behaviors, the aggregated correlations were 0.58 and 0.64.

Comparable observations were made by Eaton (1983) who assessed activity level in three- and four-year olds using single versus multiple actometers attached to the children's wrists as the criterion and teachers' and parents' ratings of the children's activity level as the predictors. The ratings predicted activity scores from single actometers relatively weakly (0.33) while predicting those aggregated across multiple actometers comparatively well (0.69).

One Problem with Experimental Studies

Failures to aggregate dependent variables in experimental situations may produce conclusions about the relative modifiability of behavior that may be incorrect. For example, with respect to social development, it is considered well established that observational learning from demonstrators has powerful effects on social behavior (Bandura, 1969, 1986). These findings have prompted governmental concern about possible inadvertent learning from television. Concerning intellectual development, it is equally well known that intervention programs designed to boost children's intelligence, some of them employing observational learning, have achieved only modest success (Brody, 1992; Locurto, 1991).

The apparent difference in the relative malleability of social and intellectual development has been explained in various ways. One leading interpretation is that intellectual development is controlled by variables that are "structural" and, therefore, minimally susceptible to learning, whereas social development is controlled by variables that are "motivational" and, therefore, more susceptible to learning. An analysis of the dependent variables used in the two types of studies, however, suggests an interpretation based on the aggregation principle.

In observational learning studies, a single dependent variable is typically used to measure the behavior; for example, the number of punches delivered to a Bo-Bo doll in the case of aggression (Bandura, 1969) or the number of tokens donated to a charity in the case of altruism (Rushton, 1980). In intellectual training studies, however, multiple-item dependent variables such as standardized intelligence tests are typically used. Throughout this discussion it has been stressed that the low reliability of nonaggregated measures can mask strong underlying relationships between variables. In the case of learning studies, it can have essentially the opposite effect. It is always easier to produce a change in some trait as a consequence of learning when a single, less stable measure of the trait is taken than when more stable, multiple measures are taken. This fact may explain why social learning studies of altruism have generally been more successful than training studies of intellectual development.

Mental Ability Tests

Intelligence has been the most researched individual difference variable since Galton (1869). In 1879, in Leipzig, Wilhelm Wundt (1832–1920) established the first psychology laboratory. He used many of the same measures as Galton although he was interested in the structure of the mind common to everybody. James McKeen Cattell (1860–1944), an American studying with Wundt, wanted to examine individual differences but was unable to interest Wundt. So, after receiving his doctorate, Cattell moved to London for a postdoctoral period with Galton and went on to become the world's first professor of psychology (at the University of Pennsylvania) and then head of the psychology department at Columbia University. He was one of the founders of the American Psychological Association and it was he who, in 1890, coined the term *mental test* to describe the series of sensory and reaction-time tasks that were burgeoning during this time.

The main outcome of the Galton-Cattell effort was negative. A study by one of Cattell's own graduate students reported that the various mental tests failed to correlate either with each other or with academic grades (Wissler, 1901). Even though several flaws can be noted about this study, including a failure to aggregate (Jensen, 1980a), it signaled the end of the Galtonian approach for several decades. Instead, the measurement of intelligence went off in a very different direction.

In 1904 the French Ministry of Education wanted to identify slow learners who needed help so they commissioned Alfred Binet (1857–1911) and Théophile Simon (1873–1961) to construct a test that would screen low-achieving students. They reasoned that a good test should include increasingly difficult items that older children could answer more easily than younger children. The test should tap higher mental functions, such as comprehension and imagination.

In 1908, Binet produced a second version of his scale with an increased number of test items. It was found that, on average, a three-year-old child can point to nose, eyes, or mouth; can repeat sentences of six syllables; and can give his family name. At the age of four he knows his sex, he can name certain objects shown to him, such as a key, knife, or penny, and can indicate which of two lines, 5 cm and 6 cm in length respectively, is the longer. At the age of five, the child can indicate the heavier of two cubes, one weighing 3 g and the other 12 g; he can copy a square, using pen and ink; and he can count four pennies. At the age of six he knows right from left as shown by indicating right hand and left ear; he can repeat sentences of 16 syllables; and he knows morning from afternoon. At the age of seven he knows the number of fingers on each hand, or both hands, without counting them; he can copy a diamond, using pen and ink; and he can describe pictures as seen.

The test worked. It identified the retarded and correlated with expected indicators of intelligence such as school marks, teacher and peer evaluations, and ease of trainability; the test was soon introduced to America. In 1910, Henry H. Goddard found the scales had predictive accuracy at his Vineland, New Jersey school for feeble-minded children. In 1916, Louis Terman and his associates at Stanford University adapted the test for American schoolchildren and established norms for average performance. The original Binet-Simon test thus became the Stanford-Binet test. The 1916 version was modified in 1937, 1960, 1972, and 1986, and the norms for average performance were updated. It became a standard by which all later intelligence tests have been judged.

In 1917, the United States entered the First World War and Robert Yerkes of Harvard, then president of the American Psychological Association, organized psychologists to help the war effort. America's leading psychometricians, including Henry Goddard and Louis Terman, began to develop group-administered tests to help select recruits. Two group tests were devised, Alpha and Beta. The Alpha was a verbal test designed for literate people, containing questions in such areas as arithmetical reasoning, number series completion, and analogies—categories similar to those found in the Stanford-Binet and many present-day intelligence tests. The Beta, intended for use with illiterate recruits, contained similar questions, but in purely pictorial form. Altogether nearly 2 million army recruits took one or the other of these tests.

Comparisons based on these data were published as an official report amounting to 890 pages (Yerkes, 1921) as well as a book (Yoakum & Yerkes, 1920). For the comparison of blacks and whites, the former included all who showed any physical evidence of Negroid ancestry, that is, all hybrids. Also, all were born in the United States, with English their native language. Of those scoring sufficiently high to be allowed into the army, a disproportionate number of blacks scored C- to D-, low average to inferior, whereas a disproportionate number of whites scored C+ to A+, average to superior.

Marked differences occurred between different states, with the largely urbanized northern states producing higher scores than the more rural south, a difference attributed to the better educational facilities in the north. Like whites, blacks also did better in the north. A special comparison was made of the races in five northern states versus four southern states. Although the northern blacks still did not score as high as the whites, their scores were distributed in a more similar pattern.

The results of this undertaking set off the first public controversy about intelligence testing. Overall, the average mental age of all army recruits was 13, meaning that the average 13-year-old could pass the tests, but not the average 12-year-old. The data also revealed that immigrant groups, on the average, scored lower than native-born Americans, and that immigrants from southern and eastern Europe scored lower than those from northern and western Europe. These data were made much of by Carl Brigham (1923), a professor of psychology at Princeton who, in his book *A Study of American Intelligence,* advocated immigration controls to keep the American gene pool from deteriorating. Yerkes wrote the foreword to Brigham's book.

The controversy over the test results began the modern version of the nature-nurture debate. Clearly test scores were not 100 percent determined by innate ability; the question became whether environmental factors alone could account for the pattern of distributions. On the environmental side, biases and problems inherent in the tests began to be identified. For example, some items

Figure 2.4: Typical Intelligence Test Items

1. *Digit span forward.*   Repeat a series of three to nine digits, after hearing them spoken at the rate of one digit per second.

2. *Digit span backward.*   Repeat three to nine digits backward, that is, in reverse order of presentation.

3. *Picture arrangement.*   Arrange a haphazard order of cartoon pictures in a row to make a logical story.

4. *Verbal analogies.*   Complete the analogy. Cat is to kitten as dog is to:

    beast   bark   puppy   chase

5. *Logical reasoning.*   In a race the dog runs faster than the horse, which is slower than the cow, and the pig runs faster than the dog. Which one finishes last?

6. *Number series.*   Write the number that most logically continues the series.   35, 28, 21, 14, ____

7. *Figure matrices.*   Indicate which alternative most logically fills the blank space.

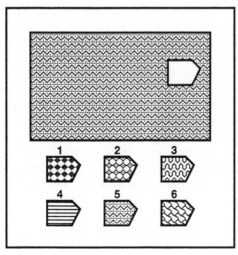

depended on highly specific cultural knowledge, a flaw that was particularly disadvantageous to recent immigrants, and those outside the educational mainstream. Moreover, testing conditions had not been standardized; for some, the tests were administered in cramped and noisy conditions. On the genetic side, adoption and twin studies for systematically examining the relative roles of heredity and environment in intelligence were begun.

Dozens of publishing firms sprang up to service industrial and clinical needs as well as educational ones. Measures of specific aptitudes and personality as well as general intelligence were produced. In 1926 the Scholastic Aptitude Test (SAT) came into being for college admissions. In 1939 David Wechsler published what was to become the Wechsler Adult Intelligence Scale (WAIS), the most widely used individually administered intelligence test for adults, and in 1949 he published the Wechsler Intelligence Scale for Children (WISC). The professionalized testing industry generated sophisticated new techniques for examining the reliability and validity of tests. The introduction of machine-scoring techniques greatly facilitated research and development.

Diverse items have become available and a large technical literature has grown on the characteristics of good items (Jensen, 1980a). They can be administered individually or given to many people simultaneously. On group tests, to make scoring easier, the subject is asked to select the correct answer from the several alternatives provided. Figure 2.4 illustrates typical item types from both individually and group administered tests (see Jensen, 1980a, for a full range). Ideally, items should not take too long to solve as there is only a limited time for testing and many must be given. Also, items must be so devised as to have a single correct answer. Preferably, items should not involve specific knowledge such as "How far is it between San Francisco and Los Angeles?" so much as problem solving where all the elements are equally known or equally unknown to the subjects. One exception is vocabulary where the subject may be asked to explain the meaning of words going from very easy and familiar words like *summer* and *strange* to more rare and difficult words like *adumbrate* and *cacophony*.

One reason for thinking that items such as those in Figure 2.4 tap intelligence is the observation that children grow more intelligent in an absolute sense as they grow older. The average ten-year-old is brighter than the average four-year-old, and can pass more test items. Thus, mental age is an index of mental ability, and in relation to chronological age gives some indication of the degree to which a child is advanced or retarded. This was the original concept on which mental testing was based. Indeed the equation for IQ, or the intelligence quotient is:

$$IQ = \frac{MA}{CA} \times 100$$

where MA stands for mental age and CA stands for chronological age and the 100 is introduced to get rid of the decimal point.

Figure 2.5: The Normal Distribution

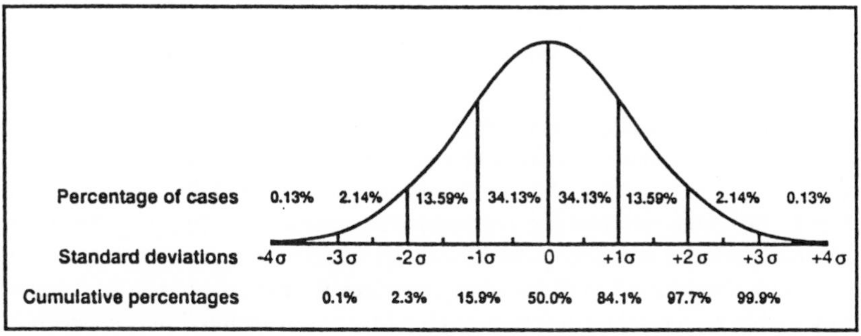

Areas (in percentages) under the normal curve and the baseline of the curve are scaled to standard deviations and cumulative percentages

The equation for IQ is no longer used. Because test scores for large numbers of representative people are more or less normally distributed (Figure 2.5) scores from almost any system can be converted into a standard score. For convenience the average IQ is set at 100 with a standard deviation of of 15.

Spearman's g

Spearman (1927) discovered that a general factor of mental ability (symbolized g) exists in any and every large collection of diverse tests of cognitive performance, regardless of its specific information content, sensory modality, or form of response. He posited that the g factor reflects whatever it is that causes individual differences in performance.

The degree to which various tests are correlated with g, or are "g-loaded," can be determined by factor analysis, a statistical procedure for grouping items. Differences in g loading, however, are not predictable from superficial features of the item. Other than performing a factor analysis, the best clue to an item's g loading is the degree of its cognitive demand. For example, backward digit span (Item 2, Figure 2.3) has a higher g loading than forward digit span (Item 1). Other highly g-loaded tests are verbal analogies (Item 4), series completions (Item 6), and figure matrices (Item 7). Several of these last items (#7), involving two-dimensional perceptual analogies with both horizontal and vertical transformations, were combined into a g-saturated test, the Raven's Progressive Matrices by Lionel Penrose, the British geneticist, and John Raven, a British psychologist, and student of Spearman (Penrose & Raven, 1936). It has become the best known and most researched of all "culture-reduced" tests (Raven & Court, 1989).

Most conventional tests of mental ability are highly *g*-loaded although they usually measure some admixture of other factors in addition to *g*, such as verbal, spatial, and memory abilities, as well as acquired information of a scholastic nature (Brody, 1992). Test scores with the *g* factor statistically removed have virtually no predictive power for scholastic performance. Hence, it is the *g* factor that is the "active ingredient." The predictive validity of *g* applies also to performance in nearly all types of jobs. Occupations differ in their complexity and *g* demands as much as do mental tests, so as the complexity of a job increases, the better cognitive ability predicts performance on it (e.g., managers and professions 0.42 to 0.87, sales clerks and vehicle operators 0.27 to 0.37; see Hunter, 1986, Table 1; Hunter & Hunter, 1984).

Gottfredson (1986, 1987) summarized meta-analyses of decades of personnel selection research and showed the following: (a) intelligence tests predict performance in training and on the job in all kinds of work; (b) job performance is more correlated with test performance in higher-level, more complex jobs than in lower-level ones; (c) the relation of tested intelligence to job performance is linear, meaning that there is no threshold above which higher levels of intelligence are not associated with higher mean levels of job performance; (d) it is almost entirely the *g* factor in psychometric tests that accounts for their validity for predicting job performance; (e) the predictive validity of intelligence tests remains largely the same but that of experience fades among workers with higher mean levels of experience; (f) intelligence tests predict job performance even after controlling for differences in job knowledge; and (g) intelligence tests predict job performance equally well for blacks and whites, whether performance is measured objectively or subjectively.

Decision-Making Speed

Convincing proof for the pervasiveness of *g* comes from recent work on brain efficiency in decision making. The Galton-Cattell type of tasks found lacking at the beginning of the century are again in the forefront. The tasks are simple, calling on very elementary cognitive processes in which there is little or no intellectual content. All subjects can easily perform the tasks, the only source of reliable individual differences being the speed (measured in milliseconds) with which the subject responds. These have been shown to be highly correlated with intelligence as measured by traditional IQ tests (Brody 1992).

One type of reaction time apparatus, described by Jensen (1993), is shown in Figure 2.6. Covers are placed on the console, exposing either one, two, four, or eight of the light button combinations. In the "simple reaction time" task (shown in A), a single light is exposed and when it comes on the subject moves his hand to switch it off. This response normally takes around half a second. In the more complicated "choice reaction time" task (shown in B), all the light buttons are exposed and when one of them comes on, the subject has

Figure 2.6: Subject's Response Console for Decision Time Studies

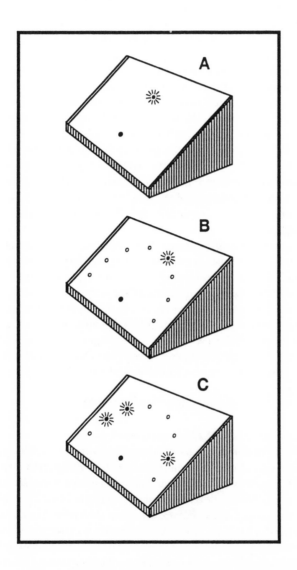

Console A is for simple reaction time, B is for choice reaction time, and C is for odd-man-out reaction time. The black dot in the lower center of each panel is the home button. The open circles, 15 cm from the home button, are green under-lighted push buttons. In conditions A and B, only one green push button lights up on each trial; in C, three push buttons light up simultaneously on each trial, with unequal distances between them, the remotest one from the other two being the odd-man-out, which the subject must touch. From Jensen (1993, p. 53, Figure 1). Copyright 1993 by Ablex Publishing Corporation. Reprinted with permission.

to "choose" which one to turn off, and the reaction time takes a little longer. In the "oddman out" task (shown in C), a still more complex version, three lights come on of which two are close together and one stands apart. The subject has to judge which is the light that stands apart and switch it off. It is more difficult than the simpler reaction time tasks and typically takes about twice as long, but still averages less than a second. Reaction time is the time taken to get off the home button after one of the lights goes on.

Another speed of information processing task that is correlated with g is known as "inspection time." It is the time that a visual or auditory stimulus must be displayed before a person is able to make a simple discrimination, such as which of two lines is the longer, when one line is double the length of the other. Inspection time is typically less than one-tenth of a second. Nonetheless it correlates with the g factor extracted from ability tests between 0.30 and 0.50, for a very wide range of ages, from childhood to old age, with longer intervals being required by people with lower levels of ability (Kranzler & Jensen, 1989).

It is interesting to ask why these reaction time and elementary cognitive tasks correlate with measures of intelligence when the earlier Galton-Cattell measures did not? One answer includes the principle of aggregation. In the reaction time task shown in Figure 2.6, 15 trials are given at each level of 1, 2, 4, or 8 light buttons of complexity. Moreover the multi-trial information-processing tasks are themselves often combined in aggregations, thus increasing still further the correlations with multi-item IQ tests. In Wissler's (1901) negative review, simple reaction times had been correlated with academic grades (not IQ tests) and then in a restricted range of subjects.

Intelligence and Brain Size

A threefold increase in the relative size of the hominid brain has occurred in the last 4 million years. It is reasonable to hypothesize that bigger brains evolved to increase intelligence. Passingham (1982) reported evidence in favor of this hypothesis using a visual discrimination learning task to measure the speed with which children and other mammals abstracted such rules as "pick the same object each time to get food." More intelligent children, assessed by standardized IQ tests, learn faster than those less intelligent, and mammals with larger brains learn faster than those with smaller brains (i.e. chimp > rhesus monkey > spider monkey > squirrel monkey > marmoset > cat > gerbil > rat = squirrel).

Georges Cuvier (1769–1832) may have been the first to formally consider that brain size proportional to body size was the determinant of intelligence across species. Galton (1888b) was the first to quantify the relationship among humans. He reported that students at Cambridge University who earned top grades averaged a 2 1/2 to 5 percent larger head volume (length x width x height of head) than others. Soon after, K. Pearson (1906) re-examined the relationship, using the newly developed correlation coefficient, and found a small positive correlation. This has remained the general observation with correlations typically ranging from 0.10 to 0.30 (Jensen & Sinha, 1993; Wickett, Vernon & Lee, 1994; Van Valen, 1974).

Table 2.2 summarizes the results from 32 studies of the relation between head size and mental ability in normal samples. Clinical samples have been excluded. The most representative or average correlation has been reported from those studies providing multiple correlations (e.g. by age and sex or by adjusting for body size). Corrections for body size have typically not been included because many studies did not report this statistic although occasionally they have been used to control for age effects. Double entries have been eliminated, particularly those emanating from the Collaborative Perinatal Project (Broman, Nichols, Shaughnessy, & Kennedy, 1987). Also not included in Table 2.2 are typological studies showing that mentally defective children have smaller heads than children of normal intelligence (Broman et al., 1987), while gifted and superior children have larger ones (Fisch, Bilek, Horrobin, & Chang, 1976; Terman, 1926/1959: 152).

The 32 studies are categorized into 3 sections. Section A sets out the results of 13 studies that took external head measurements from a total of 43,166 children and adolescents and correlated these with mental ability estimated by ratings, school grades, and standardized tests. The correlations ranged from 0.11 to 0.35 with an unweighted mean of 0.23 (when weighted by sample size, 0.21). The relationship was found in boys and girls, in whites from Australia, Europe, and the United States, in blacks from the United States, and in Amerindians from Guatemala.

Section B sets out the results from 15 studies using external head measurements from a total of 6,437 adults with intelligence estimated by ratings, university grades, and standardized tests. The correlations ranged from 0.03 to 0.39 with an unweighted mean of 0.15 (when weighted by sample size, also 0.15). The samples included both sexes, whites from Europe, Canada, and the United States, and Amerindians and Orientals from North America.

The correlations in Section A and B are low. This is partly because measuring head size by tape and ignoring skull thickness is not a perfect measure of brain size and also because intelligence tests are not perfect measures of mental ability. It is possible to correct the correlations for some of these unreliabilities. In his review Van Valen (1974) estimated that the true correlation between head size and intelligence is about 0.30. This was confirmed by R. Lynn (1990a) in three studies of 9- and 10-year-olds in schools in Northern Ireland and England measuring head perimeter by tape and intelligence by standardized tests. Before correction for attenuation due to measurement error, R. Lynn's correlations were between 0.18 and 0.26; after correction they ranged from 0.21 to 0.30.

TABLE 2.2
Intelligence and Brain Size

Source	Sample	Head measurement	Test	r
A. Children and adolescents by external head measurements				
Pearson (1906)	4,386 British children (2,198 boys, 2,188 girls) aged 3 to 20; standardized to age 12	Length	Teachers' estimate	.11
Murdock & Sullivan (1923)	595 American children aged 6 to 17; standardized by age and sex	Perimeter	IQ tests	.22
Estabrooks (1928)	251 American children of North European ancestry (102 boys, 149 girls) aged 6 years	Capacity	Binet	.19
Porteus (1937)	200 white Australian children	Perimeter	Porteus Maze	.20
Klein et al. (1972)	170 Guatemalan Indian children aged 3 to 6	Perimeter	Knowledge tests standardized with age-sex groups	.28
W. A. Weinberg et al. (1974)	334 white American boys aged 8 to 9 years	Perimeter	WISC	.35
Broman et al. (1987)	18, 907 black American boys and girls aged 7 years	Perimeter	WISC	.19
Broman et al. (1987)	17, 241 white American boys and girls aged 7 years	Perimeter	WISC	.24
R. Lynn (1990a)	310 Irish boys and girls aged 9 to 10	Perimeter	PMAT	.18
R. Lynn (1990a)	205 Irish children aged 9 years	Perimeter	Matrices	.26
R. Lynn (1990a)	91 English children aged 9 years	Perimeter	Matrices	.26
Osborne (1992)	224 white American children (106 boys, 118 girls) aged 13 to 17; controls for height and weight	Capacity	Basic	.29
Osborne (1992)	252 black American children (84 boys, 168 girls) aged 13 to 17; controls for height and weight	Capacity	Basic	.28
Summary of A	*Number of Studies:* 13 *Range of r:* .11 - .35 *Mean r:* .23			
B. Adults by external head measurements				
Pearson (1906)	1,011 British male university students	Length	Grades	.11
Pearl (1906)	935 Bavarian male soldiers	Perimeter	Officers' ratings	.14
Reid & Mulligan (1923)	449 Scottish male medical students	Capacity	Grades	.08
Sommerville (1924)	105 white American male university students	Capacity	Thorndike	.08
Wrzosek (1931; cited in Henneberg et al., 1985)	160 Polish male medical students	Capacity	Baley's Polish language IQ test	.14
Schreider (1968)	80 Otomi Indians from Mexico of unspecified sex	Perimeter	Form Board	.39
Schreider (1968)	158 French peasants of unspecified sex	Perimeter	Matrices	.23
Passingham (1979)	415 English villagers (212 men, 203 women) aged 18 to 75	Capacity	WAIS	.13
Susanne (1979)	2,071 Belgian male conscripts	Perimeter	Matrices	.19
Henneberg et al. (1985)	302 Polish medical students (151 men, 151 women) aged 18 to 30 years.	Capacity	Baley's Polish language IQ test	.14

Table 2.2 (cont.)

Source	Sample	Head measurement	Test	r
Bogaert & Rushton (1989)	216 Canadian men and women university students, adjusted for sex	Perimeter	MAB	.14
Rushton (1992c)	73 Oriental Canadian men and women university students	Perimeter	MAB	.14
Rushton (1992c)	211 white Canadian men and women university students	Perimeter	MAB	.21
Reed & Jensen (1993)	211 white American men college students	Capacity	Various	.03
Wickett et al. (1994)	40 white Canadian women university students	Perimeter	MAB	.11
Summary of B	*Number of Studies:* 15			
	Range of r: .03 - .39			
	Mean r: .15			
C. Adults by magnetic resonance imaging				
Willerman et al. (1991)	40 white American university students (20 men, 20 women); corrected for sex, body size and the extended IQ range	MRI	WAIS	.35
Andreasen et al. (1993)	67 white American adults (37 men, 30 women) with a mean age of 38	MRI	WAIS	.38
Raz et al. (1993)	29 white American adults (17 men, 12 women) aged 18 to 78	MRI	CFIT	.43
Wickett et al. (1994)	39 white Canadian women aged 20 to 30 years	MRI	MAB	.40
Summary of C	*Number of Studies:* 4			
	Range of r: .35 - .43			
	Mean r: .39			

Note. CFIT = Culture Free Intelligence Test; MAB = Multidimensional Aptitude Battery; MRI = Magnetic Resonance Imaging; PMAT = Primary Mental Abilities Test; WAIS = Wechsler Adult Intelligence Scale; WISC = Weschsler Intelligence Scale for Children.

The head size-IQ correlations reported in Table 2.2 have been reported separately for each of the three races. In a Canadian study, I found a correlation of r = 0.14 in a sample of 73 Oriental first-year university students and r = 0.21 in a sample of 211 non-Orientals, both samples taken from introductory psychology classes (Rushton, 1992c). For both black and white U.S. teenagers, Osborne (1992) found correlations of 0.28 and 0.29. In the Collaborative Perinatal Project, Broman et al. (1987) found a correlation of 0.24 for 17,000 white 7-year-olds and 0.19 for 19,000 black 7-year-olds. In a follow-up analysis of these data, Jensen and Johnson (in press) showed that the 0.20 head size-IQ correlation existed *within* families. The sibling with the larger head perimeter tended to be the more intelligent sibling, in both the black and the white samples.

Section C sets out the results of 4 studies on 175 adults with brain size estimated by magnetic resonance imaging (MRI) to create, in effect, a 3-dimensional model of the brain in *vivo*. Each of these studies used standardized tests to measure IQ. The correlations ranged from 0.35 to 0.43 with an unweighted mean of 0.39 (when weighted by sample size, also 0.39). These new-technology confirmations of Galton's (1888b) observations make it indisputable that brain size is related to intelligence.

TABLE 2.3
Correlations Between Head Circumference at Different Ages with IQ at 7 Years

| Age | Whites | | | | Blacks | | | |
	Sample size	Circumfer-ence (cm)	SD	r	Sample size	Circumfer-ence (cm)	SD	r
Birth	16,877	34.0	1.5	.13[*]	18,883	33.4	1.7	.12[*]
4 months[a]	15,905	40.9	1.4	.19[*]	17,793	40.4	1.6	.16[*]
1 year	14,724	45.8	1.5	.20[*]	16,786	45.6	1.5	.15[*]
4 years	12,454	50.1	1.5	.21[*]	14,630	49.9	1.6	.16[*]
7 years	16,949	51.5	1.5	.24[*]	18,644	51.2	1.6	.18[*]

Note. Data have been calculated from Broman, Nichols, Shaughnessy & Kennedy (1987; p. 104, Table 6-10; p. 220, Table 9-28; p. 226, Table 9-34; p. 223, Table 9-41; p. 247, Table 9-54).
[a] Contains up to 2 percent of children with damage to central nervous system.
* p<.00001.

The U.S. national Collaborative Perinatal Project (Broman et al., 1987) is worth considering in more detail. Children were followed from conception to the age of 7 years with head circumference measured at birth, 4 months, 1 year, 4 years, and 7 years, and the Bayley Mental and Motor Scales given at 8 months, the Stanford-Binet at 4 years, and the Wechsler at 7 years. For white children, head circumference at birth correlated 0.47 with head circumference at 7 years, and for black children the correlation was 0.39. For both races combined, Bayley scores at 8 months correlated about 0.25 with Wechsler scores at 7 years and the Binet IQ at age 4 correlated 0.62 with the Wechsler at age 7.

Table 2.3. summarizes data I have abstracted from several tables in Broman et al. (1987) after excluding the 2 percent with major neurological disorders, except where reported. For both the black and the white children, the correlations among the head circumference measures at all ages predicted the mental ability scores. As can be seen, the head circumference of white children is greater than that of black children in each of the age categories by a mean of 0.36 cm or approximately 0.2 SD. The greater head size of white children is not a function of greater body size because black children are taller than white children at both 4 and 7 years of age (Broman et al., 1987, Tables 7-8, 8-19). Although not shown in Table 2.3, the three tests of mental ability all favored the white children while the measure of motor ability favored the black children. These topics will be taken up in chapters 6 and 7.

Finally, the relation between brain size and intelligence is supported by the parallels with age. Both brain size and IQ increase during childhood and adolescence and then slowly and finally more quickly decrease. Table 2.3. shows the age trends with head circumference for both black and white children. At autopsy, from birth through childhood, head circumference is related to brain weight between 0.80 and 0.98 (Brandt, 1978; Bray et al., 1969; Cooke, Lucas, Yudkin, & Pryse-Davies, 1977).

In summation, the mean for the 29 head size-IQ correlations (Sections A and B in Table 2.2) is 0.20 (weighted r = 0.18). Although this correlation is not large, accounting for 4 percent of the variance, it is pervasive across numerous samples. Correcting for height and weight in some studies decreased the relationship whereas in others it increased the correlation (Wickett et al., 1994). Correcting for unreliability raises the correlation to about 0.30. Taking the four studies of magnetic resonance imaging, the correlation with intelligence is r = .40. This is the currently best estimate of the relationship between brain size and mental ability.

3

Behavioral Genetics

From an evolutionary point of view, individual differences are the alternative genetic combinations and adaptations that compete through the mechanism of natural selection. A mountain of data has now accumulated showing that genes bias the development of complex social behavior in one direction over alternatives, even of political attitudes and choice of marriage and other social partners. As Turkheimer and Gottesman (1991) proposed, it is time to enshrine $H^2 \neq 0$ as the "first law of behavior genetics" and to argue that $H^2 = 0$ is no longer an interesting null hypothesis.

Methods

The basic assumption of behavior genetic studies is that phenotypic variance in measurements can be partitioned into environmental (E) and genetic (G) components, which combine in an additive manner. A nonadditive interaction term (G x E) allows for combinations of genetic and environmental effects. Symbolically:

Phenotypic variance = G + E + (G x E)

The percentage of phenotypic variance attributable to genetic influences is often referred to as the heritability coefficient and can be represented as H^2. All procedures for estimating genetic influence involve measuring family groups and unrelated people and comparing the resultant correlations with those expected from a genetic hypothesis. Adoption studies and the comparison of twins are the most widely used procedures. In twin studies, monozygotic (MZ) or identical twins are assumed to share 100 percent of their genes and dizygotic (DZ) or fraternal twins are assumed to share, on average, 50 percent of their genes. If the correlation between scores on a trait is higher for the monozygotic than for the dizygotic twins, the difference can be attributed to genetic effects if it is assumed that the environments of each type of twin are roughly equal.

While critics have argued that the twin method is invalid for estimating heritability, detailed empirical work demonstrates the critiques to be of limited importance. For example, in cases where parents and twins misclassify zygosity, the degree of twin similarity on many traits is better predicted by true zygosity (defined by blood and fingerprint analysis) than by social definition. Moreover, when measures of the differences that do exist in the treatment of twins are correlated with personality and other scores, there is no evidence that differences in treatment have any effect (Plomin, DeFries, & McClearn, 1990).

One of the less appreciated aspects of twin studies is the information they also provide about environmental effects. If the raw data are the between-pair and within-pair sibling variances and covariances, then between-sibling mean squares reflect both sibling resemblances and sibling differences, while the within-pairs mean squares reflect only sibling differences. The genetic models are fitted to these mean squares. The total phenotypic variance can be partitioned into the following three sources: V(G), additive genetic effects; V(CE), common environmental influences that affect both siblings equally; and V(SE), specific environmental influences that affect each sibling individually. This last one is a residual term that is comprised of many sources, including measurement error and certain kinds of interaction between genotypes and environments. Thus, the total phenotypic variance is partitioned as V(G) + V(CE) + V(SE).

In many studies, the statistics used are correlations, including regressions and a special form of the correlation, the intraclass (R) correlation (Plomin et al., 1990). Heritabilities can be estimated by comparing these correlations, as in doubling the difference between monozygotic and dizygotic twin similarities, that is, $H^2 = 2(RMZ - RDZ)$. Doubling the similarity correlation among siblings presents another evaluation (or multiplying by four the correlation among half-siblings). Another estimate of heritability is obtained by taking the correlation between the "midparent" value (mean of two parents) and "midchild" value (mean of all children). These methods, however, have to assume there is no nongenetic cause of resemblance between offspring and parents; to the degree to which there are, the heritabilities may be overestimated.

Environmental influences can also be estimated from within families. In twin studies, the effects of common environment (CE) can be estimated by subtracting the monozygotic twin correlation from double the dizygotic twin correlation, that is, CE = 2RDZ − RMZ. Any specific environmental (SE), or nonshared environmental influences, including error of measurement, can be estimated from subtraction, that is, $SE = 1 - H^2 - CE$, which should agree with 1 − RMZ if certain basic assumptions of the twin method are met. Because monozygotic twins are genetically identical, RMZ in itself constitutes an upper-bound estimate of H^2 (if CE = 0), and 1 − RMZ constitutes an estimate of environmentality, that is, the proportion of individual differences in a population unexplained by genetic factors.

Adoption studies provide the human equivalent of the "cross-fostering" designs used in animal experiments and allow estimates of genetic and environmental influences under a different but overlapping set of assumptions as compared to those of the twin method. For example, assumptions are made that there is random selection but, of course, children who are placed up for adoption may not be a random sample of the population and the homes into which they are adopted are typically better than average. Nonetheless, the logic of adoption studies is straightforward. Any resemblance between birth parents and their adopted-away children will be due to genetic influences for there are no environmental factors in common; any resemblance between adopted children and their adoptive families will be due to environmental influences, for there are no genetic influences in common.

Particularly dramatic are those studies that combine the twin and adoption methods, as in the famous Minnesota Study of Twins Reared Apart (Bouchard et al., 1990). Here monozygotic and dizygotic twins are separated in infancy and reared apart (MZA and DZA), a technique that becomes even more powerful when combined with a matched group of MZ and DZ twins reared together (MZT, DZT). In addition to the Minnesota study there is the Swedish Adoption/Twin Study of Aging examining 351 pairs of middle-aged twins reared apart with 407 matched control pairs (Pedersen et al., 1991), and a Finnish investigation of 165 pairs of twins reared apart (Langinvainio, Koskenvuo, Kaprio & Sistonen, 1984).

Emergent Traits

In the case of identical twins reared apart, their correlation directly represents heritability; differences represent environmentality and measurement error. Table 3.1 presents a contrast of data from the monozygotic twins reared apart (MZA) in the Minnesota study with a group of monozygotic twins reared together (MZT) for anthropometric, psychophysiologic, intellectual, personality, and social interest variables (from Bouchard et al., 1990). Convergent results show substantial genetic effects on all the traits in question, and weak or nonexistent effects for the common environment.

The findings in Table 3.1 demonstrate remarkable similarity between MZA twins. They are often nearly equal to those for MZT twins and, as such, imply that common rearing enhances familial resemblance during adulthood only slightly. The MZ twin correlations constitute a substantial portion of the reliable variance of each trait confirming the high heritabilities involved. The MZA twin correlations were not related to how much contact the twins had as adults (Bouchard et al., 1990).

Remarkable similarities of idiosyncratic life-style and personal preference have been noted among monozygotic pairs, although not among dizygotic pairs. For example, the lives of the "Jim twins," adopted as infants into sepa-

TABLE 3.1
Similarity Correlations for Monozygotic Twins Reared Apart and Together

Variables	Reared apart		Reared together	
	r	Number of pairs	r	Number of pairs
Anthropometric				
Fingerprint ridge count	.97	54	.96	274
Height	.86	56	.93	274
Weight	.73	56	.83	274
Psychophysiological				
Brain wave alpha	.80	35	.81	42
Systolic blood pressure	.64	56	.70	34
Heart rate	.49	49	.54	160
Intelligence				
WAIS IQ-full scale	.69	48	.88	40
WAIS IQ-verbal	.64	48	.88	40
WAIS IQ-performance	.71	48	.79	40
Raven, Mill-Hill composite	.78	42	.76	37
Reaction time speed	.56	40	.73	50
g factor	.78	43	–	–
Mean of 15 Hawaii-battery scales	.45	45	–	–
Mean of 13 CAB scales	.48	41	–	–
Personality				
Mean of 11 MPQ scales	.50	44	.49	217
Mean of 18 CPI scales	.48	38	.49	99
Social attitude				
Mean of 23 SCII scales	.39	52	.48	116
Mean of 34 JVIS scales	.43	45	–	–
Mean of 17 MOII scales	.40	40	.49	376
Mean of 2 religiosity scales	.49	31	.51	458
Mean of 14 nonreligious social attitude items	.34	42	.28	421
MPQ Traditionalism scale	.53	44	.50	217

Note: Adapted from Bouchard, Lykken, McGue, Segal & Tellegen (1990, p. 226, Table 4). Copyright 1990 by the American Association for the Advancement of Science. Reprinted with permission. CAB = Comprehensive Ability Battery; CPI = California Personality Inventory; JVIS = Jackson Vocational Interest Survey; MOII = Minnesota Occupational Interest Inventory; MPQ = Multidimensional Personality Questionnaire; SCII = Strong Campbell Interest Inventory; WAIS = Wechsler Adult Intelligence Scale.

rate working-class Ohio families, have been marked by a trail of similar names. Both had childhood pets named Toy. Both married and divorced women named Linda and had second marriages with women named Betty. They named their sons James Allen and James Alan.

Lykken, McGue, Tellegen, and Bouchard (1992) describe other examples from the Minnesota study. One pair resolutely refused to express any opinions on controversial issues, since long before they discovered each other's existence this had been their habit. Another pair were helpless gigglers, although each described their adoptive parents as undemonstrative and serious in manner, and neither had known anyone who laughed as freely as she did until finally she met her twin. There were two who handled dogs; one showed them, and the other who taught obedience classes.

Lykken et al. (1992: 1565–66) continued:

> There were two gunsmith hobbyists among the group of twins; two women who habitually wore seven rings; two men who offered a (correct) diagnosis of a faulty wheel bearing on Bouchard's car; two who obsessively counted things; two who had been married five times; two captains of volunteer fire departments; two fashion designers; two who left little love notes around the house for their wives,... in each case, an MZA pair.

Lykken et al. (1992) suggest that these personal idiosyncrasies are "emergenic" traits due to chance genetic configurations and so may not run in families. Because monozygotic twins share all their genes and thus all gene configurations, they can be surprisingly concordant for unusual qualities despite being separated in infancy and reared apart. These emergent traits may explain statistical rarities such as great leadership and genius, or even just atypical selling ability, parenting success, interpersonal attractiveness, entrepreneurial ability, psychotherapeutic effectiveness and other important individual differences.

The standard assumption of behavior genetics is that traits run in families and that pairs of relatives are similar in proportion to their genetic resemblance. Yet there is evidence of traits for which the MZ correlation is high, indicating a genetic basis, when the DZ correlation and other first degree relatives are insignificant. When MZ twins are substantially more than twice as similar as DZ twins and other first-degree relatives, a nonadditive or configural genetic determination is suggested.

The Heritability of Behavior

It may come as something of a surprise to learn the range of traits that studies have shown to be genetically influenced. In the next sections, therefore, the heritability of individual differences are reviewed on several dimensions.

Anthropometric and Physiological Traits

Height, weight, and other physical attributes provide a point of comparison to behavioral data. Not surprisingly, they are usually highly heritable accounting for 50 to 90 percent of the variance. These results are found from studies of both twins and adoptees (e.g., Table 3.1). The genes also account for large portions of the variance in physiological processes such as rate of breathing, blood pressure, perspiration, pulse rate, and EEG-measured brain activity.

Obesity was studied in a sample of 540 42-year-old Danish adoptees selected so that the age and sex distribution was the same in each of four weight categories: thin, medium, overweight, and obese (Stunkard et al., 1986). Biological and adoptive parents were contacted and their current weight assessed. The weight of the adoptees was predicted from that of their biologic parents but not at all from that of the adoptive parents with whom they had been raised. The relation between biologic parents and adoptees was present across the whole range of body fatness—from very thin to very fat. Thus, genetic influences play an important role in determining human fatness, whereas the family environment alone has no apparent effect. This latter result, of course, is one that varies from popular views. Subsequent evidence shows significant genetic transmission of obesity in black as well as in white families (Ness, Laskarzewski, & Price, 1991).

Testosterone is a hormone mediating many bio-behavioral variables in both men and women. Its heritability was examined in 75 pairs of MZ twins and 88 pairs of DZ twins by Meikle, Bishop, Stringham, & West (1987). They found that genes regulated 25 to 76 percent of plasma content for testosterone, estradiol, estrone, 3 alpha-audiostanediol glucuronide, free testosterone, lutinizing hormone, follicle stimulating hormone, and other factors affecting testosterone metabolism.

Activity Level

Several investigators have found activity level to be heritable from infancy onward (Matheny, 1983). In one study, activity in 54 identical and 39 fraternal twins aged 3 to 12 years was assessed with behaviors like "gets up and down" while "watching television" and "during meals" (Willerman, 1973). The correlation for identical twins was 0.88 and for fraternal twins was 0.59, yielding a heritability of 58 percent. An investigation of 181 identical and 84 fraternal twins from 1 to 5 years of age using parent ratings found correlations for a factor of zestfulness of 0.78 for identical and 0.54 for fraternal twins, yielding a heritability of 48 percent (Cohen, Dibble, & Grawe, 1977). Data from a Swedish sample aged 59 years and including 424 twins reared together and 315 twins reared apart showed the heritability for activity level in this older sample to be 25 percent (Plomin, Pedersen, McClearn, Nesselroade, & Bergeman, 1988).

Altruism and Aggression

Several twin studies have been conducted on altruism and aggression. Loehlin and Nichols (1976) carried out cluster analyses of self-ratings made by 850 adolescent pairs on various traits. Clusters labeled kind, argumentative, and family quarrel showed the monozygotic twins to be about twice as much alike as the dizygotic twins, with heritabilities from 20 to 42 percent. Matthews, Batson, Horn, and Rosenman (1981) analyzed adult twin responses to a self-report measure of empathy and estimated a heritability of 72 percent. In the Minnesota adoption study of twins raised apart, summarized in Table 3.1, the correlations for 44 pairs of identical twins reared apart are 0.46 for aggression and 0.53 for traditionalism, a measure of following rules and authority (Tellegen et al., 1988).

In a study of 573 pairs of identical and fraternal adult twin pairs reared together, all of the twins completed separate questionnaires measuring altruistic and aggressive tendencies. The questionnaires included a 20-item self-report altruism scale, a 33-item empathy scale, a 16-item nurturance scale, and many items measuring aggressive dispositions. As shown in Table 3.2, 50 percent of the variance on each scale was associated with genetic effects, virtually 0 percent with the twin's common environment, and the remaining 50 percent with each twin's specific environment. When the estimates were corrected for unreliability of measurement, the genetic contribution increased to 60 percent (Rushton, Fulker, Neale, Nias, & Eysenck, 1986).

TABLE 3.2
Genetic and Environmental Contributions to Altruism and Aggression Questionnaires in 573 Adult Twin Pairs

Trait	Additive genetic variance		Common environmental variance		Specific environmental variance	
Altruism	51%	(60%)	2%	(2%)	47%	(38%)
Empathy	51%	(65%)	0%	(0%)	49%	(35%)
Nurturance	43%	(60%)	1%	(1%)	56%	(39%)
Aggressiveness	39%	(54%)	0%	(0%)	61%	(46%)
Assertiveness	53%	(69%)	0%	(0%)	47%	(31%)

Note. Adapted from Rushton, Fulker, Neale, Nias & Eysenck (1986, p. 1195, Table 4). Copyright 1986 by the American Psychological Association. Reprinted with permission. Estimates in parentheses are corrected for unreliability of measurement.

At 14 months of age, empathy was assessed in 200 pairs of twins by the child's response to feigned injury by experimenter and mother (Emde et al., 1992). Ratings were based on the strength of concern expressed in the child's face, the level of emotional arousal expressed in the child's body as well as prosocial intervention by the child (e.g., comforting by patting the victim or bringing the victim a toy). About 36 percent of the variance was estimated to be genetic.

Attitudes

Although social, political and religious attitudes are often thought to be environmentally determined, a twin study by Eaves and Eysenck (1974) found that radicalism-conservatism had a heritability of 54 percent, tough-mindedness had a heritability of 54 percent, and the tendency to voice extreme views had a heritability of 37 percent. In a review of this and two other British studies of conservatism, Eaves and Young (1981) found for 894 pairs of identical twins an average correlation of 0.67 and for 523 fraternal twins an average correlation of 0.52, yielding an average heritability of 30 percent.

In a cross-national study, 3,810 Australian twin pairs reared together reported their response to 50 items of conservatism such as death penalty, divorce, and jazz (Martin et al., 1986). The heritabilities ranged from 8 percent to 51 percent (see Table 4.4, next chapter). Overall correlations of 0.63 and 0.46 were found for identical and fraternal twins, respectively, yielding a heritability of 34 percent. Correcting for the high assortative mating that occurs on political attitudes raised the overall heritability to about 50 percent. Martin et al. (1986) also replicated the analyses by Eaves and Eysenck (1974) on the heritability of radicalism and tough-mindedness.

Religious attitudes also show genetic influence. Although Loehlin and Nichols (1976) found no genetic influences on belief in God or involvement in organized religious activities in their study of 850 high school twins, when religiosity items were aggregated with other items, such as present religious preference, then a genetic contribution of about 20 percent became observable (Loehlin & Nichols, 1976, Table 4-3, Cluster 15). Using a more complete assessment battery, including five well-established scales of religious attitudes, interests and values, and estimates of heritability from twins reared apart as well as together, the Minnesota study estimated the genetic contribution to the variance in their instruments to be about 50 percent (Table 3.1; also Waller, Kojetin, Bouchard, Lykken, & Tellegen, 1990).

Criminality

The earliest twin study of criminality was published in 1929 in Germany by Johannes Lange. Translated into English in 1931, *Crime as Destiny* reported on the careers of a number of criminal twins, some of them identical, others fraternal, shortly after the distinction between the two kinds had become generally accepted. Lange compared the concordance rates for 13 monozygotic and 17 dizygotic pairs of twins in which at least 1 had been convicted of a criminal offense. Ten of the 13 monozygotic pairs (77 percent) were concordant, whereas only 2 of the 17 dizygotic pairs (12 percent) were concordant. A summary of Lange's (1931) study and of the literature up to the 1960s was provided by Eysenck and Gudjonsson (1989). For 135 monozygotic twins the concordance rate was 67 percent and for 135 dizygotic twins, 30 percent.

Among subsequent studies is an investigation of the total population of 3,586 male twin pairs born on the Danish Islands from 1881 to 1910, recording serious offenses only. For this nonselected sample, identical and fraternal twin concordances are 42 percent versus 21 percent for crimes against persons and 40 percent versus 16 percent for crimes against property (Christiansen, 1977). Three small studies carried out in Japan showed similar concordance rates to those in the West (see Eysenck & Gudjonsson, 1989: 97-99).

Replicating the concordance ratios based on official statistics are those from studies based on self-reports. Sending questionnaires by mail to 265 adolescent twin pairs, Rowe (1986) sampled the eighth through twelfth grades in almost all the school districts of Ohio. The results showed that identical twins were roughly twice as much alike in their criminal behavior as fraternal twins, the heritability being about 50 percent.

Converging with the twin work are the results from several American, Danish, and Swedish adoption studies. Children who were adopted in infancy were at greater risk for criminal convictions if their biological parents had been so convicted than if their adoptive parents had been. For example, in the Danish study, based on 14,427 adoptees, for 2,492 adopted sons who had neither adoptive nor biological criminal parents, 14 percent had at least one criminal conviction. For 204 adopted sons whose adoptive (but not biological) parents were criminals, 15 percent had at least one conviction. If biological (but not adoptive) parents were criminal, 20 percent (of 1,226) adopted sons had criminal records; if both biological and adoptive parents were criminal, 25 percent (of 143) adopted sons were criminals. In addition, it was found that siblings raised apart showed 20 percent concordance and that half-siblings showed 13 percent concordance while pairs of unrelated children reared together in the same adoptive families showed 9 percent concordance (Mednick, Gabrielli, & Hutchings, 1984).

Dominance

Using a variety of assessment techniques, several studies have found individual differences in interpersonal dominance to be largely inherited (e.g.,

Gottesman, 1963, 1966; Loehlin & Nichols, 1976). In a longitudinal study of 42 twin pairs, Dworkin, Burke, Maher, and Gottesman (1976) found that individual differences in dominance, as assessed on the California Psychological Inventory, remained stable over a 12-year time period, as did the heritability estimate. Carey, Goldsmith, Tellegen, and Gottesman (1978), in a review of the literature, reported that, of all traits, dominance is one of those most reliably found to be heritable, with a weighted mean heritability coefficient, over several samples, of 56 percent. In the Minnesota study (Table 3.1) this is also the correlation for 44 pairs of identical twins reared apart for the trait of social potency (a leader who likes to be the center of attention).

Emotionality

The largest heritability study of emotional reactivity, or the speed of arousal to fear and anger, was carried out by Floderus-Myrhed, Pedersen, and Rasmuson (1980). They administered the Eysenck Personality Inventory to 12,898 adolescent twin pairs of the Swedish Twin Registry. The heritability for neuroticism was 50 percent for men and 58 percent for women. Another large twin study, carried out in Australia, involving 2,903 twin pairs, found identical and fraternal twin correlations of 0.50 and 0.23 for neuroticism (Martin & Jardine, 1986). The opposite side of the neuroticism continuum, emotional stability, as measured by the California Psychological Inventory's Sense of Well-Being scale, is also found to have a significant heritability, both in adolescence and 12 years later (Dworkin et al., 1976).

The studies of twins raised apart substantiate the genetic contribution to a neuroticism "superfactor." In the Minnesota study (Table 3.1), the correlation for the 44 MZA twins is 0.61 for the trait of stress reaction, 0.48 for alienation, and 0.49 for harm avoidance (Tellegen et al., 1988). In a Swedish study of 59-year-olds the correlation for emotionality in 90 pairs of identical twins reared apart is 0.30 (Plomin et al., 1988). Other adoption studies also confirm that the familial resemblance for neuroticism is genetically based. In a review of three adoption studies, the average correlation for nonadoptive relatives was about 0.15 and the average correlation for adoptive relatives was nearly zero, suggesting a heritability estimate of about 0.30 (Henderson, 1982).

Intelligence

Ever since Galton (1869), more genetic studies of intelligence have been carried out than for any other trait. The early data were reviewed by Erlenmeyer-Kimling and Jarvik (1963) and were compatible with a heritability as high as 80 percent. Newer data and reviews have confirmed the high heritability of intelligence, showing that it is 50 percent or greater. The most extensive review is that by Bouchard and McGue (1981) based on 111 studies identified

Figure 3.1: Familial Correlations for IQ

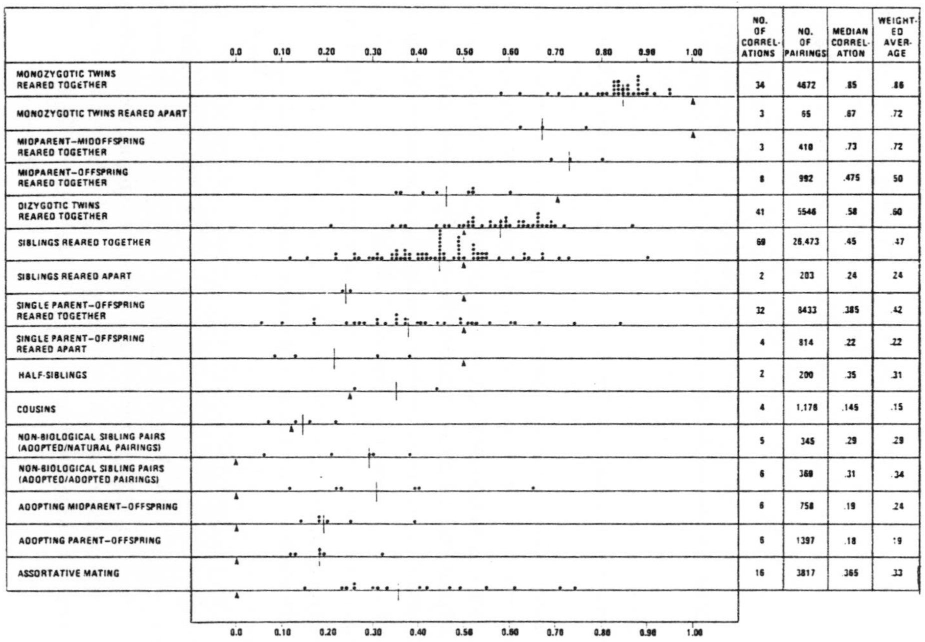

	NO. OF CORRELATIONS	NO. OF PAIRINGS	MEDIAN CORRELATION	WEIGHTED AVERAGE
MONOZYGOTIC TWINS REARED TOGETHER	34	4672	.85	.86
MONOZYGOTIC TWINS REARED APART	3	65	.67	.72
MIDPARENT-MIDOFFSPRING REARED TOGETHER	3	410	.73	.72
MIDPARENT-OFFSPRING REARED TOGETHER	8	992	.475	.50
DIZYGOTIC TWINS REARED TOGETHER	41	5546	.58	.60
SIBLINGS REARED TOGETHER	69	26,473	.45	.47
SIBLINGS REARED APART	2	203	.24	.24
SINGLE PARENT-OFFSPRING REARED TOGETHER	32	8433	.385	.42
SINGLE PARENT-OFFSPRING REARED APART	4	814	.22	.22
HALF-SIBLINGS	2	200	.35	.31
COUSINS	4	1,176	.145	.15
NON-BIOLOGICAL SIBLING PAIRS (ADOPTED/NATURAL PAIRINGS)	5	345	.29	.29
NON-BIOLOGICAL SIBLING PAIRS (ADOPTED/ADOPTED PAIRINGS)	6	369	.31	.34
ADOPTING MIDPARENT-OFFSPRING	6	758	.19	.24
ADOPTING PARENT-OFFSPRING	6	1397	.18	.19
ASSORTATIVE MATING	16	3817	.365	.33

The horizontal lines show the median correlation coefficients; the arrows show the correlations expected if IQ were entirely due to additive genetic variance; and the vertical bar in each distribution indicates the median observed correlation. From Bouchard & McGue (1981, p. 1056, Figure 1). Copyright 1981 by the American Association for the Advancement of Science. Reprinted with permission.

in a survey of the world literature. Altogether there were 652 familial correlations, including 113,942 pairings. Figure 3.1 displays the correlations between relatives, biological and adoptive, in the 111 studies.

Several heritability estimates can be calculated from Bouchard and McGue's (1981) review. Doubling the difference between the correlations for identical and fraternal twins reared together produces a heritability estimate of 52 percent. Doubling the correlation for parents and offspring adopted apart yields an estimate of 44 percent. Doubling the correlation for siblings adopted apart provides an estimate of 48 percent. Doubling the difference between the correlation for biological parents and offspring living together (0.42) and the correlation for adoptive parents and their adopted children (0.19) leads to a heritability estimate of 46 percent. Doubling the difference between the correlation for biological siblings reared together (0.47) and the correlation for adoptive siblings (0.32) provides an estimate of 30 percent. The sample of identical twins reared apart yields the highest estimate, 72 percent. As shown in Table 3.1, the ongoing study of reared-apart identical twins at the University of Minnesota also yields estimates of substantial heritability (Bouchard et al., 1990).

The Swedish Adoption/Twin Study of Aging provided corroborative data for high heritability. There were 46 pairs of identical twins reared apart, 67 pairs of identical twins reared together, 100 pairs of fraternal twins reared apart, and 89 pairs of fraternal twins reared together. Their average age was 65 years. The heritabilities for general intelligence was about 80 percent and for 13 specific abilities somewhat less. Thus, average heritabilities for verbal, spatial, perceptual speed, and memory tests were, respectively, 58 percent, 46 percent, 58 percent, and 38 percent (Pedersen, Plomin, Nesselroade, & McClearn, 1992).

It is the g factor that is the most heritable component of intelligence tests. In Bouchard et al.'s study (Table 3.1) the g factor, the first principal component extracted from several mental ability tests, had the highest heritability (78 percent). Similarly in Pedersen et al.'s (1992) study, the first principal component had a heritability of 80 percent whereas the specific abilities averaged around 50 percent.

Remarkably, the strength of the heritability varies directly as a result of a test's g loading. Jensen (1983) found a correlation of 0.81 between the g loadings of the 11 subtests of the Wechsler Intelligence Scale for Children and heritability strength assessed by genetic dominance based on inbreeding depression scores from cousin marriages in Japan. Inbreeding depression is defined as a lowered mean of the trait relative to the mean in a non-inbred population and is especially interesting because it indicates genetic dominance, which arises when a trait confers evolutionary fitness.

Jensen took the figures on inbreeding depression from a study by Schull and Neel (1965) who calculated them from 1,854 7- to 10-year-old Japanese children. Since about 50 percent of the sample involved cousin marriages, it was possible to assess the inbreeding depression on each subtest, expressed as the percentage decrement in the score per 10 percent increase in degree of inbreeding. These were calculated after statistically controlling for child's age, birth rank, month of examination, and eight different parental variables, mostly pertaining to SES. The complement of inbreeding depression was found by Nagoshi and Johnson (1986) who observed "hybrid vigor" in offspring of Caucasoid-Mongoloid matings in Hawaii.

Subsequently, Jensen (1987a) reported rank order correlations of 0.55 and 0.62 between estimates of genetic influence from two twin studies and the *g* loadings of the Wechsler Adult Intelligence Scale subtests, and P. A. Vernon (1989) found a correlation of 0.60 between the heritabilities of a variety of speed of decision time tasks and their relationship with the *g* loadings from a psychometric test of general intelligence. More detailed analyses showed that the relationship among the speed and IQ measures are mediated entirely by hereditary factors. Thus, there are common biological mechanisms underlying the association between reaction time and information-processing speed and mental ability (Baker, Vernon, & Ho, 1991).

Heritabilities for mental ability have been examined within black and Oriental populations. A study by Scarr-Salapatek (1971) suggested the heritability might be lower for black children than for white children. Subsequently, Osborne (1978, 1980) reported heritabilities of greater than 50 percent both for 123 black and for 304 white adolescent twin pairs. Japanese data for 543 monozygotic and 134 dizygotic twins tested for intelligence at the age of 12 gave correlations of 0.78 and 0.49 respectively, indicating a heritability of 58 percent (R. Lynn & Hattori, 1990).

Related to intelligence at greater than 0.50 are years of education, occupational status, and other indices of socioeconomic status (Jensen, 1980a). All of these have also been shown to be heritable. For example, a study of 1,900 pairs of 50-year-old male twins yielded MZ and DZ twin correlations of 0.42 and 0.21, respectively for occupational status, and 0.54 and 0.30 for income (Fulker & Eysenck, 1979; Taubman, 1976). An adoption study of occupational status yielded a correlation of 0.20 between biological fathers and their adult adopted-away sons (2,467 pairs; Teasdale, 1979). A study of 99 pairs of adopted-apart siblings yielded a correlation of 0.22 (Teasdale & Owen, 1981). All of these are consistent with a heritability of about 40 percent for occupational status. Years of schooling also shows substantial genetic influence; for example, MZ and DZ twin correlations are typically about 0.75 and 0.50 respectively, suggesting that heritability is about 50 percent (e.g., Taubman, 1976).

Locus of Control

The Internal-External Locus of Control Scale was developed as a continuous measure of the attitude with which individuals relate their own behavior to its contingent reward or punishment. That one's own actions are largely affected by luck or chance or some more powerful force was labeled a belief in external control. The converse attitude, that outcomes are contingent on one's own behavior, was termed internal control. A study by Miller and Rose (1982) reported a family twin study in variation of locus of control. In this study, the heritability estimates based on the comparison of MZ and DZ twins were corroborated by also estimating the heritability through the regression of offspring on parent and the correlation between non-twin siblings. The combination of results revealed heritability estimates greater than 50 percent.

Longevity and Health

Work on the genetics of longevity and senescence was pioneered by Kallman and Sander (1948, 1949). These authors carried out a survey in New York of over 1,000 pairs of twins aged 60 years or older and found that intra-pair differences for longevity, disease, and general adjustment to the aging process were consistently smaller for identical twins than for fraternal twins. For example, the average intra-pair difference in life span was 37 months for identical twins and 78 months for fraternal twins. In an adoption study of all 1,003 nonfamilial adoptions formally granted in Denmark between 1924 and 1947, age of death in the adult adoptees was predicted better by knowledge of the age of death in the biological parent than by knowledge of the age of death in the adopting parent (Sorensen, Nielsen, Andersen, & Teasdale, 1988).

Many individual difference variables associated with health are heritable. Genetic influences have been found for blood pressure, obesity, resting metabolic rate, behavior patterns such as smoking, alcohol use, and physical exercise, as well as susceptibility to infectious diseases. There is also a genetic component of from 30 to 50 percent for hospitalized illnesses in the pediatric age group including pediatric deaths (Scriver, 1984).

Psychopathology

Numerous studies have shown substantial genetic influences on reading disabilities, mental retardation, schizophrenia, affective disorders, alcoholism, and anxiety disorders. In a now classic early study, adopted-away offspring of hospitalized chronic schizophrenic women were interviewed at the average age of 36 and compared to matched adoptees whose birth parents had no known psychopathology (Heston, 1966). Of 47 adoptees whose biological parents were schizophrenic, 5 had been hospitalized for schizophrenia. None of the adoptees in the control group was schizophrenic. Studies in Denmark confirmed this finding and also found evidence for genetic influence when researchers started with schizophrenic adoptees and then searched for their adoptive and biological relatives (Rosenthal, 1972; Kety, Rosenthal, Wender,

& Schulsinger, 1976). A major review of the genetics of schizophrenia has been presented by Gottesman (1991).

Alcoholism also runs in families such that about 25 percent of the male relatives of alcoholics are themselves alcoholics, as compared with less than 5 percent of the males in the general population. In a Swedish study of middle-aged twins who had been reared apart, twin correlations for total alcohol consumed per month were 0.71 for 120 pairs of identical twins reared apart and 0.31 for 290 pairs of fraternal twins reared apart (Pedersen, Friberg, Floderus-Myrhed, McClearn, & Plomin, 1984). A Swedish adoption study of males found that 22 percent of the adopted-away sons of biological fathers who abused alcohol were alcoholic (Cloninger, Bohman, & Sigvardsson, 1981).

Sexuality

A questionnaire study of twins found genetic influence on strength of sex drive in turn predictive of age of first sexual intercourse, frequency of intercourse, number of sexual partners, and type of position preferred (Eysenck, 1976; Martin, Eaves, & Eysenck, 1977). Divorce, or the factors leading to it at least, is also heritable. Based on a survey of more than 1,500 twin pairs, their parents, and their spouses' parents, McGue and Lykken (1992) calculated a 52 percent heritability. They suggested the propensity was mediated through other heritable traits relating to sexual behavior, personality, and personal values.

Perhaps the most frequently cited study of the genetics of sexual orientation is that of Kallman (1952), in which he reported a concordance rate of 100 percent among homosexual MZ twins. Bailey and Pillard (1991) estimated the genetic component to male homosexuality to be about 50 percent. They recruited subjects through ads in gay publications and received usable questionnaire responses from 170 twin or adoptive brothers. Fifty-two percent of the identical twins, 22 percent of the fraternal twins, and 11 percent of the adoptive brothers were found to be homosexual. The distribution of sexual orientation among identical co-twins of homosexuals was bimodal, implying that homosexuality is taxonomically distinct from heterosexuality.

Subsequently, Bailey, Pillard, Neale, and Agyei (1993) carried out a twin study of lesbians and found that here, too, genes accounted for about half the variance in sexual preferences. Of the relatives whose sexual orientation could be confidently rated, 34 (48 percent) of 71 monozygotic co-twins, 6 (16 percent) of 37 dizygotic cotwins, and 2 (6 percent) of 35 adoptive sisters were homosexual.

Sociability

In one large study, Floderus-Myrhed et al. (1980) gave the Eysenck Personality Inventory to 12,898 adolescent twin pairs of the Swedish Twin Registry. The heritability for extraversion, highly related to sociability, was 54 percent for men and 66 percent for women. Another large study of extraversion involving 2,903 Australian twin pairs, found identical and fraternal twin correlations of 0.52 and 0.17 with a resultant heritability of 70 percent (Martin & Jardine, 1986). In a Swedish adoption study of middle-aged people, the correlation for sociability in 90 pairs of identical twins reared apart was 0.20 (Plomin et al., 1988).

Sociability and the related construct of shyness show up at an early age. In a study of 200 pairs of twins, Emde et al. (1992) found both sociability and shyness to be heritable at 14 months. Ratings of videotapes made of reactions to arrival at the home and the laboratory and other novel situations, such as being offered a toy, along with ratings made by both parents showed heritabilities ranging from 27 to 56 percent.

Values and Vocational Interests

Loehlin and Nichols's (1976) study of 850 twin pairs raised together provided evidence for the heritability of both values and vocational interests. Values such as the desire to be well-adjusted, popular, and kind, or having scientific, artistic, and leadership goals were found to be genetically influenced. So were a range of career preferences including those for sales, blue-collar management, teaching, banking, literature, military, social service, and sports.

As shown in Table 3.1, Bouchard et al. (1990) reported that, on measures of vocational interest, the correlations for their 40 identical twins raised apart are about 0.40. Additional analyses from the Minnesota Study of Twins Reared Apart suggest the genetic contribution to work values is pervasive. One comparison of reared-apart twins found a 40 percent heritability for preference for job outcomes such as achievement, comfort, status, safety, and autonomy (Keller, Bouchard, Arvey, Segal, & Dawis, 1992). Another study of MZAs indicated a 30 percent heritability for job satisfaction (Arvey, Bouchard, Segal, & Abraham, 1989).

Threshold Model

The genetic model typically proposed to explain the experimental results is the polygenic threshold model, which assumes that a large number of genes contribute equally and additively to the trait, and that there is a threshold point beyond which the phenotype is expressed. In addition to the genetic effects, environmental factors can act to shift the distribution, thus influencing the position of a given genotype with respect to the threshold (Falconer, 1989). This interaction of polygenic threshold inheritance with environmental influences is termed the multifactorial model.

Thus, genetic "influence," not genetic "determinism" is the appropriate catchphrase when it comes to social behavior. Although genes affect a person's threshold for activation, for some only a small stimulus is needed to activate behavior, while for others a greater stimulus is required. An analogy drawn from medicine is of someone with a genetic disposition for flu who may never succumb in a benevolent environment although even a person relatively resistant may suffer if the environment is sufficiently hostile. Often the environment may override genetic differences. About 50 percent of the variance in human social behavior seems to be of genetic origin, with the remaining 50 percent environmental.

Figure 3.2 illustrates Kimble's (1990) threshold model showing the interactions that bring expression to a variety of potentials. The underlying predisposition (x-axis) is largely genetic in origin but may have been strengthened or weakened during development. The y-axis is the strength of the environmental effect. The threshold function within these axes divides the figure into two parts: reaction and no reaction.

The threshold model has great generality, offering a unifying principle to wide areas of psychology (Kimble, 1990). Its generality is achieved by treating numerous behaviors in terms of the occurrence or nonoccurrence of responses and its incorporation of human differences that enter the model as differences in predisposition and reaction thresholds. Kimble (1990) provides several examples: (1) from sensory perception, the rule is that the greater the sensitivity of an observer, the lower the stimulus intensity required to make a signal detectable; (2) in stress models of mental disorder, the greater an individual's vulnerability, the lower the stress required to produce a pathological reaction; (3) in psychopharmacology, the greater the susceptibility of a person to a drug, the smaller the dose required to produce a specific effect; (4) in education, the greater the readiness of a child to learn, the less instruction needed to impart a given skill or bit of knowledge; and (5) with social attitudes, the more racial bias a person has, the less evidence it takes to elicit a prejudicial statement.

Whether a predisposition is activated depends upon the net effect of other tendencies that are activated with it and that encourage or discourage the expression of that potential. For example, students pass or fail their courses for reasons that depend on their abilities, but also on their willingness to work hard enough to meet the standards of a course. The ease with which new learning occurs depends on previous learning, response biases and innate stimulus preferences.

The strength of environmental effects may combine in unique ways. Additive effects may be found with stress. As stress accumulates, it takes the organism upward on the y-axis of Figure 3.2 and above the thresholds for a succession of cumulative responses—alarm, resistance, and exhaustion. Interactive complexities may also occur. A new stressor, delivered during the

Figure 3.2: Threshold Model of the Interaction of Instigation and Disposition

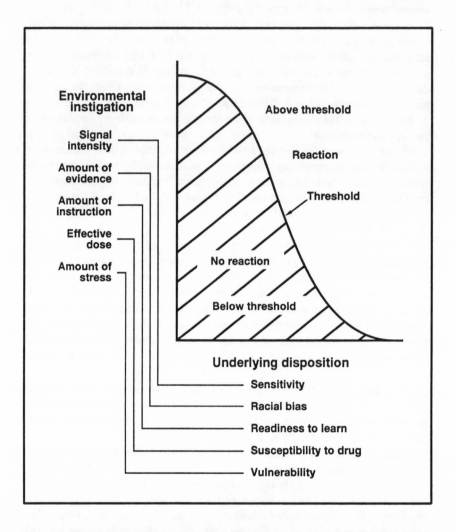

Figure 3.2 can be read as though it were a correlational scatter plot. Combinations of environmental instigation (vertical y-axis) and underlying disposition (horizontal x-axis) above the threshold produce a reaction; those below the threshold do not. Figure 3.2 tells us that, in general, the greater the underlying disposition, the less the stimulus required to evoke the response. Adapted from Kimble (1990, pp. 37, Figure 1). Copyright 1990 by the American Psychological Society. Reprinted with permission

stage of resistance when individuals are coping effectively, may bring them prematurely to the stage of exhaustion. According to the inverted-U hypothesis, up to a point increasing arousal benefits performance; beyond that point it interferes.

In cases such as this it is useful to think of the entire *behavioral scale*, not isolated points on it, as the genetically based trait that has been fixed by natural selection (E. O. Wilson, 1975: 20-21). Events may slide individual responses up or down a scale of stress (or aggression), but each of the various degrees may be adaptive at the appropriate level of instigation—short of the rarely recurring pathological level.

Genetic dispositions are simply one set of causes contributing to behavior. Alcoholism provides a good example of the qualification that must often be made to how genes and environment combine to influence behavior. No matter how strong the hereditary propensity toward alcoholism might be, no one will become alcoholic unless large quantities of alcohol are consumed over long periods of time.

Epigenesis in Development

Genes do not cause behavior directly. They code for enzymes, which, under the influence of the environment, lay down tracts in the brains and nervous systems of individuals, thus differentially affecting people's minds and the choices they make about behavioral alternatives. In regard to aggression, for example, some people may inherit temperaments that dispose them to irritability, impulsivity, or a lack of conditionability. There are many plausible routes from genes to behavior, and collectively, these routes may be referred to as epigenetic rules.

Epigenetic rules are genetically based recipes by which individual development is guided in one direction over alternatives. Their operation is probably most apparent in embryology in which the construction of anatomical and physiological features occurs (Waddington, 1957). To take a familiar example, the physical development from fertilized egg to neonate follows a preordained course in which development starts in the head region and works its way down the body. By the end of the first month, a brain and spinal cord become evident, and a heart has formed and begun to beat. By the end of the eighth week, the developing fetus has a face, arms, legs, basic trunk, and internal organs. By the sixth or seventh month, all major systems have been elaborated and the fetus may survive if born prematurely. However, development continues, and the last months of pregnancy are important for the buildup of body fat, tissue, and antibodies and for the refinement of other systems.

Average newborns weigh about 7 1/2 pounds, but they can double their birth weight by 6 months and triple it by their first birthday. After age 2 and until puberty, children grow 2 to 3 inches in height and gain 6 to 7 pounds in weight each year. The sequence of growth during infancy is rapid and uniform. Most babies in North America can sit in a highchair by 6 months, crawl by 10 months, and walk alone by 15 months.

The reason for spelling out what may seem obvious is that it so powerfully illustrates that development involves coordinated pathways of timed gene-action systems that switch off and on according to a predetermined plan. Behavioral development thus gives expression to the dynamics of preprogrammed change; and in this perspective, behavioral discontinuities (walking, adolescence) may be as strongly rooted in the epigenetic ground plan as the continuities are.

The genetics of behavioral development is illustrated in R. S. Wilson's (1978, 1983, 1984) longitudinal Louisville Twin Study, which tested some 500 pairs at 3, 6, 9, 12, 18, 24, and 30 months, then yearly from 3 through 9 years, with a final follow-up at 15 years. Measures were made of both height and mental development. Each test yielded age-adjusted standardized scores with a mean of 100. Thus, an infant of average height or IQ at every age would have scores of 100, with no variability. But if there were episodes of acceleration or lag in growth, the standardized scores would change across ages, reflecting the relative upward or downward shift of the child's height or IQ in relation to age mates. Consider the results for mental ability shown in Figure 3.3.

The results for mental development aggregated across 500 pairs of twins (Figure 3.4) show that the differentiation between the 2 zygosity groups is not very pronounced in the early years. After 3 years, however, the DZ twin correlations drop steadily to 0.59 at 6 years, while the MZ correlations remain in the upper 0.80s, thus showing a consonance proportionate with shared genes. In fact, by 6 years of age, the DZ correlations for height and intelligence are virtually the same (R = 0.57 and 0.59, respectively). Also shown in Figure 3.4 are the correlations between DZ twins and their siblings computed by pairing the sibling first with Twin A, then with Twin B, and averaging the results. The siblings were tested on a schedule that yielded age-matched tests for each twin-sibling set (R. S. Wilson, 1983).

Further strengthening these results are the correlations for non-twin sibling pairs (not shown in Figure 3.4). By 8 and 9 years these non-twin siblings had virtually the same concordance value as DZ twins at that age. In short, any two-zygote pair from the same family—whether DZ twins, a twin matched with a sibling, or two singleton siblings—showed a progressive trend to converge to a degree of similarity in cognitive performance expectable from the number of genes they shared in common.

The differentiation of monozygotic from dizygotic twin pairs is given additional perspective with data for height where the correlations can be extended back to birth. The results are presented graphically in the right hand box in Figure 3.5. They show that MZ twins are less concordant for height at birth than DZ twins, but there is a sharp rise in concordance at 3 months.

Figure 3.3: Correlated Pathways of Development

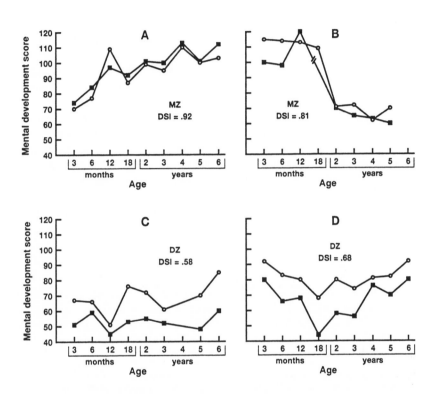

The two sets of MZ twins shown in panels A and B display quite different trends in mental development, but there is a high degree of congruence within each pair. Note especially the upward trend for the twins in panel A and how it contrasts with the downward trend in panel B. It appears that the inner programming can dictate trends in either direction, and the degree of advancement or lag in the early months has little bearing on the ultimate level reached by school age. The two sets of dizygotic twins shown in panel C and D display a greater divergence in trend during childhood, although the main directional shifts are somewhat the same. This is in accord with what would be expected from individuals who share half their genes in common. The developmental synchronies index (DSI) reflects the goodness of fit between the two curves and can be used to quantify the relative similarity of the two groups. Synchronies between lags and spurts in mental development are found to average about 0.90 for identical twins and about 0.50 for fraternal twins. From R.S. Wilson (1978, p. 942, Figure 1). Copyright 1978 by the American Association for the Advancement of Science. Reprinted with permission.

Subsequently, the MZ concordance for height moved incrementally upward while that for DZ progressively dropped. The comparative data for mental ability starting at 3 months (left box) is less pronounced, but still clear. Inci-

Figure 3.4: Correlations Proportionate with Shared Genes for Mental Development

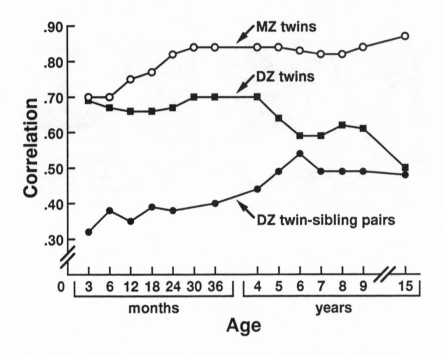

Due to common and specific environmental influences, during the first months of life the differentiation between the two zygosity groups is not very pronounced whereas that between DZ twin-sibling sets is over pronounced. Genetic influences are continually at work and by 6 years of age, while the MZ twin correlations remained in the upper 0.80s, the DZ twin correlations had dropped and the DZ twin-sibling correlations had risen and were not significantly different from each other. Adapted from R.S. Wilson (1983, p. 311, Figure 4). Copyright 1983 by the Society for Research in Child Development. Reprinted with permission.

dentally, these and similar data also suggest that, after 18 months of age, the growth gradients for height and mental development are independent of one another (R. S. Wilson, 1984).

R. S. Wilson's (1983) data are considered a benchmark for quality in human behavior genetics. They are also pivotal for the ideas presented in this book. The data show that genes are like blueprints or recipes, providing a template for propelling development forward to some targeted end point. The mechanism could be simple: If a gene produces an enzyme, then all that is required is that a switch mechanism operates to turn on when feedback informs that insufficient enzyme exists in the system and to turn off when feedback informs that the deficit has been corrected. Homeostatic mechanisms

Figure 3.5: Steady March Toward Twin Concordance

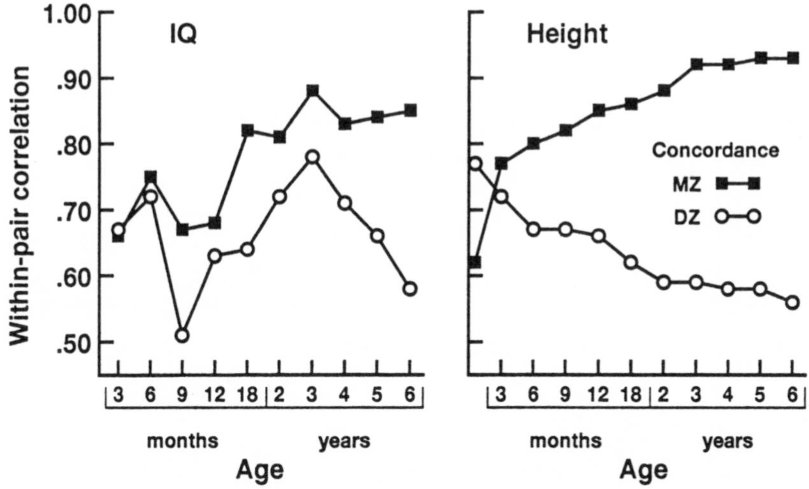

At birth the MZ twins are less concordant for height (right panel) than are DZ twins, perhaps due to monochorionicity and competition effects during gestation. By 3 months, however, the MZ concordance for height has moved sharply upward and thereafter moves incrementally upward until reaching R = 0.94 at 6 years. By contrast, the DZ pairs dropped from an initially high value of R = 0.78 at birth until they reached an intermediate value of R = 0.57 at 6 years. The comparative data for mental ability starting at 3 months (left panel) is less pronounced, but still clear. Adapted from R. S. Wilson (1984, p. 155, Figure 4).

are well established in the physiology and psychology of motivation (Toates, 1986).

"Catch-up growth" following deficits caused by malnutrition or illness also demonstrates that development requires constant self-corrections until some targeted end state is reached. Deprived children subsequently develop very rapidly to regain the growth trajectory they would have been on if the diversion had not occurred, following which growth slows down and development proceeds at the normal rate (Tanner, 1978). Developmental processes are constantly involved in a match-to-model process with an inherent growth equation.

Other genetic timing mechanisms include the age at peak height velocity, age at menarche, age of development of secondary sex characteristics, age of first sexual intercourse, and age of menopause. In all of these, identical twins, whether reared apart or together show greater concordance than dizygotic twins raised apart or together.

Gene-Culture Correlation

In *Genes, Mind and Culture,* Lumsden and Wilson (1981) outline the co-evolutionary process between genes and culture and how epigenetic rules guide psychological development from sensory filtering through perception to feature evaluation and decision making. In *Genes, Culture and Personality,* Eaves, Eysenck, and Martin (1989) describe some of the individual difference variables that play themselves out in social behavior.

The concept of geneotype-environment correlation, originally proposed by Plomin, DeFries, and Loehlin (1977), has been developed by Sandra Scarr (Scarr & McCartney, 1983; Scarr, 1992). When there is a correlation between genetic and environmental effects it means that people are exposed to environments on the basis of their genetic propensities. For example, if intelligence is heritable, then gifted children will have, on average, intellectually gifted parents who provide them with an intellectual environment as well as genes for intelligence. Alternatively, the individual might be picked out as gifted and given special opportunities. Even if no one does anything about the individual's talent, the individual might gravitate toward intellectual environments. These three scenarios represent three types of gene-environment correlation: passive, reactive, and active, respectively.

An example of how genotypes drive experience, or of active genotype-environment correlation, was provided in an analysis of television effects by Rowe and Herstand (1986). Although same-sex siblings were found to resemble one another in their exposure to violent programs, it was the most aggressive sibling who (1) identified most with aggressive characters, and (2) viewed the consequences of the aggression as positive. Within-family studies of delinquents find that both IQ and temperament distinguishes delinquent siblings from those who are nondelinquent (Hirschi & Hindelang, 1977; Rowe, 1986). It is not difficult to imagine how intellectually and temperamentally different siblings acquire alternate patterns of social responsibility. Nor to see how children with higher IQs may accumulate better language skills and greater knowledge of more diverse areas than their lower IQ peers, and how some personality types gravitate to one rather than an alternative work environment.

Genetic canalization provides an explanation for the important finding, mentioned earlier, that common family environment has little impact on longer-term intellectual and personality development. Such factors as social class, family religion, parental values, and child-rearing styles are not found to have a common effect on siblings (Plomin & Daniels, 1987). Within the same upbringing environment, the more belligerent sibling observationally learns the items from the parents' aggressive repertoire, whereas the more nurturant sibling selects from the parents' altruistic responses. As Scarr (1992) highlights, the unit of environmental transmission is not so much the family as the microenvironment within the family, and this is largely the construction of individuals in the ways "they evoke responses from others, actively select or ignore opportunities, and construct their own experiences" (p. 14).

That genes guide experience is shown in studies examining variables more often considered as environmental causes than as genetic outcomes (reviewed by Plomin & Bergeman, 1991). Thus, genes influence not only the amount of television watched but also the nurturance of parents, the nature of the peer group, the sense of well-being experienced and a host of life history events. For genetic reasons parents initiate more similar actions to MZ twins than they do to DZ twins while MZ twins reared apart retrospectively recall the warmth of their unlike environments more similarly than do their DZ counterparts. The heritability of family environment measures is about 25 percent.

Both twin and adoption studies show genetic influence on sibling gravitations to college-oriented, delinquent, or popular peer groups (Daniels & Plomin, 1985; Rowe & Osgood, 1984). Although television viewing has been used as an environmental measure in thousands of studies, the correlation for the amount of television viewing for biological siblings is 0.48, whereas the correlation for adoptive siblings is 0.26, suggesting substantial genetic influence (Waller, Kojetin, Bouchard, Lykken, & Tellegen, 1990). The Swedish Adoption Twin Study of Aging showed that life events are heritable. For reared apart monozygotic twins (MZA) the correlation for controllable life events (e.g., serious conflict) is 0.54 and for uncontrollable life events (e.g., serious illness) it is 0.22. The typical heritability for life events is 40 percent (Plomin, Lichtenstein, Pedersen, McClearn, & Nesselroade, 1990).

Dramatic evidence of how genes influence exposure to trauma comes from ongoing studies of combat experience in twin pairs who served in the U.S. military during the Vietnam era (1965–1975). The Vietnam Era Twin Registry consists of 4,042 male-male twin pairs who were born between 1939 and 1957 and served on active duty in the U.S. armed forces. A 35 percent heritability was found on the probability of serving in Vietnam, a 47 percent heritability for exposure to combat, and a 54 percent heritability for receiving a combat decoration (Lyons et al., 1993). Subsequent liability for experiencing symptoms associated with posttraumatic stress disorder had a heritability of about 30 percent (True et al., 1993).

The potential effects of epigenetic rules on behavior and society may go well beyond ontogeny. Through cognitive phenotypes and group action, altruistic inclinations may find their expression in charities and hospitals, creative and instructional dispositions in academies of learning, martial tendencies in institutes of war, and delinquent tendencies in social disorder. Thus, genes may have extended effects beyond the body in which they reside, biasing individuals toward the production of particular cultural systems (Rushton, Littlefield, & Lumsden, 1986).

That genotypes seek out maximally conducive environments is well illustrated by findings that aggressive and altruistic individuals select similar others with whom to associate, not only as friends but also as marriage partners
(Huesmann, Eron, Lefkowitz, & Walder, 1984; Rowe & Osgood, 1984). As
discussed in the next chapter, the epigenetic rules that bias people to choose
each other on the basis of similarity may be particularly fine-tuned, inclining
individuals to assort most according to the more genetically influenced of sets
of attributes.

4

Genetic Similarity Theory

Choosing mates and other social partners are among the most important decisions individuals make affecting their social environment. The tendency is to choose similarity. For example, spouses tend to resemble each other in such characteristics as age, ethnic background, socioeconomic status, physical attractiveness, religion, social attitudes, level of education, family size and structure, intelligence, and personality.

As can be seen in Figure 4.1, the median assortative mating coefficient for standardized IQ measures averaged over 16 studies involving 3,817 pairings is 0.37 (Bouchard & McGue, 1981). Correlations tend to be higher for opinions, attitudes, and values (0.40 to 0.70) and lower for personality traits and personal habits (0.02 to 0.30 with a mean of about 0.15). Spouses also resemble each other in a variety of physical features. Rushton, Russell, and Wells (1985) combined anthropometric data from a wide range of studies and found low but positive correlations for more than 60 different measures, including height (0.21), weight (0.25), hair color (0.28), eye color (0.21), chest breadth (0.20), and interpupillary breadth (0.20)—even curious outliers like 0.40 for ear lobe length, 0.55 for wrist circumference, and 0.61 for length of middle finger.

Most explanations of the role of similarity in human relationships focus on immediate, environmental effects, for example, their reinforcement value (Byrne, 1971). Recent analyses, however, suggest that genetic influences may also be involved. According to "genetic similarity theory" (Rushton, Russell, and Wells, 1984; Rushton, 1989c), genetic likeness exerts subtle effects on a variety of relationships and has implications for the study of social behavior in small groups and even in large ones, both national and international.

In this chapter, genetic similarity theory is introduced in connection with altruism. It is proposed that genetically similar people tend to seek one another out and to provide mutually supportive environments such as marriage, friendship, and social groups. This may represent a biological factor underlying ethnocentrism and group selection.

Figure 4.1: Spousal Resemblance on a Variety of Characteristics

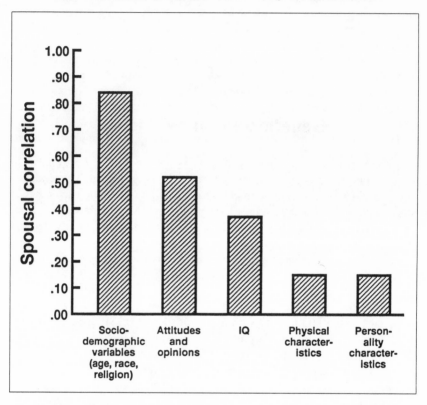

Spouses are most similar for sociodemographic variables such as age, race, and religion, next most for a variety of social attitudes and opinions, then for IQ, and finally for physical and personality characteristics. On all dimensions, spouses are more similar than is expected by chance.

The Paradox of Altruism

Altruism has long posed a serious dilemma for theories of human nature. Defined as behavior carried out to benefit others, in extreme form altruism involves self-sacrifice. In humans altruistic behavior ranges from everyday kindness, through sharing scarce resources, to giving up one's life to save others. In nonhuman animals, altruism includes parental care, warning calls, cooperative defense, rescue behavior, and food sharing; it may also involve self-sacrifice. The poisonous sting of a honeybee is an adaptation against hive robbers. The recurved barbs facing backward from the sharp tip cause the whole sting to be wrenched out of the bee's body, along with some of the bee's vital internal organs. These barbs have been described as instruments of altruistic self-sacrifice.

As recognized by Darwin (1871), however, a genetic basis for altruism would represent a paradox for theories of evolution: How could altruism evolve through "survival of the fittest" when, on the face of it, altruistic behavior diminishes personal fitness? If the most altruistic members of a group sacrifice themselves for others, they run the risk of leaving fewer offspring to pass on the very genes that govern the altruistic behavior. Hence, altruism would be selected against, and selfishness would be selected for.

The resolution of the paradox of altruism is one of the triumphs that led to the new synthesis called sociobiology. By a process known as kin selection, individuals can maximize their inclusive fitness rather than only their individual fitness by increasing the production of successful offspring by both themselves and their genetic relatives (Hamilton, 1964). According to this view, the unit of analysis for evolutionary selection is not the individual organism but its genes. Genes are what survive and are passed on, and some of the same genes will be found not only in direct offspring but in siblings, cousins, nephews/nieces, and grandchildren. If an animal sacrifices its life for its siblings' offspring, it ensures the survival of common genes because, by common descent, it shares 50 percent of its genes with each sibling and 25 percent with each sibling's offspring.

Thus, the percentage of shared genes helps determine the amount of altruism displayed. Social ants are particularly altruistic because of a special feature of their reproductive system that gives them 75 percent of their genes in common with their sisters. Ground squirrels emit more warning calls when placed near relatives than when placed near nonrelatives; "helpers" at the nest tend to be related to one member of the breeding pair; and when social groups of monkeys split, close relatives remain together. When the sting of the honey bee is torn from its body, the individual dies, but the bee's genes, shared in the colony of relatives, survive.

Thus, from an evolutionary perspective, altruism is a means of helping genes to propagate. By being most altruistic to those with whom we share genes we help copies of our own genes to replicate. This makes "altruism" ultimately "selfish" in purpose. Promulgated in the context of animal behavior this idea became known as "kin-selection" and provided a conceptual breakthrough by redefining the unit of analysis away from the individual organism to his or her genes, for it is these that survive and are passed on.

Another way sociobiologists have suggested that altruism could evolve is through reciprocity. Here there is no need for genetic relatedness; performing an altruistic act need only lead to an altruistic act in return. For example, two male baboons in coalition are able to supplant a single male consorting with a female; on any particular occasion, one of the two males copulates while the other, the "altruist," does not. On a later occasion when another female is in estrus, the same two males are likely to get together again, but this time their roles are reversed, the former beneficiary now assuming the role of the altruist.

Detecting Genetic Similarity

In order to pursue a strategy of directing altruism toward kin, the organism must be able to recognize degrees of relatedness. There is clearly no such thing as "genetic extra-sensory perception." For individuals to direct altruism selectively to genetically similar individuals, they must respond to pheno-typic cues. This is typically accomplished by detecting similarities between self and others in physical and behavioral cues. Four processes have been suggested by which animals recognize relatives: (a) innate feature detectors, (b) matching on appearance, (c) familiarity, and (d) location. They are not mutually exclusive. If there are evolutionary advantages to be gained from the ability to detect genetic similarity, all the mechanisms may be operative.

Innate Feature Detectors

Individuals may have "recognition alleles" that control the development of innate mechanisms allowing them to detect genetic similarity in strangers. Dawkins (1976) suggested a thought experiment to illustrate how this could come about, known as the "green beard effect." In this theory, a gene has two effects: It causes individuals who have it to (1) grow a green beard, and (2) behave altruistically toward green-bearded individuals. The green beard serves as a recognition cue for the altruism gene. Altruism could therefore occur without the need for individuals to be directly related.

Matching on Appearance

The individual may be genetically guided to learn its own phenotype, or those of its close kin, and then to match new, unfamiliar individuals to the template it has learned—for example, Dawkins's (1982) "armpit effect." Individuals that smell (or look or behave) like oneself or one's close kin could be distinguished from those that smell (or look or behave) differently. This mechanism would depend on the existence of a strong correlation between genotype and phenotype.

Familiarity or Association

Preferences may also depend on learning through social interaction. This may be the most common means of kin recognition in nature. Individuals that are reared together are more likely to be kin than non-kin. This may also involve a more general mechanism of short-term preference formation. Zajonc (1980) has shown experimentally that the more one is exposed to a stimulus, the more one prefers it. Based on studies of Japanese quail and of humans, respectively, Bateson (1983) and van den Berghe (1983) have suggested that sexual preferences may be established early in life through an imprinting-like process.

Location

The fourth kin recognition mechanism depends on a high correlation between an individual's location and kinship. The rule states: "If it's in your nest, it's yours." Where an individual is and whom the individual encounters can also be based on similar genes—for example, if parents exert discriminatory influence on where and with whom their offspring interact.

Kin Recognition in Animals

There is dramatic experimental evidence that many animal species recognize genetic similarity. Greenberg (1979) showed that the sweat bee, *Lasioglossum zephyrum*, can discriminate between unfamiliar conspecifics of varying degrees of relatedness. Guard bees of this species block the nest to prevent intruders from entering. In this study, bees were first bred for 14 different degrees of genealogical relationship with each other. They were then introduced near nests that contained sisters, aunts, nieces, first cousins, or more distantly related bees. In each case the guard was expected to make a binary decision—either permitting the bee that was introduced to pass or actively preventing it from doing so. There was a strong linear relationship ($r = 0.93$) between the ability to pass the guard bee and the degree of genetic relatedness. The greater the degree of genetic similarity, the greater the proportion of bees that were allowed to enter the hive. The guard bees appear to be able to detect the degree of genetic similarity between themselves and the intruder. Subsequent kin recognition studies have shown that the honeybee, *Apis mellifera*, is able to discriminate between full and half sisters raised in neighboring cells.

There is also evidence that the ability to detect genetic similarity exists in various species of plants, tadpoles, birds, rodents, and rhesus monkeys. In studies of the frog *Rana cascadae*, by Blaustein and O'Hara (1982), tadpoles were separated before hatching and reared in isolation. The individual tadpoles were then placed in a rectangular tank with two end compartments created by plastic mesh. Siblings were placed in one compartment and nonsiblings in the other. The separated tadpoles spent more time at the siblings' end of the tank. Because the tadpoles were separated as embryos and raised in complete isolation, an ability to detect genetic similarity is implicated.

Mammals are also able to detect degrees of genetic relatedness (Fletcher & Michener, 1987). For example, Belding's ground squirrels produce litters that contain both sisters and half sisters. Despite the fact that they shared the same womb and inhabit the same nest, full sisters fight less often than half sisters, come to each other's aid more, and are less prone to chase one another out of their home territory. Similar findings have been noted among captive multimale, multifemale groups of rhesus monkeys growing up outdoors in large social troops. Adults of both sexes are promiscuous, but mothers appear to chase paternal half siblings away from their infants less often than they do unrelated juveniles, and males (despite promiscuity) appear to "recognize" their own offspring, for they treat them better (Suomi, 1982). In the preceding examples, the degree of genetic relatedness was established by blood tests. Walters (1987) has reviewed well-replicated data from several primate species indicating that grooming, alliance formation, cooperative defense, and food sharing occur more readily in kinship groups.

Kin Recognition in Humans

Building on the work of Hamilton (1964), Dawkins (1976), Thiessen and Gregg (1980), and others, the kin-selection theory of altruism was extended to the human case. Rushton et al. (1984) proposed that, if a gene can better ensure its own survival by acting so as to bring about the reproduction of family members with whom it shares copies, then it can also do so by benefiting any organism in which copies of itself are to be found. This would be an alternative way for genes to propagate themselves. Rather than merely protecting kin at the expense of strangers, if organisms could identify genetically similar organisms, they could exhibit altruism toward these "strangers" as well as toward kin. Kin recognition would be just one form of genetic similarity detection.

The implication of genetic similarity theory is that the more genes are shared by organisms, the more readily reciprocal altruism and cooperation should develop because this eliminates the need for strict reciprocity. In order to pursue a strategy of directing altruism toward similar genes, the organism must be able to detect genetic similarity in others. As described in the previous section, four such mechanisms by which this could occur have been considered in the literature.

Humans are capable of learning to distinguish kin from non-kin at an early age. Infants can distinguish their mothers from other women by voice alone at 24 hours of age, know the smell of their mother's breast before they are six days of age, and recognize a photograph of their mother when they are 2 weeks old. Mothers are also able to identify their infants by smell alone after a single exposure at 6 hours of age, and to recognize their infant's cry within 48 hours of birth (see Wells, 1987, for review).

Human kin preferences also follow lines of genetic similarity. For example, among the Ye'Kwana Indians of South America, the words "brother" and "sister" cover four different categories ranging from individuals who share 50 percent of their genes (identical by descent) to individuals who share only 12.5 percent of their genes. Hames (1979) has shown that the amount of time the Ye'Kwana spend interacting with their biological relatives increases with their degree of relatedness, even though their kinship terminology does not reflect this correspondence.

Anthropological data also show that in societies where certainty of paternity is relatively low, males direct material resources to their sisters' offspring (to whom their relatedness is certain) rather than to their wives' offspring (Kurland, 1979). An analysis of the contents of 1,000 probated wills reveals that after husbands and wives, kin received about 55 percent of the total amount bequeathed whereas non-kin received only about 7 percent; offspring received more than nephews and nieces (Smith, Kish, & Crawford, 1987).

Paternity uncertainty also exerts predictable influence. Grandparents spend 35 to 42 percent more time with their daughters' children than with their sons' children (Smith, 1981). Following a bereavement they grieve more for their daughters' children than for their sons' children (Littlefield & Rushton, 1986). Family members feel only 87 percent as close to the fathers' side of the family as they do to the mothers' side (Russell & Wells, 1987). Finally, mothers of newborn children and her relatives spend more time commenting on resemblances between the baby and the putative father than they do about the resemblance between the baby and the mother (Daly & Wilson, 1982).

When the level of genetic similarity within a family is low, the consequences can be serious. Children who are unrelated to a parent are at risk; a disproportionate number of battered babies are stepchildren (Lightcap, Kurland, & Burgess, 1982). Children of preschool age are 40 times more likely to be assaulted if they are stepchildren than if they are biological children (Daly & Wilson, 1988). Also, unrelated people living together are more likely to kill each other than are related people living together. Converging evidence shows that adoptions are more likely to be successful when the parents perceive the child as similar to them (Jaffee & Fanshel, 1970).

Spouse Selection

A well-known phenomenon that is readily explained by genetic similarity theory is positive assortative mating, that is, the tendency of spouses to be nonrandomly paired in the direction of resembling each other in one or more traits more than would be expected by chance. Although the data shown in Figure 4.1 are widely accepted, it is less well known that spouses also resemble each other in socially undesirable characteristics, including aggressiveness, criminality, alcoholism, and psychiatric disorders such as schizophrenia and the affective disorders. Although alternative reasons can be proposed for this finding, such as losing the competition for the most attractive and healthiest mates (Burley, 1983), it does suggest that the tendency to seek a similar partner may override considerations such as mate quality and individual fitness.

A study of cross-racial marriages in Hawaii found more similarity in personality test scores among males and females who married across ethnic groups than among those marrying within them (Ahern, Cole, Johnson, & Wong, 1981). The researchers posit that, given the general tendency toward homogamy, couples marrying heterogamously with respect to ethnicity tend to "make up" for this dissimilarity by choosing spouses more similar to themselves in other respects than do persons marrying within their own ethnic group.

It could be argued that human assortative mating has nothing to do with questions about genetic similarity, that it results only from common environmental influences. This view cannot easily account for the incidence of assortative mating in other animals ranging from insects to birds to primates, in laboratory as well as in natural settings (Fletcher & Michener, 1987; Thiessen & Gregg, 1980). Assortative mating also occurs in many species of plants (Willson & Burley, 1983). To have evolved independently in such a wide variety of circumstances, assortative mating must confer substantial advantage. In humans these may include (1) increased marital stability, (2) increased relatedness to offspring, (3) increased within-family altruism, and (4) greater fecundity.

The upper limit on the fitness-enhancing effect of assortative mating for similarity occurs with incest. Too much genetic similarity between mates increases the chances that harmful recessive genes may combine. The negative effects of "inbreeding depression" have been demonstrated in many species, including humans (Jensen, 1983; Thiessen & Gregg, 1980). As a result, many have hypothesized that the "incest taboo" has an evolutionary basis, possibly mediated through negative imprinting on intimate associates at an early age (van den Berghe, 1983). Optimal fitness, then, may consist in selecting a mate who is genetically similar but not actually a relative. Van den Berghe (1983) speculates that the ideal percentage of relatedness is 12.5 percent identical by descent, or the same as that between first cousins. Other animal species also avoid inbreeding. For example, several experiments have been carried out with Japanese quail, birds that, although promiscuous, proved particularly sophisticated. They preferred first cousins to third cousins, and both of these relatives to either unrelated birds or siblings, thus avoiding the dangers of too much or too little inbreeding (Bateson, 1983).

Blood Tests of Sexually Interacting Couples

To directly test the hypothesis that human mating follows lines of genetic similarity, Rushton (1988a) examined blood antigen analyses from nearly 1,000 cases of disputed paternity. Seven polymorphic marker systems—ABO, Rhesus (Rh), MNSs, Kell, Duffy (Fy), Kidd (Jk), and HLA—at 10 loci across 6 chromosomes were examined in a sample limited to people of North European appearance (judged by photographs kept for legal identification). Such blood group differences provide a biological criterion sufficient to identify more than 95 percent of true relatedness in situations of paternal dispute (Bryant, 1980), and to reliably distinguish between fraternal twins raised together (Pakstis, Scarr-Salapatek, Elston, & Siervogel, 1972). They provide a less precise but still useful estimate of genetic distance among unrelated individuals.

Sexually interacting couples were found to share about 50 percent of measured genetic markers, partway between mothers and their offspring, who shared 73 percent, and randomly paired individuals from the same sample, who shared 43 percent (all comparisons were significantly different, $p < 0.001$). In the cases of disputed paternity, genetic similarity predicted whether the male was the true father of the child. Males not excluded from paternity were 52 percent similar to their partners whereas those excluded were only 44 percent similar ($p < 0.001$).

TABLE 4.1
Percentage of Genetic Similarity in 4 Types of Human Relationships,
Based on 10 Blood Loci

Relationship	Number of pairs	Mean	Standard deviation	Range
Mother-offspring	100	73	9	50-88
Sexually interacting adults (male not excluded from paternity)	799	52	12	17-90
Sexually interacting adults (male excluded from paternity)	187	44	12	15-74
Randomly paired male-female dyads	200	43	14	11-81

Note. From Rushton (1988a, p. 331, Table 1). Copyright by Elsevier Science Publishing. Reprinted with permission.

Heritability Predicts Spousal Similarity

If people choose each other on the basis of shared genes, it should be possible to demonstrate that interpersonal relationships are influenced more by genetic similarity than by similarity attributable to a similar environment. A strong test of the theory is to observe that positive assortative mating is greater on the more heritable of a set of homogeneous items. This prediction follows because more heritable items better reflect the underlying genotype.

Stronger estimates of genetic influence have been found to predict the degree of matching that marriage partners have engaged in on anthropometric, attitudinal, cognitive, and personality variables. Thus, Rushton and Nicholson (1988) examined studies using 15 subtests from the Hawaii Family Study of Cognition and 11 subtests from the Wechsler Adult Intelligence Scale. With the Hawaii battery, genetic estimates from Koreans in Korea correlated positively with those from Americans of Japanese and European ancestry (mean $r = 0.54$, $p < 0.01$). With the Wechsler scale, estimates of genetic influence correlated across three samples with a mean $r = 0.82$.

Consider the data in Table 4.2 showing heritabilities predicting the similarity of marriage partners. Note, though, that many of the estimates of genetic influence in this table are based on calculations of midparent-offspring regressions using data from intact families, thereby combining genetic and shared-family environmental effects. The latter source of variance, however, is surprisingly small (Plomin & Daniels, 1987) and has not been found to add systematic bias. Nonetheless, it should be borne in mind that many of the estimates of genetic influence shown in Table 4.2 were calculated in this way.

Reported in Table 4.2 is a study by Russell, Wells, and Rushton (1985) who used a within-subjects design to examine data from three studies reporting independent estimates of genetic influence and assortative mating. Positive correlations were found between the two sets of measures ($r = 0.36$, $p < 0.05$, for 36 anthropometric variables; $r = 0.73$, $p < 0.10$, for 5 perceptual judgment variables; and $r = 0.44$, $p < 0.01$, for 11 personality variables). In the case of the personality measures, test-retest reliabilities over a three-year period were available and were not found to influence the results.

Another test of the hypothesis reported in Table 4.2 was made by Rushton and Russell (1985) using two separate estimates of the heritabilities for 54 personality traits. Independently and when combined into an aggregate, they predicted similarity between spouses ($rs = 0.44$ and 0.55, $ps < 0.001$). Rushton and Russell (1985) reviewed other reports of similar correlations, including Kamin's (1978) calculation of $r = 0.79$ ($p < 0.001$) for 15 cognitive tests and DeFries et al.'s (1978) calculation of $r = 0.62$ ($p < 0.001$) for 13 anthropometric variables. Cattell (1982) too had noted that between-spouse correlations tended to be lower for the less heritable, more specific cognitive abilities (tests of vocabulary and arithmetic) than for the more heritable general abilities (g, from Progressive Matrices).

TABLE 4.2
Summary of Studies on Relation Between Heritability of Traits and Assortive Marriage

Study	Sample	Test type	Heritability	Correlation with assortment
Kamin (1978)	739 European-American families in Hawaii	15 subtests from HFSC	Midparent-midchild regression	.79***
DeFries et al. (1978)	73 European-American families in Hawaii	13 anthropometric variables from HFSC	Midparent-midchild regression	.62***
Cattell (1982)	Numerous twin and family studies	Cognitive abilities, specific and general	Multiple abstract variance analysis	Higher on the more heritable traits; magnitudes not reported
Russell et al. (1985)	Asians and North Africans	5 perceptual judgments	Parent-offspring correlation corrected for assortative mating	.73***
	Belgians	36 anthropometric variables	Parent-offspring correlation corrected for assortative mating	.36*
Rushton & Russell (1985)	European-Americans	11 scales from MMPI	Midparent-offspring correlation	.71**
	100-669 families in Hawaii (ethnicity not specified)	54 personality scales	Parent-offspring regression	.44***
			Doubled sibling-sibling correlation	.46***
			Composite of both above	.55***
Rushton & Nicholson (1988)	871 European-American families in Hawaii	15 subtests from HFSC	Midparent-offspring regression	Intragroup .71** Intergroup .43+
	311 Japanese-American families in Hawaii	15 subtests from HFSC	Midparent-offspring regression	Intragroup .13 Intergroup .47*
	209 families in Republic of Korea	14 subtests from HFSC	Midparent-offspring regression	Intragroup .53* Intergroup .18
	55 Canadians	11 subtests from WAIS	Midparent-offspring regression	Intragroup .23 Intergroup .60*
	240 adolescent twins in Kentucky	11 subtests from WAIS	Holsinger's H formula	Intragroup - Intergroup .68*
	120 Minnesota families	4 subtests from WAIS plus total score	Parent-offspring correlation corrected for assortative mating	Intragroup .68 Intergroup .64

Note. From Rushton (1989c, p. 509, Table 3). Copyright 1989 by Cambridge University Press. Reprinted with permission.
HFSC = Hawaii Family Study of Cognition; MMPI = Minnesota Multiphasic Personality Inventory; WAIS = Weschler Adult Intelligence Scale
*** $p < .001$; ** $p < .01$; * $p < .05$; + $p < .10$.

Also shown in Table 4.2 are analyses carried out using a between-subjects design. Rushton and Nicholson (1988) analyzed data from studies using 15 subtests from the Hawaii Family Study of Cognition (HFSC) and 11 subtests from the Wechsler Adult Intelligence Scale (WAIS); positive correlations were calculated within and between samples. For example, in the HFSC, parent-offspring regressions (corrected for reliability) using data from Americans of European ancestry in Hawaii, Americans of Japanese ancestry in Hawaii, and Koreans in Korea correlated positively with between-spouse similarity scores taken from the same samples and with those taken from two other samples: Americans of mixed ancestry in California and a group in Colorado. The overall mean r was 0.38 for the 15 tests. Aggregating across the numerous estimates to form the most reliable composite gave a substantially better prediction of mate similarity from the estimate of genetic influence ($r = 0.74$, $p < 0.001$). Similar results were found with the WAIS. Three estimates of genetic influence correlated positively with similarities between spouses based on different samples, and in the aggregate they predicted the composite of spouse similarity scores with $r = 0.52$ ($p < 0.05$).

Parenthetically, it is worth noting that statistically controlling for the effects of g in both the HFSC and the WAIS analyses led to substantially lower correlations between estimates of genetic influence and assortative mating, thus offering support for the view that marital assortment in intelligence occurs primarily with the g factor. The g factor tends to be the most heritable component of cognitive performance measures (chap. 3).

Intrafamilial Relationships

One consequence of genetic similarity between spouses is a concomitant increase of within-family altruism. Several studies have shown that not only the occurrence of relationships but also their degree of happiness and stability can be predicted by the degree of matching on personal attributes (Bentler & Newcombe, 1978; Cattell & Nesselroade, 1967; Eysenck & Wakefield, 1981; Hill, Rubin & Peplau, 1976; Meyer & Pepper, 1977; Terman & Buttenwieser, 1935a, 1935b). Because many of the traits on the basis of which spouses choose each other are about 50 percent heritable, it follows that the matching results in genetic similarity. Whereas each trait may add only a tiny amount to the total genetic variance shared by spouses, the cumulative effects could be considerable.

The quality of marriage of 94 couples was examined in a study by Russell and Wells (1991). The couples were also given the Eysenck Personality Questionnaire. On average, couples showed a significant tendency to assort on Eysenck Personality Questionnaire items. Likewise, on average, similarity between spouses at the item level was predictive of a good marriage. The degree to which similarity on an item predicted a good marriage correlated weakly but significantly ($p < 0.05$) with the heritability of the item, as estimated independently by Neale, Rushton, & Fulker (1986). Thus, some support was found for the hypothesis that quality of marriage depends on genetic similarity.

A related prediction can be made about parental care of offspring that differ in similarity. Sibling differences within families have often been overlooked as a topic of research. Positive assortative mating for genetically based traits may make some children genetically more similar to one parent or sibling than to another. For example, if a father gives his child 50 percent of his genes, 10 percent of them shared with the mother, and the mother gives the child 50 percent of her genes, 20 percent shared with the father, then the child will be 60 percent similar to the mother and 70 percent similar to the father. Genetic similarity theory predicts that parents and siblings will favor those who are most similar.

Littlefield and Rushton (1986) tested this hypothesis in a study of bereavement following the death of a child. It was predicted that the more similar the parent perceived the child to be, the greater would be that parent's grief experience. (Perceived similarity with offspring is correlated with genetic similarity measured by blood tests [Pakstis et al., 1972].) Respondents picked which side of the family the child "took after" more, their own or their spouse's. Spouses agreed 74 percent on this question. Both mothers and fathers grieved more intensely for children perceived as resembling their side of the family.

Other evidence of within-family preferences comes from a review by Segal (1993) of feelings of closeness, cooperation, and altruism in twin pairs. Compared with fraternal twins, identical twins worked harder for their co-twins on tasks, maintained greater physical proximity, expressed more affection, and suffered greater loss following bereavement.

A Genetic Basis for Friendship

Friendships also appear to be formed on the basis of similarity. This assumption holds for similarity as perceived by the friends, and for a variety of objectively measured characteristics, including activities, attitudes, needs, personality, and, also, anthropometric variables. Moreover, in the experimental literature on who likes whom, and why, one of the most influential variables is perceived similarity. Apparent similarity of personality, attitudes, or any of a wide range of beliefs has been found to generate liking in subjects of varying ages and from many different cultures.

According to genetic similarity theory, there is a genetic basis to friendship and friendship is one of the mechanisms that leads to altruism. Many social psychological studies show that altruism increases with the benefactor's actual or perceived similarity to the beneficiary. For example, Stotland (1969) had subjects observe a person who appeared to be receiving electric shocks.

When Stotland manipulated the subjects' beliefs about their similarity to that person, perceived similarity was correlated with reported empathy as well as with physiological skin conductance measures of emotional responsiveness. Krebs (1975) has found that apparent similarity not only increases physiological correlates of emotion such as skin conductance, vasoconstriction, and heart rate, but also the willingness to reward the victim. In young children, the frequency of social interactions between friends corresponds closely to the frequency of acts of altruism between them (Strayer, Wareing, & Rushton, 1979).

Data show that the tendency to choose similar individuals as friends is genetically influenced. In a study of delinquency among 530 adolescent twins by Rowe and Osgood (1984), path analysis revealed not only that antisocial behavior was about 50 percent heritable, but that the correlation of 0.56 between the delinquency of an individual and the delinquency of his friends was mediated genetically, that is, that adolescents genetically disposed to delinquency were also genetically inclined to seek each other out for friendship. In a study of 396 adolescent and young adult siblings from both adoptive and nonadoptive homes, Daniels and Plomin (1985) found that genetic influences were implicated in choice of friends: Biological siblings were more similar to each other in the types of friends they had than were adoptive siblings.

Blood Tests among Friends

I (Rushton, 1989d) used blood tests to determine whether friends are more similar to each other using methods parallel to those used in the study of heterosexual partners. Seventy-six long-term, nonrelated, nonhomosexual male Caucasian friendship pairs ranging in age from 18 to 57 years were recruited by advertisements from the general community. A control group was formed by randomly pairing individuals from the sample. At the testing session, a 12- to 14-milliliter blood sample was drawn from each person.

The best friends were 54 percent similar to each other using 10 loci from 7 polymorphic blood systems—ABO, Rhesus (Rh), MNSs, P, Duffy (Fy), Kidd (Jk), and HLA. An equal number of randomly chosen pairs were only 48 percent similar ($t[150] = 3.13$, $p < 0.05$). Stratification effects were unlikely because within-pair differences in age, education, and occupation did not correlate with the blood similarity scores (mean $r = -0.05$).

Heritability and Friendship Similarity

I also examined similarity on several questionnaire items chosen because estimates had been calculated of the degree of genetic influence on the various components. For example, 36 heritabilities were available with respect to 50 social attitude items (see Table 4.3) from data on 3,810 Australian twin pairs (Martin et al., 1986). For 90 items from the Eysenck Personality Questionnaire, two independent sets of heritability estimates were available for a

TABLE 4.3
Heritability Estimates and Similarity Between Friends on Conservatism Items
(N = 76)

Item	Heritability estimate	Friendship similarity score	Test-retest reliability	Similarity score corected for unreliability	Similarity score corrected for age, education, and occupation
1. Death penalty	.51	.28	.87	.30	.38
2. Evolution theory	—	.08	.95	.08	.20
3. School uniforms	—	.20	.99	.20	.42
4. Striptease shows	—	.13	.97	.13	.24
5. Sabbath observance	.35	.08	.91	.08	.09
6. Hippies	.27	.03	.97	.03	.15
7. Patriotism	—	.10	.89	.11	.13
8. Modern art	—	.02	.93	.02	.09
9. Self-denial	.28	.08	.79	.09	.12
10. Working mothers	.36	.07	.83	.08	.13
11. Horoscopes	—	.23	.92	.24	.20
12. Birth control	—	.04	-.01	.00	.19
13. Military drill	.40	.10	.96	.10	.22
14. Coeducation	.07	-.05	.74	-.06	-.05
15. Divine law	.22	.25	.82	.28	.20
16. Socialism	.26	.08	.83	.09	.14
17. White superiority	.40	.22	.68	.27	.11
18. Cousin marriage	.35	.04	.89	.04	.24
19. Moral training	.29	.07	.77	.08	.16
20. Suicide	—	.08	.86	.09	.08
21. Chaperones	—	.00	.94	.00	.11
22. Legalized abortion	.32	.13	.96	.13	.29
23. Empire building	—	.02	.85	.02	.05
24. Student pranks	.30	-.02	.88	-.02	.07
25. Licensing law	—	-.20	.85	-.22	-.13
26. Computer music	.26	.02	.91	.02	.16
27. Chastity	—	.00	.76	.00	.13
28. Fluoridation	.34	.08	.86	.09	.04
29. Royalty	.44	.15	.92	.16	.16
30. Women judges	.27	.03	1.00	.03	.08
31. Conventional clothes	.35	.31	.83	.34	.29
32. Teenage drivers	.26	.02	.78	.02	.20
33. Apartheid	.43	.14	.69	.17	.10
34. Nudist camps	.28	.08	.85	.09	-.09
35. Church authority	.29	.08	.86	.09	.21
36. Disarmament	.38	.07	.96	.07	.19
37. Censorship	.41	.03	.81	.03	.10
38. White lies	.35	.06	.76	.07	-.01
39. Caning	.21	.14	.83	.15	.11
40. Mixed marriage	.33	.25	.79	.28	.29
41. Strict rules	.31	.25	.81	.28	.19
42. Jazz	.45	.42	.77	.48	.40
43. Straitjackets	.09	.00	.85	.00	.00
44. Casual living	.29	.18	.63	.23	.55
45. Learning Latin	.26	.03	.97	.03	.10
46. Divorce	.40	.03	.92	.03	.09
47. Inborn conscience	—	.20	.70	.24	-.11
48. Colored immigration	—	.06	.88	.06	.10
49. Bible truth	.25	.30	.95	.31	.47
50. Pajama parties	.08	.08	.91	.08	.24

Note. From Rushton (1989d, p. 365, Table 1). Copyright 1989 by Elsevier Science Publishing. Reprinted with permission.

total of 81 of the items, one set from 3,810 Australian twin pairs (Jardine, 1985), and the other set from 627 British twin pairs (Neale et al., 1986). These intercorrelated with $r = 0.44$ ($p < 0.001$) and were aggregated to form a more reliable composite. For 13 anthropometric measures, estimates of genetic influence were available based on midparent-offspring regressions from data on 125 families in Belgium (Susanne, 1977).

Examples of varying heritabilities include: 51 percent for attitude to the death penalty versus 25 percent for attitude to the truth of the Bible (see Table 4.3), 41 percent for having a preference for reading versus 20 percent for having a preference for many different hobbies (Neale et al., 1986), and 80 percent for mid-finger length versus 50 percent for upper arm circumference (Susanne, 1977). When evaluating these results, it should be kept in mind that the friendship heritabilities were generalized from one sample (e.g., Australian twins) to another (Canadian friends). This result is a conservative test of the genetic similarity hypothesis because the predicted effect has to be sufficiently generalizable to overcome these differences.

Across the measures, close friends were found to be significantly more similar to each other than to randomly paired individuals from the same sample. Pearson product-moment correlations showed that compared with random pairs, friendship dyads are more similar in age (0.64 vs. -0.10, $p < 0.05$), education (0.42 vs. 0.11, $p < 0.05$), occupational status (0.39 vs. -0.02, $p < 0.05$), conservatism (0.36 vs. -0.02, $p < 0.05$), mutual feelings of altruism and intimacy (0.32 vs. -0.04 and 0.18 vs. -0.08, $ps < 0.05$), 13 anthropometric variables (mean = 0.12 vs. -0.03, ns), 26 personality scale scores (mean = 0.09 vs. 0.00, ns), and 20 personality self-rating scores (mean = 0.08 vs. 0.00, ns). Although these similarities are very small, significantly more are positive than could be expected by chance (13/13 of the anthropometric variables, 18/26 of the personality scale scores, and 15/20 of the personality self-rating scores, all $p < 0.05$, binomial sign test). It should be noted that these relative magnitudes parallel the between-spouse similarities (Figure 4.1).

Similarity between friends was strongest on the most heritable characteristics. For the 36 conservatism items (Table 4.3), the heritabilities correlated $r = 0.40$ ($p < 0.01$) with the degree of similarity between friends, a relationship not altered when corrected for test-retest reliability or age, education, and occupational status. For the 81 personality items, the heritabilities correlated 0.20 ($p < 0.05$) with friendship similarities, a relationship also not changed by a correction for test-retest reliability or socioeconomic similarity. For the 13 anthropometric variables, however, the correlation between heritabilities and similarities was not significant ($r = 0.15$).

Independent corroboration that attitudes with high heritability are stronger than those with low heritability has come from a series of studies by Tesser (1993). Each subject responded "agree" or "disagree" to attitudes with known heritabilities, including some of those in Table 4.3. Attitudes higher in heritability were accessed more readily as measured by response time, changed less readily when attempts were made at social influence, and predicted better in the attitude-similarity attraction relationship. Thus, Tesser (1993) found that the more heritable attitudes correlated most with attraction to a stranger imagined as a potential friend, a romantic partner, and as a spouse.

Ethnocentrism

The implications of the finding that people moderate their behavior as a function of genetic similarity are far-reaching. They suggest a biological basis for ethnocentrism. Despite enormous variance within populations, it can be expected that two individuals within an ethnic group will, on average, be more similar to each other genetically than two individuals from different ethnic groups. According to genetic similarity theory, people can be expected to favor their own group over others.

Ethnic conflict and rivalry, of course, is one of the great themes of historical and contemporary society (Horowitz, 1985; Shaw & Wong, 1989; van den Berghe, 1981). Local ethnic favoritism is also displayed by group members who prefer to congregate in the same area and to associate with each other in clubs and organizations. Understanding modern Africa, for example, is impossible without understanding tribalism there (Lamb, 1987). Many studies have found that people are more likely to help members of their own race or country than they are to help members of other races or foreigners, and that antagonism between classes and nations may be greater when a racial element is involved.

Traditionally, political scientists and historians have seldom considered intergroup conflict from an evolutionary standpoint. That fear and mistrust of strangers may have biological origins, however, is supported by evidence that animals show fear of and hostility toward strangers, even when no injury has ever been received. Direct analogies have been drawn between the way monkeys and apes resent and repel intruding strangers of the same species and the way children attack another child who is perceived as being an outsider (Gruter & Masters, 1986; Hebb & Thompson, 1968). Many influential social psychologists have pondered whether the transmission of xenophobia could be partly genetic. W. J. McGuire (1969:265) wrote:

> [I]t appears possible for specific attitudes of hostility to be transmitted genetically in such a way that hostility is directed towards strangers of one's own species to a greater extent than towards familiars of one's own species or towards members of other species. It would not be impossible for xenophobia to be a partially innate attitude in the human.

Theorists from Darwin and Spencer to Allport and Freud and now Alexander, Campbell, Eibl-Eibesfeldt, and E. O. Wilson have considered in-group/outgroup discrimination to have roots deep in evolutionary biology. (For a historical review, see van der Dennen, 1987.) Recent developmental psychological studies have found that even very young children show clear and often quite rigid disdain for children whose ethnic and racial heritages differ from their own, even in the apparent absence of experiential and socialization effects (Aboud, 1988).

Many of those who have considered nationalist and patriotic sentiment from a sociobiological perspective, however, have emphasized its apparent irrationality. Johnson (1986) formulated a theory of patriotism in which socialization and conditioning engage kin-recognition systems so that people behave altruistically toward in-group members as though they were genetically more similar than they actually are. In Johnson's analysis, for example, patriotism may often be an ideology propagated by the ruling class to induce the ruled to behave contrary to their own genetic interests, while increasing the fitness of the elite. He noted that patriotism is built by referring to the homeland as the "motherland" or "fatherland," and that bonds between people are strengthened by referring to them as "brothers" and "sisters."

According to genetic similarity theory, patriotism is more than just "manipulated" altruism working to the individual's genetic detriment. It is an epigenetically guided strategy by which genes replicate copies of themselves more effectively. The developmental processes that Johnson (1986) and others have outlined undoubtedly occur, as do other forms of manipulated altruism. However, if these were sufficient to explain the human propensity to feel strong moral obligation toward society, patriotism would remain an anomaly for evolutionary biology. From the standpoint of optimization, one might ask whether evolutionarily stable ethical systems would survive very long if they consistently led to reductions in the inclusive fitness of those believing in them.

If epigenetic rules do incline people toward constructing and learning those ideologies that generally increase their fitness, then patriotic nationalism, religious zealotry, class conflict, and other forms of ideological commitment can be seen as genetically influenced cultural choices that individuals make that, in turn, influence the replication of their genes. Religious, political, and other ideological battles may become as heated as they do partly because of implications for fitness; some genotypes may thrive more in one ideological culture than another. In this view, Karl Marx did not take the argument far enough: Ideology serves more than economic interest; it also serves genetic purpose.

Two sets of falsifiable propositions follow from this interpretation. First, individual differences in ideological preference are partly heritable. Second, ideological belief increases genetic fitness. There is evidence to support both propositions. With respect to the heritability of differences in ideological preference, it has generally been assumed that political attitudes are mostly determined by the environment; however, as discussed in chapter 3, both twin and adoption studies reveal significant heritabilities for social and political attitudes as well as for stylistic tendencies (see also Table 4.3).

Examples of ideologies that increase genetic fitness are religious beliefs that regulate dietary habits, sexual practices, marital custom, infant care, and child rearing (Lumsden & Wilson, 1981; Reynolds & Tanner, 1983). Amerindian tribes that cooked maize with alkali had higher population densities and more complex social organizations than tribes that did not, partly because cooking with alkali releases the most nutritious parts of the cereal, enabling more people to grow to reproductive maturity (Katz, Hodiger, & Valleroy, 1974). The Amerindians did not know the biochemical reasons for the benefits of alkali cooking, but their cultural beliefs had evolved for good reason, enabling them to replicate their genes more effectively than would otherwise have been the case.

By way of objection, it could be argued that although some religious ideologies confer direct benefits on the extended family, ideologies like patriotism decrease fitness (hence, most analyses of patriotism would ultimately rest entirely on social manipulation). Genetic similarity theory may provide a firmer basis for an evolutionary understanding of patriotism, for benefited genes do not have to be only those residing in kin. Members of ethnic groups, for example, often share the same ideologies, and many political differences are genetic in origin. One possible test of genetic similarity theory in this context is to calculate degrees of genetic similarity among ideologues in order to examine whether ideological "conservatives" are more homogeneous than the same ideology's "liberals." Preserving the "purity" of an ideology might be an attempt to preserve the "purity" of the gene pool.

Because ethnic conflict has defied explanation by the standard social science disciplines, genetic similarity theory may represent an advance in understanding the causes of these conflicts, as well as of ethnocentric attitudes in general. Eibl-Eibesfeldt (1989) agreed that if attraction toward similarity has a genetic component then it provides the basis for xenophobia as an innate trait in human beings, a phenomenon manifested in all cultures so far studied.

Van den Berghe (1989) also endorsed the genetic similarity perspective on ethnocentrism, stating that ethnicity has a "primordial dimension." In his 1981 book, *The Ethnic Phenomenon,* he had suggested that ethnocentrism and racism were explainable as cases of extended nepotism. He had shown that even relatively open and assimilative ethnic groups police their ethnic boundaries against invasion by strangers and he showed how they used badges as markers of group membership. These were likely to be cultural rather than physical, he argued, such as linguistic accent or even clothing style. Subsequently, it seemed to him, the ability to recognize others who shared traits of high heritability provided a better means for identifying fellow ethnics. Genetic markers would be more reliable than flexible cultural ones, although these other membership badges could also be used.

Adopting a gene-based evolutionary perspective for ethnic conflict may prove illuminating, especially in the light of the conspicuous failures of environmentalist theories. With the breakup of the Soviet Bloc, many Western analysts have been surprised at the outbreak of the fierce ethnic antagonisms long thought over. Richard Lynn (1989: 534) put it directly:

> Racial and ethnic conflict is occurring throughout the world—between Blacks and Whites in the United States, South Africa, and Britain; Basques and Spaniards in Spain; and Irish and British in Northern Ireland. These conflicts have defied explanations by the disciplines of sociology, psychology, and economics.... genetic similarity theory represents a major advance in the understanding of these conflicts.

R. Lynn (1989) raised the question of why people remain as irrationally attached as they do to languages, even almost dead ones such as Gaelic and Welsh. One function of language barriers, he suggested, was to promote inbreeding among fellow ethnics. The close mapping recently found to occur between linguistic and genetic trees supports Lynn's hypothesis. Cavalli-Sforza, Piazza, Menozzi, and Mountain (1988) grouped gene frequencies from 42 populations into a phylogenetic tree based on genetic distances and related it to a taxonomy of 17 linguistic phyla (chap. 11). Despite the apparent volatility of language and its capacity to be imposed by conquerors at will, considerable parallelism between genetic and linguistic evolution was found.

Selection of Groups

Humans have obviously been selected to live in groups, and the line of argument presented so far may have implications for determining whether group selection occurs among humans. Although the idea of group selection, defined as "selection that operates on two or more members of a lineage group as a unit" (E. O. Wilson, 1975: 585), and as "the differential reproduction of groups, often imagined to favor traits that are individually disadvantageous but evolve because they benefit the larger group" (Trivers, 1985: 456), was popular with Darwin, Spencer, and others, it is not currently thought to play a major role in evolution. Hamilton's (1964) theory of inclusive fitness, for example, is regarded as an extension of individual selection, not group selection (Dawkins, 1976, 1982). Indeed, in recent times group selection has "rivaled Lamarkianism as the most thoroughly repudiated idea in evolutionary theory," as D. S. Wilson put it (1983: 159). Mathematical models (reviewed in D. S. Wilson, 1983) show that group selection could override individual selection only under extreme conditions such as small intergroup migration rate, small group size, and large differences in fitness among groups.

In the recent past it was Wynne-Edwards (1962) who brought the altruism issue to theoretical center stage. He suggested that whole groups of animals collectively refrain from overbreeding when the density of population becomes too great—even to the point of directly killing their offspring if necessary. Such self-restraint, he argued, protects the animals' resource base and gives them an advantage over groups that do not practice restraint and become extinct as a result of their profligacy. This extreme form of the group selection claim was immediately disputed. A great deal of argument and data was subsequently marshaled against the idea (Williams, 1966). There did not seem to exist a mechanism (other than favoring kin) by which altruistic individuals could leave more genes than selfish individuals who cheated.

A compromise was offered by E. O. Wilson (1975), who suggested that although genes are the units of replication, their selection could take place through competition at both the individual and the group levels; for some purposes these can be viewed as opposite ends of a continuum of nested, ever-enlarging sets of socially interacting individuals. Kin selection is thus seen as intermediate between individual and group selection. Genetic similarity theory, according to which genes maximize their replication by benefiting any organism in which their copies are to be found, may provide a mechanism by which group selection can be enhanced.

Among humans, the possibility of conferring benefits on genetically similar individuals has been greatly increased by culture. Through language, law, religious imagery, and patriotic nationalism, all replete with kin terminology, ideological commitment enormously extends altruistic behavior. Groups made up of people who are genetically predisposed toward such moral behaviors as honesty, trust, temperence, willingness to share, loyalty, and self-sacrifice will have a distinct genetic advantage over groups that do not. In addition, if strong socialization pressure, including "mutual monitoring" and "moralistic aggression," is used to shape behavior and values within the group, a mechanism is provided for controlling, and even removing, the genes of cheaters.

Moreover, as reviewed earlier, social learning is biased by individualized epigenetic rules. Social psychological studies of cultural transmission show that people pick up trends more readily from role models who are similar (Bandura, 1986). Taken together it is likely that different ethnic groups learn from different trendsetters and the variance among groups is increased, thereby increasing the efficacy of group selection. Those groups adopting an optimum degree of ethnocentric ideology may have replicated their genes more successfully than those that did not. Evolution under bioculturally driven group selection, including migration, war, and genocide, may account for a substantial amount of change in human gene frequencies (Alexander, 1987; Ammerman & Cavalli-Sforza, 1984; Chagnon, 1988; D. S. Wilson, 1983). E. O. Wilson (1975: 573-74) put it forcefully:

> If any social predatory mammal attains a certain level of intelligence, as the early hominids, being large primates, were especially predisposed to do, one band would have the capacity to consciously ponder the significance of adjacent social groups and to deal with them in an intelligent organized fashion. A band might then dis-

pose of a neighboring band, appropriate its territory, and increase its own genetic representation in the metapopulation, retaining the tribal memory of this successful episode, repeating it, increasing the geographic range of its occurrence, and quickly spreading its influence still further in the metapopulation. Such primitive cultural capacity would be permitted by the possession of certain genes.... The only combination of genes able to confer superior fitness in contention with genocidal aggressors would be those that produce either a more effective technique of aggression or else the capacity to preempt genocide by some form of pacific manoeuvering. Either probably entails mental and cultural advance. In addition to being autocatalytic, such evolution has the interesting property of requiring a selection episode only very occasionally in order to proceed as swiftly as individual-level selection. By current theory, genocide or genosorption strongly favoring the aggressor need take place only once every few generations to direct evolution. This alone could push truly altruistic genes to a high frequency within the bands.

5

Race and Racism in History

For millennia, racism was not a word, it was a way of life. Ethnic nepotism and prohibitions against hybridization are a matter of historical record. Downgrading the importance of race not only conflicts with people's evolved tendency to classify and build histories according to putative descent, but ignores the work of biologists studying other species (Mayr, 1970). In his 1758 work, Linnaeus classified four subspecies of *Homo sapiens: europaeus, afer, asiatic,* and *americanus.* Most subsequent classifications recognize at least the three major subdivisions considered in this book: Negroid, Caucasoid, and Mongoloid (see Glossary for terminology).

Racism

The most fundamental relationship recognized by tribal man is that of blood, or descent; in many cases anyone not made a relative becomes an enemy. Primitive society often seems to be organized on two major principles: that the only effective bond is a bond of blood, and that the purpose of society is to unite for wars of offense and defense. Sometimes tribes take the name "men," meaning *we alone are men,* whereas outsiders are something else, often not defined at all.

Like groups of baboons, macaques, and chimpanzees, aboriginal tribes of people occupy territory as a closed group system. After a critical population density is reached, within-group antagonisms often lead to splits along kinship lines. Among the Yanomamo of South America, when the population reaches about 300, tensions within the village increase, arguments are more frequent, and, typically following a fight, a fission occurs (Chagnon, 1988).

Identification of racial variation in man based on differences in morphology and pigmentation is as old as recorded history. As referenced by Loehlin et al. (1975), in 1200 B.C. the Egyptians of the Nineteenth Dynasty painted polychromatic human figures on the walls of their royal tombs depicting peoples of different skin color and hair form: red (Egyptians), yellow (Asiatic and Semitic), black (sub-Saharan African), and white (western and northern European, also shown with blue eyes and blond beards).

In the Bible, from a single ancestor, the three sons of Noah are mythically divided into the descendents of Shem (Semites), Ham (non-Semitic Mediterraneans, sometimes said to include Negroids), and Japheth (northern peoples, sometimes said to mean Indo-Europeans, or Aryans). The Jews were descended from Shem and were warned by Jehovah to preserve themselves as "a special people unto himself, above all the people that are upon the face of the earth" (Deut. 7: 6). The patriarch Noah condemned Canaan, one of Ham's sons and his descendents to be "a servant of servants...unto his brethren" (Gen. 9: 25-27). This verse was used by the Israelites to sanction their subjugation of the Canaanites when they conquered the Promised Land and later by both Christians and Muslims to justify their slavery of blacks.

Other groups generated their own religious justifications for separateness. The Aryan or Indo-European people who invaded India 2,500 years ago built up a complex caste system to preserve their original physical type. They began to compose the *Rig-Veda*, a distillation of their religious beliefs. Eventually these were combined in the *Upanishads* (composed c. 800 B.C., first written c. 1300 A.D.) which, among other things, placed strong social barriers against free hybridization. The caste system may have been the most elaborate and effective barrier against the mixing of contiguous ethnic groups that the world has ever known. It continues to this day despite the attempts of governments to dismantle it. Nonetheless, the once fair complexions of the Brahmans have darkened considerably.

At the Battle of Blood River in Zululand, South Africa, on Sunday, December 16, 1838, the White Boer Voortrekkers entered into a covenant with God. If he would deliver them from the overwhelming numbers of Zulu warriors that surrounded them, they would observe the day as an anniversary every year and conduct their lives in accord with the spirit of the covenant. In the battle, 4,000 Zulu soldiers armed with assegai and shields were killed while one member of the small force of Boer soldiers, armed with rifles and a cannon, suffered a cut hand. The Boer nation had become a theocracy (Michener, 1980).

Caucasoids, of course, are not the only ethnocentrics. It is impossible to understand modern Africa without comprehending the nature of tribal rivalry (Lamb, 1987). For example, *The Times Higher Education Supplement* (August 30, 1985: 8) reported that the Kenyan government had warned lecturers and administrators at the University of Nairobi to stop awarding higher marks to students of their own tribe.

The character *yi*, "barbarian," has been the normal Chinese word applied to all non-Chinese peoples for over 2,000 years (Cameron, 1989: 13). The Chinese had always felt superior to the rest of the world, long before women of the Roman Empire craved the alluring effects of Chinese silk to the point of alarming the Roman Senate about the drain on its treasury. The European traders, priests, and soldiers who came later gave the Chinese no reason to doubt their judgment about themselves. The very name that the Chinese called their country, *Chung Kuo,* the centrally located "Middle Kingdom," from whence culture radiated outward, was ethnocentric. Today China is convinced that her communism is the only right and true communism, and that her way out of communism is the only right and true way forward.

By the late eighteenth and early nineteenth centuries, most of mankind had been categorized by white scientists according to race. Along with the classifications came value judgments. Since white people had now conquered or settled much of the earth they proposed for themselves an innately superior bloodline.

A theory of North European racial supremacy was assisted and expanded by the discovery of a surprising linguistic relationship between the Aryans, Persians, Hittites, Greeks, and Romans of the ancient world, and the peoples of modern Europe. The Indo-European languages gave rise to the hypothesis of a common race, in which a blond, light complexioned people with rare creative gifts continuously refertilizes dying and decadent civilizations.

Among the chief advocates of this "Aryan" hypothesis was Arthur de Gobineau (1816-1882), a French count who wrote the first racial interpretation of history. The Comte de Gobineau's (1853-1855) *Essays on the Inequality of Human Races* portrayed the Aryans as an ancient race of European peasants, fishermen, hunters, and shepherds who gave flower to the genius of the Greek and Roman civilizations, among many others. Gobineau felt the virtues of the European aristocracy—love of freedom, honor, and spirituality was racially ordained and from there downward went a hierarchy of capacity based partly on linguistic ability.

The bourgeoisie, for example, corrupted the nobility. The "yellow race" was bourgeois, preoccupied with a steady uncreative drive toward material prosperity. Blacks had little intelligence but had crude, overdeveloped senses. Gobineau's ideas were later incorporated with those of other theorists to provide a means of racial identification, particularly the idea that a common language rooted Europeans together. Many of these ideas were taken over by the Nazis to justify their attacks on "alien" Jews (Mosse, 1978).

Mostly anthropologists ignored Jewish people, regarding them as part of the Caucasian race and capable of assimilation into European life. Gobineau, himself, thought of the Jews as a race that had succeeded in everything it did, a free, strong, intelligent people that had produced as many men of learning as merchants. Moreover, for Gobineau, the ancient Jews demonstrated that the value of race was independent of the material conditions of the environment. Great races could flourish anywhere, and did so.

Others who supported the doctrine of Nordic superiority included: Houston Stewart Chamberlain (1855-1927), an Englishman who detected Aryan genes in almost all the great men of the past, including Jesus Christ; Madison Grant (1865-1937), American lawyer and naturalist whose book *The Passing of the Great Race* (1916) treated the decline of the Nordic people and whose arguments helped pass the restrictive U.S. immigration laws in the early 1920s; and Lothrop Stoddard (1883-1950), also active in the immigration issue, who warned in *The Rising Tide of Color* (1920) that white people would eventually be overwhelmed by the fecundity of the nonwhite, colored races.

As late as the 1950s, the word "race" was still widely used to designate peoples and national groups that today would be called ethnic groups. In Britain the word was applied to the English, Welsh, Scottish, and Irish components of the country. Winston Churchill, in his *History of the English Speaking Peoples,* habitually used the term for ethnic or "tribal" differences, as between Angles, Saxons, Danes, Jutes, and Normans. Few words in the Western world have undergone such significant changes, primarily as a result of the aftermath of World War II. For example, a survey showed that among the writers of physical anthropology textbooks in the United States, whereas 65 percent between 1932 and 1969 accepted that races of man exist, only 32 percent of those that appeared between 1970 and 1979 did so (Littlefield, Lieberman, & Reynolds, 1982).

Race as Breeding Group

Classifying animals into types is the special concern of the science of taxonomy, or systematics. To impart order to the biological world, a classificatory scheme was originated by Carolus Linnaeus (1707-1778), a Swedish naturalist at the University of Uppsala. The system that is currently in use is known as the Linnaean Hierarchy and dates in its (near) present form to 1758 and the tenth edition of Linnaeus's *Systema Naturae.* It is based on the proposition that animals with similar body construction may be regarded as members of the same classification group. Moreover, an evolutionary inference is made: the more closely two animals resemble each other, the more closely they are likely to be related. Thus, taxonomy directly correlates the structural organization of animals and indirectly their evolutionary histories.

Within a given classification group, it is often possible to distinguish several subgroups, each containing animals characterized by even greater similarity of body structure and, by inference, evolutionary history. Each such subgroup may then be further subclassified, and a whole hierarchy of classification groups can be established. In this hierarchy, from highest (most inclusive) to lowest (least inclusive) the seven main ranks are: kingdom, phylum, class, order, family, genus, and species. Intermediate ranks may also be assigned by the prefixes sub- or super- (e.g., superorder, suborder, and so on). The specific animal groups encompassed by a given category are often referred to as taxa. For example, mammals are a taxon at the class rank.

In the hierarchy as a whole, progressively lower ranks consist of progressively more but smaller groups. Thus, animals make up one kingdom, some 2 dozen phyla, and about 2 million species. Also, the groups at successively lower ranks exhibit an increasing resemblance of body forms and an increasingly similar evolutionary history. For example, the members of a class resemble each other to a great extent, but the members within one of the orders of that class resemble each other to an even greater extent. A similar correlation holds for evolutionary histories.

According to Linnaean tradition and the International Code of Zoological Nomenclature, all species (and only species) should be identified by two names, their genus name and their species name. These are in Latin or latinized form and used universally. For example, the species to which we belong is *Homo sapiens*. Such species names are always underlined or printed in italics, and the first name is capitalized. Thus, the human species belongs to the genus *Homo*. *Homo sapiens* happens to be the only presently living species within the genus *Homo*. The genus name is always a noun, and the specific name is usually an adjective.

TABLE 5.1
A Partial Taxonomic Classification of Man

Rank	Name	Characteristics
Phylum	Chordata	With notochord, dorsal hollow nerve cord, and gills in pharynx at some stage of life cycle
Class	Mammalia	Young nourished by milk glands, skin with hair; body cavity divided by diaphragm; aortic arch only on left; red corpuscles without nuclei; constant body temperature; 3 middle-ear bones; brain with well-developed cerebrum
Order	Primates	Basically tree-dwelling; usually with fingers, flat nails; sense of smell reduced
Family	Hominidae	Upright, bipedal locomotion; living on ground; hands and feet differently specialized; family and tribal social organization
Genus	Homo	Large brain; speech; life span extended, with long youth
Species	Homo sapiens	Prominent chin, high forehead, thin skull bones; spine double-curved; body hair sparse

A complete classification of an animal tells a great deal about the nature of that animal. For example, if we knew nothing else about men except their taxonomic classification, then we would know that their design characteristics are as outlined in Table 5.1. Such data already represent a substantial detailing of the body structure. We would also know by implication that the evolutionary history of men traces back to a common chordate ancestry.

There are times when a species is divided into subspecies, in which case a trinomial nomenclature is employed. Taxa lower than subspecies are sometimes employed when four words are used in the scientific name, the last one standing for *variety*. Thus, the race is a minor taxon in relation to the species.

Despite the central importance of the species concept in biology, biologists do not agree on a definition that applies to all cases. Before Darwin's time, the species was considered a primeval pattern, or archetype, divinely created. Gradually taxonomists began to think of species as groups of interbreeding natural populations that are reproductively isolated from other such groups, in which every individual is unique and may change to a greater or lesser extent when placed in a different environment.

The theoretical importance of variation within populations was discussed by Mayr (1970). For decades, it had been debated whether geographic variation was genetic in nature. Mendelian evolutionists denied it was so because their interpretation of speciation depended upon spectacular mutations, not selection operating on graded characters. Today all biologists accept the genetic uniqueness of local populations. Because no two individuals are genetically identical, no two groups of individuals will be identical. Moreover, every local population is under continuous selection pressure for maximal fitness in the particular area where it occurs. Consequently subspecies may come to differ behaviorally, as well as biometrically.

In sum, race is a biological concept. Races are recognized by a combination of geographic, ecological, and morphological factors and gene frequencies of biochemical components. However, races merge with each other through intermediate forms, while members of one race can and do interbreed with members of other races.

Most modern classifications recognize three major subdivisions, Negroid, Caucasoid, and Mongoloid. Some investigators have designated additional races, such as the Amerindians and Australoids. Within each race, several varieties or minor races have been proposed, although there is no agreed upon number. Mostly for political reasons, a majority of investigators avoid the use of the term *race* as much as possible and use, for the major human races, the word "population" and for the minor races, the phrase "ethnic group."

Islamic Ethnology

Hostility and hybridization both characterized ethnic relations among those ancient Middle Eastern groups who affected history—the Egyptians, the

Sumerians, the Akkadians, the Israelites, the Hittites, the Persians, and later, the Greeks and the Romans. The nobility and leadership of the varying factions often urged against hybridization. The Bible provides many examples of the Hebrews being enjoined to avoid it. Tribes and nations thought it natural and legitimate to despise, conquer, enslave, and displace each other. Slavery is attested from the very earliest written records among the Sumerians, the Babylonians, and the Egyptians, as well as the Greeks and the Romans. The wall paintings of ancient Egypt, for example, typically depict the gods and pharaohs as larger than life while Negroes and other outlanders were posed as servants and slaves.

In the seventh century A.D. Islam arose among the Arabs. Under them, and later under the Ottoman Turks, a universal civilization was created from the Atlantic Ocean to China, and from Europe to West Africa. The creation through conquest of far-flung empires into which different races and ethnic groups were pulled, especially through the institution of slavery, led to a considerable body of writing, extending over almost a thousand years, about the characteristics of the various groups. Written in Arabic, Persian, and Turkish, discussion focused on the suitability of various races for different tasks and occupations.

Among Arabs, where intense tribal loyalties spilled over into feuding and warfare, there existed the usual ethnocentrism. In his book *Race and Slavery in the Middle East*, Lewis (1990) examined the common stereotypes that emerged for various national groups. In early Arabic poetry, many nuances of human coloration are described. The Arabs saw their own olive coloring as generally preferable to either the redder color of the Persians, Greeks, and Europeans or to the black and brown peoples of the Horn of Africa and beyond. As Ibn al-Fagih al-Hamadani, an Iraqi Arab author put it around A.D. 902: "The Iraqis are neither half-baked dough nor burned crust but between the two" (cited in Lewis, 1990: 46). One exception was the preference for blondes as concubines; these typically brought the highest prices.

Sa'id al-Andalusi (d. 1070), writing from the then Muslim city of Toledo in Spain, classified ten nations as having achieved distinction in cultivating civilization: the Indians, Persians, Chaldees, Greeks, Romans, Egyptians, Arabs, Jews, Chinese, and Turks. But the northern as well as the southern barbarians were seen as more like beasts than men. It was thought that the Slavs and Bulgars, because of their distance from the sun, had a frigid temperament and dull intelligence. In the South Sa'id thought that the blacks, because of the hot thin air, lacked "self control and steadiness of mind and are overcome by fickleness, foolishness, and ignorance" (cited in Lewis, 1990: 47–48).

Lewis (1990) examined Arabic relations with blacks with whom the Muslims had dealt as slave traders for over 1,000 years. Although the Koran stated there were no superior and inferior races and therefore no bar to racial intermarriage, in practice this pious doctrine was disregarded. Arabs did not want their daughters to marry even hybridized blacks. The Ethiopians were the most respected, the "Zanj" (Bantu and other Negroid tribes from East and West Africa south of the Sahara) the least respected, with the Nubians occupying an intermediate position.

The negative views of black people are traced by Lewis (p. 52) to Mas'udi (d. 956) who quoted the Greek physician Galen (A.D. c. 130-c. 200) attributing to the black man "a long penis and great merriment. Galen says that merriment dominates the Black man because of his defective brain, whence also the weakness of his intelligence." This description is later repeated, with variations.

Most Arab geographers speak of the nudity, paganism, cannibalism, and primitive life of the Africans, particularly of the Bantu-speakers of East Africa alongside Zanzibar, which the Arabs had colonized in 925 A.D. Maqdisi depicted blacks as having the nature "of wild animals...most of them go naked...the child does not know his father, and they eat people" (cited in Lewis, 1990: 52). A thirteenth-century Persian writer, Nasir al-Din Tusi, remarks that Negroes differ from animals only in that "their two hands are lifted above the ground...the ape is more teachable and more intelligent" (cited in Lewis, 1990: 53). In the fourteenth century, Ibn Butlan held a musical rhythm stereotype, suggesting that if an African "were to fall from heaven to earth he would beat time as he goes down" (cited in Lewis, p. 94); another stereotype held that black people may be particularly pious because of their simplicity.

Throughout Islamic literature there is also the image of unbridled, sexual potency in blacks, as related, for example, in stories and illustrations from *The Thousand and One Nights*. Black females, as well as males, are portrayed with greatly endowed genitalia. One Persian manuscript from 1530 A.D. (Lewis, 1990: 97, and color plate no. 23) contains a pictorial illustration accompanying a poem in which a white woman watches while her black maidservant is able to accommodate to copulation with an ass; when the white woman tries do so, there are disastrous consequences.

In the main, black people are considered destined for menial occupations. Whereas slaves and their offspring from other parts of the empire were able to, and did, rise to the highest levels of office, black slaves did so rarely. Black slaves were seen as unintelligent, a view not held of non-African slaves, nor of those on the empires' borders, including the European Christians, the Indian Hindus, and the Chinese.

Racial characteristics were often attributed to the environment. Ibn Khaldun (1332-1406) whom Lewis describes as the greatest historian and social thinker of the Middle Ages, devoted a chapter to climatic effects. Even the merriment attributed to black people was considered climatic rather than genetic in origin (Lewis, p. 47). One writer, Jahiz of Basra (ca. 776-869) attributed the widely perceived low intelligence of black people to their existing socioeconomic position and asked his readers whether they would have anticipated the existence of the achievements in Indian science, philosophy, and art from their experience of Indian slaves. Since the reply was likely to be no, then the same argument might apply to black lands (cited in Lewis, p. 31).

Christian Explorers

Europeans had always known of the great glories and riches of the East. Chinese silk production from looms had long been a desired commodity and silk routes from China into central Asia and the Mediterranean had been established by 126 B.C., although sometimes forgotten, then rediscovered. The brilliance of the Chinese as inventors and artists was known to the Islamic Arabs and Persians (Lewis, 1990).

In 1275, Marco Polo (1254-1324) traveled to China from Venice with a view to opening up trade with the Mongol Empire. He came away impressed with the efficient administration of roads, bridges, cities interconnected by canals, a postal system, census, markets, standardized weights and measures, coin and paper money. The brilliance and tolerance of the Oriental court, as portrayed by Marco Polo, enthralled the Western world. Polo wrote, "Surely there is no more intelligent race on earth than the Chinese."

Christian contact with Africa began in earnest in 1441 when for the first time, slaves and gold were directly imported from West Africa into Portugal. The discovery of gold provided a great stimulus to further exploration. Later in the fifteenth Century the Portugese had rounded the Cape of Good Hope and established contact with the Arab-controlled East African areas of Mozambique and Mombassa, before continuing historic voyages that opened direct commerce between Europe and India. It was chiefly to protect their trade with India and the East that first the Portugese, and later the other European powers, established colonies on the African coast. Trade in ivory, and later, slaves for the American colonies, provided additional impetus for investigation. Through centuries of trade with Greco-Roman, Islamic, and now Christian cultures, large parts of the periphery of North, East, and West Africa had been influenced by foreigners. Other parts, however, especially the central interior regions and southern tracts, remained unexplored and unknown to outsiders.

The written impressions of seven major explorers of black Africa, including of areas uninfluenced by Arab or European cultures was collated by J. R. Baker (1974). These explorers were chosen because of their reputation for accuracy and reliability in reporting. Baker believed it improbable that a very different picture would have emerged if another set of explorers had been substituted, or a fuller number included. The explorers, with the dates of their major works and of their explorations, are:

H. F. Fynn (1950)	1824-34
D. Livingstone (1857)	1840-56

F. Galton (1853)   1850–51
B. P. Du Chaillu (1861)   1856–59
J. H. Speke (1863)   1860–63
S. W. Baker (1866)   1862–65
G. Schweinfurth (1873)   1869–71

As J. R. Baker (1974) describes it, the impression gained is of a poor level of civilization, including naked or near naked appearance, sometimes broken by an amulet or ornament rather than a covering of the genital area; self-mutilation as in filing down the teeth and piercing the ears and lips to admit large ornaments; poorly developed toilet and sanitary habits; one-story dwellings of simple construction; villages rarely reaching 6 or 7 thousand inhabitants or being interconnected with roadways; simple canoes excavated from large trees with no joining parts; no invention of the wheel for pottery or grinding corn or vehicular transport; little domestication of animals or using them for labor or transport; no written script or recording of historical events; no use of money; no invention of a numbering system, nor of a calendar.

Some explorers were struck by the absence of administration and code of law. Examples were told of chiefs despotically killing at will for minor breaches of etiquette or even for pleasure. When the explorer Speke gave Mutesa, the king of Buganda, a rifle, the king tried it out on a woman prisoner. When witchcraft was suspected, hundreds might be slaughtered often with grotesque forms of execution. When slavery was practiced, slave owners were at liberty to kill their slaves. In some places cannibalism was practiced. Nowhere did there appear to exist any formal religion with sanctified traditions, beliefs about the origin of the world, or ethical codes with sentiments of mercy.

The explorers found Africans to be of low intelligence with few words to express abstract thoughts and little interest in intellectual matters. Speke wrote that the Negro thinks only for the moment and prefers to spend the day as lazily as possible. Livingstone wrote that the tribes lacked foresight, thinking it futile of the explorer to plant date seeds in full knowledge that he would never see the fruit. S. W. Baker (1866: 396–397) thought that young black children were "in advance, in intellectual quickness, of the white child of similar age" but that "the mind does not expand—it promises fruit, but does not ripen."

Whenever a bright individual did arise, as in one story told to Livingstone about a man who built an irrigation system to his garden to help cultivate potatoes, the idea typically died with its creator. Occasional stories were told about individuals attempting to invent written scripts. The explorers tended to see the hybrid groups as being more intelligent and the darker more Negroid groups as less intelligent. Thus, Livingstone remarked that the tribes of Angola were "by no means equal to the Cape Caffires in any respect whatever" (S. W. Baker, 1866: 397). However, some tribes were notably accomplished in pottery, iron forging, wood art, and musical instrumentation.

As also reported by the Islamic writers, Africans were perceived to have great musical virtuosity in precision of timing and accuracy of pitch, whether of voice or tuning of instruments. The native dances that the explorers witnessed tended to be voluptuous, with obscene motions made to other dancers. This was not true of ceremonial war dances, particularly those given by the Zulus, where great discipline, order, sedateness, and regularity were to be observed. The Zulus had been one of the greatest warrior tribes ever known in Africa, creating a military empire from Zululand through Tanzania to the Congo for much of the nineteenth century, until being defeated finally by the British in 1879.

The Enlightenment

Europe's scientific revolution, begun with Galileo (1564–1642) and Newton (1642–1727), produced profound and far-reaching changes. Science altered in meaning from simply "knowledge" to "systematically formulated knowledge, based on observation and experiment." It became, as never before, necessary to "prove" the rules. The Enlightenment of the eighteenth century was characterized by belief in the power of human reason to comprehend the natural world. The study of human nature and human differences was brought within its ambit.

In the seventeenth century, as explorers discovered more and more about varieties of ape and human, there was much confusion about the degree of overlap. Some humans lived very simple lives as food gatherers, without knowledge of agriculture. Some apes were able to be trained to eat dinner at a table. It was possible to conjecture that apes were a lower form of man that refused to speak in order to avoid being made into slaves, while pygmies, for example because of their flat noses and short statures, were a higher form of ape. In 1699, the English physician Edward Tyson was the first to make a careful study of the anatomy of a chimpanzee, showing it to be structurally more similar to humans than to monkeys. He hypothesized that African pygmies were intermediate to apes and humans (Baker, 1974: 31–32).

Carl Linnaeus supposed that anthropoid apes were structurally not very distinguishable from humans. By 1758, in the tenth edition of his *System Naturae,* he assigned two species to the genus *Homo, H. sapiens* (man) and *H. troglodytes* (anthropoid apes). As mentioned at the beginning of this chapter, Linnaeus also classified *Homo sapiens* into four subspecies: *europaeus, afer, asiaticus,* and *americanus.* He used mental as well as physical qualities to distinguish them. Thus, *europaeus* was described as "active, very acute, a discoverer... ruled by custom" and *afer* (African blacks) were judged as "crafty, lazy, careless...ruled by caprice."

Later, Leclerc de Buffon (1707–1788), a French naturalist, and Petrus Camper (1722–1789), a Dutch anatomist, demonstrated that apes were more clearly distinguishable from man. Thus, in 1779, a study by Camper of the orangutan's vocal organs revealed that it was incapable of speech, and in later studies, he showed its inability to walk upright on two feet, a point that biologists agreed separated man from apes at a higher taxonomic level than Linnaeus had suggested.

Camper also made studies of the human races. He introduced the concept of a "facial line" to quantitatively compare the races of man with one another and with animals, thus beginning modern craniology (see Figure 5.1). Camper made it clear that the Negro was no man-ape hybrid. By a criterion established by Buffon, all human races were members of the same species because they were able to breed with each other, but not with representatives of other groups. Yet to many, it seemed inescapable that the Negro was the most apelike variety of man.

Two views of racial differences predominated before Darwin's theory of evolution: *monogenism,* the belief that despite racial differences, man was a single species with a unique origin; and *polygenism,* the view that the human races had separate origins. Although the races could clearly interbreed, the polygenist view was that hybrids from such a union possessed weak constitutions, confirming just how far the races had diverged. The crucial question was how far in the past the various branches of human evolution had begun to

Figure 5.1: Camper's (1791) Drawings of Skulls to Illustrate Facial Angle

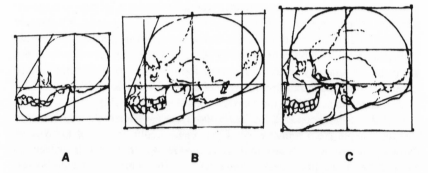

A   B   C

The skulls are of A, a young orangutan, B, a young Negro, and C, a typical European. Camper first made a drawing of the left side of a skull set up in a horizontal position and then drew a line grazing the front surface of the first incisor tooth and forehead, neglecting any nasal bone en route. The angle formed by the facial line with the horizontal plane became the "facial angle." If either the jaw projects or the forehead slopes backward, the facial angle will be small. Camper found the following facial angles: for a monkey, 42°; orangutan, 58°; a Negro, 70°; a European, 80°; and the most perfect human features, as represented in classical Greek statues, almost 90°. From Camper (1791, cited in Baker, 1974).

diverge. If the divergence had occurred very far back, the varieties may have become distinct enough to be considered as species.

Many of those supporting the inequalities of race were political liberals, opposed to the religious monarchists of their day. Jean Jacques Rousseau (1712–1778), the French political philosopher, posited in his 1775 *Discourse on the Origins of Inequality*, that whereas primitive man was solitary and there-fore knew nothing of his inequality, great civilizations necessarily threw un-equal people together thereby causing misery. Rousseau argued that it was only by accepting the great diversity that existed in society that one could construct a legitimate social order in which the citizenry would be willing to renounce their natural liberty for sake of a superior freedom. The power of law and democracy, Rousseau argued, would make men independent of one another by making them all equally dependent on the law of the republic.

Voltaire (1694–1778), too, stressed the immutable physical differences between the races, for example, emphasizing the size of the labia and external genitalia in the female Hottentot (see J. R. Baker, 1974: 313–317 for engrav-ings and details). By the seventeenth century it was recognized that skin color was not solely due to the action of the sun's rays during the life of the indi-vidual. White babies born in the tropics and black babies born in Europe were seen to resemble their parents and to keep their color throughout life. Voltaire argued that such diversity inclined against the religious belief that all human races were descended in recent time from a single Adam and Eve ancestor.

David Hume (1711–1776), Scottish philosopher and historian, wrote that the races had originated independently and those that lived beyond the polar circles or between the tropics were inferior to those of the temperate zone. The people of Africa were less intelligent and accomplished than the rest of mankind, he claimed, and that although many had been freed, none had made a major contribution to art or science. Hume held many political posts, includ-ing head of the British Colonial Office in 1766. He argued that the character of the different races was partly inborn, for he noted the uniform nature of the Chinese despite their distribution over a huge area varying in climate.

Immanuel Kant (1724–1804) wrote much about national character but only little about differences between the major races, agreeing in the main with Hume's assessment. Kant was particularly impressed by the African belief in fetishes, the teeth of leopards and the skin of snakes worn for their magical powers. Fetishistic beliefs implied intellectual inferiority, sinking "as deep in foolishness as seems to be possible for human nature" and far away from the sense of innate moral duty he called "Categorical Imperative," wherein max-ims of conduct served as universal laws.

George Wilhelm Friedrich Hegel (1770–1831) also scorned the use of fe-tishes to control the forces of nature, believing that Africans were incapable of acquiring complicated religious belief systems and that they stood outside his theory of historical development. For Hegel, Africa was "no historical part of the world; it has no movement or development to exhibit." Although Karl Marx (1818-1883) did not make it public knowledge, he was later to share Hegel's view of African people when he transformed Hegel's theory of history to fit his own political philosophy (Weyl, 1977).

Johann Friedrich Blumenbach (1752-1840), a German professor of medicine, researched the physiology and comparative anatomy of the different races and confirmed they were all members of the same species. Although he did not know about evolution, he was aware that plants and animals became modified as a result of climatic changes and domestication, a process he referred to as *degeneration* from the God-given original. Assuming the truth of the Bible, he contended that Caucasoids were the closest to Adam and Eve and that the other varieties arose by a process of degeneration through exposure to climatic extremes. Although Blumenbach thought the European forms the most beautiful, he insisted that many racial differences had been greatly exaggerated in the telling, including the size of the external genitalia of the female Hottentot, emphasized by Voltaire.

Samuel Thomas Soemmering (1755-1830), a German anatomist still known today for his work on the sympathetic nervous system, wrote on the comparative anatomy of the Negro and European. He dissected the various body parts to systematically examine the claim that, anatomically, the Negro approximated more closely to the apes than did the European. He concluded that Negroes were strikingly human, clearly distinguishable from apes and other animals, although there were many primitive features. For example, the lower jaw of the Negro is more robust than the European, and the part to which the masseter muscle is attached is very broad; also, the upper and lower incisor teeth project forward so as to meet at an angle.

It was Soemmering in 1785 (cited by Todd, 1923) who first published an estimate of cranial capacity. His method was the simple one of filling the skull with water. He reasonably assumed that the cavity of the human skull reflected the size of the brain it once contained. He reported that the cranium of a European is more capacious than that of a Negro. Saumarez (cited by Todd, 1923), also using the water method, confirmed Soemmering's statement. Vicey, too, in 1817 (cited by Todd, 1923), also using the water method, found the relationship.

Not all biologists of the time believed that Africans differed from Europeans. Franz Joseph Gall (1758-1828), the German physician most responsible for establishing that the brain was the organ of the mind, specifically rejected the view that the Negroid skull contained less brain than that of the European. On the other hand, Gall had rejected classification schemes altogether, holding that each skull was unique. He invented phrenology, a theory in which a person's talents and qualities were traced from the configurations of the skull to particular areas of the brain.

Friedrich Tiedemann (1781–1861), a German comparative anatomist and physiologist, pointed out that Camper's facial angle did not give a measure of brain size, as certain authors had supposed. Measuring endocranial volume he found no differences between Africans and Europeans. Using autopsies, however, he found African brains to be slightly smaller than those of Europeans, especially in their frontal parts. Structurally he also found the brains to be similar, except that the African brain seemed less convoluted. In facial features Tiedemann reiterated that Africans showed more similarities to the ape than did Europeans. Relative to Europeans, he found Africans had larger facial and flatter nasal bones, a more strongly projecting jaw and incisor teeth, and a less anterior foramen magnum, the position where the backbone meets the skull.

Louis Agassiz (1807–1873), the Swiss naturalist famous for studying fossil fishes, traveled to America in 1846 and was persuaded to stay on as professor of zoology at Harvard, where he founded and directed the Museum of Comparative Zoology. He theorized that the creation of species occurred in discrete geographical centers with minimum variation, a view he later applied to the human situation. Agassiz believed that God had created the races as separate species; the biblical tale of Adam referred only to the origin of Caucasians. For him, mummified remains from Egypt implied that Negroes and Caucasians were as distinct 3,000 years earlier as they were in his day, and since the biblical story of Noah's Ark had been dated only 1,000 years before that, there would not have been time for all the sons of Noah to have developed their distinct attributes. For Agassiz, these included intellectual and moral qualities, with Europeans ranking higher than Amerindians and Orientals, and Africans ranking the lowest. Agassiz lived to become America's leading opponent of the Darwinian revolution.

Samuel George Morton (1799–1851), America's great physical anthropologist, collected more than 1,000 human skulls. In his illustrated *Crania Americana,* published in 1839, Morton reported that Amerindian and Mongoloid skulls were intermediate in size to those of Caucasoids and Negroids; for 144 Amerindian skulls the mean cranial capacity was 82 in^3 as compared to the mean of 87 in^3 for whites and 78 in^3 for blacks. For a second study, the *Crania Aegyptiaca* of 1844, Morton categorized by race more than 100 skulls he had been sent from the tombs of ancient Egypt. His two Negroid groups averaged 73 and 79 in^3 and his Caucasian groups averaged from 80 to 88 in^3. By 1849, in Morton's final tabulation of 623 skulls the size ranking remained Caucasoid > Mongoloid > Negroid; among Caucasoids, North Europeans typically came out on top.

Although problematic by today's standards, Morton's work is still debated (chap. 6). One problem was that Morton often randomly combined male with female skulls. Another was his tendency to average his subsamples using a weighted rather than an unweighted procedure, thus allowing an over-representation of extreme groups. Among Indians for example, the small-sized Incas were overrepresented relative to the large-sized Iroquois, thus lowering the Amerindian average. In its time, however, Morton's was a major achievement.

Paul Broca (1824–1880), the great French neurologist who also founded the Anthropological Society of Paris in 1859, was a world leader in the field of brain-behavior relationships. He used a comparative approach, examining brains either damaged by strokes or compared across races. Today, "Broca's area" refers to that part of the left cerebral hemisphere that controls the production of speech, and the difficulty in speaking after damage to this area is called "Broca's aphasia."

Broca weighed brains at autopsy and refined the techniques for estimating endocranial volume by filling skulls with lead shot. He concluded that variation in brain size was related to intellectual achievement: skilled workers had larger brains than unskilled workers, mature adults had larger brains than either children or the very elderly, eminent individuals had larger brains than those who were less eminent, and Europeans had larger brains than Africans.

Broca was struck by the variation in the size of brains. Those of eminent men donated after their deaths ranged from about 1,000 grams for Gall, the founder of phrenology, and Walt Whitman, the American poet, through 1,492 grams for the great German mathematician Gauss, to nearly 2,000 grams for Georges Cuvier, the French naturalist. Broca's own brain was later found to weigh 1,424 grams. It began to be realized that brain size varied with several nonintellectual factors, including age, body size, health, cause of death, time after death before weighing the brain, and so on. The only way to examine the true relationship between brain size and eminence was to take an average of many brains and to try to statistically control for extraneous variables.

Broca provided additional distinctions among the brains of the races. These included the ratio of the anterior part of the brain to the posterior (Negroids had a lower ratio, with less in the front), the relative number of convolutions (Negroids had fewer), the speed and order with which sutures between the skull bones closed (Negroids closed faster), and the relative position of the foramen magnum (Negroids further back). Broca noted that in some samples of Mongoloid populations the cranial capacities surpassed those of Europeans. Also with respect to the Negro skull, Broca (1858; cited by J. R. Baker, 1974) remarked:

> In him, the bones of the cranium are conspicuously thicker than ours, and have at the same time much greater density; they scarcely contain any diploë, and their resistance is such that they can sustain truly extraordinary blows without breaking.

After Darwin

In 1859, in the first edition of *The Origin of Species*, Charles Darwin (1809–1882) was very guarded on the subject of human evolution. He merely remarked tentatively that as a result of future investigations, "Psychology will be based on a new foundation, that of the necessary acquirement of each mental power and capacity by gradation." These words were slightly strengthened in later editions, and by 1871, in *The Descent of Man*, Darwin made explicit the application of evolution to human faculties. Evolutionary thinking destroyed the creationist debate between monogenists and polygenists; it affirmed human unity but left the question open as to how far back in prehistoric time a common ancestor had been shared, and by what routes the various races had taken to their present adaptions.

Human fossil evidence had begun to enter the picture in the seventeenth century when Isaac de la Payrère, from France, discovered stone tools used by primitive men who, he claimed, lived in the time before Adam. In 1655 his findings and theory were greatly disapproved of and his books publicly burned by Church authorities. Shortly thereafter, human bones began to turn up along with those of extinct animals throughout western Europe. In 1796 Georges Cuvier, the French naturalist, found the remains of ancient mammoths and gigantic reptiles, and soon paleoanthropology was established as a scientific discipline.

In 1856, three years before Darwin propounded his theory of evolution, Neanderthal Man was discovered in Germany's Neander Valley near Dusseldorf. The skeleton possessed a number of peculiar traits that defined them as very ancient, including a low, narrow, sloping forehead, heavy eyebrow ridges, and a deep depression at the root of the nose. This began the long tradition of a club-wielding, uncouth, "caveman" ancestor and the search for a still more primitive "missing link" between man and ape.

The German biologist Ernst Haeckel (1834–1919) predicted that the sought-after link would be found in a warmer climate such as Africa or southern Asia where the living would be easier than in glaciated Europe. Toward the end of the nineteenth century, a member of the Dutch colonial army, Eugene Dubois, ventured out to Sumatra and Java in the hopes of discovering such a manlike ape. Between 1890 and 1892, Dubois found pieces of "Java Man," now dated to about 800,000 years B.P., that everyone agreed was more apelike than the Neanderthal. This meant that early humans, later named *Homo erectus*, had been in Asia before Europe. The importance of *H. erectus* was vastly increased from 1927 to 1937 as more than 40 similar fossils were found in limestone caves at Zhoukoudian, outside of Beijing. Also found were thousands of stone tools and evidence that *H. erectus* used fire. "Beijing Man" was somewhat like the Java *erectus* and has been dated at 200,000 to 500,000 years.

Homo erectus and Neanderthals were more manlike than apelike. Then, in South Africa, in 1924, Raymond Dart discovered a real apelike missing link. It was followed by the discovery of similar apelike creatures in Africa, with a brain only slightly bigger than a chimpanzee's. The nose was flat. The jaw dominated the face and the mouth thrusted forward. But the teeth were humanlike and it had a bit of a forehead. Most importantly, it walked upright! Its spinal cord entered the brain not at the back of the head, like a gorilla's, but at the bottom of the skull, suggesting bipedalism. Although that didn't make it human, it allowed it to fall into the broader category of "hominid." Later termed *Australopithecus,* these apelike creatures existed 3 million or so years before Java Man.

In all of the fossil finds, however, in the progression from the apelike *Australopithecus* to the manlike *erectus* and then Neanderthal man, there was no evidence of where and when anatomically modern humankind first arose. Although it seemed fairly certain that *Australopithecus* had turned into *erectus,* and that *erectus,* after originating in Africa, had then spread around the Old World, the question was: How had erectus turned into *Homo sapiens*?

There were two rival theories: multi-regional continuity versus single-origin. The first of these was propounded by the German anthropologist Franz von Weidenreich (1873–1948), who meticulously described fossils from around the world including those from Java and China. The theory was elaborated by his follower, the American anthropologist, Carleton S. Coon (1904–1982), of Harvard University, the Peabody Museum, and the University of Pennsylvania. Their theory postulated a separate but parallel evolution for several different groups of *Homo erectus* occurring simultaneously in various regions of the world, beginning about 1 million years ago. Half a million years ago, *Homo erectus,* already divided into geographic races, gradually evolved into the different races of *Homo sapiens.*

Living in their own territory, Coon (1962) postulated that each race could be at different points along the evolutionary path and could pass the critical threshold from primitive to *sapient* state at different times. To account for observed differences in cranial capacity and cultural attainment, Coon (1962) suggested that African populations lagged behind the other races and that living Australian aborigines still retained primitive *erectus* characteristics. Although these "racist" elements were later discarded as an embarrassment, the multiregional hypothesis has remained viable to contemporary times (see chap. 11).

Predictable consequences followed from the theory. Because each race had its own distinct rootstock, remnants of the original people should be detectable in modern populations, despite admixture and migration. Thus, the 800,000-year-old *erectus* Java Man, and his descendants, the Australian aborigines, were considered to share ridges in their skull tops and enormously thick brows above their eyes. In China, the 200,000- to 500,000-year-old *erectus,* Beijing Man, was said to share, with modern Mongoloids, a flat face and a distinct shovel-shaped incisor.

At the other extreme of the forum were those who claimed that all currently living races are but local varieties of the expansion of a single population of *Homo sapiens* that colonized the entire world. Much debate centered on the origin of this single population, many suggesting Asia as a likely contender because of its large, centrally located population. At the time, much of Europe would have been under ice. Intermediate theories suggested separate parallel evolutions from distinct Neanderthal populations, with local differences continuously modified by intermittent migration and admixture. This compromise multiregional theory was probably the most accepted view until modern genetic theories entered the debate with their "Out of Africa" hypothesis suggesting that "Eve" was a black African woman who lived only 200,000 years ago (chap. 11).

Meanwhile, in nineteenth-century Europe, the science of craniometry flourished (Topinard, 1878). Cesare Lombroso (1836–1909), an Italian physician and anthropologist who founded the discipline of criminology believed that Darwin's theory of evolution provided a biological basis for why some people were more likely to develop criminal tendencies than others, and why physical indicators may exist to allow prediction. He carried out several anthropometric surveys of the heads and bodies of criminals and noncriminals, including a sample of 383 crania from dead convicts. He claimed that, as a group, criminals averaged many primitive features including smaller brains, greater skull thickness, simplicity of cranial sutures, large jaws, preeminence of the face over the cranium, a low and narrow forehead, long arms, and large ears. He also studied African tribes in the Upper Nile region and thought they displayed so many primitive traits that criminality would be considered normal behavior among them.

Maria Montessori (1870–1952), the well-known Italian educational reformist, not only devised a system of self-education for young children, but also lectured on anthropology at the University of Rome. She accepted evolutionary-based differences in criminality and intelligence from the work of Broca and Lombroso. She also measured the circumference of children's heads in her schools and concluded that faster learning was made by children with bigger brains.

Todd (1923) gives some of the history of attempts to measure skull capacity using linear formulations and packing material. Sand was used in 1831, millet in 1837, white pepper or mustard seed in 1839, and shot in 1849. These were poured inside of a sealed skull and then emptied into a graduated cylinder to read the skull's volume in cubic centimeters. Head circumferences, lengths, breadths, and heights were measured across races to predict internal capacity. At the Western Reserve University in Cleveland, Todd (1923) found that the sex-combined cranial capacity for 198 whites was 1,312 cm^3 and for 104 blacks it was 1,286 cm^3.

The collection of wet brains and dry skulls for comparing blacks and whites was reviewed by Pearl (1934). This included the study by Samuel Morton already described and an autopsy study of soldiers who had died of pneumonia during the American Civil War (1861–1865). Pearl calculated that the brains of black soldiers weighed 1,342 grams and white soldiers 1,471 grams. Pearl also cited a study just then published by Vint (1934) of 389 adult male Kenyans with an average brain weight of 1,276 grams. Altogether, Pearl concluded, the Negro brain averaged about 100 grams, or about 8 to 10 percent lighter than the white brain.

With notable exceptions, for example, American anthropologist Franz Boas and his school, this view was dominant until World War II. Even during the war, Simmons (1942) reported a study of 2,241 skulls from the permanent collection at Western Reserve University, Cleveland, Ohio. Using a new technique of filling skulls with plastic material rather than seed or water, she found that 1,179 white men averaged 1,452 cm^3 in contrast to 661 black men who averaged 1,389 cm^3, and 182 white women averaged 1,275 cm^3 as against 219 black women who averaged 1,238 cm^3 (white and black means = 1,364 and 1,314 cm^3). Simmons was also able to show that the race differences in cranial capacity were not due to racial differences in body size because black men and women were taller than white men and women.

Bean (1906) reported that structurally, the anterior part of the Negro brain was smaller and less complexly convoluted than the Caucasian brain. He also reported that the weight of the Negro brain at autopsy varied with the amount of Caucasian admixture, from 0 admixture = 1,157 grams, 1/16 = 1,191, 1/8 = 1,335, 1/4 = 1,340, and 1/2 = 1,347. Later reports of brain complexity differences and size covariations with white admixture came from Vint (1934) and Pearl (1934). Debates were generated. Mall (1909), for example, disputed Bean's (1906) claim that whites had relatively larger frontal lobes than blacks, although he accepted that there was an overall size difference of about 100 grams.

Mongoloid populations were not as intensely studied, at least not by Europeans. Morton's (1849) craniometric data on Amerindians had suggested a capacity intermediate to whites and blacks. Analyses and reviews of 15 autopsy studies on hundreds of Japanese and Koreans by Spitzka (1903) and Shibata (1936), however, suggested that Asians and Europeans were more or less comparable in brain weight. Brains from Asia were larger than those from Africa although Asians were often smaller in height and lighter in weight than were Africans.

Regardless, during World War II (1939–1945), ethnic nepotism led to unparalleled degrees of discrimination and killing. After the Holocaust, the association with Nazism discredited even the mildest attempts to produce genetic explanations of human affairs. Craniometry became associated with extreme forms of racial prejudice. For many years, research on race differences in brain size (and intelligence) virtually ceased, and the literature underwent vigorous critiques, notably from Philip V. Tobias (1970), Leon Kamin (1974), and Stephen Jay Gould (1981). As we shall see in the next chapter, their conclusions in favor of the null hypothesis do not hold.

6

Race, Brain Size, and Intelligence

From weighing wet brains at autopsy and calculating cranial capacity from skulls and external head measurements, it will be seen from modern as well as historical studies that Mongoloids and Caucasoids average larger brains than Negroids. The Mongoloid > Negroid finding is especially striking. When adjustments are made for body size, Mongoloids have even larger and heavier brains than do Caucasoids. Although sampling and methodological difficulties may be identified in particular studies, results obtained from multimethod comparisons allow a triangulation on probable truth.

The racial differences in brain size show up early in life. Analyses of the U.S. Collaborative Perinatal Project discussed in chapter 2 showed that 17,000 white infants and 7-year-olds had significantly larger head perimeters than their 19,000 black counterparts, even though, by 7 years, black children were taller and heavier (Broman et al., 1987). In all groups, head perimeter at birth and at age 7 correlated with IQ at age 7 from 0.10 to 0.20.

Small differences in brain volume translates into greater brain efficiency and millions of excess neurons and helps to explain the global distribution of intelligence test scores. It will be seen that Caucasoids from North America, Europe, and Australasia generally obtain mean IQs of around 100. Mongoloids from both North America and Pacific Rim countries typically obtain higher means in the range of 101-111. Negroids from south of the Sahara, the Caribbean, or the United States obtain means of from 70-90. Studies of mental decision times, measured in milliseconds, which correlate with conventional IQ tests (chap. 2), show that Mongoloids have the fastest reaction times, followed by Caucasoids, and then by Negroids.

Brain Weight at Autopsy

In a review highly critical of the literature on wet brain weight measured at autopsy, Tobias (1970) claimed that all interracial comparisons were "invalid," "misleading," and "meaningless" because 14 crucial variables had been left uncontrolled. These included "sex, body size, age of death, nutritional state in early life, source of the sample, occupational group, cause of death, lapse of time after death, temperature after death, anatomical level of severance [of brain from spinal cord], presence or absence of cerebrospinal fluid, of meninges, and of blood vessels" (pp. 3 and 16). Tobias pointed out that each of these variables alone could increase or decrease brain size by 10 to 20 percent, an amount equivalent or greater than any purported race difference. He equally opposed conclusions of race differences in structural variables such as cortical thickness, size of frontal lobe, or complexity of the brain's convolutions.

Because I was curious to know what the data would show, despite methodological weaknesses, and because I believed that the principle of aggregation (chap. 2) often cancels measurement error, I calculated the mid-points of the range of scores provided by Tobias (1970: 6, Table 2) and found that Mongoloids averaged 1,368 grams, Caucasoids 1,378 grams, and Negroids 1,316 grams (Rushton, 1988b). I also averaged a related measure, the "millions of excess nerve cells" estimated by Tobias for 8 subgroups and nationalities (1970: 9, Table 3). These were the number of neurons available for general adaptive purposes over and above that necessary for maintaining bodily functioning and were derivable from equations based on brain/body weight ratios (Jerison, 1963, 1973). Tobias was skeptical of the value of this "exercise" and provided few details. Nonetheless, I found that in millions of excess neurons, Mongoloids = 8,990, Caucasoids = 8,650, and Negroids = 8,550 (Rushton, 1988c).

Subsequent to Tobias's (1970) review, a major autopsy study was carried out by Ho et al. (1980a, 1980b) who provided original brain weight data for 1,261 adult subjects aged 25 to 80 from Cleveland, Ohio. Ho et al. excluded those brains obviously damaged and avoided most of the problems cited by Tobias. Sex-combined differences were found between 811 American whites (1,323 g; SD = 146) and 450 American blacks (1,223 g; SD = 144), a difference that, according to Ho et al., remained significant after controlling for age, stature, body weight, and total body surface area.

In the introduction to their article, Ho et al. (1980a) briefly reviewed additional literature from which I calculated that Mongoloids averaged 1,334 grams, Caucasoids 1,307 grams, and Negroids 1,289 grams. Averaging the three sets of estimates (Tobias's review, Ho et al.'s review, and Ho et al.'s data), I found a sex-combined brain weight for Mongoloids of 1,351 grams, Caucasoids 1,336 grams, and Negroids 1,286 grams (Rushton, 1988b). Further, Ho et al.'s review suggested that, whereas the Caucasoid brain weight began to decline at age 25, the Mongoloid brain weight may not do so until age 35.

Endocranial Volume

Many more studies have estimated brain size from cranial capacity, for, as J. R. Baker (1974: 429) remarked, "Skulls are many, freshly removed brains are few." This literature too has undergone serious critiques, for example, by Gould, first published in *Science* (1978), and then his book, *The Mismeasure of Man* (1981). In particular, Gould re-analyzed Morton's (1849) work, mentioned in the last chapter, and alleged that the figures had been biased by "unconscious...finagling" and "juggling" (1978: 503).

Gould (1981: 65) suggested how biases could be introduced into such data:

> Plausible scenarios are easy to construct. Morton, measuring by seed, picks up a threateningly large black skull, fills it lightly and gives it a few desultory shakes. Next, he takes a distressingly small Caucasian skull, shakes hard, and pushes mightily at the foramen magnum with his thumb. It is easily done, without conscious motivation; expectation is a powerful guide to action.

TABLE 6.1
S. J. Gould's "Corrected" Final Tabulation of Morton's Assessment of Racial Differences in Cranial Capacity

Population	Cubic inches	
	1978 version	1981 version
Native Americans	86	86
Mongolians	85	87
Modern Caucasians	85	87
Malays	85	85
Ancient Caucasians	84	84
Africans	83	83

Note. From Rushton (1989a, p. 14. Table 2). Copyright 1989 by Academic Press. Reprinted with permission.

Table 6.1 represents Gould's summary of Morton's data after correcting Morton's alleged errors. The first column reports Gould's 1978 summary and the second column his 1981 summary following an admission of his own bias in calculating the 1978 figures for modern Caucasians. In both his 1978 and 1981 writings, Gould dismissed the differences between groups as "trivial."

I have averaged Gould's 1978 and 1981 figures on cranial capacity and found, on both occasions, that Mongoloids (Native Americans + Mongoloids) > Caucasoids (Modern Caucasians + Ancient Caucasians) > Negroids (Africans). After excluding "Malays" due to uncertainty as to their racial category, the figures from column 1 are 85.5, 84.5, and 83 cubic inches (1,401; 1,385; and 1,360 cm^3) and from column 2 they are 86.5, 85.5, and 83 cubic inches, respectively (1,418; 1,401; 1,360 cm^3). The figures did not change appreciably if Malays were included as either Mongoloids or Caucasoids. Clearly, despite Gould's conclusions, Mongoloids and modern Caucasians had an advantage of 4 cubic inches (64 cm^3) over Africans in these "corrected" data (Rushton, 1988b, 1989b). Differences of even 1 cubic inch (16 cm^3) should probably not be dismissed as "trivial."

In any case, Gould's charge that Morton "unconsciously" doctored his results to show Caucasian racial superiority has been refuted. A random sample of the Morton collection was remeasured by Michael (1988) who found that very few errors had been made and that these were not in the direction that Gould had asserted. Instead, errors were found in Gould's own work. Michael (1988: 353) concluded that Morton's research "was conducted with integrity...(while)...Gould is mistaken."

I also averaged other data on endocranial volume and found support for my ranking based on Gould's analyses. For example, Coon (1982) had calculated capacities for 17 populations from detailed measurements made by Howells (1973) of 2,000 skulls recorded on a tour of the world's museums. Coon had concluded that "Asiatic Mongols, Eskimoes, and Polynesians have the largest brains, European Caucasoids the next largest, Africans and Australoids still smaller, and the small or dwarfed peoples the smallest" (1982: 18). Coon's book began with a preface from Howells warning readers not to be too easily dismissive. Combining the sexes, I found that Mongoloids = 1,401 cm^3, Caucasoids = 1,381 cm^3, and Negroids = 1,321 cm^3. I also averaged capacities from a table provided by Molnar (1983: 65) based on data from Montagu (1960) and found that Mongoloids = 1,494 cm^3, Caucasoids = 1,435 cm^3, and Negroids = 1,346 cm^3. I then averaged across Coon's and Molnar's figures to find Mongoloids = 1,448 cm^3, Caucasoids = 1,408 cm^3, and Negroids = 1,334 cm^3 (Rushton, 1988b).

An international database of up to 20,000 endocranial specimens from 122 ethnic groups has been computerized and classified in terms of climate and geography by Beals et al. (1984). It showed that endocranial volume varied according to climate in various regions of the world, including the Americas.

Overall there was a 2.5 cm³ increase in brain volume with each degree of latitude. Regional differences emerged. Table 2 (p. 306) in Beals et al. shows that sex-combined brain cases from 26 populations in Asia averaged 1,380 cm³ (*SD* = 83), 10 from Europe averaged 1,362 cm³ (*SD* = 35), and 10 from Africa averaged 1,276 cm³ (*SD* = 84).

The continental areas represented heterogenous ethnic groups. For example, "Asia" included Arabs, Hindus, Tamils and Veddas, while "Africa" included Egyptians (K. Beals, personal communication, May 9, 1993). When the aforementioned groups are eliminated to reduce racial heterogeneity by identifying continental areas in relation to the presence or absence of winter frost (Beals et al., 1984: 307, Table 5), the regional differences become more pronounced (19 Asian groups = 1,415 cm³, *SD* = 51; 10 European groups = 1,362 cm³, *SD* = 35; 9 African groups = 1,268 cm³, *SD* = 85).

External Head Measurements

A third way of estimating cranial capacity is from external head measurements (Figure 6.1). For example, the length, width, and height of the head are placed in regression equations to predict cranial capacity. Lee and Pearson (1901) may have been the first to do this. They chose skulls in series of 50 to 100 from widely different races to permit generalizing the results. Capacities had been determined independently by competent observers. Altogether, skull

Figure 6.1: Cranial Capacity Estimated from External Head Measurements

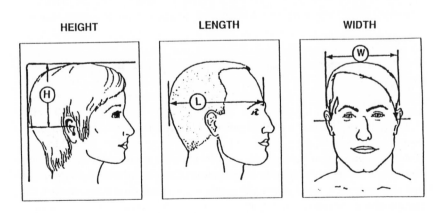

HEIGHT   LENGTH   WIDTH

H = height, *L* = length, and *W* = width. Using formulae devised by Lee and Pearson (1901), cranial capacity (cm³) for men = .000337 (*L* = 11 mm) (*W* = 11 mm) (*H* − 11 mm) + 406.01 and for women = .0004 (*L* − 11 mm) (*W* − 11 mm) (*H* − 11 mm) + 206.6, where 11 mm is subtracted for fat and skin around the skull.

dimensions based on the greatest length, the greatest breadth, and the height measured from the auricular line were examined for 941 men and 516 women including representatives of the Asian, European, and African continents (p. 246, Table XX).

Lee and Pearson (1901) showed that their equations, including a "panracial" equation (p. 252, Number 14; p. 260), provided cranial capacity estimates more accurate for the individual skull than the direct method of using sand, seed, or shot. Their equations predicted both male and female capacities with errors of less than 1 percent, or about 2 to 5 cm³ on crania of 1,300 to 1,500 cm³ (p. 244, Table XVIII), considerably less than the 30 cm³ difference typically found between two observers measuring the same series of skulls using an internal "packing" procedure.

Lee and Pearson's (1901) panracial equations were:

for men,

$$CC \text{ (cm}^3) = 0.000337 \ (L-11\text{mm})(B-11\text{mm})(H-11\text{mm}) + 406.01 \ (1)$$

for women,

$$CC \text{ (cm}^3) = 0.0004 \ (L-11\text{mm})(B-11\text{mm})(H-11\text{mm}) + 206.6 \ (2),$$

where CC is cranial capacity and L, B, and H are length, breadth, and height in millimeters and 11mm is subtracted for fat and skin around the skull. When data for height of head are missing, cranial capacity can be estimated from another equation given by Lee and Pearson (1901: 235, Table VII, Number 5; as used by Passingham (1979) and amended by Rushton (1993) to subtract 11mm for fat and skin around the skull):

for men,

$$CC \text{ (cm}^3) = 6.752 \ (L-11\text{mm}) + 11.421 \ (B-11\text{mm}) - 1434.06 \ (3)$$

for women,

$$CC \text{ (cm}^3) = 7.884 \ (L-11\text{mm}) + 10.842 \ (B-11\text{mm}) - 1593.96 \ (4).$$

I have applied these equations to four different anthropometric data sets. One set, compiled by Melville Herskovits (1930), a student of Franz Boas, has often been cited as showing an absence of racial differences because of the amount of overlap in the distributions. As can be seen in Table 6.2, a sample of 961 American Negroes had larger head measurements than a sample of Swedes. However, Herskovits's monograph actually contained information on head length and width for 26 internatioanl samples (N = 54,454; males only).

TABLE 6.2
Cranial Capacities Calculated from Head Lengths and Widths Provided
by Herskovits (1930) for Various Male Samples and Classified by
Race or Geographical Region

Race/region and group	Sample size	Length (mm)	Width (mm)	Cranial capacity (cm^3)
Mongoloids/Asian				
Pure Sioux	540	194.90	155.10	1,453
Half-blood Sioux	77	194.40	154.30	1,441
Montagnais-Naskapi	50	194.00	157.10	1,470
Marquesans	83	193.20	153.20	1,420
Hawaiians	86	191.25	158.93	1,472
Mean		*193.55*	*155.73*	*1,451*
Caucasoids/European				
Old Americans	727	197.28	153.76	1,454
Foreign-born Scotch	263	196.70	153.80	1,451
Oxford students	959	196.05	152.84	1,435
Aberdeen students	493	194.80	153.40	1,433
Swedes	46,975	193.84	150.40	1,393
Cambridge students	1,000	193.51	153.96	1,431
Cairo natives	802	190.52	144.45	1,302
Foreign-born Bohemians	450	189.80	159.10	1,465
American-born Bohemians	60	188.00	156.50	1,423
Mean		*193.39*	*153.13*	*1,421*
Negroids/African				
American Negroes	961	196.52	151.38	1,422
Masai	91	194.67	142.49	1,308
Lotuko	34	192.90	141.30	1,283
Kajiji	55	192.31	144.56	1,316
Somali	27	191.81	143.19	1,297
Ekoi	19	191.05	143.16	1,291
Vai	40	188.85	142.45	1,268
Akikuyu	384	188.72	143.25	1,276
Kagoro	72	188.19	142.43	1,263
Akamba	128	187.80	143.63	1,275
Ashanti	48	187.33	145.01	1,287
Acholi	30	187.30	141.80	1,250
Mean		*190.62*	*143.72*	*1,295*

Note. From Rushton (1993, p. 230, Table 1). Copyright 1993 by Pergamon Press. Reprinted with permission. Cranial capacity (cm^3) = [6.752 x (L − 11mm)] + [11.421 x (W − 11mm)] − 1434.06. Formula is from Lee and Pearson (1901).

Using equation 3, I calculated cranial capacities for each sample and then took averages. I found that 5 "Mongoloid" samples (in this case, mostly North American Indians) averaged 1,451 cm^3 (SD = 22), 9 Caucasoid samples averaged 1,421 cm^3 (SD = 49), and 12 Negroid samples averaged 1,295 cm^3 (SD = 44). Treating each sample mean as an independent entry, a one-way ANOVA revealed that the races differed significantly in brain size with a highly significant trend in the predicted direction (Rushton, 1990c, as amended, 1993). No information was available on body size.

Herskovits's (1930) data were gathered by different investigators from different parts of the world using different techniques. Although not too much reliance should be placed on my reanalysis of this one study, nonetheless, because Herskovits's monograph has so often been referred to by those critical of race differences, the aggregation is noteworthy. It obviously confirms the re-aggregations of the "corrected" data sets by Tobias (1970) and Gould (1978, 1981).

To examine how generalizable were the results from the reanalyses of the data sets purporting to show "no difference," I sought out additional sets. The military services turned out to be a good source because of their need to measure the body proportions of their personnel so as to provide them with uniforms, including helmets. The U.S. National Aeronautics and Space Administration (1978) made a compilation from which I abstracted the body size and head size data for 24 international male military samples totaling 57,378 individuals (Rushton, 1991b). These are shown in Table 6.3. For each sample I calculated cranial capacities using equation 3 and then the mean differences. The unadjusted cranial capacity for the 4 Mongoloid samples was 1,343 cm³ (SD = 47) and for 20 Caucasoid samples, 1,467 cm³ (SD = 58). The stature, weight, and total body surface area of the Mongoloid samples averaged significantly lower than those of the Caucasoid samples. After adjusting for the body size variables, the least-square mean for Mongoloids was 1,460 cm³, and for Caucasoids, 1,446 cm³.

Probably the best single data set is the stratified random sample of 6,325 U.S. Army personnel measured in 1988 (Rushton, 1992a). Individual and head measurements were available separately for men and women, officers and enlisted personnel, and those who had defined themselves to the U.S. Army as black, Asian or white. Because head measurements were available for length, width, and height, cranial capacities were calculated from equations (1) and (2). The means and standard errors for all the variables are shown in Table 6.4.

For the entire sample, the unadjusted size of the cranium was 1,375 cm³. The range was from 981 cm³, a black woman, to 1,795 cm³, a white man. Because the measurements had been gathered on individuals, specific adjustments could be made to the raw data for the effects of age, stature, and weight, and then sex, rank, or race.

The races differed significantly in both the unadjusted (raw) and adjusted cranial capacities. Analysis of variance of unadjusted cranial capacity showed that 543 Asian-Americans averaged 1,391 cm³ (SD = 104), 2,871 European-Americans, 1,378 cm³ (SD = 92) and 2,676 African-Americans, 1,362 cm³ (SD = 95). After adjusting for the effects of stature, weight, sex, and military rank, the differences became larger with Asian-Americans averaging 1,416

TABLE 6.3
Anthropometric Variables for Male Military Samples from NASA (1978)

Race / NASA identification number, and group	Sample size	Head length (mm)	Head breadth (mm)	Head height (mm)	Stature (cm)	Weight (gms)	Surface area (m²)	Cranial capacity (cm³)	Encephal-ization quotient
Orientals									
84. Thai military, 1963	2,950	179.0	152.0	128.0	163.40	56,300	1.60	1,340	7.33
85. Vietnam military, 1964	2,129	181.9	149.0	123.3	160.43	51,100	1.52	1,299	7.58
86. South Korean Air Force, 1961	264	184.1	154.9	130.4	168.66	62,840	1.72	1,408	7.16
87. South Korean military, 1965	3,747	179.0	153.0	125.0	165.20	59,400	1.65	1,323	6.98
Mean		*181.0*	*152.2*	*126.7*	*164.42*	*57,410*	*1.62*	*1,343*	*7.26*
SD		*2.5*	*2.5*	*3.2*	*3.38*	*4,983*	*.08*	*47*	*.26*
Caucasoids									
18. U.S. Air Force fliers, 1950	4,063	197.0	154.1	129.7	175.56	74,100	1.90	1,471	6.69
19. U.S. Air Force, 1965	3,827	196.2	153.1	131.8	175.28	70,980	1.86	1,477	6.92
24. U.S. Navy fliers, 1965	1,549	198.3	155.6	131.1	177.64	77,760	1.95	1,502	6.62
25. U.S. Air Force, 1967	2,420	198.7	156.0	134.5	177.34	78,740	1.96	1,539	6.72
30. U.S. Army, 1966	6,682	194.7	152.7	132.3	174.52	72,160	1.87	1,470	6.81
31. U.S. Navy, 1966	4,095	194.2	152.3	135.4	175.33	71,560	1.87	1,491	6.95
32. U.S. Navy divers, 1972	100	197.5	154.0	142.6	176.22	81,520	1.98	1,589	6.78
33. U.S. Marines, 1966	2,008	194.3	152.8	133.8	174.56	72,650	1.87	1,482	6.83
34. U.S. Navy aviators, 1959	500	197.3	155.4	126.7	176.52	71,100	1.87	1,455	6.81
36. U.S. Army aviators, 1970	1,482	197.0	152.6	132.9	174.56	77,630	1.93	1,488	6.56
48. NATO military, 1961	3,356	189.7	155.5	131.8	170.22	67,660	1.79	1,457	7.05
59. German Air Force, 1975	1,465	191.6	156.8	129.2	176.66	74,730	1.91	1,455	6.58
65. British soldiers, 1972	500	197.8	155.1	127.3	174.05	73,190	1.88	1,461	6.70
66. British Air Force, 1971	2,000	199.0	157.8	130.3	177.44	75,040	1.92	1,516	6.84
68. Canadian Air Force, 1961	314	193.5	152.9	131.5	177.44	76,410	1.94	1,458	6.50
69. Canadian Air Force, 1961	290	193.8	152.9	129.7	176.68	75,550	1.92	1,444	6.49
70. New Zealand Air Force, 1973	238	197.1	152.1	132.5	176.95	75,280	1.92	1,481	6.67
75. Latin American Forces, 1972	1,985	186.0	152.0	122.0	167.00	65,900	1.74	1,329	6.54
77. French young men, 1967	2,000	195.0	154.5	125.1	171.99	63,850	1.75	1,421	7.14
90. Iranian military, 1969	9,414	187.4	148.6	127.1	166.85	61,630	1.69	1,356	6.98
Mean		*195.3*	*153.9*	*130.9*	*174.66*	*72,872*	*1.88*	*1,470*	*6.76*
SD		*3.7*	*2.1*	*4.4*	*3.21*	*5,114*	*.09*	*58*	*.20*

Note. From Rushton (1991b, pp. 356–357, Table 1). Copyright 1991 by Ablex Publishing Corporation. Reprinted with permission.

Surface area (m²) = [wt (kgms)$^{0.425}$ x ht (cm)$^{0.725}$ x 0.007184].

Cranial capacity (cm³) = 0.000337 (Head length – 11 mm) (Head Breadth – 11 mm) + 406.01.

Encephalization quotient = Observed cranial capacity (cm³)/Expected cranial capacity, i.e., (0.12) (Body weight in gms)$^{0.67}$.

TABLE 6.4
Cranial Capacity, Height, and Weight by Sex, Rank, and Race for
6,325 U.S. Military Personnel

Sex, rank / race	Sample size	Cranial capacity (cm³)		Height (cm)		Weight (kg)	
		Mean	SE	Mean	SE	Mean	SE
Female, enlisted							
Negroid	1,206	1,260	2.73	163.0	.18	62.2	.23
Caucasoid	1,011	1,264	2.84	162.9	.20	61.6	.25
Mongoloid	116	1,297	9.38	158.1	.61	58.6	.91
Female, officer							
Negroid	89	1,270	10.05	164.0	.66	64.4	.85
Caucasoid	270	1,284	5.49	164.7	.37	62.3	.55
Mongoloid	16	1,319	34.20	157.1	1.44	56.2	2.20
Male, enlisted							
Negroid	1,336	1,449	2.64	175.5	.18	78.4	.31
Caucasoid	1,302	1,468	2.52	176.0	.18	77.9	.30
Mongoloid	388	1,464	4.74	168.9	.32	73.2	.60
Male, officer							
Negroid	45	1,467	14.17	176.5	1.10	80.3	1.29
Caucasoid	288	1,494	5.48	177.6	.39	80.5	.57
Mongoloid	23	1,485	17.60	169.4	1.64	71.4	2.05

Note. From Rushton (1992a, p. 405, Table 1). Copyright 1992 by Ablex Publishing Corporation. Reprinted with permission.

cm³, European-Americans 1,380 cm³, and African-Americans 1,359 cm³. Attempts to diminish the differences in cranial capacity by numerous corrections for body size were unsuccessful (Figure 6.2).

A fourth study was made possible by a 1990 review of ergonomically important body measurements compiled by the International Labour Office in Geneva (Jurgens, Aune, & Pieper, 1990). Head and body size measurements had been gathered over a 30-year period for tens of thousands of men and women aged 25 to 45 years. Some 300 references had been examined from 7 sources: handicraft workers such as tailors and shoemakers, anthropology studies, medical records, sports participation, growth surveys, forensic and legal investigations, and ergonomic studies. Notably lacking were the studies of

Figure 6.2: Cranial Capacity for a Stratified Random Sample of 6,325 U.S. Army Personnel

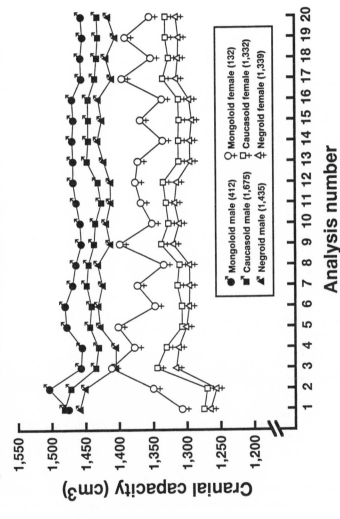

The data, grouped into six sex by race categories, are collapsed across military rank. They show, across 20 different analyses controlling for body size, men averaging larger cranial capacities than women and Asian-Americans averaging larger than European-Americans or African-Americans. Analysis 1 presents the data, unadjusted for body size. From Rushton (1992a, p. 408, Figure 1). Copyright 1992 by Ablex Publishing Corporation. Reprinted with permission.

TABLE 6.5
Cranial Capacities of World Populations of 25 to 45-Year-Olds

Region, number of references, and source countries	Men Stature (mm)	Men Head length (mm)	Men Head breadth (mm)	Men Cranial capacity (cm³)	Women Stature (mm)	Women Head length (mm)	Women Head breadth (mm)	Women Cranial capacity (cm³)
1. North America (34 refs. from Canada and U.S.A.)	1,790	195	155	1,453	1,650	180	145	1,191
2. Latin America (20 refs. from Indian populations in Bolivia, Peru, etc.)	1,620	185	150	1,328	1,480	175	145	1,152
3. Latin America (15 refs. from European-Negroid populations in Chile, the Caribbean Island States, etc.)	1,750	190	155	1,419	1,620	175	150	1,206
4. Northern Europe (28 refs. from Denmark, Sweden, etc.)	1,810	195	155	1,453	1,690	180	150	1,246
5. Central Europe (42 refs. from Austria, Switzerland, etc.)	1,770	190	155	1,419	1,660	180	145	1,191
6. Eastern Europe (14 refs. from Poland and Soviet Union)	1,750	190	155	1,419	1,630	180	150	1,246
7. South-eastern Europe (40 refs. from Bulgaria, Romania, etc.)	1,730	190	155	1,419	1,620	175	150	1,206
8. France (20 refs.)	1,770	195	155	1,453	1,630	180	140	1,137
9. Iberian Peninsula (6 refs. from Spain and Portugal)	1,710	185	155	1,385	1,600	180	150	1,246
10. North Africa (10 refs. from Algeria, Ethiopia, Sudan, etc.)	1,690	190	145	1,305	1,610	185	140	1,177
11. West Africa (10 refs. from Congo, Ghana, Nigeria, etc.)	1,670	195	145	1,339	1,530	180	135	1,083
12. South-eastern Africa (16 refs. from Angola, Kenya, etc.)	1,680	195	145	1,339	1,570	180	135	1,083
13. Near East (5 refs. from Iraq, Lebanon, Turkey, etc.)	1,710	190	150	1,362	1,610	180	140	1,137
14. North India (23 refs. from Bangladesh, Nepal, etc.)	1,670	190	145	1,305	1,540	180	135	1,083
15. South India (3 refs. from India and Sri Lanka)	1,620	180	145	1,237	1,500	175	130	989
16. North Asia (5 refs. from China, Mongolia, etc.)	1,690	190	150	1,362	1,590	180	145	1,191
17. South China (9 refs. from Macao, Taiwan, etc.)	1,660	190	150	1,362	1,520	180	145	1,191
18. South-East Asia (11 refs. from Brunei, Indonesia, Malaysia, Philippines, etc.)	1,630	185	145	1,271	1,530	175	135	1,043
19. Australia (6 refs. from European population in Australia and New Zealand)	1,770	192	155	1,433	1,670	180	145	1,191
20. Japan (26 refs. from Japan and Korea)	1,720	190	155	1,419	1,590	180	145	1,191

Note. From Rushton (1994, Table 1).

Cranial capacity for men (cm³) = [6.752 x (Head length - 11 mm) + 11.421 x (Head breadth - 11 mm)] - 1434.06.

Cranial capacity for women (cm³) = [7.884 x (Head length - 11 mm) + 10.842 x (Head breadth - 11 mm) - 1593.96. Formulas are from Lee and Pearson (1901).

military personnel examined above, thus making these new data independent of previous sets.

Jurgens et al. (1990) grouped their data into 20 world regions. Summarized in Table 6.5 are the 50th percentile measures of stature, head length, and head breadth, separately for men and women as well as the number of references cited to arrive at the summarized figures. From these I derived cranial capacities using equations (4) and (5) above (Rushton, 1994).

Because the regions were fully described in the research report with respect to the included countries (see Table 6.5), it was possible to eliminate ambiguous categories, thereby facilitating racial comparisons. Excluded from statistical analysis were 6 regions: No. 2 (Amerindians), Nos. 3 and 10 (combining Caucasoid and Negroid populations), Nos. 14 and 15 (North and South India), and No. 18 (combining Caucasoid and Mongoloid populations).

If each of the male/female sample means is treated as an independent entry for analysis, there are 6 clear Mongoloid samples (Regions 16, 17, and 20), 18 predominately Caucasoid samples (Regions 1, 4, 5, 6, 7, 8, 9, 13, and 19), and 4 clear African samples (Regions 11 and 12). Analysis of variance carried out on the unadjusted (raw) means showed that the east Asians (M = 1,286 cm³, SD = 117) and Caucasoids (M = 1,311 cm³, SD = 103) averaged larger absolute cranial capacities than Africans (M = 1,211 cm³, SD = 144). After adjusting for the effects of stature, the differences became more pronounced with east Asians averaging 1,308 cm³, Caucasians 1,297 cm³, and Africans 1,241 cm³. Subsidiary analyses weighted by the number of references or some other combination of countries did not alter the overall pattern of the results (Rushton, 1994).

Brain Size from Infancy to Adolescence

Race differences in brain size are evident in infants and young children. Ho, Roessmann, Hause, and Monroe (1981) collated brain weights at autopsy from 782 newborns. In absolute terms (unadjusted for other variables), white babies averaged heavier brains than black babies: 272 grams versus 196 grams. Many of these babies were premature (49 percent of the white sample and 78 percent of the black sample). When the criteria of a gestational age of 38 weeks and a body weight at birth of 2,500 grams was employed to define "full term" in both groups, the racial differences disappeared. Black babies, however, have a biologically based shorter gestation than white babies (chap. 7) and so the appropriateness of imposing these criteria for racial comparisons can be questioned.

The U.S. Collaborative Perinatal Project discussed in chapter 2 examined and followed up approximately 17,000 white children and 19,000 black children from conception to the age of 7 years in the United States (Broman et al., 1987). In both blacks and whites, head perimeter at birth, 4 months, 1 year, 4 years, and 7 years predicted IQ scores at age 7 from 0.12 to 0.24 (Table 2.3). I have calculated from the appropriate tables in Broman et al. (1987) that the white children are born with larger heads and larger bodies (a 16 percentile point advantage in each). However, I have also calculated that catch-up growth favors black children in height but not in head perimeter. By age 4 black children are 11 percentile points taller than white children, and by age 7 they are 16 percentile points taller, but at age 7 their head perimeter remains 8 percentile points smaller. With IQ measured at 4 and at 7 years of age, white children show a 34 percentile point advantage (1 standard deviation).

Adolescents have also been examined. R. Lynn (1993) used Lee and Pearson's (1901) equations (1) and (2) to calculate cranial capacities from external head measurements on 36 samples of 7- to 15-year-olds gathered by the Philadelphia Growth Center (Krogman, 1970). The core sample consisted of 169 white males, 224 black males, 135 white females, and 220 black females. The boys and girls had all been screened for serious illnesses or dental problems and were middle-class from "a solid, stable responsible cross section of the population" (Krogman, 1970: 4). After adjusting for the effects of age, stature, and sex, white children averaged 1,250 cm³ and black children averaged 1,236 cm³.

Summary of Brain Size Data

Table 6.6 summarizes the results from 44 studies of race differences in adult brain size from the 3 different methods discussed: wet brain weights from autopsies (grams), endocranial volume (cm³), and external head measurements (cm³). The brain size in grams can be converted to cranial capacity in cubic centimeters and vice versa. J. R. Baker (1974: 429) provided an equation for changing cm³ to grams:

Brain weight [g] = 1.065 cm³ - 195   (5)

To convert brain weight into cranial capacity, a specific gravity of 1.036 has often been assumed. Thus:

Cranial capacity (cm³) = 1.036 g   (6)

These equations do not result in the same product. Equation (6) has been used in modern studies (e.g., Hofman, 1991) and will be used here to convert the autopsy data in Table 6.6 from grams to cm³.

There are four sets of data itemized and then averaged in Table 6.6. Section A sets out the results of autopsy studies. There were 38 of these, including 16 reports of data from Korea and Japan, 18 from Caucasoids in Europe and the United States, and 8 from Negroids in Africa and the United States. The results are shown for men and women separately where possible. For some studies, key reviews were used because the originals were unpublished, in a foreign language, or otherwise difficult to obtain. In the studies cited by Dekaban and Sadowsky (1978) I calculated the mean as the midpoint of a range. Double entries have been eliminated whenever found. After the 38th autopsy study, summary statistics are provided for each racial group showing the number of studies, the range, the mean, and the median. The sex-combined averages are calculated by adding the mean and median figures for men and women and dividing by two. Following this, the mean is transformed into cm³ using equation (6).

TABLE 6.6
Summary of Race Differences in Brain Size: Multimethod Comparisons

Data type / source	Samples and procedures	Mongoloids			Caucasoids			Negroids		
		Men	Women	Both	Men	Women	Both	Men	Women	Both
A. Autopsy data (grams)										
1. Peacock (1865, cited and averaged by Pearl, 1934)	5 Negro men	–	–	–	–	–	–	1,257	–	–
2. Russell (1869, analyzed by Pearl, 1934)	379 black soldiers and 24 white soldiers most of whom died of pneumonia during U.S. Civil War	–	–	–	1,471	–	–	1,342	–	–
3. Doenitz (1874, cited in Spitzka, 1903)	10 Japanese men executed by decapitation	1,337	–	–	–	–	–	–	–	–
4. Bischoff (1880, cited in Pakkenberg & Voigt, 1964)	906 Europeans measured at pathology institute	–	–	–	1,362	1,219	(1,291)	–	–	–
5. Taguchi (1881, cited in Spitzka, 1903)	100 Japanese men executed by decapitation	1,356	–	–	–	–	–	–	–	–
6. Topinard (1885, cited in Pearl, 1934)	29 unspecified Negro men, collected from the literature	–	–	–	–	–	–	1,234	–	–
7. Suzuki (1892, cited in Shibata, 1936)	27 Japanese (24 men, 3 women) aged 35 to 73	1,348	1,120	(1,234)	–	–	–	–	–	–
8. Taguchi (1892, cited in Shibata, 1936)	524 Japanese (374 men, 150 women) aged 21 to 95	1,367	1,214	(1,291)	–	–	–	–	–	–
9. Marshall (1892)	2,012 British (972 men, 1,040 women) aged 20 to 90 years; reanalysis of 1861 data published with breakdowns for age, height, weight, sane/insane	–	–	–	1,329	1,194	(1,262)	–	–	–
10. Waldeyer (1894, cited in Pearl, 1934)	12 African men aged 15+	–	–	–	–	–	–	1,148	–	–
11. Retzius (1900, cited in Pakkenberg & Voigt, 1964)	700 Swedes at a pathological institute	–	–	–	1,399	1,248	(1,324)	–	–	–
12. Matiegka (1902, cited in Pakkenberg & Voigt, 1964)	416 Europeans at a pathological institute	–	–	–	1,347	1,204	(1,276)	–	–	–
13. Matiegka (1902, cited in Pakkenberg & Voigt, 1964)	581 Europeans at the Institute of Forensic Medicine in Prague	–	–	–	1,450	1,306	(1,378)	–	–	–
14. Marchand (1902, cited in Pakkenberg & Voigt, 1964)	1,169 Europeans aged 18 to 50 at a pathological institute in Marburg	–	–	–	1,400	1,275	(1,338)	–	–	–
15. Spitzka (1903)	597 Japanese (421 men, 176 women) aged 21 to 95 from hospitals around Tokyo; ten years of records including data on age, stature, weight	1,367	1,214	(1,291)	–	–	–	–	–	–
16. Bean (1906)	Review of records for 22 Negro men and 10 Negro women	–	–	–	–	–	–	1,256	980	(1,118)
17. Bean (1906)	125 Americans from an anatomical laboratory in Baltimore (37 white men, 9 white women, 51 black men, 28 black women)	–	–	–	1,341	1,103	(1,222)	1,292	1,108	(1,200)
18. Chernyshev (1911, cited in Dekaban & Sadowsky, 1978)	Unspecified number of men and women (probably Russian) aged 20 to 80 years	–	–	–	1,346	1,210	(1,278)	–	–	–

TABLE 6.6 (cont.)

Data type / source	Samples and procedures	Mongoloids			Caucasoids			Negroids		
		Men	Women	Both	Men	Women	Both	Men	Women	Both
19. Nagayo (1919, 1925, cited in Shibata, 1936)	485 Japanese (329 men, 156 women) aged 16 to 60	1,362	1,242	(1,302)	–	–	–	–	–	–
20. Kurokawa (1920, cited in Shibata, 1936).	440 Japanese (240 men, 200 women) aged 15 to 50	1,402	1,256	(1,329)	–	–	–	–	–	–
21. Kubo (1922, cited in Shibata, 1936)	60 Koreans (56 men, 4 women) aged 21 to 74	1,353	1,206	(1,280)	–	–	–	–	–	–
22. Kimura (1925, cited in Shibata, 1936)	405 Japanese (243 men, 162 women) aged 15 to 50	1,402	1,249	(1,326)	–	–	–	–	–	–
23. Muhlmann (1927, cited in Dekaban & Sadowsky, 1978)	Unspecified number of men and women (probably German) aged 20 to 80 years	–	–	–	1,346	1,205	(1,276)	–	–	–
24. Yoshizawa (1929, 1930, cited in Shibata, 1936)	315 Japanese (211 men, 104 women) aged 16 to 80	1,361	1,231	(1,296)	–	–	–	–	–	–
25. Hoshi (1930, cited in Shibata, 1936)	954 Japanese (551 men, 403 women) aged 16+	1,396	1,255	(1,326)	–	–	–	–	–	–
26. Hoshi (1930, cited in Shibata, 1936)	Unknown number of Japanese of both sexes aged 15 to 50	1,406	1,261	(1,334)	–	–	–	–	–	–
27. Amano-Hayashi (1933, cited in Shibata, 1936)	1,817 Japanese (1,074 men, 743 women) aged 16+	1,375	1,244	(1,310)	–	–	–	–	–	–
28. Kusumoto (1934, cited in Shibata, 1936)	522 Japanese (342 men, 180 women) of unknown age	1,360	1,241	(1,301)	–	–	–	–	–	–
29. Vint (1934)	389 adult Kenyans of Bantu and Nilotic stock autopsied by author from native hospitals in Nairobi; only brains judged normal used; weights validated against cranial capacity using water technique and compared to data published on Europeans	–	–	–	1,428	–	–	1,276	–	–
30. Shibata (1936)	153 Koreans (136 men, 17 women) aged 17 to 78; those who died of diseases known to influence brain weight were excluded	1,370	1,277	(1,324)	–	–	–	–	–	–
31. Roessle & Roulet (1938, cited in Pakkenberg & Voigt, 1964)	456 German soldiers	–	–	–	1,405	–	–	–	–	–
32. Appel & Appel (1942)	2,080 white U.S. men aged 12 to 96 at a mental hospital in Washington, DC; weights recorded from hospital records; brains with lesions and abnormalities excluded	–	–	–	1,305	–	–	–	–	–
33. Takahashi & Suzuki (1961)	470 Japanese (301 men, 169 women) aged 30 to 69	1,397	1,229	(1,313)	–	–	–	–	–	–
34. Pakkenberg & Voigt (1964)	1,026 Danes (724 men, 302 women) aged 19 to 95 at the Forensic Institute in Copenhagen between 1959 and 1962; age, height, weight, and cause of death examined	–	–	–	1,440	1,282	(1,361)	–	–	–

TABLE 6.6 (cont.)

Data type / source	Samples and procedures	Mongoloids			Caucasoids			Negroids		
		Men	Women	Both	Men	Women	Both	Men	Women	Both
35. Spann & Dustmann (1965, cited in Dekaban & Sadowsky, 1978)	Unspecified number of (German men and women aged 15 to 94	–	–	–	1,403	1,268	(1,336)	–	–	–
36. Chrzanowska & Beben (1973, cited in Dekaban & Sadowsky, 1978)	1,670 Poles (896 men, 774 women) aged 20 to 89	–	–	–	1,413	1,266	(1,340)	–	–	–
37. Dekaban & Sadowsky (1978)	4,736 U.S. whites (2,733 males, 1,963 females) from hospitals around Washington, D.C., aged birth to 86+; figures calculated for 16 to 86 years (2,036 men, 1,411 women)	–	–	–	1,392	1,254	(1,323)	–	–	–
38. Ho et al. (1980a, 1980b)	1,261 white and black Americans aged 25 to 80 (416 white men, 228 black men, 395 white women, 222 black women); weights taken from 5 years of records at Case Western Reserve University	–	–	–	1,392	1,252	(1,322)	1,286	1,158	(1,222)
Summary of A	*Number of studies*	*16*	*14*	*14*	*18*	*14*	*14*	*8*	*3*	*3*
	Range	*1,337-1,406*	*1,120-1,277*	*1,234-1,334*	*1,305-1,471*	*1,103-1,306*	*1,222-1,378*	*1,148-1,342*	*980-1,158*	*1,118-1,222*
	Mean in grams	*1,372*	*1,231*	*1,304*	*1,387*	*1,235*	*1,309*	*1,261*	*1,082*	*1,180*
	Median in grams	*1,367*	*1,242*	*1,306*	*1,396*	*1,250*	*1,333*	*1,267*	*1,108*	*1,200*
	Mean in cm^3	*1,421*	*1,275*	*1,351*	*1,437*	*1,280*	*1,356*	*1,306*	*1,121*	*1,223*
B. Endocranial volume (cm^3)										
39. Beals et al. (1984)	Sex-combined endocranial volume from 122 populations based on up to 20,000 specimens from around the world and their geographic and climatic coordinates; packing was made with mustard seed; a standard 6% reduction made for studies reporting results based on lead shot	1,491	1,340	(1,415)	1,441	1,283	(1,362)	1,338	1,191	(1,268)
C. Cranium size from external head measurements (cm^3)										
40. Rushton (1990c; amended 1993)	26 male populations (5 "Mongoloid" -- mostly Amerindian, 9 European and European-American and 12 African and African-American; 54,454 individuals); measurements compiled by Herskovits (1930)	1,451	–	–	1,421	–	–	1,295	–	–
41. Rushton (1991b)	24 international male military samples (4 Mongoloid, 20 Caucasoid; 57,378 individuals); measurements compiled by NASA (United States, 1978)	1,343 1,460*	–	–	1,467 1,446*	–	–	–	–	–

TABLE 6.6 (cont.)

Data type / source	Samples and procedures	Mongoloids			Caucasoids			Negroids		
		Men	Women	Both	Men	Women	Both	Men	Women	Both
42. Rushton (1992a)	6,325 U.S. military personnel from a stratified random sample including officers and enlisted personnel (411 Asian men, 132 Asian women, 1,590 white men, 1,281 white women, 1,381 black men, 1,295 black women); measurements gathered by Army	1,465 / 1,486*	1,300 / 1,319*	(1,383) / (1,403)*	1,473 / 1,462*	1,268 / 1,259*	(1,371) / (1,361)*	1,450 / 1,441*	1,261 / 1,250*	(1,356) / (1,346)*
43. Rushton (1994)	28 world samples (3 of Asian men, 3 of Asian women, 9 of Caucasian men, 9 of Caucasian women, 2 of African men, 2 of African women; tens of thousands of individuals); measurements compiled by the International Labour Office in Geneva	1,381 / 1,371*	1,191 / 1,244*	(1,286) / (1,308)*	1,422 / 1,378*	1,199 / 1,215*	(1,311) / (1,297)*	1,339 / 1,337*	1,083 / 1,144*	(1,211) / (1,241)*
Summary of C										
	Number of studies (uncorrected)	4	2	2	4	2	2	3	2	2
	Range	1,343- 1,465	1,191- 1,300	1,286- 1,383	1,421- 1,473	1,199- 1,268	1,311- 1,371	1,293- 1,450	1,083- 1,261	1,211- 1,356
	Mean in cm³	1,410	1,246	1,335	1,446	1,234	1,341	1,361	1,172	1,284
	Median in cm³	1,416	1,246	1,335	1,445	1,234	1,341	1,339	1,172	1,284
	Number of studies (corrected)	3	2	2	3	2	2	2	2	2
	Range	1,371- 1,486	1,244- 1,319	1,308- 1,403	1,378- 1,462	1,215- 1,259	1,297- 1,361	1,337- 1,441	1,144- 1,250	1,241- 1,346
	Mean in cm³	1,439	1,282	1,356	1,425	1,237	1,329	1,389	1,197	1,294
	Median in cm³	1,460	1,282	1,356	1,446	1,237	1,329	1,389	1,197	1,294
D. Grand summary: Mean of means (cm³)										
	Autopsies	1,421	1,275	1,351	1,437	1,280	1,356	1,306	1,121	1,223
	Endocranial volume	1,491	1,340	1,415	1,446	1,283	1,362	1,338	1,191	1,268
	External head measures	1,410	1,246	1,335	1,446	1,234	1,341	1,361	1,172	1,284
	Corrected external head measures	1,439	1,282	1,356	1,425	1,237	1,329	1,389	1,197	1,294
	GRAND MEAN in cm³	1,440	1,286	1,364	1,437	1,259	1,347	1,349	1,170	1,267

Note. *Adjustments made for body size.

The results in section A show that the sex-combined mean brain weight of Mongoloids is almost as heavy (1,304 g) as that of Caucasoids (1,309 g) and that both of these are higher than those of Negroids (1,180 g). The statistical significance of these differences can be gauged from the fact that in no case is the brain weight of a Negroid sample of men or women above the mean or median of those of Mongoloids or Caucasoids ($p < .001$). Translating the grams into cm^3 the Mongoloids, Caucasoids, and Negroids average, respectively 1,351; 1,356; and 1,223 cm^3.

Section B sets out the endocranial data. Here the global review by Beals et al. (1984) based on up to 20,000 endocranial specimens from 122 ethnic groups is relied on. The sex-combined mean for Mongoloids is 1,415 cm^3, for Caucasoids 1,362 cm^3, and for Negroids 1,268 cm^3 (Figures from Table 5 of Beals et al., 1984; sex differences from K. Beals, personal communication, May 9, 1993). Several endocranial studies carried out within the United States, described at the end of chapter 5 (e.g. Todd, 1923, Simmons, 1942), have not been included, nor has the subsequent confirmation of the Beals et al. figures for Negroid crania in the independent review by Ricklan and Tobias (1986). Ricklan and Tobias (1986), for example, found that 917 males averaged 1,342 cm^3 and 320 females averaged 1,280 cm^3 for a sex-combined Negroid mean of 1,280 cm^3. Because of the degree of overlap in some series, I took Beals et al. (1984) to be sufficient.

Section C sets out four studies estimating cranial capacity from external head measurements. The non-asterisked figures are uncorrected for body size while the asterisked figures have been corrected. As in Section A, the number of studies, the range, the mean, and the median are provided. The uncorrected sex-combined mean cranial capacity of Mongoloids (1,335 cm^3) is virtually the same as for Caucasoids (1,341 cm^3), both of which average larger than Negroids (1,284 cm^3). Using the body size corrected figures in Section C shows Mongoloids average 1,356 cm^3, Caucasoids 1,329 cm^3, and Negroids 1,294 cm^3. These differences are highly significant within studies.

Noteworthy is the consistency of the results shown across the different methods. In cm^3 the data from (a) autopsies, (b) endocranial volume, (c) head measurements, and (d) head measurements corrected for body size show: Mongoloids = 1,351; 1,415; 1,335; 1,356 (mean = 1,364); Caucasoids = 1,356; 1,362; 1,341; 1,329 (mean = 1,347); and Negroids = 1,223; 1,268; 1,284; 1,294 (mean = 1,267). From these a world average brain size can be calculated of 1,326 cm^3, comparable to one of 1,349 cm^3 computed by Beals et al. (1984).

The primary conclusion to be made is that whereas the Mongoloid-Caucasoid difference in brain size is quite small, amounting to an average of 17 cm^3 favoring Mongoloids overall (14 cm^3 on uncorrected measures and 27 cm^3 on measures corrected for body size), those between Mongoloids and Negroids average an overall 97 cm^3. The Mongoloid-Negroid difference based on autopsy data is 128 cm^3, on endocranial volume 147 cm^3, on uncorrected external head measurements 51 cm^3, and on head measurements corrected for body size 62 cm^3. The mean difference between Caucasoids and Negroids is 80 cm^3.

No exact solution is possible, of course, to the problem of how large the difference in cranium size is among the races. The magnitudes depend on which samples are included, whether the craniums are adjusted for body size, and which methods are used for computing the average. For example, one might hold that brain size should be weighted by sample size because larger samples provide more stable estimates than do smaller samples, at least when the samples are homogeneous with respect to methods employed. With approximate solutions the only way is to use as many estimates as possible and see if they triangulate. Many of the figures can be recalculated using sample weighted means, mid-points of ranges, medians, and other procedures. These make no difference to the rank orderings, especially of Mongoloid and Caucasoid greater than Negroid. Whether Mongoloids average higher than Caucasoids, however, sometimes depends on correction for body size.

The pervasive sex difference in brain size so clearly observed throughout Table 6.6 has been known since Paul Broca in the nineteenth century. As with race differences, however, critics have suggested the differences "disappear" when variables such as age and body size are controlled for (Gould, 1981:105-6). A decisive reanalysis of Ho et al.'s (1980) autopsy data by Ankney (1992) now makes clear that even after controlling for body size and other variables, a 100 gram difference remains between men and women. My own research using external head measurements confirmed Ankney's results, including in the stratified sample of 6,325 U.S. Army personnel. Ankney (1992) proposed that the sex difference in brain size is related to those intellectual qualities at which men excel, that is, in spatial and mathematical reasoning.

Differences due to method of estimation within a race are smaller than the differences between Mongoloids and Negroids. Based on the sex-combined averages, discrepancies due to methods within race average 31 cm^3. Within Mongoloids the discrepancies range from 5 to 80 cm^3, with a mean of 41 cm^3; within Caucasoids they range from 6 to 33 cm^3, with a mean of 19 cm^3; and within Negroids they range from 10 to 71 cm^3, with a mean of 38 cm^3.

Problems of sampling and lack of control over extraneous variables can be cited for many of the individual studies (Tobias, 1970). These difficulties, of course, apply to data from all three racial groups and there is no special reason to believe they are systematically in favor of one race over another. Body size differences cannot be the cause of the racial differences because Mongoloids have a greater cranial capacity than Negroids although they are often shorter in height and lighter in weight (Eveleth & Tanner, 1990). The racial ordering remains constant even in samples where Negroids are taller than Caucasoids, as in the study by Simmons (1942) cited at the end of the last chapter, or when the races are statistically equated by adjusting for body size.

Within humans, Haug (1987: 135) has reported a correlation of $r = .479$ ($n = 81$, $p < .001$) between the number of neurons in the human cerebral cortex and brain volume in cm^3, including both men and women in the sample. The regression equating the two is given as: (# of cortical neurons [in billions] = $5.583 + 0.006$ [cm^3 brain volume]). This means that on this estimate, Mongoloids, who average 1,364 cm^3 have 13.767 billion cortical neurons (13.767 x 10^9). Caucasoids who average 1,347 cm^3 have 13.665 billion such neurons, 102 million less than Mongoloids. Negroids who average 1,267 cm^3, have 13.185 billion cerebral neurons, 582 million less than Mongoloids and 480 million less than Caucasoids.

Overall the human brain has been estimated to contain up to 100 billion (10^{11}) nerve cells classifiable into about 10,000 different types (Kandel, 1991). There may be 100,000 billion synapses. Even storing information at the low average rate of one bit per synapse, which would require two levels of synaptic activity (high and low), the structure as a whole would generate 10^{14} bits. Contemporary supercomputers, by comparison, command a memory of about 10^9 bits of information.

Most neural tissue goes to maintain bodily functions. Over and above this are "excess neurons" available for general adaptive purposes (Jerison, 1973). However crude the current estimates, hundreds of millions of cerebral cortex neurons differentiate Mongoloids from Negroids (582 x 10^6 based on those just calculated; 440 x 10^6 based on those averaged from Tobias as described on page 114). These are probably sufficient to underlie the proportionate achievements in intelligence and social organization. The half-billion neuron difference between Mongoloids and Negroids are probably all "excess neurons" because, as mentioned, Mongoloids are often shorter in height and lighter in weight than Negroids. The Mongoloid-Negroid difference in brain size across so many estimation procedures is striking.

Intelligence Test Scores

Since the time of World War I, when widespread testing began, African-descended people have scored lower than whites on assessments of intelligence and educational attainment (Loehlin et al., 1975). Fewer people are aware that Orientals often score higher than whites on the same tests whether assessed in Canada and the United States, or in their home countries (P. E. Vernon, 1982). In an overview of mathematics education, for example, Steen (1987) showed that within the United States, the proportion of Oriental-American students who achieve high mathematics scores (above 650) on the Scholastic Aptitude Test is twice the national average while the proportion of black students who do so is much less than one-fourth the national average.

A review of the global distribution of intelligence test scores has been provided by Richard Lynn (1991c). The mean IQs for whites in the United States,

Britain, Continental Europe, Australia, and New Zealand were presented relative to an American IQ set at 100, with a standard deviation of 15. Caucasoids in the United States and Britain obtained virtually identical mean IQs. This was first demonstrated in a 1932 Scottish survey of 11-year-olds who obtained a mean IQ of 99 on the American Stanford-Binet. Subsequent studies in Scotland and Britain confirmed this result.

The earlier standardization of tests in the United States were generally based on normative samples of Caucasoids only, such as the early Stanford-Binet and Wechsler tests, but the later standardizations such as the WISC-R included blacks. For this reason R. Lynn adjusted the American means for later tests, because when the mean of the American total population is set at 100, the mean of American whites is 102.25, as derived from the standardization sample of the WISC-R (Jensen & Reynolds, 1982).

The mean IQs from all the Caucasoid populations reviewed lay in the range of 85 to 107. R. Lynn discussed some of the reasons for the variation between and within countries, such as sampling accuracy and procedures as well as differences in education and living standards. For example, in the case of children, those in private schools may or may not be included in the samples. The IQs of Indians from the Indian subcontinent and Britain ranged from 85 to 96. A mean of 86 in India was derived from a review by Sinha (1968) of 17 studies of children aged between 9 and 15 years and totaling in excess of 5,000. The ethnic Indians in Britain obtained a mean of 96.

The Mongoloid mean IQs are set out in Table 6.7. It will be seen that for general intelligence the Mongoloid peoples tend in the majority of studies to obtain somewhat higher means than Caucasoids. This is the case in the United States, Canada, Europe, Japan, Hong Kong, Taiwan, Singapore, and the People's Republic of China. The range is from 97 to 116, with a mean of around 105.

A striking feature of the result for Mongoloids is that their verbal IQs are consistently lower than their visuospatial IQs. In most studies the differences are substantial, amounting to between 10 to 15 IQ points. This pattern is present in Japan, Hong Kong, the United States, and Canada. This difference also shows up in the United States on the Scholastic Aptitude Test, in which Mongoloids invariably do better than Caucasoids on the mathematics test (largely a measure of general intelligence and visuospatial ability) but also less well than Caucasoids on the verbal test (Wainer, 1988).

Research on the academic accomplishments of Mongoloids in the United States continues to grow. Caplan, Choy, and Whitmore (1992) gathered survey and test score data on 536 school-age children of Indochinese refugees in five urban areas around the United States. Unlike some of the previously studied populations of "boat people," these refugees had had limited exposure to Western culture, knew virtually no English when they arrived, and often had a history of physical and emotional trauma. Often they came with nothing more

TABLE 6.7
Mean IQ Scores for Various Mongoloid Samples

Sample	Age	Sample size	Test	Intelligence General	Verbal	Visuo-spatial	Source
Japan	5-16	1,070	WISC	–	–	103	Lynn, 1977b
Japan	6	240	Vocabulary-spatial	97	89	105	Stevenson et al., 1985
Japan	11	240	Vocabulary-spatial	102	98	107	Stevenson et al., 1985
Japan	4-6	600	WPPSI	103	98	108	Lynn & Hampson, 1986a
Japan	2-8	550	McCarthy	100	92	108	Lynn & Hampson, 1986b
Japan	6-16	1,100	WISC-R	103	101	107	Lynn & Hampson, 1986c
Japan	13-15	178	Differential Aptitude	104	–	114	Lynn, Hampson & Iwawaki, 1987
Japan	13-14	216	Kyoto NX	101	100	103	Lynn, Hampson & Bingham, 1987
Japan	3-9	347	CMMS	110	–	–	Misawa et al., 1984
Japan	9	444	Progressive Matrices	110	–	–	Shigehisa & Lynn, 1991
Hong Kong	6-15	4,500	Progressive Matrices	110	–	–	Lynn, Pagliari & Chan, 1988
Hong Kong	10	197	PM, Space Relations	108	92	114	Lynn, Pagliari & Chan, 1988
Hong Kong	9	376	Cattell Culture Fair	113	–	–	Lynn, Hampson & Lee, 1988
Hong Kong	6	4,858	Coloured PM	116	–	–	Chan & Lynn, 1989
China	6-16	5,108	Progressive Matrices	101	–	–	Lynn, 1991b
Taiwan	16	1,290	Culture Fair	105	–	–	Rodd, 1959
Singapore	13	147	Progressive Matrices	110	–	–	Lynn, 1977a
Belgium	6-14	19	WISC	110	102	115	Frydman & Lynn, 1989
United States	6-17	4,994	Various	100	97	–	Coleman et al., 1966; Flynn, 1991
United States	6-11	478	Various	101	–	–	Jensen & Inouye, 1980
United States	6-10	2,000	Figure copying	–	–	105	Jensen, 1973
United States	6	80	Hunter Aptitude	106	97	106	Lesser, Fifer & Clark, 1965
United States	6-14	112	Various	107	–	–	Winick et al., 1975
Canada	15	122	Differential Aptitude	105	97	108	P. E. Vernon, 1982
Canada	6-8	38	WISC	100	94	107	Kline & Lee, 1972

Note. From R. Lynn (1991c, pp. 264–265, Table 2). Copyright 1991 by The Institute for the Study of Man. Reprinted with permission. CMMS = Columbia Mental Maturity Scale; WISC = Wechsler Intelligence Scale for Children; WPPSI = Wechsler Preschool and Primary Scale of Intelligence.

than the clothes they wore. All the children attended schools in low-income metropolitan areas. The results showed that whether measured by school grades or nationally normed standardized tests, the children were above average overall, "spectacularly" so in mathematics.

The mean IQs of Negroids are invariably found to be lower than those of Caucasoids. Three hundred and sixty-two investigations done in the United States were presented by Shuey (1966) who reported the overall mean IQ of Afro-Americans to be approximately 85. Subsequent studies in the United States such as those by Coleman et al. (1966), Broman et al. (1987), and others have confirmed this figure. Many of these studies are shown in Table 6.8. For the United States, seven major post-Shuey (1966) studies were chosen because of their special interest by virtue of the large number of subjects, because they yield IQs for the verbal and visuospatial abilities, or because they are derived from young children. These show that the Negroid mean IQ of approximately 85 is present among children as young as 2 to 6 years old. In Britain, three studies of Afro-Caribbeans obtained mean IQs of 86, 94, and 87, broadly similar to those in the United States. Figures are available for two of the Caribbean islands, namely Barbados (mean IQ = 82) and Jamaica (mean IQ = 66–75).

As a result of these studies, carried out across different intelligence tests and cohorts, it is sometimes assumed that the mean IQ of all Negroids is approximately 85. R. Lynn noted, however, that most African-Americans are Negroid-Caucasoid hybrids with about 25 percent Caucasian admixture (Chakraborty, Kamboh, Nwankwo, & Ferrell, 1992) and he believed a similar proportion was probably true of blacks in the West Indies and Britain. It is possible, therefore, that the mean IQs of non-mixed Africans will be lower than that of the hybrids. R. Lynn tested this hypothesis by examining the literature from Africa (see Table 6.9).

TABLE 6.8
Mean IQ Scores for Various Negroid-Caucasold Mixed-Race Samples

				Intelligence			
Sample	Age	Sample size	Test	General	Verbal	Visuo-spatial	Source
United States	–	–	362 Studies	85	–	–	Shuey, 1966
United States	7	19,000	Wechsler	90	89	93	Broman et al., 1987
United States	2	46	Stanford-Binet	86	–	–	Montie & Fagan, 1988
United States	6-18	4,995	Verbal and non-verbal	84	89	–	Coleman et al., 1966
United States	6	111	WISC	81	86	80	Miele, 1979
United States	6-16	305	WISC-Revised	84	87	88	Jensen & Reynolds, 1982
United States	7-14	642	PMA	77	77	83	Baughman & Dahlstrom, 1968
United States	6-11	2,518	Various	84	–	–	Jensen & Inouye, 1980
S. Africa colored	10-14	4,721	Army Beta	84	–	–	Fick, 1929
Barbados	9-15	108	WISC-Revised	82	84	84	Galler et al., 1986
Britain	11	113	NFER	86	87	–	Mackintosh & Mascie-Taylor,1985
Britain	10	125	British Ability Scales	94	92	–	Mackintosh & Mascie-Taylor,1985
Britain	8-12	205	NFER	87	–	–	Scarr et al., 1983
Jamaica	10-11	50	Various	75	82	90	P. E. Vernon, 1969
Jamaica	11	1,730	Moray House	72	72	–	Manley, 1963; P. E. Vernon, 1969
Jamaica	5-12	71	WISC	66	74	64	Hertzig et al., 1972

Note. From R. Lynn (1991c, p. 269, Table 4). Copyright 1991 by The Institute for the Study of Man. Reprinted with permission. NFER = National Federation of Educational Research; PMA = Primary Mental Abilities; WISC = Wechsler Intelligence Scale for Children.

TABLE 6.9
Mean IQ Scores for Various Negroid Samples

Sample	Age	Sample size	Test	Intelligence General	Verbal	Visuo-spatial	Source
Congo	adults	320	Progressive Matrices	65	–	–	Ombredane et al., 1952
Ghana	adults	225	Culture Fair	80	–	–	Buj, 1981
Nigeria	6-13	87	Colored Matrices, PMA	75	–	81	Fahrmeier, 1975
Nigeria	adults	–	Progressive Matrices	86	–	–	Wober, 1969
South Africa	8-16	1,220	Progressive Matrices	81	–	–	Notcutt, 1950
South Africa	adults	703	Progressive Matrices	75	–	–	Notcutt, 1950
South Africa	10-14	293	Army Beta	65	–	–	Fick, 1929
South Africa	9	350	Progressive Matrices	67	–	–	Lynn & Holmshaw, 1990
South Africa	16	1,093	Junior Aptitude	69	60	69	Owen, 1989
Uganda	12	50	Various	80	–	–	P. E. Vernon, 1969
Zambia	adults	1,011	Progressive Matrices	75	–	–	Pons, 1974; Crawford Nutt, 1976

Note. From R. Lynn (1991c, pp. 267, Table 3). Copyright 1991 by The Institute for the Study of Man. Reprinted with permission. PMA = Primary Mental Abilities.

An early study of the intelligence of "pure" African Negroids was carried out in South Africa by Fick (1929). He administered the American Army Beta Test, a nonverbal test designed for those who could not speak English, to 10- to 14-year-old white, black African, and mixed-race (mainly Negroid-Caucasoid hybrid) schoolchildren. In relation to the white mean of 100, based on more than 10,000 children, largely urban black African children obtained a mean IQ of 65, while urban mixed-race children obtained a mean IQ of 84. Thus South African mixed races obtained a mean IQ virtually identical to that of African-Americans.

The other studies of the IQs of black Africans summarized in Table 6.9 show means in the range of 65 to 86, with a mean of about 75. R. Lynn cited the work of Owen (1989) as the best single study. Owen presented results for 1,093 16-year-olds in the eighth grade who had been in school for around eight years and should have been knowledgable about paper and pencil tests. The test used was the South African Junior Aptitude, which provides measures of verbal and nonverbal reasoning, spatial ability, verbal comprehension, perceptual speed, and memory. The mean IQ of the sample in comparison with white South African norms is 69, which is also around the median of the studies listed in Table 6.6. R. Lynn rounded this figure to 70 and took it as the approximate mean for pure Negroids.

Since R. Lynn's review, Owen (1992) has published another South African study. He gave Raven's Standard Progressive Matrices to four groups of high school students. The results showed clear racial mean differences with 1,065 whites = 45.27 (SD = 6.34); 1,063 East Indians = 41.99 (SD = 8.24); 778 mixed races = 36.69 (SD = 8.89); and 1,093 pure Negroids = 27.65 (SD = 10.72). Thus, Negroids are from 1.5 to 2.7 standard deviations below the two Caucasoid populations and about 1 standard deviation lower than the mixed races. The four groups showed little difference in test reliabilities, the rank order of item difficulties, item discrimination values, and the loadings of items on the first principal component. Owen (1992: 149) concluded: "Consequently, from a psychometric point of view, the [test] is not culturally biased."

R. Lynn also summarized the results of studies of the intelligence of Amerindians. The mean IQs have invariably been found to be somewhat below that of Caucasoids. The largest study is that of Coleman et al. (1966), which obtained a mean of 94, but a number of studies have reported means in the 70 to 90 range. The median of the 15 studies listed is 89, which Lynn took as a reasonable approximation, indicating that the Amerindian mean IQ falls somewhere between that of Caucasoids and Negroid-Caucasoid hybrids. The same intermediate position is occupied by Amerindians in performance on the Scholastic Aptitude Test (Wainer, 1988).

In addition, all the studies of Amerindians have found that they have higher visuospatial than verbal IQs. The studies listed are those where the Amerindians speak English as their first language, so this pattern of results is unlikely to be solely due to the difficulty of taking the verbal tests in an unfamiliar language. The verbal-visuospatial disparity is also picked up in the Scholastic Aptitude Test, where Amerindians invariably score higher on the mathematical test than on the verbal (Wainer, 1988).

Finally, R. Lynn examined the published IQ scores for several Southeast Asian peoples, including Polynesians, Micronesians, Melanesians, Maoris, and Australian aborigines. Apart from the low mean of 67 for a small sample of Australian aborigine children, all the mean IQs lie in the range of 80-95. The one study to include measures of general, verbal, and visuospatial abilities for New Zealand Maoris shows that this population does not share the strong visuospatial-weak verbal ability profile of Mongoloids and Amerindians. Although the intelligence of this group of peoples has not been extensively researched, R. Lynn suggested there are sufficient studies to suggest a mean IQ of about 90.

Spearman's g

Although the black and white populations in the United States differ, on average, by about 15 IQ points, they differ by various amounts on different tests. These relative differences are directly related to the g loadings of the particular tests, g being the general factor common to all complex tests of mental ability (chap. 2). Jensen (1985) termed this important discovery about black-white differences *Spearman's hypothesis,* because it was first suggested by Charles Spearman (1927: 379), the English psychologist who invented factor analysis and discovered g. In a series of studies, Jensen investigated and found support for Spearman's hypothesis.

Thus, Jensen (1985) examined 11 large-scale studies, each comprising anywhere from 6 to 13 diverse tests administered to large black and white samples aged 6 to 16 1/2, with a total sample size of 40,000, and showed that a significant and substantial correlation was found in each between the test's g loadings and the mean black-white difference on the same tests. In a follow up, Jensen (1987b; Naglieri & Jensen, 1987) matched 86 black and 86 white 10- to 11-year-olds for age, school, sex, and socioeconomic status and tested them with the Wechsler Intelligence Scale for Children-Revised and the Kaufman Assessment Battery for Children for a total of 24 subtests. The results showed that the black-white differences on the various tests correlated $r = 0.78$ with the test's g loading.

Hence, Jensen concluded, in accord with Spearman's hypothesis, the average black-white difference on diverse mental tests may be interpreted as chiefly a difference in g, rather than as a difference in the more specific sources of test score variance associated with any particular informational content, scholastic knowledge, acquired skill, or type of test.

Decision Times

As described in chapter 2, speed of information processing in decision time or on elementary cognitive tasks rests on the neurological efficiency of the brain in analysis and decision making. Early studies of black-white differences in speed of reaction time were reviewed by Jensen (1980a) who concluded that the more complex the task, the more it loaded on Spearman's g, the more it tapped neurological efficiency, and the faster whites performed relative to blacks.

To further examine the racial difference in reaction times and their relationship to g, P. A. Vernon and Jensen (1984) gave a battery of eight tasks to 50 black and 50 white college students who were also tested on the Armed Services Vocational Aptitude Battery (ASVAB). Despite markedly different content, the reaction time measures correlated significantly at about 0.50 with the ASVAB in both the black and the white samples. Blacks had significantly slower reaction time scores than whites, as well as lower scores on the ASVAB. The greater the complexity of the reaction time task, measured in milliseconds, the stronger its relationship to the g factor extracted from the ASVAB, and the greater the magnitude of the black-white difference.

In his global review, R. Lynn (1991c) summarized several of his own cross-cultural investigations of reaction times with 9-year-old children from five countries (R. Lynn, Chan, & Eysenck, 1991; R. Lynn & Holmshaw, 1990; R. Lynn & Shigehisa, 1991). There were Mongoloids from Hong Kong (N = 118) and Japan (N = 444), Caucasoids from Britain (N = 239) and Ireland (N = 317), and Negroids from South Africa (N = 350). All the children were drawn from typical primary schools in their respective countries, except the Irish children who came from rural areas. All 1,468 children were administered the Raven Progressive Matrices intelligence test.

Three reaction time tasks were used for different degrees of difficulty from "simple" through "complex" to "odd-man-out," all taking under a second to perform (chap. 2). The results are shown in Table 6.10. It will be seen that the Mongoloid children are consistently faster in decision times than the Caucasoid, who in turn are consistently faster than the Negroid. All the differences are statistically significant. The figures given are the times in milliseconds, so that the Mongoloids have the shortest times and the Negroids the longest. The table also gives the IQ scores on the Progressive Matrices. R. Lynn concluded

TABLE 6.10
IQ Scores and Decision Times for 9-Year-Old Children from Five Countries

Racial type / country	Sample size	Progressive matrices IQ score	Decision time (msecs) Simple	Complex	Odd-man-out
Mongoloid					
Hong Kong	118	113	361	423	787
Japan	444	110	348	433	818
Caucasoid					
Britain	239	100	371	480	898
Ireland	317	89	388	485	902
Negroid					
South Africa	350	67	398 [a]	489 [a]	924 [a]
		SD	64	67	187

Note. From R. Lynn (1991c, pp. 275, Table 7). Copyright 1991 by The Institute for the Study of Man. Reprinted with permission.
[a] Errata, *The Mankind Quarterly,* Vol. 31, No. 3, Spring 1991, p. 192.

that the racial differences lie at the neurological level, reflecting the efficiency of the brain in analysis and decision making.

Meanwhile, Jensen (1993; Jensen & Whang, 1993) used similar decision time tasks as R. Lynn to extend his test of Spearman's hypothesis. Thus, Jensen (1993) gave 585 white and 235 black 9- to 11-year-old children from middle-class suburban schools in California a battery of 12 reaction time tasks based on the simple, choice, and oddman procedures. The response time loadings on psychometric g were estimated by their correlations with scores on Raven's Progressive Matrices. In another procedure, the chronometric tasks assessed speed of retrieval of easy number facts such as addition, subtraction, or multiplication of single digit numbers. These have typically been learned before the children are 9 years old, and all children in the study were able to perform them correctly.

In both studies, Spearman's hypothesis was borne out as strongly as in the previous studies using conventional psychometric tests. Blacks scored lower than whites on the Raven's Matrices and were slower than whites in decision time. In addition, the size of the black-white difference on the decision time variables was directly related to the variables' loadings on psychometric g. Moreover, when the response time was separated into a cognitive decision component and a physical movement component, blacks were found to be slower than whites on the cognitive part and faster than whites on the physical part.

Using the same procedures as in the study just described, Jensen and Whang (1993), also in California, compared 167 9- to 11-year-old Chinese American children with the 585 white children. On Raven's Matrices there was a 0.32 standard deviation advantage to the Oriental children (about 5 IQ points), although they were lower in socioeconomic status. Also, compared to the white American children, the Chinese American children were faster in the cognitive aspects of information processing (decision time) but slower in the motor aspects of response execution (movement time).

Cultural Achievement

The third focus of R. Lynn's (1991c) review of intelligence around the world was on discoveries and inventions. Here R. Lynn followed Galton and other early psychologists who proposed that civilization results from the presence in a population of very talented people. Because there will be more of these in a population where the average level of intelligence is high, the intelligence levels of populations can be inferred from their intellectual achievements.

Twenty-one criteria by which a civilization could be judged were set up by J. R. Baker (1974), some of whose work was described in chapter 5. J. R. Baker suggested that in civilized societies, the majority of people complied with most of the requirements set out in Table 6.11. He then proceeded to analyze the historical record to ascertain which races have originated civilizations. His conclusion was that the Caucasoid peoples developed all 21 components of civilization in four independent locations, the Sumerian in the valley of the Tigris and the Euphrates, the Cretan, the Indus Valley, and the ancient Egyptian. The Mongoloids also developed a full civilization in the Sinic civilization in China. The Amerindians achieved about half of the 21 components in the Maya society of Guatemala, a little less in the Inca and Aztec societies, but these peoples never invented a written script, the wheel (except possibly in children's toys), the principle of the arch in their architecture, metal working, or money for the exchange of goods. The Negroids and the Australian aborigines achieved virtually none of the criteria of civilization.

While J. R. Baker confined his analysis to the achievements of the races in originating civilizations, parallel racial differences occur in later cultural development. During the last 3,000 years the many discoveries required for developed civilizations have been made primarily by Caucasoid and Mongoloid

TABLE 6.11
Criteria for Civilization

1. In the ordinary circumstances of life in public places, they cover the greater part of the trunk with clothes.
2. They keep the body clean and take care to dispose of its waste products.
3. They do not practice severe mutilation or deformation of the body, except for medical reasons.
4. They have knowledge of building in brick or stone, if the necessary materials are available in their territory.
5. Many of them live in towns or cities, which are linked by roads.
6. They cultivate food plants.
7. They domesticate animals and use some of the larger ones for transport (or have in the past so used them), if suitable species are available.
8. They have knowledge of the use of metals, if these are available.
9. They use wheels.
10. They exchange property by the use of money.
11. They order their society by a system of laws, which are enforced in such a way that they ordinarily go about their various concerns in times of peace without danger of attack or arbitrary arrest.
12. They permit accused persons to defend themselves and to bring witnesses for their defense.
13. They do not use torture to extract information or for punishment.
14. They do not practice cannibalism.
15. Their religious systems include ethical elements and are not purely or grossly superstitious.
16. They use a script (not simply a succession of pictures) to communicate ideas.
17. There is some facility in the abstract use of numbers, without consideration of actual objects (or, in other words, at least a start has been made in mathematics).
18. A calendar is in use, accurate to within a few days in the year.
19. Arrangements are made for the instruction of the young in intellectual subjects.
20. There is some appreciation of the fine arts.
21. Knowledge and understanding are valued as ends in themselves.

Note. Adapted from J. R. Baker (1974, pp. 507–508). Copyright 1974 by J. R. Baker.

peoples. As mentioned in chapter 5, during much of this period the Mongoloid civilization in China was equal to or in advance of the Caucasoid civilizations in Europe.

As early as 360 B.C., the Chinese had invented the cross bow and transformed the nature of warfare. The key to its effectiveness is the pressure sensitive trigger that releases the string of the bow mounted crosswise on a wooden stock. Cities became transformed for the manufacture and trade in weaponry.

Around 200–100 B.C. the Han period saw the introduction of written examinations for candidates for the Mandarin civil service, an idea that was considered an advance when it was introduced into Britain some 2,000 years later (Klitgaard, 1986; Bowman, 1989). Printing was invented in China by about 800, some 600 years before it was developed in Germany. Paper money was used in China in 1300 but not in Europe until the nineteenth and twentieth centuries. By 1050 A.D. Chinese knowledge of chemistry allowed them to invent gunpowder, along with hand grenades, fire arrows, and rockets of oil and poison gas. By 1100 A.D. there were industrially organized complexes involving upward of 40,000 workers making rockets in factories. Flame throwers, guns, and cannons were used by the thirteenth century, meaning that the Chinese had the cannon at least a century before Europe did.

The Chinese were the first to invent the principle of the magnetic compass. In 1422 the Chinese reached the east coast of Africa with a great fleet of sixty or more ships provisioned for ocean cruising, carrying 27,000 men, and their horses, and a year's supply of grain, herds of pigs, and jars of fermenting wine. There was nothing comparable in Europe, and certainly not in Africa. With gunpowder weapons, great navigational and organizational skills, the latest charts and magnetic compasses, the Chinese could have gone around the Cape of Good Hope and "discovered" Europe! The Chinese may have had the compass as early as 100 A.D.; it is not mentioned in European writing until 1190.

For centuries China was the richest and most powerful nation on earth. The Chinese technology for the manufacture of high quality porcelain was ahead of Europe until the late eighteenth century. However, the Chinese were an inward-looking people. The earlier sailing expedition had been for bringing back giraffes, lions, and rhinoceroses to the emperor. After the voyage, Confucian civil servants destroyed many records of the travels including the building plans of the vessels. In place of foreign voyages, they began the task of rebuilding the Great Wall, constructed from rammed earth some 1700 years earlier. When completed it was planned to wind across northern China for 1400 miles, 25 feet high, faced with brick, and with a 12-foot wide cobbled road running along the top between guard houses—one of the greatest man-made structures ever built. The goal was to keep foreigners out.

During the last five centuries the Caucasoids have pulled ahead of the Mongoloids in science and technology. Nevertheless, although the Europeans have generally been ahead of the Mongoloids during the last five centuries, since 1950 the Japanese have provided a major challenge and have surpassed the West in the production of high quality technological goods. Other Pacific Rim countries are similarly rising to prominence relative to the United States and Europe, let alone to the Third World and Africa (McCord, 1991).

Another source noted by R. Lynn (1991c) for evaluating racial contributions to science and technology, is Isaac Asimov's (1989) *Chronology of Science and Discovery*. This lists approximately 1,500 of the most important scientific and technological discoveries and inventions that have ever been made. Virtually every one was made by the Caucasian or Mongoloid peoples, thus confirming the historical record.

Finer grain analysis within the United States suggests that the differences in cultural achievement may be far-reaching. The relatively strong visuospatial and weak verbal abilities of Oriental Americans may result in a tendency to do well in professions like science, architecture, and engineering, which call for strong visuospatial abilities, and less well in law, which calls for strong verbal abilities. This is the pattern of occupational achievement documented by Weyl (1989) in studies of American ethnic populations.

Weyl's method involves the analysis of the frequencies of ethnic names among those who have achieved occupational distinction calculated in relation to their frequencies in the general population. Thus, he finds that typical Chinese names like Chang and Yee are greatly overrepresented in *American Men and Women of Science* as compared with their frequency in the general population, but they are underrepresented in *Who's Who in American Law*. On the basis of this method Weyl constructs a performance coefficient for which average achievement is 100. A coefficient of 200 means that an ethnic group appears twice as frequently in reference works of occupational distinction as would be expected from its numbers in the total population, while a coefficient of 50 means that it appears half as often. In the 1980s, ethnic Chinese obtained performance coefficients of over 600 for science, while for law their performance coefficient was only 24. (African-American representation was negligible on all rosters.)

Gottfredson (1986, 1987) suggested that occupations be viewed as analogous to differentially *g*-loaded mental tests. Large-scale studies from World War I through the 1980s have shown that occupations differ considerably in the mean intelligence levels of their incumbents. The mean level of intelligence of the occupation, in turn, correlates highly with the prestige level of the occupation. Gottfredson reasoned that the overall intellectual complexity of the work should effect the percentage of workers who are black. Figure 6.3 provides data relevant to this conjecture.

Gottfredson first determined the IQ ranges from which workers have most often been recruited to different occupations. Then, she used nationally representative mental test data to determine the proportions of blacks and whites

Figure 6.3: Percentage of Blacks and Whites in the United States Above
Minimum IQ Required for Various Occupations

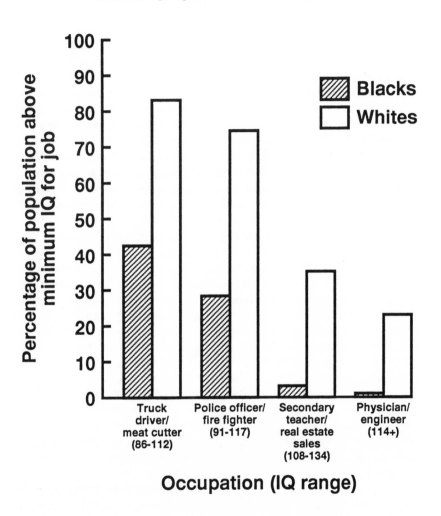

The lower average distribution of IQ among blacks leads to a disproportionate underrepresentation
in occupations selected on the basis of high IQ. Drawn from data in Gottfredson (1986, 1987).

falling within each of those IQ recruitment ranges. Third, she computed the
ratio of blacks to whites who would be eligible for each occupation on the
basis of intelligence alone. Black-white parity in employment is represented
by a ratio of 1.00. She found that the ratios ranged from 0.72 for truck drivers
to 0.05 for physicians, proportional to the actually observed black/white ra-

tios of 0.98 to 0.30. Note that observed black-white differences in employment are smaller than those expected on the basis of intelligence alone, a finding consistent with data showing that mean IQs are lower for blacks than for whites in the same occupational category and for black versus white applicants for the same jobs.

Gottfredson (1987) noted that different assumptions about the distribution of intelligence in the black and white populations and about the intelligence requirements of occupations would produce somewhat different estimated black-white ratios for individual occupations, but the overall pattern of ratios would probably be the same under any set of reasonable assumptions. For example, even when recruitment standards are set half a standard deviation (7.5 IQ points) lower for blacks, the ratios are only 1 to 5 for physicians and engineers and 1 to 3 for secondary school teachers and real estate salespersons. She concluded that "racially blind worker selection can be expected to produce especially striking deviations from black-white parity in higher level jobs" (p. 512).

7

Speed of Maturation, Personality, and Social Organization

In this chapter there are fewer stratified random samples than in the previous chapter and more errors in collecting information on small groups. Some studies, often with poorly standardized methodologies, fail to show a racial difference. When differences are found, however, they support the Mongoloid-Caucasoid-Negroid gradient. The racial pattern is discernible in speed of development, mortality rates, personality, family functioning, mental durability, law abidingness, social organization, and other variables.

Speed of Maturation

Table 7.1 summarizes the racial differences on several measures of life span development. In the United States, black babies have a shorter gestation period than white babies. By week 39, 51 percent of black children have been born while the figure for white children is 33 percent; by week 40, the figures are 70 and 55 percent respectively (Niswander & Gordon, 1972). Similar results have been obtained in Paris. Collating data over several years, Papiernik, Cohen, Richard, de Oca, and Feingold (1986) found that French women of European ancestry had longer pregnancies than those of mixed black-white ancestry from the French Antilles, or black African women with no European admixture. These differences persisted after adjustments for socioeconomic status.

Other observations, made within equivalent gestational age groups established by ultrasonography, find that black babies are physiologically more mature than white babies as measured by pulmonary function, amniotic fluid, fetal birth weight between 24 and 36 weeks of gestation, and weight-specific neonatal mortality (reviewed in Papiernik et al., 1986). I am unaware of data on gestation time for Mongoloids.

Black precocity continues throughout life. Revised forms of Bayley's Scales of Mental and Motor Development administered in 12 metropolitan areas of the United States to 1,409 representative infants aged 1–15 months showed black babies scored consistently above whites on the Motor Scale (Bayley, 1965). This difference was not limited to any one class of behavior, but in-

TABLE 7.1
Relative Ranking of Races on Speed of Maturation

Speed of maturation variable	Orientals	Whites	Blacks
Gestation period	?	Intermediate	Earlier
Fetal maturity	?	Intermediate	Earlier
Skeletal development at birth	?	Intermediate	Earlier
Head lifting at 24 hours	?	Intermediate	Earlier
Muscular development	Later	Intermediate	Earlier
Reaching and eye-hand coordination at 2 months	Later	Intermediate	Earlier
Turning self over at 3 to 5 months	Later	Intermediate	Earlier
Age to crawl	Later	Intermediate	Earlier
Age to walk	Later	Intermediate	Earlier
Ability to remove clothing at 15-20 months	Later	Intermediate	Earlier
Dental maturity	Later	Intermediate	Earlier
Age of puberty and first sexual intercourse	Later	Intermediate	Earlier
Age at first pregnancy	Later	Intermediate	Earlier
Age at death	Later	Intermediate	Earlier

Note. Adapted from Rushton (1992b, p. 814, Table 3). Copyright 1992 by Psychological Reports. Reprinted with permission.

cluded: coordination (arm and hand); muscular strength and tonus (holds head steady, balances head when carried, sits alone steadily, and stands alone); and locomotion (turns from side to back, raises self to sitting, makes stepping movements, walks with help, and walks alone).

Similar results have been found for children up to about age 3 elsewhere in the United States, in Jamaica, and in sub-Saharan Africa (Curti, Marshall, Steggerda, & Henderson, 1935; Knobloch & Pasamanik, 1953; Williams & Scott, 1953; Walters, 1967). In a review critical of the literature Warren (1972) nonetheless reported evidence for African motor precocity in 10 out of 12 studies. For example, Geber (1958: 186) had examined 308 children in Uganda and reported an "all-round advance of development over European standards which was greater the younger the child." Freedman (1974, 1979) found similar results in studies of newborns in Nigeria using the Cambridge Neonatal Scales (Brazelton & Freedman, 1971).

Mongoloid children are motorically delayed relative to Caucasoids. In a series of studies carried out on second- through fifth-generation Chinese-Americans in San Francisco, on third- and fourth-generation Japanese-Americans in Hawaii, and on Navajo Amerindians in New Mexico and Arizona, consistent differences were found between these groups and second- to fourth-generation European-Americans using the Cambridge Neonatal Scales (Freedman, 1974, 1979; Freedman & Freedman, 1969). One measure involved pressing the baby's nose with a cloth, forcing it to breathe with its mouth. Whereas the average Chinese baby fails to exhibit a coordinated "defense reaction," most Caucasian babies turn away or swipe at the cloth with the hands, a response reported in Western pediatric textbooks as the normal one.

On other measures including "automatic walk," "head turning," and "walking alone," Mongoloid children are more delayed than Caucasoid children. Mongoloid samples, including the Navajo Amerindians, typically do not walk until 13 months, compared to the Caucasian 12 months and Negro 11 months (Freedman, 1979). In a standardization of the Denver Developmental Screening Test in Japan, Ueda (1978) found slower rates of motoric maturation in Japanese as compared with Caucasoid norms derived from the United States, with tests made from birth to 2 months in coordination and head lifting, from 3 to 5 months in muscular strength and rolling over, at 6 to 13 months in locomotion, and at 15 to 20 months in removing garments.

Eveleth and Tanner (1990) discuss race differences in terms of skeletal maturity, dental maturity, and pubertal maturity. Problems include poorly standardized methods, inadequate sampling, and many age/race/method interactions. Nonetheless, when many null and idiosyncratic findings are averaged out the data suggest that African-descended people have a faster tempo than others.

With skeletal maturity, the clearest evidence comes from the genetically timed age at which bone centers first become visible. Africans and African-Americans, even those with low incomes, mature faster up to 7 years. Mongoloids are reported to be more delayed at early ages than Caucasoids but later catch up, although there is some contradictory data. Subsequent skeletal growth varies widely and is best predicted by nutrition and socioeconomic status.

With dental development, the clearest pattern comes from examining the first phase of permanent tooth eruption. For beginning the first phase, a composite of first molar and first and second incisors in both upper and lower jaws showed an average for 8 sex-combined African series of 5.8 years compared to 6.1 years each for 20 European and 8 east Asian series (Eveleth & Tanner, 1990, Appendix 80, after excluding east Indians and Amerindian samples from the category "Asiatics"). For completion of the first phase, Africans averaged 7.6, Europeans 7.7, and east Asians 7.8 years. (The significance of this pattern will be discussed in chapter 10, where the predictive value of age of first molar for traits like brain size has been shown in other primate species.) No clear racial pattern emerged with the onset of deciduous teeth nor with the second phase of permanent tooth eruption.

In speed of sexual maturation, the older literature and ethnographic record suggested that Africans were the fastest to mature and Orientals slowest with Caucasian people intermediate (e.g., French Army Surgeon, 1898/1972). Despite some complexities this remains the general finding. For example, in the United States, blacks are more precocious than whites as indexed by age at menarche, first sexual experience, and first pregnancy (Malina, 1979). A national probability sample of American youth found that by age 12, 19 percent of black girls had reached the highest stages of breast and pubic hair development, compared to 5 percent of white girls (Harlan, Harlan, & Grillo, 1980). The same survey, however, found white and black boys to be similar (Harlan, Grillo, Coroni-Huntley, & Leaverton, 1979).

Subsequently, Westney, Jenkins, Butts, and Williams (1984) found that 60 percent of 11-year-old black boys had reached the stage of accelerated penis growth in contrast to the white norm of 50 percent of 12.5-year-olds. This genital stage significantly predicted onset of sexual interest, with over 2 percent of black boys experiencing intercourse by age 11. While some surveys find that Oriental girls enter puberty as early as whites (Eveleth & Tanner, 1990), others suggest that in both physical development and onset of interest in sex, the Japanese, on the average, lag one to two years behind their American counterparts (Asayama, 1975).

Mortality Rates

Death rates between blacks and other populations in the United States are substantial (National Center for Health Statistics, 1991). For example, the 1980 annual age-adjusted death rate per 1,000 resident population was 3.5 for Chinese Americans in contrast to 5.6 for white Americans, and more for black Americans (Yu, 1986). In numerous specific studies these statistics are borne out. For example, in a study of 2,687 deaths among U.S. Navy personnel between 1974 and 1979, blacks had higher mortality rates than whites for numerous types of accidental and violent occurrences, improper use of medication, toxic effects, accidental drownings, and shootings (Palinkas, 1984). The gap in the death rate between blacks and whites has widened over the last 26 years (Angel, 1993; Pappas, Queen, Hadden, & Fisher, 1993).

Black babies in the United States show a greater mortality rate than white babies. In 1950, a black infant was 1.6 times as likely to die as a white infant. By 1988, the relative risk had increased to 2.1. Controlling for some maternal risk factors associated with infant mortality or premature birth, such as age, parity, marital status, and education, does not eliminate the gap between blacks and whites within those risk groups. For instance, in the general population, black infants with normal birth weights have almost twice the mortality of their white counterparts.

One recent study examined infants whose parents were both college graduates in a belief that such a study would eliminate obvious inequalities in access to medical care. The researchers compared 865,128 white and 42,230 black children but they found that the mortality rate among black infants was 10.2 per 1,000 live births as against 5.4 per 1,000 among white infants (Schoendorf, Carol, Hogue, Kleinman, & Rowley, 1992).

The reason for the disparity appears to be that the black women give birth to greater numbers of low birth weight babies. When statistics are adjusted to compensate for the birth weight of the babies, the death rates for the two groups become virtually identical. Newborns who are not underweight, born to black and white college-educated parents, had an equal chance of surviving the first year. Thus, in contrast to black infants in the general population, black infants born to college-educated parents have higher mortality rates than similar white infants only because of their higher rates of low birth weight.

The racial differences in mortality persist into adulthood. Polednak (1989) examined mortality rates for black and white adults in the United States from various National Health Surveys. For most causes of death, including cancers, hypertensive and ischemic heart disease, cerebrovascular diseases, pneumonia, tuberculosis, and chronic liver diseases, at most ages (15–24, 25–34, 35–44, 45–54, 55–64, 65–74, 75–84), blacks had higher mortality rates than whites. For all causes of death combined and across all age groups, using an age-standardized procedure, Polednak (1989) calculated that in 1980 the death rate per 100,000 for whites was 1,018 and for blacks was 1,344.

The summary statistics obviously obscure particular patterns, such as the death rate for black adults being highest in young adults (ages 25–54) and lower at age 75 years and older than among whites when death rates are typically the highest. Also the death rate differentials were highest of all for blacks at all ages from 15 to 85 and older for homicide with a reversal at all ages for suicide. With motor vehicle accidents, more whites died than blacks at very young and very old ages with a reversal in the middle age range. This latter statistic has been replicated with infant deaths and may be due to lower access by blacks to motor vehicles and a greater reliance on public transport (Schoendorf et al., 1992).

Polednak (1989) also examined the international data by compiling mortality rates from various sourcebooks. The total annual death rates were consistently higher for African countries (18 per 1,000) than for other least developed countries (17.1 per 1,000) and the rest of the world (11.3 per 1,000). For 52 reporting countries from the World Health Organization's *World Health Statistics* Annual of 1987, Polednak (1989) calculated age-standardized mortality rates per 100,000 for selected causes of death (infectious and parasitic diseases, cancers, circulatory diseases, ischemic heart disease, stroke, etc.).

I have aggregated Polednak's data on "all causes" of death and found that 8 Carribbean countries (mostly black) averaged an age-standardized mortality rate of about 713 per 100,000, 34 European and North American countries (mostly white) averaged about 615 per 100,000, and Japan and Singapore averaged about 550 per 100,000. Interestingly, the racial pattern showed a reversal for suicide with Caribbean countries lowest (about 4 per 100,000), Pacific countries highest (about 15 per 100,000), and European countries intermediate (about 12 per 100,000).

TABLE 7.2
Relative Ranking of Races on Personality and Temperament Traits

Trait	Orientals	Whites	Blacks
Activity level	Low	Medium	High
Aggressiveness	Low	Medium	High
Cautiousness	High	Medium	Low
Dominance	Low	Medium	High
Excitability	Low	Medium	High
Impulsivity	Low	Medium	High
Self-concept	Low	Medium	High
Sociability	Low	Medium	High

Note. Adapted from Rushton (1992b, p. 815, Table 5). Copyright 1992 by Psychological Reports. Reprinted with permission.

Personality

Across ages (24-hour-old infants, children, high school students, university students, and adults), across traits (activity level, aggressiveness, cautiousness, dominance, excitability, impulsiveness, and sociability), and across methods (archival statistics, naturalistic observation, ratings, and self-reports), data show that, in terms of behavioral restraint, Mongoloids average higher than do Caucasoids who, in turn, average higher than Negroids (Table 7.2). With infants and young children, observer ratings are the main method employed, whereas with adults the use of standardized tests are more frequent.

Freedman and Freedman (1969) compared Chinese-American newborns with European-American newborns on 25 items of behavior. Analysis indicated that the main differences came from items tapping excitability/imperturbability. Thus, the European-American infants had a greater tendency to be changeable, moving back and forth between states of contentment and upset, as well as reaching the peak of excitement sooner, while the Chinese-American infants were calmer and more consolable when upset.

In a study of Amerindian infants, Brazelton, Robey, and Collier (1969) reported that Amerindian neonates exhibited almost none of the normally occurring spasmodic movements common in Caucasian newborns, and maintained smoother gross motor movements throughout the first year. By 3 and 4 years of age, Caucasoid children engage in more approach and interaction behavior, whereas Mongoloid children spend more time on individual projects and generally demonstrate low noise levels, quiet serenity, and few aggressive or disruptive behaviors (Freedman, 1974, 1979). Eskimos (Inuit), also of Mongoloid origin, are perceived by Europeans as behaviorally restrained (LeVine, 1975: 19) while to Eskimos, Euro-Americans appear "emotionally volatile" (LeVine, 1975: 19), as they do also to Chinese Americans (Freedman, 1979: 156).

With preschoolers, a study carried out in Quebec, Canada, suggests that the racial pattern in temperament is generalizable. A sample of 825 4- to 6-year-old children from 66 different countries speaking 30 different languages were assessed by 50 teachers. All the children were in preschool French language immersion classes for immigrant children in Montreal to enable better integration into the school system. Only 20 percent of the children were born in Canada, with the black children typically coming from French language countries like Haiti, the white children from Spanish-speaking countries like Chile, and the Oriental children from what used to be French Indochina (Vietnam, Kampuchea). Teachers reported better social adjustment and less hostility-aggression from Mongoloid than from Caucasoid children; and Caucasoid children were better adjusted and less hostile than Negroid children (Tremblay & Baillargeon, 1984).

Using continuous observation for four separate 2 1/2 hour time periods, Orlick, Zhou, & Partington (1990) compared three groups of Chinese 5-year-olds in Beijing (N = 77) with three groups of their white Canadian counterparts in Ottawa (N = 89). Whereas 85 percent of peer interactions documented in China were cooperative in nature, 78 percent of those in Canada involved conflict. With 10-year-olds, Ekblad and Olweus (1986) gave the Olweus' Aggression Inventory to 290 10-year-old children in the People's Republic of China and found that the Chinese were less aggressive and higher in prosocial behavior than the Swedish children.

Studies of adults show parallel differences. Researchers have investigated the personality of the Chinese and Japanese, both in their homelands and in North America, giving university students standardized tests such as Cattell's Sixteen Personality Factor Questionnaire, the Eysenck Personality Questionnaire, the Edwards Personal Preference Schedule, and the Minnesota Multiphasic Personality Inventory (P. E. Vernon, 1982). The evidence consistently favored the hypothesis that, on average, Orientals were more introverted and more anxious than Euro-Americans and less dominant and less aggressive. While fewer systematic studies have been carried out on Africans and black Americans, many imply greater aggressiveness, dominance, impulsivity, and displays of masculinity compared to whites (Dreger & Miller, 1960; J. Q. Wilson & Herrnstein, 1985).

I (Rushton, 1985b) indexed behavioral restraint by low extraversion (sociability) and high neuroticism (anxiety) scores from the Eysenck Personality Questionnaire. Data collected from 25 countries around the world were summarized by Barrett and Eysenck (1984). Averaging across these I found that eight Mongoloid samples (N = 4,044) were less extraverted and more neurotic than 38 Caucasian samples (N = 19,807), who were less extraverted and more neurotic than four African samples (N = 1,906).

Self-Concept

African American youth have higher general self-esteem than whites or Orientals. In one study, a sample of 637 (299 African Americans and 338 white Americans) 11- to 16-year-olds were examined in two small southern towns (Tashakkori, 1993). Respondents read along on each question while the teacher was reading it aloud. Items measuring self-esteem were from the Rosenberg Self-Esteem Scale and included: "I take a positive attitude toward myself"; "I feel I am a person of worth, on an equal basis with others"; "At times I think I am no good at all"; "On the whole, I am satisfied with myself"; "I feel I do not have much to be proud of"; and "I am able to do things as well as most people."

Several other general competence and specific self-beliefs were assessed. Thus, general competence beliefs were assessed by items such as "I am intelligent" and "I can learn almost anything if I set my mind on it." More specific beliefs tapped attractive appearance, physical ability, and academic self-perceptions like reading and mathematics and personal control over events.

Tashakkori (1993) found the general self-esteem scores on the Rosenberg Scale as well as other indices of self-attitudes showed African Americans scored from one-half to two-thirds of a standard deviation higher than white Americans. This finding joined those from older adolescents in national studies (Tashakkori & Thompson, 1991). African American groups have consistently more positive scores on the majority of specific self-belief indices, particularly regarding appearance and attractiveness but also including competence in reading, science, and social studies (but not mathematics), despite their lower self-reported (and actual) academic achievement. The only beliefs in which the blacks scored lower than the whites were those that reflected self-efficacy and control of events that happened to self.

Many results now confirm Hare's (1985:41) conclusion that "African American adolescents can be theorized to be feeling relatively better, but doing relatively worse, lending importance to study of the *sources* as well as the *levels* of self-esteem" (his italics). Nyborg (1994) proposes that self-esteem is partly a function of steroid action and that African-Americans have more testosterone than whites (chapters 8 and 13).

Family Functioning

Marital stability can be assessed by rate of divorce, out-of-wedlock birthing, child abuse, and delinquency. On each of these measures, the rank ordering of marital stability within American populations is Oriental > white > black (Jaynes & Williams, 1989). For example, it has been noted that while there are approximately 1.5 million individuals of Northeast Asian descent living in the United States, they tend not to be an object of family research, partly because they are not perceived as a "problem," having significantly fewer divorces, out-of-wedlock births, or incidences of child abuse than whites, even when controlling for social class, on which they are higher (Garbarino and Ebata, 1983). Black family structure, on the other hand, has been studied intensively.

Much research has emphasized the instability of black marriages and family ties, the matriarchal family structure, and the lack of authority of fathers (DuBois, 1908; Frazier, 1948). Subsequently, Moynihan (1965) wrote the report that is the most frequently cited discussion of black families in the United States. Moynihan observed high rates of marital dissolution, frequent heading of families by women, and numerous illegitimate births in black families, in contrast to white families. Some 25 years later the figures cited as evidence for the instability of the black family have doubled and tripled (Jaynes & Williams, 1989). While one out of two white marriages will end in divorce, two out of three black marriages will eventually dissolve. Out-of-wedlock births have increased among whites from 2 percent in 1960 to 8 percent in 1982, whereas among blacks it increased from 22 percent in 1960 to 52 percent in 1982. About 75 percent of births to black teenagers are out of wedlock compared with 25 percent of births to white teenagers, an age group constituting over 50 percent of new mothers (Jaynes & Williams, 1989).

A family pattern similar to that of black Americans is found in Africa, south of the Sahara. Draper (1989) described the unique pattern of African marriage, mating, and family organization that predates the colonial period and differentiates the Negro racial majority from elsewhere in the world. For example, biological parents do not expect to be the major providers for their children.

The African pattern typically contains some or all of the following distinctions: (1) the early onset of sexual activity; (2) loose emotional ties between spouses; (3) the expectation of sexual union with many partners, and children by them; (4) lowered maternal nurturing with long-term "fostering" of children, sometimes for several years, to nonprimary caretakers, with the stated reason sometimes being to remain sexually attractive to future sexual partners; (5) increased male-male competitiveness for females and lowered paternal involvement in child rearing or maintenance of single pair bonds; and (6) higher fertility, despite education and urbanization, that in other regions lead to a decline in fertility. Among the Herero of South West Africa among whom Draper lived, men typically do not marry until 35 or 40 years of age. However, nearly all will have sired several children by unmarried women. Children from such unions suffer no social stigmata.

Africa is characterized by the continued high prevalence of polygyny, a status not only the preserve of elite men, but one to which men of moderate means aspire at some point in their lives. Women are the mainstays of the rural economy and they and their children tend to be self-supporting. Africa is primarily a continent of female farming. African men do not have a tradition of working for the family; when they work, separate bookkeeping by husband and wife is the norm. Women rarely receive, and do not expect to receive full support from husbands, even in cities. Men expect to have substantial leisure and the general male pattern of low parental investment is as true in the pastoral and mixed pastoral/horticultural economies of East Africa as it is in the agricultural areas of Central and West Africa: "Male reproductive effort was not channeled into parenting...but into mating" (Draper, 1989: 154).

The use of surrogate caretakers relieves both men and women from full responsibility for their offspring, thus opening the way for greater emphasis on mating effort and increased fertility. Relative to others in the developing world, African women terminate intensive care of the child early in the child's life. Once a child is a year or so old, the mother enlists the help of various surrogate caretakers for her children. Young children and grandparents do much of the normal upbringing. Children learn to look to older children for satisfaction of basic needs during the day, and pre-teen and teenage peer groups exist relatively independently of the family unit. With reduction of weaning, ovulation is restored and the mother is capable of conceiving again. Large numbers of births per women at relatively short birth intervals results.

The persistence of adult mating and parenting strategies in the face of countervailing environmental cues is to be found in the literature on West African couples living in London, England. As summarized by Draper (1989), young couples who migrate to England for postsecondary education often foster their children to European families in the larger metropolitan region. The foster parents interpret the infrequent visiting of their wards by the parents as signs of parental neglect; the African parents consider that they have made safe and responsible arrangements for the care of their children.

Mental Durability

Indices of social breakdown are also to be gained from figures of those confined to mental institutions or who are otherwise behaviorally unstable. Most of the data to be reviewed come from the United States. In 1970, 240 blacks per 100,000 population were confined to mental institutions, compared with 162 whites per 100,000 population (Staples, 1985). Blacks also use community mental health centers at a rate almost twice their proportion in the general population. The rate of drug and alcohol abuse is much greater among the black population, based on their overrepresentation among patients receiving treatment services. Moreover, it is estimated that over one-third of young black males in the inner city have serious drug problems (Jaynes & Williams, 1989).

Kessler and Neighbors (1986) have demonstrated, using cross-validation on eight different surveys encompassing more than 20,000 respondents, that the effect of race on psychological disorders is independent of class. They observed an interaction between race and class such that the true effect of race was suppressed and the true effect of social class was magnified in models that failed to take the interaction into consideration. Again, in contrast, Orientals are underrepresented in the incidence of mental health problems (P. E. Vernon, 1982).

Law Abidingness

With respect to crime, J. Q. Wilson and Herrnstein (1985) review much of the relevant literature. Afro-Americans currently account for about half of all arrests for assault and murder and two-thirds of all arrests for robbery in the United States, even though they constitute less than one-eighth of the population. Since about the same proportion of victims say their assailant was black, the arrest statistics cannot be attributed to police prejudice. Blacks are also overrepresented among persons arrested for most white-collar offenses. For example, in 1980 blacks made up about one-third of those arrested for fraud, forgery, counterfeiting, and receiving stolen property, and about one-fourth of those arrested for embezzlement. Blacks are underrepresented only among those white-collar offenses that ordinarily require, for their commission, access to high status occupations (tax fraud, securities violations).

A similar racial pattern is to be found in other industrialized Western countries. In London, England, for example, while comprising 13 percent of the population, African-descended people account for 50 percent of the crime (*Daily Telegraph*, March 24, 1983). The dark-skinned Caucasoids from Pakistan, India, and Bangladesh, however, who are also recent immigrants, do not appear to be higher in crime than white populations. In Toronto, Canada, unofficial figures suggest that recent Afro-Caribbean immigrants, while making up 2 to 5 percent of the population, are responsible for between 32 and 40 percent of the crime (*The Globe and Mail*, February 8, 1989). Immigrants from the Pacific Rim, however, are underrepresented in crime.

In the 1920s the underrepresentation of the Chinese in the U.S. crime figures led American criminologists to consider the ghetto as a place that *protected* members from the disruptive tendencies of the outside society (J. Q. Wilson & Herrnstein, 1985: 473). Among blacks the ghetto is said to foster crime. Detailed analyses made in the United States show that currently one in four black males between the ages of 20 and 29 is either in jail, on probation, or on parole and that this is not due to bias in the criminal justice system (Klein, Petersilia, & Turner, 1990).

I have found that, internationally, African and Caribbean countries report twice the amount of violent crime (murder, rape, and serious assault) as do European countries and three times more than do countries from the Pacific Rim (Rushton, 1990b). Summing crime data from the International Police Organization (INTERPOL) and averaging across years gives figures per 100,000 population, respectively, of 142, 74, and 43. These proportionate racial differences are similar to those found using statistics from within the United States. It is worth considering these data in more detail.

I consulted the published statistics provided by INTERPOL (Rushton, 1990b). INTERPOL's crime statistics for 1983–1984 and 1985–1986 provided data on nearly 100 countries in 14 crime categories. Because the figures for some crimes are highly dependent on a country's laws (e.g., sex offenses) or on availability (e.g., theft of motor cars), I focused on the three most serious crimes, which were relatively well defined: murder, rape, and serious assault.

I collated the figures per 100,000 population for 1984 and 1986 (or the next nearest year) and aggregated across the three categories (see Table 7.3). Countries for which data could not be found in all three categories were dropped. Countries were then grouped by primary racial composition with only Fiji and Papua, New Guinea being eliminated due to uncertainty as to

TABLE 7.3
International Crime Rates per 100,000 Population for Countries
Categorized by Predominant Racial Type

Year / racial type	Number of countries	Homicide		Rape		Serious assault		Total	
		Mean	SD	Mean	SD	Mean	SD	Mean	SD
1984									
Mongoloid	9	8.0	14.1	3.7	2.6	37.1	46.8	48.8	50.3
Caucasoid	40	4.4	4.3	6.3	6.5	61.6	66.9	72.4	72.5
Negroid	22	8.7	11.8	12.8	15.3	110.8	124.6	132.3	139.3
$F(2,69)$		1.92		3.99*		3.16*		3.59*	
1986									
Mongoloid	12	5.8	10.9	3.2	2.7	29.4	40.2	38.4	42.7
Caucasoid	48	4.5	4.6	6.2	6.3	65.7	91.2	76.4	95.4
Negroid	28	9.4	10.6	14.4	15.9	129.6	212.4	153.3	223.8
$F(2,86)$		3.04		7.54*		2.87		3.55*	

Note. From Rushton (1990b, p. 320, Table 2). Copyright 1990 by the Canadian Criminal Justice Association. Reprinted with permission.
* $p < 0.05$

their racial status. For 1984, complete data were available for 71 countries: 9 Mongoloid (including Indonesia, Malaysia, and the Philippines), 40 Caucasoid (including Arabic North Africa, the Middle East, and Latin America), and 22 Negroid (sub-Saharan Africa including Sudan and the Caribbean); for 1986, complete data were available for 88 countries (12 Mongoloid, 48 Caucasoid, and 28 Negroid).

Obviously the groupings shown in Table 7.3 do not represent in any sense "pure types" and there is enormous racial and ethnic variation within almost every country; moreover, each country undoubtedly differs in the procedures used to collect and disseminate the crime figures. Certainly within each racial grouping are to be found countries reporting both high and low crime rates. The Philippines, for example, a country grouped as Mongoloid, reported one of the highest homicide rates in the world, 43 per 100,000 in 1984; Togo, a country grouped as Negroid, had the lowest reported crime rate in the world, a "rounded down" 0 per 100,000 in all 3 crime categories in 1984.

The means and standard deviations for the three racial groups broken down by type of crime are shown in Table 7.3. If each country is treated as an independent entry, the results of one-way ANOVAS reveal that the races differ significantly in crime production. Using the aggregates, significant linear trends show Mongoloids < Caucasoids $<$ Negroids for both 1984 [F (1, 69) = 5.20, p < 0.05] and 1986 [F (1, 86) = 4.99, p < 0.05]. A nonparametric analysis of these ratio figures shows that the exact probability of getting this particular ranking twice in a row is 1/6 x 1/6 = 0.027.

Social Organization

A similar racial pattern is found when assessing administrative cohesion and political organization, either contemporaneously or historically. Twenty-five hundred years ago, China governed 50 million people via an imperial bureaucracy with universally administered entrance exams leading to the Inner Cabinet, an achievement that surpassed those of equivalent European civilizations, including that of the Roman Empire. In Africa, however, written languages were not invented and the degree of bureaucratic organization therefore necessarily limited.

One way of assessing a government's administrative ability is its capacity for conducting an accurate census. The United States conducts one of these every ten years and there is, of course, a margin of error. The amount of error in the U.S. census is considered small relative to African and Caribbean countries whose population statistics are notoriously poor, but large compared to a census conducted over ten days beginning July 1, 1990 in the People's Republic of China. There were over 1 million census takers organized for the population of 1 billion people.

The disorganization of African and African-American societies relative to those elsewhere in the world is increasingly the focus of concerned commentary. In the United States, the optimism generated by the Civil Rights movement of the 1950s, culminating in the Civil Rights Act of 1964 has almost completely dissipated. The abysmal social and financial conditions of poverty and unemployment, drugs and crime, teenage parenthood, and wretched educational achievement in black urban centers provide problems of gigantic proportion for the future (Jaynes & Williams, 1989).

Some see the city of Detroit as a harbinger of what is to come. In the early 1960s Detroit seemed like a model American city. Industry was booming as both blacks and whites found steady work in the automobile industry. But in 1967 the worst race riot in American history erupted. Overnight, Detroit was violently jerked from being a prosperous, integrated industrial center to that of a chaotic, seething ghetto. The anarchic conditions and political rhetoric surrounding black city-states like Detroit have been recorded by the Israeli

writer, Ze'ev Chafets (1990) in *Devil's Night and Other True Tales of Detroit,*
an account of, among other events, how local citizens burn down houses, abandoned buildings, and unused factories each Halloween night. Chafets refers to
Detroit as "America's first Third World City."

In Africa, as the imperial powers of Europe began decolonization after World
War II there were high hopes and intensive, forward-looking interest in the
countries of sub-Saharan Africa. Hundreds of billions of dollars of foreign aid
and private investment poured in. However, unlike South Asia, a region generally considered to be in a somewhat similar situation thirty-five years ago,
Africa's economy has substantially declined in size and dereliction and decay
are everywhere. The crumbling infrastructure often forces companies to provide their own generators for electricity, their own water for drinking and
their own radio transmitters for communication. In an age of computers and
fax machines, it is difficult to raise a dial tone in many African cities (Duncan,
1990; Lamb, 1987). Studies by the World Bank and others show that by every
indicator conditions will only worsen in the 1990s and that the relentless
peripheralization of Africa from the world economy will continue.

One ominous feature is Africa's inability to control its population growth,
currently at 3.2 percent a year, the highest rate in Africa's known history or in
the world (Caldwell & Caldwell, 1990). South Asia and Latin America, whose
rates stand at 2.1 percent and 2.5 percent respectively, have reduced population growth since 1960. In the United States the average woman will be a
source of 14 children, grandchildren, and great-grandchildren; the comparable figure for an African woman is 258. As a result, the African continent,
which accounted for 9 percent of the world's population in 1950, accounts for
12 percent today.

If these trends continue, Africans will constitute more than a quarter of the
human race by late in the next century and for a long time thereafter (Caldwell
& Caldwell, 1990). In spite of a staggering death toll from AIDS of about 20
million people, the United Nations world population projections say that
Africa's population will double by the year 2015 (Briefings, *Science,* September 18, 1992, vol. 257, p. 1627).

Racial Rankings

Table 1.1 summarized the results for some 6 categories of variables reported in the empirical literature. I have found that general rankings made
by Orientals, as well as by whites reflect these racial orderings (Rushton,
1992c). As shown in Table 7.4, whites and Orientals rank whites intermediate
to Orientals and blacks on measures of industriousness, activity, sociability,
rule following, strength of the sex drive, genital size, intelligence, and brain
size.

TABLE 7.4
Ranking of Races on Various Dimensions Made by Orientals and Whites

| | Oriental ranking of | | | White ranking of | | |
	Blacks	Whites	Orientals	Blacks	Whites	Orientals
Intelligence	3c	2b	1a	3c	2b	1a
Brain size	3c	2b	1a	3b	1a	2a
Industriousness	3b	2b	1a	3c	2b	1a
Activity	1a	2b	3c	1a	2b	3c
Anxiety	3b	2b	1a	3	2	1
Sociability	3b	1a	3c	2b	1a	3c
Aggressiveness	2	1	3	1a	2b	3c
Rule-following	3c	2b	1a	3c	2b	1a
Strength of sex drive	2a	1a	3b	1a	2b	3c
Size of genitalia	1a	2b	3c	1a	2b	3c

Note. From Rushton (1992c, p. 441, Table 2). Copyright 1992 by Pergamon Press. Reprinted with permission. Different superscripts indicate significant differences ($p < .05$).

Other Variables

Many other variables distinguish the races, some anecdotal, but surely worthy of study. African rhythm from Burkino Faso to South Africa enables Africans to sing in unison while they work. A visitor will often note that when a group is working in the fields, one person sits off to the side and beats a drum so all can sing and work in unison. African American rhythm music has conquered the adolescent population from Toronto to Tokyo. Is there a racial gradient on this dimension from Africans to Asians? If so, what is the neuro-hormonal mediator?

There are racial differences in the production of odor produced by the apocrine glands (J. R. Baker, 1974). These glands are associated with underarm and genital hair and become active when people are frightened or aroused. Blacks have more and larger apocrine glands than Caucasians and Caucasians more than Orientals. The Sino-Japanese are very sensitive to smell and doctors specialize in treatment for body odors. In Japan, a strong odor used to be sufficient in the early part of this century to warrant the sufferer being exempt from military service (J. R. Baker, 1974: 173).

Blacks have deeper voices than whites. In one study, Hudson and Holbrook (1982) gave a reading task to 100 black men and 100 black women volunteers ranging in age from 18 to 29 years. The fundamental vocal frequencies were measured and compared to white norms. The frequency for black men was 110 Hz, lower than the 117 Hz for white men, and the frequency for black women was 193 Hz, lower than the frequency of 217 Hz for white women.

Differences in bone density between blacks and whites have been noted at a variety of ages and skeletal sites and remain even after adjusting for body mass (Pollitzer & Anderson, 1989). Racial differences in bone begin even before birth. Divergence in the length and weight of the bones of the black and white fetus is followed by greater weight of the skeleton of black infants compared with white infants. Blacks have not only greater skeletal calcium content, but also greater total body potassium and muscle mass. These findings are important for osteoporosis and fractures, especially in elderly people.

Body structure differences likely account for the differential success of blacks at sporting events. Blacks are disproportionately successful in sports involving running and jumping but not at all successful at sports such as swimming. For example in the 1992 Olympic Games in Barcelona, blacks won every men's running race. On the other hand, no black swimmer has ever qualified for the U.S. Olympic swim team. The bone density differences mentioned above may be a handicap for swimming.

The physique and physiology of blacks may give them a genetic advantage in running and jumping, as discussed in *Runner's World* by long time editor Amby Burfoot (1992). For example, blacks have less body fat, narrower hips, thicker thighs, longer legs, and lighter calves. From a biomechanical perspective, this is a useful package. Narrow hips allow for efficient, straight-ahead running. Strong quadricep muscles provide horsepower, and light calves reduce resistance.

With respect to physiology, West Africans are found to have significantly more fast-twitch fibers and anaerobic enzymes than whites. Fast-twitch muscle fibers are thought to confer an advantage in explosive, short duration power events such as sprinting. East and South African blacks, by contrast, have muscles that provide great endurance by producing little lactic acid and other products of muscle fatigue.

A number of direct performance studies have shown a distinct black superiority in simple physical tasks such as running and jumping. Often, the subjects in these studies were very young children who had no special training. Blacks also have a significantly faster patellar tendon reflex time (the familiar knee-jerk response) than white students. Reflex time is obviously an important variable for sports that require lightning reflexes. It would be interesting to know if the measures on which blacks performed best were the ones on which Orientals performed poorest, and vice versa. Do reflex times and percentage of fast-twitch muscle show a racial gradient, and is it one opposite to that of cognitive decision time? Is this ultimately a physiological tradeoff?

8

Sexual Potency, Hormones, and AIDS

An inverse relation is found between the racial pattern reported on brain size and intelligence and that reported in this chapter on gamete production and sexual behavior. Mongoloid populations, who average highest in brain size and intelligence, are lowest in egg production and reproductive effort. Caucasoids average intermediately. The racial gradient is found on numerous physiological, anatomical, and behavioral measures, including AIDS. Sex hormones may mediate this pattern.

Reproductive Potency

The average woman produces one egg every 28 days in the middle of the menstrual cycle. Some women, however, have shorter cycles than others and some produce two eggs in a cycle. Both events translate into greater fecundity because of the greater opportunities they provide for a conception. Occasionally double ovulation results in the birth of dizygotic (two-egg) twins.

The races differ in the rate at which they double ovulate. Among Mongoloids, the frequency of dizygotic twins per 1,000 births is less than 4, among Caucasoids the rate is 8 per 1,000, and among Negroids the figure is greater than 16 per 1,000, with some African populations having twin frequencies of more than 57 per 1,000 (Bulmer, 1970). Recent reviews of twinning rates in the United States (Allen, 1988) and Japan (Imaizumi, 1992) confirm the racial differences. Note that the frequency of monozygotic twinning is nearly constant at about 4 per 1,000 in all groups. Monozygotic twinning is the result of a single fertilized egg splitting into two identical parts.

The frequency of three-egg triplets and four-egg quadruplets shows a comparable racial ordering. For triplets, the rate per million births among Mongoloids is 10, among Caucasoids 100, and among Negroids 1,700; and for quadruplets, per million births, among Mongoloids 0, among Caucasoids 1, and among Negroids, 60 (Allen, 1987; Nylander, 1975). Data from racially mixed matings show that multiple births are largely determined by the race of the mother, independently of the race of the father, as found in Mongoloid-Caucasoid crosses in Hawaii, and Caucasoid-Negroid crosses in Brazil (Bulmer, 1970).

165

TABLE 8.1
Relative Ranking of Races in Reproductive Potency

Reproductive potency variable	Orientals	Whites	Blacks
Gamete production and multiple birthing	3	2	1
Speed of menstrual cycle	?	2	1
Speed of sexual maturation	?	2	1
Age of first sexual intercourse	3	2	1
Number of premarital partners	3	2	1
Frequency of premarital intercourse	3	2	1
Frequency of sexual fantasies	3	2	1
Frequency of marital intercourse	3	2	1
Number of extramarital partners	3	2	1
Permissive attitudes, low guilt	3	2	1
Primary sexual characteristics (size of penis, testis, vulva, vagina, clitoris, ovaries)	3	2	1
Secondary sexual characteristics (salient voice, breasts, buttocks, muscles)	3	2	1
Biologic control of sexual behavior (periodicity of sexual response; predictability of sexual life history from age of onset of puberty)	3	2	1
Androgen levels	3	2	1
Sexually transmitted diseases	3	2	1

Note. From Rushton (1992b, p. 814, Table 3). Copyright 1992 by Psychological Reports. Reprinted with permission.

Sexual Anatomy

Anatomical differences have often been referred to in the ethnographic record (chap. 5; see also French Army Surgeon, 1898/1972; J. R. Baker, 1974; Lewis, 1990). Reference has been made to the placement of female genitals

(Orientals highest, blacks lowest); the angle and texture of erection (Orientals parallel to body and stiff, blacks at right angles to the body and flexible); the size of genitalia (Orientals smallest, blacks largest); and the salience of muscularity, buttocks, and breasts (Orientals least, blacks most).

Rushton and Bogaert (1987) averaged the ethnographic data on erect penis size and estimated them to approximate: Orientals, 4 to 5.5 inches in length (10–14 cm) and 1.25 inches in diameter (3.2 cm); Caucasians, 5.5 to 6 inches in length (14–15.3 cm) and 1.3 to 1.6 inches in diameter (3.3–4.1 cm); blacks, 6.25 to 8 inches in length (15.9–20.3 cm) and 2 inches in diameter (5.1 cm). Women were proportionate to men, with Orientals having smaller vaginas and blacks larger ones, relative to Caucasians. Variations were noted: in the French West Indies, the size of the penis and vagina covaried with amount of black admixture.

New focus on penis size has come in the wake of the AIDS crisis. It has become increasingly obvious that one size of condom does not fit all. Because condom use is considered an essential element of AIDS prevention, and because condom size is a critical determinant in user satisfaction, both the World Health Organization's *Specifications and Guidelines for Condom Procurement* and the United Nations' International Organization for Standardization have recommended a 49-mm flat width condom for Asia, a 52-mm flat width for North America and Europe, and a 53-mm size for Africa (e.g., World Health Organization, 1991). China is reported to be manufacturing its own condoms— 49 mm, plus or minus 2 mm.

In Thailand, where several ergonomic studies have been conducted, female prostitutes say that size 52 mm condoms bunch up during intercourse causing irritation and adolescent male users report that even 49 mm slip off during intercourse. Other indications are that size 52 mm condoms may be too small for some Caucasian and African men. As a result of such information, studies are currently underway to establish typical penis size and shape in various parts of the world (e.g., Program for Appropriate Technology in Health, 1992).

The research currently available suggests that at least three sizes are needed to cover the 10th to 90th percentile, based on Kinsey Institute (see 8.6 below) and Thailand data (Table 8.2). These sizes would be: (1) 45 mm flat width, (2) 52 mm flat width, and (3) 57 mm flat width. It seems evident, based on penile size data collected in Thailand, that the current "Asian" size of 49 mm flat width is too large for approximately 15 percent of the male population. It also seems possible, assuming the Kinsey data for African American males are relevant, that the 52 mm nominal flat width condom is too small for at least 25 percent of the African population, and that flat widths of 55–56 mm would be more suitable for that region (Program for Appropriate Technology in Health, 1991).

Another aspect of size—length—poses less of a problem for universal fit. Condoms that rely on general elasticity to prevent slip-off can be unrolled to

TABLE 8.2
Racial Differences in Erect Penis Size

	Percentage of sample		
Penis size	Thailand[a]	White/U.S.[b]	Black/U.S.[b]
Length (mm)			
75-100	3	0	0
100-125	27	3	0
126-150	51	27	15
151-175	17	53	59
176-200	2	15	20
> 200	0	2	5
Circumference (mm)			
< 75	0	2	2
76-100	16	3	2
101-112	37	13	9
113-127	30	53	53
128-137	14	10	11
138-150	3	15	15
>150	0	5	9

Note. From World Health Organization Global Programme on AIDS Specifications and Guidelines for Condom Procurement (1991, p. 33, Table 5). Data are in the public domain.
[a] Measured at point of maximum circumference; [b] Measured at base

any of a variety of lengths, provided that the condom is sufficiently long to accommodate at least the 95th percentile. Based on Kinsey Institute data for African American and white males in the United States and additional data from Thailand, the optimum lengths might be 180 mm for the Asian populations, 190 mm for the Caucasian populations, and 200 mm for the African populations (Program for Appropriate Technology in Health, 1991).

Data provided by the Kinsey Institute have confirmed the black-white difference in penis size (Table 8.2, and items 70–72 of Table 8.4). Alfred Kinsey and his colleagues instructed their respondents on how to measure their penis along the top surface, from belly to tip. The respondents were given cards to fill out and return in preaddressed stamped envelopes. Nobile (1982) published the first averages of these data finding the length and circumferences of the penis for the white samples was smaller than for the black sample. (Flaccid length = 3.86 inches [9.80 cm] vs. 4.34 inches [11.02 cm]; erect length = 6.15 inches [15.62 cm] vs. 6.44 inches [16.36 cm]; erect circumference = 4.83 inches [12.27 cm] vs. 4.96 inches [12.60 cm] respectively.)

Measures of the size of the testes, either taken from living subjects or from those at autopsy, show that this is twofold lower in Asian men than Europeans (9 vs. 21 g). These differences are too large to be accounted for in terms of body size (Harvey & May, 1989; Short, 1979, 1984). According to Harvey and May (1989) this size differential means that individual Caucasians produce about twice the number of spermatozoa per day than do Chinese (185–253 x 10^6 compared with 84 x 10^6). Larger scrotal circumferences have sometimes been reported in Africans than in Europeans (Short, 1979; Ajmani, Jain, & Saxena, 1985).

Sex Hormones

In an early study by W. Freeman (1934), racial-group differences in the weight of the hypophysis (pituitary) were suggested, with blacks having the heaviest (800 mg), whites being intermediate (700 mg), and Orientals having the lightest (600 mg). The pituitary is directly involved with the release of gonadotropins, which stimulate the testicles and ovaries in their functions (the release of testosterone, estradiol, and progesterone on the one hand, and sperm and eggs on the other). This would order the population differences in rate of multiple birthing, for gonadotropin levels differentiate the races in the predicted direction (Soma, Takayama, Kiyokawa, Akaeda, & Tokoro, 1975), as well as distinguish mothers of dizygotic twins from mothers with no dizygotic twins (Martin, Olsen, Thiele, Beaini, Handelsman, & Bhatnager, 1984).

The proposition of a Negroid-Caucasoid-Mongoloid gradient for maternal gonadotropin was supported by R. Lynn (1990b) in a review of the medical literature. He provided indirect evidence from racial differences in the sex ratio, that is, the proportion of male to female infants. It is known that the sex ratio is low in black populations, moderate in Caucasoids, and high in Mongoloids, and there is also evidence that high levels of gonadotropin lowers the sex ratio, suggesting that high gonadotropin levels in black women are partially responsible for the low sex ratio (James, 1986). The maternal hormonal gradient may also be the explanation for the same racial pattern that exists for premenstrual syndrome (Janiger, Riffenburgh, & Kersh, 1972).

R. Lynn (1990b) suggested that paralleling the gonadotropin gradient in women is a testosterone gradient in men. One study of matched groups of 50 black and 50 white male college students in California found that testosterone levels were 19 percent higher in blacks than in whites (Ross, Bernstein, Judd, Hanisch, Pike, & Henderson, 1986). A 3 percent difference favoring blacks has been found among an older group of 3, 654 white and 525 black U.S. male Vietnam era military veterans (Ellis & Nyborg, 1992).

The incidence of cancer of the prostate provides indirect evidence. Numerous medical surveys show that Oriental populations experience less than half the U.S. incidence whereas U.S. blacks have a much higher lifetime risk than U.S. whites (Hixson, 1992; Polednak, 1989). By turning over cells in the prostate, the conversion of testosterone to dihydrostestosterone by the enzyme 5-alpha reductase is most widely considered to be one major source of the mutations leading to cancer. Measurements of two metabolites of dihydrostestosterone show markedly lower levels in the serum of Japanese natives and 10 to 15 percent higher concentrations in American blacks (Hixson, 1992).

There is also evidence that biological factors differentially influence sexual behavior across the races, the direction being blacks > whites > Orientals. Inspection of Figures 1 vs. 2 and 3 in Udry and Morris (1968), for example, shows a higher periodicity, or greater frequency of intercourse at midcycle, the time that is most likely to result in pregnancy, among black women than among white women. In a recent comparison of Oriental and white students at a Canadian university, Oriental women reported less periodicity of sexual response than white women (Rushton, 1992c).

Biological factors similarly predict the onset of sexual interest, dating, first intercourse, and first pregnancy better for blacks than for whites or for Orientals (Presser, 1978; Goodman, Grove, & Gilbert, 1980; Westney et al., 1984). The converse may also be true. Social factors such as religious beliefs and sex-role attitudes predict the sexual behavior of white women better than that of black women (Tanfer & Cubbins, 1992).

Intercourse Frequency and Attitudes

Racial differences exist in frequency of sexual intercourse. Examining Hofmann's (1984) review of the extent of premarital coitus among young

TABLE 8.3
World Health Surveys Showing Proportion of Population
Aged 11–21 Experiencing Premarital Coitus

	% sexually experienced		
Population	Men	Women	Both
Asians	12	5	9
Europeans	46	35	40
Africans	74	53	64

Note. From Rushton & Bogaert (1987, p. 535, Table 2).
Copyright 1987 by Academic Press. Reprinted with
permission. The table summarizes a review by Hofmann
(1984).

people around the world, Rushton and Bogaert (1987) categorized the 27 countries by primary racial composition and averaged the figures. The results showed that African adolescents are more sexually active than Europeans, who are more sexually active than Asians (see Table 8.3). While some variation occurs from country to country, consistency is found within groups. As is typical of such surveys, young men report a greater degree of sexual experiences than young women (Symons, 1979). It is clear from Table 8.3, however, that the population differences are replicable across sex, with the men of the more restrained group having less experience than the women of the less restrained.

A confirmatory study was carried out in Los Angeles which held the setting constant and fully sampled the ethnic mix. Of 594 adolescent and young adults, 20 percent were classified as Oriental, 33 percent as white, 21 percent as Hispanic, and 19 percent as black. The average age at first intercourse was 16.4 for Orientals and 14.4 for blacks, with whites and Hispanics intermediate, and the percentage sexually active was 32 percent for Orientals and 81 percent for blacks, with whites and Hispanics intermediate (Moore & Erickson, 1985).

A Youth Risk Behavior Survey with a reading level for 12-year-olds was developed by the Centers for Disease Control in the United States to examine health-risk behaviors including sexual behaviors. In 1990, a representative sample of 11,631 students in grades 9–12 (ages 14 to 17) from across the United States anonymously completed the questionnaire during a 40-minute class period. Students were asked whether they had ever had sexual intercourse, with how many people they had had sexual intercourse, and with how many people they had had sexual intercourse during the past 3 months. They were also asked about their use of condoms and other methods of preventing pregnancy (Centers for Disease Control, 1992a).

Of all students in grades 9–12, 54 percent reported ever having had sexual intercourse and 39 percent reported having had sexual intercourse during the 3 months preceding the survey. Male students were significantly more likely than female students to ever have had sexual intercourse (61 percent and 48 percent, respectively) and to have had sexual intercourse during the 3 months preceding the survey (43 percent and 36 percent, respectively). Black students were significantly more likely than white students to ever have had sexual intercourse (72 percent and 52 percent, respectively), to have had sexual intercourse during the 3 months preceding the survey (54 percent and 38 percent, respectively), and to have had four or more sex partners in their lifetime (38 percent and 16 percent, respectively). Four percent of all students reported having had a sexually transmitted disease. Black students (8 percent vs. 3 percent) were significantly more likely to report having had a sexually transmitted disease than white students (Centers for Disease Control, 1992a, 1992b).

The rate of premarital intercourse is matched by that following marriage. Rushton and Bogaert (1987) inspected a section on cross-cultural intercourse frequency in a review by Ford and Beach (1951) and categorized the tribal peoples listed into three main groups. The Oceanic and Amerindian people tended to have a lower rate of sexual intercourse per week average (1–4) than U.S. whites (2–4) and Africans (3–10). Subsequent surveys tend to support the same conclusion. For married couples in their twenties, the average frequency of intercourse per week for the Japanese approximates 2 (Asayama, 1975), for American whites 4, and for American blacks 5 (Fisher, 1980).

Sex surveys are also beginning in the People's Republic of China where, according to *Time Magazine* (May 14, 1990), a new era of relative permissiveness is beginning. According to the *Time* account, in one survey, 500 volunteer social workers have interviewed 23,000 people in 15 provinces using a 240-question survey. Results from a smaller survey, of about 2,000 men and women from urban centers throughout China have now been published (Bo & Wenxiu, 1992). The results show much restraint relative to that in the West. For example, over 50 percent of the men and women reported never having discussed sex with others and over 20 percent of spouses had never talked about sex with each other. This compared to less than 5 percent of respondents in England (Eysenck, 1976).

Over 50 percent thought that masturbation (and even loss of semen) was debilitating. Only 19 percent of males who admitted masturbating had engaged in the practice before the age of 17 years, and no female masturbators reported that they had done it before that age, while over 90 percent of the women stated that they had commenced after the age of 20. One reason for the older average age of masturbation is a later puberty. Of the males, about 50 percent reported that they had experienced their first seminal emission above the age of 17.

The frequency of reported intercourse may also be slightly lower in urban China than in the urban West. For married couples aged 20–30 the average is about 12 times a month or 3 times a week (Bo & Wenxiu, 1992, Table 7). Only 5 percent of the males and 3 percent of the females reported frequencies of one or more sexual outlets a day. The incidence of reported extramarital intercourse is also lower in China. About 29 percent of the males and 23 percent of the females admitted that they had been or were engaged in it. In the United States, one set of figures indicate 45 percent and 34 percent, respectively (*Playboy Magazine*, 1983).

Not all surveys find racial differences in the predicted direction. Tanfer and Cubbins (1992) found that 20- to 29-year-old single black women cohabiting with a sexual partner reported only 4.3 occasions of intercourse in the previous four weeks as compared with 6.9 among cohabiting white women ($p <$ .05). The authors suggested that these black women's partners had other sexual partners as well and were less available than the white women's partners. Another possible reason was that more of the black sample were pregnant (Tanfer & Cubbins, 1992, Table 3).

Concomitant racial differences are found in sexual attitudes. In Ford and Beach's (1951) survey, the Asian groups were the most likely to endorse beliefs concerning the weakening effects of intercourse. A review by P. E. Vernon (1982) led him to conclude that both the Chinese and the Japanese were not only less experienced in premarital sex, but were also less permissive, and less concerned with sexual display than Caucasians. Thus, Connor (1975, 1976) had found that three generations of Japanese Americans, as well as Japanese students in Japan, reported less interest in sex than Caucasian samples. Abramson and Imari-Marquez (1982) observed that each of three generations of Japanese Americans showed more sex guilt than matched Caucasian Americans. In studies carried out in Britain and Japan using a sex fantasy questionnaire, Iwawaki and Wilson (1983) found that British men reported twice as many fantasies as Japanese men, and British women admitted to four times as much sex fantasy as Japanese women.

In contrast, African-descended people are more permissive than Caucasians. Reiss (1967) observed this with several hundred black and white university students in the United States on scales measuring premarital sexual attitudes (e.g., approving of or feeling guilt about petting and intercourse in casual and romantic relationships); results replicated with other samples and measuring instruments (Heltsley & Broderick, 1969; Sutker & Gilliard, 1970). Johnson (1978) also compared black and white premarital sexual attitudes and behavior and included a Swedish sample who were expected to be (and were) more permissive than American whites. The black sample (particularly males) was found to have had intercourse earlier and with a greater number of casual partners, and with less feelings of distaste, than either white sample.

The Kinsey Data

To explore racial differences in behavior, Rushton and Bogaert (1987, 1988) examined the Kinsey data. As is generally known, Kinsey, Pomeroy, Martin, and Gebhard created the Institute for Sex Research at Indiana University in 1947. In 1948 they published *Sexual Behavior in the Human Male* and in 1953 *Sexual Behavior in the Human Female*. In these books they did not address the issue of group differences but did leave a promissory note:

> The present volume is confined to a record on American and Canadian whites, but we have begun accumulating material which will make it possible to include the American and Canadian Negro groups in later publications. Several hundred histories from still other race cultural groups begin to show the fundamental differences which exist between American and other patterns of sexual behavior, but the material is not yet sufficient for publication. (1948: 76)

Early impressions based on some of these data suggested that if blacks were found to be sexually precocious compared to whites on some measures (Gebhard, Pomeroy, Martin, & Christenson, 1958), the differences would probably be small and overstated (Bell, 1978). Only recently has it become possible to provide tests of significance on a full range of variables.

In 1979, Gebhard and Johnson published a supplementary volume containing novel information, as well as a "cleaning" of the original data (eliminating individuals derived from sources with a known sexual bias such as prostitutes). This volume presented nearly 600 tables of percentages for a range of sexual practices and morphological data by race, socioeconomic status, sexual orientation, etc. From these data, we chose 41 items to compare black-white differences. Because the black sample was a privileged group, consisting of university students from 1938 to 1963, a period of time during which it was more difficult for blacks in the United States to go to a university than it is today, and because they were also of high socioeconomic and religiously devout background (Gebhard & Johnson, 1979: Tables 3-6, 9, 295), it was possible to compare social class differences. The white sample was divided into those who were college-educated and those who were not.

The Kinsey interview method along with some of its strengths and weaknesses has been described by Gebhard and Johnson (1979). Personal interviews were conducted from 1938 to 1963 assessing some 300 items of demographic, physical, and sexual information on over 10,000 white and 400 black respondents. It is not a random sample, as most respondents were college educated and between 20 and 25 years of age when interviewed. They are most representative of the middle classes and the Midwest of the United States at the time (Indiana and Illinois, including Chicago). Because the black sample was a relatively elite group, a restricted test of race differences is made. If more normative samples of black people had been used, it is likely that the differences would be greater.

Rushton and Bogaert examined the 600 tables in Gebhard and Johnson (1979) to choose those that seemed most relevant. As often as possible, a cutoff was chosen at the place where 50 percent of the black respondents had fallen. For example, if 10 percent of the black sample's fathers were under age 20 when the respondent was born, 20 percent were between the ages of 20 and 26, and 35 percent were between the ages of 26 and 30, the 50th percentile would be found in the category of age 26–30. It was then possible to calculate the percentage of the two white samples falling in this category to see if they differed from the black percentage. Where feasible, data was collapsed across males and females, thus providing the most reliable number of data points. The percentages were turned into proportions based on the number who had answered the question and a z test was calculated for the significance of differences between proportions. Analysis in terms of dichotomous proportions rather than means and standard deviations was necessitated by the limitations of the archival data.

It is worth noting that the proportions of females in the black and white groups were not entirely equivalent. For example, considering the item concerning year of birth (Gebhard & Johnson, 1979, Table 2) for which fairly complete data were available, males comprised 52 percent of the 9023 white college students responding, 44 percent of the 399 black college students, and 43 percent of the 1794 noncollege whites. Because females comprised a significantly higher percentage of black than of white students ($X^2 = 9.2$) the results were biased *against* finding race differences since females typically are more restrained in their sexual behavior than males (Symons, 1979). Although we did not report it in our papers, most of the racial differences were replicated across sex.

Table 8.4 presents the items and the table numbers from Gebhard and Johnson (1979), the proportions for the three samples, along with the tests of significance. The hypothesis that the white college-educated sample was more sexually restrained than the white noncollege-educated sample, which, in turn, was more sexually restrained than the black college-educated was supported on 24 out of 41 occasions (items 19, 31, 70, 72, 74, 90, 91, 100, 135, 199, 218, 227, 228, 239, 268, 297, 301, 322, 323, 326, 329, 348, 351, 367), with the majority being statistically significant. The probability of taking three items at a time and getting this ordering on 24 out of 41 occasions is itself greater than chance on a test of direct probabilities ($p < 0.001$). When the comparisons are made pairwise, the black college-educated sample is found to be more different from college-educated whites than are whites without a college education on 31 out of 41 occasions (items 19, 20, 28, 29, 69, 70, 71, 74, 90, 91, 100, 135, 183, 199, 218, 227, 228, 239, 268, 291, 297, 322, 323, 324, 326, 342, 348, 351, 355, 367, 374).

These results imply that race is more important than social class in determining sexual behavior. Social class did, however, have effects. Comparing the white college-educated sample with the white noncollege-educated sample showed statistically significant differences favoring the college-educated in terms of sexual restraint on 23 out of 41 occasions (items 19, 30, 31, 90, 91, 99, 100, 135, 183, 199, 218, 227, 228, 239, 268, 297, 301, 308, 322, 323, 326, 329, 367). Results not in accord with expectation were also observed (items 28, 29, 30, 53, 99, 291, 308).

In sum, college-educated whites tended to be the most sexually restrained and college-educated blacks the least sexually restrained, with noncollege-educated whites intermediate. This pattern was observed on measures made of the speed of occurrence of premarital, marital, and extramarital sexual experiences, number of sexual partners, and frequency of intercourse. For women, measures of the speed and incidence of pregnancy, the rapidity of the menstrual cycle, and the number of orgasms per act of coitus also differentiated the groups.

Subsequently, M. S. Weinberg and Williams (1988) confirmed many of Rushton and Bogaert's (1987, 1988) observations with respect to black-white differences in sexuality. They reanalyzed evidence from three independent sources: the Kinsey data, which formed the basis of Rushton and Bogaert's studies, except that they used the original raw data rather than the published marginal totals; a 1970 National Opinion Research Center poll of sexual attitudes; and a study carried out in San Francisco. All three reanalyses showed the racial effects on sexuality while statistically holding education and social class constant.

TABLE 8.4
Analysis of Kinsey Data on Race and Socioeconomic Status Differences in Sexual Behavior

		Sample sizes and proportion		
Number	Item	Black college	White non-college	White college
19	Genetic father's age at respondent's birth: "26-30 and under"	189 / 313 = .60[a]	677 / 1,471 = .46[b]	3,385 / 7,872 = .43[c]
20	Genetic mother's age at respondent's birth: "26-30 and under"	275 / 348 = .79[a]	1,026 / 1,532 = .67[b]	5,415 / 8,082 = .67[b]
28	Respondent's age at genetic father's death: "18 and under"	65 / 123 = .53[a]	243 / 695 = .35[b]	966 / 2,300 = .42[c]
29	Respondent's age at genetic mother's death: "19 and under"	49 / 93 = .53[a]	175 / 472 = .37[b]	663 / 1,441 = .46[a]
30	Age respondent left parental home: "21 years or under"	104 / 186 = .56[a]	639 / 1,048 = .61[a]	1,767 / 3,606 = .49[b]
31	Number of siblings: "2 and under"	215 / 399 = .54[a]	977 / 1,777 = .55[a]	6,423 / 9,047 = .71[b]
53	Age at puberty (aggregate measure): "13 years and under"	292 / 400 = .73[a]	1,238 / 1,794 = .69[a]	6,970 / 9,052 = .77[b]
69	Estimated length of erect penis: "Less than or equal to 6.50 inches"	105 / 161 = .65[a]	403 / 791 = .82[b]	3,059 / 3,777 = .81[b]
70	Measured length of erect penis: "Less than or equal to 6.25 inches"	30 / 59 = .51[a]	86 / 143 = .60[a,b]	1,497 / 2,376 = .63[b]
71	Measured length of flaccid penis: "Less than or equal to 4.50 inches"	40 / 59 = .68[a]	126 / 142 = .89[b]	2,117 / 2,379 = .89[b]
72	Measured circumference of flaccid penis: "Less than or equal to 4.00 inches"	41 / 59 = .70[a]	104 / 137 = .76[a,b]	1,825 / 2,310 = .79[b]
74	Angle of penile erection: "Penis almost vertical or down from vertical as much as... 85°"	102 / 164 = .62[a]	450 / 585 = .77[b]	3,473 / 4,396 = .79[b]
90	Average length of menstrual cycle: "28 days or less"	129 /155 = .83[a]	428 / 595 = .72[b]	1,983 / 2,916 = .68[c]
91	Average length of menstrual flow: "4 days or under"	80 / 148 = .54[a]	230 / 574 = .40[b]	1,044 / 2,983 = .35[c]
99	Periodicity of female sexual response: "No periodicity"	36 / 173 = .21[a,b]	153 / 767 = .20[b]	710 / 2,839 = .25[a]
100	Age hymen broken: "18 years or under"	67 / 126 = .53[a]	175 / 546 = .32[b]	414 / 1,594 = .26[c]
135	Incidence of prepubertal heterosexual techniques: "Coitus"	116 / 400 = .29[a]	215 / 1,789 = .12[b]	814 / 9,045 = .09[c]
183	Reason for worry about masturbation: "Moral (guilt, shame)"	13 / 41 = .32[a,b]	56 / 206 = .27[b]	390 / 1,027 = .38[a]
199	Age of first premarital petting: "15 years and under"	241 / 388 = .62[a]	931 / 1,663 = .56[b]	3,929 / 8,731 = .45[c]
218	Age of first postpubertal coitus: "17 years and under"	171 / 335 = .51[a]	514 / 1,286 = .40[b]	1,186 / 5,651 = .21[c]
227	Intention to have premarital coitus: "No intention"	81 / 368 = .22[a]	654 / 1,487 = .44[b]	3,509 / 7,311 = .48[c]
228	Moral restraint on premarital coitus: "Much"	195 / 397 = .49[a]	993 / 1,655 = .60[b]	5,926 / 8,845 = .67[c]
239	Number of premarital coital companions: "5 partners or fewer"	169 / 307 = .55[a]	550 / 786 = .70[b]	3,068 / 4,202 = .73[c]
268	Incidence and type of nonmarital pregnancy: "Never"	102 / 310 = .68[a]	665 / 864 = .77[b]	3,938 / 4,633 = .85[c]
291	Duration of first marriage: "Under 5 years"	93 / 176 = .53[a]	326 / 1,053 = .31[b]	1,446 / 3,443 = .42[c]
297	Time between first marriage and first marital coitus in first marriage: "One day or less"	53 / 67 = .79[a]	428 / 620 = .69[b]	1,108 / 1,705 = .65[c]

TABLE 8.4 (cont.)

Number	Item	Black college	White non-college	White college
301	Time before first birth in first marriage: "9-11 months"	14 / 62 = .23[a]	86 / 574 = .15[a]	218 / 1,815 = .12[b]
308	Clarity of contraceptive data for first marriage: "Clearly none used in this marriage"	25 / 176 = .14[a]	147 / 1,051 = .14[a]	172 / 3,432 = .05[b]
322	Frequency of cunnilingus in foreplay in first marriage: "None"	139 / 174 = .80[a]	636 / 1,043 = .61[b]	1,576 / 3,426 = .46[c]
323	Frequency of fellatio in foreplay in first marriage: "None"	146 / 174 = .84[a]	679 / 1,044 = .65[b]	1,710 / 3,420 = .50[c]
324	Time between intromission and ejaculation in coitus in first marriage: "<6 minutes"	89 /158 = .56[a]	675 / 951 = .71[b]	2,057 / 3,164 = .65[c]
326	Frequency (mean) per week of marital coitus in first marriage: "Age 21-25"	3.83	3.32	3.11
327	Maximum frequency of marital coitus in first marriage: "7 per week or less"	110 / 167 = .66[a,b]	616 / 934 = .66[a]	2,043 / 3,349 = .61[b]
329	Frequency of positions in coitus in first marriage: female above, male supine: "Much"	16 / 172 = .09[a]	134 / 1,033 = .13[a]	546 / 3,415 = .16[b]
340	Average number of wife's orgasms per act of coitus in first marriage: ">1"	23 / 173 = .13[a]	92 / 1,026 = .09[a,b]	304 / 3,376 = .09[b]
342	Incidence of extramarital sexual activity in first marriage: "None"	31 / 175 = .17[a]	390 / 1,053 = .37[b]	1,047 / 3,439 = .30[c]
348	Year of first marriage in which first extra-marital coitus occurred: "Within first 2 years"	40 / 78 = .51[a]	112 / 448 = .25[b]	199 / 867 = .23[b]
351	Number of extramarital companions during first marriage: "Zero"	93 / 173 = .54[a]	763 / 1,045 = .73[b]	2,573 / 3,431 = .75[b]
355	Expectation of future extramarital coitus: "Will not have"	50 /131 = .38[a]	445 / 695 = .64[b]	1,751 / 2,779 = .63[b]
367	Incidence of sexual contact with prostitutes: "Never"	96 / 177 = .54[a]	506 / 766 = .66[b]	3,285 / 4,693 = .70[c]
374	Incidence of fellatio with prostitutes: "Never"	44 / 70 = .63[a]	116 / 228 = .51[b]	605 / 1,164 = .52[b]

Note. From Rushton & Bogaert (1988, pp. 265-268, Table 1). Copyright 1988 by Academic Press. Reprinted with permission. Within each item, those proportions of respondents answering in each category having different superscripts are significantly different ($p < .05$). The table number and item are from the "cleaned" Kinsey data by Gebhard & Johnson (1979).

AIDS

Differences in sexual activity translate into consequences. Teenage fertility rates around the world show Negroids > Caucasoids > Mongoloids (Hofmann, 1984). So does the pattern of sexually transmitted diseases. World Health Organization Technical Reports and other studies examining the worldwide prevalence of syphilis, gonorrhea, herpes, and chlamydia typically find low levels in China and Japan and high levels in Africa, with European countries intermediate. Africa is known to be unusual compared to other areas of the world in having sexually transmitted diseases as the major cause of infertility (Cates, Farley, & Rowe, 1985). The worldwide racial pattern in these diseases is replicated within the United States.

The 100,410 cases of acquired immunodeficiency syndrome (AIDS) reported to the World Health Organization as of July 1, 1988 were examined by Rushton and Bogaert (1989). While the modes of transmission were universally the same—through sex and blood and from mother to fetus—it was clear that the virus had entered and spread disproportionately among the racial groups. Because of political sensitivities, many African and Caribbean countries report only a fraction of their actual number of AIDS cases and strenuously deny that AIDS may have originated in Africa (Norman, 1985; Palca, 1991). Negroid countries, relative to others, have an enormous AIDS problem. In some areas, 25 percent or more of the 20–40-year age group are infected with the human immunodeficiency virus (HIV).

In African and Caribbean countries the AIDS virus is transmitted predominantly through heterosexual intercourse (Figure 8.1). The age and sex distributions of HIV infection rates is similar to that of other sexually transmitted diseases with higher prevalence among younger sexually active women. At the other extreme, it is a characteristic feature of AIDS in China and Japan that most sufferers are hemophiliacs. An intermediate amount of HIV infection is apparent in Europe and the Americas, where it has occurred predominantly among homosexual men.

The pattern of whites intermediate to blacks and Orientals is also well documented within the United States (Figure 8.2). As of July 1, 1988, blacks amounted to 12 percent of the U.S. population and accounted for 26 percent of adult and 53 percent of pediatric cases of AIDS. Whites amounted to 80 percent of the population and accounted for 59 percent of adult and 23 percent of child cases, with Hispanic populations intermediate. Oriental populations did not exist in the figures, which included those from California and Hawaii.

By April 1, 1990, the global figures had grown to 237,110 showing an 18-month doubling time and a crystallization of the racial pattern. I (Rushton 1990a) calculated the figures on a per capita basis to find that blacks in Caribbean countries had developed as large an AIDS problem as had Africans and African-Americans, a point ignored by most commentators. The three most affected countries in the world were Bermuda, the Bahamas, and French Guiana. Moreover, within the United States, blacks had increased their total share of the figures from 26 to 27 percent, whites had decreased, and Orientals remained at less than 1 percent.

I have collated the most recent data as of January 4, 1994 in Table 8.5 (World Health Organization, 1994). The official statistics show a cumulative global total of 851,628 cases reported from 187 countries. The number of cases per 1,000 population are computed to give an indication of the relative seriousness of the epidemic between countries with different sizes of populations after excluding countries reporting fewer than 200 cases. The population size of the country is taken from estimates standardized for mid-1991 (United Nations, 1992). On this measure Canada has a rate of .320 per 1,000 making it the 33rd most affected country in the world. Of the other leading countries, 17 are in Africa, 10 are in the Caribbean, 4 are in Europe, and the other is the United States.

Figure 8.1: Three Infection Patterns of the AIDS Virus Are Apparent Worldwide

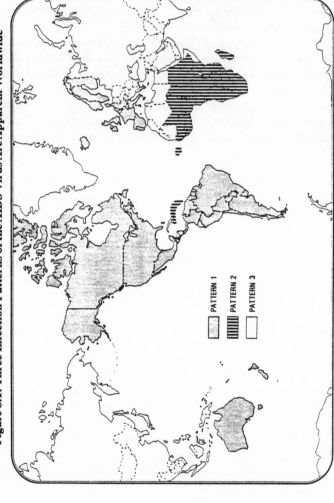

Pattern 1 is found in North and South America, Western Europe, and Australasia where 90% of the cases are homosexual males or users of intravenous drugs. Pattern 2 is found in Africa and the Caribbean where the primary mode of transmission is heterosexual sex and the number of infected females and males is approximately equal. Pattern 3 is typical of the rest of the world where relatively few cases have been reported. Adapted from Piot et al. (1988, Figure 3). Data are in the public domain.

Figure 8.2: Racial and Ethnic Classification of U.S. Adult AIDS cases in 1988

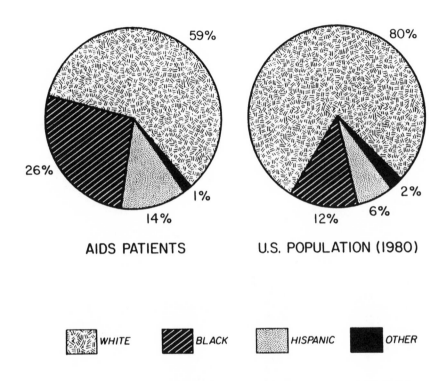

Orientals were underrepresented in cases of AIDS relative to their numbers in the population. Since 1988 the racial differences have grown larger. Adapted from Heyward & Curran (1988, p. 80). Data are in the public domain.

The most recent figures from the United States confirm that blacks are overrepresented in every exposure category (data as of September 30, 1993; Centers for Disease Control and Prevention, 1993). If the population of the United States is divided up racially, the 30 million African-Americans with a cumulative total of 106,585 adult/adolescent cases have a rate of 3.553 per 1,000, equivalent to the black populations of Africa and the Caribbean (Table 8.5). The white and Oriental populations of the United States have rates of .861 and .000 per 1,000, comparable to the white and Oriental populations of Europe and Asia.

One suggestion often made is that blacks in the United States have such a high prevalence of AIDS because of intravenous drug use. Among black men, 36 to 43 percent acquired the disease through drug use, but between 50 and 57

TABLE 8.5
The 33 Countries Most Affected by AIDS Based on Per Capita Cumulative
Cases Reported to the World Health Organization as of January 1994

Country	Date of report (y.m.d)	Cumulative number of cases	Population in millions (as of mid-1991)	Cases per thousand
1. Bahamas	93.09.20	1,329	.259	5.131
2. Bermuda	93.06.30	223	.061	3.656
3. Malawi	93.08.20	29,194	8.556	3.412
4. Zambia	93.10.20	29,734	8.780	3.387
5. Zimbabwe	93.09.30	26,332	10.019	2.628
6. French Guiana	93.09.30	232	.101	2.297
7. Congo	92.12.31	5,267	2.346	2.245
8. Uganda	93.09.30	34,611	19.517	1.773
9. Barbados	93.09.30	397	.255	1.557
10. Kenya	93.07.09	38,220	25.905	1.475
11. Tanzania	93.01.07	38,719	28.359	1.365
12. Rwanda	93.12.10	10,138	7.491	1.353
13. U.S.A.	93.09.30	339,250	252.688	1.343
14. Burundi	93.12.10	7,225	5.620	1.286
15. Central African Republic	92.11.30	3,730	3.127	1.193
16. Cote d'Ivoire	93.07.05	14,555	12.464	1.168
17. Trinidad	93.09.30	1,404	1.253	1.121
18. Guadeloupe	93.03.21	353	.345	1.023
19. Botswana	93.11.24	1,151	1.348	.854
20. Martinique	93.09.30	266	.343	.776
21. Ghana	93.04.30	11,044	15.509	.712
22. Togo	93.12.10	2,391	3.643	.656
23. Zaire	93.06.10	21,008	35.672	.589
24. Spain	93.09.30	21,205	39.025	.543
25. Switzerland	93.09.20	3,415	6.792	.503
26. France	93.09.30	26,970	57.049	.473
27. Haiti	90.12.31	3,086	6.625	.466
28. Honduras	93.09.30	2,365	5.265	.449
29. Guyana	93.03.31	359	.800	.449
30. Gabon	93.12.10	472	1.212	.389
31. Guinea-Bissau	93.12.10	380	.984	.386
32. Italy	93.09.30	19,832	57.052	.348
33. Canada	93.09.30	8,640	27.034	.320

percent acquired it through sexual transmission, 8 percent heterosexually (compared to 1 percent of whites). Of all 24,358 adult cases transmitted heterosexually (7 percent of total), 14,143 or 58 percent involve blacks, with another 20 percent being Hispanic. Hispanics, of course, are a linguistic group; racially, a proportion is black or partly black, especially in New York. Blacks are also overrepresented in the "men who have sex with men" exposure category (19 % versus a population expectation of 12 %). Overall, in the last six years, blacks in the United States increased their total share of the AIDS figures from 26 to 31 percent, Hispanics increased from 14 to 17 percent, Asians and American Indians combined stayed at less than 1 percent, and whites decreased from 59 to 51 percent.

The racially distinct mode of AIDS transmission is particularly marked for women and children, with blacks accounting for 53 and 55 percent of all cases and whites 25 and 20 percent respectively. Whereas among white Americans 94 percent of cases are in men, with a sex ratio of 16:1, among black Americans it is 79 percent with a ratio of 4:1. Black Americans approximate the pattern in Africa and the Caribbean and white Americans the pattern in Europe (Figure 8.1).

9

Genes Plus Environment

Could the observed racial differences be entirely due to cultural modes of transmission? Because the Chinese and Japanese are known to come from tightly integrated family backgrounds, strong socialization is deemed to produce conformity, restraint, and respect for traditional values. An opposite pattern of results is then typically expected from blacks who come from less cohesive family systems and who are undersocialized for achievement.

The racial differences in family unity, however, themselves need explanation. What caused Caucasians to average intermediately in this respect to Africans and Orientals? In any case, socialization cannot account for the early onset of the traits, the speed of dental and other maturational variables, the size of the brain, the number of gametes produced, the physiological differences in testosterone, nor the evidence on cross-cultural consistency. All of these strongly implicate the role of genetic and evolutionary influences. Although purely environmental explanations are therefore unparsimonious from the outset, it is useful to consider the heritability of the racial group differences more fully.

Genetic Weights Predict Racial Differences

High heritabilities are stronger predictors across samples and tests than low heritabilities, probably because they better reflect the enduring biological substrate. As described in chapter 4, items higher in heritability are more consequential for assortment between spouses and best friends than are those with low heritabilities (Rushton, 1989c). Attitudes higher in heritability are shown to be responded to more quickly, to be more resistant to change, and to be more predictive in the attitude similarity attraction relationship (Tesser, 1993).

To my knowledge, Jensen (1973, chapter 4) was the first to apply the idea of differential heritability to race differences. Jensen deduced diametrically opposite predictions from genetic and environmental perspectives. He reasoned that if racial differences in cognitive performance are genetically based, then black-white differences should be greatest on those tests with higher heritabilities. But if racial differences are caused by the environment, then black-white differences should be greatest on those tests more environmentally influenced, and so would have lower heritability.

Jensen (1973) tested these predictions by calculating "environmentability" for various tests through the degree to which sibling correlations departed from the pure genetic expectation of 0.50. These showed an inverse relation with the magnitude of the black-white differences. That is, the most environmentally influenced tests were the ones that least differentiated between blacks and whites. Then, Jensen (1973) cited an unpublished study by Nichols (1972) who estimated the heritability of 13 tests from 543 siblings and found that the correlation between these heritabilities and the black-white difference scores on the same tests was 0.67. In other words, the more heritable the test, the more it discriminated between the races.

The genetic hypothesis is indirectly supported by studies using a test's g loading rather than its heritability. As described in chapters 2, 3, and 6, the higher a test's g loading, the more predictive of intelligent behavior it tends to be, the more heritable it is, and the more it differentiates between the races. Thus, Jensen (1985, 1987b) examined 12 large-scale studies, each comprising anywhere from 6 to 13 tests administered to over 40,000 elementary and high school students and found that the test's g loading consistently predicted the magnitude of the black-white difference.

Prompted by Jensen's approaches I showed a direct genetic effect on the black-white differences using inbreeding depression scores, a measure of genetic dominance (Rushton, 1989e). As described by Jensen (1983), inbreeding depression is an effect for which there is no really satisfactory explanation other than a genetic one. It depends on the presence of dominant genes that enhance fitness in the Darwinian sense.

Inbreeding depression scores had been calculated by Schull and Neel (1965) in a study of 1,854 7 to 10-year-old Japanese cousins tested in 1958 and 1960 and shown to be related to the g factor scores for 11 subtests of the Wechsler Intelligence Scale for Children by Jensen (1983).

I correlated these inbreeding depression scores with standardized black-white differences on the same subtests from five of the studies used by Jensen. Because the Japanese children had been tested in the 1950s on the original Wechsler Scale, while the American children were tested in the 1970s on the revised version of Wechsler Scale, the predicted effect had to be sufficiently strong to overcome these differences.

Set out in Table 9.1 is a summary of the data used in the studies by Jensen (1985, 1987b) and Rushton (1989e). As mentioned, the g factor loadings are indirect estimates of genetic penetrance and the inbreeding depression scores direct estimates. I have calculated a weighted average for the five sets of black-white differences (in σ units, based on raw scores from a total N = 4,848) as well as a weighted average for the 10 sets of g loadings. Also in Table 9.1 are the reliabilities of the tests.

TABLE 9.1

Subtests of the Wechsler Intelligence Scale for Children-Revised (WISC-R) Arranged in Ascending Order of Black-White Differences in the United States, with Each Subtest's g loading, Inbreeding Depression Score, and Reliability

WISC-R subtest	Black-White difference (N = 4,848)	g loading (N = 4,848)	Inbreeding depression (N = 1,854)	Reliability (N = 2,173)
1. Coding	.45	.37	4.45	.72
2. Arithmetic	.61	.61	5.05	.77
3. Picture completion	.70	.53	5.90	.77
4. Mazes	.73	.40	5.35	.72
5. Picture arrangement	.75	.52	9.40	.73
6. Similarities	.77	.65	9.95	.81
7. Comprehension	.79	.62	6.05	.77
8. Object assembly	.79	.53	6.05	.70
9. Vocabulary	.84	.72	11.45	.86
10. Information	.86	.68	8.30	.85
11. Block design	.90	.63	5.35	.85

Note. Based on data from Jensen (1983, 1985, 1987; Naglieri & Jensen 1987) and Rushton (1989e).

Figure 9.1 shows the regression of black-white differences on the g factor loadings and on the inbreeding depression scores. Clearly, as the g loading and inbreeding depression scores increase, so do the magnitudes of the black-white differences. The racial differences are significantly predicted by the genetic penetrance of each of the subtests. The genetic contribution to racial differences in mental ability is robust across populations, languages, time periods, and measurement specifics.

Adoption Studies

A well-known adoption study of 7-year-old black, interracial, and white children by middle-class white families was conducted by Scarr and Weinberg (1976), with a 10-year follow-up by R. A. Weinberg, Scarr, & Waldman (1992).

Figure 9.1: Regression of Black-White Differences on _g_ Loadings (Panel A) and on Inbreeding Depression Scores (Panel B) Calculated from a Japanese Sample

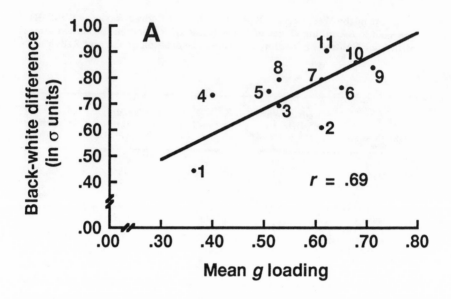

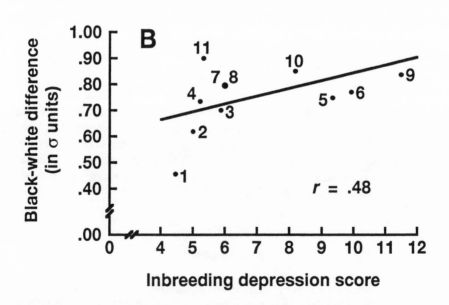

The numbers indicate subtests from the Wechsler Intelligence Scale for Children—Revised: 1 Coding, 2 Arithmetic, 3 Picture completion, 4 Mazes, 5 Picture arrangement, 6 Similarities, 7 Comprehension, 8 Object assembly, 9 Vocabulary, 10 Information, 11 Block design. The results show that the magnitude of the black-white difference in IQ increases with the genetic penetrance of the subtest, either measured indirectly by the _g_ factor, or directly by inbreeding depression.

Designed specifically to separate genetic factors from rearing conditions as causal influences on the poor cognitive performance of black children, Scarr and Weinberg (1976: 726) noted:

> Transracial adoption is the human analog of the cross-fostering design, commonly used in animal behavior genetics research.... There is no question that adoption constitutes a massive intervention.

Presented in the first column of Table 9.2 are some of the results from the study when the children were aged 7. The 29 adopted children whose biological parents were both black achieved a mean IQ of 97; the 68 adopted children with one black and one white biological parent scored 109; the 25 adopted children whose biological parents were both white scored 112; and the 143 white nonadopted children with whom they were raised scored 117. (A mixed group of 21 Asians, North American Indians and Latin American Indians scored 100.)

Also set out in Table 9.2 are some of the follow-up results when the children were aged 17. The 21 adopted children whose biological parents were both black achieved a mean IQ of 89 and an average school aptitude percentile of 42 across four measures; the 55 adopted children with one black and one white biological parent had an IQ of 99 and a school percentile of 53; the 16 adopted children with two white parents had an IQ of 106 and a school percentile of 59; and the 104 nonadopted white children had an IQ of 109 and

TABLE 9.2

Comparison of Black, Mixed-Race, and White Adopted and Biological Children Raised In White Middle-Class Families

Children's background	Age 7 IQ	Age 17 IQ	Age 17 school achievement		Age 17 school aptitude based on national norms (weighted mean of 4 percentiles)
			Grade point average	Class rank	
Adopted, with 2 black biological parents	97	89	2.1	36	42
Adopted, with 1 white, 1 black biological parent	109	99	2.2	40	53
Adopted, with 2 white biological parents	112	106	2.8	54	59
Nonadopted, with 2 white biological parents	117	109	3.0	64	69

Note. Based on data from R.A. Weinberg, Scarr & Waldman (1992).

a school percentile of 69. (The 12 adopted mixed group of Asian/Amerindian children had an IQ of 96 with no data provided of school achievement.)

Expectancy effects, that adoptive parents' beliefs about the child's racial background could influence the child's intellectual development were ruled out, at least at age 7, by the finding that scores from 12 interracial children believed by their adoptive parents to be black/black scored at virtually the same level as interracial children correctly classified by their adoptive parents (Scarr & Weinberg, 1976).

Scarr and Weinberg (1976) and R. A. Weinberg et al. (1992) did not interpret their results with the genetic-racial hypothesis. The poorer performance of the all-black children was attributed to their experience of later and more difficult placements in the adoption process and to the fact that these children had both natural and adoptive parents with somewhat lower educational levels and abilities (two points lower in adoptive parents' IQ). The authors emphasized the beneficial effects of the rearing environment, pointing out that at both age 7 and 17 all groups of adopted children performed above their expected population means. Their analyses frequently combined the two "socially classified black" groups with "other" black children with one parent of unknown, Asian, Indian, or other racial background.

At age 7 this combined interracial group had an IQ of 106 and a mean school achievement percentile across 3 measures of 56, significantly higher than the regional black mean, although not as high as the nonadopted white children with whom they were raised. At age 17, the combined interracial sample had a mean IQ of 97 and a school performance at the 41st percentile, still higher than the regional black mean, but now lower than the regional white mean.

Although in their age 17 breakdowns, R. A. Weinberg et al. (1992: 132) found that "[b]iological mothers' race remained the best single predictor of adopted child's IQ when other variables were controlled," this was largely attributed to "unmeasured social characteristics." Their overall conclusion (p. 133) was that

> the social environment maintains a dominant role in determining the average IQ level of black and interracial children and that both social and genetic variables contribute to individual variations among them.

A more straightforward interpretation of the results consistent with the other data presented in this book, is that blacks have lower mental ability than whites because of their African ancestry. At both age 7 and 17 the adopted children with one black and one white biological parent had an IQ and aptitude percentile intermediate to the adopted children with two black or two white parents. Because school achievement and school aptitude tests are not affected by the potential biases that may have influenced the individual IQ testing, the convergence of results is striking.

It will be interesting to examine the remaining data from Scarr and Weinberg's 10-year follow-up when it is eventually published. Preliminary analyses suggest that the black 17-year-olds display greater amounts of social deviance and psychopathology than do the white 17-year-olds (Scarr, Weinberg, & Gargiulo, 1987).

Two other adoption studies, however, show mixed results, either with no relative deficiency in the IQs of black or mixed-race children when compared to white children or what appear to be effects for the social environment. In the first of these, Eyferth (1961, cited in Loehlin et al., 1975) compared 83 offspring from German mothers and white occupation troops with 181 offspring whose fathers were U.S. blacks or French North Africans. The results showed no overall difference in average IQ between the two groups when tested at about 10 years of age on a German version of the Wechsler Intelligence Scale for Children. In the second, Moore (1986) reported that 23 black children adopted by white middle-class families had a mean IQ of 117 and 23 black children adopted by black middle-class families had a mean IQ of 104. No difference in IQ existed between children with one or two black parents. In neither study was information available on the biological parents, so selective factors could not be ruled out.

Although the Asian/Amerindian children in Scarr and Weinberg's (1976) study showed little evidence of having IQs above the white mean, four studies of Korean children adopted by white families do support the racial hypothesis. In the first, 25 four-year-olds from Vietnam, Korea, Cambodia and Thailand, all adopted into white American homes prior to 3 years of age, excelled in academic ability with a mean IQ score of 120, as opposed to a U.S. national norm of 100 (Clark & Hanisee, 1982). Prior to placement half the babies had required hospitalization for malnutrition.

In the second, Winick, Meyer, and Harris (1975) found 141 Korean children adopted as infants by American families exceeded American children in both IQ and achievement scores when they reached 10 years of age. Many of these Korean infants were malnourished and the interest of the investigators was on the possible effects of early malnutrition on later intelligence. When tested, those who had been severely malnourished as infants obtained a mean IQ of 102; a moderately well nourished group obtained a mean IQ of 106; and an adequately nourished group obtained a mean IQ of 112.

A study by Frydman and Lynn (1989) examined 19 Korean infants adopted by families in Belgium. At about 10 years of age, their mean IQ was 119, the verbal IQ was 111, and the performance IQ was 124. Because the Belgian norms had been established in 1954 and Flynn's (1984) evidence suggested that mean IQs in all economically developed nations had been increasing over time by about 3 IQ points a decade, Lynn corrected the Belgian norms upward to 109. This still left the Korean children with a statistically significant 10 point advantage over indigenous Belgian children. Neither the social class of the adopting parent nor the number of years the child spent in the adopted family had any effect on the child's IQ.

A study by Brooks (1989) examined a group of Korean children raised by white American families. She compared their activity level and temperament with white infants raised in white families and Oriental infants raised in Oriental families. The adopted children scored partway between the other two groups suggesting that both genetic and environmental factors were operative.

Generalizing Heritabilities

A less direct line of reasoning for the heritability of racial group differences is to show that many of the variables on which the populations differ are substantially heritable. Chapter 3 reviewed the behavioral genetic literature on intelligence, rate of maturation, strength of sex drive, altruism, family structure, and law abidingness. Occasionally heritabilities have been calculated for races other than Caucasoids, although their number is small. Thus, for tests of mental ability, data for 543 monozygotic and 134 dizygotic Japanese 12-year-old twins gave correlations of 0.78 and 0.49 respectively, indicating a heritability of 58 percent (R. Lynn & Hattori, 1990). Similarly the genetic and cultural transmission of obesity in black families is similar to that among white families, which led the authors of the study to conclude that the greater obesity in black people is probably mediated genetically (Ness et al., 1991).

By a process of inductive generalization, it is reasonable to estimate the heritability of the differences between groups to be roughly the same as that within groups, or about 50 percent. A formal relation of within-group to between-group heritability was proposed by DeFries (1972), but, to the best of my knowledge, this has not been developed further. However, as the geneticist Theodosius Dobzhansky (1970: Preface) wrote, "does one need nowadays to convince the reader that...differences between subspecies... are mostly genetic?" He was writing about wild animals and plants, but, as natural scientists, how can we afford not to extrapolate this to humans? Many heritabilities have been found to be generalizable across distinct cultural and racial groups, that is, to correlate with the magnitudes of heritabilities calculated in other groups, as well as to predict behavioral phenomena in those groups (Rushton, 1989b; Figure 9.1 and chap. 4).

A standard objection, however, exists to the effect that one cannot apply observations *within* populations to valid comparisons *between* them until such time as we know conclusively that the two populations being compared have been exposed to exactly the same environmental conditions. This argument was made most explicit in an influential article by Bodmer and Cavalli-Sforza (1970) following the controversy generated by Jensen's (1969) classic monograph. Bodmer and Cavalli-Sforza (1970: 29) concluded:

[T]he question of a possible genetic basis for the race I.Q. difference will be almost impossible to answer satisfactorily before the environmental differences between U.S. blacks and whites have been substantially reduced...no good case can be made for such studies on either scientific or practical grounds.

Many have reiterated Bodmer and Cavalli-Sforza's (1970) perspective. Thus, Weizmann, Wiener, Wiesenthal, and Ziegler (1990:4) insisted that "[o]ne cannot generalize heritabilities...a point disputed to our knowledge only by Rushton 1989[b]." Weizmann et al. (1990:5) went on to state that "if substantial changes within a population are due to environmental changes, then similar explanations may also apply to differences between groups." However, it is a narrowly conceived argument to expect environmental relationships to generalize and genetic ones not to. As Maynard-Smith (1978: 150) contended, "it is a good common sense principle that if environmental factors can affect some characteristic, it is likely that genes will do so also."

The animal data shows a degree of genetic generalizability. Similar characters tend to have similar heritabilities. Two extensive literature surveys of this question were conducted by Roff and Mousseau (1987) for drosophila and by Mousseau and Roff (1987) for nondrosophila. Both showed, for example, that morphological traits are consistently more heritable than physiological variables. Such findings have led an important caveat to be added to textbook conclusions: "Whenever a value is stated for the heritability of a given character it must be understood to refer to a particular population under particular conditions.... Nevertheless, within the range of sampling errors, estimates tend to be similar in different populations" (Falconer, 1989: 164).

Regression to the Mean

In the 1970s several "indirect" approaches were proposed to test the genetic explanation of race differences (Loehlin et al., 1975; Scarr, 1981). One was to examine parent-child regression effects, which are predicted to differ for black and white samples if they are drawn from genetically different populations. If the population mean for blacks is 15 IQ points lower than for whites, then the offspring of high-IQ black parents should show more regression toward a lower population mean than the offspring of high-IQ white parents. Similarly, the offspring of low-IQ black parents should show less regression than those of low-IQ white parents.

Although not having parent-child comparisons, Jensen (1973, chapter 4) tested the prediction with even better data, from siblings. Sibling comparisons provide a better test than parent-offspring comparisons because siblings share more similar environments than do parents and offspring. Jensen found that black and white children matched for IQ have siblings who regress approximately halfway to their respective population means rather than to the mean of the combined populations.

For example, if black and white children are matched with IQs of 120, the black siblings will average close to 100 and the white siblings close to 110. A reverse effect is found with children matched at the lower end of the IQ scale. If black and white children are matched for IQs of 70, the black siblings will average about 78 and the white siblings about 85. The regression line shows no significant departure from linearity throughout the range of IQ from 50 to 150. As Jensen (1973) pointed out, this amount of regression directly fits a genetic model and not an environmental one. The same effect occurs for height, or number of fingerprint ridges, or any other polygenically inherited characteristic.

Jensen (1974) provided additional results explained by a genetic-regression hypothesis. Black and white parents matched for high socioeconomic status produce children with different levels of IQ. Upper-status black children average two to four IQ points below lower-status white children, despite the environmental advantage and even though it is likely that the upper-status black parents were of higher IQ than the lower-status white parents. The regression-to-the-mean phenomenon could account for the cross-over of the average IQs of the children from the two racial groups.

Between versus Within Family Effects

Other adoption and twin designs show that the environmental variables influencing behavior are primarily those that occur within families rather than between them (Plomin & Daniels, 1987). This is one of the more important discoveries made using behavior genetic procedures; it appears to hold even for variables such as altruism, obesity, and law abidingness, which parents are thought to strongly socialize. One implication of this finding is that because the variables usually proposed to explain racial differences, such as social class, religious beliefs, cultural practices, father absence, and parenting styles account for so little variance *within* a race, they are unlikely to account for the differences *among* races.

Using similar reasoning, Jensen (1980b) described how data from siblings could be used to determine whether relationships between variables are caused by factors "extrinsic" to the family, such as social class. Such factors serve to make family members similar to one another and different from people in other families. Strong social class effects can be presumed operative, therefore, if the covariance structures that emerge from between-family data disappear when using "intrinsic" within-family data. If the covariance structures remain constant regardless of whether they are calculated on the basis of within-family or between-family data, then social class effects must be less operative, and genetic and within-family effects more operative. Research shows that the general factor of intelligence, *g,* is constant across all three major racial groups from both within-family and between-family analyses (Jensen,

1987a; Nagoshi, Phillips, & Johnson, 1987). The implication is that the differences in *g* found between races are primarily due to within-family effects, such as genetics, rather than to between-family effects such as socioeconomic background.

Additional evidence for the within-family, intrinsic nature of *g* comes from data on the head size-IQ correlation (chap. 2). Jensen and Johnson (in press) showed a significant positive correlation between head size and IQ in both black and white, male and female samples of 4- and 7-year-olds. In all cases, the sibling with the larger head perimeter tends to be the more intelligent sibling.

Race versus Social Class

One challenge for purely environmental theories is to explain upward and downward within-family mobility. For example, Weinrich (1977) reviewed data showing that those adolescents moving from one SES level to another showed the sexual patterns of their *to be acquired* class, not the class they were raised in by their parents. More recent research confirms the importance of within-family variation with some siblings more often adopting the syndrome of early sexuality, delinquency, and low educational attainment than others (Rowe, Rodgers, Meseck-Bushey, & St. John, 1989).

Within-family social mobility has been known for some time in the IQ literature. In one study Waller (1971) obtained the IQ scores of 130 fathers and their 172 adult sons, all of whom had been routinely tested during their high school year in Minnesota. The IQs ranged from below 80 to above 130 and were related to social class. Children with lower IQs than their fathers went down in social class as adults, and those with higher IQs went up (r = 0.37 between difference in father-son social class and difference in father-son IQ). Such intergenerational social mobility has subsequently been confirmed (Mascie-Taylor & Gibson, 1978).

Socioeconomic effects often appear to confound those of race because, as will be discussed in chapter 13, lower socioeconomic groups more often engage in *r*-strategies than do higher socioeconomic groups. Dizygotic twinning (the *r*-strategy) is greater among lower than upper socioeconomic women in both European and African samples, as are differences in family size, intelligence, law abidingness, health, longevity, and sexuality. The question then arises as to whether social class or race is more predictive of behavior.

With brain size, in the stratified random sample of 6,325 military personnel (Rushton, 1992a), the 18 cm^3 (1 percent) difference in rank between officers and enlisted personnel was smaller than either the 21 cm^3 (1.5 percent) difference between Caucasoids and Negroids, or the 36 cm^3 (2.6 percent) difference between Mongoloids and Caucasoids. Other data (summarized in Table 6.6) suggests a 4 to 6 percent Negroid-Caucasoid difference and a 1 to 2.8

percent Mongoloid-Caucasoid difference in brain size. Race may be the more important variable.

In the study just referred to on regression effects, Jensen (1974) found that black children from high socioeconomic status homes scored lower on IQ tests than white children from low socioeconomic homes. The study examined virtually all the white (N = 1,489) and black (n = 1,123) children enrolled in regular classes of the fourth, fifth, and sixth grades of the Berkeley elementary school district in California. The black children's parents were high-level administrators, supervisors, college teachers, and professionals; the white children's parents were manual and unskilled workers. The racial differences showed up on both the verbal and the nonverbal parts of the nationally standardized Thorndike-Lorge Intelligence Test.

In a similar study of the Scholastic Aptitude Test, the results from 1984 showed that the median scores of black college applicants from families earning over $50,000 were lower than those of whites from families earning less than $6,000. The scores were monotonically related to income within both races (R. A. Gordon, 1987a). Race was more powerful than income in determining test scores.

Although it is well known that test scores are correlated with socioeconomic status within racial groups, this does not, in fact, explain black-white ability differences. The pattern of black-white differences is different in factorial composition from the pattern of social class differences within the black and the white groups (Jensen & Reynolds, 1982). For example, the SES differences tend to be largest on tests of verbal ability rather than on tests of spatial visualization. This is just the opposite of the pattern of black-white differences on verbal and spatial tests.

To examine race versus social class differences in sexual behavior, Rushton and Bogaert (1988) contrasted noncollege-educated whites with college-educated blacks. Table 8.4 shows the results. Noncollege-educated whites were more restrained than college-educated blacks on such measures as speed of occurrence of premarital, marital, and extramarital experiences, number of partners, frequency of intercourse, speed and incidence of pregnancy, and length of the menstrual cycle, although they were not as restrained as the college-educated whites. The black sample, consisting of university students from 1938 to 1963 was atypical in the direction of being religiously devout and of high socioeconomic status.

The race/social class findings of Rushton and Bogaert (1988) depicted in Table 8.4 were independently replicated with additional samples by M. S. Weinberg and Williams (1988). These authors reanalyzed evidence from three independent sources: the original Kinsey data, which formed the basis of Rushton and Bogaert's studies; a 1970 National Opinion Research Center poll of sexual attitudes; and a study carried out in San Francisco. All three reanalyses showed the predicted racial effects on sexuality while holding education and social class constant. Moreover, with dizygotic twinning, while both race and social class are predictive, race is the source of the larger portion of variance (Rushton, 1987b).

In other domains, too, race has been found to have strong effects independent of class. With psychological illness, Kessler and Neighbors (1986) used cross-validation on eight different surveys encompassing more than 20,000 respondents to demonstrate an interaction between race and class such that the true effect of race was suppressed and the true effect of social class was magnified in models that failed to take the interaction into consideration.

With crime, figures show that even at the time when they were lower in socioeconomic status, the Chinese in the United States were more law abiding than the Caucasoids. In the 1920s this led American criminologists to consider the ghetto as a place that protected members from the disruptive tendencies of the outside society (J. Q. Wilson & Herrnstein, 1985).

Gene-Culture Coevolution

Why is there such a strong correlation between poor social and economic conditions, low intelligence, and high social pathologies such as crime? Environmentalists have argued that the Negroid peoples in Africa, the Caribbean, the United States, and Britain all live in socially and economically impoverished backgrounds, as compared with Caucasoids and Mongoloids, and that these conditions are responsible for some or perhaps all of their low intelligence. R. Lynn (1991c) met this argument with the concept of genotype-environment correlation introduced in chapter 3.

Theorists have proposed that, particularly after puberty, an increasingly active organism is capable of shaping its own environment in a direction canalized by its underlying genotype. Scarr and McCartney (1983) call this "niche building," and the two races most successful in building socially and economically developed niches in which to live and rear their children have been the Caucasoids and the Mongoloids.

The argument that poor social and economic conditions are responsible for the lower intelligence of the Negroids places the cart before the horse. It assumes that the impoverished environments are simply the result of external circumstances over which people have no control. Such a claim does not stand up to examination. There are too many cases that it does not explain, such as the achievements of immigrants to the United States from the Pacific Rim and to Britain and South Africa from the Indian subcontinent.

Genetic theories help to explain why some people have succeeded where others, initially more advantageously placed, have failed in the same way that they explain upward and downward mobility effects among siblings within a family. Some have the right genotypes for building socially and economically prosperous environments for themselves and their families. Within the constraints allowed by the total spectrum of cultural alternatives, people create environments maximally compatible with their genotypes (Rushton et al., 1986).

10

Life-History Theory

Explaining the total array of international evidence summarized in Table 1.1 necessitates a more powerful theory than would be required to explain any single dimension from the set. It also requires going beyond the particulars of any one country. Mongoloids and Caucasoids have the largest brains, whether indexed by weight at autopsy, endocranial volume, or externally measured head circumference, but they have the slowest rate of dental development, indexed by onset of permanent molar teeth, and they produce the fewest gametes, indexed by double ovulation and frequency of twin birthing. I proposed that the explanation for the racial pattern lay in primate life-history theory.

Evolutionary biologists assume that each species (or subspecies, such as a race) has evolved a characteristic life history adapted to the particular ecological problems encountered by its ancestors (E. O. Wilson, 1975). A life history is a genetically organized suite of characters that evolved in a coordinated manner so as to allocate energy to survival, growth, and reproduction. These strategies may be organized along a scale.

At one end of this scale are "r-strategies" that emphasize gamete production, mating behavior, and high reproductive rates and, at the other, "K-strategies" that emphasize high levels of parental care, resource acquisition, kin provisioning, and social complexity. The K-strategy requires more complex nervous systems and larger brains. Johanson and Edey (1981: 326) succinctly summarized, quoting Owen Lovejoy: "More brains, fewer eggs, more 'K'."

The thesis to be advanced in this and the next chapter is that archaic versions of what were to become the modern Caucasoid and Mongoloid peoples dispersed out of Africa about 100,000 years ago and adapted to the problem of survival in predictably cold environments. This evolutionary process required a bioenergetic tradeoff that increased brain size and parenting behavior ("K") at the expense of egg production and sexual behavior ("r"). In other words, Mongoloids are more K-selected than Caucasoids, who in turn are more K-selected than Negroids.

Reproductive Strategies

Life cycle traits and their variations began to receive increasing study after a paper by Cole (1954) questioned why some species engaged in the extreme reproductive strategy of semelparity, expending all energy in a burst of reproductive effort and dying shortly thereafter, while other species engaged in iteroparity, reproducing at regular intervals over the life span. Since then much additional information on life histories has been amassed.

The fundamental axiom of sociobiology is that an organism is just a gene's way of making another gene (Dawkins, 1976; E. O. Wilson, 1975). Because certain gene combinations will be reproductively more successful than others in a particular environment, they will increase in relative number in the population. An organism's body and behavior are mechanisms by which genes maintain and replicate themselves more efficiently.

Sometimes it is advantageous for genes to build large bodies in which to live, while at other times small bodies are more effective. Large bodies take longer to build at each developmental stage and the cycle from one generation to the next becomes extended along with increased life span (Figure 10.1). Larger bodies also lead to lowered reproductive capacities due to increased interbirth intervals and lower average litter sizes. With fewer offspring comes increased parental care and social organizational skills and a concomitant increase in brain size. Life-history variables tend to be selected together.

r-K Reproductive Strategies

A whole new canon of theory came into being with MacArthur and Wilson's (1967) r-K analysis of how species colonize islands and become equilibriated. Their models emphasized birth rates, death rates, and population size. The symbol r stands for the maximum rate of increase in a population and is aided by prolific breeding; K is a symbol for the carrying capacity of the environment, or the largest number of organisms of a particular species that can be maintained indefinitely in a given part of the environment.

Thus, there are two alternative strategies by which to produce offspring. At one extreme organisms can produce a very large number of offspring but give little parental care to any of them. This is the r-strategy. At the other extreme organisms can produce very few offspring, but lavish intensive parental care and protection on each. This is the K-strategy. Thus, the symbols r and K have been used to designate two ends of a hypothetical continuum involving trade-offs between offspring production and parental care (Figure 10.2).

Shortly after MacArthur and Wilson (1967) formulated their r-K analysis, Pianka (1970) codified a number of life-cycle traits thought to be selected for, and to covary with, the r- and K- reproductive strategies. These are summarized in Table 10.1. While each of the traits might independently contribute to

Figure 10.1: Length of an Organism Plotted Logarithmically Against Age of First Reproduction

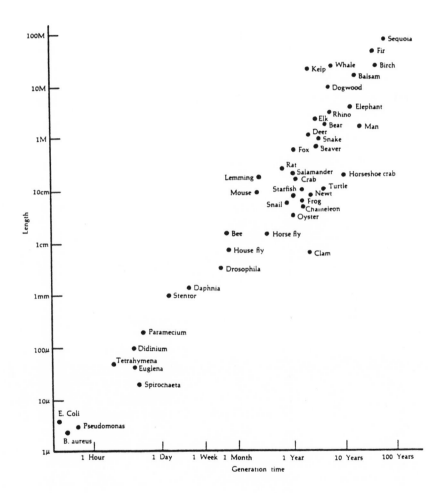

In general, smaller organisms have a shorter period of development, partly because they are simpler to build. At the other extreme, giant sequoia trees do not reproduce until they are 80 meters tall, which takes 60 years to achieve. Putting energy resources into reproductive structures is something a sapling can ill afford when it is struggling desperately to grow more rapidly than other rival saplings. Only the fastest growers will win in the competition for sun, and any plant that diverts its precious resources toward cones or flowers and seeds may lose. From Bonner (1965, p. 17, Figure 1). Copyright 1965 by Princeton University Press. Reprinted with permission.

Figure 10.2: The *r-K* Continuum of Reproductive Strategies Balancing Egg Output with Parent Care

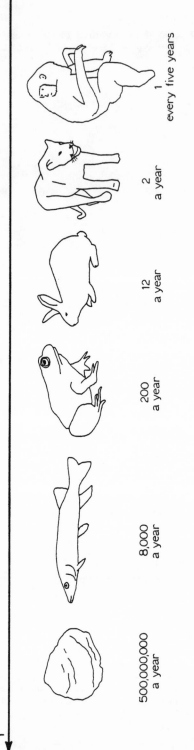

Shown on this macro-scale, oysters producing 500 million eggs a year but providing no care exemplify the *r*-strategy. The great apes, producing one infant every five or six years and providing extensive care, exemplify the *K*-strategy. After Johanson & Edey (1981).

TABLE 10.1

Some Life-History Differences Between *r* and *K* Strategists

r-strategist	*K*-strategist
Family characteristics	
Large litter size	Small litter size
Short birth spacing	Long birth spacing
Many offspring	Few offspring
High infant mortality	Low infant mortality
Little parental care	Much parental care
Individual characteristics	
Rapid maturation	Slow maturation
Early sexual reproduction	Delayed sexual reproduction
Short life	Long life
High reproductive effort	Low reproductive effort
High energy utilization	Efficient energy utilization
Low encephalization	High encephalization
Population characteristics	
Opportunistic exploiters	Consistent exploiters
Dispersing colonizers	Stable occupiers
Variable population size	Stable population size
Lax competition	Keen competition
Social system characteristics	
Low social organization	High social organization
Low altruism	High altruism

Note. Modified from Pianka (1970, p. 593, Table 1), E. O. Wilson (1975, p. 101, Table 4-2), Eisenberg (1981, p. 442, Figure 156), and Barash (1982, p. 307, Table 13.1).

fitness, the important point is that they are expected to correlate with and select for other features of the life history (E. O. Wilson, 1975). These have been codified by a number of workers (see Barash, 1982: 307; Daly & Wilson, 1983: 201; Eisenberg, 1981: 438ff; Pianka, 1970: 593; E. O. Wilson, 1975: 101).

From Table 10.1, it can be seen that, in terms of *family characteristics*, r- and K-strategists differ in terms of litter size (number of offspring produced at one time), birth spacing, total number of offspring, rate of infant mortality, and degree of parental care. In regard to *individual characteristics*, r- and K- strategists differ in rate of physical maturation, sexual precocity, life span, body size, reproductive effort, energy use, and brain size. In terms of *population and social system characteristics*, they differ in their treatment of the environment, their tendency to geographically disperse, the stability of their population size, their ability to compete under scarce resources, their degree of social organization, and their altruism.

Species are, of course, only relatively r and K. Thus, rabbits are K-strategists compared to fish but r-strategists compared to primates. Primates are all relatively K-strategists, and humans may be the most K of all. But primates vary enormously. Following Harvey and Clutton-Brock (1985, Table 1) the following figures are provided for nonhuman primate species (with those for *Homo sapiens* in parentheses). Gestation lengths range from 60 to 250 days (267); birth weight from less than 10 to over 2000 g (3300 g); litter size typically is 1, but twinning is very common in some species (1); weaning age from less than 50 to over 1500 days (720); female age at first breeding from less than 1 to over 9 years (>10); adult brain weight from less than 10 to over 500 g (1250); and longevity from less than 10 to over 40 years (70). Most of the life-history measures are positively correlated, although the relationships are not perfect.

The life phases and gestation times of primates display a natural scale of prolongation going from lemur to macaque to gibbon to chimp to early humans to modern humans (see Figure 10.3), with a consistent trend toward K (Schultz, 1960; Lovejoy, 1981). For example, a female gorilla will have her first pregnancy at about 10 years of age and can expect to live to the age of 40. A female mouse lemur, at the other end of the primate scale, produces her first offspring at 9 months of age and has a life expectancy of 15 years. A mouse lemur may mature, have offspring, and die before a gorilla has her first offspring.

Note the suggestion in Figure 10.3 (from Schultz, 1960) that earlier human ancestors lived on a shorter time scale than present-day humans. Also note the proportionality of the four indicated phases. The postreproductive phase is restricted to humans. With each step in the natural scale, populations devote a greater proportion of their reproductive energy to subadult care, with increased investment in the survival of offspring. As a species, humans are at the K end of the continuum.

Figure 10.3: Progressive Prolongation of Life Phases and Gestation in Primates

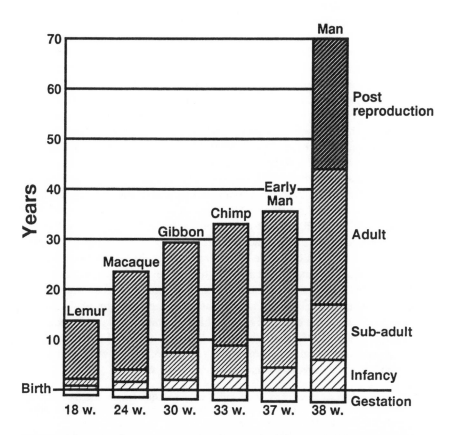

Note the proportionality of the indicated phases. With each step in the natural scale, populations devote a greater proportion of their reproductive energy to subadult care, with increased investment in the survival of offspring. The post-reproductive phase is restricted to humans. After Schultz (1960) and Lovejoy (1981).

Even tooth development accurately reflects primate life histories. B. H. Smith (1989) correlated the age of eruption of the first molar with the life-history factors tabulated by Harvey and Clutton-Brock (1985). First molars are the earliest permanent teeth to erupt in primates and in many other mammals and they are stable in many aspects of their growth. Smith found that across 21 primate species, age of eruption of first molar correlated 0.89, 0.85, 0.93, 0.82, 0.86, and 0.85 with the life-history variables of body weight, length of gestation, age of weaning, birth interval, sexual maturity, and life span. The highest correlation was 0.98 with brain size.

Brain size, even more than body size, is the key factor, acting as the biological constant determining many variables. These include the upper limit on the size of the group cohesively maintained through time (Dunbar, 1992). It also includes other variables like speed of physical maturation, degree of infant dependency, and maximum recorded life span (Harvey & Krebs, 1990; Hofman, 1993).

The hominid brain has tripled in size over the last 4 million years. *Australopithecenes* averaged about 500 cm³, the size of a chimpanzee. *Homo habilis* averaged about 800 cm³, *Homo erectus* about 1,000 cm³, and modern *Homo sapiens* about 1,400 cm³. If the encephalization quotient, the expected brain ratio given a certain body size, is plotted over the same evolutionary time frame, the increase is proportionately less, although still substantial: 3.0 to 6.9 (Jerison, 1973; Passingham, 1982). On the most recent calculations, the figures go from 2.4 to 5.8 (McHenry, 1992).

Metabolically the brain is a very expensive organ. Representing only 2 percent of body mass, the brain uses about 5 percent of the body's basal metabolic rate in cats and dogs, about 10 percent in rhesus monkeys and other primates, and about 20 percent in humans. Across primates large brains are also expensive in life-history trade-offs, requiring a more stable environment, a longer gestation, a slower rate of maturation, a higher offspring survival, a lower reproductive output, and a longer life (Pagel & Harvey, 1988; Harvey & Krebs, 1990). Unless large brains substantially contributed to fitness, therefore, they would not have evolved. Increasing encephalization likely adds fitness by increasing the efficiency with which information is processed.

Bonner (1980, 1988) hierarchically arranged the facts of animal behavior and the evolution of culture according to a continuous increase in brain size or complexity of the nervous system. Bonner (1980) wrote:

> There is a direct inverse correlation with the time of appearance of a group in earth history and the size of its brain. At one end of the spectrum fish have small brains, while at the other end mammals have the largest. This suggests a trend toward increase in the ability to learn, toward an increase in the flexibility of the response.

One influential scheme proposed to account for the evolution of *r*- and *K*-strategies is *r*- and *K*-selection (E. O. Wilson, 1975). The symbols *r* and *K* originate in the mathematics of population biology: *r* refers to the natural *rate of increase* in a population temporarily freed from resource limitations. In *r*-selected species, the population is usually kept at a low density by unpredictable features of the environment such as the weather, or predators. Under such circumstances a selective advantage is hypothesized to accrue to speedy, prolific breeders who maximally replicate their genes before conditions change and their lives are ended. On the other hand, *K* refers to the *carrying capacity* of a particular habitat, or the maximum population a species can maintain under certain fixed conditions. In *K*-selected species, the population is usually at a high density and competitive interactions among individuals are expected to be important. Selection, therefore, is hypothesized to favor large individuals with high competitive ability who produce small numbers of intensely cared for offspring rather than engage in high reproductive output. K-strategies are thought to evolve in predictable environments.

Consider the animals and plants depicted on the continuum in Figure 10.1 from the perspective of r-K theory. The smallest bacteria are archetypal r-strategists, having a maximally intense rate of reproduction and an enormously fluctuating population size as the environment alternates. The largest mammals and trees, on the other hand, because they are so large, prevail over many environmental perturbations and their populations remain steady over time.

Criticisms of and refinements to the MacArthur and Wilson (1967) and Pianka (1970) formulations began immediately. While some claimed that Pianka's extension was an inappropriate overgeneralization (Stearns, 1977; Boyce, 1984), others found it useful, including E. O. Wilson (1975), the co-founder of the r-K perspective. Some argued that r- and K-strategies are not properly organized as bipolar ends of a continuum but, rather, describe orthogonal axes in a multidimensional space where additional strategies also operate (e.g., alpha-strategies, based on extreme competitiveness). "Bet-hedging" theory and other possibilities were also proposed as alternative explanations for patterns in life-history variation (Boyce, 1984; Stearns, 1984).

At the empirical level, deviations occur from the positive correlations expected. A negative correlation between body size and parental care, for example, has been found in a variety of marine taxa. Despite such anomalies, however, the r-K continuum usefully organized information on life-history traits. As Dawkins (1982: 293) wrote: "Ecologists enjoy a curious love/hate relationship with the r-K concept, often pretending to disapprove of it while finding it indispensible."

r-K Strategies Within Species

Sociobiologists focus primarily on the evolutionary origins of between-species differences. Yet the theory of evolution also requires that there be a genetic basis to within-species differences. Several studies suggest that the r-K continuum applies within species.

Gadgil and Solbrig (1972) examined within species differences in plants, specifically in the common weedy dandelion *Taraxacum officinale sensu latu*. They measured an important characteristic of r and K, the proportion of resources devoted to reproductive tissues. These individual differences were examined under a variety of growth chamber, greenhouse, and experimental field conditions. Among populations of naturally occurring dandelions it was found that those biotypes growing on lawns more frequently walked on, mowed, or otherwise unpredictably disturbed (i.e., subjected to r-selection) had, as expected, a higher seed output and a higher proportion of biomass devoted to reproduction than those dandelions growing in less disturbed areas. When the plants were subsequently grown from seed under greenhouse experimental conditions using a variety of temperatures and soils, it was demonstrated that the differences were genetically fixed. Whereas the *r*-selected biotypes allocated more resources to the production of seeds and reached reproductive maturity faster (they bloomed a year earlier), the more *K*-selected biotypes allocated resources to leaf biomass at the expense of seed production, thus gaining a direct competitive advantage in conditions of higher density through their capacity to shade out the *r*-types.

In a five-year examination of the fluctuating population cycles of field mice, demographic changes were demonstrated to be related to genetic markers predictive of *r*- and *K*-behaviors (Krebs, Gaines, Keller, Myers, & Tamarin, 1973). Examining two species of *Microtus* (*M. pennsylvanius* and *M. orchragaster*) through a combination of naturalistic observation, fencing experiments, dispersal studies, and polymorphic serum protein analysis, the authors showed that the genotype most responsible for speedy population growth tended to be the earliest breeders and most dispersing when population density was high (*r*-strategists). The segment of the population that remained behind were individuals selected for competitive spacing behavior under high population density (*K*-strategists).

In a study on fish, five populations of American shad (*Alosa sapidissima*) were observed at different latitudes on the Atlantic coast (Leggett & Carscadden, 1978). Reproductive strategies were found to vary: Northern populations, spawning in environments that are thermally harsh but predictably variable, allocate a greater proportion of their energy reserves to migration, thereby ensuring higher post-spawning survival. This was accomplished by reducing energy allocated to gonads. These *K*-shad were larger, older at maturity, more iteroparus (repeat spawners), and less fecund (producing three to five times fewer eggs), than the semelparous (dying after reproduction) *r*-shad.

In a selective breeding experiment, Taylor and Condra (1980) chose *Drosophila pseudoobscura* (flies) either for rapid development in an uncrowded environment and early oviposition of many eggs (*r*-selection), or for the ability to withstand crowding and intense competition for food (*K*-selection). After 10 months and approximately 17 generations, significant differences were found in chromosome frequencies, egg-adult development rates (*r*-selected lines developed one day faster than *K*-selected ones), survivorship (as preadults, *K*-selected flies were 14 percent to 22 percent more viable than *r*-selected flies), and longevity. Contrary to prediction, however, no differences were observed in body size, overall fecundity, or carrying capacity (population size).

In another breeding experiment, Hegmann and Dingle (1982) examined a set of life-history variables in the milkweed bug, *Oncopeltus fasciatus*. They indexed body size, age at first reproduction, number of eggs per clutch, interclutch interval, and developmental time to adulthood. To estimate the additive genetic variance for each of these characteristics and the additive genetic covariances among them, they employed half-sibling comparisons. The results indicated that each of the individual traits was heritable, and moreover, because significant genetic covariances were found among traits, that selection for any one trait in the set was likely to lead to selection for the others.

In an eleven-year study of differences in the guppy (*Poecilia reticulata*), genetic changes in life histories were shown over 30 to 60 generations (Reznik, Bryga, & Endler, 1990). Earlier maturing fish allocated a greater proportion of the body mass to reproduction (embryo weight/total body weight) and produced more and smaller offspring per brood, while late maturing fish produced a smaller number of larger offspring. Using experimental procedures and the transplanting of populations to a common environment, the differences were shown to be heritable. Other evidence for within-species variation in life histories was found with snow geese by Lessells, Cooke, and Rockwell (1989) and with ground squirrels by Zammuto and Millar (1985), among others.

K and Hominid Life Histories

Two hundred and fifty million years ago, the mammalian grade was reached by descendants of reptiles. Subsequent mammalian evolution was explained from an *r-K* perspective by Eisenberg (1981). Competition over resources selected for longer lives, smaller litters, and trends toward iteroparity, which, if the resource base then varied predictably within years, selected for an increased percentage of life span spent in social learning. The increased need for social learning selected for higher encephalization, a longer gestation, and continuing growth after birth. Larger brains in turn led to delayed sexual maturation and the creation of a complex interdependent social grouping with high degrees of altruism. The first primitive primates emerged 70 million years ago, in the form of shrewlike creatures. Twenty-five million years ago, primates were well established and the higher primates had split into three types: the New World monkeys, the Old World monkeys, and the apes. By 5 billion years ago, the human evolutionary line had diverged from the African apes (chimpanzees and gorillas).

Approximately 4 million years ago, several species of *Australopithecus*, apelike hominids, walked upright in regions of East Africa with small brains not much larger than those of apes (about 500 cm^3) and large canine teeth. There is disagreement on what the life history and family structure of the australopithecenes was like. Strong sexual dimorphism suggests these earliest hominids were more apelike than humanlike in their sexual behavior, with males physically fighting each other for estrous females (Leakey & Lewin, 1992). Some australopithecenes, however, may already have begun to differentiate from apes employing something more akin to humanlike pair-bonding, family structure, and social organization (Johanson & O'Farrell, 1990). In this scenario, by walking erect, males had their hands free to carry food back to their families. This would have enabled the simultaneous raising of more offspring than could be managed by other primates. It required a move toward pair-bonding so that the food the males brought back was being used by their own genetic offspring (Lovejoy, 1981; Johanson & Edey, 1981).

After 2.3 million years ago, the australopithecenes were joined on the East African savanna by *Homo habilis,* a more advanced hominid with a larger brain, a higher and rounder head, and a less protruding face. These were the first representatives of the genus *Homo* and their name, "handy man," follows the opposable thumbs that enabled them to grip and manipulate fine objects and make stone tools. Their hands, more curved than those of modern people, were still adapted for grasping and climbing trees. They probably ate a broad-based diet and lived in a food-sharing social group of some 20 or 30 individuals, males and females, young and sexually mature.

Almost 2 million years ago, *Homo erectus* emerged in Africa, fully adapted to an upright posture and standing taller than their predecessors. The males were about 180 cm (5'9") and the females about 160 cm (5'3") (McHenry, 1992). Their hands were capable of precision gripping and many kinds of tool making. Their skulls were also larger, with a brain of about 1,000 cm^3. However, they still had a receding forehead, big front teeth, huge brow ridges over the eyes, and extremely thick neck muscles.

H. erectus probably lived in small bands of perhaps 100 members, most of whom were genetically related. Time was spent hunting and gathering along the banks of streams or on the shores of lakes. Weapons and implements were made from bone and stone. Fire was discovered, enabling movement from open encampments to caves. Able to keep warm, *erectus* started to migrate throughout Eurasia, perhaps as long as 1.8 million years ago. In Europe and Western Asia, Neanderthals evolved. Neanderthals developed clothing, constructed simple winter shelters, stored food, and buried their dead. They had brain volumes comparable to early *H. sapiens* and may have shared a similar stone age technology in regions of the Middle East as recently as 50,000 years ago.

H. erectus was likely a hunter practicing cannibalism and head hunting. Meat from the hunt, however, would have formed only a small part of the diet. Other edible forms of life were snakes, birds and their eggs, and mice and other rodents. Many of these even children might have caught, as with present-day hunters like the Kalahari Bushmen and the Australian aborigines. Vegetable food was a particularly large part of the diet in the form of fleshy leaves, fruits, nuts, and roots.

H. erectus may not have used language as fully as modern humans (Milo & Quiatt, 1993). Neanderthal vocal anatomy seems to have precluded them from generating the full range of human speech sounds (Lieberman, 1991). The less advanced linguistic and cognitive skills of *H. erectus* may eventually have given modern humans an evolutionary advantage in communicating and in competing for food. Neanderthals no longer existed after 32,000 B.P.

Because *H. erectus* used weapons and was a prey-killing animal, some theorists have speculated that they were "killer-apes," engaging in murder and warfare. This view was popularized most by Robert Ardrey (1961: 31) in his book, *African Genesis*. Ardrey wrote:

> Man emerged from the anthropoid background for one reason only: because he was a killer. Long ago, perhaps many millions of years ago, a line of killer apes branched off from the nonaggressive primate background. For reasons of predatory necessity the line advanced. We learned to stand erect in the first place as a necessity of the hunting life. We learned to run in our pursuit of game across the yellowing African savannah...

> A rock, a stick, a heavy stone—to our ancestral killer ape it meant the margin of survival. But the use of the weapon meant new and multiplying demands on the nervous system for the coordination of muscle and touch and sight. And so at last came the enlarged brain; so at last came man.

> Far from the truth lay the antique assumption that man had fathered the weapon. *The weapon, instead, had fathered man.* (Emphasis added)

If killing, through hunting or battle, did provide some of the impetus for humans' evolution to a bipedal erect gait and larger brain, then the ability and desire to wield clubs certainly was not sufficient. As important was the necessity to learn to cooperate and work as a group. Humans were not only hunters. They also were hunter-*gatherers* with up to two-thirds of their diet being plant foods.

With increasing complexity of social organization would have come the social rules necessary to keep the individual's personal drives and emotions concerning jealousy, fear, sex, and aggression under control. Language developed to enhance cooperation. Thus, humans became religious, loyal, and altruistic to the group, and capable of abstract theorizing about their nature and the society of which they were part. Altruism and society both arose out of evolutionary necessity, as much as did any killer instincts.

Human nature, therefore, even at the level of *Homo erectus*, is far more complex and positive than that suggested by such terms as *killer ape*. Even if killing does turn out to have been one of humans' evolutionary pacemakers, there can be little doubt that cooperation and altruism toward group members was another. A tendency toward hostility to and suspicion of outgroups, and loyalty and identification to ingroups appears to be the fuller story of this earlier development.

Lovejoy (1981) provided a more complete scenario of how *K*-selection led the evolving hominid line to develop the unique reproductive and other characteristics that separated it from apes, including bipedality, reduced anterior dentition, a large neocortex, and material culture. Although the K-strategy of adaptation is a general mammalian trait, and well developed among the primates, Lovejoy argued that hominids diverged from pongids through an adaptive strategy that involved the r-selected trait of a shorter period between births.

Because K-selection normally increases the length of time between births, a species adopting an extreme K-strategy may risk extinction. Great apes, for example, produce only one infant every five or six years, a dangerously low reproductive rate for ensuring survival. To produce a greater number of offspring while otherwise increasing a K-strategy, Lovejoy (1981) proposed that early hominids made a move to pair-bonding. This set in motion a series of feedback loops. Pair-bonding resulted in females and infants being provided with food by males, which resulted in females not having to be so mobile, which resulted in females being able to raise more children at a time. This required males to carry food back to their families, which required a bipedal gait to free the hands for carrying, which required pair-bonding so that the food the males brought back was used by their own genetic offspring. Pair-bonding may also have resulted in a reduction in male-male competition for mates, thus making cooperation and wider social bonding possible.

Lovejoy's (1981) ideas challenged the consensus of opinion, ever since Darwin, that bipedality and a large neocortex arose out of tool use and hunting. The hominid fossils found in Ethiopia and attributed to *Australopithecus,* together with the 4 million-year-old footprint discovered at Laeotali in Tanzania, made the hunting hypothesis unlikely. Study of the crania and pelvis suggested that bipedality had arisen while the brain size was no larger than a modern chimpanzee, about 2 million years before the widespread use of material culture (Johanson & Edey, 1981).

Because tooth development accurately reflects extant primate life histories, it can be used to give insight into extinct hominids known only through the fossil record. B. H. Smith (1989) generated predictions for age of first molar eruption and life span. She divided the resultant life-history patterns into three grades. The first, a "chimpanzee grade" she applied to australopithecenes. Here the data suggested a little over three years for the first molar eruption, and a life span of about 40. Next, an *"erectus* grade" included *Homo habilis* and early *Homo erectus,* with figures of 4.6 years for first molar and 52 years for life span. Finally, modern humans constituted a third grade along with later *erectus* and Neanderthals in which first molar eruptions took place at 5.9 years and life span was 66 years.

Falk (1992) and Leakey and Lewin (1992), among others, hold that other dental research confirms that the australopithecenes were more apelike than humanlike. This was suggested by the pattern of development. In apes, the canine erupts after the second molar whereas in humans, it precedes it. Apes and humans also differ in the relation between the development of the anterior and posterior teeth. Research using computerized tomography (CAT scans) to produce three-dimensional X-ray pictures of fossil skulls suggested that the australopithecenes were bipedal apes, with apelike life histories and apelike facial and dental developments. Nonetheless some hominid-like features existed, including the lack of a gap between the canine and premolar teeth and the overall shape of the brain.

To reiterate, by a series of adaptations, large brained modern humans have become the most K of all the primates. As shown in Figure 10.3, there is a consistent trend toward prolonged life span, prolonged gestation, single births, successively longer periods between pregnancies, and developmental delay. With each step in the natural scale, populations devote a greater proportion of their reproductive energy to subadult care, with increased investment in the survival of fewer offspring.

The possible family life and social organization of *Homo* was further described by R. L. Smith (1984). He suggested that 1 to 2 million years ago, the degree of male bonding and female promiscuity may have been more similar to chimpanzees. In such a situation, where ejaculates from more than one male occur in the vicinity of ova, sperm competition leads to enlarged penises and testes to make deeper and more voluminous ejaculations possible. With increased weaponry and individual male command of food resources, female promiscuity would be supplemented by temporary courtship, which would be adaptive for females in leading to more paternal investment in offspring, and for males in leading to greater paternity confidence. Evolutionary competition among females may have led to continuous female attractiveness, with perennial pendulous breasts, ongoing sexual receptivity, and hidden ovulation. Competition among males may have selected for increased capacity to provide resources and paternal investment. Slowly a move occurred toward pair-bonding.

The further consequences of human pair-bonding were described by Lovejoy (1981). With greater pair-bonding, fewer male-male agonistic interactions need occur in competition for mates. With the decreased emphasis on sexual competitiveness would come a reduction in the need for anterior dentition, heavy musculature, and general robustness, and an increase in the complexity of social organization. This, too, would increment the number of children able to be raised to reproductive maturity. Indeed, Lovejoy (1981) suggested that an evolutionary process was set in motion that led to a lengthening of the juvenile stage of human development, a greater degree of overall parental care, and the creation of the uniquely human life history.

Race Differences in *r-K* Strategies

It is time to consider whether *r-K* theory explains the race differences among modern humans. The pervasiveness of the pattern of traits summarized in Table

1.1 suggests that the underlying mechanisms are powerful. Racial differences in brain size from autopsies, endocranial volume, and externally measured craniums before and after correction for body size were reviewed in chapter 6. These showed that Mongoloids averaged 1,364 cm³, Caucasoids 1,347 cm³, and Negroids 1,267 cm³. Then, in chapter 7, an inverse relation was found between brain size and speed of physical maturation, including the age of first molar eruption. Eveleth and Tanner (1990) had compiled the data on the first phase of permanent tooth eruption from worldwide information. Eight sex-combined African series averaged 5.8 years compared to 6.1 years for 20 European and 8 East Asian series. A parallel racial difference also occurred for age of completion of this first phase: Africans at age 7.6, Europeans at age 7.7, and East Asians at 7.8.

Chapter 8 reviewed the differences among the races in number of two-egg twins per 1,000 births, caused by the production of two eggs in the same menstrual cycle. The rate per 1,000 births among Mongoloids is less than 4, among Caucasoids it is approximately 8, and among Negroids it is greater than 16, with some African populations having rates as high as 57 per 1,000 (Bulmer, 1970). Many subsequent surveys from around the world have confirmed the racial pattern, and have also shown that the incidence of non-monozygotic triplets and quadruplets shows the same rank ordering (Allen, 1987, 1988; Imaizumi, 1992; Nylander, 1975). The pattern occurs because the tendency to double ovulate is inherited largely through the race of the mother, independently of the race of the father, as observed in Mongoloid-Caucasoid crosses in Hawaii and Caucasoid-Negroid crosses in Brazil (Bulmer, 1970).

Populations adopting the lesser K-strategy to egg production (i.e., more eggs) are predicted to also allocate a larger percentage of bodily resources to other aspects of reproductive effort. Chapter 8 presented additional data on reproductive effort and sexual investment. Mongoloid and Negroid populations were at opposite extremes with Caucasoids intermediate. This pattern occurred consistently over traits such as:

1. Intercourse frequencies (premarital, marital, extramarital).
2. Developmental precocity (age of first intercourse, age at first pregnancy, number of pregnancies).
3. Primary sexual characteristics (size of penis, vagina, testes, ovaries).
4. Secondary sexual characteristics (salient voice, muscularity, buttocks, breasts).
5. Biological control of behavior (length of menstrual cycle, periodicity of sexual response, predictability of life history from onset of puberty).
6. Sex hormones (testosterone, gonadotropins, follicle stimulating hormone).
7. Attitudes (permissiveness to premarital sex, expectation of extramarital sex).

The racial differences in intelligence, law abidingness, health, and longevity, reviewed in chapters 6, 7, and 8 seem similarly to be ordered by r-K theory.

This is also the view of Lee Ellis (1987) who carried out an r-K analysis of race differences in crime. After drawing a distinction between intentional victimizing acts in which someone is obviously harmed and nonvictimizing acts, such as prostitution and drug taking, Ellis conceptualized victimizing criminal behavior as the opposite of altruism and therefore an r-selected trait.

Reviewing the literature, Ellis (1987) looked for universal demographic correlates of criminal behavior and found the following traits suggestive of r-selection:

1. Number of siblings. (Victimizers came from families with large numbers of siblings, or half siblings).
2. Intactness of parents' marital bond. (Victimizers came from families in which parents no longer lived together).
3. Shorter gestation periods. (Victimizers had more premature births).
4. Victimizers had more rapid development to sexual functioning.
5. Victimizers had a greater frequency of copulation outside of bonded relationships (or at least had a stated preference for such).
6. Victimizers had less stable bonding.
7. Victimizers had a lower parental investment in offspring (as evidenced by higher rates of child abandonment, neglect, and abuse).
8. Victimizers had a shorter life expectancy.

Ellis (1987) then examined the evidence on race differences in these characteristics and concluded that blacks are more r-selected than whites and both are more r-selected than Orientals. Because, across societies, blacks had higher victimizing crime rates than whites, and whites, in turn, had higher rates than Orientals, he also concluded that the racial differences in crime rates were likely the result of underlying neurhormonal mechanisms mediating the differences in reproductive strategies.

In a later extrapolation, Ellis (1989: 94) incorporated reproductive strategies and neurohormonal factors into a theory of rape. In this he made explicit (1989: 94) the prediction that "blacks should have higher rape rates than whites, and whites in turn should have higher rates than Orientals." As described in chapter 7 and Table 7.3, African and Caribbean countries report twice the amount of rape as do European countries and four times more than do countries from the Pacific Rim. Summing crime data from INTERPOL and averaging across years gives figures for rape per 100,000 population, respectively, for Negroids, 13; for Caucasoids, 6; and for Mongoloids, 3. These proportionate racial differences are similar to those found within the United States and they confirm Ellis's predictions.

In summary, when the pattern of traits summarized in Table 1.1 are evaluated against the attributes of Table 10.1, they suggest that the Mongoloids are more K-selected than Caucasoids, who in turn are more K-selected than Negroids. This view of r-K theory is precise enough to generate new research and to throw anomalies into relief. For example, from Table 10.1 it would be predicted that Mongoloids would be larger in body size than Caucasoids, who, in turn, would be larger in body size than Negroids, and yet, this pattern does not appear to be true (Eveleth & Tanner, 1990).

A formidable challenge for alternative theories to the r-K formulation is the inverse relation to be observed empirically between brain size and gamete production across human racial groups and their association with other bio-behavioral variables. No environmental factor is known to account for the trade-off between brain size, speed of maturation, and reproductive potency nor to cause so many diverse variables to correlate in so comprehensive a fashion. There is, however, a genetic factor: evolution.

11

Out of Africa

Race differences in reproductive strategies map onto modern theories of human evolution in an interesting way. Genetic distance estimates, including those from DNA sequencing, indicate that archaic versions of the three races emerged from the ancestral hominid line in the following order: Africans less than 200,000 years ago, with an African/non-African split about 110,000 years ago, and a Caucasoid/Mongoloid about 41,000 years ago (Stringer & Andrews, 1988). Such an ordering would fit with and explain the way in which the variables were found to cluster: Negroids, the earliest to emerge, were least K-selected; Caucasoids, emerging later, were next least K-selected; and Mongoloids, emerging latest, were the most K-selected.

Racial Origins

Australopithecus, Homo habilis, and *Homo erectus* all made their first appearances on the African continent. Thus, Africa, as Charles Darwin correctly surmised, is "the cradle of mankind." However, two very different theories are competing to explain how racial differentiation occurred during the final stages of hominid evolution. At the extremes (Figure 11.1), these are the Multiregional and the Single Origin theories (Sussman, 1993). The Multiregional model requires that many racial characteristics be traceable backward in time over very long periods whereas this is not a requirement of the Single Origin model, which holds that a common female ancestor to all humans, dubbed "Eve," arose only recently in Africa.

Both theories agree that between 1 million and 2 million years ago *Homo erectus* emerged out of Africa to populate Eurasia. They are divided on whether the descendants of these *erectus* populations (the Neanderthals in Europe, Beijing Man in China, and Java Man in Indonesia) gave rise to modern ancestors, or whether the *erectus* groups were evolutionary dead ends supplanted by a wave of anatomically modern people arising in Africa less than 200,000 years ago.

The Multiregional theory holds that over a 1 million-year-period, modern human races evolved in parallel in Africa, Europe, and Asia through intermediate stages from *Homo erectus.* Thus, modern Europeans evolved from Ne-

217

Figure 11.1: Alternative Models for the Evolution of the Human Races

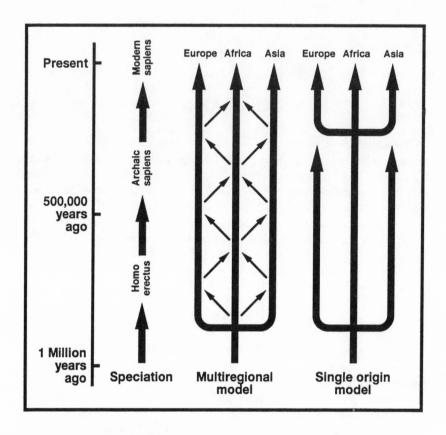

Both models assume that early man originated in Africa. They differ in how long ago the dispersal into Eurasia occurred. The single origin model (right) holds that modern humans evolved first in Africa, and then migrated to other continents around 100,000 years ago, eventually replacing earlier *Homo erectus* populations. The multiregional model (left) holds that after the migration of *Homo erectus* out of Africa around 1 million years ago, people evolved into modern humans independently in different parts of the world, with some gene flow occurring between the evolving lines to keep them from becoming too far apart (indicated by small arrows).

anderthals, the Chinese people from Beijing Man, and Australian aborigines from Java Man. Unique morphological features are claimed to persist from the archaic populations through to modern ones (Wolpoff, 1989; Thorne & Wolpoff, 1992; Frayer, Wolpoff, Thorne, Smith, & Pope, 1993). These continuing features include the prominent noses of modern Europeans with those of the Neanderthals (200,000 to 35,000 years ago), the flat faces and shovel-shaped incisor teeth of modern Chinese with those of Beijing Man and the Zhoukoudian fossils (500,000 to 200,000 years ago), and the continuous brow ridge of modern Australians with those of Java Man and the Ngandong fossils (700,000 to 100,000 years ago). Necessary to this view, much gene transfer must have occurred among the various groups to keep them evolving in concert.

The Single Origin theory, in contrast, proposes that fully modern humans emerged recently, perhaps only 140,000 years ago, from a primeval African population, and then migrated into all corners of the world. In the process, specific racial features developed while existing Neanderthals and *Homo erectus* populations were replaced (A. C. Wilson & Cann, 1992). A strong version of this theory holds that no genetic mixture took place between the modern and the older populations. An African/non-African split is envisaged as occurring 110,000 years ago following a dispersal event in the Middle East, the pathway out of Africa, with a Caucasoid/Mongoloid split occurring 41,000 years ago (Stringer & Andrews, 1988).

The main debating point between the two theories is whether there is regional continuity in the fossil record. In their review paper supporting the Single Origin model, Stringer and Andrews (1988) maintained that the fossil evidence claimed by the Multiregionalists is so incomplete that no possibility existed of consensus on the fossil record alone, even among paleontologists. Their analysis suggested that the Asian *erectus* populations were evolutionarily separate from those in Africa. These Asian forms then became extinct, and the African species of *Homo*, which should no longer be called *Homo erectus*, was the ancestor of anatomically modern humans.

The consensus of opinion seems increasingly favorable to the Single Origin perspective. Because of its parsimonious alignment with the data set out in Table 1.1, this author preferred Single Origin theory from the outset (Rushton, 1989a, 1992b). However, it is not crucial for the thesis which of the two approaches to racial origins turns out to be correct. Many literate accounts have been provided of the debate and its evidential base (Brown, 1990; Diamond, 1991; Fagan, 1990; Howells, 1993; Leakey & Lewin, 1992; Sussman, 1993). Here the topic will be considered primarily from the Single Origin perspective, based on genetic, paleontological, archaeological, linguistic, and behavioral sources of data.

Genetic Evidence

For many Single Origin theorists, the preferred mode of evidence is at the molecular, genetic level partly because genes and by-products like blood proteins are plentiful. Existing human populations can be compared by measuring similarities and differences and estimating the dates of divergence. Large genetic samples help to smooth minor, often local, variations. A. C. Wilson and Cann (1992: 68) explain the advantage of genes over fossils for evidence:

[L]iving genes must have ancestors, whereas dead fossils may not have descendants. Molecular biologists know that the genes they are examining must have been passed through lineages that survived to the present; paleontologists cannot be sure that the fossils they examine do not lead down an evolutionary blind alley.

In an early breakthrough using molecular evidence, Sarich and Wilson (1967) had shown that the human lineage had diverged from African apes only 5 to 8 million years ago rather than the 25 million years ago claimed by paleontologists. This meant that the African apes (chimpanzees and gorillas) were genetically more closely related to human beings than they were to Asian apes (orangutans) from whom they separated 10 to 13 million years ago. Further, humans and chimpanzees were each other's closest relatives; chimpanzees and humans were more similar to each other than either were to gorillas. These conclusions on relatedness contradicted both superficial physical similarity and more formal anatomical analysis in which chimpanzees and gorillas appear to be each other's closest relative.

Sarich and Wilson's (1967) molecular clock used blood-group systems and proteins. Subsequent lines of evidence involved DNA hybridization, mitochondrial (mt) DNA sequencing, and nuclear DNA sequencing. All clocks rest on the assumption that if the rate of mutation that occurs is more or less a constant, then by counting the number of differences between two populations it is possible to estimate their time of divergence from a common ancestor.

Only 1 to 5 percent of the DNA genome is expressed as proteins. Between 95 and 99 percent consists of introns, pseudogenes, or "junk" DNA that goes along for the ride, replicating from generation to generation without affecting morphology at all. This superfluous DNA may not be of much use to the organism, but is of great value for researchers. Because it is not impeded by natural selection, mutations accumulate at an even faster rate in this "neutral" DNA than in the coding sequences of DNA, and so provides a "fast clock" for timing evolutionary divergences.

Using DNA hybridization, comparisons can be made of entire genomes (or major portions of them) consisting of billions of base pairs. In the DNA double helix, long strands wind about each other with each base pair attaching to its complementary base in the other strand. A double strand can be "melted" by heat into a single strand and compared with a similarly produced single strand from another species. These "hybrid" strands melt apart at a lower temperature than the originals because of the mismatches in the base pairs, like gaps in a zip. A difference of 1 degree in temperature represents roughly a 1 percent difference in the sequence. Human-chimp DNA comparisons are about 20 percent more stable than human-gorilla or chimp-gorilla comparisons.

Mitochondrial DNA lies outside the nucleus of the cell and contains only about 15,000 base pairs, contrasted with the 3 billion base pairs of the nucleus. Mitochondrial DNA is easier to analyze than nuclear DNA, not only because it has fewer nucleotide sites, but because it has a rate of change 5 to 10 times that of nuclear DNA. Moreover, because it is inherited only through the female line and so is immune to change by sexual recombination, it provides a purer measure of rate of change by mutation alone. It has been "clocked" at a rate of about 2 or 4 percent (or about 330 to 660 mutations) per million years.

Genetic trees, representing the relatedness of modern humans, reflect one fundamental split: sub-Saharan Africans and all other human populations. A classic study by Cann, Stoneking, and Wilson (1987) examined mtDNA gathered from 147 placentas from children whose ancestors lived in five parts of the world: Africa, Asia, Europe, Australia, and New Guinea. Cann et al.'s (1987) evolutionary tree showed that Africans could trace their ancestry to the base of the tree without running into any non-African ancestors. The descendants of the other areas, however, had at least one African ancestor. Moreover, the African-only branch contained more diverse types of mtDNA than the other geographic groups, showing that most evolutionary change had occurred among Africans. Africans had the oldest ancestry because their mtDNA had accumulated the most mutations. Asians, on the other hand, had relatively homogeneous mitochondrial DNA, suggesting they are of more recent ancestry.

Later studies supported and extended the African origin hypothesis, using more refined techniques, broader based populations, and chimpanzee mtDNAs as outgroup anchor points. In one study, mtDNA in single hairs plucked from 15 !Kung hunter-gatherers from the Kalahari Desert in southern Africa were sequenced and compared to 68 other humans, including African pygmies (Vigilant, Pennington, Harpending, Kocher, & Wilson, 1989). The genealogical tree showed the deepest branches occurring amongst the !Kung bushmen.

In a subsequent, confirmatory study, 189 people of diverse geographic origin, including 121 native Africans, produced a tree having many deep branches leading exclusively to African mtDNAs. The deepest branches occurred for pygmies and !Kung bushmen (Vigilant, Stoneking, Harpending, Hawkes, & Wilson, 1991). That the human DNA closest to that of the apes occurs most commonly in Africa implies an African origin for human mtDNA.

These studies give a date for the origin of anatomically modern human mitochondrial DNA to be between 166,000 and 249,000 years ago, or, more simply, about 200,000 years ago. One response of the Multiregionalists has been to question the assumption of the rate of change; they argue that a slower mutation rate is more appropriate and if adopted would place the origin of modern populations at about 850,000 years ago. A slower rate, however, does not seem to fit with the calibrations tested against archaeological data on known human colonization events or known divergence times made with other species such as the chimpanzee (A. C. Wilson & Cann, 1992).

The mitochondrial DNA research does not stand alone in supporting the Single Origin model. The patterns of genetic differences based on the coded sequences of DNA carried in the cell nucleus show similar results to those of mitochondrial DNA as, too, do "classical" data sets based on the proteins that the genes express (Cavalli-Sforza et al., 1993; Nei and Roychoudhury, 1993; Stoneking, 1993). Cavalli-Sforza's support for a recent African origin is a reversal of opinion, for, earlier, on more limited data, he had held that human populations can be divided into two major groups: the Eurafrican (European and African) and the greater Asian. From this observation he had proposed that anatomically modern humans had originated in western Asia (Cavalli-Sforza & Edwards, 1964).

Whereas the work with DNA clocks assumes that mutations accumulate at a constant rate, the work with blood proteins assumes that populations drift apart at a constant rate. These genetic distances show a closer relation between Europeans and Asians than between Europeans and Africans or between Asians and Africans. Thus, Nei and Livshits (1989) examined the three major races using four different sets of genetic loci (84 protein loci, 33 blood group loci, 8 HLA and immunoglobin loci, and 61 DNA markers) to calculate genetic distances. They concluded in favor of the recent African origin based on the assumption that the population that is most distinct has remained in the place of origin and other populations have migrated to other parts of the world.

Subsequently, Nei and Roychoudhury (1993) examined 121 alleles for 26 distinct populations from around the world and statistically allowed the rate of evolution to vary. They confirmed Nei and Livshit's (1989) results indicating an extremely high probability that the first major split of the phylogenetic tree separated Africans from non-Africans and that the genetic distance between Caucasians and Orientals is significantly smaller than either that between Caucasians and Africans or that between Orientals and Africans. Nei and Roychoudhury (1993) noted that to root a tree it is customary to use an outgroup species but that a useful alternative is to put the root to the midpoint of the longest branch between a pair of populations. This was the procedure they used and they went on to support the Out of Africa model and provide a plausible scenario of subsequent migrations and the origins of human populations.

Following the dubbing of mitochondrial Eve as "the mother of us all" some researchers began to search for Adam, "the father of us all." Work with DNA hybridization of the Y chromosome suggested that Adam was also an African. One team suggested that genetic Adam's closest modern counterpart is an Aka pygmy in the Central African Republic (Gibbons, 1991). Polymorphisms on the long arm of the Y chromosome were identified and the most ancestral version found in the pygmies. Other teams have traced the origin of polymorphisms from the Y chromosome to !Kung bushmen, two different groups of pygmies, and Africans in Ethiopia.

The studies described above proceeded independently, using quite different sets of data, yet each strongly implied the Single Origin out of Africa model. Genetic distances calculated from protein systems suggested divergence times of about 110,000 years ago for the African/non-African split and about 41,000 years ago for the Caucasoid/Mongoloid split (Stringer & Andrews, 1988). Nonetheless, detailed critiques of the molecular evidence for the African "Eve" hypothesis continue to appear (Templeton, 1993).

Paleontological Evidence

Proponents of the Multiregional model claim evidence of regional continuity between old and recent forms in anatomical features, particularly in Asia and Australia (Frayer et al., 1993). The Single Origin implies a divide between older and more modern forms (Aiello, 1993). Debate remained especially speculative until new dating procedures became available adding power to the traditional radiocarbon techniques, which cannot reliably date materials older than 30,000 to 40,000 years. Now uranium series techniques are used to date cave sediments such as stalagmites; thermoluminescence procedures are used on sediments or on flints burned by ancient fires; and electron-spin resonance on a variety of materials, particularly animal teeth. In each case a date is assigned to hominid remains by determining the age of the materials with which the remains are associated.

Together the new techniques confirm that all the major steps in human evolution took place in Africa and that *Homo sapiens* lived in Africa between 200,000 and 100,000 years ago, and in the Middle East about 100,000 years ago (Aiello, 1993). In the Middle East there is some evidence that *H. sapiens* and Neanderthals lived in the same region and shared the same Middle Stone Age "tool kit" about 50,000 to 100,000 years ago. The Neanderthals appear to have continued to occupy the area until the moderns took over completely about 40,000 years ago. The persistence of two populations with separate identities over a long period, with no signs of hybridization, suggests that they belonged to separate species. Also, in contrast to the continuity of the fossil record in sub-Saharan Africa, the record in North Africa can be divided into two widely separated groups, non-*Homo sapiens* between 500,000 and 200,000 years ago, and *H. sapiens* after 50,000 years ago.

A review of the physical differences between Neanderthals, who may have arisen in northern Eurasia, and moderns subsequently entering Eurasia from Africa, was provided by Simons (1989). Like earlier *H. erectus,* Neanderthals have dense skeletal bones and thick skulls with projecting brow ridges, and both sexes are extraordinarily muscular. The face juts forward and holds large front teeth. Robust hind limbs and dense bone suggests high levels of endurance and an adaptation to long hours of walking. Early modern humans in Europe have longer distal limb segments than do Neanderthals, which might imply more recent equatorial ancestry. Allen's rule, a principle of zoology, predicts that mammals generally have longer extremities in warm climates. There is ongoing debate about whether, anatomically, in brain localization and vocal tract, Neanderthalers were as capable of speech as moderns (Lieberman, 1991; Milo & Quiatt, 1993).

Craniometric analyses have shown that divergence in face and cranium among modern races is highly limited compared with the distance separating any of them from Neanderthals or *erectus* populations (Howells, 1973, 1989, 1993). Modern European skulls are much more similar to modern Africans and Chinese than they are to fossils of 100,000-year-old Neanderthals. Results such as these provide no evidence of regional continuity. Thus, Howells (1989) concluded that the data supported a recent Single Origin model. Although Howells's analyses often placed Africans (and Australoids) at the polar opposite of East Asians (and American Indians), a result consistent with a recent out of Africa migration, he was unable to show a specific sub-Saharan first source.

Dental research shows that features of the crowns and roots also outline the relationship among prehistoric populations. Dental features are more stable than many evolutionary traits, with a high genetic component that minimizes the effects of environmental differences, sexual dimorphism, and age variations. Among the features found in all modern humans are their number, 32, and their division into quarters: three incisors, one canine, two premolars, and two molars.

Turner (1989) has shown that Mongoloid populations are differentiated from the generalized pattern existing elsewhere in the world in several features, including shovel-shaped incisors, the result of extra ridges in the crown. There is also an important subdivision within the Mongoloid population. Sinodonts, the modern Chinese and Japanese, the Siberians, and the peoples of the Americas have the most shoveling and Sundadonts, southeast Asians, Thais, Malays, Javanese, Polynesians, Jomonese, and Ainu have the least. Sinodonts also display a greater frequency of single-rooted upper first premolars, and triple-rooted first molars. Turner conjectures that these changes were adaptations to life in the dentally demanding colder north.

Turner (1989) used the dental patterns to reconstruct the prehistoric migrations that peopled the Pacific Basin, East Asia, and the New World. The generalized pattern, thought common to all modern humans, entered southeast Asia sometime around 50,000 B.P. Sundadonty evolved from this pattern sometime after 30,000 B.P. and Sinodonty sometime after 20,000 B.P. Turner noted that his type of dental analysis is still in its infancy as a scientific discipline but that future work must link world populations together in a global framework.

Archaeological Evidence

During the 1.5 million years that spanned the emergence of *H. erectus* and *H. sapiens*, the stone implements were crude. Hand axes, choppers, and cleavers were not sufficiently differentiated in shape to imply distinctive function. Wear marks on the tools show they were variously used to cut meat, bone, hides, wood, and nonwoody parts of plants. Moreover, there is no evidence that the tools were ever mounted on other materials for increased leverage and there were no tools made of bone, no ropes to make nets, and no fishhooks. The stone tools remained unchanged for thousands of years. In fact, minimalists have held that there is no good evidence of hunting skills until around 100,000 years ago and even then humans would have been relatively ineffective hunters. Calvin (1990), however, has suggested that some of the stone axes used by *erectus* populations may have been effective throwing instruments aimed at animal herds as they watered.

It is only in the northern Eurasian land mass, particularly the arctic, where little plant food was available, that big-game hunting clearly became the dominant food source. And humans didn't reach the Arctic until around 30,000 years ago. Neanderthal tools found in Europe were similar to earlier human tools found in Africa, being simple hand-held axes not mounted on separate parts such as handles. There were no standardized bone tools and no bows and arrows. Shelters were apparently crude; all that remains of them are postholes and simple stone piles. There is no evidence of art, sewing, boating, or trade, and no variation of tools over time and space suggesting little in the way of innovation.

One hundred thousand years ago, in Africa, at the time when modern-looking Africans had evolved, the stone tool implements suddenly became more specialized. Carefully prepared stone cores enabled numerous thin blades about two inches (five cm) long to be struck off and turned into knives, spear barbs, scrapers, borers, and cutters. This blade technology allowed many more flakes to be struck off than previously and the stone workers relied more heavily on nonlocal rocks, choosing to bring in fine-grained rocks of many types from miles away.

Although the anatomically modern Africans had somewhat superior tools to their predecessors, they are still characterizable as Middle Stone Age in culture. They continued to lack standardized bone tools, bows and arrows, art, and cultural variation. These Africans can barely be considered big-game hunters because their weapons were still spears for thrusting rather than bows and arrows.

Evidence for a more abrupt change doesn't occur until the last Ice Age in Europe (France and Spain) around 35,000 years ago. Anatomically modern people, known as Cro-Magnons, appeared on the scene with dramatically more specialized tools. Standardized bone and antler tools appear for the first time, including needles used for sewing, as do compound tools of several parts tied or glued together, such as spear points set in shafts or ax heads hafted to handles. Rope, used in nets or snares, accounts for the frequent bones of foxes, weasels, and rabbits at Cro-Magnon sites.

Sophisticated weapons for killing dangerous animals at a distance now appear also—weapons such as barbed harpoons, darts, spear throwers, and bows and arrows. European caves are full of bones of bison, elk, reindeer, horse, and ibex. By this time South African caves also yield bones of buffalo and pigs.

Several types of evidence testify to the effectiveness of late Cro-Magnon people as big-game hunters. Their sites are more numerous than those of Neanderthals or Middle Stone Age Africans, implying more success at obtaining food. Moreover, numerous species of big animals that had survived many previous ice ages became extinct toward the end of the last ice age, suggesting that they were exterminated by the human hunters' new skills. Likely victims include Europe's woolly rhino and giant deer, and southern Africa's giant buffalo and giant Cape horse. With watercraft capable of crossing the 60 miles from eastern Indonesia to Australia, and tailored clothing enabling the crossing of the Bering straits, the giant kangaroos of Australia and the mammoths of North America were exterminated.

The occupation of Northeast Asia about 30,000 years ago depended on many advances: tailored clothing, as evidenced by eyed needles, cave paintings of parkas, and grave ornaments marking outlines of shirts and trousers; warm furs, indicated by fox and wolf skeletons minus the paws (removed in skinning and found in a separate pile); elaborate houses (partially dug into the ground for insulation and marked by postholes, pavements, and walls of mammoth bones) with intricate fireplaces; and stone lamps to hold animal fat and light the long Arctic nights.

Whereas Neanderthals obtained their raw materials within a few miles of home, Cro-Magnons and their contemporaries throughout Eurasia practiced long-distance trade, not only for raw material for tools but also for ornaments. Tools of obsidian, jasper, and flint have been found hundreds of miles from where those stones were quarried. Baltic amber reached southeast Europe, while Mediterranean shells and the teeth from sharks were carried to inland parts of France, Spain, and the Ukraine. Burial displays reflect great variation, with skeletons wearing necklaces, bracelets, and head bands of shell beads and bear and lion teeth.

The artwork of anatomically modern humans also shows a clear discontinuity with what went before. Well known are the rock paintings, with polychrome depictions of now extinct animals and the relief carvings and clay sculptures deep within caves in France and Spain that hinted at shamanistic rituals. On the Eurasian plains are "Venus" figurines of women with enormous breasts and buttocks, made from a mixture of clay and bone powder. Ivory carvings of eagles, mammoths, and arctic waterbirds, as well as female figurines have been found in Siberia and dated to 35,000 years ago.

Analysis of amino acids in ostrich eggshells, once used as food and as containers, also bolsters the case that the first modern humans originated in

Africa. Change in amino acids take place in eggshells at a steady rate and, once anchored to radiocarbon dating, enable dating back to 200,000 years ago, and up to 1 million years in colder climates (Gibbons, 1992). The eggshells turn up at camp sites in South Africa between 105,000 and 125,000 years ago, before the earliest dates on other continents. Not long afterward, ostrich shells appear in the Middle East along with anatomically modern human remains.

Linguistic Evidence

Converging with the genetic, paleontological, and archaeological data is that from linguistics. Trees of relatedness constructed from 17 linguistic affinities were found to be related to those based on blood protein affinities in 42 aboriginal peoples who had had little or no mixing with outsiders (Cavalli-Sforza et al., 1988). As with other studies the first split in the genetic tree separated Africans from non-Africans, and the second separated two major clusters, one corresponding to Caucasoids, northeast Asians, Arctic populations, and Amerindians, and the other to southeast Asians, Pacific Islanders, and New Guineans and Australians. Average genetic distances between the most important clusters are proportional to archaeological separation times. Strikingly, the genetic clustering closely matched that of the major language families, indicating considerable parallelism between genetic and linguistic evolution.

Behavioral Evidence

The apparent stepwise sequence of behavioral data summarized in Table 1.1, with Caucasoids averaging consistently between Negroids and Mongoloids, appears to coincide with the dates for the succession of the three races in earth history. The three races emerged from the ancestral hominid line in roughly the following sequence: archaic Africans (later, Negroids) about 200,000 years ago, archaic non-Africans (later, Caucasoids) about 110,000 years ago, and archaic non-Caucasoids (later, Mongoloids) about 41,000 years ago. Such an ordering would fit with and explain the way in which the variables are found to cluster. The clustering thus supports the Single Origin model but is not clearly predictable from the Multiregional Model, based on long periods of separation, in which no consistent pattern of character appearance is expected.

Evidence from behavioral genetics is also relevant. For example, as reviewed in chapter 4, genetic estimates for mental ability subtests are often generalizable across populations, whether calculated on Mongoloid or Caucasoid samples. As was seen in Figure 9.1, inbreeding depression scores on IQ subtests calculated from Japanese families are predictive of the magnitude of black-white differences on the same tests in the United States. These findings support the Single Origin model because they suggest that the underlying genetic substructure of mental ability is the same across the races and thus that substantial genetic relatedness exists.

Racial Differentiation

Given an African origin of less than 200,000 years ago, a dispersal event out of Africa about 100,000 years ago, and a peopling of the rest of the world thereafter, the question arises as to how these events led to the behavioral profiles found among the races. Why would Mongoloids have ended up the most K-selected? I agree with those who have proposed that colonizing temperate and cold environments leads to increased cognitive demands to solve the problems of gathering food and gaining shelter and general survival in cold winters (e.g., Calvin, 1990; R. Lynn, 1987, 1991a).

From time to time populations move into new niches which entails increased cognitive demands for survival. When this occurs populations respond by evolving larger brains in relation to body size. Larger brains have the capacity for greater intelligence and enable the populations to deal with the cognitive demands of the new niche. The Caucasoid and Mongoloid peoples who evolved in Eurasia were subjected to pressures for improved intelligence to deal with the problems of survival in the cold northern latitudes. Most of the last 80,000 years has been colder than today. During the main Wurm glaciation of approximately 24-10,000 B.P. winter temperatures in Europe and northeast Asia fell by 5-15°C. The terrain became cold grasslands and tundra with only a few trees in sheltered river valleys; the environment was broadly similar to that of present-day Alaska.

Obtaining food and keeping warm in these conditions posed a problem. Unlike the tropics and subtropics, plant foods were seasonal and not available for many months during the winter and spring. People therefore became wholly reliant on hunting large herbivores such as mammoth, horse, and reindeer to secure their food supply. Even among near-contemporary hunter-gatherers, the proportions of foods obtained by hunting and by gathering varies according to latitude. Peoples in tropical and subtropical latitudes were largely gatherers, while peoples in temperate environments relied more on hunting. Peoples in arctic and subarctic environments relied almost exclusively on hunting, together with fishing, and did so of necessity because plant foods were unavailable for much of the time.

Hunting in the open grasslands of northern Eurasia was also more difficult than hunting in the woodlands of the tropics and subtropics where there is plenty of cover for hunters to hide in. The only way of hunting animals in open grasslands is to make use of natural traps into which the animals could be driven. One of the most common traps was the narrow ravine where some of the beasts would stumble and could be speared by members of the group waiting in ambush. In addition, the herbivores could be surrounded and driven over cliffs, into bogs or into the loops of rivers.

For effective hunting of large herbivores people would have needed to manufacture a variety of tools from stone, wood, and bone for making spearheads and for cutting. When these peoples had killed a large herbivore they would have to skin and butcher it into pieces of a size that could be carried back to the base camp. For this it was necessary to manufacture a variety of sophisticated cutting and skinning tools.

Another set of problems in the northern latitudes would have centered on keeping warm. People had to solve the problems of making fires, clothes, and shelters. It would have been much harder to make fires in Eurasia than in Africa, where spontaneous bush fires would have been frequent. In Eurasia during the glaciations there would have been no spontaneous bush fires. People would have had to make fires by friction or percussion in a terrain where there was little wood. Probably dry grass had to be stored in caves for use as tinder and the main fuel would have been dung, animal fat, and bones. In addition, clothing and shelters were unnecessary in sub-Saharan Africa but were made in Europe during the main Wurm glaciation. Needles were manufactured from bone for sewing together animal skins, and shelters were constructed from large bones and skins. Torrence (1983) has demonstrated an association between latitude and the number and complexity of tools used by contemporary hunter-gatherers.

Thus, the cognitive demands of manufacturing sophisticated tools and making fires, clothing, and shelters (as well as regulating the storage of food; Miller, 1991) would have selected for higher average intelligence levels than in the less cognitively demanding environment in sub-Saharan Africa. Those individuals who could not solve these problems of survival would have died out, leaving those with alleles for higher intelligence as the survivors.

In the data set out in chapter 6, general, verbal, and visuospatial abilities are all higher in Caucasoids compared with Negroids. The magnitude of the Caucasoid advantage was about the same for all three abilities, namely, about 30 IQ points for the comparison with Africans and about 15 IQ points for the comparison with African Americans and African Caribbeans. It is likely that all three abilities came under selection pressure for enhancement in Eurasia to about the same extent.

The intelligence of the Mongoloids are held to have evolved somewhat differently. While the Mongoloid peoples have only slightly higher general intelligence than the Caucasoids, they have markedly higher visuospatial abilities and, indeed, somewhat weaker verbal abilities. R. Lynn (1987, 1991a) attributed the evolution of this pattern of abilities to the even colder winters that Mongoloids experienced relative to Caucasoids. Evolving in Siberia where, in the main Wurm glaciation, the temperatures were some 5-15°C colder than today, the people of northeast Asia would have found themselves between the encroaching ice from the Himalayas in the south and from the Arctic region in the north. In response to this extreme cold, Mongoloids evolved distinctive adaptations to reduce heat loss, including the flattened face and shortened limbs and epicanthic fold and narrow eyes that afford protection against the cold and the glare of the sunlight on the snow. Under these adverse conditions natural selection increased general intelligence and a trade-off in favor of visuospatial abilities over verbal because of the crucial role of strong visuospatial abilities for making sophisticated tools and weapons, and for the planning and execution of group hunting strategies.

R. Lynn (1991a) also provided a scenario for the evolution of intelligence in southeast Asians and Amerindians. Although southeast Asians had some exposure to cold winters before they migrated southward, and so were selected for some enhanced intelligence, this would have been less than that experienced by the northern Caucasoids and Mongoloids. Hence, their intelligence levels were raised above those of Negroids but not to as high a level as the Caucasoids and Mongoloids. With respect to Amerindians, they are descendants of an archaic Mongoloid people that entered the Americas prior to the main Wurm glaciation of approximately 24-10,000 years ago that produced the "classical" Mongoloid features with their highly elevated cognitive abilities. Thus, the first Wurm glaciation at 40,000 B.P. set in place the archaic Mongoloid cognitive profile of relatively strong visuospatial and weak verbal abilities, and then some subsequent selection pressure, such as the main Wurm glaciation, raised the whole profile in the Mongoloids, leaving that of the Amerindians at a lower level.

Once proto-Mongoloids had crossed the Bering Strait and made their way down into the Americas they would have found life easier than their ancestors had been accustomed to in northeast Asia. They would have found a number of herbivorous mammals such as mammoth, horse, antelope, and bison who were quite unused to being hunted by man. With no experience of predation by man they would have been easy game for the skilled hunters who had evolved for many thousands of years in the more difficult environment of northeast Asia. As they moved southward proto-Mongoloids would have found that plant foods were readily available. Thus, survival would have been easier and selection for further increase in cognitive abilities would have relaxed.

K-Selection and Brain Size

R. Lynn is not the first to argue that the benefits of intelligence were greatest for those populations living in cold climates during the ice ages, but he has certainly provided the most detailed modern exposition. Lynn's (1991a) analysis went beyond his earlier (1987) account by also focusing on the racial differences in brain size that I had described (Rushton, 1988b, 1990c). As reviewed in chapter 2, a direct relation exists of about 0.40 between brain size and intelligence. The human brain is a metabolically expensive organ, using 20 percent of the body's supply of energy while representing only 2 percent of its body mass. Unless large brains substantially contribute to fitness, therefore, they would not have evolved. Increasing encephalization likely adds fitness by increasing the efficiency with which information is processed, as measured using conventional tests of intelligence.

The evolution of a larger brain is expected to lead to the selection of other K-characteristics. As discussed in chapter 10, with regard to within-species r-K selection, life-history traits tend to be selected together. Culling for one life-history characteristic typically pulls in related traits. Across species, building a bigger brain demands a longer gestation, higher offspring survival, a delayed maturity, a lower reproductive output, and a longer life (Harvey & Krebs, 1990).

As populations moved north, out of Africa, they encountered not only more cognitively demanding but also more predictable environments. Predictable environments are an ecological precondition for K-selection. Although the Arctic climate varies greatly over 1 year, it is highly predictably harsh among years. Temperate zones are also quite predictable but subtropical savannahs, where humans evolved, because of sudden droughts and devastating viral, bacterial, and parasitic diseases, are generally less predictable.

Noncognitive personal qualities were likely selected along with intelligence, either as a necessary concomitant feature or because additional advantages were conferred. In the most K-selected populations there would not only be increased brain size and intelligence, but also a reduction in personal and sexual competitiveness including the size of breasts, buttocks, and male genitalia. Decreased emphasis on personal and sexual competitiveness and more emphasis on parenting and personal restraint would allow greater complexity of social organization and increment the number of children successfully raised to reproductive maturity.

K-strategy populations generate centralized social systems with regulated communication networks in which individuals initially compete for position but subsequently gain access to resources dependent on their place in the hierarchy. Less K-strategy populations generate relatively less centralized organizations in which the important lines of communication are face-to-face and in which personal dominance matters, because each time resources become available they are competed for anew, in an opportunistic scrambling fashion. Thus may the suite of correlated characteristics shown in Table 1.1 have come into being.

Agriculture and the Modern Era

By 12,000 or so years ago, modern *H. sapiens* dominated the land masses of Africa, Europe, and Asia, and had crossed into the Americas. The semitropical savanna of Africa, the arid tundra of the Eurasian steppes, and the cold glacial landscapes of Siberia had been conquered. Evolutionary challenges continued, however, not least of which was the retreat of the glaciers that began some 10,000 years ago from as far south as London and New York. The global warming threatened a whole way of life developed over thousands of years, destroying many forms of animals and allowing new ones to develop, one of which, largely because of the extension of grasslands, was the horse. In addition, it produced enormous changes in the distribution of plants and animals, especially in the Northern Hemisphere. It was the retreat of the polar ice cap that brought the next, revolutionary, stage of human development—agricultural settlements.

R. Lynn (1991a) suggested that although warm interglacial interludes had occurred previously, the transition to agricultural societies wasn't possible until people became sufficiently intelligent to take advantage of the wild grasses. According to Lynn, it was only after people had been through the last Wurm glaciation that they were cognitively able to do so. Lynn's view provides an explanation for why these advances were never made by Negroids or those southeast Asian populations who escaped the rigors of the last glaciation.

The invention of agriculture, 10,000 years ago, may have speeded up human evolution. It certainly increased cultural innovation. Humans shifted from an essentially mobile, hunting, and gathering existence, to a more sedentary one. Agriculture opened the way to an unprecedented expansion of food supplies and of human populations that, in turn, made cities and civilization possible. Those populations that were most capable of adopting an urban, agricultural way, increased enormously in numbers and social organization, and finally in military power. Smaller bands of hunter-gatherers were swamped by force of numbers and were either absorbed or extinquished.

Agriculture exerted enormous pressure on the human gene pool. Individuals who were members of successful agricultural settlements reproduced themselves at a far greater rate than did those who remained outside such settlements. The stable year-round food supply allowed for large population increases. Agricultural settlements made possible a complex urban society, the development of metallurgy, the invention of writing, and ultimately, civilization.

The earliest archeological sites with evidence of domesticated grain lie in the Middle East, at the north end of the Dead Sea, and date to about 10,000 years ago. Long before that, people in the region had gathered and eaten wild grain. Population growth, possibly combined with climatic change causing summertime food scarcity, might have forced people to plant wild cereals to tide them over. Once begun, the transition from wild to domesticated cereals could have occurred quite quickly.

The domestication of wheat, barley, peas, and beans spread northward into Turkey and eventually into Mesopotamia, moving at about one kilometer a year as the expanding population moved into new territory. The domestication of animals came about 1,000 years after the domestication of plants. Pottery and polished stone implements increased in frequency with the beginning of agriculture and completed the neolithic transition, the final part of the Stone Age.

The slow movement of the spread of agriculture implies demic diffusion, a process in which "it is not the idea of farming that spreads but the farmers themselves" (Ammerman & Cavalli-Sforza, 1984: 61). Integrating information from the archaeological record, radiocarbon dating, and the distribution of genetic polymorphisms from blood-group and other blood-based systems, a southeasterly-northwesterly progression is seen, being as early as 8,000 years ago in Greece and as late as 5,000 years ago in parts of the United Kingdom and Scandinavia. The diffusion is one of people, not cultural knowledge passed passively from static group to group. Population replacement is clearly implied.

Just as hunter-gatherer groups differentially survived, so have cultures and civilizations and the gene pools associated with them. In Western Europe alone, between the years A.D. 275 and A.D. 1025, it has been estimated that there was a war every two years on the average. Some of these wars substantially affected the gene pool, particularly when genocide was practiced. Genocide has probably not been uncommon during human history (Diamond, 1991; E. O. Wilson, 1975). Wars also changed social structures, as when one ideology replaced alternatives. Cultures that put a high premium on trade and exploration, as in Western Europe over the last several hundred years, produced movements of gene pools through migration. Substantial population movements continue, of course, to this day.

12

Challenges and Rejoinders

Holding that the use of racial terminology is poorly justified, opponents of the race concept successfully substituted the phrase "ethnic group" and thereby shifted the emphasis away from a "question begging...biologistic bias" (Montagu, 1960: 697; see also Lewontin et al., 1984: 119–29). The main empirical reason given for denying the importance of race is poor predictive utility. Critics point to enormous variance within races, the blurring of racial distinctions at category edges, and the lack of agreement as to how many races there are (Yee, Fairchild, Weizmann, & Wyatt, 1993).

Is Race a Useful Concept?

The view that race is only a social construct is contradicted by biological evidence. Along with blood protein and DNA data discussed in chapter 11, forensic scientists are able to classify skulls by race. Narrow nasal passages and a short distance between eye sockets mark a Caucasian, distinct cheekbones identify a Mongoloid and nasal openings shaped like an upside down heart typify a Negroid (Ubelaker & Scammell, 1992).

Of course it is simplified to divide all the world's peoples into just three major races. This ignores "Negritoes" and "Australoids," but also subdivisions within the macro races. Within the Mongoloid population distinctions might be drawn between east Asians like the Sino-Japanese and Koreans, and Amerindians and south Asians like the Filipinos and Malays. Similarly, the classification "Negroid" includes Bantu-speaking Africans, pygmies, Khoisan bushmen, and the socially classifiable blacks in the Americas who are hybridized with whites and Amerindians (in the United States by about 25 percent, Chakraborty et al., 1992). Caucasoids include Europeans, Middle Easterners, and members of the Indian subcontinent. It is unclear where still other groups belong. Are Polynesians Caucasian, Mongoloid, or some degree of admixture between them?

The histories of global populations are genetically complex and linked by intervening gradients. Intermediate populations may have come into being due to living in intermediate environments or they may be the result of inter-

235

breeding between formerly disparate groups. Future research using genetic information sequences will determine more precisely genetic affiliations and their behavioral correlates.

Constructs in science are only useful if they have explanatory power. The three macro racial categories show much predictive and construct validity. As has been shown, racial categories better organize disparate data than is possible using only ethnicity, religion, or sociopolitical grouping. In each category of Table 1.1, Caucasoids fall *between* Negroids and Mongoloids. The efficient unit of analysis, therefore, is the higher order concept of race, within which cluster the different subdivisions, ethnic groups, and, ultimately, individuals. Ignoring the concept of race not only obscures predictive order of internationally based data, but also neglects the approach of population biologists studying other species (Mayr, 1970: 186–204).

Are the Race Differences as Described?

Many critics have disputed my characterization of the pattern of racial differences. Some have charged that the data presented were misleadingly selected. Weizmann et al. (1991: 49) were among the most explicit:

> Rushton scavenges whatever materials lay at hand, whether ecology, anthropology, psychology or paleontology. His tendentious borrowing of materials, often themselves tainted by racism, is quite unscholarly. Libraries are full of so-called data which can be used to support almost any point of view about the causes of differences among people.

Similarly, Silverman (1990: 1) worried that the studies reviewed led to conclusions that "so precisely parallel racist stereotypes that it is difficult to dismiss the possibility of bias in the theory and/or the data."

A complaint by M. Lynn (1989a: 3) may be nearer the truth:

> [M]any of the race differences reported by Rushton and Bogaert (1987) have not been consistently found. The authors themselves acknowledged that some studies have failed to replicate the reported race differences in testes size, age at onset of puberty, and biologic control of sexual interest. Other failures to replicate the reported race differences were not acknowledged.

My response is that critics have failed to show an opposite to predicted ordering in brain size, intelligence, sexual restraint, law abidingness, and social organizational skills. If the null hypothesis was correct, then racial differences would be randomly distributed around a mean of zero with an equal number of negative as positive instances. Although critics have discussed the reliability of the data sources, the variability within the races, the overlap of the distributions, the size of the samples, the magnitude of the differences, and the change of scores over time, they have not provided contradictory data.

Aggregation versus Deconstruction

The principle of aggregation, a major methodological point discussed at length in chapter 2 must now be reconsidered in the present context. The principle states that the sum of a set of measurements is more stable and unbiased an estimator than any single measurement from the set. One reason is that there is always error associated with measurement. When several measurements are combined, these errors tend to average out. Errors made in one direction are considered to be offset by errors in another. Disregarding "outliers" and intragroup variance is inherent in, and is the purpose of, taking an average.

It is necessary to belabor this obvious principle, made explicit for psychological measurement in the nineteenth century, because it is so easily forgotten when discussing racial differences. What too often occurs is that a subset of the data is identified, deconstructed into particulars, and special explanations given for the scattered fragments. These deconstructed particulars, when re-aggregated, typically show the now familiar pattern of racial differences.

This view of the importance of aggregation has been contested. Zuckerman and Brody (1988: 1032) concluded a critique by saying:

> In sum, we find Rushton's paper flawed in terms of its obscure logic…ignoring of large group differences within the three major races (that are often larger than those between the three racial groupings) and aggregating that which should not be aggregated.

Zuckerman (1991: 985) elaborated this position: "[T]he variability within the three 'races' makes the general comparisons among them meaningless, and aggregation only serves to hide the variability."

Others have made similar points. In the context of U.S. crime statistics, Roberts and Gabor (1990: 299–300) stated: "Any examination of aggregate crime statistics is going to over-estimate the true incidence of crime committed by blacks relative to the amount of crime committed by whites." Yee et al. (1993: 1134) state that I interpret all within group variation as "error" but the next chapter shows how untrue this is. Rather, it represents natural variation, likely genetically based, that is common to all studied animal populations. Finally, Weizmann, Wiener, Wiesenthal, & Ziegler (1991: 46) wrote:

> Rushton's discussion of aggregation reveals his continued misunderstanding of the limited value of averaging multiple items, multiple instances and multiple samples. Aggregation provides a more unbiased estimator of true population values only where they are obscured by random error variance. It is of no use in reducing systematic error.

The principle of aggregation is pivotal. It's implications were discussed at length in chapter 2 for a wide variety of nonracial domains; it is central to other debates. Let us consider some of the examples that have been contested.

Aggregation and Brain Size

Many nineteenth-century scientists including Broca, Darwin, Galton, Lombroso, and Morton concluded that there were racial differences in brain size (chap. 5). With some exceptions, for example, American anthropologists Boas and Mead, this view was probably dominant until World War II (Pearl, 1934). As discussed in chapter 6, following the war, the literature on brain size and race underwent vigorous critiques. Thus, Tobias (1970) cited 14 potentially confounding variables that he argued made the data on black-white differences in brain weight measured at autopsy highly problematic; and Gould (1978) alleged that many of the data on racial differences in endocranial volume were due to "unconscious...finagling" and "juggling" of figures. Together, these authors claimed to have dismantled the "myth" of racial group differences in brain size.

As discussed in chapter 6, however, when the autopsy data debunked by Tobias (1970) were aggregated, racial group differences were found, with Mongoloids and Caucasoids having heavier brains than Negroids (1,368 g, 1,378 g vs. 1,316 g, respectively). When Tobias's number of "excess neurons" were averaged, Negroids had 8.55 billion, Caucasoids had 8.65 billion, and Mongoloids had 8.99 billion. Similarly, re-aggregating Gould's (1978, 1981) "corrected" analyses of nineteenth-century endocranial data showed that about 1 in^3 (16 cm^3) of cranial capacity differentiated the races such that Mongoloids > Caucasoids > Negroids.

These re-assemblages did not convince all the critics. Cain and Vanderwolf (1990) countered that the averaging method I had used for Tobias's data was inappropriate because, for example, the midpoint of a range of means had been used. This procedure, they suggested, could yield misleading results unless the distribution was symmetrical. They did not say why it was reasonable to assume that the distributions were skewed.

Cain and Vanderwolf (1990) and M. Lynn (1989b) also objected to the inclusion of the data from the ancient Caucasians in the category "Caucasoid" in my aggregation of Gould's data because of their small bodies and dried skulls. But if one accepted this position and excluded the ancient Caucasians from analysis, a 4 in^3 difference in internally measured cranial capacity would be left between Mongoloids and Caucasoids on the one hand and Negroids on the other (see Table 6.1). Even if this magnitude is somewhat overestimated, the residual cannot be ignored. Moreover, if body size is controlled, the rank ordering is indeed Mongoloids > Caucasoids > Negroids because Mongoloids are often smaller in body size than Caucasoids.

Critics also brought "new" data to bear on the debate from a monograph by Herskovits (1930) who had collected external head measurements of American blacks and other populations. From this table, Zuckerman and Brody (1988: 1027) separated out a sample of 46,975 Swedes with a smaller cranial capacity than the American blacks and argued that if this kind of overlap was possible, then it was meaningless to make comparisons across races. This position was subsequently cited by other critics (e.g., Cain & Vanderwolf, 1990; Weizmann et al., 1990).

As discussed in chapter 6, Herskovits (1930) actually collated head size data for 36 male populations made by several investigators (Table 6.2). By choosing among the samples, any racial ranking can be artificially created. It is more appropriate to use the principle of aggregation and combine samples. When Herskovits's (1930) data were aggregated, as we have seen, statistically significant differences in brain size were found, with Mongoloids (in this case North American Indians) and Caucasoids averaging larger than Negroids.

Other tabulations provided by critics to support the null hypothesis turn out on closer examination to support the racial hypothesis. Thus, Cain and Vanderwolf (1990: 782) set out 20 data points including a 1923 series of Caucasoid crania and a 1986 Negroid series (Table 12.1). Their purpose was "to illustrate that by drawing from other studies one can arrive at different conclusions than Rushton did" and to show that Negroid crania are "sometimes" greater than Caucasoid crania. They concluded: "Depending on the studies one chooses to cite, one can arrive at a variety of orderings of brain size or cranial capacity."

TABLE 12.1
Adult Brain Size Data Assembled by Cain and Vanderwolf (1990)

Brain size variable / references	Number of cases	Caucasian		Black		Oriental	
		Men	Women	Men	Women	Men	Women
Birth weight data (grams)							
Ho et al., 1980a	1,261	1,392	1,252	1,286	1,158	-	-
Holloway, 1980	330	1,457	1,318	-	-	-	-
Shibata, 1936	153	-	-	-	-	1,370	1,277
Studies reviewed by Shibata	>3,388	-	-	-	-	1,348-1,406	1,120-1,261
Cranial capacity data (cm^3)							
Ricklan & Tobias, 1986	100	-	-	1,373	1,251	-	-
Todd, 1923	302	1,391	1,232	1,350	1,221	-	-

Note. From Cain & Vanderwolf (1990, p. 782, Table 1). Copyright 1990 by Pergamon Press. Reprinted with permission.

Figure 12.1: Adult Cranial Capacities Plotted From Data Assembled by Groves (1991)

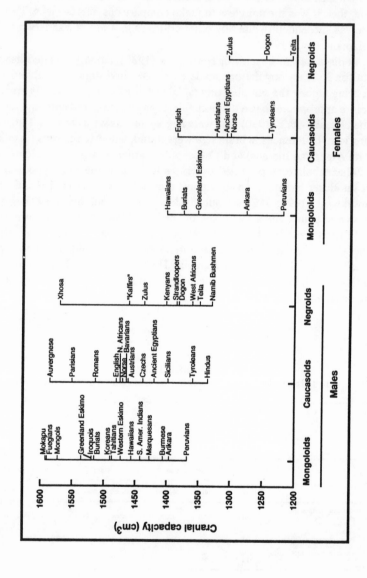

Adapted with permission of the Australasian Society for Human Biology.

Yet, Cain and Vanderwolf's data show that Negroid adults average the smallest brains. I converted to grams the data in cubic centimeters in Table 12.1 using equation (5) from chapter 6 and aggregated the data across the sexes and measures (Rushton 1990c). Mongoloids averaged 1,297 g, Caucasoids averaged 1,304 g, and Negroids averaged 1,199 g, a difference of 100 g between Negroids and the other two populations. In a reply, Vanderwolf and Cain (1991) acknowledged that "some" of the data are "trustworthy" and in the direction claimed.

A similar sort of table was created by Groves (1991) who entered 21 Mongoloid populations (16 male, 5 females), 18 Caucasoid populations (13 male, 5 female), and 12 Negroid populations (9 male, 3 female). Among those having the largest cranial capacity were the Mokapu, a Mongoloid tribe in Hawaii, and the Xhosa, a tribe from Africa. Groves focused discussion on these outliers and ignored the remainder of his own table. I have plotted the data from his table in Figure 12.1, which, in aggregation, clearly shows the racial pattern. For males, the Mongoloids, Caucasoids, and Negroids average 1,487 cm^3, 1,458 cm^3, and 1,408 cm^3, respectively, and for females they average 1,325 cm^3, 1,312 cm^3, and 1,254 cm^3 respectively. An unweighted sex-combined average of these figures results in 1,406 cm^3, 1,385 cm^3, and 1,331 cm^3, respectively.

Aggregation and Crime

Some claim that crime statistics only reflect police prejudice and biases in the criminal justice system. Some have gone so far as to claim that when the self-reports of adolescents are used, no racial differences in crime exist. Others sidestep crime statistics and focus on those surveys failing to show racial differences in antisocial personality disorder, psychopathy, and psychotic tendency (Zuckerman & Brody, 1988: 1030).

It is true that self-report measures typically show less racial disproportionality than arrest data. This is because they emphasize lesser, even trivial, offenses, that almost all males have engaged in at least once (e.g., "Have you ever been in a fight?") or because they include items of marginal relation to crime (e.g., "Would being in debt worry you?"). It is also because few of the questionnaires assess the frequency of activities.

Self-report measures do, however, show the same general pattern of group differences (age, sex, socioeconomic, and race) as do official statistics. J. Q. Wilson and Herrnstein (1985) review the literature. One study, involving a U.S. national sample of 1,726 youth aged 11 to 17, found clear evidence that African Americans engage in more crime than European-American, and particularly in predatory crimes, with the difference most apparent among high-rate offenders (Elliott & Ageton, 1980). Other studies showed that black males scored higher (that is, were less "normal") than white males on personality tests such as the Minnesota Multiphasic Personality Inventory, particularly on the Psychopathic Deviate (Pd) scale, which is predictive of criminal behavior in both racial groups.

Because crime figures vary enormously over type, region, generation, and subpopulation, Roberts and Gabor (1990) proposed they could only be explained using "situational" and "interaction" factors. Thus Roberts and Gabor (1990) pointed out that whereas arrest data from the U.S. Federal Bureau of Investigation indicated that 47 percent of violent crimes were committed by blacks, another set based on the reports of victims, by the U.S. Department of Justice, observed that only 24 percent of such crimes were committed by blacks. The figures were also shown to change with time and geographic area. Thus, the involvement of blacks in crime had increased over the last thirty years and for one year in the state of Delaware, the homicide rate for blacks was 16.7 per 100,000 whereas in Missouri the rate was 65 per 100,000.

Roberts and Gabor (1990) also pointed out that American blacks had a higher homicide rate than their more racially pure counterparts in Africa. They cited rates of 0.01 per 100,000 in Mali and 8 per 100,000 in Tanzania. Moreover, homicide rates in the Far East varied considerably, from 39 per 100,000 residents in the Philippines to 1.3 per 100,000 in Hong Kong.

As discussed in chapter 7, however, I tested the generalizability of racial differences in crime by aggregating the international crime statistics reported to INTERPOL for 1983–1984 and 1985–1986, which provided data on nearly 100 countries in 14 crime categories. For both 1984 and 1986 African and Caribbean countries reported twice the amount of violent crime (rape, murder, and serious assault) as did European countries, and about three times as much as did countries from the Pacific Rim (Table 7.3).

In reply, Gabor and Roberts (1990: 338) argued that the international statistics are "an unstandardized data base which is highly sensitive to the differential legal definitions, reporting, and recording practices of the countries around the world." In many countries, they pointed out, politically motivated killings are included in the homicide data. Rape, they go on to say, is notoriously underreported and highly sensitive to public attitudes, victim services available, the status of women, and the practices of the police and courts prevailing in a given society. Gabor and Roberts (1990) did not say why, despite all the sources of error they had enumerated, so clear a racial pattern could be calculated.

Many critics of the work on crime and race point out that African Americans are typically the victims of crime. For example, Roberts and Gabor (1990) showed that in the United States, black men are 20 times more likely than white men to be shot, cut, or stabbed, and black women are 18 times more likely to be raped than white women. Black people are also more likely than white people to be the victims of burglary, motor vehicle theft, assaults, robbery, and many other offenses.

To this argument two points may be made. First, as J. Q. Wilson and Herrnstein (1985: 463) cogently remarked:

> To believe that blacks do not commit such offenses at greater rates than whites, one would have to believe that the higher rates of victimization are caused by whites entering black neighborhoods in order to break into homes and hold up citizens. While that is possible, it seems unlikely.

Second, there is an asymmetry to interracial crime. The problem of interracial violence is overwhelmingly one of black assaults on whites. While more than 97 percent of white criminals victimize white people, up to 67 percent of black criminals also victimize white people. According to U.S. Department of Justice statistics for 1987, 200 million whites committed 87,029 violent assaults on blacks while nearly 30 million blacks committed 786,660 violent attacks on whites. This averages out to 1 out of every 38 blacks violently assaulting a white in one year, and only 1 out of every 2,298 whites assaulting a black. The black criminal's preference for white victims is at least 60 times that of the white criminal's preference for black victims. Levin (1992) has discussed some of the social implications of racial discrepancies in crime production.

Aggregation and Reproductive Behavior

In a critique, Silverman (1990) made a suggestion that I have adopted (chap. 8) of differentiating the races in terms of "reproductive potency" rather than, as I had previously been doing, in terms of "sexual restraint." Silverman (1990: 6) noted:

> Rushton has performed a novel synthesis in pulling together an array of anatomical, physiological, maturational, and behavioral differences among races, converging on the same pattern, which seems unquestionably rooted in evolutionary processes.

Generally, however, more *ad hominem* attacks have been levelled for the work on sexual behavior than any other. Zuckerman and Brody (1988: 1031) referred to a "strange naivete," an "ethnocentric bias," and a "puritanical esthetic sensibility"; Leslie (1990: 891) labeled it "transparent racist pseudoscience"; and Weizmann et al. (1990: 8) referred to it as "anthroporn." Weizmann et al. ridiculed one reference in particular (French Army Surgeon, 1898/1972) for containing "a recipe for do-it-yourself penis enlargement employing an eggplant and hot peppers!" They alleged this reference was the only source for some of the data, including an item on erect penile angle being parallel to the body in Orientals and at right angles in blacks.

Perhaps it is because data on genital size and sexual potency imply a link with animal reproductive systems that so many reacted with outrage. The interesting question, hardly addressed, is why these differences originated and what purpose they serve. A French Army Surgeon (1898/1972) was only one of several ethnographic sources. He had spent 30 years as a specialist in venereal disease in the French Foreign Legion stationed in Africa, the Middle East, the Caribbean, and French Indochina. Although it was a minor item, the black-white difference in the angle of erection reported by him was confirmed in the Kinsey data (Table 8.4, item 74) as were many other items on penis size and sexual habits (chap. 8).

In a reply to the critique by Weizmann et al. (1990), I pointed to the extensive itemization and re-analysis of the Kinsey data, the reviews of the international surveys carried out by the World Health Organization, and the surveys carried out within the United States since Kinsey, all of which showed that, in reproductive activities, Mongoloids were more restrained than Caucasoids who, in turn, were more restrained than Negroids (Rushton, 1991a). I also discussed the world wide prevalence of AIDS and other sexually transmitted diseases. Unfortunately, the tone of Weizmann et al.'s (1991: 49), counter-response was captured in their labeling of another of the citations as "ethnopornography."

Nevertheless, many legitimate concerns can be raised about the data on sexuality. M. Lynn (1989a, 1989b) and Cunningham and Barbee (1991) questioned the representativeness of Kinsey's samples, the validity of self-report measures, the degree of experimental control over possible confounding variables, and the modifiability of reproductive behavior as indexed by changes from one generation to another. These issues can only be dealt with by the collection of more data and by aggregating over different types of study.

M. Lynn (1989a, 1989b) responded that aggregation cannot overcome any initial selectivity in choosing studies. He emphasized the importance of locating *all* the relevant research on a topic and then cited several studies failing to replicate the race differences. These included reports that sexually experienced blacks had intercourse less often than whites, that on a measure of fertility in Brazil the three races ranked exactly opposite to prediction, and that infertility in the United States was higher for blacks than for whites.

Debate can go back and forth on particulars. Thus, I pointed out that the reason that blacks suffer higher infertility than whites is because of their higher proportion of sexually transmitted diseases, a problem for Negroid populations worldwide (Rushton, 1989a, 1989f). Africa is known to be differentiated from other areas of the world in having these diseases as the major cause of infertility (Cates et al., 1985).

Some critics have suggested that even if all the data were to be included in a gigantic meta-analysis, and the results shown to be as I claim, the outcome would still be a biased one because only those studies consonant with pre-existing stereotypes have been published (Fairchild, 1991; M. Lynn, 1989b;

Weizmann et al., 1991). The best response here is to reiterate that better data must be collected. In collecting these data, however, we must be just as alert to the possibility of bias toward the null hypothesis as toward "pre-existing stereotypes." Cunningham and Barbee (1991), for example, suggested that many of the gender differences that had seemed well established in the 1950s had vanished by the 1980s. However, Cunningham and Barbee (1991) failed to consider the possibility that this was because strong "politically correct" feminist pressure had biased the publication process toward data consistent with the null hypothesis (Levin, 1987).

Aggregation and Other Variables

Similar rejoinders to those made against brain size, sex, and crime have been made to other data sets. With respect to personality, Zuckerman (1990) deconstructed the ordered data from cross-cultural studies into national and even tribal particulars and made the pattern disappear. With respect to developmental status, counter-examples have been provided showing that girls from Hong Kong have an average age of menarche of 12 years and girls from Africa an average age of 15 years (Groves, 1991; M. Lynn, 1989a).

With cognitive performance, Flynn (1984, 1987, 1989, 1991) has discussed how, because IQ in the developed world has been rising for 30 years, it is premature to assume that environmental factors cannot account for racial differences. Flynn (1991) calculated that when generational changes in test scores are taken into account, the Mongoloid-Caucasoid difference disappears. Even the data on black-white differences in IQ contain anomalous studies. Scarr (1987), for example, claimed that black children in Britain are not educationally disadvantaged until age 8, and that in Bermuda at 12 years of age they score two years above U.S. whites on tests of school achievement.

Much disputed also is the contention that the pattern of racial differences in behavior show up historically. Some have suggested that blacks played a significant intellectual role in the civilization of ancient Egypt (Weizmann et al., 1991). Some proponents of Afro-centrism have gone so far as to claim that Aristotle and other geniuses from ancient Greece stole their ideas from black Africa (James, 1992). Flynn (1989) challenged the evidence of history on law abidingness, pointing to the authority-driven criminality of this century in China, Japan, Germany, and Russia. Gabor and Roberts (1990: 343) dismissed the entire effort of examining such data as "idle speculation" with "no place" in the scientific enterprise.

Is the Genetic Evidence Flawed?

Some critics hold to the position that until the genes themselves are mapped, inferences about their effects on behavior are unwarranted. Lovejoy (1990: 909–910) wrote:

> I am particularly interested in Rushton and Bogaert's (presumably) polygenic models for the inheritance of "social organizational complexity," and their projections as to the prospect of identifying which chromosome bears the loci which lead to "decentralized organizations with weak power structures." Perhaps these are pleiotropic characters of a single dominant gene?

If taken seriously, such reasoning would undermine the value of any epidemiological research, a prerequisite for detailed genetic analyses. It would even have denied the strategy of Charles Darwin who, of course, never knew the mechanism by which characters were inherited. Genetic effects were not discovered until years after Darwin's death and the biochemical structure of genes not until decades after. I can only refer such critics to the discussion of distal-proximal explanations in chapter 1.

Some who disapprovingly reviewed the early behavior genetic literature held that the heritability of intelligence should be set at zero (e.g., Kamin, 1974). A 100 percent denial of genetic influence continues to be promoted, most forcefully by Lewontin (1991; Lewontin et al., 1984). One argument is that because development is so complicated and genetic x environment interactions are so ubiquitous it is impossible to disentangle causality and apportion variance separately to genes and environment (Hirsch, 1991; Wahlsten, 1990). These complexities are considered to undermine theorizing on race differences. Lewontin (1992, ix) continues to call for the "dialectical relation" elaborated by Karl Marx in which organism and environment are somehow "fused" as subject and object, a point elaborated on by Lerner (1992) in his account of "developmental contextualism."

In general response to the complexity discussion Bouchard (1984: 182) made a forceful point: If context and interaction effects are so ubiquitous and genetic effects so complicated, how can it be that monozygotic twins reared apart grow to be so similar in so many ways? Siblings raised away from each other grow to be significantly similar to each other, with their degree of similarity being predicted by the number of genes they share. This implies the presence of genetically based stabilizing systems driving development into a common channel (see Table 3.1 and Figures 3.3 to 3.5).

The specific analyses presented for the heritability of race differences have also been debated. M. Lynn (1989a: 30) attributed the findings in Table 9.2, showing that black children raised by white middle-class families regress to their population mean in IQ scores and educational level, to "self-fulfilling prophecies." There is, however, scant (if any) evidence for such effects (Jensen, 1980a).

M. Lynn (1989a: 31) dismissed as "faulty logic" the discussion of how combining within-family and between-family analyses ruled out between-family sources of variance such as social class, thereby leaving in genetic and within-family sources of environmental variance. He similarly dismissed regression to the mean effects and attributed them to environmental effects and called the finding that Japanese inbreeding depression scores predict the magnitude of the black-white difference on the same tests (Figure 9.1) as a "coincidence" (p. 32).

Evidence against the genetic hypothesis was marshaled by Sandra Scarr (1987) who summarized her 20-year program of research on black-white differences in a presidential address to the Behavior Genetics Association. First, using the twin method, she reported lower heritabilities among blacks than among whites, suggesting that among blacks, environmental effects had a more repressive effect. (Willerman, 1979: 440–44, has reviewed other studies showing a lower heritability of IQ in blacks.) Second, using blood groups as genetic markers of African ancestry, Scarr reported that degree of African ancestry did not correlate with IQ test scores. Third, her study of transracial adoption analyzed to that point in time had found that 7-year-old black and mixed-race children reared by upper-middle-class white parents scored above the IQ norm for white children in the same area. Fourth, cross-cultural studies showed that black children in Britain did not become educationally disadvantaged until after age 8, and that black children in Bermuda scored two years above U.S. white children on tests of vocabulary, reading, and mathematics at age 12. Fifth, preschool intervention programs remedied early disparities.

Scarr (1987) concluded that, although for whites, genes strongly influenced individual and social class differences, for blacks, culture imposed limitations on individual mobility and so causal relationships were different. She maintained that racial categories were more rigidly prescribed statuses than social classes. More generally her theory of how people made their own environments was held not to apply to people with few opportunities (Scarr, 1992). Additional evidence against the genetic hypothesis was cited by Zuckerman and Brody (1988) who referred to Eyferth's work showing that the IQs of children fathered by U.S. troops and reared by their white German mothers were the same, irrespective of whether their biological fathers were black or white.

Problems exist in the counter-research too, of course. First, in Scarr's study comparing black and white twins, no tests of zygosity were made (see commentaries in Scarr, 1981). Instead, Scarr inferred monozygotic and dizygotic variances from knowledge of the relationship between opposite-sex pairs who are necessarily dizygotic but who are overrepresented in black samples because of the greater production of female offspring among blacks. Her procedures underestimated heritabilities for all samples, including the whites, among whom the heritabilities ranged from 4 to 44 percent, lower than the 50 to 80 percent more typically estimated. Moreover, Osborne (1978, 1980) subsequently showed heritabilities of greater than 50 percent for a sample of 123 pairs of black adolescent twins, similar to those calculated for a comparison group of 304 pairs of white twins.

Second, with the study of African ancestry, as discussed by Jensen (1981), a positive correlation existed between skin color and blood group ancestry, suggesting that skin color was as good an indicator of African ancestry as were blood groups. But the effects of skin color were statistically controlled for in Scarr's study. If they had not been, African blood groups would have correlated with test scores, as predicted by genetic theory. A significant statistical relation between skin color and IQ among Negroid-Caucasoid hybrids was calculated by Shockley (1973; see also Shuey, 1966). He estimated that for low IQ black populations there is a one-point increase in average "genetic" IQ for each 1 percent of Caucasian ancestry, with diminishing returns as an IQ of 100 is reached.

With the adoption, cross-cultural, and early intervention studies, it is accepted that environments affect IQ and scholastic attainment to a magnitude of 6 to 10 IQ points, even when the heritability is as high as 70 percent (Jensen, 1989). However, the strongest intervention and between-family environments effects are observed among pre-adolescents and not among post-adolescents. The results from the adoption studies cited by Scarr (1987) and Zuckerman and Brody (1988) are based on children who were no older than 13 years of age. The results are thus comparable to those from several American adoption studies showing that the common family environment can affect development up until puberty, after which it is less likely to do so (Plomin & Daniels, 1987).

Post-puberty, causal influences on behavior are increasingly of the genetic and within-family variety. Thus, it would be interesting to know what happened after puberty to the black and white German children in the studies by Eyferth cited by Zuckerman and Brody (1988). The results of the 10-year follow-up to the transracial adoption study conducted by Scarr and her colleagues (Table 9.2), not available to Scarr (1987) at the time of her address to the Behavior Genetics Association, is problematic to the environmentalist perspective because it suggests that the black children regressed to their population mean in IQ.

Is *r-K* Theory Correct?

Several writers have claimed that my theoretical account ignored ecological processes and assumptions that are central to the *r-* and *K*-selection concept (Anderson, 1991; Lerner, 1992; Miller, 1993; Weizmann et al., 1990, 1991). One reason for widespread confusion even among ecologists has centered on the climatic conditions most likely to produce *r*-selection. For example, Barash (1982: 306) wrote, in his textbook *Sociobiology and Behavior*:

> Although the distinction between *r* and *K*-selection was first made explicit by MacArthur and Wilson (1967), it was actually suggested nearly 20 years previously by the great evolutionary geneticist Theodosius Dobzhansky (1950). He noted that, in general, inhabitants of the temperate and arctic zones suffered mortality that was largely independent of their population density, occurring because of large-scale environmental fluctuations, such as drought, storms, sudden influx of large

numbers of predators. In such conditions, mortality was relatively independent of individual characteristics, so parents ensured their reproductive success by generating a large number of offspring (that is, *r*-selection). By contrast, Dobzhansky emphasized that tropical species competed most intensely with one another rather than with the environment. The relatively benign habitat was virtually filled with organisms, so the difference between success and failure was by producing not a large number of offspring but rather a smaller number of well-endowed descendents (that is, *K*-selection).

Barash, however, is incorrect. *Predictability* is the ecological necessity for *K*-selection. This can occur in either a stable environment or a predictably variable one. What has apparently been misunderstood is that subtropical savannahs, where humans evolved, because of sudden droughts and devastating viral, bacterial, and parasitic diseases, are less predictable for long-lived species than are temperate and especially Arctic environments. Although the Arctic climate varies greatly over one year, it is highly predictable, but harsh, over many years (Rushton & Ankney, 1993).

Many critics have made the classic mistake (many ecologists do also) of confusing variable and unpredictable. Weizmann et al. (1990: 2) claimed that, because of their longer ancestry in stable tropical climates, blacks should be more *K*-selected than other human groups. Miller (1993) also suggested that the converse might be true, that arctic animals with variable winter cycles, would be *r*-selected. But, of course, they are not. Long-lived arctic mammals like polar bears, caribou, muskox, seals, and walruses are highly *K*-selected, as are Arctic people. The reason is that the Arctic environment is not only highly variable, but more importantly, is highly predictable as well. (More generally, data show that plants, lizards, and mammals become more *K*-selected with increasing elevation and latitude [Zammuto & Millar, 1985].)

Annual food shortage in the arctic is predictable, that is, people knew that it would be difficult to find food for 4 to 6 months every year. Thus, this selected for *K*-traits. If an individual had the traits necessary to plan ahead well, the individual's genes survived. Contrast this with tropical savannahs where disease epidemics and prolonged droughts were (and are) unpredictable. Under such conditions an individual that produced many descendants during favorable conditions would be most likely to have some that survived (unpredictable) catastrophes. Alternatively, if an arctic-dwelling person put maximal effort into mating/reproduction he or she likely wouldn't survive for one year; their offspring certainly would not.

Additional criticisms have been made of my (Rushton, 1985a, 1988b) version of *r-K* theory (originally termed "differential *K* theory" to emphasize that all human beings are *K*-selected relative to other animals). Some have insisted that *r-K* theory is applicable only at the level of the species or, at best, to well-defined local populations, but is not applicable to variation within species (Anderson, 1991; Lerner, 1992; Weizmann et al. 1990, 1991). This criticism ignores both the origins of the theory (MacArthur & Wilson, 1967) and the within-species studies of plants, insects, fish, and nonhuman mammals (chap. 10). Other complaints that predictions about altruism, law abidingness, and sexuality are arbitrary and do not derive from r-K theory, rest on an incomplete understanding of what the original codifiers of the theory have written (see chap. 10 for references and page numbers).

Are Environmental Explanations Sufficient?

Many environmental theories have been proposed to explain racial differences. Typically the theories are sociological in nature and specify global and diffuse processes such as poverty and systemic white racism. Evidence then often consists of zero-order correlations such as those between race and socioeconomic indicators. Psychological theories have also been proposed. The most detailed and powerful of these I will refer to as "environmental r-K theory," to be presented shortly. First, let us consider alternatives.

Freudian Theory

In *Civilization and It's Discontents,* Freud (1930/1962) noted a positive correlation between restrained sexuality and the production of culture. He proposed that repressing aggressive and sexual instincts led them to be sublimated into higher cultural products. Because African children are raised more permissively than are European or American children, their instincts are less subject to being repressed and thus blacks develop uninhibited personalities but lowered economic success.

The toilet training variant of Freud's theory was found in the literature of the early 1950s. This held that African children, not trained to control their bowels until a considerably later age than European children, developed an extraverted culture with values of sensual self-expression and a relaxed heterosexual attitude to sex. At the other end of the scale were Orientals who were toilet trained at a very early age, and thereby became puritanically self-disciplined and oriented toward achievement.

Ice versus Sun People

An evolutionary-based psychological theory of "ice" versus "sun" people by Bradley (1978) was promoted by Leonard Jeffries, Jr., chair of the Black Studies Department at the City College of New York. He held that people of European ancestry, whom he called "ice people," were intrinsically greedy and intent on domination, while people of African descent, or "sun people," were humanistic and communal. Jeffries suggested that abundant skin pigment in African Americans gave them intellectual and physical advantages over whites ("White Professor Wins Court Ruling," *New York Times*, September 5, 1991).

Sex Ratio Theory

Cunningham and Barbee (1991) proposed an ecological analysis based on high infant mortality rates and a scarcity of black males. They hypothesized that a stressful environment led to high black infant mortality rates, particularly *male* infant mortality. The subsequent shortage of adult black males undermined female sexual restrictiveness and encouraged sexual behavior. Males would be reluctant to marry and invest in parenthood and, instead, would mate with a number of women sequentially; single mother births would be common and male attitudes would be misogynistic. Attitudes of sexual permissiveness combined with a high infant mortality rate would encourage high rates of reproduction.

Messner and Sampson (1991) elaborated on this general model to explain the disproportionate amount of crime committed by blacks. It might have been predicted that, because males are more involved in violent crime than females, populations with fewer male births (i.e., blacks) would produce less crime per capita than populations with more male births (i.e., Orientals). But, the opposite occurs. Messner and Sampson (1991) explained the paradox by suggesting that a shortage of men necessarily increases the number of female-headed households, which in turn leads, through poor socialization, to higher levels of underachievement and crime. Crime in turn leads more black men to go to prison, which exacerbates the cycle.

If reproductive patterns are ecologically induced states, rather than genetically maintained traits, then as an ecological setting became more supportive and the infant mortality and unbalanced sex ratio were reduced, the high reproduction rates should also be reduced. Cunningham and Barbee (1991) analyzed the 1960–1985 U.S. fertility data to test this hypothesis. Differences in black/white birth rates were indeed associated with differences in infant mortality rates. As black mortality rates declined, birth rates also declined at rates parallel to that of whites. Thus, it was reasoned, sexual behavior in blacks and whites were equally responsive to their ecologies and there was no necessity to postulate genetic differences.

Further supporting Cunningham and Barbee's (1991) analysis are recent data from the U.S. census on infant mortality. The U.S. National Center for Health Statistics provided breakdowns on infant mortality for 1988. By race, per 1,000 live births, blacks = 18, whites = 9, and Orientals = 5. On the other hand, babies born to college-educated blacks have a higher mortality rate than those born to similarly educated whites, a finding that seems to undermine the idea that poverty and poor medical care are mostly to blame for the difference (Schoendorf et al., 1992).

One reason for the racial disparity in infant mortality is that black women give birth to greater numbers of low-birth weight babies who are considered premature. However the thesis advanced in this book is that the lower birth weight and shorter gestation of blacks is part of a genetically based racial difference in life history (chap. 10). The environmentalist case is that premature births are due to the stress brought on by "complex discriminatory effects" (Wise & Pursley, 1992). On the other hand, predictably, Orientals have a greater number of male births than Caucasoids (James, 1986) and there is at least some evidence that the sex ratio is partly heritable (J. S. Watson, 1992), perhaps mediated hormonally (James, 1986).

Environmental r-K Theory

Prior to my (Rushton, 1984, 1985a) application of r-K analyses to human variation, others had explained group differences using an r-K approach *without* recourse to genetic factors (Weinrich, 1977; Cunningham, 1981; Draper and Harpending, 1982; Reynolds and Tanner, 1983; Masters, 1984; Weigel and Blurton Jones, 1983). All of these authors postulated that individuals living in unpredictable environments with consequent resource scarcity and uncertainty that offspring would survive to reproductive maturity, would be induced to opportunistically produce as many children as possible while giving less parental care.

Draper and Harpending (1982, 1988) proposed that father absence was a critical determinant of later reproductive strategy. Due to learned perceptions about the predictability of the environment, low-income and father-absent families were said to adopt an opportunistically oriented r-strategy of high "mating effort" whereas high-income and father-present families adopted a future-oriented K-strategy of "parenting effort." The more predictable an environment is learned to be, the more a K-strategy would be adopted. Draper and Harpending reviewed the correlates of the "mating effort" strategy and its culmination in the father-absent child: poor school performance, antiauthoritarianism, aggressiveness, sexual precocity, and criminality. They concluded that "father-present societies are those where most males act like dads and father-absent societies are those where most males act like cads" (1988: 349).

Building on the earlier work by Draper and Harpending, environmental theories of the development of reproductive strategies have been proposed by Belsky, Steinberg, and Draper (1991) and Chisholm (1993). Thus, two diverging pathways (Figure 12.2) were succinctly described by Belsky et al. (1991: 647):

> One is characterized, in childhood, by a stressful rearing environment and the development of insecure attachments to parents and subsequent behavior problems;

in adolescence by early pubertal development and precocious sexuality; and in adulthood, by unstable pair bonds and limited investment in child rearing, whereas the other is characterized by the opposite.

These predictions have been confimed in several longitudinal studies. In one, over 900 16-year-old New Zealand girls were assessed with a diverse battery of psychological, medical, and sociological measures every 2 years from age 3 to age 15 (Moffit, Caspi, Belsky, & Silva, 1992). Family conflict and father absence in childhood predicted an earlier age of menarche, independent of body weight. In longitudinal studies in the United States, Jessor, Donovan, and Costa (1991) predicted onset of sexual intercourse among adolescents from knowledge of whether they had low scores in academic achievement and religiosity, and high scores on measures of deviance and "problem

Figure 12.2: Developmental Pathways of Divergent Reproductive Strategies

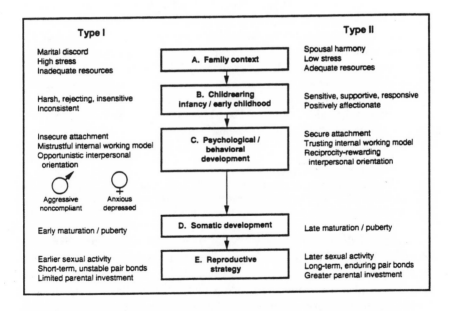

In pathway 1, a discordant, stressful, or otherwise unpredictable early environment leads to insecure attachment, an early onset of sexual activity, an opportunistic interpersonal orientation, and limited parental investment. In pathway 2, a harmonious and predictable early environment leads to a delayed onset of sexual activity, a reciprocally rewarding interpersonal orientation and large amounts of parental investment. From Belsky, Steinberg & Draper (1991, p. 651, Figure 1). Copyright 1991 by the Society for Research in Child Development. Reprinted with permission.

behavior." Multiple correlations reached predictive levels greater than 0.50 accounting for approximately 30 percent of the variance over a 9-year interval.

Additional aspects of sexuality are predictive. Age of menarche is related to adult orgastic capacity and sexual activity in both women (Raboch & Bartak, 1981) and men (Raboch & Mellan, 1979). In a review of the literature on early menarche, Surbey (1990) found a significant positive correlation between mothers and daughters' menarcheal ages and for early menarche to be associated with a cluster of social and sexual behaviors related to a woman losing her mate or never living with the father of her child. Promiscuity, high school drop out, and other problem behaviors were also more likely.

In a longitudinal Swedish study of 1,400 individuals, Magnusson (1992) found that early-maturing girls had cheated, been truants, got drunk, and tried marijuana more often than late-maturing girls. Conflicts with parents and teachers were more common and the early-maturing girls were less interested in school and future education. The early-maturing girls entered pair relationships earlier, married earlier, had children earlier, and entered the labor market earlier.

Environmental r-K theories could be integrated with the genetic polymorphism perspective that individuals are genetically inclined to one developmental pathway over another. Many have insisted, however, that the racial pattern can be explained, even from a reproductive strategy perspective, "without necessitating any underlying genetic variability" (Mealey, 1990: 387). For example, Mealey reported international findings on infant mortality showing the pattern of Negroids most, Caucasoids intermediate, and Mongoloids least. But, she held that this pattern could be parsimoniously explained through poor maternal nutrition leading to high overall mortality. She concluded:

> All in all, I find the pattern that Rushton presents interesting and worth pursuing; but his interpretation is not the only one compatible with existing data. Differential utilization of reproductive strategies may be environmentally contingent rather than genetic, and apparent group differences a result, therefore, of the segregation of different human groups into different environments.

Certainly the potency of nutrition as an environmental factor seems reasonable. It has recently been advanced as an important variable for consideration by R. Lynn (1990b) and by Eysenck (1991a, 1991b). Across ages and settings, studies have shown that adding a vitamin and mineral supplement to normal diets increased intelligence and positive social behavior such as paying attention, keeping one's temper, and refraining from fighting (Eysenck & Eysenck, 1991). Eysenck elaborated (1991b: 329): "The possibility needs at least to be considered that there may be *biological* ways of improving brain function, including giving the brain additional nourishment to enable it to function at an optimal level." R. Lynn (1990b) suggested that improved nutrition may have been the crucial factor underlying the massive rise in mental test scores over the past 50 years in 14 European and American nations, as documented by Flynn (1984, 1987).

Eysenck (1991a: 124) applied a nutrient deficiency hypothesis to the pattern of race differences:

> [I]t may be useful to point to ways of testing some of the consequences which would seem to follow from my hypothesis. It would seem that Negroid children should benefit significantly more from dietary supplementation than Caucasoid, and Caucasoid slightly more than Mongoloid. Equally, determination of vitamin and mineral deficiencies should find these more plentiful in Negroid than in Caucasoid, and in Caucasoid than in Mongoloid children. African blacks should come out worst, and benefit most. These suggestions are easily testable and findings should be of obvious social and scientific importance.

However, there is no evidence to show that nutrition causes an inverse relation between brain size and gamete production. Postulating some genetic variance seems indispensable to explain the consistency of the racial ordering across so many attributes, including the macrophysiological variables of brain size, egg production, and hormone level. A mixed 50 percent evolutionary and 50 percent environmental model fits the data better than either the 100 percent environmental or the 100 percent genetic alternatives.

It is always easy to hypothesize poorly defined causal factors to explain race differences for which there is actually no scientific evidence. Jensen (1973) labeled these "X-factors," that is, factors that can account for anything, but cannot be proved or disproved. Most analyses of racial differences are superficial and diffuse. If understanding in this area is to advance, it is essential that hypotheses be made with greater clarity and with the capacity for generating differential predictions.

The mechanism of paternal provisioning has been postulated by E. M. Miller (1993, 1994) to be a more exact specification of the evolutionary process by which the races became differentiated. A continuum of male paternal effort is focused on, ranging from none to maximum. Miller proposed that, in warm climates, females can typically gather enough food to support themselves and their children. In cold climates, however, hunting is required, and females typically do not hunt. Thus, males in cold climates were selected to devote more of their effort to provisioning and less to seeking matings. Thus, for males, during the hunter-gatherer period of human evolution, the optimal combination of mating effort and paternal investment varied with the severity of the winters. In Africa, a strong sex drive, aggression, dominance seeking, impulsivity, low anxiety, sociability, extraversion, and a morphology and muscle enzyme suitable for fighting lead to mating success, whereas in northeast Asia, altruism, empathy, behavioral restraint, and a long life assisted success in provisioning. Although Rushton and Ankney (1993) suggested that Miller's account is not different from r-K theory, Miller's work does show the value of highlighting particular processes.

Is Race Science Immoral?

Some have claimed that human sociobiology is not a science and exists only to justify existing social inequalities; they attack sociobiology for viewing war and xenophobia as inevitable parts of human nature. It is claimed that a socially just society is impossible if "selfish" genes truly act to influence, in the service of their reproduction, our mores, our social institutions, and our culture. As Lewontin et al. (1984: 18) put it:

> Biological determinism is, then, a reductionist explanation of human life in which the arrows of causality run from genes to humans and from humans to humanity. But that is more than mere explanation: It is politics. For if human social organization, including the inequalities of status, wealth, and power, are a direct consequence of our biologies, then, except for some gigantic program of genetic engineering, no practice can make a significant alteration of social structure or of the position of individuals or groups within it.

At the extreme, sociobiological work, especially on race, is associated with the Nazis. It is held that the Nazis would not have achieved power if their general ideology had not been widely accepted in Germany. They could not have realized their racial program—including the murder of Jews, Gypsies, and the insane—without the help of an ideology of biological determinism (Lerner, 1992; Lewontin, 1992; Muller-Hill, 1988, 1992). This is the position taken by Richard Lerner (1992: 147) in *Final Solutions:*

> Rushton's thinking, so redolent of Nazi-era political and scientific pronouncements about advances in cures of genetic disease, is nothing more than the most recent instance of genetic determinist ideology promoted as science. His work, and that of many other contemporary sociobiologists, is poor science and represents a fatally flawed basis for prescribing social policy. Scientists and citizens alike must confront both these domains of shortcomings. If we do otherwise, we are allowing history to repeat itself.

The underlying logic of these political critiques is grievously flawed. Scientific theories do not cause people to commit murder. Nonetheless, all ideas can be used to justify hatred. But here, religious and egalitarian ideas have just as bad a history. The Reign of Terror following the French Revolution (1789) and the 70 years of Communist dictatorship following the Russian Revolution (1917) show how readily idealism can be perverted. Thus, it is totalitarianism in the service of fanaticism that causes people to be murdered, not theories of human nature.

Opponents of the genetic study of racial differences are either unable or unwilling to separate their political agendas from the scholarly pursuit of truth; many seem to deny that it is even possible, a view that stems from nihilistic ideas of the relativity of truth and Marxist claims that even scientists are motivated by class interests. Perhaps there is some reality here and one could go further and postulate that ideologies also reflect genetic interests (chap. 4). Obviously, abundant sources of bias operate. The scholars we should try to emulate, however, are the ones who have managed to transcend the particulars of their individual circumstances in order to discern truth more closely.

There are no necessary policies that flow from race research. The findings are compatible with a wide range of recommendations: from social segregation, through laissez-faire, to programs for the disadvantaged. Yet effective public policies must be based on sound scientific conclusions rather than popular assumptions or misconceptions. Social problems of poverty, crime, drug abuse, and unemployment often have an ethnic dimension, whether examined in "developing," "ex-communist," or "developed" countries (Klitgaard, 1986). As the world continues a trend toward a global village it will be more necessary than ever to come to terms with the degree of genetic variation within the human species.

From an evolutionary point of view it is to be expected that separate breeding populations will come to differ, genetically, in the mechanisms underlying their behavior. This is because behavior, like morphology, represents at least in part, the adaptation of gene pools to particular environments. The existence of genetic variance both within and between populations is, in fact, the first postulate of Darwinian theory. (The second is that some parts of this variance are more successful at replication than are other parts.)

Rejection of a genetic basis for human variation is not only poor science, it is likely to be injurious to both unique individuals and complexly structured societies. Nor does adopting an evolutionary outlook disconfirm the democratic ideal. As E. O. Wilson (1978) put it: "We are not compelled to believe in biological uniformity in order to affirm human freedom and dignity" (p. 52). He went on to quote the sociologist Bressler (1968):

> An ideology that tacitly appeals to biological equality as a condition for human emancipation corrupts the idea of freedom. Moreover, it encourages decent men to tremble at the prospect of "inconvenient" findings that may emerge in future scientific research.

The deeply pious Blaise Pascal said, regarding the condemnation of the Copernican hypothesis: "If the earth moves, a decree from Rome cannot stop it." As Enrico Fermi remarked, "Whatever Nature has in store for mankind, unpleasant as it may be, men must accept, for ignorance is never better than knowledge." The danger comes when we violate Fermi's adjuration (often with humanitarian arguments), not when honest scholars discuss ideas freely and openly. Ultimately, the study of racial differences may help us to appreciate more fully the nature of human diversity as well as the binding commonalities we share with other species (E. O. Wilson, 1992). That, too, would be one of the legacies of the Darwinian perspective.

13

Conclusions and Discussion

Across time, country, and circumstance, African descended people show similarities that differentiate them from Caucasoids who, in turn, show similarities differentiating them from Orientals. Although variation occurs from country to country, consistency is found within racial groups with Chinese, Koreans, and Japanese being similar to each other and different from Israelis, Swedes, and American whites, who, in turn, are similar to each other but are different from Kenyans, Nigerians, and American blacks.

The stepwise function of racial characteristics are summarized in Table 1.1. Mongoloids and Caucasoids have the largest brains, the slowest rate of dental development, and produce the fewest gametes. No environmental factor is known to cause an inverse relation between brain size and gamete production nor cause so many diverse variables to cohere in so comprehensive a fashion. There is, however, a genetic factor: evolution.

The Main Findings

Brain Size

The size of the brain has been estimated using three main procedures: weight at autopsy, within-skull (endocranial) volume, and external head volume. Data collected over 150 years were summarized in chapter 6 and averaged. Mongoloids were found to have a sex-combined brain volume of 1,364 cm^3, Caucasoids 1,347 cm^3, and Negroids 1,267 cm^3. While sampling and methodological difficulties may be identified in each source, results obtained from diverse procedures allow a triangulation on probable truth. The sex-combined world average brain size was estimated to be 1,326 cm^3.

The racial differences in brain size show up early in life. At birth, 17,000 white infants in a U.S. national study had significantly larger head perimeters than 19,000 black infants even though, by 7 years, black children were taller and heavier (Broman et al., 1987). In all groups, head perimeter at birth and at age 7 correlated with IQ at age 7 from 0.10 to 0.20. Small differences in brain volume translate into millions of excess neurons.

259

Intelligence

Among humans there is a small but robust correlation between brain size and intelligence. Using a simple tape measure, head perimeter reliably correlates between 0.10 and 0.30 with intelligence test scores for children, university students, and military conscripts (Table 2.2). The relationship has been found among Oriental students as among white students (Rushton, 1992c) and among black children as among white children (Broman et al., 1987). Correlations of about 0.40 between brain size and IQ have been confirmed in studies using magnetic resonance imaging to measure adult brain size *in vivo* (Andreasen et al., 1993; Raz et al., 1993; Wickett et al., 1994; Willerman et al., 1991).

Race differences in intelligence have been noted since the time of World War I when widespread testing began with blacks scoring about 15 IQ points lower than whites in the United States, the United Kingdom, the Caribbean, and in sub-Saharan Africa. Orientals score higher than whites on exactly the same measuring instruments, whether tested in Canada and the United States, or in their home countries. A major review of the global distribution of intelligence by R. Lynn (1991c) found the racial pattern to occur whether assessed by standard tests, by cognitive decision times, or by contributions to civilization. Lynn also reported that nonhybridized African blacks scored significantly lower than the hybridized blacks in the United States and Caribbean.

Speed of Maturation

On numerous measures of dental and physiological maturation, the distinct racial pattern emerges across the life span. Blacks are fast, compared with Caucasians, while Orientals are slow. For example, black babies have a shorter gestation period than white babies and yet are born physiologically more mature with superior muscular strength and eye-hand coordination. As infants they are able to crawl, walk, and dress earlier than whites and Orientals. Black toddlers typically begin to walk at 11 months, compared to Caucasians at 12 months, and Mongoloids at 13 months. Speed of dental development, indexed by onset of permanent molar teeth shows Africans to average about 5.8 years and Europeans and northeast Asians at 6.1 years. Other life-cycle traits, including age at first intercourse and age at first pregnancy, as well as longevity, show a similar set of differences among the three populations.

Personality

In personality, blacks are less inhibited than whites who are less inhibited than Orientals. With infants and young children, observer ratings are the main method employed, whereas with adults the use of standardized tests are more frequent. One study carried out in Quebec examined 825 4-to 6-year-olds in French language classes for immigrant children. Teachers consistently reported better social adjustment and less hostility-aggression from Asian children than from Caucasian children than from black children. With adults, Rushton (1985b) aggregated the results from 25 countries using the Eysenck Personality Questionnaire and found 8 Oriental samples (N = 4,044) to be less sociable and more anxious than 30 Caucasoid samples (N = 19,807) who were less sociable and more anxious than 4 African samples (N = 1,906).

Marital Relations

Marital stability can be assessed by rate of divorce, out-of-wedlock birthing, child abuse, and delinquency. On each of these measures, the rank ordering within American populations is Oriental < white < black. The unique African-American pattern is also to be found in Africa, south of the Sahara, and to predate the colonial period (Draper, 1989). In Africa, biological parents do not expect to act as a unit to be the major provider for their children. The African pattern typically contains some or all of the following distinctions: (1) the early onset of sexual activity; (2) loose emotional ties between spouses; (3) the expectation of sexual union with many partners, and children by them; (4) lowered maternal nurturing with long-term "fostering" of children, sometimes for several years, to nonprimary caretakers, with the stated reason sometimes being to remain sexually attractive to future sexual partners; (5) increased male-male competitiveness for females and lowered paternal involvement in child rearing or maintenance of single pair-bonds; and (6) higher fertility, despite education and urbanization.

Crime

In law abidingness, Asian Americans are underrepresented and African Americans overrepresented in crime. Internationally, African and Caribbean countries report twice the amount of violent crime (murder, rape, and serious assault) as do European or Middle East countries and three times more than do countries in the Pacific Rim. Summing crime data from INTERPOL and averaging across years gives figures per 100,000 population, respectively of 142, 74, and 43. A similar disproportionate racial pattern is to be found within industrialized Western cities such as London, England, and Toronto, Canada, as well as cities within the USA.

Reproductive Behavior

Differences in reproductive anatomy and physiology exist, including in the rate of gamete production caused in part by differential rates of ovulation.

Data collected from the Kinsey Institute for Sex Research, the World Health Organization, and from around the world consistently show a racial pattern for intercourse frequencies (whether assessed maritally, premaritally, or extramaritally), secondary sexual characteristics (salient voice, muscularity, buttocks, and breasts), biologic control of behavior (periodicity of sexual response, predictability of life history from onset of puberty), as well as in androgen levels and sexual attitudes.

Differences in sexual activity translate into consequences. Teenage fertility rates around the world show the racial gradient. So does the pattern of sexually transmitted diseases. World Health Organization Technical Reports and other studies examining the worldwide prevalence of AIDS, syphilis, gonorrhea, herpes, and chlamydia typically find low levels in China and Japan and high levels in Africa, with European countries intermediate.

Conclusion

In sum, the racial gradient of Oriental-white-black occurs on multifariously complex dimensions. From brain size, intelligence, and personality to law abidingness, social organization, and reproductive morphology, Africans and Asians average at opposite ends of the continuum, with Caucasian populations falling intermediately. This racial ordering is reflected in global rankings made by Orientals, as well as by whites. In a social perception study, Orientals viewed themselves as having more intelligence, industry, anxiety, and rule-following behavior than whites or blacks, while being significantly lower in activity level, sociability, aggressiveness, strength of the sex drive, and genital size (Table 7.4).

Reproductive Strategies

The ultimate aim of science is to causally explain the natural world rather than only to describe it. Accounting for the total array of international evidence summarized above necessitates a more powerful theory than would be required to explain any single dimension from the set. It also requires going beyond the particulars of any one country.

My thesis is that archaic versions of what were to become the modern Caucasoid and Mongoloid peoples dispersed out of Africa about 100,000 years ago and adapted to the problem of survival in predictably cold environments. The evolutionary process required a bioenergetic trade-off that increased brain size and social organization (K) at the expense of egg production and sexual behavior (r).

The r-K scale is generally used to compare what are often widely disparate species, but I (Rushton, 1992b: 817-18) used it to describe the immensely smaller variations within the human species:

Generalizing from the animal literature to human differences, the more K the family, the greater should be the spacing between births, the fewer the number of offspring, the lower the rate of infant mortality, the more stable the family system, and the better developed the parental care. The more K the person, the longer should be the period of gestation, the higher the birthweight, the more delayed the onset of sexual activity, the older the age at first reproduction, the longer the life, the more physiologically efficient the use of energy, the higher the intelligence, the more social rule-following the behavior, and the greater the altruism. Thus, diverse organismic characteristics, not otherwise relatable, are presumed to covary along a single dimension.

Because the races differ on many of the K characteristics, I hypothesized that Orientals are more K-selected than Caucasoids, who in turn are more K-selected than Negroids. Thus, the posited racial differences in behavior belong in a broader evolutionary context than had been considered to date.

An African Origin

The ancestors of modern humans, the australopithecenes, *Homo habilis,* and *Homo erectus* all made their first appearances on the African continent. Thus, Africa is the cradle of humankind. There are two competing theories, however, to explain how racial differentiation occurred during the final stages of hominid evolution. These are the Multiregional and the Single Origin theories.

Both theories agree that by a million or more years ago *Homo erectus* had emerged out of Africa to populate Eurasia. They are divided on whether the descendants of these *erectus* populations (the Neanderthals in Europe, Beijing Man in China, and Java Man in Indonesia) gave rise to modern ancestors, or whether these were evolutionary dead ends supplanted by a wave of anatomically modern people arising in Africa only 200,000 years ago.

The position taken in this book has been to favor the single origin "Out of Africa" model. Chapter 11 reviewed the genetic, paleontological, archaeological, linguistic, and behavioral data supporting this conclusion. However, it is not crucial for the general position whether the races began their divergence 1 million years ago or only 100,000 years ago.

Given an African origin of less than 200,000 years ago, a dispersal event out of Africa about 100,000 years ago, and a peopling of the rest of the world thereafter, the question arises as to how these events led to the behavioral profiles found among the races. The suggestion is made that colonizing temperate and cold environments led to increased cognitive demands to solve the problems of gathering and storing food, gaining shelter, and raising children successfully in cold winters, including the ice ages, which ended only about 10,000 years ago. As the original African populations evolved into Caucasoids and Mongoloids, they did so in the direction of larger brains, slower rates of maturation, and lower levels of sex hormone with concomitant reductions in sexual potency, aggressiveness and impulsivity, and increases in family stability, forward planning, self-control, rule-following and longevity.

Genes in Addition to Environment

Many of the observed racial correlations are said to be due to purely cultural modes of transmission. The Chinese and Japanese are known to provide intact family backgrounds where they socialize conformity, restraint, and tradition. An opposite pattern is found among African-descended people who come from less integrated families and who are undersocialized for achievement. However, the physiological data on the size of the brain, the rate of maturation, and the production of gametes, as well as the cross-cultural consistency of the racial pattern, shows that genetic and evolutionary influences also play a role.

Purely environmental explanations of the differences cannot explain the complete pattern of the life history. Also impossible to explain from an environmental perspective is why the group differences are strongest on those items with the greatest heritability. For example, the most heritable subtests of the Wechsler Intelligence Scale for Children predicts best the magnitudes of the black-white differences (Rushton, 1989e). Similarly, the higher a test's g loading, the more predictive it is of black-white differences (Jensen, 1985, 1987b). These are *differential* expectations. Heritable g would only predict difference scores if those difference scores were under genetic influence.

The results from a longitudinal study of black children adopted by white families also supports the genetic perspective (R. A. Weinberg et al., 1992). After being raised for 17 years in white families, the black children do not resemble their white siblings. At 7 years of age the black children's IQ was comparable to those of their white siblings, but 10 years later the black children had reverted to their population mean in IQ and educational achievement.

Another line of reasoning for the heritability of racial group differences is that many of the variables on which the races differ are substantially heritable. Chapter 3 reviewed the behavior genetic literature on intelligence, rate of maturation, strength of the sex drive, altruism, family structure, and law abidingness. Occasionally heritabilities have been calculated for races other than Caucasoids and found to be comparable. Thus, a greater than 50 percent heritability for mental ability was calculated for 123 pairs of black adolescent twins by Osborne (1978, 1980) and a heritability of 58 percent was reported for several hundred Japanese 12-year-old pairs by R. Lynn & Hattori (1990).

Generalizing the *r-K* Formulation

If one generalizes the information from the macro-scale characteristics outlined in Table 10.1 and Figure 10.3 to the within-race human variation,

TABLE 13.1
Direction of Correlations Among Human Life–History Variables Found to Date

Life-history variables	Heritability	SES	Race	1	2	3	4	5	6	7	8	9	10	11	12	13	14	15	16
1. Dizygotic twinning	+	+	+															
2. Birth spacing	0	+	0	+														
3. Family size	+	+	+	+	+													
4. Marital stability	0	+	+	+	0	0												
5. Parental care	0	+	+	0	0	0	+											
6. Infant mortality	0	+	+	+	0	0	+	+										
7. Gestation period	0	+	+	+	0	0	0	0	+									
8. Birth weight	+	+	+	+	0	0	0	0	0	+								
9. Age of puberty	+	-	+	+	0	0	+	+	0	0	0							
10. Age of first coitus	+	+	+	+	0	0	+	+	0	0	0	+						
11. Age of reproduction	+	+	+	+	0	0	0	0	0	0	0	+	+					
12. Stature	+	+	-	+	0	0	+	+	0	0	0	0	0	0				
13. Longevity	+	+	+	+	0	0	+	+	+	+	+	0	0	0	0			
14. Intelligence	+	+	+	+	+	+	+	+	+	0	0	-	+	+	+	+		
15. Law abidingness	+	+	+	+	0	+	+	+	+	0	0	0	+	+	0	+	+	
16. Sex drive	+	0	+	+	0	0	0	0	+	0	0	0	0	0	0	0	0	+

several falsifiable predictions can be derived. A summary of the variables expected to intercorrelate is shown in Table 13.1, along with positive and negative evidence and identification of those variables not yet examined.

From Table 13.1 it can be seen that while many variables remain to be investigated, of those that have been, most are in the expected direction. There are some anomalies. Although it is predicted that the higher a person's socioeconomic status, the later he or she would enter puberty, the opposite appears to be true (Malina, 1979). Another contradictory finding occurs with body size. Because large body size is indicative of a K-strategy, Mongoloids should be larger than Caucasoids or Negroids, and yet the opposite is true. Large body size should dispose to law abidingness, and yet the evidence here too is in the opposite direction. Perhaps the most striking aspect of Table 13.1, however, is the infrequency of such lapses. Additional relationships among the variables can be considered. While some of the ideas are speculative, they may be worthy of further investigation.

Family Structure

Double ovulation and the production of two-egg twins has been related to several r-K traits. Mothers of dizygotic twins can be considered to represent the r-strategy. Their characteristics have been contrasted with mothers of singletons representing the K-strategy (Rushton, 1987b). Predictably, the mothers of dizygotic twins are found to have, on average, a lower age of menarche, a shorter menstrual cycle, a higher number of marriages, a higher rate of coitus, more illegitimate children, a closer spacing of births, a greater fecundity, more wasted pregnancies, a larger family, an earlier menopause, and an earlier mortality. Further, twins typically have a shorter gestation, a lower birth weight, a greater incidence of infant mortality, and a lowered IQ.

Other family structure variables such as marital breakup and single parenting are related to r-characteristics such as child abuse, lower intelligence, educational dropout, sexual precocity, and juvenile delinquency (Draper & Harpending, 1988; J. Q. Wilson & Herrnstein, 1985). To quote again the distinction made by Draper and Harpending (1988: 349): "Father-present societies are those where most males act like dads and father absent societies are those where most males act like cads."

Sexuality

The developmental transition in the lives of most young people from virginity to nonvirginity takes place within a network of individual, social, and behavioral factors that go beyond mere covariation. In two longitudinal studies, Jessor et al. (1991) found that early onset of sexual intercourse was predicted from knowledge of whether adolescents had low scores in academic achievement and religiosity, and high scores on measures of deviance and "problem behavior." Multiple correlations reached predictive levels greater than 0.50 accounting for approximately 30 percent of the variance over a 9-year interval.

Personality and sexuality have been related. Eysenck (1976) found that, compared to introverts, extroverts typically have intercourse earlier, more frequently, and with more different partners. These findings were replicated by Barnes, Malamuth, and Check (1984). More historically, in *Civilization and Its Discontents,* Freud (1930) explained the existence of a positive correlation between restrained sexuality and the production of culture through the psychodynamics of repression and sublimation. The perspective being outlined here explains it in terms of genetically correlated traits. Energy can be allocated to reproductive effort either directly through sexual behavior or indirectly through the ability to produce complex social institutions and thereby compete when resources are scarce.

Sexual behavior varies by social class. Weinrich (1977) examined over 20 studies from the world literature and concluded that the lower the socioeconomic status, the earlier the age of first coitus, the greater the likelihood of premarital coitus and coitus with prostitutes, the shorter the time before engaging in extramarital affairs, and the less stable the marriage bond. Weinrich (1977) also found that the higher the socioeconomic status, the more likely the individual was to engage in sexual activities beyond those directly leading to conception, including fellatio, cunnilingus, petting, and affection, and coitus during menstruation. Moreover, although lower socioeconomic status adolescents apparently knew as much about birth control devices as upper socioeconomic status adolescents, they used them less frequently.

Of interest are social class differences in the production of two-egg twins. Monozygotic twinning is nearly constant at about 3 1/2 per 1,000 in all groups. Dizygotic twinning, however, is greater among lower than among upper social-class women in both European and African samples (Golding, 1986; Nylander, 1981).

Altruism and Law Abidingness

Because they are lower in altruism and disrupt rather than maintain social organization, criminals are considered to represent the *r*-strategy. Ellis (1987) found that criminals have the following *r*-strategy traits: large numbers of siblings (or half-siblings); families in which parents no longer live together; shorter gestation periods (more premature births); more rapid sexual maturation; greater copulatory frequency outside of bonded relationships (or at least a preference for such); less stable bonding; lower parental investment in offspring (as evidenced by higher rates of child abandonment, neglect, and abuse); and a shorter life expectancy.

Antisocial and other problem behaviors like alcohol and drug abuse are linked to early onset of sexual intercourse (Jessor et al., 1991). Among adolescents, 36 to 49 percent of the variance in nonsexual forms of deviance in siblings of either sex could be explained by the amount of sexual behavior engaged in by the other (Rowe et al., 1989).

Conscientiousness at work, as well as more obvious criminal behavior, has also been linked to temperament and intelligence (Elander, West, & French, 1993). Some evidence has suggested that introverts are more punctual, absent less often, and stay longer at a job, whereas extroverts spend more time talking to their workmates, drinking coffee, and generally seeking diversion from routine. Accidents by bus drivers have also been found to be predicted by intelligence and extraversion (Shaw & Sichel, 1970).

Health and Longevity

As shown in Figure 10.3, humans are the only primates with a post-reproductive phase. One explanation for menopause is that since the human body becomes weaker with age, women eventually reach a point where continued childbearing would endanger their lives. While there is no equivalent pressure on men, sperm production declines with age. By 45 years of age, a man is producing only 50 percent of the sperm he was producing at 18 years of age, and most older men have difficulty attracting fertile females. Thus, in the evolutionary past, older people better aided copies of their genes by caring for grandchildren and the extended family than by producing additional offspring themselves. With increasing K, grandparents will have to remain healthier and live longer to be able to do this effectively since both their own offspring and their children's offspring will be delaying reproduction to later ages. In both developed and developing countries early maternal death is associated with short spacing of births and total number of children.

Lower socioeconomic classes have higher death rates than upper socioeconomic classes and these differences have increased in the past several decades. *The Black Report* and other studies record a growing disparity in death rates between occupational classes in England and Wales (Black et al., 1982; Whitehead, 1988; Marmot et al., 1991). For example, in 1930 people in the lowest social class had a 23 percent higher chance of dying at every age than people in the highest social class. By 1970, this excess risk had grown to 61 percent. A decade later it had jumped to 150 percent (Black et al., 1982). This increasing disparity presents a paradox especially when a national health service system has long existed in Britain to minimize inequalities in health-related services.

Similar gaps have been noted in France and Hungary during the past two decades (Black et al., 1982). The inverse relation between mortality and socioeconomic status has also been increasing in the United States. One large study showed that over the 26-year period between 1960 and 1986, health inequalities according to educational level increased for whites and blacks by over 20 percent with respect to women and by over 100 percent with respect to men (Pappas et al., 1993).

The increasing correlation of health and social class is explainable from an r-K perspective when it is appreciated that removing environmental barriers to health increases the variance accounted for by genetic factors (Scriver, 1984). In a parallel way, increasing equality of educational opportunity leads to an increase in the heritability of educational attainment (Heath et al., 1985). Generally, removing environmental impediments makes individual-difference variance more dependent on innate characteristics. This implies that, in the 1990s at least, and on average, more genes coding for good health and longevity exist in persons of the upper classes than in persons of the lower classes (Rushton, 1987a).

Intelligence

Many studies show a negative relation between intelligence and family size (Vining, 1986). Others have found that when family size is held constant, birth spacing is important: the greater the spacing between births, the higher the intelligence of the children (Zajonc, Markus, & Markus, 1979; Lancer & Rim, 1984). Intelligence is also related to speed of maturation, temperament, social organization, health, and longevity (Jensen, 1980a).

The central role of intelligence in law abidingness is demonstrated by the finding that IQ has an effect on delinquency independent of family background, race, or class. Siblings reared together in the same families show almost the same degree of association between IQ and delinquency as is found in the general population (Hirschi & Hindelang, 1977). The relation between IQ and delinquency was measured by self-reports as well as by incarcerations, so the result is not just due to clever people evading capture. Less intelligent people often lack behavioral restraint, marriage-bonding techniques, adequate parenting styles, and moral rules, and are less capable of creating stable personal circumstances or of predicting their environment.

Personality

Extroverts may be less K than introverts for they are described as "active," "impulsive," and "changeable" while introverts are "careful," "thoughtful," and "reliable" (Eysenck & Eysenck, 1975). With respect to academic success, some evidence suggests that while extraverted children may perform better in school up until puberty, after this introverts gain a progressive advantage (Anthony, 1977; Eysenck & Cookson, 1969). Jensen (1980a) reported a tendency for introverts to perform faster on reaction-time measures of intelligence than extroverts. Finally, there is the evidence that extroverts are less conditionable and more criminal than introverts (Eysenck & Gudjonsson, 1989). An underlying dimension of "behavioral restraint" may be involved (Gray, 1987).

Masters (1989) suggested an *r-K* integration of Cloninger's (1986) three-dimensional system of personality based on neurotransmitter functions. According to Cloninger, harm avoidant vs. risk-taking is associated with serotonergic transmission, novelty-seeking vs. stereotyping rests on dopaminergic transmission, and reward dependence vs. social independence rests on noradrenergic transmission. Masters hypothesized that *r*-strategists are those with risk-taking, novelty-seeking, and reward-dependent personalities while *K*-strategists are those with harm-avoidant, conventional, socially-independent personalities.

Masters went on to connect *r-K* strategies with preferences in assortative mating (chapter 4). *K*-strategists were said to prefer others who were genetically similar, in part, because they are not risk takers, whereas *r*-strategists do not necessarily prefer similarity, in part, because they seek novelty. Thus, spousal similarity will be less in *r*-strategists. Masters used *r-K* theory to explain why interethnic dating is more frequent among poorer *r*-groups (e.g., in Hawaii) than in wealthier *K*-groups.

Social Class Differences

Sociobiological theorizing leads to the expectation that terrestrial primates such as *Homo sapiens* will form themselves into dominance hierarchies with those at the top exhibiting higher levels of whatever traits make for success in that culture and in turn get a greater than equal share of whatever scarce resources are available. In hunting societies those at the top will be the best hunters; in warrior societies those at the top will be the best warriors, and so on. As the last few pages and Table 13.1 show, socioeconomic status correlates substantially with most of the variables psychologists are interested in, including intelligence, health, sexuality, crime, aggression, family structure, and social attitudes. It seems reasonable to suggest that within races higher socioeconomic groups are more *K*-strategists than lower socioeconomic groups (Rushton, 1985a).

With regard to intelligence the socioeconomic hierarchies of technological societies are built on intelligence, measured by standard IQ tests. Several reviews of this literature have appeared (Herrnstein, 1973; Jensen, 1980a). The basic finding is that there is a difference of nearly 3 standard deviations (45 IQ points) between average members of the professional and the unskilled classes. These are group-mean differences, with considerable overlap of distributions. Nonetheless, the overall correlation between IQ and social class is about 0.50.

Within-family variation has been known for some time in the literature on intelligence. In studies of intergenerational social mobility, Mascie-Taylor and

Gibson (1978) and Waller (1971) obtained the IQ scores of both fathers and their adult sons. They found that children with lower test scores than their fathers had gone down in social class as adults while those with higher test scores had gone up. Within-family differences also occur in sexuality with some siblings adopting the early onset syndrome (Rowe et al., 1989). As Weinrich (1977) noted, adolescents moving from one social class to another behave like their acquired class rather than the class they were socialized in by their parents.

In the study of external head measurements from a stratified random sample of 6,325 U.S. Army personnel, Rushton (1992a) found that after adjusting for the effects of stature, weight, sex, and race, the cranial capacity of officers averaged 1,393 cm^3 and that of enlisted personnel, 1,375 cm^3.

Biological Mediators

One advantage of an evolutionary perspective is the focus it brings to underlying physiology including the endocrine system. As indicated in chapter 8, there are reliable differences among the races in testosterone. Relative to whites, blacks have more and Orientals have less.

Testosterone may order many of the racial differences, for it has been related to self-concept, temperament, sexuality, aggression, and altruism, in women as well as in men (Baucom, Besch, & Callahan, 1985; Dabbs, Ruback, Frady, Hopper, & Sgoutas, 1988). In a study of 4,462 U.S. male veterans, where extensive archival records were available, Dabbs and Morris (1990) found testosterone correlated with reports of childhood delinquency, adult delinquency, drug use, alcohol abuse, military misconduct, and having many sex partners. Testosterone is also involved in the development of secondary sexual characteristics such as muscularity and depth of voice (Haeberle, 1978; Hudson & Holbrook, 1982) as well as the organization and structure of the brain.

A person's position on the r-K dimension might be set by a hormonal switch mechanism. Reproductive strategies need to be coherent and harmonized, not with some traits going to one pole and other traits going to the opposite pole. Inasmuch as the switch regulator is genetically based, it suggests a functional polymorphism within populations, with extreme r-strategists at one end and extreme K-strategists at the other, with most people being normally distributed between the two and environmental factors modifying and fine-tuning the system.

A sex hormone model to explain r-K strategies was provided by Nyborg (1987). He extrapolated for life-history traits the optimum level of estradiol that he had previously proposed to explain spatial ability. Because hormones go everywhere in the body they are uniquely able to exert more or less simultaneous effects and coordinate widespread development and functioning.

Figure 13.1: Sex Hormone Model for Coordinating Development Across Body, Brain, and Behavioral Traits

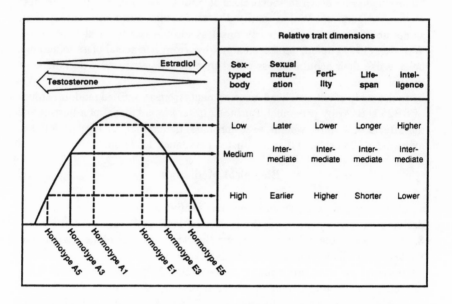

	Relative trait dimensions				
	Sex-typed body	Sexual matur-ation	Ferti-lity	Life-span	Intel-ligence
Estradiol / Testosterone	Low	Later	Lower	Longer	Higher
	Medium	Inter-mediate	Inter-mediate	Inter-mediate	Inter-mediate
	High	Earlier	Higher	Shorter	Lower

Hormotype A5 Hormotype A3 Hormotype A1 Hormotype E1 Hormotype E3 Hormotype E5

Men are classified in accordance with testosterone concentration into hormotypes A5 (high testosterone) to A1 (low testosterone) and women are classified into hormotypes ranging from E1 (low estradiol) to E5 (high estradiol). Men with high testosterone and women with high estradiol are the most sex-typed. Men with low testosterone and women with low estradiol are most similar to each other (androgenous). In this model Mongoloids are A2/E2, Caucasoids A3/E3, and Negroids A4/E4. After Nyborg (1987).

Nyborg's model provided an explanation of covariant trait development based on "hormotyping."

Hormotyping classifies people in accordance with the balance among their plasma concentration of androgens such as testosterone and estradiol. As shown in Figure 13.1, an inverse relation between testosterone and estradiol is assumed. Males can be hierarchically ordered with 5 levels of androgen from A5 (most) to A1 (least) and females can be classified by levels of estradiol from E1 (least) to E5 (most). Hormotypes A3 and E3 represent individuals with close to average male testosterone values or average female estradiol values, respectively. Hormotypes A1 and E1 represent so-called androgynous males and females, that is, males who in addition to ordinary masculine traits also show some clearly feminine traits, or females who in addition to the usual feminine traits show some clearly masculine attributes as well.

Figure 13.1 shows that at the beginning of the inverted U-shaped curve, the most androgenized males (A5) would be furthest from the zenith of K with intermediately androgenized males (A3) closer and the least androgenized males (A1) closest. With increasing degrees of estrogenization (E1 to E5) females move away from zenith. Nyborg (1987, 1994) proposed that Orientals are typically hormotype A2/E2 and Africans are hormotype A4/E4. The graphics to the right of the curve show the direction of effects on various traits of increasing testosterone.

Nyborg (1994) predicts that blacks should be more sexually dimorphic than whites who should be more sexually dimorphic than Orientals. Numerous other falsifiable predictions are possible from this heuristic model. If this, or some other hypothesis like it was eventually confirmed, it would provide a commanding proximal explanation of how the various traits distribute themselves as they do.

A model like the one shown in Figure 13.1 can readily accommodate bidirectional causality. So far it has been implied that optimal neurohormonal balances are inherent. As Kemper (1990), among others, has pointed out, hormonal processes are themselves susceptible to social influence. For example, testosterone in both men and women is affected by dominance acquired through valued social attainments. Kemper reviewed several studies showing that testosterone levels became elevated in young men who won tennis matches, wrestling matches, or entry to medical school, but they showed a decline in the losers. Similarly, Masters (1989) cited work on the effects of many environmental factors, including carbohydrate intake, exposure to light, and social interaction on neurotransmitter levels, such as serotonin. In chapter 12, the hypotheses of Eysenck and R. Lynn were discussed on the importance of nutrition.

A central locus for research attention is brain functioning. Brain size has become the key factor in life-history theory, acting as the biological constant determining many variables, including the upper limit on the size of the group cohesively maintained through time (Dunbar, 1992), as well as such life history variables as speed of physical maturation, degree of infant dependency, and maximum recorded life span (Harvey & Krebs, 1990; Hofman, 1993).

It is of interest to wonder where the 90 cm^3 difference between Mongoloids and Negroids (perhaps 500 million neurons) is located. The relation between brain size and intelligence was discussed in chapter 2. The brain obviously mediates other variables too. Gray (1987) has described the cytoarchitecture and functioning of the behavioral inhibition and other systems that he postulates underlie such relevant components of temperament as cautiousness and sociability, which also differentiate the races. Recently initiated Magnetic Resonance Imaging studies, and other mapping techniques, in conjunction with tests of various mental abilities, are certain to illuminate further these fascinating aspects of human biology.

The Fertility Paradox

The main theme of this book is that human behavior is determined by a biological imperative to preserve and replicate DNA. The means by which this will be accomplished will differ as a function of both genetic and ecological circumstance. Only recently has the importance of individual variation in the control of reproductive behavior begun to be investigated. Previously, it was assumed that fluctuations in population size were essentially an ecological problem, not a genetic one. The application of such analyses to human behavior may be especially novel.

One application of r-K theory is to the "fertility paradox." Vining (1986) asked why, if the replication of genetically similar genes is as strong a biological imperative as sociobiological theorizing suggests, are so many European populations experiencing negative growth? He reviewed data to show that, apart from a few cohorts who bore their children during the unique period of rising fertility from 1936 to 1960, there is a characteristically inverse relationship between fertility and "endowment" (wealth, success, and measured aptitudes).

The fertility paradox has been analyzed over centuries. Gobineau (1853–1855) had asked why great civilizations seemed destined to decay. He considered the reasons put forward by others—decline of religion, fanaticism, corruption of morals, luxury, bad government—and rejected them all on the evidence of history. Instead he provided an answer in terms of ethnicity and race. The character of a civilization was determined by the traits of the dominant race, often created by the union of several related tribes. If wealth grows, cities develop, and an international society forms. Among the new arrivals are persons belonging to ethnic taxa that have never initiated a civilization. Degeneration sets in and the intrinsic worth the people originally possessed becomes lost, for the population no longer has in its veins the same quality blood with which it began.

R. A. Fisher, who synthesized Mendelian genetics with Darwinian evolution, also discussed the question of why civilizations decay. In his book *The Genetical Theory of Natural Selection* (2nd ed., 1958), he showed that ruling groups fail to reproduce themselves because of low fertility. Fisher (1958) hypothesized a trade-off between the capacity for economic success and fertility. As discussed, this trade-off is more profound than Fisher realized, being related to a whole complex of characteristics partly genetic in origin. When there are abundant resources, selection pressures are off and natural selection favors r-genotypes so that segment of the population expands. Eventually, saturation point is reached and the population crashes (Malthus, 1798). With selection pressures back on, selection again favors K-genotypes. This occurs with rodents (C. J. Krebs et al., 1973) and a direct parallel is suggested with humans. With humans the situation is complicated by culture, which must also be taken into account.

If a gene-culture coevolutionary framework is correct (Lumsden & Wilson, 1983), then many interesting questions can be raised about the relation between genes, culture, and population growth. As discussed in chapters 3 and 4, epigenetic rules guide development over the life span, biasing individuals to learn or to produce those patterns of culture, from the available array, maximally compatible with their genotypes. The consequences, of course, feed back to affect the gene frequencies of subsequent generations.

Given that efficient energy use is a K-strategy (Table 10.1), does metabolic rate covary with body build and a preference for restrained social behavior? Given that colonization is an r-strategy (Table 10.1), are people who frequently move their habitat less K than those who do not? Given that degree of social organization varies with K (Table 10.1), are people who prefer less-structured interpersonal social systems less K than those organizing themselves into more formal ones? Assuming similar genotypes detect and seek each other out for friendship and marriage (chap. 4), is there social assortment on the K dimension? And, if people create cultures compatible with their genotypes, are all these tendencies not only related to each other but also to sociopolitical attitudes (e.g., order vs. freedom) and ultimately, to demographic trends and the very sweep of history?

Glossary

No definition is absolute and scientific constructs are always subject to controversy and debate. They are proposed in order to classify and coordinate large numbers of facts. It is hoped that the following definitions may be of use.

ADAPTATION. In biology, a particular anatomical structure, physiological process, or behavior that improves an organism's fitness to survive and reproduce. Also, the evolutionary process that leads to the acquisition of such a trait.

AGGREGATION. Formed by the collection of particulars into a sum total.

AGGRESSION. A physical act or threat of action by one individual intended to reduce the freedom or genetic fitness of another.

ALLELE. A particular form of a gene, where multiple such forms occur. Sickle-cell anemia is caused by one such variant of a gene; another variant of the same gene contributes to the normal hemoglobin.

ALTRUISM. Self-destructive behavior performed for the benefit of others.

ASSORTATIVE MATING. Mating of individuals that are more similar phenotypically than if they were mating at random.

AUSTRALOPITHECUS. The genus of early hominids known from 4 million to 2 million years ago before the appearance of the genus *Homo*. These "man-apes" lived during the Pleistocene Epoch and possessed postures similar to those of modern men but brains not much larger than those of modern apes.

BASE PAIR. A pair of organic bases constituting a letter of the genetic code; usually adenine (A) paired with thymine (T), or cytosine (C) paired with guanine (G). Each base is found on one strand of the DNA double helix and opposes the other base at the same position on the second strand. The code is then read off as a sequence of four possible letters on the double helix, AT, TA, CG, and GC. Versions of the same gene differ by the sequence of these four letters.

BEHAVIOR GENETICS. The scientific study of the genetic and environmental contributions to behavior.

BEHAVIORISM. A school of psychology founded by John B. Watson in which psychology is defined solely as the study of behavior; all data therefore must come from observable behavior.

BRAIN. The part of the central nervous system enclosed in the cranium of man and other vertebrates, consisting of a soft, convoluted mass of gray and white matter and serving to control and coordinate the mental and physical actions.

BROW RIDGES. Constituting a bar of bone over the eyes in apes and early hominids, these are varied in development in later hominids and diminished in modern people to slight-to-moderate bony swellings over each eye.

CARRYING CAPACITY. Usually symbolized by K, the largest number of organisms of a particular species that can be maintained indefinitely in a given part of the environment.

CAUCASOID RACE. A major racial division of mankind originally inhabiting Europe, North Africa, western Asia, and India. Individuals are depigmented to a greater or lesser degree. Hair in males is generally well developed on the face and body, and is mostly fine and wavy or straight. A narrow face, prominent narrow nose, and narrow lips are typical.

CHROMOSOMES. Paired sections of the DNA in the nucleus of a cell bearing genes in a linear order. The number varies in different species: in *Homo* the number of pairs is 23.

CLASSIFICATION. The categories of life form a hierarchical system going from higher to lower: Kingdom, Phylum, Class, Order, Family, Genus, Species, with further subdivisions being possible, such as superfamilies and subspecies. Living humanity is placed in the preceding categories as follows: Animalia, Vertebrata, Mammalia, Primates, Hominidae, *Homo sapiens.*

COEVOLUTION. The evolution of two or more species due to mutual influence; for example, many species of flowering plants and their insect pollinators have coevolved in a way that makes the relationship more effective. *See also* GENE-CULTURE COEVOLUTION.

CORRELATION. An index of the degree of relationship between two variables, expressed as a coefficient of correlation, which ranges from 0 to ±1.

CRANIOMETRY. The science of measuring skulls.

CRANIUM. The skull of a vertebrate. The part of the skull that encloses the brain.

DARWINISM. Evolution by natural selection, originally proposed by Charles Darwin. The modern interpretation of the process is called neo-Darwinism; it incorporates all we know about evolution from genetics, ecology, and other disciplines.

DEMOGRAPHY. The study of birth rates, death rates, age distributions, sex ratios, and size of populations—a fundamental discipline within the larger field of ecology.

DENSITY DEPENDENCE. The increasing severity by which factors in the environment slow down growth of a population as the organisms become more numerous and hence densely concentrated. Density-dependent factors include competition, food shortage, disease, predation, and emigration.

DETERMINISM. A fixed-cause effect model usually implying that an outcome is narrowly constrained by very few variables. Thus, "genetic determinism" means to many that behavior is rigidly constrained by the genes, while "cultural determinism" means that behavior depends almost entirely on the particularities of the surrounding culture.

DEVELOPMENT. The process of coming into being, unfolding, maturing, being built up.

DNA (DEOXYRIBONUCLEIC ACID). The fundamental hereditary material of all living organisms. The carrier of the genes. It consists of extremely long paired sugar-phosphate chains (the "double helix"), which are joined by pairs of four kinds of organic bases. The order of these last gives the codes by which the genes (segments of the DNA chains) control the formation of proteins.

DIZYGOTIC (DZ) TWINS. Fraternal twins, arising from the fertilization of two eggs by two sperm.

DOMINANCE. In genetics, the expression of one form of a gene (allele) over another form of the same gene when both occur on the same chromosome; the gene for normal blood clotting, for example, is dominant over the one for hemophilia (failure to clot). In ecology, the abundance and ecological influence of one species or group of species over others: pines are dominant plants and beetles are dominant animals. In animal behavior, the control of one individual over another in social groupings.

ECOLOGY. The scientific study of the interaction of organisms with their environment, including both the physical environment and the other organisms that live in it.

EMERGENIC. Arising as a novel or emergent property resulting from the interaction of more elementary properties. The distinctive feature of emergenesis is the notion of configurality, which implies that change of any one component results in a qualitative, or a large quantitative, change in the emergenic trait.

ENDOCRANIAL. Within the cranium or brain case. The endocranial volume of a chimpanzee is about 500 cm^3 and that of a modern human about 1,300 cm^3.

ENVIRONMENT. The surroundings of an organism or a species: the ecosystem in which it lives, including both the physical environment and the other organisms with which it comes in contact.

ENVIRONMENTALISM. The form of analysis that stresses the role of environmental influences in the development of behavioral or other biological traits. Also, the point of view that such influences tend to be paramount in behavioral development.

EPIGENESIS. The process of interaction between genes and environment that ultimately results in the distinctive behavioral, cognitive, and morphological traits of the organism.

EPIGENETIC RULE. Any regularity during epigenesis that channels development of a trait in a particular direction. Epigenetic rules are ultimately genetic in basis and depend on the DNA developmental blueprint.

ETHNOCENTRISM. A complex of attitudes whereby members of σ:.e ethnic group consider themselves superior or at least preferablɐ to another ethnic group on the basis of their own conception of what is socially, culturally, biologically good or right. *See also* RACISM.

EVOLUTION. Any change in the genetic constitution of a population of organisms. Evolution can vary in degree from small shifts in the frequencies of minor genes to the origins of complexes of new species. Changes of lesser magnitude are called microevolution, and changes at or near the upper extreme are called macro-evolution.

EVOLUTIONARY BIOLOGY. An umbrella term for a broad array of disciplines that have in common their focus on the evolutionary process.

FECUND. Bearing or capable of producing offspring in abundance.

FERTILE. Bearing or capable of bearing offspring.

FITNESS. *See* GENETIC FITNESS.

G. The first principal component or general factor of intelligence that emerges when factor analysis is carried out on any diverse set of mental tests. The higher a subtest loads on *g* the more reflective of mental ability it is. Black-white differences in mental ability are largest on the *g* factor.

GAMETE. The mature sexual reproductive cell: the egg or the sperm.

GENE. The basic unit of heredity; a section of the giant DNA molecule long enough to code for one protein.

GENE-CULTURE COEVOLUTION. The coupled evolution of genes and culture.

GENE FREQUENCY. For the population as a whole, the percentage of genes at a particular locus that are of one form (allele) as opposed to another, such as the allele for sickle-cell hemoglobin that can be distinguished from the allele for normal hemoglobin.

GENETIC CODE. *See* BASE PAIR.

GENETIC FITNESS. The contribution to the next generation of one genotype in a population relative to the contributions of other genotypes.

GENOTYPE. The genetic constitution of an organism.

GONAD. An organ that produces sex cells; ordinarily either an ovary (female gonad) or testis (male gonad).

GROUP SELECTION. Any process, such as competition, the effects of disease, or the ability to reproduce, that results in one group of individuals leaving more descendants than another group. Selected groups can range in size from kin to tribe to population to species.

HERITABILITY. The proportion of variance in a trait within a population that is attributable to genetic variance among the individuals composing the population.

HOMINID. Any member of the human family Hominidae (all species of *Australopithecus* and *Homo*).

HOMO. The genus of true men, including several extinct forms (*H. habilis, H. erectus, H. neanderthalis*) as well as modern man (*H. sapiens*), who are or were primates characterized by completely erect stature, bipedal locomotion, reduced dentition, and above all an enlarged brain size.

HOMO ERECTUS. The species recognized as including fossils dated from about 2 million to 400,000 years ago from Africa, the Middle East, Java, and China, with brains varying around 1,000 cm³ and with robust skulls, but skeletons generally modern in size and shape.

HOMO HABILIS. The earliest recognized species of *Homo*, appearing 2.4 million years ago in East Africa and associated with the first recognizable stone tools. Distinguished from australopithecenes by enlarged brain and reduced face, the skeleton, however, retained primitive traits not seen in later *Homo*.

HOMO SAPIENS. The formal species name for living mankind. It is also extended to cover populations known from fossils that are distinguished as being above the evolutionary level of *Homo erectus*. There is debate over whether Neanderthals are to be included as a subspecies of *Homo sapiens* or made into a separate species.

HORMONE. Any of various internally secreted compounds such as insulin or testosterone, formed in the endocrine glands, that affect the functions of specifically receptive organs or tissues when carried to them by the body fluids.

HUMAN NATURE. In the broader sense, the full set of genetically based behavioral predispositions or traits evolved by natural selection that characterize the human species; and in the narrower sense, those predispositions that affect social behavior.

INBREEDING. The mating of kin.

INTELLIGENCE. General mental ability. *See* G. The capacity for reasoning, understanding, and for similar forms of mental activity. Quick to understand.

IQ *or* INTELLIGENCE QUOTIENT. A person's mental age divided by chronological age, expressed as a multiple of 100. The IQ of a 10-year-old child whose mental age equals that of the average 12-year-old is 120.

K. Symbol for the carrying capacity of the environment.

KIN SELECTION. Selection of genes causing individuals to favor the survival and reproduction of relatives (in addition to offspring) who possess the same genes by common descent. Kin selection is one way in which altruistic behavior can evolve as a biological trait.

K-SELECTION. Selection favoring the qualities needed to succeed in stable, predictable environments where there is likely to be heavy competition for limited resources between individuals well equipped to compete, at population sizes close to the maximum that the habitat can bear. A variety of qualities are thought to be favored by K-selection, including in mammals, long life, large brains, and small numbers of intensively cared-for offspring. Contrast with r-selection. K and r are symbols in the conventional algebra of population biologists.

K-STRATEGY. A set of reproductive characteristics that tends to maximize use of resources by emphasizing intensive nurture and a slow reproductive rate, with concomitant increase in complexity of nervous system and larger brain (cf. *r*-strategy).

LIFE CYCLE. The entire life span of an organism from the moment it is conceived to the time it reproduces and on to the time that it dies.

LIFE HISTORY. A genetically organized suite of characters that have evolved so as to allocate energy to survival, growth, and reproduction.

MATURATION. The automatic development of a pattern of behavior that becomes increasingly complex or precise as the animal matures.

MEAN. The numerical average.

MONGOLOID RACE. A major racial division of mankind found in all Asia except the west and south (India), in the northern and eastern Pacific, and in the Americas. The skin is brown to light often with a yellowish tinge; hair is coarse, straight to wavy, and sparse on the face and body. The face is broad and tends to flatness. The eyelid is covered by an internal skinfold. The teeth often have crowns more complex than in other peoples, and the inner surfaces of the upper incisors frequently have a shovel appearance.

MONOZYGOTIC (MZ) TWINS. Identical twins, arising from the fertilization of one egg by one sperm.

NATURAL SELECTION. The differential contribution of offspring to the next generation by various genetic types belonging to the same population. This mechanism of evolution was proposed by Charles Darwin and is thus also called Darwinism. Distinguished from artificial selection, the same process but carried out with human guidance.

NEANDERTHALS. A type of powerfully built, cold-adapted Paleolithic man who inhabited Europe and central Asia from about 125,000 to about 30,000 years ago. Some call them a subspecies of modern humans but others, who believe they are not directly ancestral to modern humans, see them as a distinct species.

NEGROID RACE. A major racial division of mankind originating and predominating in sub-Saharan Africa. Skin pigmentation is dense, hair wooly, nose broad, face generally short, lips thick, and ears squarish and lobeless. Stature varies greatly, from pygmy to very tall. The most divergent group are the Khoisan (Bushman and Hottentot) peoples of southern Africa.

PALEOLITHIC. The Stone Age, a cultural period during which hominids were dependent entirely upon hunting and gathering using subsistence techniques. A division has often been made into the lower, middle, and upper paleolithic based on improvements in stone-working techniques.

PALEONTOLOGY. The scientific study of fossils and all aspects of extinct life.

PERSONALITY. The more or less stable and enduring organization of a person's character, temperament, intellect, and physique, which determines his unique adjustment to the environment. Character suggests will power and conscious decision making; temperament suggests emotionality; intellect implies intelligence; and physique includes bodily configuration and neuroendocrine endowment.

PHENOTYPE. The observed traits of an organism created by an interaction of the organism's genotype (hereditary material) and the environment in which it developed.

PLEISTOCENE. "Almost recent." The period beginning 1.7 million years ago and ending about 10,000 years ago with the last glacial retreat, loosely called the "Ice Age," consisting of a series of glacial and interglacial periods. It is associated with rapid hominid evolution.

POPULATION. In biology, any group of organisms belonging to the same species at the same time and place.

PRIMATE. Any mammal of the order primates, such as a lemur, monkey, ape, or man.

PRIMITIVE. Referring to a trait that appeared first in evolution and gave rise to other, more "advanced" traits later. Primitive traits are often but not always less complex than the advanced ones.

PROGRESS. Cumulative improvement. Increasing differentiation and movement forward in the course of development.

PROTO-. Used as a prefix, the term implies an early form of either a biological or a cultural organism, out of which later (usually more complex) varieties can be demonstrated to have evolved.

r. The symbol used to designate the intrinsic rate of increase of a population.

RACE. A group related by common descent, blood, or heredity. A variety, a subspecies, a subdivision of a species characterized by a more or less distinctive combination of physical traits transmitted in descent. A genetically distinct inbreeding division within a species. Often used interchangeably with the term subspecies. In humans the 3 major races of Caucasoid, Mongoloid, and Negroid can be distinguished on the basis of skeletal morphology, hair and facial features, and molecular genetic information.

RACISM. Hatred or intolerance of another race. The treatment of all members of another race as though they were all the same, usually in order to do them harm.

REPRODUCTIVE STRATEGY. *See r-* and *K*-strategy.

r-SELECTION. Selection for the qualities needed to succeed in unstable, unpredictable environments, where ability to reproduce rapidly and opportunistically is at a premium, and where there is little value in adaptations to succeed in competition. A variety of qualities are thought to be favored by r-selection, including high fecundity and, in mammals, short life and small brains. Contrasted with K-selection. It is customary to emphasize that r-selection and K-selection are the extremes of a continuum, most real cases lying somewhere between.

r-STRATEGY. A set of reproductive characteristics that tends to maximize the potential rate of population increase at the expense of intensive nurture of young and efficient resource utilization (cf. *K*-STRATEGY).

SELECTION. *See* NATURAL SELECTION.

SELECTION PRESSURE. Any feature of the environment that results in natural selection; for example, food shortage, the activity of a predator, or competition from other members of the same sex for a mate.

SEX RATIO. The ratio of males to females (for example, 3:1 equals 3 males to 1 female).

SOCIOBIOLOGY. The systematic study of the biological basis of all social behavior.

SPECIES. The basic unit of biological classification, consisting of a population or series of populations of closely related organisms that freely interbreed with one another in natural conditions but not with members of other species.

STANDARD DEVIATION. A measure of dispersion of a frequency distribution. It is equal to the square root of the variance.

TESTOSTERONE. The sex hormone $C_{19}H_{28}O_2$, secreted mainly by the testes, that stimulates the development of masculine characteristics.

THRESHOLD. The point at which a stimulus is of sufficient intensity to begin to produce an effect.

TRAIT. An inherited or acquired characteristic that is considered consistent, persistent, and stable.

VARIANCE. The most commonly used statistical measure of variation (dispersion) of a trait within a population. It is the mean squared deviation of all individuals from the sample mean.

ZOOLOGY. The scientific study of animals.

ZYGOTE. The cell created by the union of two gametes (sex cells), in which the gamete nuclei are also fused.

References

Aboud, F. (1988). *Children and Prejudice.* Oxford: Blackwell.

Abramson, P. R., & Imari-Marquez, J. (1982). The Japanese-American: A cross-cultural, cross-sectional study of sex guilt. *Journal of Research in Personality, 16,* 227-37.

Ahern, F. M., Cole, R. E., Johnson, R. C., & Wong, B. (1981). Personality attributes of males and females marrying within vs. across racial/ethnic groups. *Behavior Genetics, 11,* 181-94.

Aiello, L. C. (1993). The fossil evidence for modern human origins in Africa: A revised view. *American Anthropologist, 95,* 73-96.

Ajmani, M. L., Jain, S. P., & Saxena, S. K. (1985). Anthropometric study of male extended genitalia of 320 healthy Nigerian adults. *Anthropoligisher Anzeiger, 43,* 179-86.

Alexander, R. D. (1987). *The Biology of Moral Systems.* New York: Aldine de Gruyter.

Allen, G. (1987). The nondecline in U.S. twin birth rates, 1964-1983. *Acta Geneticae Medicae et Gemellologiae, 36,* 313-23.

Allen, G. (1988). Frequency of triplets and triplet zygosity types among U.S. births, 1964. *Acta Geneticae Medicae et Gemellologiae, 37,* 299-306.

Ammerman, A. J., & Cavalli-Sforza, L. L. (1984). *The Neolithic Transition and the Genetics of Populations in Europe.* Princeton, NJ: Princeton University Press.

Anderson, J. L. (1991). Rushton's racial comparisons: An ecological critique of theory and method. *Canadian Psychology, 32,* 51-60.

Andreasen, N. C., Flaum, M., Swayze, V., O'Leary, D. S., Alliger, R., Cohen, G., Ehrhardt, J., & Yuh, W. T. C. (1993). Intelligence and brain structure in normal individuals. *American Journal of Psychiatry, 150,* 130-34.

Angel, M. (1993). Privilege and health—what is the connection? *New England Journal of Medicine, 329,* 126-27.

Ankney, C. D. (1992). Sex differences in relative brain size: The mismeasure of woman, too? *Intelligence, 16,* 329-36.

Anthony, W. S. (1977). The development of extraversion and ability. *British Journal of Educational Psychology, 47,* 193-96.

Appel, F. W., & Appel, E. M. (1942). Intracranial variation in the weight of the human brain. *Human Biology, 14,* 235-50.

Ardrey, R. (1961). *African Genesis.* New York: Bantam.

Arvey, R. D., Bouchard, T. J., Jr., Segal, N. L., & Abraham, L. M. (1989). Job satisfaction: Environmental and genetic components. *Journal of Applied Psychology, 74,* 187-92.

Asayama, S. (1975). Adolescent sex development and adult sex behavior in Japan. *Journal of Sex Research, 11,* 91-122.

Asimov, I. (1989). *Chronology of Science and Discovery.* London: Grafton Books.

Bailey, J. M., & Pillard, R. C. (1991). A genetic study of male sexual orientation. *Archives of General Psychiatry, 48,* 1089-96.

Bailey, J. M., Pillard, R. C., Neale, M. C., & Agyei, Y. (1993). Heritable factors influence sexual orientation in women. *Archives of General Psychiatry, 50,* 217-23.

Baker, J. R. (1974). *Race.* Oxford: Oxford University Press.

Baker, L. A., Vernon, P. A., & Ho, H-Z. (1991). The genetic correlation between intelligence and speed of information processing. *Behavior Genetics, 21,* 351-67.

Baker, S. W. (1866). *The Albert N'Yanza, Great Basin of the Nile, and Explorations of the Nile Sources.* London: Macmillan.

Bandura, A. (1969). *Principles of Behavior Modification.* New York: Holt, Rinehart & Winston.

Bandura, A. (1986). *Social Foundations of Thought and Action.* Englewood Cliffs, NJ: Prentice-Hall.

Barash, D. P. (1982). *Sociobiology and Behavior* (2nd ed.). New York: Elsevier.

Barnes, G. E., Malamuth, N. M., & Check, J. V. P. (1984). Personality and sexuality. *Personality and Individual Differences, 5,* 159-72.

Barrett, P., & Eysenck, S. B. G. (1984). The assessment of personality factors across 25 countries. *Personality and Individual Differences, 5,* 615-32.

Bateson, P. P. G. (1983). *Mate Choice.* Cambridge University Press.

Baucom, D. H., Besch, P. K., & Callahan, S. (1985). Relation between testosterone concentration, sex role identity, and personality among females. *Journal of Personality and Social Psychology, 48,* 1218-26.

Baughman, E. E., & Dahlstrom, W. G. (1968). *Negro and White Children.* New York: Academic Press.

Bayley, N. (1965). Comparisons of mental and motor test scores for ages 1-15 months by sex, birth order, race, geographic location, and education of parents. *Child Development, 36,* 379-411.

Beals, K. L., Smith, C. L., & Dodd, S. M. (1984). Brain size, cranial morphology, climate and time machines (with commentaries and authors' response). *Current Anthropology, 25,* 301-30.

Bean, R. B. (1906). Some racial peculiarities of the Negro brain. *American Journal of Anatomy, 5,* 353-432.

Bell, A. P. (1978). Black sexuality: Fact and fancy. In R. Staples (Ed.), *The Black Family: Essays and Studies* (2nd ed.). Belmont, CA: Wadsworth.

Belsky, J., Steinberg, L., & Draper, P. (1991). Childhood experience, interpersonal development, and reproductive strategy: An evolutionary theory of socialization. *Child Development, 62,* 647-70.

Bentler, P. M., & Newcombe, M. D. (1978). Longitudinal study of marital success and failure. *Journal of Consulting and Clinical Psychology, 46,* 1053-70.

Black, D., Morris, J. N., Smith, C., Townsend, P. (1982). *The Black Report.* London: Pelican.

Blaustein, A. R., & O'Hara, R. K. (1982). Kin recognition in Rana cascadae tadpoles: Maternal and paternal effects. *Animal Behaviour, 30,* 1151-57.

Block, J. (1971). *Lives Through Time.* Berkeley, CA: Bancroft Books.

Block, J. (1981). Some enduring and consequential structures of personality. In A. I. Rabin, J. Aronoff, A. M. Barclay, & R. A. Zucker (Eds.), *Further Explorations in Personality.* New York: Wiley.

Bo, Z., & Wenxiu, G. (1992). Sexuality in urban China. *Australian Journal of Chinese Affairs, 28,* 1-20.

Boas, F. (1912). *Changes in Bodily Form of Descendents of Immigrants.* New York: Columbia University Press.

Boas, F. (1940). *Race, Language and Culture.* New York: Macmillan.

Bodmer, W. F., & Cavalli-Sforza, L. L. (1970). Intelligence and race. *Scientific American, 223*(4), 19-29.

Bogaert, A. F., & Rushton, J. P. (1989). Sexuality, delinquency and r/K reproductive strategies: Data from a Canadian university sample. *Personality and Individual Differences, 10,* 1071-77.

Bonner, J. T. (1965). *Size and Cycle.* Princeton, NJ: Princeton University Press.

Bonner, J. T. (1980). *The Evolution of Culture in Animals.* Princeton, NJ: Princeton University Press.

Bonner, J. T. (1988). *The Evolution of Complexity.* Princeton, NJ: Princeton University Press.

Bouchard, T. J., Jr. (1984). Twins reared together and apart: What they tell us about human diversity. In S. W. Fox (Ed.), *Individuality and Determinism.* New York: Plenum.

Bouchard, T. J., Jr., Lykken, D. T., McGue, M., Segal, N. L., & Tellegen, A. (1990). Sources of human psychological differences: The Minnesota study of twins reared apart. *Science, 250,* 223-28.

Bouchard, T. J., Jr., & McGue, M. (1981). Familial studies of intelligence: A review. *Science, 212,* 1055-59.

Bowman, M. L. (1989). Testing individual differences in ancient China. *American Psychologist, 44,* 576-78.

Boyce, M. S. (1984). Restitution of r and K-selection as a model of density-dependent natural selection. *Annual Review of Ecology and Systematics, 15,* 427-47.

Bradley, M. (1978). *The Iceman Inheritance: Prehistoric Sources of Western Man's Racism, Sexism and Aggression.* Toronto: Dorset.

Brandt, I. (1978). Growth dynamics of low-birth weight infants with emphasis on the perinatal period. In F. Falkner & J. M. Tanner (Eds.), *Human Growth, Vol. 2* (pp. 557-617). New York: Plenum Press.

Bray, P. F., Shields, W. D., Wolcott, G. J., & Madsen, J. A. (1969). Occipitofrontal head circumference—an accurate measure of intracranial volume. *Journal of Pediatrics, 75,* 303-305.

Brazelton, T. B., & Freedman, D. G. (1971). The Cambridge neonatal scales. In J. J. van der Werf ten Bosch (Ed.), *Normal and Abnormal Development of Brain and Behavior.* Leiden: Leiden University Press.

Brazelton, T. B., Robey, J. S., & Collier, G. A. (1969). Infant development in the Zinacanteco Indians of Southern Mexico. *Paediatrics, 44,* 274-90.

Bressler, M. (1968). Sociobiology, biology and ideology. In D. Glass (Ed.), *Genetics* (pp. 178-210). New York: Rockefeller University Press.

Brigham, C. C. (1923). *A Study of American Intelligence.* Princeton, NJ: Princeton University Press.

Broca, P. (1858). Memoire sur l'hybridite en general, sur la distinction des especes animales et sur les metis obtenus par le croisement du lievre et du lapin. *Journal de la Physiologie, 7,* 433-71, 684-729.

Brody, N. (1992). *Intelligence* (2nd ed.). New York: Academic.

Broman, S. H., Nichols, P. L., Shaughnessy, P., & Kennedy, W. (1987). *Retardation in Young Children.* Hillsdale, NJ: Erlbaum.

Brooks, L. (1989). *Adopted Korean Children Compared with Korean and Caucasian Non-Adopted Children.* Unpublished doctoral dissertation, University of Chicago.

Brown, M. H. (1990). *The Search for Eve.* New York: Harper & Row.

Bryant, N. J. (1980). *Disputed Paternity.* New York: Thieme-Stratton.

Buj, V. (1981). Average IQ values in various European countries. *Personality and Individual Differences, 2,* 168-69.

Bulmer, M. G. (1970). *The Biology of Twinning in Man.* Oxford: Clarendon Press.

Burfoot, A. (1992). White men can't run. *Runner's World,* August, pp. 89-95.

Burley, N. (1983). The meaning of assortative mating. *Ethology and Sociobiology, 4,* 191-203.

Burton, R. V. (1963). Generality of honesty reconsidered. *Psychological Review, 70,* 481-99.

Buss, D. M. (1984). Evolutionary biology and personality psychology: Toward a conception of human nature and individual differences. *American Psychologist, 39,* 1135–47.

Byrne, D. (1971). *The Attraction Paradigm.* New York: Academic Press.

Cain, D. P., & Vanderwolf, C. H. (1990). A critique of Rushton on race, brain size and intelligence. *Personality and Individual Differences, 11,* 777–84.

Caldwell, J. C., & Caldwell, P. (1990). High fertility in sub-Saharan Africa. *Scientific American, 267* (No. 3), 119–25.

Calvin, W. H. (1990). *The Ascent of Mind.* New York: Bantam Books.

Cameron, N. (1989). *Barbarians and Mandarins.* Hong Kong: Oxford University Press. (Original work published in 1970.)

Cann, R. L., Stoneking, M., & Wilson, A. C. (1987). Mitochondrial DNA and human evolution. *Nature, 325,* 31–36.

Caplan, N., Choy, M. H., & Whitmore, J. K. (1992). Indochinese refugee families and academic achievement. *Scientific American, 266*(2), 18–24.

Caporael, L. R., & Brewer, M. B. (1991). The quest for human nature: Social and scientific issues in evolutionary psychology. *Journal of Social Issues, 47,* 1–9.

Carey, G., Goldsmith, H. H., Tellegen, A., & Gottesman, I. I. (1978). Genetics and personality inventories: The limits of replication with twin data. *Behavior Genetics, 8,* 299–313.

Cates, W., Farley, T. M. M., & Rowe, P. J. (1985). Worldwide patterns of infertility: Is Africa different? *Lancet,* 1985–II, 596–98.

Caton, H. (Ed.). (1990). *The Samoa Reader.* London: University Press of America.

Cattell, R. B. (1982). *The Inheritance of Personality and Ability.* New York: Academic Press.

Cattell, R. B., & Nesselroade, J. R. (1967). Likeness and completeness theories examined by Sixteen Personality Factor measures on stably and unstably married couples. *Journal of Personality and Social Psychology, 7,* 351–61.

Cavalli-Sforza, L. L., & Edwards, A. W. F. (1964). Analysis of human evolution. In *Proceedings of the 11th International Congress of Genetics* (pp. 923–33). Oxford: Pergamon Press.

Cavalli-Sforza, L. L., Menozzi, P., & Piazza, A. (1993). Demic expansions and human evolution. *Science, 259,* 639–46.

Cavalli-Sforza, L. L., Piazza, A., Menozzi, P., & Mountain, J. (1988). Reconstruction of human evolution: Bringing together genetic, archaeological, and linguistic data. *Proceedings of the National Academy of Sciences of the U.S.A., 85,* 6002–6.

Centers for Disease Control and Prevention. (1992a). Sexual behavior among high school students—United States, 1990. *Morbidity and Mortality Weekly Report, 40* (Nos. 51 & 52), 885–88.

Centers for Disease Control and Prevention. (1992b). Selected behaviors that increase risk for HIV infection among high school students—United States, 1990. *Morbidity and Mortality Weekly Report, 41* (No. 14), 231–40.

Centers for Disease Control and Prevention. (1993). *HIV/AIDS Surveillance Report, 5,* (no. 3), 1–20.

Chafets, Z. (1990). *Devil's Night, and Other True Tales of Detroit.* New York: Random House.

Chagnon, N. A. (1988). Life histories, blood revenge, and warfare in a tribal population. *Science, 239,* 985–92.

Chaillu, P. B. Du (1861). *Explorations and Adventures in Equatorial Africa.* London: Murray.

Chakraborty, R., Kamboh, M. I., Nwankwo, M., & Ferrell, R. E. (1992). Caucasian genes in American blacks: New data. *American Journal of Human Genetics, 50,* 145–55.

Chan, J., & Lynn, R. (1989). The intelligence of 6-year-olds in Hong Kong. *Journal of Biosocial Science, 21,* 461-64.

Chisholm, J. S. (1993). Death, hope, and sex: Life history theory and the development of reproductive strategies. *Current Anthropology, 34,* 1-24.

Christiansen, K. O. (1977). A preliminary study of criminality among twins. In S. A. Mednick & K. O. Christiansen (Eds.), *Biosocial Bases of Criminal Behavior.* New York: Gardner.

Clark, E. A., & Hanisee, J. (1982). Intellectual and adaptive performance of Asian children in adoptive American settings. *Developmental Psychology, 18,* 595-599.

Clark, R. W. (1984). *The Survival of Charles Darwin.* New York: Random House.

Cloninger, C. R. (1986). A unified biosocial theory of personality and its role in the development of anxiety states. *Psychiatric Developments, 3,* 167-226.

Cloninger, C. R., Bohman, M., & Sigvardsson, S. (1981). Inheritance of alcohol abuse: Cross-fostering analysis of adopted men. *Archives of General Psychiatry, 38,* 861-69.

Cohen, D. J., Dibble, E., & Grawe, J. M. (1977). Fathers' and mothers' perceptions of children's personality. *Archives of General Psychiatry, 34,* 480-87.

Cole, L. C. (1954). The population consequences of life history phenomena. *Quarterly Review of Biology, 29,* 103-37.

Coleman, J. S., Campbell, E. Q., Hobson, C. J., McPortland, J., Mood, A. M., Weinfeld, F. D., & York, R. L. (1966). *Equality of Educational Opportunity,* 2 vols. Washington, DC: U.S. Office of Education.

Conley, J. J. (1984). The hierarchy of consistency: A review and model of longitudinal findings on adult individual differences in intelligence, personality and self opinion. *Personality and Individual Differences, 5,* 11-25.

Conley, J. J. (1985). Longitudinal stability of personality traits: A multitrait-multimethod-multioccasion analysis. *Journal of Personality and Social Psychology, 49,* 1266-82.

Connor, J. W. (1975). Value changes in third generation Japanese Americans. *Journal of Personality Assessment, 39,* 597-600.

Connor, J. W. (1976). Family bonds, maternal closeness and suppression of sexuality in three generations of Japanese Americans. *Ethos, 4,* 189-221.

Cooke, R. W. I., Lucas, A., Yudkin, P. L. N., & Pryse-Davies, J. (1977). Head circumference as an index of brain weight in the fetus and newborn. *Early Human Development, 1/2,* 145-49.

Coon, C. S. (1962). *The Origin of Races.* New York: Knopf.

Coon, C. S. (1982). *Racial Adaptations.* Chicago: Nelson-Hall.

Costa, P. T., Jr., & McCrae, R. R. (1992). Trait psychology comes of age. In T. B. Sonderegger (Ed.), *Nebraska Symposium on Motivation: Psychology and Aging.* Lincoln, NE: University of Nebraska Press.

Costa, P. T., Jr., & McCrae, R. R. (1994). Set like plaster? Evidence for the stability of adult personality. In T. F. Heatherton & J. L. Weinberger (Eds.), *Can Personality Change?* Washington, DC: American Psychological Association.

Crawford Nutt. (1976). African IQ in Zambia. Cited in R. Lynn (1991c).

Cunningham, M. R. (1981). Sociobiology as a supplementary paradigm for social psychological research. In L. Wheeler (Ed.), *Review of Personality and Social Psychology, Vol. 2.* Beverly Hills, CA: Sage.

Cunningham, M. R., & Barbee, A. P. (1991). Differential *K*-selection versus ecological determinants of race differences in sexual behavior. *Journal of Research in Personality, 25,* 205-17.

Curti, M., Marshall, F. B., Steggerda, M., & Henderson, E. M. (1935). The Gesell schedules applied to one-, two-, and three-year old Negro children of Jamaica, B.W.I. *Journal of Comparative and Physiological Psychology, 20,* 152-56.

Dabbs, J. M., Jr., & Morris, R. (1990). Testosterone, social class, and antisocial behavior in a sample of 4,462 men. *Psychological Science, 1*, 209–11.

Dabbs, J. M., Jr., Ruback, R. B., Frady, R. L., Hopper, C. H., & Sgoutas, D. S. (1988). Saliva testosterone and criminal violence among women. *Personality and Individual Differences, 9*, 269–75.

Daly, M., & Wilson, M. (1982). Whom are newborn babies said to resemble? *Ethology and Sociobiology, 3*, 69–78.

Daly, M., & Wilson, M. (1983). *Sex, Evolution, and Behavior* (2nd ed.). Boston, MA: Willard Grant.

Daly, M., & Wilson, M. (1988). *Homicide.* New York: Aldine de Gruyter.

Daniels, D., & Plomin, R. (1985). Differential experience of siblings in the same family. *Developmental Psychology, 21*, 747–60.

Darwin, C. (1859). *The Origin of Species.* London: Murray.

Darwin, C. (1871). *The Descent of Man.* London: Murray.

Dawkins, R. (1976). *The Selfish Gene.* Oxford: Oxford University Press.

Dawkins, R. (1982). *The Extended Phenotype.* San Francisco, CA: Freeman.

DeFries, J. C. (1972). Quantitative aspects of genetics and environment in the determination of behavior. In L. Ehrman, G. S. Omenn, & E. Caspari (Eds.), *Genetics, Environment, and Behavior.* New York: Academic.

DeFries, J. C., Ashton, G. C., Johnson, R. C., Kuse, A. R., McClearn, G. E., Mi, M. P., Rashad, M. N., Vandenberg, S. G., & Wilson, J. R. (1978). The Hawaii Family Study of Cognition: A reply. *Behavior Genetics, 8*, 281–88.

Degler, C. N. (1991). *In Search of Human Nature.* New York: Oxford University Press.

Dekaban, A. S., & Sadowsky, D. (1978). Changes in brain weights during the span of human life: Relation of brain weights to body heights and body weights. *Annals of Neurology, 4*, 345–56.

Diamond, J. (1991). *The Rise and Fall of the Third Chimpanzee.* London: Radius.

Dobzhansky, T. (1970). *Genetics of the Evolutionary Process.* New York: Columbia University Press.

Draper, P. (1989). African marriage systems: Perspectives from evolutionary ecology. *Ethology and Sociobiology, 10*, 145–69.

Draper, P., & Harpending, H. (1982). Father absence and reproductive strategy: An evolutionary perspective. *Journal of Anthropological Research, 38*, 255–73.

Draper, P., & Harpending, H. (1988). A sociobiological perspective on the development of human reproductive strategies. In K. B. MacDonald (Ed.), *Sociobiological Perspectives on Human Development.* New York: Springer-Verlag.

Dreger, R. M., & Miller, K. S. (1960). Comparative psychological studies of Negroes and whites in the United States. *Psychological Bulletin, 57*, 361–402.

DuBois, W. E. B. (1908). *The North American Family.* Atlanta, GA: Atlanta University Publication No. 13. Atlanta University Press.

Dunbar, R. I. M. (1992). Neocortex size as a constraint on group size in primates. *Journal of Human Evolution, 20*, 469–93.

Duncan, D. E. (1990). The long goodbye. *The Atlantic Monthly,* July, pp. 20–24.

Dworkin, R. H., Burke, B. W., Maher, B. A., & Gottesman, I. I. (1976). A longitudinal study of the genetics of personality. *Journal of Personality and Social Psychology, 34*, 510–18.

Eaton, W. O. (1983). Measuring activity level with actometers: Reliability, validity, and arm length. *Child Development, 54*, 720–26.

Eaves, L. J., & Eysenck, H. J. (1974). Genetics and the development of social attitudes. *Nature, 249*, 288–89.

Eaves, L. J., Eysenck, H. J., & Martin, N. G. (1989). *Genes, Culture and Personality.* London: Academic.

Eaves, L. J., & Young, P. A. (1981). Genetical theory and personality differences. In R. Lynn (Ed.), *Dimensions of Personality.* Oxford: Pergamon.

Eibl-Eibesfeldt, I. (1989). Familiality, xenophobia, and group selection. *Behavioral and Brain Sciences, 12,* 523.

Eisenberg, J. F. (1981). *The Mammalian Radiations.* Chicago: University of Chicago Press.

Ekblad, S., & Olweus, D. (1986). Applicability of Olweus' Aggression Inventory in a sample of Chinese primary school children. *Aggressive Behavior, 12,* 315-25.

Elander, J., West, R., & French, D. (1993). Behavioral correlates of individual differences in road-traffic crash risk: An examination of methods and findings. *Psychological Bulletin, 113,* 279-94.

Elliott, D. S., & Ageton, S. S. (1980). Reconciling race and class differences in self-reported and official estimates of delinquency. *American Sociological Review, 45,* 95-110.

Ellis, L. (1987). Criminal behavior and r- vs. K-selection: An extension of gene-based evolutionary theory. *Deviant Behavior, 8,* 149-76.

Ellis, L. (1989). *Theories of Rape.* New York: Hemisphere.

Ellis, L., & Nyborg, H. (1992). Racial/ethnic variations in male testosterone levels: A probable contributor to group differences in health. *Steroids, 57,* 72-75.

Emde, R. N., Plomin, R., Robinson, J., Corley, R., DeFries, J., Fulker, D. W., Reznik, J. S., Campos, J., Kagan, J., & Zahn-Waxler, C. (1992). Temperament, emotion, and cognition at fourteen months: The MacArthur Longitudinal Twin Study. *Child Development, 63,* 1437-55.

Epstein, S. (1977). Traits are alive and well. In D. Magnusson & N.S. Endler (Eds.), *Personality at the Crossroads: Current Issues in Interactional Psychology.* Hillsdale, NJ: Erlbaum.

Epstein, S. (1979). The stability of behavior: I. On predicting most of the people much of the time. *Journal of Personality and Social Psychology, 37,* 1097-1126.

Epstein, S. (1980). The stability of behavior: II. Implications for psychological research. *American Psychologist, 35,* 790-806.

Epstein, S., & O'Brien, E. J. (1985). The person-situation debate in historical and current perspective. *Psychological Bulletin, 98,* 513-37.

Erlenmeyer-Kimling, L., & Jarvik, L. R. (1963). Genetics and intelligence: A review. *Science, 142,* 1477-79.

Eron, L. D. (1987). The development of aggressive behavior from the perspective of a developing behaviorism. *American Psychologist, 42,* 435-42.

Estabrooks, G. H. (1928). The relation between cranial capacity, relative cranial capacity and intelligence in school children. *Journal of Applied Psychology, 12,* 524-29.

Eveleth, P. B., & Tanner, J. M. (1990). *Worldwide Variation in Human Growth* (2nd ed.). London: Cambridge University Press.

Eysenck, H. J. (1970). *Crime and Personality* (2nd ed.). London: Granada.

Eysenck, H. J. (1971). *Race, Intelligence and Education.* London: Temple Smith.

Eysenck, H. J. (1976). *Sex and Personality.* London: Open Books.

Eysenck, H. J. (Ed.). (1981). *A Model for Personality.* New York: Springer.

Eysenck, H. J. (1991a). Race and intelligence: An alternative hypothesis. *Mankind Quarterly, 32,* 133-36.

Eysenck, H. J. (1991b). Raising I.Q. through vitamin and mineral supplementation: An introduction. *Personality and Individual Differences, 12,* 329-33.

Eysenck, H. J., & Cookson, D. (1969). Personality in primary school. *British Journal of Educational Psychology, 39,* 109-22.

Eysenck, H. J., & Eysenck, S. B. G. (1975). *Manual of the Eysenck Personality Questionnaire.* San Diego, CA: Educational and Industrial Testing Service.

Eysenck, H. J., & Eysenck, S. B. G. (Eds.). (1991). Improvement of I.Q. and behavior as a function of dietary supplementation: A symposium. *Personality and Individual Differences, 12,* 329-65.

Eysenck, H. J., & Gudjonsson, G. H. (1989). *The Causes and Cures of Criminality.* New York: Plenum.

Eysenck, H. J., & Kamin, L. (1981). *The Intelligence Controversy.* New York: Wiley.

Eysenck, H. J., & Wakefield, J. A. (1981). Psychological factors as predictors of marital satisfaction. *Advances in Behaviour Research and Therapy, 3,* 151-92.

Fagan, B. M. (1990). *The Journey from Eden.* New York: Thames and Hudson.

Fahrmeier, E. D. (1975). The effect of school attendance on intellectual development in Northern Nigeria. *Child Development, 46,* 281-85.

Fairchild, H. H. (1991). Scientific racism: The cloak of objectivity. *Journal of Social Issues, 47,* 101-15.

Falconer, D. S. (1989). *Introduction to Quantitative Genetics* (3rd ed.). London: Longman.

Falk, D. (1992). *Braindance.* New York: Holt.

Fick, M. L. (1929). Intelligence test results of poor white, native (Zulu), coloured and Indian school children and the educational and social implications. *South African Journal of Science, 26,* 904-20.

Fisch, R. O., Bilek, M. K., Horrobin, J. M., & Chang, P. N. (1976). Children with superior intelligence at 7 years of age. *American Journal of Diseases in Children, 130,* 481-87.

Fishbein, M., & Ajzen, I. (1974). Attitudes towards objects as predictors of single and multiple behavioral criteria. *Psychological Review, 81,* 59-74.

Fisher, R. A. (1958). *The Genetical Theory of Natural Selection* (2nd ed.). New York: Dover.

Fisher, S. (1980). Personality correlates of sexual behavior in black women. *Archives of Sexual Behavior, 9,* 27-35.

Fletcher, D. J. C., & Michener, C. D. (Eds.). (1987). *Kin Recognition in Animals.* New York: Wiley.

Floderus-Myrhed, B., Pedersen, N., & Rasmuson, I. (1980). Assessment of heritability for personality based on a short form of the Eysenck Personality Inventory: A study of 12,898 twin pairs. *Behavior Genetics, 10,* 153-62.

Flynn, J. R. (1984). The mean IQ of Americans: Massive gains 1932 to 1978. *Psychological Bulletin, 95,* 29-51.

Flynn, J. R. (1987). Massive IQ gains in 14 nations: What IQ tests really measure. *Psychological Bulletin, 101,* 171-91.

Flynn, J. R. (1989). Rushton, evolution, and race: An essay on intelligence and virtue. *The Psychologist: Bulletin of the British Psychological Society, 2,* 363-66.

Flynn, J. R. (1991). *Asian Americans: Achievement Beyond IQ.* Hillsdale, NJ: Erlbaum.

Ford, C. S., & Beach, F. A. (1951). *Patterns of Sexual Behavior.* New York: Harper & Row.

Forrest, D. W. (1974). *Francis Galton: The Life and Work of a Victorian Genius.* New York: Halsted.

Frayer, D. W., Wolpoff, M. H., Thorne, A. G., Smith, F. H., & Pope, G. G. (1993). Theories of modern human origins: The paleontological test. *American Anthropologist, 95,* 14-50.

Frazier, E. F. (1948). *The Negro Family in the United States.* New York: Dryden.

Freedman, D. G. (1974). *Human Infancy.* New York: Halsted.

Freedman, D. G. (1979). *Human Sociobiology.* New York: Free Press.

Freedman, D. G., & Freedman, N. C. (1969). Behavioral differences between Chinese-American and European-American newborns. *Nature, 224,* 1227.

Freeman, D. (1984). *Margaret Mead and Samoa*. New York: Penguin.

Freeman, W. (1934). The weight of the endocrine glands: Biometrical studies in psychiatry, No. 8. *Human Biology, 6*, 489–523.

French Army Surgeon. (1898/1972). *Untrodden Fields of Anthropology* (2 vols.). Paris, France: Carington. (Reprinted in Huntington, New York: Krieger).

Freud, S. (1930/1962). *Civilization and its Discontents*. (Ed. and Trans. J. Strachey.) New York: Norton.

Frydman, M., & Lynn, R. (1989). The intelligence of Korean children adopted in Belgium. *Personality and Individual Differences, 10*, 1323–26.

Fulker, D. W., & Eysenck, H. J. (1979). Nature and nurture: Heredity. In H. J. Eysenck (Ed.), *The Structure and Measurement of Intelligence*. Berlin: Springer-Verlag.

Fynn, H. F. (1950). *The Diary of Henry Francis Fynn*. (Ed. J. Stuart.) Pietermaritzburg: Shooter & Shooter.

Gabor, T., & Roberts, J. V. (1990). Rushton on race and crime: The evidence remains unconvincing. *Canadian Journal of Criminology, 32*, 335–43.

Gadgil, M., & Solbrig, O. T. (1972). The concept of *r*- and *K*- selection: Evidence from wild flowers and some theoretical considerations. *American Naturalist, 106*, 14–31.

Galler, J. R., Ramsey, F., & Forde, V. (1986). A follow up study in the influence of early malnutrition on subsequent development. *Nutrition and Behavior, 3*, 211–22.

Galton, F. (1853). *The Narrative of an Explorer in Tropical South Africa*. London: Murray.

Galton, F. (1865). Hereditary talents and character. *Macmillan's Magazine, 12*, 157–66, 318–27.

Galton, F. (1869). *Hereditary Genius*. London: Macmillan.

Galton, F. (1874). *English Men of Science*. London: Macmillan.

Galton, F. (1879). Psychometric experiments. *Brain, 2*, 149–62.

Galton, F. (1883). *Inquiries into Human Faculty and Its Development*. London: Macmillan.

Galton, F. (1888a). Co-relations and their measurement, chiefly from anthropometric data. *Proceedings of the Royal Society, 45*, 135–45.

Galton, F. (1888b). Head growth in students at the University of Cambridge. *Nature, 38*, 14–15.

Galton, F. (1889). *Natural Inheritance*. London: Macmillan.

Galton, F. (1908). *Memories of My Life*. London: Methuen.

Garbarino, J., & Ebata, A. (1983). The significance of ethnic and cultural differences in child maltreatment. *Journal of Marriage and the Family, 45*, 773–83.

Geber, M. (1958). The psycho-motor development of African children in the first year, and the influence of maternal behavior. *Journal of Social Psychology, 47*, 185–95.

Gebhard, P. H., & Johnson, A. B. (1979). *The Kinsey data: Marginal Tabulations of the 1938–1963 Interviews Conducted by the Institute for Sex Research*. Philadelphia, PA: Saunders.

Gebhard, P. H., Pomeroy, W. B., Martin, C. E., & Christenson, C. V. (1958). *Pregnancy, Birth, and Abortion*. New York: Harper-Hoeber.

Gibbons, A. (1991). Looking for the father of us all. *Science, 251*, 378–80.

Gibbons, A. (1992). Following a trail of old ostrich eggshells. *Science, 256*, 1281–82.

Gobineau, A. de, (1853–1855). *Essai sur L'inegalite des Races Humaines*. Paris: Didot.

Golding, J. (1986). Social class and twinning. *Acta Geneticae Medicae et Gemellologiae, 35*, 207 (Abstracts, p. 29).

Goodman, M. J., Grove, J. S., & Gilbert, F. (1980). Age at first pregnancy in relation to age at menarche and year of birth in Caucasian, Japanese, Chinese, and part-Hawaiian women living in Hawaii. *Annals of Human Biology, 7*, 29–33.

Gordon, K. (1924). Group judgments in the field of lifted weights. *Journal of Experimental Psychology, 7,* 398-400.

Gordon R. A. (1987a). Jensen's contributions concerning test bias: A contextual view. In S. Modgil & C. Modgil (Eds.), *Arthur Jensen: Consensus and Controversy.* New York: The Falmer Press.

Gordon, R. A. (1987b). SES versus IQ in the race-IQ-delinquency model. *International Journal of Sociology and Social Policy, 7,* 30-96.

Gottesman, I. I. (1963). Heritability of personality: A demonstration. *Psychological Monographs, 77* (No. 9) (Whole No. 572).

Gottesman, I. I. (1966). Genetic variance in adaptive personality traits. *Journal of Child Psychology and Psychiatry and Allied Disciplines, 7,* 199-208.

Gottesman, I. I. (1991). *Schizophrenia Genesis: The Origins of Madness.* San Francisco, CA: Freeman.

Gottfredson, L. S. (1986). Societal consequences of the *g* factor in employment. *Journal of Vocational Behavior, 29,* 379-410.

Gottfredson, L. S. (1987). The practical significance of black-white differences in intelligence. *Behavioral and Brain Sciences, 10,* 510-12.

Gould, S. J. (1978). Morton's ranking of races by cranial capacity. *Science, 200,* 503-9.

Gould, S. J. (1981). *The Mismeasure of Man.* New York: Norton.

Grant, M. (1916). *The Passing of the Great Race.* New York: Scribner.

Gray, J. A. (1987). *The Psychology of Fear and Stress* (2nd ed.). Cambridge: Cambridge University Press.

Greenberg, L. (1979). Genetic component of bee odor in kin recognition. *Science, 206,* 1095-97.

Groves, C. P. (1991). Genes, genitals and genius: The evolutionary ecology of race. In P. O'Higgins & R. N. Pervan (Eds.), *Human Biology: An Integrative Science.* Nedlands, Australia: University of Western Australia, Centre for Human Biology.

Gruter, M., & Masters, R. D. (Eds.). (1986). Ostracism: A social and biological phenomenon. *Ethology and Sociobiology, 7,* 149-256.

Haeberle, E. W. (1978). *The Sex Atlas.* New York: Seabury.

Hames, R. B. (1979). Relatedness and interaction among Ye'Kwana: A preliminary analysis. In N. A. Chagnon & W. Irons (Eds.), *Evolutionary Biology and Human Social Behavior.* North Scituate, MA: Duxbury.

Hamilton, W. D. (1964). The genetical evolution of social behaviour: I and II. *Journal of Theoretical Biology, 7,* 1-52.

Hare, B. R. (1985). Stability and change in self-perception and achievement among black adolescents: A longitudinal study. *Journal of Black Psychology, 11,* 29-42.

Harlan, W. R., Grillo, G. P., Coroni-Huntley, J., & Leaverton, P. E. (1979). Secondary sex characteristics of boys 12 to 17 years of age: The U.S. Health Examination Survey. *Adolescent Medicine, 95,* 293-97.

Harlan, W. R., Harlan, E. A., & Grillo, G. P. (1980). Secondary sex characteristics of girls 12 to 17 years of age: The U.S. Health Examination Survey. *Adolescent Medicine, 96,* 1074-78.

Hartshorne, H., & May, M. A. (1928). *Studies in the Nature of Character: Vol. 1. Studies in Deceit.* New York: Macmillan.

Hartshorne, H., May, M. A., & Maller, J. B. (1929). *Studies in the Nature of Character: Vol. 2. Studies in Self-Control.* New York: Macmillan.

Hartshorne, H., May, M. A., & Shuttleworth, F. K. (1930). *Studies in the Nature of Character: Vol. 3. Studies in the Organization of Character.* New York: Macmillan.

Harvey, P. H., & Clutton-Brock, T. H. (1985). Life history variation in primates. *Evolution, 39,* 559-81.

Harvey, P. H., & Krebs, J. R. (1990). Comparing brains. *Science, 249,* 140-45.

Harvey, P. H., & May, R. M. (1989). Out for the sperm count. *Nature, 337,* 508-9.

Haug, H. (1987). Brain sizes, surfaces, and neuronal sizes of the cortex cerebri: A stereological investigation of man and his variability and a comparison with some species of mammals (primates, whales, marsupials, insectivores, and one elephant). *American Journal of Anatomy, 180,* 126-42.

Heath, A. C., Berg, K., Eaves, L. J., Solaas, M. H., Corey, L. A., Sundet, J., Magnus, P., & Nance, W. E. (1985). Education policy and the heritability of educational attainment. *Nature, 314,* 734-36.

Hebb, D. O., & Thompson, W. R. (1968). The social significance of animal studies. In G. Lindzey & W. R. Thompson (Eds.), *The Handbook of Social Psychology, Vol. 2.* New York: Addison-Wesley.

Hegmann, J. P., & Dingle, H. (1982). Phenotypic and genetic covariance structure in milkweed bug life history traits. In J. P. Hegmann & H. Dingle (Eds.), *Evolution and Genetics of Life Histories.* New York: Springer.

Heltsley, M. E., & Broderick, C. B. (1969). Religiosity and premarital sexual permissiveness. *Journal of Marriage and the Family, 21,* 441-43.

Henderson, N. D. (1982). Human behavior genetics. *Annual Review of Psychology, 33,* 403-40.

Henneberg, M., Budnik, A., Pezacka, M., & Puch, A. E. (1985). Head size, body size and intelligence: Intraspecific correlations in *Homo sapiens sapiens. Homo, 36,* 207-18.

Herrnstein, R. J. (1973). *IQ in the Meritocracy.* Boston, MA: Little, Brown.

Herskovits, M. J. (1930). *The Anthropometry of the American Negro.* New York: Columbia University Press.

Hertzig, M. E., Birch, H. G., Richardson, S. A., & Tizard, J. (1972). Intellectual levels of school children severely malnourished during the first two years of life. *Pediatrics, 49,* 814-24.

Heston, L. L. (1966). Psychiatric disorders in foster home reared children of schizophrenic mothers. *British Journal of Psychiatry, 112,* 819-25.

Heyward, W. L., & Curran, J. W. (1988). The epidemiology of AIDS in the U.S. *Scientific American, 258,* 272-81.

Hill, C. T., Rubin, Z., & Peplau, L. A. (1976). Breakups before marriage: The end of 103 affairs. *Journal of Social Issues, 32,* 147-68.

Hirsch, J. (1991). Obfuscation of interaction. *Behavioral and Brain Sciences, 14,* 397-98.

Hirschi, T., & Hindelang, M. J. (1977). Intelligence and delinquency: A revisionist review. *American Sociological Review, 42,* 571-87.

Hixson, J. R. (1992, October 20). Benign prostatic hypertrophy drug to be tested in prostate CA prevention. *The Medical Post.*

Ho, K-C., Roessmann, U., Straumfjord, J. V., & Monroe, G. (1980a). Analysis of brain weight: I. Adult brain weight in relation to sex, race, and age. *Archives of Pathology and Laboratory Medicine, 104,* 635-39.

Ho, K-C., Roessmann, U., Straumfjord, J. V., & Monroe, G. (1980b). Analysis of brain weight: II. Adult brain weight in relation to body height, weight, and surface area. *Archives of Pathology and Laboratory Medicine, 104,* 640-45.

Ho, K-C., Roessmann, U., Hause, L., & Monroe, G. (1981). Newborn brain weight in relation to maturity, sex, and race. *Annals of Neurology, 10,* 243-46.

Hofman, M. A. (1991). The fractal geometry of convoluted brains. *Journal fur Hirnforschung, 32,* 103-11.

Hofman, M. A. (1993). Encephalization and the evolution of longevity in mammals. *Journal of Evolutionary Biology, 6,* 209-27.

Hofmann, A. D. (1984). Contraception in adolescence: A review. 1. Psychosocial aspects. *Bulletin of the World Health Organization, 63,* 151-62.

Horowitz, D. L. (1985). *Ethnic Groups in Conflict.* University of California Press.

Howells, W. W. (1973). *Cranial Variation in Man.* (Papers of the Peabody Museum of Archaeology and Ethnology, Volume 67.) Cambridge, MA: Harvard University Press.

Howells, W. W. (1989). *Skull Shapes and the Map.* (Papers of the Peabody Museum of Archaeology and Ethnology, Volume 79.) Cambridge, MA: Harvard University Press.

Howells, W. (1993). *Getting Here: The Story of Human Evolution.* Washington, DC: The Compass Press.

Hudson, A. I., & Holbrook, A. (1982). Fundamental frequency characteristics of young black adults: Spontaneous speaking and oral reading. *Journal of Speech and Hearing Research, 25,* 25-28.

Huesmann, L. R., Eron, L. D., Lefkowitz, M. M., & Walder, L. O. (1984). Stability of aggression over time and generations. *Developmental Psychology, 20,* 1120-34.

Hunter, J. E. (1986). Cognitive ability, cognitive aptitudes, job knowledge, and job performance. *Journal of Vocational Behavior, 29,* 340-62.

Hunter, J. E., & Hunter, R. F. (1984). Validity and utility of alternate predictors of job performance. *Psychological Bulletin, 96,* 72-98.

Imaizumi, Y. (1992). Twinning rates in Japan, 1951-1990. *Acta Geneticae Medicae et Gemellologiae, 41,* 165-75.

Iwawaki, S., & Wilson, G. D. (1983). Sex fantasies in Japan. *Personality and Individual Differences, 4,* 543-45.

Jaccard, J. J. (1974). Predicting social behavior from personality traits. *Journal of Research in Personality, 7,* 358-67.

Jackson, D. N. (1984). *Multidimensional Aptitude Battery Manual.* Port Huron, MI: Research Psychologists Press.

Jaffee, B., & Fanshel, D. (1970). *How They Fared in Adoption: A Follow-up Study.* New York: Columbia.

James, G. G. M. (1992). *Stolen Legacy.* Trenton, NJ: Africa World Press. (Original work published 1954).

James, W. (1981). *The Principles of Psychology, Vol. 1.* Cambridge, MA: Harvard University Press. (Original work published in 1890.)

James, W. H. (1986). Hormonal control of sex ratio. *Journal of Theoretical Biology, 118,* 427-41.

Janiger, O., Riffenburgh, R., & Kersh, R. (1972). Cross-cultural study of premenstrual symptoms. *Psychosomatics, 13,* 226-35.

Jardine, R. (1985). *A Twin Study of Personality, Social Attitudes and Drinking Behaviour.* Unpublished doctoral dissertation, Australian National University, Canberra, Australia.

Jaynes, G. D., & Williams, Jr., R. M. (Eds.). (1989). *A Common Destiny: Blacks and American Society.* Washington, DC: National Academy Press.

Jensen, A. R. (1969). How much can we boost IQ and scholastic achievement? *Harvard Educational Review, 39,* 1-123.

Jensen, A. R. (1973). *Educability and Group Differences.* London: Methuen.

Jensen, A. R. (1974). Interaction of level I and level II abilities with race and socioeconomic status. *Journal of Educational Psychology, 66,* 99-111.

Jensen, A. R. (1980a). *Bias in Mental Testing.* New York: Free Press.

Jensen, A. R. (1980b). Uses of sibling data in educational and psychological research. *American Educational Research Journal, 17,* 153-70.

Jensen, A. R. (1981). Obstacles, problems, and pitfalls in differential psychology. In S. Scarr (Ed.), *Race, Social Class and Individual Differences in IQ.* Hillsdale, NJ: Erlbaum.

Jensen, A. R. (1983). The effects of inbreeding on mental ability factors. *Personality and Individual Differences, 4,* 71-87.

Jensen, A. R. (1985). The nature of the black-white difference on various psychometric tests: Spearman's hypothesis. *Behavioral and Brain Sciences, 8,* 193-263.

Jensen, A. R. (1987a). The *g* beyond factor analysis. In R. R. Ronning, J. A. Gover, J. C. Conoley, & J. C. Witt (Eds.), *The Influence of Cognitive Psychology on Testing.* Hillsdale, NJ: Erlbaum.

Jensen, A. R. (1987b). The nature of the black-white difference on various psychometric tests: Spearman's hypothesis. *Behavioral and Brain Sciences, 10,* 507-37.

Jensen, A. R. (1989). Raising IQ without increasing *g*? *Developmental Review, 9,* 234-58.

Jensen, A. R. (1993). Spearman's hypothesis tested with chronometric information-processing tasks. *Intelligence, 17,* 47-77.

Jensen, A. R., & Inouye, A. R. (1980). Level I and Level II abilities in Asian, white and black children. *Intelligence, 4,* 41-49.

Jensen, A. R., & Johnson, F. W. (in press). Race and sex differences in head size and IQ. *Intelligence.*

Jensen, A. R., & Reynolds, C. R. (1982). Race, social class and ability patterns on the WISC-R. *Personality and Individual Differences, 3,* 423-38.

Jensen, A. R., & Sinha, S. N. (1993). Physical correlates of human intelligence. In P. A. Vernon (Ed.), *Biological Approaches to the Study of Human Intelligence.* Norwood, NJ: Ablex.

Jensen, A. R., & Whang, P. A. (1993). Reaction times and intelligence: A comparison of Chinese-American and Anglo-American children. *Journal of Biosocial Science, 25,* 397-410.

Jerison, H. J. (1963). Interpreting the evolution of the brain. *Human Biology, 35,* 263-91.

Jerison, H. J. (1973). *Evolution of the Brain and Intelligence.* New York: Academic.

Jessor, R., Donovan, J. E., & Costa, F. M. (1991). *Beyond Adolescence: Problem Behavior and Young Adult Development.* Cambridge: Cambridge University Press.

Johanson, D. C., & Edey, M. A. (1981). *Lucy: The Beginnings of Humankind.* New York: Simon & Schuster.

Johanson, D. C., & O'Farrell, K. (1990). *Journey from the Dawn.* New York: Villard.

Johnson, G. R. (1986). Kin selection, socialization, and patriotism: An integrating theory (with commentaries and response). *Politics and the Life Sciences, 4,* 127-54.

Johnson, L. B. (1978). Sexual behavior of southern blacks. In R. Staples (Ed.), *The Black Family: Essays and Studies* (2nd ed.). Belmont, CA: Wadsworth.

Johnson, R. C., McClearn, G. E., Yuen, S., Nagoshi, C. T., Ahern, F. M., & Cole, R. E. (1985). Galton's data a century later. *American Psychologist, 40,* 875-92.

Jurgens, H. W., Aune, I. A., & Pieper, U. (1990). *International Data on Anthropometry.* Geneva, Switzerland: International Labour Office.

Kallman, F. J. (1952). Comparative twin study on the genetic aspects of male homosexuality. *Journal of Nervous and Mental Diseases, 115,* 283-98.

Kallman, F. J., & Sander, G. (1948). Twin studies on aging and longevity. *Journal of Heredity, 39,* 349-57.

Kallman, F. J., & Sander, G. (1949). Twin studies on senescence. *American Journal of Psychiatry, 106,* 29-36.

Kamin, L. J. (1974). *The Science and Politics of IQ.* Hillsdale, NJ: Erlbaum.

Kamin, L. J. (1978). The Hawaii Family Study of Cognitive Abilities: A comment. *Behavior Genetics, 8,* 275-79.

Kandel, E. R. (1991). Nerve cells and behavior. In E. R. Kandel, J. H. Schwartz, & T. M. Jessell (Eds.), *Principles of Neural Science* (3rd ed.). New York: Elsevier.

Katz, S. H., Hodiger, M. L., & Valleroy, L. A. (1974). Traditional maize processing techniques in the new world. *Science, 223,* 1049-51.

Keller, L. M., Bouchard, T. J. Jr., Arvey, R. D., Segal, N. L., & Dawis, R. V. (1992). Work values: Genetic and environmental influences. *Journal of Applied Psychology, 77,* 79–88.

Kemper, T. D. (1990). *Social Structure and Testosterone.* New Brunswick, NJ: Rutgers University Press.

Kessler, R. C., & Neighbors, H. W. (1986). A new perspective on the relationships among race, social class, and psychological distress. *Journal of Health and Social Behavior, 27,* 107–55.

Kety, S. S., Rosenthal, D., Wender, P. H., & Schulsinger, F. (1976). Studies based on a total sample of adopted individuals and their relatives: Why they were necessary, what they demonstrated and failed to demonstrate. *Schizophrenia Bulletin, 2,* 413–38.

Kevles, D. J. (1985). *In the Name of Eugenics.* New York: Knopf.

Kimble, G. A. (1990). Mother nature's bag of tricks is small. *Psychological Science, 1,* 36–41.

Kinsey, A. C., Pomeroy, W. B., & Martin, C. E. (1948). *Sexual Behavior in the Human Male.* Philadelphia, PA: Saunders.

Kinsey, A. C., Pomeroy, W. B., Martin, C. E., & Gebhard, P. H. (1953). *Sexual Behavior in the Human Female.* Philadelphia, PA: Saunders.

Klein, R. E., Freeman, H. E., Kagan, J., Yarborough, C., & Habicht, J. P. (1972). Is big smart? The relation of growth to cognition. *Journal of Health and Social Behavior, 13,* 219–50.

Klein, S., Petersilia, J., & Turner, S. (1990). Race and imprisonment decisions in California. *Science, 247,* 812–16.

Kline, C. L., & Lee, N. (1972). A transcultural study of dyslexia: Analysis of language disabilities in 277 Chinese children simultaneously learning to read and write in English and Chinese. *Journal of Special Education, 6,* 9–26.

Klitgaard, R. (1986). *Elitism and Meritocracy in Developing Countries.* Baltimore, MD: The Johns Hopkins University Press.

Knobloch, H., & Pasamanik, B. (1953). Further observations on the behavioral development of Negro children. *Journal of Genetic Psychology, 83,* 137–57.

Kranzler, J. H., & Jensen, A. R. (1989). Inspection time and intelligence: A meta-analysis. *Intelligence, 13,* 329–47.

Krebs, C. J., Gaines, M. S., Keller, B. L., Myers, J. H., & Tamarin, R. H. (1973). Population cycles in small rodents. *Science, 179,* 35–41.

Krebs, D. L. (1975). Empathy and altruism. *Journal of Personality and Social Psychology, 32,* 1134–46.

Krogman, W. M. (1970). Growth of head, face, trunk and limbs in Philadelphia white and Negro children of elementary and high school age. *Monographs of the Society for Research in Child Development, 35,* No. 136.

Kurland, J.A. (1979). Paternity, mother's brother, and human sociality. In N. A. Chagnon & W. Irons (Eds.), *Evolutionary Biology and Human Social Behavior.* North Scituate, MA: Duxbury.

Lamb, D. (1987). *The Africans.* New York: Vintage.

Lancer, I., & Rim, Y. (1984). Intelligence, family size and sibling age spacing. *Personality and Individual Differences, 5,* 151–57.

Lange, J. (1931). *Crime as Destiny.* London: Unwin.

Langinvainio, H., Koskenvuo, M., Kaprio, J., & Sistonen, P. (1984). Finnish twins reared apart II. *Acta Geneticae Medicae et Gemellologiae, 33,* 251–58.

Leakey, R., & Lewin, R. (1992). *Origins Reconsidered.* New York: Doubleday.

Lee, A., & Pearson, K. (1901). Data for the problem of evolution in man. VI. A first study of the correlation of the human skull. *Philosophical Transactions of the Royal Society of London, 196A,* 225–64.

Leggett, W. C., & Carscadden, J. E. (1978). Latitudinal variation in reproductive characteristics of American shad (*Alosa sapidissima*): Evidence for population specific life history strategies in fish. *Journal of Fish Research Board of Canada, 35,* 1469-78.

Lerner, R. M. (1992). *Final Solutions: Biology, Prejudice, and Genocide.* University Park, PA: Pennsylvania State University Press.

Leslie, C. (1990). Scientific racism: Reflections on peer review, science and ideology. *Social Science and Medicine, 31,* 891-912.

Lessells, C. M., Cooke, F., & Rockwell, R. F. (1989). Is there a trade-off between egg weight and clutch size in wild Lesser Snow Geese (*Anser C. caerulescens*)? *Journal of Evolutionary Biology, 2,* 457-72.

Lesser, G. S., Fifer, F., & Clark, H. (1965). Mental abilities of children from different social class and cultural groups. *Monographs of the Society for Research in Child Development, 30,* serial no. 102.

Levin, M. (1987). *Feminism and Freedom.* New Brunswick, NJ: Transaction Publishers.

Levin, M. (1992). Responses to race differences in crime. *Journal of Social Philosophy, 23,* 6-29.

LeVine, R. A. (1975). *Culture, Behavior, and Personality.* Chicago: Aldine.

Levy, R. A. (1993). Ethnic and racial differences in response to medicines: Preserving individualized therapy in managed pharmaceutical programmes. *Pharmaceutical Medicine, 7,* 139-65.

Lewis, B. (1990). *Race and Slavery in the Middle East.* New York: Oxford University Press.

Lewontin, R. C. (1991). *Biology as Ideology: The Doctrine of DNA.* Concord, Ontario: Anansi Press.

Lewontin, R. C. (1992). Foreword. In R. M. Lerner (1992), *Final Solutions: Biology, Prejudice, and Genocide.* University Park, PA: Pennsylvania State University Press.

Lewontin, R. C., Rose, S., & Kamin, L. J. (1984). *Not in Our Genes.* New York: Pantheon.

Lieberman, P. (1991). *Uniquely Human.* Cambridge, MA: Harvard University Press.

Lightcap, J. L., Kurland, J. A., & Burgess, R. L. (1982). Child abuse: A test of some predictions from evolutionary theory. *Ethology and Sociobiology, 3,* 797-802.

Littlefield, A., Lieberman, L., & Reynolds, L. T. (1982). Redefining race: The potential demise of a concept in physical anthropology. *Current Anthropology, 23,* 641-55.

Littlefield, C. H., & Rushton, J. P. (1986). When a child dies: The sociobiology of bereavement. *Journal of Personality and Social Psychology, 51,* 797-802.

Livingstone, D. (1857). *Missionary Travels and Researches in South Africa.* London: Murray.

Locurto, C. (1991). Beyond IQ in preschool programs? *Intelligence, 15,* 295-312.

Loehlin, J. C., Lindzey, G., & Spuhler, J. N. (1975). *Race Differences in Intelligence.* San Francisco, CA: Freeman.

Loehlin, J. C., & Nichols, R. C. (1976). *Heredity, Environment, and Personality.* Austin, TX: University of Texas.

Lovejoy, C. O. (1981). The origin of man. *Science, 211,* 341-50.

Lovejoy, C. O. (1990). Comment on "scientific racism." *Social Science and Medicine, 31,* 909-10.

Lumsden, C. J., & Wilson, E. O. (1981). *Genes, Mind and Culture: The Coevolutionary Process.* Cambridge, MA: Harvard University Press.

Lumsden, C. J., & Wilson, E. O. (1983). *Promethean Fire.* Cambridge, MA: Harvard University Press.

Lykken, D. T., McGue, M., Tellegen, A., & Bouchard, T. J., Jr. (1992). Emergenesis: Genetic traits that may not run in families. *American Psychologist, 47,* 1565-77.

Lynn, M. (1989a). Criticism of an evolutionary hypothesis about race differences: A rebuttal to Rushton's reply. *Journal of Research in Personality, 23,* 21-34.

Lynn, M. (1989b). Race differences in sexual behavior: A critique of Rushton and Bogaert's evolutionary hypothesis. *Journal of Research in Personality, 23,* 1-6.

Lynn, R. (1977a). The intelligence of the Chinese and Malays in Singapore. *Mankind Quarterly, 18,* 125-28.

Lynn, R. (1977b). The intelligence of the Japanese. *Bulletin of the British Psychological Society, 30,* 69-72.

Lynn, R. (1982). IQ in Japan and the United States shows a growing disparity. *Nature, 297,* 222-23.

Lynn, R. (1987). The intelligence of the Mongoloids: A psychometric, evolutionary and neurological theory. *Personality and Individual Differences, 8,* 813-44.

Lynn, R. (1989). Balanced polymorphism for ethnocentric and nonethnocentric alleles. *Behavioral and Brain Sciences, 12,* 535.

Lynn, R. (1990a). New evidence on brain size and intelligence: A comment on Rushton and Cain and Vanderwolf. *Personality and Individual Differences, 11,* 795-97.

Lynn, R. (1990b). The role of nutrition in secular increases in intelligence. *Personality and Individual Differences, 11,* 273-85.

Lynn, R. (1990c). Testosterone and gonadotropin levels and r/K reproductive strategies. *Psychological Reports, 67,* 1203-6.

Lynn, R. (1991a). The evolution of racial differences in intelligence (with commentaries and author's response). *Mankind Quarterly, 32,* 99-173.

Lynn, R. (1991b). Intelligence in China. *Social Behavior and Personality, 19,* 1-4.

Lynn, R. (1991c). Race differences in intelligence: A global perspective. *Mankind Quarterly, 31,* 255-96.

Lynn, R. (1993). Further evidence for the existence of race and sex differences in cranial capacity. *Social Behavior and Personality, 21,* 89-92.

Lynn, R., Chan, J. W. C., & Eysenck, H. J. (1991). Reaction times and intelligence in Chinese and British children. *Perceptual and Motor Skills, 72,* 443-52.

Lynn, R., & Hampson, S. (1986a). Further evidence on the cognitive abilities of the Japanese: Data from the WPPSI. *International Journal of Behavioral Development, 10,* 23-36.

Lynn, R., & Hampson, S. (1986b). Intellectual abilities of Japanese children: An assessment of 2 1/2 - 8 1/2 year olds derived from the McCarthy Scales of Children's Abilities. *Intelligence, 10,* 41-58.

Lynn, R., & Hampson, S. (1986c). The structure of Japanese abilities: An analysis in terms of the hierarchical model of intelligence. *Current Psychological Research and Reviews, 4,* 309-22.

Lynn, R., Hampson, S., & Bingham, R. (1987). Japanese, British and American adolescents compared for Spearman's g and for the verbal, numerical and visuo-spatial abilities. *Psychologia, 30,* 137-44.

Lynn, R., Hampson, S. L., & Iwawaki, S. (1987). Abstract reasoning and spatial abilities among American, British and Japanese adolescents. *Mankind Quarterly, 27,* 397-434.

Lynn, R., Hampson, S., & Lee, M. (1988). The intelligence of Chinese children in Hong Kong. *Social Psychology International, 9,* 29-32.

Lynn, R., & Hattori, K. (1990). The heritability of intelligence in Japan. *Behavior Genetics, 20,* 545-46.

Lynn, R., & Holmshaw, M. (1990). Black-white differences in reaction times and intelligence. *Social Behavior and Personality, 18,* 299-308.

Lynn, R., Pagliari, C., & Chan, J. (1988). Intelligence in Hong Kong measured for Spearman's g and the visuospatial and verbal primaries. *Intelligence, 12,* 423-33.

Lynn R., & Shigehisa, T. (1991). Reaction times and intelligence: A comparison of Japanese and British children. *Journal of Biosocial Science, 23,* 409–16.

Lyons, M. J., Goldberg, J., Eisen, S. A., True, W., Tsuang, M. T., Meyer, J. M., & Henderson, W. G. (1993). Do genes influence exposure to trauma? A twin study of combat. *American Journal of Medical Genetics (Neuropsychiatric Genetics), 48,* 22–27.

MacArthur, R. H., & Wilson, E. O. (1967). *The Theory of Island Biogeography.* Princeton, NJ: Princeton University Press.

Mackintosh, N. J., & Mascie-Taylor, C. G. N. (1985). The IQ question. In *Education For All* (The Swann Report). Cmnd paper 4453. London: HMSO.

Magnusson, D. (1992). Individual development: A longitudinal perspective. *European Journal of Personality, 6,* 119–38.

Malina, R. M. (1979). Secular changes in size and maturity: Causes and effects. *Monographs of the Society for Research in Child Development, 44,* Serial No. 179, Nos. 3–4.

Mall, F. P. (1909). On several anatomical characters of the human brain, said to vary according to race and sex, with especial reference to the weight of the frontal lobe. *American Journal of Anatomy, 9,* 1–32.

Maller, J. B. (1934). General and specific factors in character. *Journal of Social Psychology, 5,* 97–102.

Malthus, T. R. (1798/1817). *An Essay on the Principle of Population.* London: Murray.

Manley, D. R. (1963). Mental ability in Jamaica. *Social and Economic Studies, 12,* 51–77.

Marmot, M. G., Smith, G. D., Stansfeld, S., Patel, C., North, F., Head, J., White, I., Brunner, E., & Feeney, A. (1991). Health inequalities among British civil servants: The Whitehall II study. *Lancet, 337,* 1387–93.

Marshall, J. (1892). On the relations between the weight of the brain and its parts, and the stature and mass of the body, in man. *Journal of Anatomy and Physiology, 26,* 445–500.

Martin, N. G., Eaves, L. J., & Eysenck, H. J. (1977). Genetical, environmental and personality factors influencing the age of first sexual intercourse in twins. *Journal of Biosocial Science, 9,* 91–97.

Martin, N. G., Eaves, L. J., Heath, A. C., Jardine, R., Feingold, L. M., & Eysenck, H. J. (1986). The transmission of social attitudes. *Proceedings of the National Academy of Sciences of the U.S.A., 83,* 4365–68.

Martin, N. G., & Jardine, R. (1986). Eysenck's contributions to behavior genetics. In S. Modgil and C. Modgil (Eds.), *Hans Eysenck: Consensus and Controversy.* Philadelphia, PA: Falmer.

Martin, N. G., Olsen, M. E., Thiele, H., Beaini, J. L. E., Handelsman, D., & Bhatnager, A. S. (1984). Pituitary-ovarian function in mothers who have had two sets of dizygotic twins. *Fertility and Sterility, 41,* 878–80.

Mascie-Taylor, C. G. N., & Gibson, J. B. (1978). Social mobility and IQ components. *Journal of Biosocial Science, 10,* 263–76.

Masters, R. D. (1984). Explaining "male chauvinism" and "feminism": Cultural differences in male and female reproductive strategies. In M. Watts (Ed.), *Biopolitics and Gender.* Haworth.

Masters, R. D. (1989). If "birds of a feather...," why do "opposites attract"? *Behavioral and Brain Sciences, 12,* 535–37.

Matheny, A. P., Jr. (1983). A longitudinal twin study of stability of components from Bayley's Infant Behavior Record. *Child Development, 54,* 356–60.

Matthews, K. A., Batson, C. D., Horn, J., & Rosenman, R. H. (1981). "Principles in his nature which interest him in the fortune of others..." The heritability of empathic concern for others. *Journal of Personality, 49,* 237–47.

Maynard-Smith, J. (1978). *The Evolution of Sex.* Cambridge: Cambridge University Press.

Mayr, E. (1970). *Populations, Species, and Evolution.* Cambridge, MA: Harvard University Press.

McCall, R. B., & Carriger, M. S. (1993). A meta-analysis of infant habituation and recognition memory performance as predictors of later IQ. *Child Development, 64,* 57–79.

McCord, W. (1991). *The Dawn of the Pacific Century.* New Brunswick, NJ: Transaction Publishers.

McCrae, R. R., & Costa, P. T., Jr. (1990). *Personality in Adulthood.* New York: Guilford Press.

McGue, M., & Lykken, D. T. (1992). Genetic influence on risk of divorce. *Psychological Science, 3,* 368–73.

McGuire, W. J. (1969). The nature of attitudes and attitude change. In G. Lindzey & E. Aronson (Eds.), *The Handbook of Social Psychology.* Addison-Wesley.

McHenry, H. M. (1992). How big were the early hominids? *Evolutionary Anthropology, 1,* 15–20.

Mead, M. (1928). *Coming of Age in Samoa.* New York: Morrow.

Mealey, L. (1990). Differential use of reproductive strategies by human groups? *Psychological Science, 1,* 385–87.

Mednick, S. A., Gabrielli, W. F., & Hutchings, B. (1984). Genetic influences in criminal convictions: Evidence from an adoption cohort. *Science, 224,* 891–94.

Meikle, A. W., Bishop, D. T., Stringham, J. D., & West, D. W. (1987). Quantitating genetic and nongenetic factors that determine plasma sex steriod variation in normal male twins. *Metabolism, 35,* 1090–95.

Messner, S. F., & Sampson, R. J. (1991). The sex ratio, family disruption, and rate of violent crime: The paradox of demographic structure. *Social Forces, 69,* 693–713.

Meyer, J. P. & Pepper, S. (1977). Need compatibility and marital adjustment in young married couples. *Journal of Personality and Social Psychology, 35,* 331–42.

Michael, J. S. (1988). A new look at Morton's craniological research. *Current Anthropology, 29,* 349–54.

Michener, J. A. (1980). *The Covenant.* New York: Ballantine.

Miele, F. (1979). Cultural bias in the WISC. *Intelligence, 3,* 149–64.

Miller, E. M. (1991). Climate and intelligence. *Mankind Quarterly, 32,* 127–32.

Miller, E. M. (1993). Could *r*-selection account for the African personality and life cycle? *Personality and Individual Differences, 15,* 665–75.

Miller, E. M. (1994). Paternal provisioning versus mate seeking in human populations. *Personality and Individual Differences, 17,* 691–719.

Miller, J. Z., & Rose, R. J. (1982). Familial resemblance in locus of control: A twin-family study of the Internal-External Scale. *Journal of Personality and Social Psychology, 42,* 535–40.

Milo, R. G., & Quiatt, D. (1993). Glottogenesis and anatomically modern *Homo sapiens:* The evidence for and implications of a late origin of vocal language. *Current Anthropology, 34,* 569–598.

Misawa, G., Motegi, M., Fujita, K., & Hattori, K. (1984). A comparative study of intellectual abilities of Japanese and American children on the Columbia Mental Maturity Scale (CMMS). *Personality and Individual Differences, 5,* 173–81.

Mischel, W. (1968). *Personality and Assessment.* New York: Wiley.

Moffitt, T. E., Caspi, A., Belsky, J., & Silva, P. A. (1992). Childhood experience and the onset of menarche: A test of a sociobiological model. *Child Development, 63,* 47–58.

Molnar, S. (1983). *Human Variation: Races, Types, and Ethnic Groups* (2nd ed.). Englewood Cliffs, NJ: Prentice-Hall.

Montagu, M. F. A. (1960). *An Introduction to Physical Anthropology* (3rd ed.). Springfield, IL: Charles C. Thomas.

Montie, J. E., & Fagan, J. F. (1988). Racial differences in IQ: Item analysis of the Stanford-Binet at 3 years. *Intelligence, 12,* 315-32.

Moore, D. S., & Erickson, P. I. (1985). Age, gender, and ethnic differences in sexual and contraceptive knowledge, attitudes, and behaviors. *Family and Community Health, 8,* 38-51.

Moore, E. G. J. (1986). Family socialization and the IQ test performance of traditionally and trans-racially adopted black children. *Developmental Psychology, 22,* 317-26.

Morton, S. G. (1849). Observations on the size of the brain in various races and families of man. *Proceedings of the Academy of Natural Sciences Philadelphia, 4,* 221-24.

Mosse, G. L. (1978). *Toward the Final Solution: A History of European Racism.* New York: Harper & Row.

Mousseau, T. A., & Roff, D. A. (1987). Natural selection and the heritability of fitness components. *Heredity, 59,* 181-97.

Moynihan, D. (1965). *The Negro Family: The Case for National Action.* Washington, DC: United States.

Muller-Hill, B. (1988). *Murderous Science.* (Trans. G. R. Fraser.) Oxford: Oxford University Press.

Muller-Hill, B. (1992). Foreword. In R. M. Lerner (1992), *Final Solutions: Biology, Prejudice, and Genocide.* University Park, PA: Pennsylvania State University Press.

Murdock, J., & Sullivan, L. R. (1923). A contribution to the study of mental and physical measurements in normal school children. *American Physical Education Review, 28,* 209-330.

Naglieri, J. A., & Jensen, A. R. (1987). Comparison of black-white differences on the WISC-R and the K-ABC: Spearman's hypothesis. *Intelligence, 11,* 21-43.

Nagoshi, C. T., & Johnson, R. C. (1986). The ubiquity of *g. Personality and Individual Differences, 7,* 201-7.

Nagoshi, C. T., Phillips, K., & Johnson, R. C. (1987). Between-versus within-family factor analyses of cognitive abilities. *Intelligence, 11,* 305-16.

National Center for Health Statistics (1991). *Health, United States, 1990.* Hyattsville, MD. U.S. Public Health Service: Author.

Neale, M. C., Rushton, J. P., & Fulker, D. W. (1986). Heritability of item responses on the Eysenck Personality Questionnaire. *Personality and Individual Differences, 7,* 771-79.

Nei, M., & Livshits, G. (1989). Genetic relationships of Europeans, Asians and Africans and the origin of modern *Homo sapiens. Human Heredity, 39,* 276-81.

Nei, M., & Roychoudhury, A. K. (1993). Evolutionary relationships of human populations on a global scale. *Molecular Biology and Evolution, 10,* 927-43.

Ness, R., Laskarzewski, P., & Price, R. A. (1991). Inheritance of extreme overweight in black families. *Human Biology, 63,* 39-52.

Nichols, P. L. (1972). *The Effects of Heredity and Environment on Intelligence Test Performance in 4- and 7-year-old White and Negro Sibling Pairs.* Unpublished doctoral dissertation, University of Minnesota.

Niswander, K. R., & Gordon, M. (1972). *The Women and Their Pregnancies.* Philadelphia, PA: Saunders.

Nobile, P. (1982). Penis size: The difference between blacks and whites. *Forum: International Journal of Human Relations, 11*, 21-28.

Norman, C. (1985). Politics and science clash on African AIDS. *Science, 230*, 1140-42.

Notcutt, B. (1950). The measurement of Zulu intelligence. *Journal of Social Research, 1*, 195-206.

Nyborg, H. (1987). *Covariant Trait Development Across Species, Races, and Within Individuals: Differential K Theory, Genes, and Hormones.* Paper presented at the 3rd Meeting of the International Society for the Study of Individual Differences, Toronto, Ontario, Canada, June 18-22, 1987.

Nyborg, H. (1994). *Hormones, Sex, and Society.* Westport, CT: Praeger.

Nylander, P. P. S. (1975). Frequency of multiple births. In I. MacGillivray, P. P. S. Nylander, & G. Corney (Eds.), *Human Multiple Reproduction.* Philadelphia: Saunders.

Nylander, P. P. S. (1981). The factors that influence twinning rates. *Acta Geneticae Medicae et Gemellologiae, 30*, 189-202.

Olweus, D. (1979). The stability of aggressive reaction pattern in human males: A review. *Psychological Bulletin, 86*, 852-75.

Ombredane, A., Robaye, F., & Robaye, E. (1952). Analyse des résultats d'une application experimentale du matrix 38 à 485 noirs Baluba. *Bulletin contre d'études et reserches psychotechniques, 7*, 235-55.

Orlick, T., Zhou, Q-Y., & Partington, J. (1990). Co-operation and conflict within Chinese and Canadian kindergarten settings. *Canadian Journal of Behavioural Sciences, 22*, 20-25.

Osborne, R. T. (1978). Race and sex differences in heritability of mental test performance: A study of Negroid and Caucasoid twins. In R. T. Osborne, C. E. Noble, & N. Weyl (Eds.), *Human Variation: The Biopsychology of Age, Race, and Sex.* New York: Academic.

Osborne, R. T. (1980). *Twins: Black and White.* Athens, Georgia: Foundation for Human Understanding.

Osborne, R. T. (1992). Cranial capacity and IQ. *Mankind Quarterly, 32*, 275-80.

Owen, K. (1989). *Test and Item Bias: The Suitability of the Junior Aptitude Tests as a Common Test Battery for White, Indian and Black Pupils in Standard 7.* Pretoria, South Africa: Human Science Research Council.

Owen, K. (1992). The suitability of Raven's Standard Progressive Matrices for various groups in South Africa. *Personality and Individual Differences, 13*, 149-59.

Pagel, M. D. & Harvey, P. H. (1988). How mammals produce large-brained offspring. *Evolution, 42*, 948-57.

Pakkenberg, H., & Voigt, J. (1964). Brain weight of the Danes: Forensic material. *Acta Anatomica, 56*, 297-307.

Pakstis, A., Scarr-Salapatek, S., Elston, R. C., & Siervogel, R. (1972). Genetic contributions to morphological and behavioural similarities among sibs and dizygotic twins: Linkages and allelic differences. *Social Biology, 19*, 185-92.

Palca, J. (1991). The sobering geography of AIDS. *Science, 18*, 371-73.

Palinkas, L. A. (1984). Racial differences in accidental and violent deaths among U.S. Navy personnel. *U.S. Naval Health Research Center Report*, Rep. No. 84-85.

Papiernik, E., Cohen, H., Richard, A., de Oca, M. M., & Feingold, J. (1986). Ethnic differences in duration of pregnancy. *Annals of Human Biology, 13*, 259-65.

Pappas, G., Queen, S., Hadden, W., & Fisher, G. (1993). The increasing disparity in mortality between socioeconomic groups in the United States, 1960 and 1986. *New England Journal of Medicine, 329*, 103-9.

Passingham, R. E. (1979). Brain size and intelligence in man. *Brain, Behavior and Evolution, 16*, 253-70.

Passingham, R. E. (1982). *The Human Primate*. San Francisco, CA: Freeman.

Pearl, R. (1906). On the correlation between intelligence and the size of the head. *Journal of Comparative Neurology and Psychology, 16,* 189–99.

Pearl, R. (1934). The weight of the Negro brain. *Science, 80,* 431–34.

Pearson, K. (1906). On the relationship of intelligence to size and shape of head, and to other physical and mental characters. *Biometrika, 5,* 105–46.

Pearson, K. (1914–30). *The Life, Letters and Labours of Francis Galton, Vols. 1–3.* London: Cambridge University Press.

Pedersen, N. L., Friberg, B., Floderus-Myrhed, B., McClearn, G. E., & Plomin, R. (1984). Swedish early separated twins: Identification and characterization. *Acta Geneticae Medicae et Gemellologiae, 33,* 243–50.

Pedersen, N. L., McClearn, G. E., Plomin, R., Nesselroade, J. R., Berg, S., & DeFaire, U. (1991). The Swedish Adoption Twin Study of Aging: An update. *Acta Geneticae Medicae et Gemellologiae, 40,* 7–20.

Pedersen, N. L., Plomin, R., Nesselroade, J. R., & McClearn, G. E. (1992). A quantitative genetic analysis of cognitive abilities during the second half of the life span. *Psychological Science, 3,* 346–53.

Penrose, L. S., & Raven, J. C. (1936). A new series of perceptual tests: Preliminary communication. *British Journal of Medical Psychology, 16,* 97–104.

Pianka, E. R. (1970). On "r" and "K" selection. *American Naturalist, 104,* 592–97.

Pinneau, S. R. (1961). *Changes in Intelligence Quotient: Infancy to Maturity.* Boston: Houghton-Mifflin.

Piot, P., Plummer, F. A., Mhalu, F. S., Lamboray, J. L., Chin, J., & Mann, J. M. (1988). AIDS: An international perspective. *Science, 239,* 573–79.

Playboy Magazine. (1983). The *Playboy* Readers' Sex Survey, Part 2. March Issue, pp. 90–92. Author.

Plomin, R., & Bergeman, C. S. (1991). The nature of nurture: Genetic influence on "environmental" measures. *Behavioral and Brain Sciences, 14,* 373–427.

Plomin, R., & Daniels, D. (1987). Why are children in the same family so different from one another? (with commentaries and authors' response). *Behavioral and Brain Sciences, 10,* 1–60.

Plomin, R., DeFries, J. C., & Loehlin, J. C. (1977). Genotype-environment interaction and correlation in the analysis of human behavior. *Psychological Bulletin, 84,* 309–22.

Plomin, R., DeFries, J. C., & McClearn, G. E. (1990). *Behavioral Genetics: A Primer* (2nd ed.). San Francisco: Freeman.

Plomin, R., Lichtenstein, P., Pedersen, N. L., McClearn, G. E., & Nesselroade, J. R. (1990). Genetic influence on life events during the last half of the life span. *Psychology and Aging, 5,* 25–30.

Plomin, R., Pedersen, N. L., McClearn, G. E., Nesselroade, J. R., & Bergeman, C. S. (1988). EAS temperaments during the last half of the life span: Twins reared apart and twins reared together. *Psychology and Aging, 3,* 43–50.

Polednak, A. P. (1989). *Racial and Ethnic Differences in Disease.* Oxford: Oxford University Press.

Pollitzer, W. S., & Anderson, J. J. B. (1989). Ethnic and genetic differences in bone mass: A review with a hereditary vs environmental perspective. *American Journal of Clinical Nutrition, 50,* 1244–59.

Pons, A. L. (1974). Administration of tests outside the cultures of their origin. 26th Congress South African Psychological Association.

Porteus, S. D. (1937). *Primitive Intelligence and Environment.* New York: Macmillan.

Presser, H. B. (1978). Age at menarche, socio-sexual behavior, and fertility. *Social Biology, 25,* 94–101.

Program for Appropriate Technology in Health (PATH). (1991). *Adapting Condoms for the Developing World.* Seattle, Washington: Author.

Program for Appropriate Technology in Health (PATH). (1992). *The Correlation of Penis Size to Condom Satisfaction*. Discussion paper. Seattle, Washington: Author.

Raboch, J., & Bartak, V. (1981). Menarche and orgastic capacity. *Archives of Sexual Behavior, 10*, 379-82.

Raboch, J., & Mellan, J. (1979). Sexual development and activity of men with disturbances of somatic development. *Andrologia, 11*, 263-71.

Raven, J., & Court, J. H. (1989). *Manual for Raven's Progressive Matrices and Vocabulary Scales*. Research Supplement 4. London: Lewis.

Raz, N., Torres, I. J., Spencer, W. D., Millman, D., Baertschi, J. C., & Sarpel, G. (1993). Neuroanatomical correlates of age-sensitive and age-invariant cognitive abilities: An *in vivo* MRI investigation. *Intelligence, 17*, 407-22.

Reed, T. E., & Jensen, A. R. (1993). Cranial capacity: New Caucasian data and comments on Rushton's claimed Mongoloid-Caucasoid brain-size differences. *Intelligence, 17*, 423-31.

Reid, R. W., & Mulligan, J. H. (1923). Relation of cranial capacity to intelligence. *Journal of the Royal Anthropological Institute, 53*, 322-31.

Reiss, I. L. (1967). *The Social Context of Premarital Sexual Permissiveness*. New York: Holt, Rinehart & Winston.

Reynolds, V., Falger, V. S. E., & Vine, I. (Eds.). (1987). *The Sociobiology of Ethnocentrism*. London: Croom Helm.

Reynolds, V., & Tanner, R. E. S. (1983). *The Biology of Religion*. New York: Longman.

Reznick, D. A., Bryga, H., & Endler, J. A. (1990). Experimentally induced life-history evolution in a natural population. *Nature, 346*, 357-59.

Ricklan, D. E., & Tobias, P. V. (1986). Unusually low sexual dimorphism of endocranial capacity in Zulu cranial series. *American Journal of Physical Anthropology, 71*, 285-93.

Roberts, J. V., & Gabor, T. (1990). Lombrosian wine in a new bottle: Research on crime and race. *Canadian Journal of Criminology, 32*, 291-313.

Rodd, W. G. (1959). A cross cultural study of Taiwan's Schools. *Journal of Social Psychology, 50*, 3-36.

Roff, D. A., & Mousseau, T. A. (1987). Quantitative genetics and fitness: Lessons from *Drosophila*. *Heredity, 58*, 103-18.

Rosenthal, D. (1972). Three adoption studies of heredity in the schizophrenic disorders. *International Journal of Mental Health, 1*, 63-75.

Ross, R., Bernstein, L., Judd, H., Hanisch, R., Pike, M., & Henderson, B. (1986). Serum testosterone levels in healthy young black and white men. *Journal of the National Cancer Institute, 76*, 45-48.

Rowe, D. C. (1986). Genetic and environmental components of antisocial behaviour: A study of 265 twin pairs. *Criminology, 24*, 513-32.

Rowe, D. C. & Herstand, S. E. (1986). Familial influences on television viewing and aggression: A sibling study. *Aggressive Behavior, 12*, 111-20.

Rowe, D. C. & Osgood, D. W. (1984). Heredity and sociological theories of delinquency: A reconsideration. *American Sociological Review, 49*, 526-40.

Rowe, D. C., Rodgers, J. L., Meseck-Bushey, S., & St. John, C. (1989). Sexual behavior and nonsexual deviance: A sibling study of their relationship. *Developmental Psychology, 25*, 61-69.

Rushton, J. P. (1976). Socialization and the altruistic behavior of children. *Psychological Bulletin, 83*, 898-913.

Rushton, J. P. (1980). *Altruism, Socialization, and Society*. Englewood Cliffs, NJ: Prentice-Hall.

Rushton, J. P. (1984). Sociobiology: Toward a theory of individual and group differences in personality and social behavior (with commentaries and author's response).

In J. R. Royce & L. P. Mos (Eds.), *Annals of Theoretical Psychology, Vol. 2* (pp. 1–81). New York: Plenum.

Rushton, J. P. (1985a) Differential *K* theory: The sociobiology of individual and group differences. *Personality and Individual Differences, 6,* 441–52.

Rushton, J. P. (1985b) Differential *K* theory and race differences in E and N. *Personality and Individual Differences, 6,* 769–70.

Rushton, J. P. (1987a) An evolutionary theory of health, longevity, and personality: Sociobiology and *r/K* reproductive strategies. *Psychological Reports, 60,* 539–49.

Rushton, J. P. (1987b) An evolutionary theory of human multiple birthing: Sociobiology and *r/K* reproductive strategies. *Acta Geneticae Medicae et Gemellologiae, 36,* 289–96.

Rushton, J. P. (1988a). Genetic similarity, mate choice, and fecundity in humans. *Ethology and Sociobiology, 9,* 329–33.

Rushton, J. P. (1988b) Race differences in behaviour: A review and evolutionary analysis. *Personality and Individual Differences, 9,* 1009–24.

Rushton, J. P. (1988c) The reality of racial differences: A rejoinder with new evidence. *Personality and Individual Differences, 9,* 1035–40.

Rushton, J. P. (1989a). The evolution of racial differences: A response to M. Lynn. *Journal of Research in Personality, 23,* 7–20.

Rushton, J. P. (1989b). The generalizability of genetic estimates. *Personality and Individual Differences, 10,* 985–89.

Rushton, J. P. (1989c). Genetic similarity, human altruism, and group selection (with commentaries and author's response). *Behavioral and Brain Sciences, 12,* 503–59.

Rushton, J. P. (1989d). Genetic similarity in male friendships. *Ethology and Sociobiology, 10,* 361–73.

Rushton, J. P. (1989e). Japanese inbreeding depression scores: Predictors of cognitive differences between blacks and whites. *Intelligence, 13,* 43–51.

Rushton, J. P. (1989f). Race differences in sexuality and their correlates: Another look and physiological models. *Journal of Research in Personality, 23,* 35–54.

Rushton, J. P. (1990a). Comment on "scientific racism." *Social Science and Medicine, 31,* 905–9.

Rushton, J. P. (1990b). Race and crime: A reply to Roberts and Gabor. *Canadian Journal of Criminology, 32,* 315–34.

Rushton, J. P. (1990c). Race, brain size and intelligence: A rejoinder to Cain and Vanderwolf. *Personality and Individual Differences, 11,* 785–94.

Rushton, J. P. (1991a). Do r-K strategies underlie human race differences? *Canadian Psychology, 32,* 29–42.

Rushton, J. P. (1991b). Mongoloid-Caucasoid differences in brain size from military samples. *Intelligence, 15,* 351–59.

Rushton, J. P. (1992a). Cranial capacity related to sex, rank and race in a stratified random sample of 6,325 U.S. military personnel. *Intelligence, 16,* 401–13.

Rushton, J. P. (1992b). Contributions to the history of psychology: XC. Evolutionary biology and heritable traits (with reference to Oriental-white-black differences): The 1989 AAAS paper. *Psychological Reports, 71,* 811–21.

Rushton, J. P. (1992c). Life history comparisons between Orientals and whites at a Canadian university. *Personality and Individual Differences, 13,* 439–42.

Rushton, J. P. (1993). Corrections to a paper on race and sex differences in brain size and intelligence. *Personality and Individual Differences, 15,* 229–31.

Rushton, J. P. (1994). Sex and race differences in cranial capacity from International Labour Office data. *Intelligence,* in press.

Rushton, J. P., & Ankney, C. D. (1993). The evolutionary selection of human races: A response to Miller. *Personality and Individual Differences, 15,* 677–80.

Rushton, J. P., & Bogaert, A. F. (1987). Race differences in sexual behavior: Testing an evolutionary hypothesis. *Journal of Research in Personality, 21,* 529-51.

Rushton, J. P., & Bogaert, A. F. (1988). Race versus social class differences in sexual behavior: A follow-up of the r/K dimension. *Journal of Research in Personality, 22,* 259-72.

Rushton, J. P., & Bogaert, A. F. (1989). Population differences in susceptibility to AIDS: An evolutionary analysis. *Social Science and Medicine, 28,* 1211-20.

Rushton, J. P., Brainerd, C. J., & Pressley, M. (1983). Behavioral development and construct validity: The principle of aggregation. *Psychological Bulletin, 94,* 18-38.

Rushton, J. P., & Erdle, S. (1987). Evidence for an aggressive (and delinquent) personality. *British Journal of Social Psychology, 26,* 87-89.

Rushton, J. P., Fulker, D. W., Neale, M. C., Nias, D. K. B., & Eysenck, H. J. (1986). Altruism and aggression: The heritability of individual differences. *Journal of Personality and Social Psychology, 50,* 1192-98.

Rushton, J. P., Littlefield, C. H., & Lumsden, C. J. (1986). Gene-culture coevolution of complex social behavior: Human altruism and mate choice. *Proceedings of the National Academy of Sciences of the U.S.A., 83,* 7340-43.

Rushton, J. P., & Nicholson, I. R. (1988). Genetic similarity theory, intelligence, and human mate choice. *Ethology and Sociobiology, 9,* 45-57.

Rushton, J. P. & Russell, R. J. H. (1985). Genetic similarity theory: A reply to Mealey and new evidence. *Behavior Genetics, 15,* 575-82.

Rushton, J. P., Russell, R. J. H., & Wells, P. A. (1984). Genetic similarity theory: Beyond kin selection. *Behavior Genetics, 14,* 179-93.

Rushton, J. P., Russell, R. J. H., & Wells, P. A. (1985). Personality and genetic similarity theory. *Journal of Social and Biological Structures, 8,* 174-97.

Russell, R. J. H., & Wells, P. A. (1987). Estimating paternity confidence. *Ethology and Sociobiology, 8,* 215-20.

Russell, R. J. H., & Wells, P. A. (1991). Personality similarity and quality of marriage. *Personality and Individual Differences, 12,* 407-12.

Russell, R. J. H., Wells, P. A., & Rushton, J. P. (1985). Evidence for genetic similarity detection in human marriage. *Ethology and Sociobiology, 6,* 183-87.

Sarich, V., & Wilson, A. C. (1967). Immunological time scale for human evolution. *Science, 158,* 1200-4.

Scarr, S. (Ed.). (1981). *Race, Social Class and Individual Differences in IQ.* Hillsdale, NJ: Erlbaum.

Scarr, S. (1987). Three cheers for behavior genetics: Winning the war and losing our identity. *Behavior Genetics, 17,* 219-28.

Scarr, S. (1992). Developmental theories for the 1990s: Development and individual differences. *Child Development, 63,* 1-19.

Scarr, S., Caparulo, B. K., Ferdman, B. M., Tower, R. B., & Caplan, J. (1983). Developmental status and school achievements of minority and non-minority children from birth to 18 years in a British Midlands town. *British Journal of Developmental Psychology, 1,* 31-48.

Scarr, S., & McCartney, K. (1983). How people make their own environments: A theory of genotype-environment effects. *Child Development, 54,* 424-35.

Scarr, S., & Weinberg, R. A. (1976). IQ test performance of black children adopted by white families. *American Psychologist, 31,* 726-39.

Scarr, S., Weinberg, R. A., & Gargiulo, J. (1987). Transracial adoption: A ten year follow-up. Abstract in Program of the 17th Annual Meeting of the Behavior Genetics Association, Minneapolis, Minnesota, U.S.A.

Scarr-Salapatek, S. (1971). Race, social class and IQ. *Science, 174,* 1285-95.

Schoendorf, K. C., Carol, M. P. H., Hogue, C. J. R., Kleinman, J. C., & Rowley, D. (1992). Mortality among infants of black as compared with white college-educated parents. *New England Journal of Medicine, 326,* 1522-26.

Schreider, E. (1968). Quelques corrélations somatiques des tests mentaux. *Homo, 19,* 38-43.

Schull, W. J., & Neel, J. V. (1965). *The Effects of Inbreeding on Japanese Children.* New York: Harper & Row.

Schultz, A. H. (1960). Age changes in primates and their modification in man. In J. M. Tanner (Ed.), *Human Growth* (pp. 1-20). Oxford: Pergamon.

Schweinfurth, G. (1873). *The Heart of Africa: From 1868 to 1871* (2 vols). London: Sampson Low, Marston, Low & Searle.

Scriver, C. R. (1984). An evolutionary view of disease in man. *Proceedings of the Royal Society of London, B, 220,* 273-98.

Segal, N. L. (1993). Twin, sibling, and adoption methods: Test of evolutionary hypotheses. *American Psychologist, 48,* 943-56.

Shaw L., & Sichel, H. (1970). *Accident Proneness.* Oxford: Pergamon.

Shaw, R. P., & Wong, Y. (1989). *Genetic Seeds of Warfare.* Boston: Unwin Hyman.

Shibata, I. (1936). Brain weight of the Korean. *American Journal of Physical Anthropology, 22,* 27-35.

Shigehisa, T., & Lynn, R. (1991). Reaction times and intelligence in Japanese children. *International Journal of Psychology, 26,* 195-202.

Shockley, W. (1973). Variance of Caucasian admixture in Negro populations, pigmentation variability, and IQ. *Proceedings of the National Academy of Sciences, U.S.A., 70,* 2180a.

Short, R. V. (1979). Sexual selection and its component parts, somatic and genital selection, as illustrated by man and the great apes. In J. S. Rosenblatt, R. A. Hinde, C. Beer, & M-C Busnel (Eds.), *Advances in the Study of Behavior, Vol. 9.* New York: Academic.

Short, R. V. (1984). Testis size, ovulation rate, and breast cancer. In O. A. Ryder, & M. L. Byrd (Eds.), *One Medicine.* Berlin: Springer-Verlag.

Shuey, A. M. (1966). *The Testing of Negro Intelligence.* New York: Social Science Press.

Silverman, I. (1990). The r/K theory of human individual differences: Scientific and social issues. *Ethology and Sociobiology, 11,* 1-10.

Simmons, K. (1942). Cranial capacities by both plastic and water techniques with cranial linear measurements of the Reserve Collection; white and Negro. *Human Biology, 14,* 473-98.

Simons, E. L. (1989). Human origins. *Science, 245,* 1343-50.

Sinha, U. (1968). The use of Raven's Progressive Matrices in India. *Indian Educational Review, 3,* 75-88.

Smith, B. H. (1989). Dental development as a measure of life-history in primates. *Evolution, 43,* 683-88.

Smith, M. (1981). *Kin Investment in Grandchildren.* Unpublished doctoral dissertation, York University, Toronto, Ontario, Canada.

Smith, M. S., Kish, B. J., & Crawford, C. B. (1987). Inheritance of wealth as human kin investment. *Ethology and Sociobiology, 8,* 171-82.

Smith, R. L. (1984). Human sperm competition. In R. L. Smith (Ed.), *Sperm Competition and the Evolution of Animal Mating Systems.* New York: Academic.

Snyderman, M., & Rothman, S. (1987). Survey of expert opinion on intelligence and aptitude testing. *American Psychologist, 42,* 137-44.

Snyderman, M., & Rothman, S. (1988). *The IQ Controversy, the Media and Public Policy.* New Brunswick, NJ: Transaction Publishers.

Soma, H., Takayama, M., Kiyokawa, T., Akaeda, T., & Tokoro, K. (1975). Serum gonadotropin levels in Japanese women. *Obstetrics and Gynecology, 46,* 311-12.

Sommerville, R. C. (1924). Physical, motor and sensory traits. *Archives of Psychology, 12,* 1-108.

Sorensen, T. I. A., Nielsen, G. G., Andersen, P. K., & Teasdale, T. W. (1988). Genetic and environmental influences on premature death in adult adoptees. *New England Journal of Medicine, 318,* 727-32.

Spearman, C. (1910). Correlation calculated from faulty data. *British Journal of Psychology, 3,* 271-95.

Spearman, C. (1927). *The Abilities of Man.* New York: Macmillan.

Speke, J. H. (1863). *Journal of the Discovery of the Source of the Nile.* Edinburgh: Blackwood.

Spitzka, E. A. (1903). The brain-weight of the Japanese. *Science, 18,* 371-73.

Staples, R. (1985). Changes in black family structure: The conflict between family ideology and structural conditions. *Journal of Marriage and the Family, 47,* 1005-13.

Stearns, S. C. (1977). The evolution of life history traits: A critique of the theory and a review of the data. *Annual Review of Ecology and Systematics, 8,* 145-71.

Stearns, S. C. (1984). The effects of size and phylogeny on patterns of covariation in the life history traits of lizards and snakes. *American Naturalist, 123,* 56-72.

Steen, L. A. (1987). Mathematics education: A predictor of scientific competitiveness. *Science, 237,* 251-53.

Stevenson, H. W., Stigler, J. W., Lee, S., Lucker, G. W., Kitanawa, S., & Hsu, C. (1985). Cognitive performance and academic achievement of Japanese, Chinese and American children. *Child Development, 56,* 718-34.

Stoddard, T. L. (1920). *The Rising Tide of Color.* New York: Scribner.

Stoneking, M. (1993). DNA and recent human evolution. *Evolutionary Anthropology, 2,* 60-73.

Stotland, E. (1969). Exploratory investigations of empathy. In L. Berkowitz (Ed.), *Advances in Experimental Social Psychology, Vol. 4.* New York: Academic.

Strayer, F. F., Wareing, S., & Rushton, J. P. (1979). Social constraints on naturally occurring preschool altruism. *Ethology and Sociobiology, 1,* 3-11.

Stringer, C. B., & Andrews, P. (1988). Genetic and fossil evidence for the origin of modern humans. *Science, 239,* 1263-68.

Stunkard, A. J., Sorensen, T. I. A., Hanis, C., Teasdale, T. W., Chakraborty, R., Schull, W. J., & Schulsinger, F. (1986). An adoption study of human obesity. *New England Journal of Medicine, 314,* 193-98.

Suomi, S. J. (1982). Sibling relationships in nonhuman primates. In M. E. Lamb & B. Sutton-Smith (Eds.), *Sibling Relationships.* Hillsdale, NJ: Erlbaum.

Surbey, M. K. (1990). Family composition, stress, and human menarche. In F. B. Bercovitch & T. E. Zeigler (Eds.), *The Socioendocrinology of Primate Reproduction.* New York: Alan R. Liss.

Susanne, C. (1977). Heritability of anthropological characters. *Human Biology, 49,* 573-80.

Susanne, C. (1979). On the relationship between psychometric and anthropometric traits. *American Journal of Physical Anthropology, 51,* 421-23.

Sussman, R. W. (1993). A current controversy in human evolution. *American Anthropologist, 95,* 9-13.

Sutker, P. B., & Gilliard, R. S. (1970). Personal sexual attitudes and behavior in blacks and whites. *Psychological Reports, 27,* 753-54.

Symons, D. (1979). *The Evolution of Human Sexuality.* New York: Oxford University Press.

Takahashi, K., & Suzuki, I. (1961). On the brain weight of recent Japanese. *Sapporo Medical Journal, 20,* 179-84.

Tanfer, K., & Cubbins, L. A. (1992). Coital frequency among single women: Normative constraints and situational opportunities. *Journal of Sex Research, 29,* 221-50.

Tanner, J. M. (1978). *Fetus into Man: Physical Growth from Conception to Maturity.* Cambridge, MA: Harvard University Press.

Tashakkori, A. (1993). Race, gender and pre-adolescent self-structure: A test of construct-specificity hypothesis. *Personality and Individual Differences, 14,* 591-98.

Tashakkori, A., & Thompson, V. D. (1991). Race differences in self-perception and locus of control during adolescence and early adulthood. *Genetic, Social, and General Psychology Monographs, 117,* 135-52.

Taubman, P. (1976). The determinants of earnings: Genetics, family and other environments: A study of white male twins. *American Economic Review, 66,* 858-70.

Taylor, C. E., & Condra, C. (1980). r- and K- selection in *Drosophila pseudoobscura. Evolution, 34,* 1183-93.

Teasdale, T. W. (1979). Social class correlations among adoptees and their biological and adoptive parents. *Behavior Genetics, 9,* 103-14.

Teasdale, T. W., & Owen, D. R. (1981). Social class correlations among separately adopted siblings and unrelated individuals adopted together. *Behavior Genetics, 11,* 577-88.

Tellegen, A., Lykken, D. T., Bouchard, T. J., Jr., Wilcox, K. J., Segal, N. L., & Rich, S. (1988). Personality similarity in twins reared apart and together. *Journal of Personality and Social Psychology, 54,* 1031-39.

Templeton, A. R. (1993). The "Eve" hypotheses: A genetic critique and reanalysis. *American Anthropologist, 95,* 51-72.

Terman, L. M. (1926/1959). *Genetic Studies of Genius: Vol 1. Mental and Physical Traits of a Thousand Gifted Children,* 2d ed. Stanford, CA: Stanford University Press.

Terman, L. M. & Buttenwieser, P. (1935a). Personality factors in marital compatibility. Part I. *Journal of Social Psychology, 6,* 143-71.

Terman, L. M. & Buttenwieser, P. (1935b). Personality factors in marital compatibility. Part II. *Journal of Social Psychology, 6,* 267-89.

Tesser, A. (1993). The importance of heritability in psychological research: The case of attitudes. *Psychological Review, 93,* 129-42.

Thiessen, D. & Gregg, B. (1980). Human assortative mating and genetic equilibrium: An evolutionary perspective. *Ethology and Sociobiology, 1,* 111-40.

Thorne, A. G., & Wolpoff, M. H. (1992). The multiregional evolution of humans. *Scientific American, 266* (4), 76-83.

Toates, F. (1986). *Motivational Systems.* Cambridge: Cambridge University Press.

Tobias, P. V. (1970). Brain-size, grey matter and race—fact or fiction? *American Journal of Physical Anthropology, 32,* 3-26.

Todd, T. W. (1923). Cranial capacity and linear dimensions in white and Negro. *American Journal of Physical Anthropology, 6,* 97-194.

Topinard, P. (1878). *Anthropology.* London: Chapman and Hall.

Torrence, R. (1983). Time budgeting and hunter-gatherer technology. In G. Bailey (Ed.), *Hunter-Gatherer Economy in Prehistory.* Cambridge: Cambridge University Press.

Tremblay, R. E., & Baillargeon, L. (1984). Les difficultés de comportement d'enfants immigrants dans les classes d'accueil, au préscolaire. *Canadian Journal of Education, 9,* 154-70.

Trivers, R. L. (1985). *Social Evolution*. Menlo Park, CA: Benjamin/Cummings.

True, W. R., Rice, J., Eisen, S. A., Heath, A. C., Goldberg, J., Lyons, M. J., & Nowak, J. (1993). A twin study of genetic and environmental contributions to liability for posttraumatic stress symptoms. *Archives of General Psychiatry, 50,* 257-264.

Turkheimer, E., & Gottesman, I. I. (1991). Is $H^2 = 0$ a null hypothesis anymore? *Behavioral and Brain Sciences, 14,* 410-11.

Turner, C. G. (1989). Teeth and prehistory in Asia. *Scientific American, 260*(2), 88-96.

Ubelaker, D., & Scammell, H. (1992). *Bones: A Forensic Detective's Casebook.* New York: Harper Collins

Udry, J. R., & Morris, N. M. (1968). Distribution of coitus in the menstrual cycle. *Nature, 220,* 593-96.

Ueda, R. (1978). Standardization of the Denver Devlopment Screening Test on Tokyo children. *Developmental Medicine and Child Neurology, 20,* 647-56.

United Nations. Department of Economic and Social Development, Statistical Division. (1992). *Population and Vital Statistics Report. Data Available as of 1 October 1992.* Series A. Vol. 44, no. 4. New York, United Nations.

United States. National Aeronautics and Space Administration. (1978). *Anthropometric Source Book: Vol. 2. A Handbook of Anthropometric Data* (NASA Reference Publication No. 1024). Washington, D.C.: Author.

van den Berghe, P. L. (1981). *The Ethnic Phenomenon.* New York: Elsevier.

van den Berghe, P. L. (1983). Human inbreeding avoidance: Culture in nature (with commentaries and author's response). *Behavioral and Brain Sciences, 6,* 91-123.

van den Berghe, P. L. (1989). Heritable phenotypes and ethnicity. *Behavioral and Brain Sciences, 12,* 544-45.

van der Dennen, J. M. G. (1987). Ethnocentrism and in-group/out-group differentiation. In V. Reynolds, V. S. E. Falger, & I. Vine (Eds.), *The Sociobiology of Ethnocentrism.* London: Croom Helm.

Vanderwolf, C. H., & Cain, D. P. (1991). The neurobiology of race and Kipling's cat. *Personality and Individual Differences, 12,* 97-98.

Van Valen, L. (1974). Brain size and intelligence in man. *American Journal of Physical Anthropology, 40,* 417-24.

Vernon, P. A. (1989). The heritability of measures of speed of information-processing. *Personality and Individual Differences, 10,* 573-76.

Vernon, P. A., & Jensen, A. R. (1984). Individual and group differences in intelligence and speed of information processing. *Personality and Individual Differences, 5,* 411-23.

Vernon, P. E. (1964). *Personality Assessment: A Critical Survey.* New York: Wiley.

Vernon, P. E. (1969). *Intelligence and Cultural Environment.* London: Methuen.

Vernon, P. E. (1982). *The Abilities and Achievements of Orientals in North America.* New York: Academic.

Vigilant, L., Pennington, R., Harpending, H., Kocher, T. D., & Wilson, A. C. (1989). Mitochondrial DNA sequences in single hairs from a southern African population. *Proceedings of the National Academy of Sciences of the U.S.A., 86,* 9350-54.

Vigilant, L., Stoneking, M., Harpending, H., Hawkes, K., & Wilson, A. C. (1991). African populations and the evolution of human mitochondrial DNA. *Science, 253,* 1503-7.

Vining, D. R. (1986). Social versus reproductive success: The central theoretical problem of human sociobiology (with commentaries). *Behavioral and Brain Sciences, 9,* 167-216.

Vint, F. W. (1934). The brain of the Kenya native. *Journal of Anatomy, 48,* 216-23.

Waddington, C. H. (1957). *The Strategy of the Genes.* London: Allen and Unwin.

Wahlsten, D. (1990). Insensitivity of the analysis of variance to heredity-environment interaction. *Behavioral and Brain Sciences, 13,* 109-61.

Wainer, H. (1988). How accurately can we assess changes in minority performance on the SAT? *American Psychologist, 43,* 774-78.

Waller, J. H. (1971). Achievement and social mobility: Relationships among IQ score, education, and occupation in two generations. *Social Biology, 18,* 252-59.

Waller, N. G., Kojetin, B. A., Bouchard, T. J., Jr., Lykken, D. T., & Tellegen, A. (1990). Genetic and environmental influences on religious interests, attitudes, and values: A study of twins reared apart and together. *Psychological Science, 1,* 138-42.

Walters, C. E. (1967). Comparative development of Negro and white infants. *Journal of Genetic Psychology, 110,* 243-51.

Walters, J. R. (1987). Kin recognition in non-human primates. In D. J. C. Fletcher and C. D. Michener (Eds.), *Kin Recognition in Animals.* Wiley.

Warren, N. (1972). African infant precocity. *Psychological Bulletin, 78,* 353-67.

Watson, J. B. (1924). *Behaviorism.* Chicago: The People's Institute.

Watson, J. S. (1992). On artificially selecting for the sex ratio. *Ethology and Sociobiology, 13,* 1-2.

Weigel, R. W., & Blurton Jones, N. G. (1983). Workshop report: Evolutionary life-history analysis of human behavior. *Ethology and Sociobiology, 4,* 233-35.

Weinberg, M. S., & Williams, C. J. (1988). Black sexuality: A test of two theories. *Journal of Sex Research, 25,* 197-218.

Weinberg, R. A., Scarr, S., & Waldman, I. D. (1992). The Minnesota Transracial Adoption Study: A follow-up of IQ test performance at adolescence. *Intelligence, 16,* 117-35.

Weinberg, W. A., Dietz, S. G., Penick, E. C., & McAlister, W. H. (1974). Intelligence, reading achievement, physical size and social class. *Journal of Pediatrics, 85,* 482-89.

Weinrich, J. D. (1977). Human sociobiology: Pair bonding and resource predictability (effects of social class and race). *Behavioral Ecology and Sociobiology, 2,* 91-118.

Weizmann, F., Wiener, N. I., Wiesenthal, D. L., & Ziegler, M. (1990). Differential *K* theory and racial hierarchies. *Canadian Psychology, 31,* 1-13.

Weizmann, F., Wiener, N. I., Wiesenthal, D. L., & Ziegler, M. (1991). Eggs, eggplants and eggheads: A rejoinder to Rushton. *Canadian Psychology, 32,* 43-50.

Wells, P. A. (1987). Kin recognition in humans. In D. J. C. Fletcher and C. D. Michener (Eds.), *Kin Recognition in Animals.* Wiley.

Westney, O. E., Jenkins, R. R., Butts, J. D., & Williams, I. (1984). Sexual development and behavior in black preadolescents. *Adolescence, 19,* 557-68.

Weyl, N. (1977). *Karl Marx: Racist.* New Rochelle, NY: Arlington House.

Weyl, N. (1989). *The Geography of American Achievement.* Washington, DC: Scott-Townsend.

Whitehead, M. (1988). *The Health Divide.* London: Penguin.

"White Professor Wins Court Ruling." (1991, September 5). *New York Times,* A20.

Wickett, J. C., Vernon, P. A., & Lee, D. H. (1994). *In vivo* brain size, head perimeter, and intelligence in a sample of healthy adult females. *Personality and Individual Differences, 16,* 831-38.

Willerman, L. (1973). Activity level and hyperactivity in twins. *Child Development, 44,* 288-93.

Willerman, L. (1979). *The Psychology of Individual and Group Differences.* San Francisco, CA: Freeman.

Willerman, L., Schultz, R., Rutledge, J. N., & Bigler, E. D. (1991). *In vivo* brain size and intelligence. *Intelligence, 15,* 223-28.

Williams, G. C. (1966). *Adaptation and Natural Selection.* Princeton, NJ: Princeton University Press.

Williams, J. R., & Scott, R. B. (1953). Growth and development of Negro infants. *Child Development, 24,* 103-21.

Willson, M. F., & Burley, N. (1983). *Mate Choice in Plants*. Princeton, NJ: Princeton University Press.

Wilson, A. C., & Cann, R. L. (1992). The recent African genesis of humans. *Scientific American, 266* (4), 68–73.

Wilson, D. S. (1983). The group selection controversy: History and current status. *Annual Review of Ecology and Systematics, 14,* 159–87.

Wilson, E. O. (1975). *Sociobiology: The New Synthesis*. Cambridge, MA: Harvard University Press.

Wilson, E. O. (1978). *On Human Nature*. Cambridge, MA: Harvard University Press.

Wilson, E. O. (1992). *The Diversity of Life*. Cambridge, MA: Harvard University Press.

Wilson, J. Q., & Herrnstein, R. J. (1985). *Crime and Human Nature*. New York: Simon & Schuster.

Wilson, R. S. (1978). Synchronies in mental development: An epigenetic perspective. *Science, 202,* 939–48.

Wilson, R. S. (1983). The Louisville Twin Study: Developmental synchronies in behavior. *Child Development, 54,* 298–316.

Wilson, R. S. (1984). Twins and chronogenetics: Correlated pathways of development. *Acta Geneticae Medicae et Gemellologiae, 33,* 149–57.

Winick, M., Meyer, K. K., & Harris, R. C. (1975). Malnutrition and environmental enrichment by early adoption. *Science, 190,* 1173–75.

Wise, P. H., & Pursley, D. M. (1992). Infant mortality as a social mirror. *New England Journal of Medicine, 326,* 1558–60.

Wissler, C. (1901). The correlation of mental and physical tests. *Psychological Review, Monograph Supplement, 3* (6).

Wober, M. (1969). The meaning and stability of Raven's Matrices Test among Africans. *International Journal of Psychology, 4,* 229–35.

Wolpoff, M. H. (1989). Multiregional evolution: The fossil alternative to Eden. In P. Mellars and C. Stringer (Eds.), *The Human Revolution* (pp. 62–108). Edinburgh: Edinburgh University Press.

World Health Organization. Global Programme on AIDS. (1991). *WHO Specifications and Guidelines for Condom Procurement*. Geneva, Switzerland: World Health Organization.

World Health Organization. Global Programme on AIDS. (1994). *The Current Global Situation of the HIV/AIDS Pandemic*. Geneva, Switzerland: World Health Organization.

Wynne-Edwards, V. C. (1962). *Animal Dispersion in Relation to Social Behaviour*. Edinburgh: Oliver and Boyd.

Yee, A. H., Fairchild, H. H., Weizmann, F., & Wyatt, G. E. (1993). Addressing psychology's problems with race. *American Psychologist, 48,* 1132–40.

Yerkes, R. M. (Ed.). (1921). Psychological examining in the United States Army. *Mem. National Academy of Sciences, 15,* 1–890.

Yoakum, C. S., & Yerkes, R. M. (1920). *Mental Tests in the American Army*. London: Sidgwick & Jackson.

Yu, E. S. H. (1986). Health of the Chinese elderly in America. *Research in Aging, 8,* 84–109.

Zajonc, R. B. (1980). Feeling and thinking: Preferences need no inferences. *American Psychologist, 35,* 151–75.

Zajonc, R. B., Markus, H., & Markus, G. B. (1979). The birth order puzzle. *Journal of Personality and Social Psychology, 37,* 1325–41.

Zammuto, R. M., & Millar, J. S. (1985). Environmental predictability, variability, and *Spermophilus Columbianus* life history over an elevational gradient. *Ecology, 66,* 1784–94.

Zuckerman, M. (1990). Some dubious premises in research and theory on racial differences. *American Psychologist, 45,* 1297–1303.

Zuckerman, M. (1991). Truth and consequences: Responses to Rushton and Kendler. *American Psychologist, 46,* 984–86.

Zuckerman, M., & Brody, N. (1988). Oysters, rabbits and people: A critique of "Race Differences in Behaviour" by J. P. Rushton. *Personality and Individual Differences, 9,* 1025–33.

Author Index

Subject Index

Race, Evolution, and Behavior

A Life History Perspective

J. Philippe Rushton

Testing for racial differences in behavior has been much neglected over the past sixty years. And when not subject to neglect, to strongly negative imputations among professionals and politicians alike. According to J. Philippe Rushton, substantial racial differences do exist and their pattern can only be explained adequately from an evolutionary perspective. In *Race, Evolution, and Behavior* he reviews international data and finds a distinct pattern. People of East Asian ancestry and people of African ancestry are at opposite ends of a continuum, with people of European ancestry intermediate, albeit with much variability within each broad grouping.

Rushton's thesis is that when fully modern humans migrated out of Africa, perhaps only 100,000 years ago, the colder Eurasian climate selected for larger brains, more forward planning, greater family stability, and increased longevity with concomitant reductions in sex hormone, speed of maturation, reproductive potency, and aggressiveness. Rushton's theory emphasizes a trade-off between parenting and mating and brings into focus the concept of a coordinated life history of characteristics, evolving together, to replicate genes more effectively. The selection for large brains and parenting skills was taken furthest in east Asia. Rushton's theory explains differentiation in intelligence and predicts other, seemingly unrelated race effects, such as differences in frequency of twinning. The capacity to unify disparate phenomena is usually considered a virtue in theories. Rushton's gene-based evolutionary models explain ethnocentrism and racial group differences, and may provide a catalyst for understanding individual differences and human nature.

Fodor's

BEIJING

1st Edition

**Where to Stay and Eat
for All Budgets**

**Must-See Sights
and Local Secrets**

Ratings You Can Trust

Fodor's Travel Publications   New York, Toronto, London, Sydney, Auckland
www.fodors.com

FODOR'S BEIJING

Editors: Heidi Leigh Johansen, Jennifer Doerr, Emmanuelle Alspaugh

Editorial Production: Bethany Cassin Beckerlegge
Editorial Contributors: Dinah Gardner, Alex Miller, Katharine Mitchell, Eileen Wen Mooney, Paul Mooney, Alfredo Paris, Alex Pasternack, Victoria Patience
Maps and Illustrations: David Lindroth, *cartographer*; William Wu; with additional cartography provided Henry Columb, Mark Stroud, and Ali Baird, Moon Street Cartography; Bob Blake and Rebecca Baer, *map editors*
Design: Fabrizio La Rocca, *creative director*; Siobhan O'Hare, *art director*; Tina Malaney and Chie Ushio, *designers;* Melanie Marin, *senior picture editor*
Production/Manufacturing: Angela L. McLean
Cover Photo (Chinese New Year, Beijing): Keren Su/danitadelimont.com

First Edition

ISBN 978–1–4000–1739–3

ISSN 1934–5518

SPECIAL SALES

This book is available for special discounts for bulk purchases for sales promotions or premiums. Special editions, including personalized covers, excerpts of existing books, and corporate imprints, can be created in large quantities for special needs. For more information, write to Special Markets/ Premium Sales, 1745 Broadway, MD 6-2, New York, New York 10019 or e-mail specialmarkets@ randomhouse.com.

AN IMPORTANT TIP & AN INVITATION

Although all prices, opening times, and other details in this book are based on information supplied to us at press time, changes occur all the time in the travel world, and Fodor's cannot accept responsibility for facts that become outdated or for inadvertent errors or omissions. So **always confirm information when it matters,** especially if you're making a detour to visit a specific place. Your experiences—positive and negative—matter to us. If we have missed or misstated something, **please write to us.** We follow up on all suggestions. Contact the Beijing editor at editors@fodors. com or c/o Fodor's at 1745 Broadway, New York, New York 10019.

PRINTED IN THE UNITED STATES OF AMERICA

10 9 8 7 6 5 4 3 2 1

Be a Fodor's Correspondent

Your opinion matters. It matters to us. It matters to your fellow Fodor's travelers, too. And we'd like to hear it. In fact, we *need* to hear it.

When you share your experiences and opinions, you become an active member of the Fodor's community. That means we'll not only use your feedback to make our books better, but we'll publish your names and comments whenever possible. Throughout our guides, look for "Word of Mouth," excerpts of your unvarnished feedback.

Here's how you can help improve Fodor's for all of us.

Tell us when we're right. We rely on local writers to give you an insider's perspective. But our writers and staff editors—who are the best in the business—depend on you. Your positive feedback is a vote to renew our recommendations for the next edition.

Tell us when we're wrong. We're proud that we update most of our guides every year. But we're not perfect. Things change. Hotels cut services. Museums change hours. Charming cafés lose charm. If our writer didn't quite capture the essence of a place, tell us how you'd do it differently. If any of our descriptions are inaccurate or inadequate, we'll incorporate your changes in the next edition and will correct factual errors at fodors.com *immediately.*

Tell us what to include. You probably have had fantastic travel experiences that aren't yet in Fodor's. Why not share them with a community of like-minded travelers? Maybe you chanced upon a beach or bistro or B&B that you don't want to keep to yourself. Tell us why we should include it. And share your discoveries and experiences with everyone directly at fodors.com. Your input may lead us to add a new listing or highlight a place we cover with a "Highly Recommended" star or with our highest rating, "Fodor's Choice."

Give us your opinion instantly at our feedback center at www.fodors.com/feedback. You may also e-mail editors@fodors.com with the subject line "Beijing Editor." Or send your nominations, comments, and complaints by mail to Beijing Editor, Fodor's, 1745 Broadway, New York, NY 10019.

You and travelers like you are the heart of the Fodor's community. Make our community richer by sharing your experiences. Be a Fodor's correspondent.

Happy traveling!

Tim Jarrell, Publisher

CONTENTS

BEIJING IN FOCUS

CLOSEUPS

MAPS

ABOUT THIS BOOK

Our Ratings

Sometimes you find terrific travel experiences and sometimes they just find you. But usually the burden is on you to select the right combination of experiences. That's where our ratings come in.

As travelers we've all discovered a place so wonderful that its worthiness is obvious. And sometimes that place is so unique that superlatives don't do it justice: you just have to be there to know. These sights, properties, and experiences get our highest rating, **Fodor's Choice,** indicated by orange stars throughout this book.

Black stars highlight sights and properties we deem **Highly Recommended,** places that our writers, editors, and readers praise again and again for consistency and excellence.

By default, there's another category: any place we include in this book is by definition worth your time, unless we say otherwise. And we will.

Disagree with any of our choices? Care to nominate a place or suggest that we rate one more highly? Visit our feedback center at www.fodors.com/feedback.

Budget Well

Hotel and restaurant price categories from ¢ to **$$$$** are defined in the opening pages of each chapter. For attractions, we always give standard adult admission fees; reductions are usually available for children, students, and senior citizens. Want to pay with plastic? **AE, D, DC, MC, V** following restaurant and hotel listings indicate whether American Express, Discover, Diner's Club, MasterCard, and Visa are accepted.

Restaurants

Unless we state otherwise, restaurants are open for lunch and dinner daily. We mention dress only when there's a specific requirement and reservations only when they're essential or not accepted—it's always best to book ahead.

Hotels

Hotels have private bath, phone, TV, and air-conditioning and operate on the European Plan (aka EP, meaning without meals), unless we specify that they use the Continental Plan (CP, with a Continental breakfast), Breakfast Plan (BP, with a full breakfast), or Modified American Plan (MAP, with breakfast and dinner) or are all-inclusive (including all meals and most activities). We always

list facilities but not whether you'll be charged an extra fee to use them, so when pricing accommodations, find out what's included.

Many Listings	
★	Fodor's Choice
★	Highly recommended
⊠	Physical address
↔	Directions
⌂	Mailing address
☎	Telephone
🖶	Fax
⊕	On the Web
✉	E-mail
☜	Admission fee
☉	Open/closed times
▶	Start of walk/itinerary
Ⓜ	Metro stations
▤	Credit cards

Hotels & Restaurants	
🏨	Hotel
🛏	Number of rooms
♨	Facilities
⑩	Meal plans
✕	Restaurant
⌂	Reservations
🏛	Dress code
⌇	Smoking
🍸	BYOB
✕🏨	Hotel with restaurant that warrants a visit

Outdoors	
🏌	Golf
⛺	Camping

Other	
☺	Family-friendly
🗣	Contact information
⇨	See also
⊠	Branch address
☞	Take note

Experience
Beijing
THE HEART OF THE DRAGON

Welcome to Beijing, a city of dramatic contrasts between the ancient and the sparkling new.

WORD OF MOUTH

"Have fun! China is great and the people make it that way."
—Michael Thompson

"Beijing is easy to walk around (bring a map), cabs are cheap and plentiful (and, if you have your destinations written in Chinese, it's pretty hard to get lost). We found the great majority of Beijingers (and Chinese everywhere) open, friendly and good-humoured—even more so if you give them a good laugh by trying out a few words in Mandarin."
—Neil_Oz

BEIJING PLANNER

When to Go

The best time to visit Beijing is spring or early fall, when the weather is pleasant and crowds are a bit smaller. Book at least one month in advance for travel during these two times of year. In winter, Beijing's Forbidden City and Summer Palace can look fantastical and majestic when the traditional tiled roofs are covered with a light dusting of snow and the venues are devoid of tourists.

Avoid the three long national holidays: Chinese New Year, which ranges from mid-January to mid-February; Labor Day holiday, the first week of May; and National Day holiday, the first week of October. Millions of Chinese travel during these weeks, making it difficult to book hotels, tours, and transportation.

Beijing Temperatures

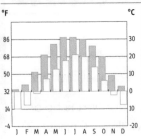

Visitor Centers

China International Travel Service (CITS), an official government agency, maintains offices in many hotels and at some tourist venues. The Beijing Tourism Administration maintains a 24-hour hotline for tourist inquiries and complaints, with operators fluent in English.

Beijing Tourism Administration Hotline (☎ 010/6513–0828)

China International Travel Service (✉ 28 Jianguomenwai Dajie, Chaoyang District ☎ 010/6515–8565 🖷 010/6515–8603 ⊕ www.citsusa.com)

How's the Weather?

The weather in Beijing is at its best in September and October, with a good chance of sunny days and mild temperatures. Winters are cold, but it seldom snows. Although hotels are usually well heated, some restaurants may be poorly heated, so be prepared with a warm sweater when dining out. Late April through June is lovely, but come July the days are hot and excruciatingly humid, with a greater chance of rain. Spring is also the time of year for Beijing's famous dust storms.

Getting Around

On Foot: Though traffic and modernization has put a bit of a cramp in Beijing's walking style, meandering remains one of the best ways of experiencing the capital—especially the old hutongs that are rich with culture and sights.

By Bike: The proliferation of cars (some 1,000 new automobiles take to the streets of the capital every day) has made biking less pleasant and more dangerous here. Fortunately, most streets have wide, well-defined bike lanes often separated from other traffic by an island of hedges. If a flat tire or sudden brake failure strikes, seek out the nearest street-side mechanic, easily identified by the bike parts and pumps. Bikes can be rented at many hotels.

By Subway: The subway is a good way to avoid Beijing's frequent traffic jams. And, with the opening of new lines, Beijing's subway service is becoming increasingly convenient. Beijing now has four lines (with more in the works for the Olympics), including a light rail that runs out to the Haidian district and another that travels to the east of the city. One line circles Beijing beneath the Second Ring Road and the other runs east–west from the city center to the western and eastern suburbs. The latter lines meet at Fuxingmen and Jianguomen. The subway runs from 5 AM to midnight daily. Fares are Y3 per ride for any distance, and an additional Y2 for transfers to the light rail. Stations are marked in both Chinese and English, and stops are also announced in both languages.

By Taxi: The taxi experience in Beijing has improved significantly as the city's taxi companies gradually shift to cleaner, more comfortable new cars. Flagfall for taxis is Y10 for the first 4 km (2½ mi) and Y2 per km thereafter. For all taxis, a 20% nighttime surcharge kicks in at 11 PM and lasts until 5 AM. ⚠ **Be sure to check that the meter has been engaged to avoid fare negotiations at your destination.** Taxis are easy to hail during the day, but can be difficult during evening rush hour, especially when it's raining. If you're having difficulty, go to the closest hotel and wait in line there. Few taxi drivers speak English, so ask your hotel concierge to write down your destination in Chinese. ■ **TIP→ You can also use the end-of-chapter glossaries throughout this book; simply point at the Chinese character and your cabbie will know where to go. Be sure to take a hotel card with you for the return trip.**

Street Vocabulary

Below are some terms you'll see over and over again. These words will appear on maps and street signs, and they are part of the name of just about every place you go:

Dong is east, **xi** is west, **nan** is south, **bei** is north, and **zhong** means middle. **Jie** and **lu** mean street and road respectively, and **da** means big.

Gongyuan means park. Jingshan Park is Jingshan Gongyuan.

Men, meaning door or gate, indicates a street that once passed through an entrance in the old wall that surrounded the city until it was torn down in the 1960s. The entrances to parks and some other places are also referred to as *men.*

Nei means inside and **wai** means outside. You will often come across streets that used to pass through a gate. Andingmen Nei Dajie, for example, is the section of the street located inside the Second Ring Road (where the gate used to be), whereas Andingmen Wai Dajie is the section outside the gate.

Qiao, or bridge, is part of the place name at just about every entrance and exit on the ring roads.

TOP ATTRACTIONS

Forbidden City

(A) The Forbidden City has been home to a long line of emperors, beginning with Yongle, in 1420, and ending with Puyi (made famous by Bernardo Bertolucci's film *The Last Emperor*), who was forced out of the complex by a warlord in 1924. The structure, which was built by more than 200,000 workers, is the best preserved and most complete collection of imperial architecture in China.

Lama Temple

(C) The sweet smell of incense permeates one of the few functioning Buddhist temples in Beijing. When Emperor Yongzheng took the throne in 1723, his former residence was converted into this Lamaistic temple. During the Qianlong Period (1736–1795), it became a center of the Yellow Hat sect of Tibetan Buddhism. At its high point, 1,500 lamas lived here. The Hall of Celestial Kings houses a statue of the Maitreya, and the Wanfu Pavilion has

a 23-meter (75½-foot) Buddha carved from one piece of sandalwood.

Magnificent Markets

(B) It's hard to resist: so much to bargain for, so little time! Beijing's markets offer a wide variety of goods, from "Maomorabilia" to silk slippers. Visit outdoor Panjiayuan (aka the Dirt Market), where some 3,000 vendors sell factory knockoffs, antiques, Cultural Revolution memorabilia, and handicrafts. For freshwater pearls, and *more* knockoffs, try the Silk Alley Market or the Hongqiao Market.

Summer Palace

(D) Snapshot: the Summer Palace glowing at dusk. Is there a more authentic Beijing experience? This garden complex dates back eight centuries, to when the first emperor of the Jin Dynasty built the Gold Mountain Palace on Longevity Hill. Notable sights are the Long Corridor (a covered wooden walkway) and the Hall of Benevolent Longevity. At the west end of

the lake is the famous Marble Boat that Cixi built with money intended to create a Chinese navy. The palace, which served as an imperial retreat from dripping summer heat, was ransacked by British and French soldiers in 1860 and later burned by Western soldiers seeking revenge for the Boxer Rebellion.

Confucius Temple

(E) This temple, with its towering cypress and pine trees, offers a serene escape from the crowds at nearby Lama Temple. This is the second largest Confucian temple after that of Qufu, the master's hometown in Shandong province. First built in the 13th century, the Confucius Temple was renovated in the 18th century.

Temple of Heaven

(F) The Temple of Heaven is one of the best examples of religious architecture in China. Construction began in the early 15th century under the order of Yongle. The com-

plex took 14 years to complete; it contains three main buildings where the emperor, as the "Son of Heaven," offered prayers. The sprawling complex is a pleasant place for wandering: watch locals practicing martial arts, playing traditional instruments, and enjoying ballroom dancing on the grass.

Tiananmen Square

(G) Walking beneath the red flags of Tiananmen Square is quintessential Beijing. The political heart of modern China, the square covers 100 acres, making it the largest public square in the world. It was from the Gate of Heavenly Peace that Mao Zedong pronounced the People's Republic of China in 1949. Many Westerners think only of the massive student protests here in the 1980s; in fact, it has been the site of protests throughout modern history.

SIGHTSEEING TOURS

Taking a tour will make it easier to sightsee without the hassle. However, if you're adventurous, you can easily explore the city on your own, even if you don't speak Chinese. Taxi drivers know the names of the major tourist sights, and armed with the names in Chinese in this guide, you should have few or no problems getting around. If you do opt for an organized tour, keep in mind that a little research pays off.

General Tours

Beijing Panda Tour. Offering a variety of private and group tours to historical sites and cultural venues in Beijing, the folks at Panda Tour also offer trips to various parts of the Great Wall. Group tours range from Y300 to Y445. ⊠ *Grand Rock Plaza, 5th fl., 13 Xinzhong Xili, Dongcheng District* ☎ *010/6417–0468.*

China International Travel Service. CITS is China's largest and oldest travel agency, dating to 1954. In Beijing, the company offers everything from customized tours to group tours and business trips, starting from around Y238. ⊠ *28 Jianguomenwai Dajie, Chaoyang District* ☎ *010/6515–8565* 🖷 *010/6515–8603* ⊕ *www.citsusa.com.*

Dragon Bus. A division of China International Travel Service, Dragon Bus offers inexpensive group city tours with English-language guides. Tours include several Great Wall sites (Y250 to Y330). Another tour features the Summer Palace, Lama Temple, and a *hutong* (alleyway neighborhood) pedicab tour for Y380, or Tiananmen Square, the Forbidden City, Summer Palace, and Temple of Heaven for Y360. ⊠ *28 Jianguomenwai Dajie (behind the Gloria Plaza Hotel), Chaoyang District* ☎ *010/6515–8565* ⊕ *www.dragontour.com.cn.*

★ **Fodor's Choice** **WildChina.** This foreign-managed travel company is probably the best in China. WildChina has excellent guides who know the city well and who don't waste your time taking you to souvenir shops. The company offers a three-day tour of Beijing that includes major historical sites, a hike on a wild part of the Great Wall, a visit to the hutongs, and an introduction to the cuisines of the capital city. It's pricey but worth it: a 3-day tour, including courtyard hotel or 5-star hotel, costs Y6,708. ⊠ *Room 801, Oriental Place, 9 East Dongfang Lu, North Dongsanhuan Lu, Chaoyang District* ☎ *010/6465–6602* ⊕ *www.wildchina.com.*

Bike Tours

Many of Beijing's pleasures are best sampled off the subway and out of taxis. In other words, pedal! Rent bikes (available at many hotels) and take an impromptu sightseeing tour. Beijing is flat, and bike lanes exist on most main roads. Pedaling among the city's cyclists isn't as challenging as it looks: copy the locals—keep it slow and ring your bell often. And, of course, be very careful and wear a helmet. Punctured tire? Not to worry: curbside repairmen line most streets. Remember to park your bike (and lock it to something stationary, as bike theft is common) only in designated areas. There are designated bike-parking lots throughout the city with attendants.

CycleChina. If a guided three-hour afternoon bicycle tour of a hutong (Y150) or a trip through Beijing sitting in a motorbike sidecar (Y795 per person) sounds like fun, call CycleChina. ☎ *139/1188–6524* ⊕ *www.cyclechina.com.*

Kingdom Bike Rental. Offering bicycle rentals and suggested itineraries covering some

of Beijing's lesser known historical sites, Kingdom is a great resource. A variety of bikes are available for rent here from Y35 to Y120 per day (or Y300 to Y600 per week). Helmets are available for Y10 per day. ☒ *North Garden office, B402, Oriental Plaza, Wangfujing, Dongcheng District* ☎ *133/8140-0738* ⊕ *www.bicyclekingdom.com.*

Pedicab Tours

Pedicabs (basically large tricycles with room for passengers behind a pedaling driver) were once the vehicle of choice for Beijingers laden with a week's worth of groceries or tourists eager for a street's-eye city tour. Today many residents are wealthy enough to bundle their purchases into taxis or their own cars, and the tourist trade has moved on to the tight schedules of air-conditioned buses. But pedicabs have made a big comeback in Beijing in recent years and can now be hired near major tourist sites such as Liulichang and Houhai. In fact, more and more Chinese are using pedicabs as a cheaper form of transportation for short trips. ■ TIP➔ Be absolutely sure to negotiate the fare in advance, clarifying which currency will be used (Yuan or dollars), whether the fare is considered a one-way or round-trip (some drivers will demand payment for a round-trip whether or not you use the pedicab for the return journey), and whether it is for one person or two. Fares start at Y10.

★ Fodor's Choice | **Beijing Hutong Tourist Agency.** This agency was one of the first to offer guided pedicab tours of Beijing's backalleys, with glimpses of old courtyard houses and daily Beijing life. This half-day trip winds its way through what was once Beijing's most prestigious neighborhood (Houhai), stops at the Drum and Bell Towers, and finishes with tea at Prince Gong's Palace. It's also possible to arrange

WORD OF MOUTH

"You can easily do Tiananmen Square and Forbidden City on your own. There is a flag-raising ceremony at dawn at Tiananmen Square that is interesting and worth it. In the Forbidden City, there's an excellent audio tour that you can rent in English. I think it is worthwhile to have a guide at Temple of Heaven and Summer Palace. A guide is helpful in explaining the various areas, especially at the Temple of Heaven, which is so ceremonial."   –Nancy

to visit the home of a local family. Advance reservations are recommended. Tours, which begin on Qianhai Xijie directly opposite the north entrance of Beihai Park, start at 9 and 2 daily, and cost about Y180 per person. ☒ *26 Di'anmen Xidajie, Dongcheng District* ☎ *010/6615-9097* 📠 *010/6400-2787.*

Hiking Tours

Beijing Hikers. This outfitter offers guided hiking trips aimed at expat hikers and tourists. The trips are rated from 1 to 5 in terms of difficulty, and they take you into the hills around Beijing. You might visit a rural village, historic temple, or the Great Wall. Groups depart from the Starbucks in the Lido Hotel. ☎ *139/1002–5516 or 010/6779–9365* ⊕ *www.beijinghikers.com* 🎫 *Y200, including round-trip transportation, park-entrance fees, and end-of-hike refreshments* ☉ *Weekends 8:30 or 9–4:30.*

CITY
ITINERARIES

Be curious: Beijing rewards the explorer. Most temples and palaces have gardens and lesser courtyards that are seldom visited. Even at the height of the summer tourist rush, the Forbidden City's peripheral courtyards offer ample breathing room, even seclusion. The Temple of Heaven's vast grounds are a pleasure year-round—and enchanting after a snowfall.

The Best of Beijing in 5 Days

On Day 1, start at **Tiananmen Square,** the heart of modern China and the entry point to the spectacular **Forbidden City.** Explore the former imperial palace to your heart's content. In the afternoon, take a guided pedicab ride through a hutong to the **Drum and Bell Towers.** Have Peking duck for dinner, perhaps at the **Li Qun Roast Duck Restaurant,** located in an old courtyard house a few blocks southeast of Tiananmen Square.

On Day 2, head straight for the vast grounds of the **Temple of Heaven,** one of Beijing's most important historical sights. Visit the **Lama Temple** and the nearby **Confucius Temple,** too. Save two or three hours in the afternoon for shopping at **Beijing Curio City** and the **Silk Alley Market** in the Chaoyang District. Have dinner or enjoy a nightcap in the Sanlitun area.

Set aside Day 3 for a tour to the **Thirteen Ming Tombs** and the **Great Wall** at Mutianyu, where a cable car offers a dramatic ride to the summit.

On Day 4, visit the rambling **Summer Palace,** and then spend a few hours at the nearby **Old Summer Palace,** an intriguing ruin. In the evening, plan to see a **Beijing Opera** performance, or hit the restaurants and bars in the bustling Houhai area.
■ TIP→ For more information about Beijing Opera, *see* Chapter 5.

On Day 5, hire a car and visit the spectacular **Eastern Qing Tombs,** where a "spirit way" lined with carved stone animals and unrestored templelike grave sites rest in a beautiful rural setting. Wear walking shoes and bring a lunch. The drive takes five hours round-trip, so get an early start.

■ TIP→ Although the Forbidden City and Tiananmen Square represent the heart of Beijing, the capital lacks a definitive downtown area in terms of shopping or business, as commercial and entertainment districts have cropped up all over.

If You Have 1 Day

Begin your day in **Tiananmen Square**—you may want to catch the flag-raising ceremony at dawn—to admire the Communist icons of modern China. Then, heading north, walk back through time into the vast **Forbidden City.** Keep in mind that in 1420, when the imperial palace was built, its structures were the tallest in Asia. You can spend the morning leisurely examining the many palaces and gardens here. Next head north into **Jingshan Park** and climb Coal Hill to get a panoramic view of the city. Then jump in a cab and head to Lotus Lane, where you can have a drink overlooking the waters of **Qianhai.**

In the afternoon, take a trip outside the city. Hire a car and driver to take you on the one-hour journey to the Badaling section of the **Great Wall,** which is the closest to Beijing. On your way back, stop at either the **Thirteen Ming Tombs** or the **Summer Palace.** The Ming Tombs are en route; the Summer Palace will add an additional half hour to your journey.

■ TIP→ Tickets are sold until one hour before closing time at the Ming Tombs and Summer Palace.

Itinerary on Two Wheels

A great way to explore Beijing is by bicycle. A ride between Ditan Park and the lake district includes some of the city's most famous sights and finest hutongs.

Begin at **Ditan Park,** just north of the Second Ring Road on Yonghegong Jie. Park your bike in the lot outside the south gate and take a walk around the park. Next, ride south along Yonghegong Jie until you come to the main entrance of **Lama Temple.** Running west across the street from the temple's main gate is Guozijian Jie (Imperial Academy Street). Shops near the intersection sell Buddhist statues, incense, texts (in Chinese), and tapes of traditional Chinese Buddhist music. Browse them before riding west to the **Confucius Temple** and the neighboring **Imperial Academy.** The arches spanning Guozijian Jie are one of the few of their kind remaining in Beijing.

Follow Guozijian Jie west until it empties onto Andingmennei Dajie. Enter this busy road with care (there's no traffic signal) and ride south to Gulou Dong Dajie, another major thoroughfare. Turn right (west) and ride to the **Drum Tower.** From here detour through the alleys just north of the **Bell Tower.** A small public square, crowded with city residents flying kites, playing badminton or chess, and chatting, links the two landmarks.

If you need a rest, stop in at the **Drum and Bell** (☎ 010/8403–3600), a rustic-looking bar and restaurant on the west side of the square; it has a nice rooftop terrace with views of the two towers and the square below. Retrace your route south to Di'anmenwai Dajie (the road running south from the Drum Tower), turning onto Yandai Xie Jie, the first lane on the right. Makers of long-stem pipes once lined the lane's narrow way (one small pipe shop still does). There are a number of shops and street vendors here selling handicrafts, ethnic clothing, and folk arts. You can also sample some of Beijing's famous old street snacks such as candied haw, sweet potatoes, roast corn, and much more.

Wind southwest on Yandai Xie Jie past guesthouses, bicycle-repair shops, tiny restaurants, and crumbling traditional courtyard houses toward Houhai, or the Rear Lake. Turn left onto Xiaoqiaoli Hutong and pass the arched **Silver Ingot Bridge,** which separates **Houhai** and **Qianhai** lakes. Before the bridge, follow the trail along Houhai's north shore, traveling toward **Soong Ching-ling's Former Residence.**

Continue around the lake until you arrive at Deshengmennei Dajie. Follow it south to the second alley, turning east (left) onto **Yangfang Hutong,** which leads back to the arched bridge. Ride along Yangfang Hutong past the stone bridge and follow Qianhai's west bank. Sip a soda, beer, or tea at one of the lakeside venues. Continue along the lane to Qianhai Xi Jie. Nearby is **Prince Gong's Palace,** 300 yards north of the China Conservatory of Music—look for the brass plaque.

■ TIP➔ Love to walk? So do we! You can also do this itinerary, or parts of it, on two feet if you're so inclined.

MUSEUMS & MONUMENTS

With its historical sites as the major attractions, Beijing has a variety of museums and monuments that often get overlooked. Our favorites, listed below, are worth the time, especially if you're already in the neighborhood visiting a nearby temple or palace.

Beijing Ancient Architecture Museum. This little-known museum, located inside a Ming dynasty temple, exhibits photos, objects, and elaborate models of ancient Chinese architecture from ancient huts and mud homes up to Ming and Qing dynasty palaces. ⊠ *21 Dongjing Lu, Xuanwu District* ☎ *010/6301–7620* 🎟 *Y15* ☉ *Daily 9 AM–4 PM.*

Great Hall of the People. This solid edifice owes its Stalinist weight to the last years of the Sino-Soviet pact. Its gargantuan dimensions (205,712 square yards of floor space) exceed that of the Forbidden City. It was built by 14,000 laborers who worked around the clock for eight months. China's legislature meets in the aptly named Ten Thousand People Assembly Hall, beneath a panoply of 500 starlights revolving around a giant red star. Thirty-one reception rooms are distinguished by the arts and crafts of the provinces they represent. Call a day ahead to confirm that it's open. ⊠ *West side of Tiananmen Sq., Dongcheng District* ☎ *010/6309–6156* 🎟 *Y30* ☉ *Daily 8:15 AM–3 PM.*

Lu Xun House and Museum. Lu Xun, one of China's most celebrated modern writers, lived here in the 1920s. His best-known works are *Diary of a Madman* and *The True Story of Ah Q*. In the small courtyard garden, he wrote novels and short stories that typically depict the plight of poor, uneducated people in prerevolutionary China.

The rooms around the courtyard display documents and artifacts relating to Lu Xun's life and literature. ⊠ *19 Gongmenkou Ertiao, Fuchengmennei, next to Baita Si, Xicheng District* ☎ *010/6615–6549* 🎟 *Y15* ☉ *Tues.–Sun. 9–4.*

Mao Zedong Memorial Hall. Sentries here will assure that your communion with the Great Helmsman is brief. After waiting in a long winding line, you'll be guided into a spacious lobby dominated by a marble Mao statue and then to the Hall of Reverence, where his embalmed body lies in state, wrapped in the red flag of the Communist Party of China inside a crystal coffin that is lowered each night into a subterranean freezer. In a bid to limit Mao's deification, a second-story museum was added in 1983; it's dedicated to the former Premier Zhou Enlai, former general Zhu De, and China's president before the Cultural Revolution, Liu Shaoqi (who was persecuted to death during the Cultural Revolution). The hall's builders willfully ignored Tiananmen Square's geomancy: the mausoleum faces north, boldly contra-

WORD OF MOUTH

"Beijing is changing rapidly with many building projects in preparation for the Olympics. The streets are congested with cars, mostly taxis. Taxis are inexpensive and the best means of transportation. Younger people who speak English are friendly, but be watchful for potential scams artists. The little children, learning to speak English, are curious and so very cute." —Love4Travel

dicting centuries of imperial ritual. ⊠ *Tiananmen Sq., Dongcheng District* ☎ *010/6513–2277* ⊠ *Free* ⊙ *Tues.–Sun. 8 AM–11:30 AM.*

Museum of Antique Currency. This museum in a tiny courtyard house showcases a small but impressive selection of rare Chinese coins. Explanations are in Chinese only. Also in the courtyard are coin and curio dealers. ⊠*Deshengmen Tower south bldgs., Bei'erhuan Jie, Xicheng District* ☎ *010/ 6201–8073* ⊠ *Y10* ⊙ *Tues.–Sun. 9–4.*

★ **The National Museum of China.** On the east side of Tiananmen Square stands a grandiose structure: the national museum. Until 2003 this iconic building housed both the massive China History Museum and the rather tired Museum of the Chinese Revolution. In honor of the 2008 Olympics, city authorities have embarked on a renovation and expansion program. The museum has an exquisite collection of bronze, ceramics, and jade pieces, as well as a newer waxworks exhibition. International exhibits are regularly held here. Bags must be checked (Y1) before you enter.

⊠ *Central entrance on building on east side of Tiananmen Sq., Dongcheng District* ☎ *010/6512–8901* ⊠ *Y30* ⊙ *Daily 8:30 AM–4:30 PM except May 1–May 7, July and Aug., and Oct. 1–Oct. 7, 8 AM–6 PM; ticket office closes at 5.*

The Poly Art Museum. This very impressive museum, located on the second floor of the Poly Plaza Hotel, was established in 1998 to promote traditional art and to protect Chinese art from being lost to foreign countries. The museum has focused on the overseas acquisition of ancient bronzes, sculpture, and painting. The museum is divided into two galleries, one for the display of early Chinese bronzes, and the other for Buddhist scriptures carved in stone. Also on display here are four bronze animal heads that were once located in the Old Summer Palace. ⊠ *Poly Plaza, 14 Dongzhimen Nan Dajie, Dongcheng District* ☎ *010/6500–8117* ⊠ *Y50* ⊙ *Daily 9:30 AM–4:30 PM.*

Xu Beihong Memorial Museum. This small space is dedicated to the work of the famous Chinese artist Xu Beihong (1895– 1953), known for his vivid Chinese-style paintings of galloping horses. The museum houses a collection of Xu's oil paintings, water colors, and sketches. His picture books and replicas of his paintings are for sale in the museum shop. ⊠ *53 Xinjiekou Bei Dajie, Xicheng District* ☎ *010/6225–2187* ⊠ *Y5* ⊙ *Tues.–Sun. 9 AM–noon.*

GETTING OUTSIDE: PARKS & LAKES

Thanks to Beijing's former imperial families, who had a proclivity for lush green playgrounds, the Chinese capital is dotted with beautiful parks, which remain very popular with today's residents, who come here to do anything from martial arts to disco dancing.

★ **Beihai Park.** This park is immediately north of Zhongnanhai, the tightly guarded former residential compound of China's senior leaders. A white Tibetan dagoba perches on a hill just north of the south gate. Also at the south entrance is the **Round City,** which contains a white-jade Buddha and an enormous jade bowl given to Kublai Khan. Nearby, the well-restored **Temple of Eternal Peace** houses a variety of Buddhas. Climb to the dagoba from Yongan Temple. Once there, you can pay an extra Y1 to ascend the Buddha-bedecked **Shanyin Hall.**

The lake is Beijing's largest and most beautiful public waterway. On summer weekends the lake teems with paddle boats. The **Five Dragon Pavilion,** on Beihai's northwest shore, was built in 1602 by a Ming dynasty emperor who liked to fish under the moon. ⊠ *South Gate, Weijin Lu, Xicheng District* ☏ *010/6404–0610* ✉ *Y10; extra fees for some sights* ☉ *Daily 6 AM–10 PM.*

Ditan Park (Temple of Earth Park). In the 16th-century park are the square altar where emperors once made sacrifices to the earth god and the Hall of Deities. This is a lovely place for a stroll. ⊠ *Yonghegong Jie, just north of Second Ring Rd., Dongcheng District* ☏ *010/6421–4657* ✉ *Y2* ☉ *Daily 6–9.*

Jingshan Park (Prospect Hill Park). This park was built around Coal Hill (Meishan), a small peak formed from earth excavated

for the Forbidden City's moats. The hill was named for an imperial coal supply supposedly buried beneath it. Climb a winding stone staircase past peach and apple trees to Wanchun Pavilion, the park's highest point. It overlooks the Forbidden City and the Bell and Drum Towers. Chongzhen, the last Ming emperor, is said to have hanged himself at the foot of Coal Hill as his dynasty collapsed in 1644. ⊠ *Jingshanqian Dajie, opposite the north gate of the Forbidden City, Dongcheng District* ☏ *010/ 6404–4071 or 010/6403–2244* ✉ *Y5* ☉ *Daily 6 AM–10 PM.*

Qianhai and Houhai. Most people come to these lakes, along with Xihai in the northwest, to stroll and enjoy the shoreside bars and restaurants. In summer you can boat, swim, fish, and even, on occasion, windsurf. In winter sections of the frozen surfaces are fenced off for skating. ⊠ *North of Beihai Lake, Xicheng District.*

Xiangshan Park (Fragrant Hills Park). This hillside park west of Beijing was once an imperial retreat. From the eastern gate you can hike to the summit on a trail dotted with small temples. If you're short on time, ride a cable car to the top. ⊠ *Haidian District* ☏ *010/6259–1155* ✉ *Y10; cable car, Y50* ☉ *Daily 6–6.*

SILVER INGOT BRIDGE

Known as **Yin Ding Qiao** in Chinese, this Ming Dynasty bridge is named for its shape, which resembles a silver ingot turned upside down. It divides Qianhai and Houhai at the lakes' most narrow point. ⊠ *Xicheng District.*

DISCOVER
THE HUTONG

Beijing's *hutong* areas are ancient, twisting alley neighborhoods that simply beg to be explored—whether on foot, by bicycle, or by pedicab, we promise you'll learn a thing or two about the real life-blood and culture of this fascinating city.

For long time residents of Beijing, there is probably nothing more emblematic of the city than these idyllic—but quickly disappearing—courtyard houses and hutongs. This is Old Peking. See it before it vanishes. Never bypass an intriguing alleyway: strolls into the hutong frequently reveal ancient neighborhoods; brick and timber homes; courtyards full of children, *laobaixing* (ordinary folk), and, in winter, mountains of cabbage and coal—not to mention walkways so narrow pedestrians can't pass two abreast.

Despite the radical changes that are taking place around the city, time seems to stand still in these tiny alleyways. Hutongs have been around for more than 700 years. During imperial days, there were no signs marking the hutongs, whose names were only passed on orally. Some are named after national heroes, some for their geographical location, and others for the businesses that were once based there.

Traditional courtyard houses are also an important part of the allure of hutongs. The designs of the houses were a symbol of the owner's rank and social status. Homes with elaborate Chinese-style gates with spreading eaves are the former residences of imperial officials or businessmen. The homes of commoners have simple square-topped gates.

One of the best places to explore Beijing's hutongs is the Houhai area, which was home to nobles during the Qing Dynasty, and where you can still find some of their

homes and gardens. Walk around the lake and plunge into any small lane and just keep wandering around this maze of alleyways. ■ TIP➔ **The Silver Ingot Bridge, which separates the front and rear lakes, is a good place to start.** Or wander around the hutongs that surround the nearby Drum Tower.

An easy way to visit the hutongs is with the **Beijing Hutong Tourist Agency** (*see* "Sightseeing Tours," p. 15). To experience the inside of one of the beautiful *siheyuan*, or courtyard houses of the Qing dynasty, have dinner at the Red Capital Club, the Source, Baijia Dazhaimen, or Gui Gongfu (*see* Chapter 6), which are located in old houses once belonging to Manchu officials.

BEIJING THEN & NOW

Since the birth of Chinese civilization, different towns of varying size and import have existed at or near the site where Beijing is now. For example, the delicious local beer, Yanjing, refers to a city–kingdom based here 3,000 years ago. With this in mind, it is not unreasonable to describe Beijing's modern history as beginning with the Jin Dynasty, approximately 800 years ago. Led by nine generations of the Jurchen tribe, the Jin Dynasty eventually fell in a war against the Mongol horde.

Few armies had been able to withstand the wild onslaught of the armed Mongol cavalry, under the command of the legendary warrior Genghis Khan. The Jurchen tribe proved no exception, and the magnificent city of the Jin was almost completely destroyed. A few decades later in 1260, when Kublai Khan, the grandson of Genghis Khan, returned to use the city as an operational base for his conquest of southern China, reconstruction was the order of the day. By 1271, Kublai Khan had achieved his goal, declaring himself emperor of China under the Yuan Dynasty (1271–1368), with Beijing (or Dadu, as it was then known) as its capital.

The new capital was built on a scale befitting the world's then superpower. Its palaces were founded around Zhonghai and Beihai lakes. Beijing's current layout still reflects the Mongolian design.

Like today, a limiting factor on Beijing's growth seven centuries ago was its remoteness from water. To ensure an adequate water supply, the famous hydraulic engineer Guo Shoujing (1231–1316) designed a canal that brought water from the mountains in the west. Then, to improve communications and increase trade, he designed another canal that extended to eastern China's Great Canal.

About 100 years after the Mongolians settled Beijing, they suffered a devastating attack by rebels from the south. Originally nomadic, the Mongolians had softened with the ease of city life and were easily overwhelmed by the rebel coalition, which drove out the emperor and wrecked Beijing, thus ending the Yuan Dynasty. The southern roots of the quickly unified Ming Dynasty (1368–1644) deprived Beijing of its capital status for a half century. But in 1405, the third Ming emperor, Yongle, began construction on a magnificent new palace in Beijing; 16 years later, he relocated his court there. In the interim, the emperor had mobilized 200,000 corvée laborers to build his new palace, an enormous maze of interlinking halls, gates, and courtyard homes, known as the Forbidden City. The city was further embellished with the stately Bell and Drum Towers.

The Ming also contributed mightily to China's grandest public works project: the Great Wall. The Ming Great Wall linked or reinforced several existing walls, especially near the capital, and traversed seemingly impassable mountains. Most of the most spectacular stretches of the wall that can be visited near Beijing were built by the Ming. But wall-building drained Ming coffers and in the end failed to prevent Manchu horsemen from taking the capital—and China—in 1644.

This foreign dynasty, the Qing, inherited the Ming palaces, built their own retreats (most notably, the Old and New Summer palaces), and perpetuated feudalism in China for another 267 years. In its

decline, the Qing proved impotent to stop humiliating foreign encroachment. It lost the first Opium War to Great Britain in 1842 and was forced to cede Hong Kong "in perpetuity" as a result. In 1860 a combined British and French force stormed Beijing and razed the Old Summer Palace.

After the Qing crumbled in 1911, its successor, Sun Yat-sen's Nationalist Party, struggled to consolidate power. Beijing became a cauldron of social activism. On May 4, 1919, students marched on Tiananmen Square to protest humiliations in Versailles, where Allied commanders negotiating an end to World War I gave Germany's extraterritorial holdings in China to Japan, not Sun's infant republic. Patriotism intensified. In 1937 Japanese imperial armies stormed across Beijing's Marco Polo Bridge to launch a brutal eight-year occupation. Civil war followed close on the heels of Tokyo's 1945 surrender and raged until the Communist victory. Chairman Mao himself declared the founding of a new nation, the People's Republic of China, from the rostrum atop the Gate of Heavenly Peace on October 1, 1949.

Like Emperor Yongle, Mao built a capital that conformed to his own vision. Soviet-inspired institutions rose up around—and in—Tiananmen Square. Beijing's city wall was demolished to make way for a ring road. Temples were torn down, closed, or turned into factories during the 1966–76 Cultural Revolution.

In more recent years the city has suffered most, ironically, from prosperity. Many ancient neighborhoods have been bulldozed to make room for a new city of glitzy commercial developments. Preservationism has slowly begun to take hold, but *chai* (to pull down) and *qian* (to move elsewhere) remain common threats to historic neighborhoods.

Today, Beijing's 15-million official residents—including 3-million migrant workers—enjoy a fascinating mix of old and new. Early morning *taiqi* (tai chi) enthusiasts, ballroom and disco dancers, old men with caged songbirds, and amateur Beijing opera crooners frequent the city's many parks. Cyclists clog the roadways, competing for space on the city's thoroughfares, the result of the steadily increasing number of affluent people who are fast becoming car owners. Beijing traffic has gone from nonexistent to nightmarish in less than a decade.

As the seat of China's immense national bureaucracy, Beijing still carries a political charge. The Communist Party, whose self-described goal is "a dictatorship of the proletariat," has yet to relinquish its political monopoly. In 1989 student protesters in Tiananmen Square dared to challenge the party. The government's brutal response remains etched in global memory. Nearly 20 years later, secret police still mingle with tourists and kite fliers on the square. Mao-style propaganda persists. Slogans that preach unity among China's national minorities and patriotism still festoon the city on occasion. Yet as Beijing's robust economy is boosted even further by the massive influx of investment prompted by the 2008 Olympics, such campaigns appear increasingly out of touch with the cell-phone-primed generation. The result is an incongruous mixture of new prosperity and throwback politics: socialist slogans adorn shopping centers selling Gucci and Big Macs. Beijing is truly a land of opposites where the ancient and the sparkling new collide.

FABULOUS FESTIVALS

The majority of China's holidays and festivals are calculated according to the lunar calendar and can vary by as much as a few weeks from year to year. Check a lunar calendar or with the China International Travel Service for dates more specific than those below.

Chinese New Year, China's most celebrated and important holiday, follows the lunar calendar and falls between mid-January to mid-February. Also called Spring Festival, it gives the Chinese an official three-day—or longer—holiday to visit family and relatives, eat special meals, and set off firecrackers to celebrate the New Year and its respective Chinese zodiac animal. Students and teachers get up to four weeks off, and some factory workers don't have to work for as long as a month. ⚠ **It's a particularly crowded time to travel in China.** Many offices and services reduce their hours or close altogether.

The **Spring Lantern Festival** marks the end of the Chinese New Year on the 15th day of the first moon.

Not so much a holiday as a day of worship, **Qing Ming** (literally, "clean and bright"), or Remembrance of the Dead, gathers relatives at the graves of the deceased on April 5th to clean the surfaces and leave fresh flowers.

Labor Day falls on May 1, and is another busy travel time, as the Chinese get a weeklong holiday from work.

The **Dragon Boat Festival,** on the fifth day of the fifth moon (falling sometime in May or June), celebrates the national hero Qu Yuan, who drowned himself in the third century in protest against the corrupt emperor. Legend has it that people attempted to rescue him by throwing rice dumplings wrapped in bamboo leaves into the river and frightening fish away by beating drums. Today crews in narrow dragon boats race to the beat of heavy drums, and rice wrapped in bamboo leaves is consumed.

On October 1st, **National Day** celebrates the founding of the People's Republic of China. Tiananmen Square fills up with a hefty crowd of visitors on this official holiday. This is a weeklong holiday, and the city fills with domestic tourists from around the country.

Mid-Autumn Festival is celebrated on the 15th day of the eighth moon, which generally falls in mid-September to mid-October. The Chinese spend this time gazing at the full moon and exchanging tasty moon cakes (so named because they resemble the full moon) filled with meat, red-bean paste, lotus paste, salted egg, date paste, and other delectable surprises.

WESTERN INFLUENCE

Christmas and New Year's Day are becoming good excuses for the Chinese to exchange cards, buy colorful decorations (made in China), and eat out banquet style, too.

THE 2008 OLYMPIC GAMES

Beijing is undergoing a major makeover as it prepares to host the 2008 Summer Olympics: just about everywhere you look, you'll find feverish activity. Whole city blocks have been razed to make way for state-of-the-art Olympic venues, new hotels, and modern buildings. Subway lines are being expanded, including a welcome new line that will link downtown Beijing with the airport; overpasses are being built seemingly overnight; and roads are being widened. Furthermore, the Capital International Airport, already badly strained by the large number of passengers passing through, is working on a major expansion.

Some 2½ million visitors, including 500,000 foreigners and 20,000 journalists, are expected to descend on the Chinese capital in 2008, and the Chinese are determined to put on the best games ever. The government moved so fast to complete Olympic structures that the International Olympic Committee (IOC) actually had to ask them to slow down. IOC officials were afraid the high-tech sporting venues would lose some of their luster before the August 8, 2008, opening ceremony rolls around.

The projects, many designed by top international architects, are impressive to say the least. Twelve brand-new Olympic venues are being built from scratch, with another 11 existing structures being renovated. All will be ready in time for the Olympic trial runs. Check out ⊕ en.beijing2008.com for more details.

The Mascots, Fanfare & Anticipation

Bringing the Olympics to Beijing is not just about new sports venues and quickly changing urban infrastructure. The Olympic mascots are on sale around the country, with Olympic officials determined to keep them out of the counterfeit stands at the Silk Alley Market. According to the Olympic Web site, the five mascots embody the natural characteristics of four of China's most popular animals—the Fish, the Panda, the Tibetan Antelope, the Swallow—and the Olympic flame.

A plan has been approved that will see the Olympic Torch pass through all 31 provinces, municipalities, and autonomous regions, as well as Hong Kong and Macao. It will then make its way to the top of Mt. Everest.

Efforts are also being made to reduce the serious pollution that grips the city. Wang Wei, secretary general of the Beijing Organizing Group for the Games, says that Beijing's environment has improved, explaining that "blue sky" days in Beijing accounted for 64.1% of the days in 2005, up 15.7% from 2000.

The city's Communist Party secretary has promised to "re-educate" people who cheer and jeer players at sporting events. To raise Beijing's "civility" level, Secretary Liu Qi will crack down on people who use *jing ma*, a Chinese phrase loosely translated as "Beijing cursing." It's said there's even a

---

WEATHER WOES

The government is even trying to deal with a problem of weather. Officials are hard at work on a project that they say could delay or push away rain clouds that might disrupt the Games. What may prove to be much more difficult, however, is changing people's behavior, another stated goal of the Olympic organizers.

THE 2008 OLYMPIC GAMES

big push to discourage the habit of spitting. Millions of brochures are being distributed to convince citizens that the habit is unhygienic. Anyone found expectorating on the sidewalk will either have to clean up after himself or cough up a Y50 fine.

The Olympics will have an enormous impact on Chinese society—some say spurring the development of rule of law, government efficiency, and legislation. There is certainly hope that it will give the Chinese more opportunities to have international exchanges with the rest of the world. "China is on a fast track of development toward modernization," Wang Wei said, "and the Olympic Games will act as a catalyst." (Source for quote: ChinaDaily.com.cn)

Growing Up: Beijing Under Construction

The skyline of Beijing is famously flat—except for the forest of cranes busily rising above the remnants of traditional hutong neighborhoods. Some say that since Beijing won its bid to host the 2008 Olympics, "the world's largest construction site" has quickly become a rowdy playground for international architects who have shown little regard for traditional Chinese design. Others predict that Beijing will be the scene of a brash, breathtaking architecture that will further open the country—and the world's eyes.

Beijing Capital Airport, Terminal 3

With its lantern-red roof shaped like a dragon, Beijing's airport expansion embraces traditional Chinese motifs with a 21st-century twist: its architect calls it the "world's largest and most advanced airport building." And with a team of 50,000 con-struction workers sweating since 2004, it promises to be the world's fastest built, too. Scheduled to open late 2007.

Address: Beijing Capital Airport

Architect: Norman Foster, the preeminent British architect responsible for Hong Kong's widely respected airport

Beijing Linked Hybrid

With 700 apartments in eight bridge-linked towers surrounding a plethora of shopping and cultural options, the Linked Hybrid has been applauded for parting from the sterility of typical Chinese housing. The elegant complex also features an impressive set of green credentials such as geothermal heating and a waste-water recycling system.

Address: Adjacent to the northeast corner of the Second Ring Road

Architects: New York–based Steven Holl, who won awards for his Museum of Contemporary Art in Helsinki, Finland, and Li Hu, who helped design China's first contemporary museum in Nanjing

CCTV (Central Chinese Television) Tower

The most remarkable of China's new architecture, China's new central television headquarters twists the idea of a skyscraper quite literally into a 40-story-tall gravity-defying loop. What some have called the world's most complex building may also be, at $750 million, the world's priciest. An accompanying cultural center will include a hotel, a visitor center, and a public theater. Scheduled to open summer 2008.

Address: 32 Dong San Huan Zhong Lu (32 East Third Ring Middle Road)

Architects: Rem Koolhaas (a Dutch mastermind known for his outlandish ideas and successful Seattle Public Library) and Ole Scheeren (Koolhaas's thirty-something German protégé)

National Stadium ("Bird's Nest")

Though its exterior lattice structure is said to resemble the twigs of a nest, the 42,000 tons of steel bending around its center make this 80,000-seat stadium look more like a Martian mothership. It must be seen to be believed. Scheduled to open summer 2008.

Address: Beijing Olympic Park at Bei Si Huan Lu (North Fourth Ring Road).

Architects: Herzog and de Meuron of Switzerland, who won the prestigious Pritzker Prize for work at London's Tate Modern and the Ricola Marketing Building in Laufen, Switzerland

---

GOT PLANS?

To see models of these buildings and others—and to see Beijing as it will look in 2008—stop by the **Beijing Urban Planning Museum** (✉ 20 East Qianmen, Chongwen District ☎ 0 10/6702-4559 ⊙ Tues.-Sun. 9-4 🚇 Y30). You can't (and shouldn't) miss the centerpiece, an impressive 1:750 scale model of the city.

National Swimming Center ("the Watercube")

The translucent skin and hexagonal hi-tech "pillows" that define this 17,000-seat stadium create the impression of a building fashioned entirely out of bubbles. The structure is based on the premise that bubbles are the most effective way to divide a three-dimensional space—and they help keep the building earthquake proof.

Address: Beijing Olympic Park

Architects: PTW, the Australian firm that cut its teeth on venues for the 2000 Games in Sydney

Grand National Theater ("the Egg")

Like the so-called Bird's Nest, "the Egg," as this bulbous glass-draped opera house is called, might cause passersby to think yet another spaceship has landed in the capital—this one near Tiananmen Square. Indeed, its close proximity to the Forbidden City and the Monument to the People's Heroes coupled with its un–feng shui design and soaring costs ($324.6 million) have earned it the sort of hostile welcome reserved for an alien invasion.

Address: Xi Chang'an Jie (just west of Tiananmen Square)

Architect: French-born Paul Andreu, who designed the groundbreaking Terminal 1 of Paris's Charles de Gaulle airport in 1974.

–Alex Pasternack & Paul Mooney

21ST ★ CENTURY CHINA

Since the late 1970s, China and its billion-plus population have been moving from a centrally planned socialist economy to a market-oriented consumer society on a scale and at a speed unparalleled in history.

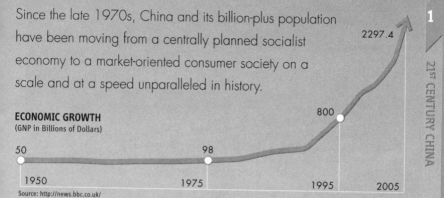

ECONOMIC GROWTH
(GNP in Billions of Dollars)

2297.4

800

50

98

1950

1975

1995

2005

Source: http://news.bbc.co.uk/

开利空调

Carrier

SHANGHAI

BEIJING

A Chinese Century?

The SARS hiccup aside, China's economy has been red hot since joining the World Trade Organization in 2001. One of the engines driving the global economy, it helped revive Japan's sagging economy and the slumping international shipping industry. Worldwide commodities markets have also been boosted by China's increasing hunger for everything from copper to coffee.

The country that was long written off as just a cheap exporter is now a net importer. It's the fourth-largest economy in the world after the United States, Japan, and Germany, whose economies are growing at less than half the rate.

Such development is nothing short of remarkable, but national problems such as energy, the environment, and wealth inequality are threatening the country.

Internationally, it's how China and the United States cooperate on global issues, and how they manage their own complex relationship, that may have the greatest impact on the rest of the century. Since Nixon first opened the door in 1972, the two countries have managed to forge a working relationship. But Yuan revaluation, trade issues, energy supply (especially oil), and both countries' military role in the Asia-Pacific region are all issues that could sour this budding friendship.

GDP-ANNUAL GROWTH RATE

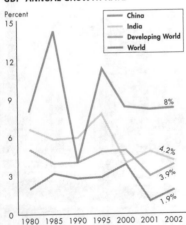

Percent

- China
- India
- Developing World
- World

15

12

9

8%

6

4.2%

3

3.9%

1.9%

0

1980 1985 1990 1995 2000 2001 2002

Source: World Bank/Earth Trends

(top) Architectural stars (or starchitects) like Rem Koolhaas, Li Hu, Paul Andreu, and Jacques Herzog and Pierre de Meuron (Olympic Stadium, above) are descending on Beijing for construction of state-of-the-art Olympic venues. (right) Hong Kong skyline.

HONG KONG

Fueling the Chinese Dream

China is now the number two energy consumer in the world, after the United States. Its consumption has exploded by an average of 5% yearly since 1998. This thirst for fuel is evident on roads all over the country. The land of the bicycle is now car-crazy. Three million vehicles were recently sold, and higher sales are predicted in the coming years.

Back in 2005, the country consumed 320 million tons of crude oil, roughly one-third of which was imported. It's expecting to import 500 million tons by 2020, two-thirds of its projected total imports.

Where will China get this oil? Much comes from countries with troubled relations with the west such as Iran and Sudan, but it is also working on importing more from traditional U.S. suppliers such as Saudi Arabia.

There's also a growing demand for electricity, 75% of which comes from coal. In the coming 25 years, the greenhouse gases produced by China's coal burning will probably exceed that of all industrial nations combined. And the country will continue to rely on coal for electricity in the years to come, despite large hydropower projects and a plan to increase the number of nuclear power plants.

Aside from developing clean, renewable energy sources, China needs to improve its poor energy efficiency—it uses nine times the energy Japan does to produce one GDP unit. But plans are being made to improve energy efficiency by 20% from 2006 to 2010.

WORLD OIL CONSUMPTION

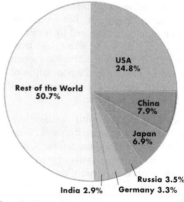

USA 24.8%

Rest of the World 50.7%

China 7.9%

Japan 6.9%

Russia 3.5%

Germany 3.3%

India 2.9%

Source: http://www.nationmaster.com/

Can China Go Green?

A devastated environment is a major result of China's economic transformation. For example, because of deforestation around the capital, Beijing is threatened by the encroaching Gobi Desert, which dumped 300,000 tons of sand on the city in one week in 2006. Industrial carelessness and lack of regulation result in accidents such as the 50-mile benzene spill in a river near Harbin in late 2005.

Cities have been smoggy for decades because of pollution from factories, vehicles, and especially coal. But air quality is now becoming obscured by water issues. In mid-2006, the Water Resources Ministry reported that 320 million urban residents—more than the population of the United States—did not have access to clean drinking water.

Much of this is the result of a development-at-any-cost mentality, particularly in the wake of economic reform. Companies and factories, many of which are foreign-owned, have only recently had to deal with environmental laws— "scoff laws"—that are often circumvented by

bribing local officials. And average citizens don't have freedom of speech or access to political tools to fight environmentally damaging projects.

Is the central government waking up? In 2006, the vice-chairman of China's increasingly outspoken State Environmental Protection Agency put it bluntly: "We will face tremendous problems if we do not change our development patterns."

Mind the Gap

China has come a long way from the days when everyone had an "iron rice bowl," or a state-appointed job that was basically guaranteed regardless of one's abilities or work performance.

Since 1980, the country has quadrupled per capita income and raised more than 220 million of its citizens out of poverty. A belt of prosperity is emerging along the coast, but hundreds of millions still live on less than $1 per day.

(left) Owning a car is the new Chinese dream. (top right) The Three Gorges Dam will be the largest in the world, supplying the hydroelectric power of 18 nuclear plants. (bottom right) China's cities are some of the most polluted in the world.

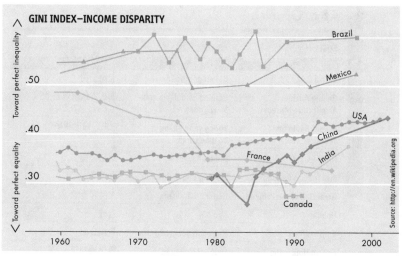

GINI INDEX—INCOME DISPARITY

Toward perfect inequality ∧

.50

.40

.30

Toward perfect equality ∨

Brazil
Mexico
USA
China
France
India
Canada

1960   1970   1980   1990   2000

Source: http://en.wikipedia.org

Economists use a statistical yardstick known as the Gini coefficient to measure wealth inequality in a society, with zero being perfect equality and one being perfect inequality. The World Bank estimates that China's national Gini coefficient rose from 0.30 to 0.45 from 1982, a 50% jump in two decades. In 2006, some academics estimated China's current Gini coefficient to be closer to, or even higher, than Latin America's 0.52.

As economic inequality has grown, so has discontent, particularly in rural areas. The country recorded 87,000 public protests in 2005, an increase of 11,000 over the year before.

Many of these protests are incited by the acts of local, particularly rural, officials whose corruption policies are sometimes beyond Beijing's sphere of influence.

Most protests are focused on specific incidents or officials rather than general dissent against the government, but the growing frequency of such events is not going unnoticed by the central government. In 2005, 8,400 officials were arrested on corruption-related charges.

CHINA IN NUMBERS

	CHINA	U.S.
Area in sq km:	9,560,960	9,631,420
Population	1.3 bil	300 mil
Men (15–64 yrs)	482 mil	100 mil
Women (15–64 yrs)	456 mil	101 mil
Population growth	0.59%	0.91%
Life expectancy: men	70.8	75
Life expectancy: women	74.6	80.8
GDP per head	$1,090	$37,240
Health spending, % GDP	5.8	14.6
Doctors per 1000 pop.	1.6	2.8
Hospital beds per 1000 pop.	1.6	3.0
Infant mortality rate per 1000 births	23.12	6.43
Education spending, % GDP	2.1	5.7
Adult literacy: men	95.1%	99%
Adult literacy: women	86.5%	99%
Internet users	111 mil	204 mil

At a Glance

ENGLISH	PINYIN	CHINESE CHARACTERS
POINTS OF INTEREST		
Beihai Park	Běihǎi gōngyuán	北海公园
Beijing Ancient Architecture Museum	Běi jīng gǔ dài jiàn zhù bó wù guǎn	北京古代建筑博物馆
Central Radio and Television Tower	Zhōng yāng guǎng bō diàn shì tǎ	中央广播电视塔
Ditan Park	Dìtán gōngyuán	地坛公园
Five Dragon Pavilion	wě lóng tíng	五龙亭
Great Hall of the People	Rénmín Dàhuìtáng	人民大会堂
Houhai	hòu hǎi	后海
Jingshan Park	jǐng shān gōngyuán	景山公园
Lu Xun House and Museum	Lǔ Xùn bówùguǎn	鲁迅博物馆
Mao Zedong Memorial Hall	Máo zhǔ xí jì nìan táng	毛主席纪念堂
Museum of Antique Currency	gǔdài qiánbì zhǎnlǎnguǎn	古代钱币展览馆
National Museum of China	Zhōngguó guójiā bówùguǎn	中国国家博物馆
Poly Art Museum	Bǎo lì yì shù bó wù guǎn	保利艺术博物馆
Qianhai	qián hǎi	前海
Silver Ingot Bridge	yíndìng qiáo	银锭桥
Xiangshan Park	Xiāng shān gōng yuán	香山公园
Xu Beihong Memorial Museum	Xú bēi hóng jì nìan guǎn	徐悲鸿纪念馆

See corresponding chapters for more pinyin and Chinese character translations. (For example, see Chapter 3, Historical Sights, for Tiananmen Square and the Summer Palace.)

Neighborhoods

Young Beijing residents play soccer in Dongcheng's Jingshan Park.

WORD OF MOUTH

"Getting around Beijing is easy. We visited the Great Wall at Mutianyu, the Ming tombs, and the Summer Palace. We woke early and watched the raising of the flag in Tiananmen Square, then strolled to a nearby park and watched morning exercises. Don't miss the Lama Temple!"

—Marija

By Alex Miller,
Eileen Wen
Mooney &
Paul Mooney

BEIJING IS A VIBRANT JUMBLE of neighborhoods and districts. It's a city in transition: construction is rampant in preparation for the 2008 Olympics, often leveling lively old *hutongs* (alleyway neighborhoods) to make way for the glittering towers that are fast dwarfing their surroundings. Still, day-to-day life seems to pulse the lifeblood of a Beijing that once was.

Laid out like a target with ring roads revolving around a bull's eye, with **Chang'an Jie** ("Eternal Peace Street") cutting across the middle, Beijing is a bustling metropolis sprawling outward from the central point of the **Forbidden City**. The ring roads are its main arteries and, along with Chang'an Jie, you will find yourself traveling them just about anytime you go from one place to another above ground. As you explore Beijing, you'll find that taxis are often the best way to get around. However, if the subway goes where you're headed, it's often a faster option than dealing with traffic, which has become increasingly congested in recent years with the rise of private automobiles.

The city is divided into 18 municipal and suburban districts (*qu*). Only six of these districts are the central stomping grounds for most visitors; this chapter focuses on those districts. **Dongcheng** ("east district") encompasses the Forbidden City, Tiananmen Square, Wangfujing (a major shopping street), the Lama Temple, and many other historical sights dating back to imperial times. **Xicheng** ("west district"), directly west of Dongcheng, is a lovely lake district that includes Beihai Park, former playground of the imperial family, and a series of connected lakes bordered by willow trees and courtyard-lined hutongs. The southern districts include **Chongwen** in the southeast and **Xuanwu** in the southwest. These areas have some of the oldest neighborhoods in the city, and a long history of traditional folk arts, with opera theaters and acrobatic shows still staged here. The Chongwen District is also home to some of the city's most famous restaurants, some more than 100 years old. **Chaoyang** is the biggest and busiest district, occupying the areas north, east, and south of the eastern Second Ring Road. It's home to foreign embassies, multinational companies, and the newly rising Central Business District, with its gleaming skyscrapers. **Haidian**, the technology and university district, is northwest of the Third Ring Road; it's packed with shops selling electronics.

> **WORD OF MOUTH**
>
> "Don't hesitate, GO! You can easily explore without being in a tour group (hire a car out to the Great Wall and watch the sun come up). You can always get a guide at your hotel, from which, if it is downtown, you can walk to many sites. Beijing is safe, but watch your purse on buses."   –beaker

BEIJING'S SUBWAY

The subway in Beijing can be faster and cheaper than a taxi, but it's also limited. There are only four subway lines—though five more are in the works for the 2008 Olympics. **Line 1** follows Jianguo Lu, starting at Sihui Dong, and passing the China World Trade Center, Jianguomen (one of the embassy districts), the Wangfujing shopping area, Tiananmen Square, the Forbidden City, and Xidan (another major shopping location), all the way to Pingguoyuan ("Apple Orchard") in the far western suburbs. **Line 2** (the loop line) runs along a sort of circular route around the center of the city. **Line 13** is a commuter rail that runs from Dongzhimen into the northern suburbs and back down to Xizhimen in a crooked upside-down U; the **Batong Line** (also a light rail) runs from Sihui, just west of the China World Trade Center, to the eastern suburbs. ■ TIP➔ **Need a visual? Flip to the inside back cover of this book for a helpful subway map.**

If both you and your final destination are near the Second Ring Road, or on Chang'an Jie, the best way to get there is probably by subway. It stops just about every mile, and you'll easily spot the entrances (with blue subway logos) dotting the streets. Each stop is announced in both English and Chinese, and there are clearly marked signs in English or pinyin at each station. Transferring between Lines 1 and 2 is easy and free, with the standard Y3 ticket including travel between any two destinations. Tickets for Line 13 and the Batong Line are Y5, with

transfer to the subway included in this price. ■ TIP➔ **When planning a trip on Line 13, make sure you are transferring from the correct station. If your destination is on the west side of the line, leave from Xizhimen; if it's on the east side of the line, leave from Dongzhimen.**

Subway tickets can be purchased at a window either at street-entrance level, or above the steps leading down to the tracks. Just follow the crowd. People unfamiliar with travel in Beijing may find buying a ticket exasperating. There is no line; instead, people crowd around the ticket window and shove their money in. When you get to the front of the line, push your money (exact change if possible) to the attendant.

In the middle of each subway platform you'll find a map of Beijing and all its subway lines. Most subway cars also have a simplified diagram above the doors.

Trains can be very crowded, especially during rush hour, and it's not uncommon for people to push onto the train before exiting passengers can get off. The crowds also make the subway system an ideal place for pickpockets to work, so be sure to keep your money and wallet in a safe place.

⚠ Unfortunately, the subway system is not convenient for handicapped people. In some stations, there are no escalators, and sometimes the only entrance or exit is via steep steps.

DONGCHENG DISTRICT

Sightseeing:
★ ★ ★ ★

Dining:
★ ★ ★ ★

Lodging:
★ ★ ★ ★

Shopping:
★ ★ ★

Nightlife:
★ ★ ★

Dongcheng district, with its idyllic hutongs and plethora of historical sights, is one of Beijing's most pleasant areas. It's also one of the smaller districts in the city, which makes it easy to get around. A day exploring Dongcheng will leave you feeling like you've been introduced to the character of the capital. From the old men playing chess in the hutongs to the sleek, chauffeured Mercedes driving down Chang'an Jie, to the colorful shopping on Wangfujing, Dongcheng offers visitors a thousand little tastes of what makes Beijing a fascinating city.

What's Here

From **Wangfujing's** glitzy mall at **Oriental Plaza** to the incense-laden **Lama Temple** and immense **Ditan Park,** Dongcheng has plenty to offer visitors looking for closely packed Beijing thrills. The district is situated north and east of the **Forbidden City,** which is not to be missed by any first-time visitor. The great palace is fronted by **Tiananmen Square,** where you'll find **Mao Zedong's Mausoleum** along with **Monument to the People's Heroes.** Aside from its historic sites and the massive hotels and office buildings that line major thoroughfares, Dongcheng is a mostly residential district increasingly made up of shiny high-rises, whose prime real estate is obtained by tearing down ancient hutongs. Many of the sites in this district are accessible by subway, as the district is hemmed in by parts of Lines 1 and 2.

**FEELING
PECKISH?** Crunchy deep-fried scorpions are sold at the **Donghuamen Night Market,** at the northern end of Wangfujing's wide walking boulevard. We'll admit: this is more of a place to look at and perhaps photograph food rather than devour it. In addition to standard street foods, hawkers here also serve up deep-fried starfish, plus a variety of insects and other hard-to-identify food items. Most street-market food is usually safe to eat as long as it's hot. The row of interesting outdoor evening stalls here makes for an intriguing walk with great photo ops.

On the western side of the district stand the **Drum and Bell Towers,** which were an integral part of the imperial city. The Ming Dynasty Drum Tower was where 24 drums were beat to mark the night watches; at the Bell Tower, a huge brass bell was rung every evening at 7. The serene **Confucius Temple,** built in the Yuan Dynasty, contains the ancestral tablets of China's great sage as well as stones inscribed with the names of successful candidates in the imperial exams. For a short climb to a great view, go to **Jingshan Park,** just north of the Forbidden City, and hike up Coal Hill to the central pavilion for a panorama of the Forbidden City and surrounding areas.

In the evening, catch a Beijing opera performance at the **Chang'an Grand Theater.** Some say it's cacophonous, some say it's beautiful; we think it's a truly authentic Beijing experience. (To find out more, *see* "Beijing Opera" *in* Chapter 5.) Next check out **Brown's** (⇨ Chapter 5), a posh Western-style restaurant in nearby Chaoyang that turns into a bar and dance floor every evening after the kitchen closes at 10 PM. If it's late at night and you're hungry, make a beeline for **Guijie** (Ghost Street), a cheap taxi ride south of Ditan Park, with restaurant after restaurant that stays open until the wee hours. The specialty in many eateries here is spicy crawfish eaten by the hundreds.

If you have a few hours, visit **Nanxincang,** China's oldest existing granary dating back to the Yongle period (1403–24). Located on Dongsi Shitiao, it is just one block west of the Second Ring Road. This valuable historical site is now Beijing's latest entertainment venue, the new home to three art galleries, a teahouse, and several bars and restaurants.

The structures at Nanxincang—just 10 years younger than those of the Forbidden City—were among the more than 300 granaries that existed in this area during imperial days to meet the increasing demands of the capital. Have a glass of wine in the second floor of Yuefu, an audio and book shop, where you can admire the old interior, then have dinner at one of the excellent restaurants in the compound. **Sifang Jie** (☎ 010/6409–6403) specializes in dishes from southwest China. **Fanqian Fanhou** (☎ 010/6409–6510) has wonderful Taiwanese cuisine. **Rain Club** (☎ 010/6409–6922 Ⓜ Dongsi Shitiao) offers East-meets-West fusion cuisine.

GETTING ORIENTED

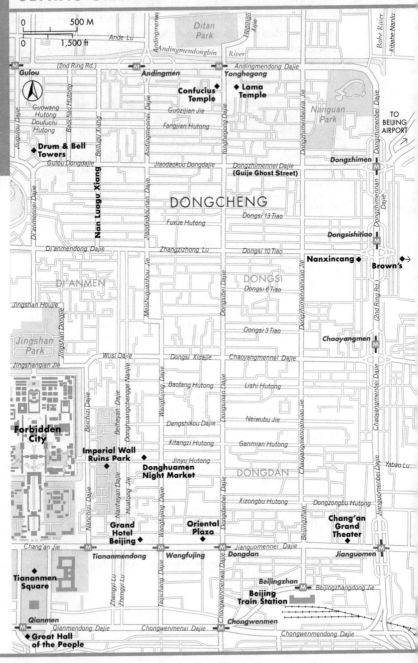

QUICK BITES

If you're feeling adventurous one evening, check out **Nan Luogu Xiang,** a beautiful old street a short ride east of Houhai, lined with boutiques, small restaurants, bars, and coffee shops. Have a cup of fresh yogurt at **Wenyu Nailao** (✉ 49 Nan Luogu Xiang ☎ 010/6405-7621), which makes its yogurt the traditional Chinese way.

For a nighttime-munchies cure, head to **Guijie** (Ghost Street), which is full of restaurants serving up every Chinese specialty, from noodles to hotpot to fried delights. One of the most popular dishes here is *malaxia*, or spicy crawfish.

In Wangfujing and looking for something good and quick to eat? Check out **Shun Yi Fu** (✉ 2 Xila Hutong, Wangfu-jing ☎ 010/6525-1360 Ⓜ Wangfujing), which serves about a dozen different types of boiled and fried dumplings.

NEIGHBORHOOD TOP 5

1. Explore the wonders of the **Forbidden City** and **Tiananmen Square.** Then climb the hill in **Jingshan Park** for a view of the golden rooftops of the Forbidden City.

2. Visit the **Lama Temple,** Beijing's most famous Tibetan Buddhist temple, then the **Confucius Temple;** finally, cross the street for a stroll through **Ditan Park.**

3. Have dinner in the renovated courtyard of **The Source** (⇨ Chapter 6), then walk to **Nan Luogu Xiang,** one of the city's best hutongs.

4. Walk up **Wangfujing,** Beijing's premier shopping spot, and check out the shops at **Oriental Plaza.**

5. Walk along the well-landscaped **Imperial Wall Ruins Park,** on Nan Heyan Dajie (one block north of the street that runs along the west side of the Grand Hotel).

GETTING HERE

Dongcheng is easily accessible by subway, with stops along most of its perimeter: Tiananmen to Jian-guomen on Line 1 forms the south side of this district; Jianguomen to Andingmen on Line 2 forms the district's north and east sides. Line 2 stops at the Lama Temple, the Ancient Observatory, Wangfujing, and Tiananmen Square. Taxi travel during peak hours (7 to 9 AM and 4 to 7 PM) is difficult. At other times, traveling by taxi is affordable, convenient, and the fastest option (especially at noon, when much of the city is at lunch, and after 10 PM). Renting a bike to see the sites is also a good option. ⚠ **If you do rent a bike, be extremely cautious of traffic.** Bus travel within the city, especially during rush hours, is laborious and should be avoided unless you speak or read Chinese.

MAKING THE MOST OF YOUR TIME

Most of Dongcheng can be seen in a day, but it's best to set aside two, because the **Forbidden City** and **Tiananmen Square** will likely take the better part of one day. The climb up Coal Hill (also called Prospect Hill) in **Jingshan Park** will take about 20 minutes for an average walker. From there, hop a taxi to the **Lama Temple,** which is worth a good two hours, then visit the nearby **Confucius Temple.** Finally, take a peaceful stroll around **Ditan Park** before dinner.

XICHENG DISTRICT

Sightseeing:
★ ★

Dining:
★ ★ ★

Lodging:
★

Shopping:
★

Nightlife:
★ ★ ★

Xicheng district is home to an eclectic mix of a few of Beijing's favorite things: delicious food, venerable hutongs and old courtyard houses, charming lakes, and engaging nightlife. The lakes at Shichahai are fun for all ages, both day and night. Take a boat ride on the lake in the warmer months, or ice skate here in the cold winter months when the lakes are crowded with parents taking their children out for a day of fun.

Our top experience? Taking a walk or bicycle tour of the surrounding hutongs: there is no better way to scratch the surface of this sprawling city (before it disappears!) than by exploring the hutongs lined by courtyard houses. Wander in and out of historical sites in the area, such as Prince Gong's palace, the courtyard house of famed opera legend Mei Lanfang (*see* "Beijing Opera" *in* Chapter 5), and the Drum and Bell Towers (which fall right between Dongcheng and Xicheng). In the evening, find a table at a restaurant or bar with a view of the lake.

Snapshot

Time seems to be standing still in the Yangfang Hutong. A street stand sells steamed meat buns beside a parked cart piled high with watermelons. Peddlers shout out while, at the corner, boys crowd around a hawker with dozens of small woven baskets the size of plums. Inside are crickets. A gaggle of grandmothers sit on short stools nearby, some holding grandchildren, others snoozing in the sun. One woman hangs her thick cotton blanket to air out. Pedicabs glide by, on constant prowl for passengers. Along the lake, elderly men are absorbed in the same pastimes that their ancestors enjoyed a century ago. One group, sitting beneath a willow tree, is playing Chinese chess, another mah-jongg—the sound of clicking tiles can be heard long before you reach the spot. Elsewhere, a group of men admire birds perched in cages hanging from trees.

What's Here

The district to the north and west of the Forbidden City, Xicheng is a natural hop, skip, and a jump from Dongcheng. **Shichahai**, a collection of lakes, comprises Xicheng's foremost attractions. Shichahai's southernmost lake, **Nanhai** ("south lake") is just west of Tiananmen Square; **Zhonghai** ("middle lake") is north of Nanhai and due west of the Forbidden City; and **Beihai** ("north lake") is located in Beihai Park, north of Zhonghai. Beihai Park was once an imperial playground: it's a well-kept, landscaped attraction featuring classic imperial gardens and murky lotus-flower-filled waters traversed by walkways of intricate woodwork. The structures are great examples of classical Chinese architecture, with rounded doorways and sloping tiled roofs.

To the north of Beihai is **Qianhai** ("front lake"). ■ TIP→ **Cross Di'anmen Xi Dajie and you will be at the entrance to the Qianhai and Houhai area, where you can easily arrange a pedicab hutong tour.** **Houhai** ("rear lake") is a commercialized yet wonderful lake surrounded by chic and cheap bars, good restaurants, and tempting shops. **Soong Ching-ling's former residence** (a lovely spot once inhabited by the wife of the father of modern China, Sun Yat-sen) is on the northeastern side of **Houhai**. The ancient **Drum and Bell Towers** are just southeast of there.

Xicheng's other main attraction is **Xidan**, an area full of shopping malls and boutiques selling clothing and accessories. There is also **Tushu Dasha** (aka Beijing Book Building), said to be the biggest bookstore in China, which has a small selection of English books in the basement. Xidan is easily accessible by the Line 1 subway (get off at the Xidan stop).

A GOOD TOUR

Start just north of the Forbidden City at **Jingshan Park**. From here you can walk several blocks west to **Beihai Park**, which is particularly beautiful during August's lotus season. Exit at the north gate; after crossing Di'anmen Xi Dajie, you'll arrive at **Qianhai**, or "front lake."

Walk on the right, or east, side of the lake for about 10 minutes until you reach the famous Ming Dynasty **Silver Ingot Bridge**. Take a side trip to the **Bell Tower**, which is a short walk northeast of the bridge. (To get there, head down Yandai Xiejie, turn left at the end and you'll see the tower. Directly behind it is the Drum Tower.) Return to the Silver Ingot Bridge and follow the lake's northern shore until you arrive at **Soong Ching-ling's Former Residence**. Next, take a short cab ride to **Prince Gong's Palace** behind the opposite side of the lake, to see how imperial relatives once lived. An alternative to those lavish interiors is the **Museum of Antique Currency**, where you can feast your eyes on rare Chinese coins.

GETTING ORIENTED

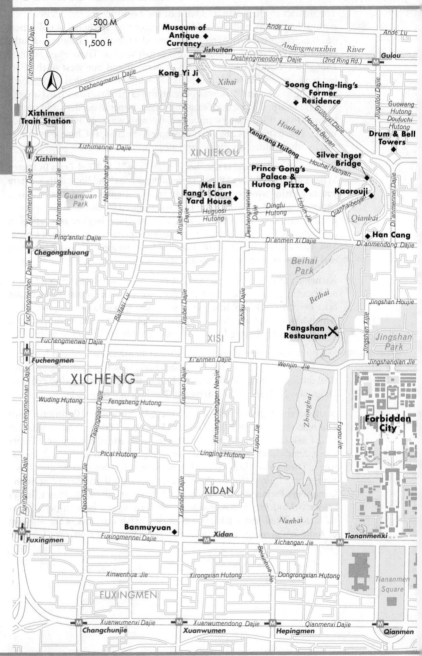

MAKING THE MOST OF YOUR TIME

Xicheng's sites are few but special. Walk around **Beihai Park** in the early afternoon. When you get tired either retire to one of Houhai's many cafés or take a pedicab hutong tour. If you come to Beijing in the winter, **Qianhai** will be frozen and you can rent skates or, the local favorite, a chair with runners welded to the bottom and a pair of metal sticks with which to propel yourself—quite a sport. Dinner along the shores of **Houhai** is a great option—stick around into the evening to enjoy the booming bar scene. Plan to spend a few hours shopping at **Xidan** on your last day in Beijing; this is great place to pick up funky, cheap gifts.

QUICK BITES

The shores of Houhai and Qianhai are lined with great restaurants. Try **Kong Yi Ji** (✉ Deshengmennei Dajie ☎ 010/6404-0507), named after a story by famous writer Lu Xun, which serves some of the dishes mentioned in the story.

Rustic **Han Cang** (☎ 010/6404-2259) specializes in the hearty dishes of the Hakkas, or China's Guest People. It's located at the southeast corner of Qianhai, on the east side of the lake just two minutes north of Di'anmen Xi Dajie, with a great view of the lake from the second floor.

Hutong Pizza (✉ 9 Yindingqiao Hutong ☎ 010/6617-5916) is a great choice for a quick bite. It's located in a renovated courtyard house just west of the Silver Ingot Bridge.

For a simple meal in the Xidan area, try **Banmuyuan** (✉ 45 Fuxingmen Nei Dajie ☎ 010/5851-8208 Ⓜ Xidan), a Taiwan-owned restaurant that serves chewy *zhajiang* noodles, tasty beef, and vegetarian pies. It's located directly behind the Bank of China headquarters (which was designed by I. M. Pei).

GETTING HERE

The Line 1 subway stops include Tiananmen, Xidan, and Fuxingmen while Line 2 makes stops from Fuxingmen to the Drum Tower (Gulou), following Xicheng's perimeter. Xizhimen is a major terminus with access to the northwest via subway. ■ TIP➔ **Shichahai and Beihai Park are more conveniently reached by taxi.**

NEIGHBORHOOD TOP 5

1. Sipping coffee or an evening cocktail lakeside at **Houhai** or on one of the rooftop restaurants or bars overlooking the lake.

2. Exploring Houhai's preserved hutongs and historical sights by pedicab or bicycle.

3. Skating on **Houhai Lake** in winter or, in the warmer months, taking an evening boat tour of the lake, dining on board on barbecued lamb provided by **Kaorouji** (✉ 14 Qianhai Dongyan, just southeast of the Silver Ingot Bridge ☎ 010/6404-2554), an old lakeside restaurant. Romantics, take note: you'll be serenaded by your own personal *pipa* musician.

4. Wandering the hills and temples of historic Beihai Park. In the evening, eat the way the emperors did with an imperial banquet at **Fangshan Restaurant** (⇨ Chapter 6) in the park.

5. Shopping for great gifts and snazzy clothes on the cheap at **Xidan.**

SOUTHERN DISTRICTS: CHONGWEN & XUANWU

Sightseeing:
★ ★ ★ ★

Dining:
★ ★

Lodging:
★

Shopping:
★ ★ ★

Nightlife:
★

Life in the southern part of Beijing has a completely different rhythm. The sights in this part of town are ancient reminders of the Beijing that once was—a more religious and artistically inspired Beijing, a Beijing as rich in culture and history as it was rich in resources and political power. This area is crowded with small shops, European architecture, opera and acrobatic theaters, and street performers and magicians. A lazy stroll through Source of Law Temple or Liulichang on a quiet afternoon is sure to remind you of the city's past.

Snapshot

Dazhalan, a street and neighborhood in Xuanwu, immediately southwest of the Forbidden City, is packed with people, cars, and bicycles—each competing for the limited space on its narrow streets, already crowded with hawkers' stands and overflowing restaurants. Dive into the hutong and you are immediately rubbing elbows with the masses. Many *laozihao,* or old brand-name shops, continue to do a booming business here. The **Ruifuxiang Silk Shop** (⊠ 5 Dazhalan Dajie ☎ 010/ 6303–5313), established in 1893, has thick bolts of silk, cotton, cashmere, and wool piled high, in more colors than you'll find in a box of crayons: chartreuse, candy-pink, chocolate brown, fresh-cut-grass green—you name it. Clerks deftly cut yards of cloth while tailors take measurements for colorful *qipaos* (traditional gowns). In this corner of Beijing, life seems to continue much as it did a century ago.

What's Here

South of the Forbidden City, the Chongwen and Xuanwu districts occupy the area enclosed by the Second Ring Road and Chang'an Jie. **Qianmen Dajie** (a walking street) runs north–south from Qianmen ("Front Gate") at Tiananmen Square, separating the two districts. Rich in history, these two districts have many great temples and historical sites, as well as some pleasant streets for strolling. The ancient, breathtaking **Temple of Heaven**, which has wonderful examples of traditional imperial architecture, is a must-visit for first timers to Beijing. The **Source of Law Temple** is a peaceful old Zen temple that's still operational. **Ox Street** and the **Niujie Mosque** are just about all that remains of Beijing's old Muslim neighborhoods, which have been torn down to make way for development.

MUSLIM QUARTER

Recent urban renewal has wiped out much of Beijing's old Muslim Quarter, an area that dates back to the 900s. The main survivor is the Niujie (Ox Street) Mosque, which was built in 996; it is often crowded with members of Beijing's Muslim community. Like other mosques in China, the Niujie Mosque looks like a traditional Buddhist temple. The Tower for Observing the Moon and the main hall have restricted entry, and women can only visit certain areas. A few Muslim shops—mainly halal restaurants and butchers—remain in the neighborhood, which is now dominated by high-rise apartment buildings.

Liulichang is Beijing's historical art street, where the Ming- and Qing-dynasty literati used to swap stories and books. Now a bustling antiques market, Liulichang has great shopping if you're looking for Chinese art or art supplies (though it's rather crammed with tourists). The **Ming Dynasty City Wall Ruins Park**, which follows Chongwenmen Dong Dajie, makes for an enlightening walk. This rebuilt section of Beijing's grand old inner city wall was reconstructed with the original bricks returned by Beijing residents who had taken them to build their own structures when the city wall was torn down in the 1960s. It's a well-lit area, flanked by a wide strip of grass with paths full of city residents walking dogs, flying kites, and practicing tai chi. The eastern terminus is the imposing **Dongbianmen Watchtower**, which houses several art galleries.

> ### WORD OF MOUTH
>
> "You can have chops [decorated, carved stamps] made at shops along Liulichang, as well as at many other tourist sites. They can be carved in a very short time, usually while you are shopping, and they also usually have premade chops with symbols such as happiness, wealth, and good health."   —Cicerone

GETTING ORIENTED

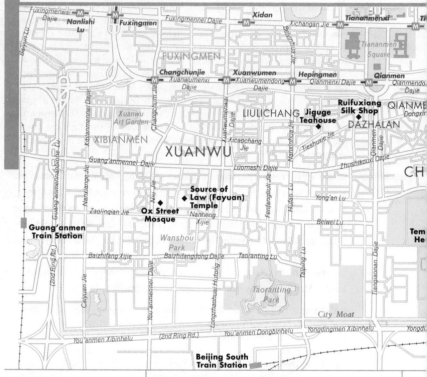

The southern portion of the Line 2 subway runs across the northern fringe of the southern district, making stops at Chongwenmen, Qianmen, Hepingmen, Xuanwumen, Changchun Jie, and Xidan.

For destinations in the south of Chongwen and Xuanwu, it's advisable to take a taxi as things are a bit more spread out and it may be hard to find your way on foot.

The southern districts of Beijing have some great attractions beyond the major players like the **Temple of Heaven.** **Liulichang** is renowned for paintings and Chinese art supplies; it's worth spending a few hours browsing here. The **Source of Law Temple** and the **Niujie Mosque** are laid-back, interesting temples; a trip to one makes visiting the other quite easy, as they are very close together. Visiting the reconstructed **Ming Dynasty City Wall Ruins** makes for a pleasant stroll before dinner.

"In Beijing, both Liulichang and Wangfujing have some interesting shopping. However, more and more of the old buildings are being torn down. Of the two Liulichang is probably more charming. I assume you will be doing a tour of the old hutongs and Bell/Drum towers. That is one of the best ways to see the old Beijing." —Cicerone

2

QUICK BITES

Old shops line the sides of Liulichang, where high-rises are juxtaposed with ancient courtyards and teahouses.

You can get a bowl of noodles and a cup of tea upstairs at the **Jiguge Teahouse** (✉ 136 Liulichang Dong Jie 136 ☎ 010/6301–7846), next to the stone pedestrian bridge. Every nonvegetarian visitor to the city should sample Beijing duck at least once during their trip.

Though it's not the most well known spot, **Li Qun Roast Duck Restaurant** (⇨ Chapter 6) has the most succulent, tasty duck around; it's located in an old courtyard house and has interesting 1950s decor.

NEIGHBORHOOD TOP 5

1. Exploring the sprawling grounds of the **Temple of Heaven**.

2. Checking out the old art supply shops and galleries at **Liulichang**.

3. Walking down Ox Street with a visit to the **Niujie Mosque** and the **Source of Law Temple**.

4. A walk along the rebuilt section of the **Ming Dynasty City Wall Ruins** along Chongwenmen Dajie and a visit to the **Red Gate Gallery** in the Dongbianmen Watch Tower.

5. Eating Beijing duck and other toothsome treats at one of the many restaurants around **Qianmen**.

CHAOYANG DISTRICT

Sightseeing:
★

Dining:
★ ★ ★ ★

Lodging:
★ ★ ★ ★

Shopping:
★ ★ ★ ★

Nightlife:
★ ★ ★ ★

Chaoyang is where you'll find a lot of the action in Beijing: the nightlife in this district is positively sizzling. The bars and clubs are vibrant and full of Chinese office workers and university students as well as foreigners including expats, English teachers, and embassy staff. During the day, all these people work in this area, as it's home to the Central Business District (CBD), as well as the embassies and the residences of the people who run Beijing's portion of the global economy.

Snapshot

A steady stream of Beijing's beautiful people passes through the north gate of the **Workers' Stadium,** drawn toward the hip-hop music that throbs from several of the bars that have displaced spaces once devoted to basketball and Ping-Pong. The crowd runs the gamut from Chinese college kids to well-heeled Beijing tycoons to Mongolian prostitutes, plus expats and foreign diplomats. Downstairs in Vics it's wall-to-wall people: drinking, dancing, or lost in conversation. A young woman, French beret pulled down over her eyes, leans against her boyfriend; an older woman straight from the society pages of Hong Kong's newspapers sips wine. There's even a Chinese Elvis, his hair defying physics to remain aloft inches into the air. Welcome to the new China.

What's Here

From shopping at **Guomao** (the World Trade Center) to partying in **Sanlitun,** Chaoyang has a little of everything. **Jianguomen** is the embassy area, with some good foreign restaurants, but mostly quiet blocks of gated embassy compounds; in the center there is lovely **Ritan Park,** with its winding paths, lotus-flower ponds, climbing wall, and even a few restaurants and bars.

If you're near Ritan Park and need a nighttime pick-me-up, check out **The Stone Boat,** located on the west side of the park alongside the lake. In a beautiful location overlooking the lake, it offers coffee, tea, juices, and mixed drinks along with some simple food. On the weekends during the warmer months, it also features local music talent. If that's not your cup of tea, try **Vics** (☎ 010/6593-6215) or **Mix** (☎ 010/6530-02889), both just inside the north gate of the Workers' Stadium.

The fast-rising **Central Business District** (CBD) encompasses the China World Trade Center and a slew of new and impressive skyscrapers, some designed by internationally known architects. One example is the new CCTV Tower. The multi-million-dollar complex will employ a continuous loop of horizontal and vertical sections, and will be the tallest skyscraper in Beijing (though several other buildings still on the drawing board could soon surpass it). Opposite the China World Trade Center is Jianwai Soho, a collection of gleaming white high-rises in a nicely laid-out complex with dozens of restaurants and shops. The jewel in the crown of the CBD is the new Beijing Yintai Centre, which includes the Park Hyatt, a 63-story, 237-room boutique hotel, condo residence, and retail complex flanked by two office buildings. The hotel's rooftop bar, designed to resemble a Chinese lantern, has dramatic views of the city.

North of Ritan Park is the **Workers' Stadium** complex, where many of the biggest visiting acts (including Britney Spears) perform. The famous Sanlitun Bar Street is several blocks east of Workers' Stadium and runs north–south; this is the area that's known for great bars catering to foreigners, expats, and young Chinese. The hottest clubs are always changing, but **Vics** and **Mix** at the north gate of the Workers' Stadium are popular places. **The World of Suzie Wong,** named after the 1957 novel by Richard Mason, and complete with stylish opium beds to lean back on with a drink, is located beside the west gate of Chaoyang Park. A few doors down is **Souk,** a laid-back restaurant with a simple but good menu serving North African and Middle Eastern snacks.

If it's shopping you're looking for, check out **Yaxiu Market** (also called Yashow Market), a former department store that's been turned into five floors of small shops mainly selling pirated products. Or head to the so-called **Silk Alley Market,** which is no longer an alley; a mall has been erected near the Yonganli subway station. There's a street of restaurants and bars growing up next to the flower market at **Nurenjie** (aka Ladies' Street). At nearby Lucky Street, there's a string of Asian, Western, and Chinese restaurants and coffee shops. Also, be sure to check out the **Panjiayuan Antique Market,** which is known for more than just antiques—it's a great place to shop for knickknacks, old books, art, posters, baskets, and gifts. For the artsy visitors, check out the **Dashanzi Art District** (aka 798 Factory), which is located in an old factory complex now full of galleries and nightlife spots.

GETTING ORIENTED

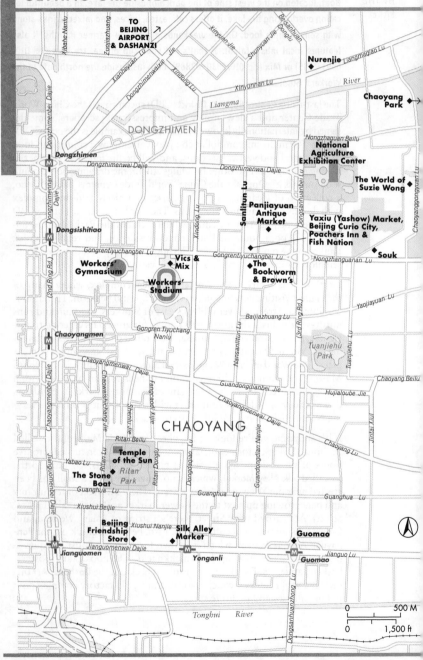

TO
BEIJING
AIRPORT
& DASHANZI

Xibahe Nanlu

Zuojiazhuang

Dongzhimennei Dajie

Xianheyuan Lu

Dongzhimenwaidie Jie

Xindong Lu

Shunyuan Jie

Xinyuan Jie

Beisanhuan Donglu

Nurenjie   Liangmaqiao Lu

Xinyunnan Lu

River

**Chaoyang
Park**

Liangma

DONGZHIMEN

Nongzhaguan Beilu

Dongzhimennan Dajie

Dongzhimennan Dajie (2nd Ring Rd.)

Dongzhimen

Dongzhimenwai Dajie

Dongzhimenwai Dajie

**National
Agriculture
Exhibition Center**

Dongsanhuanbei Lu

Chaoyanggongyuan Lu

**The World of
Suzie Wong**

Xindong Lu

Sanlitun Lu

Dongsishitiaa

**Panjiayuan
Antique
Market**

**Yaxiu (Yashow) Market,
Beijing Curio City,
Poachers Inn &
Fish Nation**

Gongrentiyuchangbei Lu

**Vics &
Mix**

Gongrentiyuchangbei Lu

Nongzhanguanan Lu

Souk

**Workers'
Gymnasium**

**Workers'
Stadium**

**The
Bookworm
& Brown's**

Yaojiayuan Lu

Gongren Tiyuchang
Nanlu

Baijiazhuang Lu

Nansantun Lu

(3rd Ring Rd.)

Tuanjiehu Lu

**Tuanjiehú
Park**

Chaoyangmen

Chaoyangmenwai Dajie

Guandongdianbei Jie

Chaoyang Beilu

Chaoyangmenbei Dajie

Chaowashichang Jie

Fangcaodi Xijie

Shenti Jie

Chaoyangmenwai Dajie

Guandongdian Nanjie

Hujialoube Jie

Jintai Xilu

Chaoyang Lu

CHAOYANG

Ritan Beilu

Ritan Donglu

Dongdaqiao Lu

Yabao Lu

**Temple
of the Sun**

**The Stone
Boat**   *Ritan
Park*

Guanghua Lu

Guanghua Lu

Guanghua Lu

Xiushui Beijie

Jianguomenbei Dajie

**Beijing
Friendship
Store**

Xiushui Nanjie

**Silk Alley
Market**

Guomao

Jianguomen

Jianguomenwai Dajie

Yonganli

Jianguo Lu

Guomao

Dongsanhuanzhong Lu

Tonghui River

0   500 M

0   1,500 ft

QUICK BITES

If you're looking for Western food, check out the restaurants surrounding **Poachers Inn** (✉ 43 Bei Sanlitun Lu ☎ 010/6417–2632 Ext. 8506), which is behind the Yaxiu Market. **Fish Nation** (✉ On the north side of the Poachers Inn ☎ 010/6415–0119) has great fish-and-chips. The Serbian-owned **Kiosk** (✉ On Nali St., a lane off the Sanlitun), serves excellent chicken and sausage gyros on crisp baguettes.

Famous for delivering all over town, **Annie's Café** (✉ Chaoyang Park West Gate ☎ 010/6951–1931 ✉ 88 Jianguo Lu, west side of SOHO New Town) has two locations serving up great pizza, delicious lasagna, and other Italian specialties in a family-friendly atmosphere.

NEIGHBORHOOD TOP 5

1. Grab dinner in Sanlitun and then wander over to **Brown's** (✉ 4 Gongti Bei Lu ☎ 010/6591–2717) to sample one of their 500 shooters.

2. Check out what's really going on in Chinese art today in the **Dashanzi Art District.** After strolling through the galleries, grab something to eat or a drink at one of the many hip bars or cafés within the factory complex.

3. Do some shopping at the **Yaxiu Market,** where you can buy anything from knockoff jeans to a custom-tailored suit. Then walk toward the end of the **Sanlitun North Street** for an espresso—or get your nails done.

4. Enjoy a drink or meal, along with some great books, at **The Bookworm** in the first alley on Sanlitun South Street. Readings and musical events take place throughout the week, usually in the evenings.

5. Go for an early-morning stroll in **Ritan Park** or **Chaoyang Park** and watch the traditional Chinese exercises.

GETTING HERE

The heart of Chaoyang district is accessible via Lines 1 and 2, but the district is huge and the sites are broadly distributed. Taking taxis between sites is usually the easiest way to get around. Dashanzi is especially far away from central Beijing, and so a taxi is also the best bet (about Y25 from the center of town). Buses go everywhere, but they are slow and amazingly crowded.

MAKING THE MOST OF YOUR TIME

Many expats spend years lost in the Chaoyang district and never get bored. There's plenty to do, but very few historical sights to see here. Spend a morning shopping at the **Silk Alley Market** or **Panjiayuan Antique Market** and the afternoon cooling off at **Ritan Park** or **Chaoyang Park,** the latter a large and pleasant park with a lot of activities for kids, from boating to simple rides. Then head to one of the numerous bar streets in the evening. If you are an art lover, or just want to see some of the hipper aspects of Chinese culture, go to **Dashanzi** one late afternoon, browse the galleries until it gets dark, have some dinner there at **Vincent Café & Creperie** (☎ 010/8456–4823) which serves a variety of crepes and fondues. On weekends, try **Cafe Pause** in Dashanzi, which has great coffee, a modest but good wine selection, and great atmosphere.

HAIDIAN DISTRICT

Sightseeing:
★★★★

Dining:
★

Lodging:
★★

Shopping:
★

Nightlife:
★

In the last decade or so, with the Chinese Internet and tech booms, the rise of the middle class, and, with it, university education, Haidian has become an education- and techno-mecca. The major IT players are all located here (including offices of Microsoft, Siemens, NEC, and Sun). If you want to escape modern life, never fear: Haidian is a huge district, and the outer areas house many interesting cultural sites—in fact, it's the juxtaposition of the Summer Palace, and, say, nearby Zhongguancun (the technology hub) that really makes the Haidian district the exemplification of new China.

Snapshot

It's just after lunch and almost every table in **Sculpting in Time**—a popular student hangout in Wudaokou—is full. Some Korean students are carefully writing Chinese in their practice books; a group laughs as they watch a rerun of *Friends*. American-language students sit with their exchange partners; beside them people chat happily while surfing wireless Internet. Among all this, young waitresses wearing aprons glide around the room with cappuccinos, sodas, and pizzas, shouting above the loud music to deliver their orders to the kitchen.

What's Here

Occupying the northwest corner of the city, the sprawling district of Haidian is Beijing's science, technology, and university district; it also houses numerous cultural sites. **Zhongguancun** is the technology neighborhood, with dozens of big-name corporate headquarters next to malls (such as

Hailong Shopping Mall) offering cheap shopping and high-quality computer components and electronics. **Peking University** (also called Beida) and **Tsinghua (Qinghua) University** (sometimes respectively referred to as China's Harvard and MIT), are both in Haidian and date back about 100 years. Visit Peking University and take a walk around the sleepy but pleasant Weiming Lake, the banks of which are lined with benches, sculptures, and heavy-limbed willow trees. The many universities in Haidian have lent a huge, energetic student presence and an international atmosphere to the entire district, and to the **Wudaokou** area in particular, which has a vibrant nightlife and dining scene dominated by students.

In addition to the new China of universities and high-tech culture, you'll also find lots of fascinating sites in Haidian. The **Summer Palace**, the **Old Summer Palace**, the **Fragrant Hills**, and the **Beijing Botanical Garden** all call this district home; these are just a few of the more popular ones. The **Beijing Zoo** is here, too. As you plan your visit to this district, keep in mind that Haidian is geographically large, and traveling between sites may require a taxi ride.

A GOOD TOUR

Haidian may be Beijing's technology and university district, but there's a lot of old Beijing left here. Before you leave your hotel, ask for a boxed lunch (or grab some food at the nearby supermarket). Jump in a cab and head for the **Summer Palace**. Saunter around the lakes and ancient pavilions, and finally settle down somewhere secluded to enjoy a picnic.

When you're done with lunch and sightseeing, hop a cab to **Hailong Shopping Mall:** go in and explore—the five-story shopping mall has every kind of computer or electronic device you could possibly want, often at deep discounts. ■ TIP→ **Be careful when buying software, though, as most of it is pirated and is illegal to bring it back to the United States.**

After you've shopped and you're ready to drop, head over to the **Wudaokou Binguan** for a selection of wonderful "snacks" that usually add up to a great dinner, and don't miss the *zhapi,* or mugs of fresh-from-the-tap beer. Taxi it on home in the wee hours.

> **WORD OF MOUTH**
>
> "It's a good idea not to accept an offer of a cab outside tourist attractions, as they'll probably be unlicensed. Hail them in the street, or ask the hotel doorman to hail one. Don't accept unsolicited offers of any kind (such as a "tea ceremony" or the helpful guys who offer to wheel your bags at the airport). Other than that, we found Beijing held few challenges for an independent traveler."   –Neil_Oz

GETTING ORIENTED

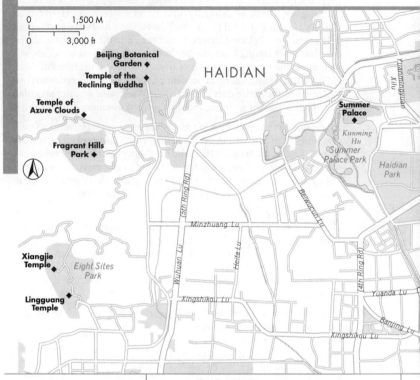

0 1,500 M
0 3,000 ft

Beijing Botanical Garden ◆

Temple of the Reclining Buddha ◆

HAIDIAN

Temple of Azure Clouds ◆

Fragrant Hills Park ◆

Summer Palace ◆

Kunming Hu

Summer Palace Park

Haidian Park

Yuanmingyuan Xilu

5th Ring Rd

Beiwuhuan Lu

Minzhuang Lu

Wuhuan Lu

Heita Lu

4th Ring Rd

Xiangjie Temple

Eight Sites Park

Yuanda Lu

Lingguang Temple

Xingshikou Lu

Banjing Lu

Xingshikou Lu

GETTING HERE

The Beijing Zoo is located near Xizhimen, which you can reach by the Line 2 subway. The Summer Palace, the Old Summer Palace, Fragrant Hills, and the Beijing Botanical Garden are all rather far away in the northwest of the city and are best reached by taxi. To save money, take the train to the Xizhimen subway station and take a taxi from there. Line 4, which is still under construction, will eventually make stops at the Beijing Zoo, the Old Summer Palace, and the Summer Palace.

MAKING THE MOST OF YOUR TIME

Because the **Summer Palace** is so large, with its lovely lakes and ancient pavilions, it makes for an entire morning of great exploring. The **Old Summer Palace** is close by, so visiting the two sites together is ideal.

The **Fragrant Hills** make for a charming outing, but keep in mind that it takes at least an hour and a half to get there from the city center. The **Botanical Garden,** with some 2,000 types of orchids, bonsai, and peach and pear blossoms, along with the **Temple of the Reclining Buddha,** is also fun, especially for green-thumbs. Plan to spend most of a day if you go to either of these sites.

If you want to shop for electronics, spend an afternoon wandering the five floors of the **Hailong Shopping Mall** (⊠ 1 Zhongguancun Dajie).

Evenings in Wudaokou are a pleasure. After dinner, take advantage of the hopping beer gardens. A mug of Tsingtao is a great way to start a summer night off right.

NEIGHBORHOOD TOP 5

1. Spending a low-key day at the vast **Summer Palace** and **Old Summer Palace**.

2. Eating and chatting all evening at the **Wudaokou Binguan** beer garden.

3. Browsing the biggest selection of electronics and computer goods this side of the Pacific at **Hailong Shopping Mall**.

4. Exploring the lovely campus at **Peking University,** with its tree-lined lanes, old architecture, and pleasant lake.

5. Getting out of town with a day trip to the **Fragrant Hills** or the **Beijing Botanical Garden**.

QUICK BITES

There are plenty of restaurants on campus and around Zhongguancun, but the coolest places to eat in Haidian are in Wudaokou. Try excellent and innovative Korean BBQ at **Hanguokeli** (✉ 35 Chengfu Lu ☎ 010/6256-3749 Ⓜ Wudaokou). Another hopping eatery is **Youle** (✉ On Shuangqing Lu, just off Chengfu Lu ☎ 010/5872-2028), a Japanese noodlehouse on the first floor of Weixin Guoji Dasha, or the Weixin International Mansion.

Not to be missed is the beer garden at the **Wudaokou Hotel** on Chengfu Lu, one block east of the subway station. The **Lily Vegetarian Restaurant** (☎ 010/6202-5284), behind the Jimen Hotel at Jimenqiao, serves up awesome "faux-meat" dishes.

At a Glance

ENGLISH	PINYIN	CHINESE CHARACTERS
POINTS OF INTEREST		
Batong Line	bā tōngxiàn	八通线
Beihai ("north lake")	Běihǎi	北海
Beijing Botanical Gardens	Běijǐng zhíwùyuán	北京植物园
Beijing Zoo	Běi jīng dòng wù yuán	北京动物园
Chang'an Jie	Cháng'ān jiē	长安街
Chaoyang District	cháoyáng qū	朝阳区
China World Trade Center	zhōng guó guó jì mào yì zhōng xīn	中国国际贸易中心
Chongwen District	chóng wén qū	崇文区
Dongcheng District	dōngchéngqū	东城区
Donghuamen Night Market	Dōnghuámén yèshì	东华门夜市
Fragrant Hills	xiāng shān	香山
Ghost Street	guǐ jiē	鬼街
Haidian District	hǎi diàn qū	海淀区
Houhai (rear lake)	hòu hǎi	后海
Jianguomen	jiànguó mén	建国门
Jiguge Teahouse	jí gǔ gé cháyuán	汲古阁茶园
Jingshan Park	jǐngshān gōngyuán	景山公园
Line 1	yīhào xiàn	一号线
Line 2	èr hào xiàn	二号线
Line 13	shísān hào xiàn	十三号线
Liulichang	Liúlichǎng	琉璃厂
Mao Zedong Memorial Hall	Máo zhǔ xí jì niàn táng	毛主席纪念堂
Ming Dynasty City Wall Ruins Park	Míng chéng qiáng yí zhǐ gōng yuán	明城墙遗址公园
Monument to the People's Heroes	rénmín yīngxióng jìniànbēi	人民英雄纪念碑
Nanhai ("south lake")	Nánhǎi	南海
Oriental Plaza	dōngfāng guǎngchǎng	东方广场
Peking University	Běi jīng dà xué	北京大学
Prince Gong's Palace	gōng wángfǔ	恭王府
Qianhai ("front lake")	qián hǎi	前海
Sanlitun	sān lǐ tún	三里屯
Second Ring Road	èr huán	二环

Shichahai	Shíchàhǎi	什刹海
Silver Ingot Bridge	yíndìng qiáo	银锭桥
Soong Ching-ling's Former Residence	sòng qìng líng gùjū	宋庆龄故居
Subway	dìtiě	地铁
Tsinghua (Qinghua) University	Qīng huá dà xué	清华大学
Wangfujing	Wángfǔjǐng	王府井
Workers' Stadium	gōngrén tǐyùchǎng	工人体育场
Xicheng District	xīchéngqū	西城区
Xidan	Xīdān	西单
Xuanwu District	xuān wǔ qū	宣武区
Zhongguancun	Zhōngguāncūn	中关村
Zhonghai ("middle lake")	zhōng hǎi	中海

2

Historical
Sights

Empress Dowager Cixi's favorite route to the vast, lavish Summer Palace was by boat.

WORD OF MOUTH

"I've been a visitor to Beijing several times, sometimes with guides and sometimes without. My personal opinion is that much of the touring can be done on your own—you just need to arrange for transportation. Hiring a driver or taking taxis is not expensive. There is generally signage in English." —Nancy

"Bring warm clothes. The wind comes off the Siberian plain and the weather can get very cold. Believe it." —Michael Thompson

www.fodors.com/forums

HISTORICAL SIGHTS PLANNER

Getting Around

A few of Beijing's major historical sights are clustered in the same district, making it easy to combine two or three in a single day. For example, the Forbidden City adjoins Tiananmen Square; the two Summer Palaces are next to each other; and the Lama Temple is just streets away from the Confucius Temple, and a few subway stops from the Drum and Bell Towers.

Although taxis are plentiful and cheap, some of the sights are conveniently near subway stops. Take one of the Tiananmen stations (Tiananmen East or Tiananmen West) to visit the square and the Forbidden City; the Lama Temple is next to Yonghegong station; the Bell and Drum Towers are a short walk from the Gulou station; and the Ancient Observatory is on top of Jiangguomen station.

It's worthwhile to take a taxi to sights in the northwestern district of Haidian and the temples around the Xuanwu and Xicheng districts. Outside of the winter months, it's possible to reach the Summer Palace by boat, either from Xizhimen or behind Beijing Zoo.

Editor's Picks

■ **The Forbidden City.** The world's largest palace complex, originally built for the "Son of Heaven," now bares its throne-stocked halls to the masses.

■ **Temple of Heaven.** This sprawling park, once used for sacrifices, has some of the most beautiful Ming-designed Taoist temples, with moody blue roofs and gilt details.

■ **Summer Palace.** A Qing Dynasty royal retreat that takes on wonderland qualities under new-fallen snow, this palace has a lake, temple-topped hills, and a stone steamboat that goes nowhere.

■ **Lama Temple.** A slice of Lhasa in Beijing: this colorful, flag-strung monastery is home to brown-robed monks and a breathtaking sandalwood Buddha.

■ **Tiananmen Square.** The ultimate symbol of modern China—no visitor should fail to visit the world's largest public square and gaze up at the face of Chairman Mao.

Beijing's Hutongs

Aside from the obvious attractions, such as the Forbidden City and the Temple of Heaven, Beijing has a network of ancient alleyways that are living museums of the old city. These alleyways, called *hutongs*, are still-used streets of courtyard houses and shops. They are full of life: washing is strung out from windows and telephone poles, vegetables and flowers are planted in any available space, old folks play chess, drink beer or tea, and sit on stools and gossip. Although they first appeared in the Yuan Dynasty, most of the surviving hutongs date from the Ming and Qing dynasties. Unfortunately, many of these tree-lined alleyways have been destroyed to make way for gleaming new office blocks. The most atmospheric hutongs still standing are around Houhai and Jiadaokou (a few streets northeast of the Forbidden City). Anyone can stroll through—or you can spring for a pedicab tour!

Reading Up

If you have time before your trip, you might brush up on a little Chinese history. Here are some recommendations:

- *Imperial China: 900–1800* by Frederick W. Mote. A trusty and not-so-stuffy tome that spans seven dynasties in over 1,000 pages. It's big but worth it.

- *The Search for Modern China* by Jonathan D. Spence. A fresh, readable, comprehensive history by an expert.

- *Empress Orchid* by Anchee Min. A fictional rework that softens the picture of oft-reviled Cixi, China's last empress.

- *The Last Emperor* by Edward Behr. The book version of the movie is a light retelling of the final years of dynastic China.

Important Dates in Beijing History

1271   Mongol leader Kublai Khan establishes Dadu as the capital, at the site of present-day Beijing.

1421   Ming emperor Yongle moves capital back to Beijing from Nanjing, and completes work on the Forbidden City.

1911   The last emperor Puyi announces his abdication from the Forbidden City.

1937   Chinese and Japanese troops clash during the Marco Polo Bridge Incident just north of the capital, sparking war.

1949   Mao Zedong proclaims People's Republic of China from the Gate of Heavenly Peace.

1989   Massive democracy demonstrations by students in Tiananmen Square are crushed by the Chinese army. Thousands are believed to have died.

2001   Beijing is chosen in July as the site of the 2008 Olympic Games.

2003   Severe Acute Respiratory Syndrome (SARS) hits the city; dozens of people die and tens of thousands are quarantined.

2006   A direct rail link opens between Beijing and Lhasa in Tibet costing $4.2 billion. The journey takes around 48 hours.

Hours

Most of Beijing's tourist sites are open daily, year-round. Hours of business vary, but sites are usually open 9 AM to 5 PM. Some ticket offices stop selling tickets an hour or so before closing time. Perennial favorites, like the Forbidden City, Temple of Heaven, and Summer Palace, are perpetually packed but unbearably so on public holidays.

Admission

China has embraced some capitalist principles feverishly, especially when it comes to tourism. You will pay an entrance fee for everything in Beijing except for Tiananmen Square and some city walls. That said, tickets are relatively inexpensive considering the age, scale, and magnificence of some of the city's points of interest. Admission prices range from Y10 to Y60.

Etiquette

China is less sensitive than, say, Thailand, about dress when it comes to visiting royal palaces and temples. Even so, it is respectful to dress modestly: cover your shoulders and don't wear short skirts or shorts when you're visiting religious buildings. ⚠ **Note that indoor photography in many temples and sites like the Forbidden City is not permitted.** Keep in mind that authorities are very sensitive about public behavior in Tiananmen Square.

By Dinah
Gardner

Hidden behind Beijing's pressing search for modernity is an intriguing historical core. Many of the city's ancient sights were built under the Mongols during the Yuan Dynasty. A number of the capital's imperial palaces, halls of power, mansions, and temples were rebuilt and refurbished during the Ming and Qing dynasties. Despite the ravages of time and the Cultural Revolution, most sights are in good shape, from the Niujie Mosque, with Koranic verse curled around its arches, to Tiananmen Square, the bold brainchild of Mao Zedong.

If You Visit Only Three Sites
The famous modern-day image of Beijing is of a June 1989 student protest being crushed by the army in **Tiananmen Square.** It's hard to reconcile those pictures of tanks on fire with this fascinating open expanse. Across the road, the **Forbidden City** occupies the exact heart of Beijing. The **Lama Temple** is a living monastery with multiple Buddha statues to smile at.

Best for Kids
Make touring Beijing fun by taking photos of your children decked out in traditional Chinese costumes at the **Summer Palace.** Let them run free at the **Temple of Heaven** with a kite: paper-and-wooden birds and beasts can be bought all over the park. The staff at the **Drum Tower** have been known to permit children to play the drums from time to time.

Best for Avoiding Summer Crowds
The city's many hutongs offer plenty of opportunities to sit and have a cold beer. The **Old Summer Palace** is often overlooked by tourists who flock in droves instead to the **Summer Palace** next door. The old gardens, though, are equally worthwhile—their ruins are fascinating. As the world's largest public space, there's enough room for everyone at **Tiananmen Square.**

TIANANMEN SQUARE

✉ Bounded by Chang'an Jie to the north and Qianmen Dajie to the south, Dongcheng District

🎫 Free

🕐 24-hours year-round

Ⓜ Tiananmen East

TIPS & TRIVIA

■ You can access a 360-degree panorama of the square online at ⊕ www.roundtiananmensquare.com.

■ The only way to cross Chang'an Jie between Tiananmen Square and the Forbidden City is to use the underpasses.

■ On October 1, 1949, Mao Zedong announced the establishment of the People's Republic of China from the Gate of Heavenly Peace.

■ A network of tunnels is rumored to lie beneath Tiananmen Square. Mao Zedong is thought to have ordered them dug in the late 1960s after China–USSR relations soured. They are said to extend across Beijing.

★ Fodor's Choice The world's largest public square, and the very heart of modern China, Tiananmen Square owes little to grand imperial designs and everything to Mao Zedong. Young protesters who assembled here in the 1919 May Fourth Movement established a tradition of patriotic dissent, which was repeated in 1989. Today the square is packed with sightseers, families, and undercover policemen. Although formidable, the square is a little bleak, with no shade, benches, or trees. Come here at night for an eerie experience—it's a little like being on a film set.

HIGHLIGHTS

Watch the military guard raise China's flag at dawn. Wide-eyed visitors converge on Tiananmen Square each day at dawn to watch the ceremony. As soldiers march forth from the Forbidden City, hundreds of visitors begin to take pictures.

Take in the surrounding sights. Tiananmen is sandwiched between two grand gates: the Gate of Heavenly Peace to the north, where a portrait of Mao gazes across the square, and Qianmen ("front gate") in the south. The stern Communist-style block along the western edge is the Great Hall of the People, while the National Museum of China and an Olympic "countdown clock" are along the eastern side.

Try your hand at flying a kite. Itinerant vendors sell kites of all kinds.

Visit the Monument to the People's Heroes. At the square's center stands the tallest monument in China, a 125-foot granite obelisk commemorating those who died for the revolutionary cause of the Chinese people.

Contemplate history. At the height of the Cultural Revolution, hundreds of thousands Red Guards crowded the square; in June 1989, the square was the scene of tragedy when hundreds of student demonstrators were killed.

THE FORBIDDEN CITY

Undeniably sumptuous, the Forbidden City, once home to a long line of emperors, is Beijing's most enduring emblem. Magnificent halls, winding lanes, and stately courtyards await you—welcome to the world's largest palace complex.

As you gaze up at roofs of glazed-yellow tiles—a symbol of royalty—try to imagine a time when only the emperor ("the son of God") was permitted to enter this palace, accompanied by select family members, concubines, and eunuch-servants. Now, with its doors flung open, the Forbidden City's mysteries beckon.

The sheer grandeur of the site—with 800 buildings and more than 8,000 rooms—conveys the pomp and circumstance of Imperial China. The shady palaces, musty with age, recall life at court, where corrupt eunuchs and palace officials schemed and bored concubines gossiped.

Building to Glory

Under the third Ming emperor, Yongle, 200,000 laborers built this complex over the course of 14 years, finishing in 1420. Yongle relocated the Ming capital to Beijing (from Nanjing in the south) to strengthen China's northern frontier. After Yongle, the palace was home to 23 Ming and Qing emperors, until the dynastic system crumbled in 1911.

In imperial times, no buildings were allowed to exceed the height of the palace. Moats and massive timber doors

protected the emperor. Gleaming yellow roof tiles marked the vast complex as the royal court's exclusive dominion. Ornate interiors displayed China's most exquisite artisanship, including ceilings covered with turquoise-and-blue dragons, walls draped with priceless scrolls, intricate cloisonné screens, sandalwood thrones padded in delicate silks, and floors of golden-hued bricks. Miraculously, the palace survived fire, war, and imperial China's collapse.

More Than Feng Shui
The Forbidden City embodies Feng Shui, architectural principles used for thousands of years throughout China. Each main hall faces south, opening to a courtyard flanked by lesser buildings. This symmetry repeats itself along a north–south axis that bisects the imperial palace, with a broad walkway paved

in marble. This path was reserved exclusively for the emperor's sedan chair. Even court ministers, the empress, and favored concubines were required to trod on pathways and pass through doors set to either side of the Imperial Way.

Take a close look at gates, doors, and woodwork here: most structures have nails in a 9 x 9 formation. Nine is the largest odd number less than the number 10, so it's considered both lucky and important.

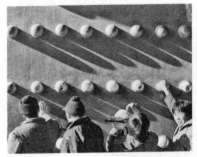

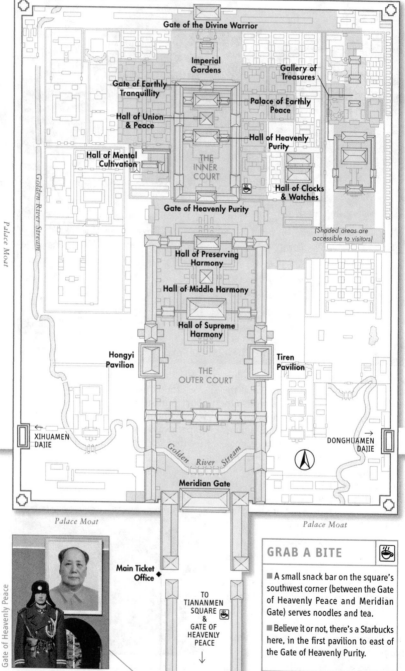

Palace Moat

Palace Moat

Gate of the Divine Warrior

Imperial Gardens

Gallery of Treasures

Gate of Earthly Tranquillity

Palace of Earthly Peace

Hall of Union & Peace

Hall of Heavenly Purity

Hall of Mental Cultivation

THE INNER COURT

Hall of Clocks & Watches

Gate of Heavenly Purity

[Shaded areas are accessible to visitors]

Hall of Preserving Harmony

Hall of Middle Harmony

Hall of Supreme Harmony

Hongyi Pavilion

Tiren Pavilion

THE OUTER COURT

← XIHUAMEN DAJIE

DONGHUAMEN DAJIE →

Golden River Stream

Meridian Gate

Palace Moat

Palace Moat

Palace Moat

Golden River Stream

Gate of Heavenly Peace

Main Ticket Office ◆

TO TIANANMEN SQUARE & GATE OF HEAVENLY PEACE ↓

GRAB A BITE

■ A small snack bar on the square's southwest corner (between the Gate of Heavenly Peace and Meridian Gate) serves noodles and tea.

■ Believe it or not, there's a Starbucks here, in the first pavilion to east of the Gate of Heavenly Purity.

WHAT TO SEE

The most impressive way to reach the Forbidden City is through the **Gate of Heavenly Peace** (Tiananmen), connected to Tiananmen Square. The Great Helmsman himself stood here to establish the People's Republic of China on October 1, 1949.

The **Meridian Gate** (Wumen), sometimes called Five Phoenix Tower, is the main southern entrance to the palace. Here, the emperor announced yearly planting schedules according to the lunar calendar; it's also where errant officials were flogged. The main ticket office and audio-guide rentals are just west of this gate.

THE OUTER COURT

The **Hall of Supreme Harmony** (Taihedian) was used for coronations, royal birthdays, and weddings. Bronze vats, once kept brimming with water to fight fires, ring this vast expanse. The hall sits atop three stone tiers with an elaborate drainage system with 1,000 carved dragons. On the top tier, bronze cranes symbolize longevity. Inside, cloisonné cranes flank the imperial throne, above which hangs a heavy bronze ball—placed there to crush any pretender to the throne.

Emperors greeted audiences in the **Hall of Middle Harmony** (Zhonghedian). It also housed the royal plow, with which the emperor would turn a furrow to commence spring planting.

The highest civil service examinations, which were personally conducted by the emperor, were once administered in the **Hall of Preserving Harmony** (Baohedian). Behind the hall, a 200-ton marble relief of dragons, the palace's most treasured stone carving, adorns the staircase.

A short jaunt to the right is **Hall of Clocks and Watches** (Zhongbiaoguan), where you'll find a collection of early timepieces. It's pure opulence: there's a plethora of jeweled, enameled, and lacquered timepieces (some astride elephants, others implanted in ceramic trees). Our favorites? Those crafted from red sandalwood. *(Admission: Y10)*

You'll see that lions in the palace live in pairs. A female lion playing with a cub symbolizes imperial fertility. A male lion, sitting majestically with a sphere beneath his paw, represents power.

The central entrance of the Meridian was reserved for the emperor. The one day the empress was allowed to walk through it was her wedding day.

Take a close look at the bronze vats and you'll see the telltale scratch marks of greedy foreign soldiers who scraped the gold with their bayonets.

The Hall of Supreme Harmony was the site of many imperial weddings.

Marble dragons will greet you behind the Hall of Preserving Harmony.

DID YOU KNOW?

- 24 emperors and two dynasties ruled from within these labyrinthine halls.

- The emperor was the only non-castrated male allowed in the eastern and western palaces. This served as proof that any pregnant concubine was carrying the royal one's baby.

- If you prepared for your trip by watching Bertolucci's *The Last Emperor*, you may recognize the passage outside the Hall of Mental Cultivation: this is where young Puyi rode his bike in the film.

- Women can enter the Forbidden City for half price on March 8, International Women's Day.

- When it was first built in the 15th century, the palace was called the Purple Forbidden City; today, its official name is the Ancient Palace Museum (Gugong Bowuguan); often it's shortened simply to Gugong.

The Hall of Heavenly Purity

THE INNER COURT

Now you're approaching the very core of the palace. Several emperors chose to live in the Inner Palace with their families. The **Hall of Heavenly Purity** (Qianqinggong) holds another imperial throne; the **Hall of Union and Peace** (Jiaotaidian) was the venue for the empress's annual birthday party; and the **Palace of Earthly Peace** (Kunninggong) was where royal couples consummated their marriages. The banner above the throne bizarrely reads DOING NOTHING.

On either side of the Inner Palace are six western and six eastern palaces—the former living quarters of concubines, eunuchs, and servants. The last building on the western side, the **Hall of Mental Cultivation** (Yangxindian), is the most important of these; starting with Emperor Yongzheng, all Qing Dynasty emperors attended to daily state business in this hall.

AN EMPEROR CHEAT SHEET

JIAJING (1507–1567)

Ming Emperor Jiajing was obsessed with Taoism, which he hoped would give him longevity, but which also led him to ignore state affairs for 25 years. His other fixation was the pursuit of girls: his 18 concubines conspired to strangle him in his sleep, but their plot was uncovered. Nearly all of the girls, and their families, were killed.

YONGZHENG (1678–1735)

The third emperor of the Qing Dynasty, Yongzheng was tyrannical but efficient. He became emperor amidst rumors that he had forged his father's will. He appeased his brothers by promoting them, but then proceeded to murder and imprison anyone who posed a challenge, including his own brothers, two of whom died in prison.

Animal ornaments decorate the corners of many roofs—the more animals, the more important the building.

The Gallery of Treasures (Zhenbaoguan), actually a series of halls, has breathtaking examples of imperial ornamentation. The first room displays candleholders, wine vessels, tea sets, and a golden pagoda commissioned by Qing emperor Qian Long in honor of his mother. A cabinet on one wall contains the 25 imperial seals. Jade bracelets, golden hair pins, and coral fill the second hall; carved jade landscapes a third. *(Admission: Y10)*

HEAD FOR THE GREEN

North of the Forbidden City's private palaces, beyond the **Gate of Earthly Tranquillity**, lie the most pleasant parts of the Forbidden City: the **Imperial Gardens** (Yuhuayuan), composed of ancient cypress trees and stone mosaic pathways. During festivals, palace inhabitants climbed the Hill of Accumulated Elegance. You can exit the palace at the back of the gardens through the park's **Gate of the Divine Warrior** (Shenwumen).

FAST FACTS

Address: The main entrance is just north of the Gate of Heavenly Peace, which faces Tiananmen Square on Chang'an Jie.

Web site: www.dpm.org.cn

Admission: Y30

Hours: Oct. 16–Apr. 15, daily 8:30–4:30; Apr. 16–Oct. 15, daily 8:30–5

UNESCO Status: Declared a World Heritage Site in 1987.

■ You must check your bags prior to entry and also pass through a metal detector.

■ Note that the Forbidden City is undergoing major renovations through 2008.

■ The palace is always packed with visitors, but it's impossibly crowded on national holidays.

■ Allow 2–4 hours to explore the palace. There are souvenir shops and restaurants inside.

■ You can hire automated audio guides at the Meridian Gate for Y40 and a Y100 returnable deposit.

3

THE FORBIDDEN CITY

CIXI (1835–1908)

The Empress Dowager served as de facto ruler of China from 1861 until 1908. She entered the court as a concubine at 16 and soon became Emperor Xianfeng's favorite. She gave birth to his only son to survive: the heir apparent. Ruthless and ambitious, she learned the workings of the imperial court and used every means to gain power.

PUYI (1906–1967)

Puyi, whose life was depicted in Bertolucci's classic *The Last Emperor*, took the throne at age two. The Qing dynasty's last emperor, he was forced to abdicate after the dynasty fell. During an attempted restoration in 1917, he held the throne for 12 days. Puyi was forced out of the Imperial City in 1924 by a warlord.

TEMPLE OF HEAVEN

✉ Yongdingmen Dajie
(South Gate), Chongwen
District

☎ 010/6702-8866

🎫 All-inclusive ticket Apr.–
Oct. Y35, Oct.–Apr. Y30;
entrance to park only
Y15

🕐 Daily 8–4:30

TIPS

■ The Temple of Heaven isn't just a tourist sight–it's a living, functional park. Take time to stroll around the tree-lined avenues and watch Beijingers relaxing in this green haven.

■ It is much cheaper to buy an all-inclusive ticket. If you only buy a ticket into the park, you will need to pay Y20 to get into each building.

■ Enter the park through the southern entrance. This way you approach the beautiful Hall of Prayer for Good Harvests via the Danbi Bridge– the same route the emperor favored.

■ It's a 20-minute walk from Qianmen or Chongwenmen subway stops, so it's probably best to take a taxi to the park. That way you can head straight to the southern entrance.

■ Automatic audio guides (Y40) are available at stalls inside all four entrances.

★ **Fodor's Choice** The Temple of Heaven, where emperors once performed important rites, is a prime example of Chinese religious architecture. Construction began in the early 15th century under Yongle, whom many call the "architect of Beijing." Set in a huge, serene, mushroom-shaped park, the Temple of Heaven is surrounded by splendid examples of Ming Dynasty architecture, including curved cobalt-blue roofs layered with yellow and green tiles. The Temple of Heaven was a site for imperial sacrifices, meant to please the gods so they would generate bumper harvests.

Shaped like a semicircle on the northern rim to represent heaven and square on the south for the earth, the grounds were once believed to be the meeting point of the two. The area is double the size of the Forbidden City and is still laid out to divine rule: buildings and paths are positioned to represent the right directions for heaven and earth. This means, for example, that the northern part is higher than the south.

HIGHLIGHTS

Check out the architecture. The temple's hallmark structure is a magnificent blue-roofed wooden tower, built in 1420. It burned to the ground in 1889 and was immediately rebuilt using Ming architectural methods (and timber imported from Oregon). The building's design is based on the calendar: 4 center pillars represent the seasons, the next 12 pillars represent months, and 12 outer pillars signify the parts of a day. Together these 28 poles, which correspond to the 28 constellations of heaven, support the structure without nails. A carved dragon swirling down from the ceiling represents the emperor.

Cross the divine pathway on the Danbi Bridge. This will take you to the Hall of Prayer for Good Harvests. The middle section was once reserved for the Emperor of Heaven, who was the only one allowed to step foot on the eastern side, while aristocrats and high-ranking officials walked on the western strip.

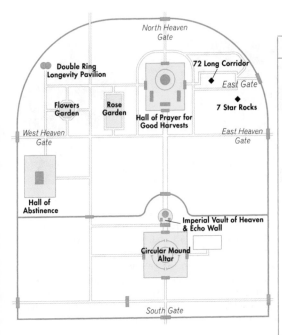

IMPERIAL SACRIFICES

To understand the significance of the harvest sacrifice at the Temple of Heaven, it is important to keep in mind that the legitimacy of a Chinese emperor's rule depended on what is known as the *tian ming,* or mandate of heaven, essentially the emperor's relationship with the gods.

A succession of bad harvests, for example, could be interpreted as the emperor losing the favor of heaven and could be used to justify a change in emperor or even in dynasty.

Hence, when the emperor came to the Temple of Heaven to pray for good harvests and to pay homage to his ancestors, there may have been a good measure of self-interest to his fervor.

The sacrifices consisted mainly of animals and fruit placed on altars surrounded by candles. Many Chinese still make sacrifices on special occasions, such as births, deaths, and weddings.

Whisper a secret into the Echo Wall. A wall encircling the Imperial Vault of Heaven, this structure allows anyone to eavesdrop. Extreme quiet is needed to hear the effect.

Stroll along the Long Corridor. A long, twisting platform, which once enclosed the animal-killing pavilion, the Long Corridor was traditionally hung with lanterns on the eve of sacrifices. Today it plays host to scores of Beijingers singing opera, playing cards and chess, and fan dancing.

Count the number of slabs on the top of the Round Altar. Just inside the south gate, this three-tiered, white-marble structure was where the emperor worshipped the winter solstice; it is based around the divine number nine.

The Hall of Abstinence. On the western edge of the grounds, this is where the emperor would retreat three days before the ritual sacrifice.

THE MAGIC NUMBER

Nine was regarded as a symbol of the power of the emperor, as it is the biggest single-digit odd number, and odd numbers are masculine and were therefore considered more powerful.

SUMMER PALACE

✉ Yiheyuan Lu and Kunminghu Lu, Haidian District, 12 km (7½ mi) northwest of downtown Beijing

☎ 010/6288-1144

🌐 www.summerpalace-china.com (Chinese only)

🎫 Apr.–Oct. Y50 and Nov.–Mar. Y40 for all exhibits, Apr.–Oct. Y30 and Nov.–Mar. Y20 for everything except the Garden of Virtue & Harmony, Suzhou Street Hall of Serenity, and Wenchang Gallery

🕐 Daily 6:30–8 (ticket office closes at 6 PM)

TIPS

■ There isn't a subway nearby, so your best option is taking a taxi to the palace. If you want to save some cash, take the overland Line 13 to Wudaokou and then take a taxi for the remainder (Y15).

■ Come early in the morning to get a head start before the coachloads of visitors arrive. You'll need the better part of a day to explore the grounds.

■ Automatic audio guides can be rented for Y40 at stalls near the ticket booth.

■ Arrive like Cixi did: come to the park by boat. In summer, craft leave from near the Millennium Monument in Xizhimen (on Fuxing Lu) or from near Beijing Zoo. Call 010/6858-9215 for times and prices. The journey takes about an hour.

★ **Fodor's Choice** Emperor Qianlong commissioned this giant royal retreat for his mother's 60th birthday in 1750. Anglo–French forces plundered, then burned, many of the palaces in 1860 and funds were diverted from China's naval budget for the renovations. Empress Dowager Cixi retired here in 1889. Nine years later, she imprisoned her nephew, Emperor Guangxu, after his reform movement failed. In 1903, she moved the seat of government from the Forbidden City to Yiheyuan from which she controlled China until her death in 1908.

Nowadays, the place is undoubtedly romantic. Pagodas and temples perch on hillsides; rowboats dip under arched stone bridges; and willows branches brush the water. The greenery provides a welcome relief from the loud, bustling city. It's also a fabulous history lesson. You can see firsthand the results of corruption: the opulence here was bought with siphoned money. The entire gardens were for Dowager's exclusive use. UNESCO placed the Summer Palace on its World Heritage list in 1998.

NAUTICAL THEME

At the west end of the lake you'll find the Marble Boat, which Cixi built with money meant for the navy.

HIGHLIGHTS

Peer inside the Hall of Benevolent Longevity. This is where Cixi held court and received foreign dignitaries. It is said that the first electric lights in China shone here. Just behind the hall and next to the lake is Hall of Jade Ripples, where Cixi kept the hapless Guangxu under guard while she ran China in his name.

Hire a boat on Kunming Lake. This giant body of water extends southward for 3 km (2 mi); it's ringed by tree-lined dikes, arched stone bridges, and numerous gazebos. In winter, you can skate on the ice. The less-traveled southern shore near Humpbacked Bridge is an ideal picnic spot.

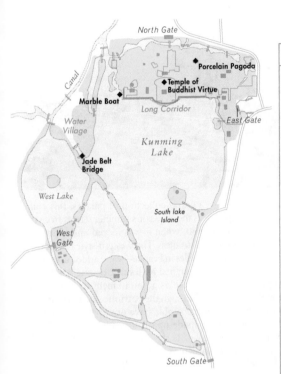

Stroll down the Long Corridor. The ceiling and wooden rafters here are richly painted with thousands of scenes from legends and nature—be on the lookout for Sun Wukong (the monkey king). The wooden walkway skirts the northern shoreline of Kunming Lake for about half a mile until it reaches the marble boat.

Longevity Hill. Strung with pagodas and temples, including the impressive Tower of the Fragrance of Buddha, Glazed Tile Pagoda, and the Hall that Dispels Clouds, this is the place where you can escape the hordes of visitors—take your time exploring the lovely northern side of the hill.

See how Cixi lived. Her home, in the Hall of Joyful Longevity, is near the beginning of the Long Corridor. The residence is furnished and decorated as Cixi left it. Her private theater, called the Grand Theater Building, just east of the hall, was constructed for her 60th birthday and cost 700,000 taels of silver.

DID YOU KNOW?

Most of this 290-hectare park is under water. Kunming Lake makes up around three-fourths of the palace.

OLD SUMMER PALACE

✉ Qinghuan Xi Lu, Haidian District (just northeast of the Summer Palace)

☎ 010/6255–1488 or 010/6254–3673

💺 Park Y10; extra Y15 fee for sites

🕐 Daily 7–7

TIPS & TRIVIA

■ The park and ruins take on a ghostly beauty if you come after a fresh snowfall. There's also skating on the lake when it's frozen over.

■ It's a long trek to the European ruins from the main gate. Electric carts buzz around the park; hop on one heading to Changchunyuan if you feel tired. Tickets are Y5.

■ The Old Summer Palace is about the same size as New York City's Central Park.

★ **Fodor's Choice** Once a grand collection of palaces, this complex was the emperor's summer retreat from the 15th century to 1860, when it was looted and blown up by British and French soldiers. The Western-style buildings—patterned after Versailles in France—were added during the Qing Dynasty and designed by Jesuits. Beijing has chosen to preserve the vast ruin as a "monument to China's national humiliation," though the patriotic slogans that were once scrawled on the rubble have now been cleaned off. The palace is now made up of three idyllic parks: Yuanmingyuan (Garden of Perfection and Light) in the west, Wanchunyuan (Garden of 10,000 Springs) in the south, and Changchunyuan (Garden of Everlasting Spring), where the European ruins of marble palaces can be found, in the east. After you explore the ruins, the gardens are great for picnicking, scrambling over rocks, and rowing on the lake.

HIGHLIGHTS

Lose yourself in the Labyrinth. This engraved concrete wall maze, known as Huanghuazhen (Yellow Flower), twists and turns around a European-style pavilion. Recently restored and located just to the left of the west gate of Changchunyuan, it was once the site of lantern parties during mid-autumn festivals. Palace maids would race each other to the pavilion carrying lotus lanterns of yellow silk.

Scramble over the stones of Changchunyuan, which are like a surreal graveyard to European architecture. The ruins of ornately carved columns, squat lion statues, and crumbling stone blocks bearing frescoes lie like fallen dominoes. The park costs an extra Y15 to enter, but it's well worth it.

Take a boat out on Fuhai Lake. Paddle your way around this charming lake, thick with pink lilies, the occasional sunken fountain, island pavilions, and stone-arched bridges. Stop off and try wild vegetable *baozi* (Chinese steamed buns) at one of the lakeside snack stores and watch the plump carp gobble up tourist-bought tidbits.

NIUJIE (OX STREET) MOSQUE

✉ 88 Niu Jie, Xuanwu
District

🎫 Y10

🕐 Daily 8–sunset

TIPS & TRIVIA

■ It's most convenient to get to the mosque by taxi. If you want to take a subway, it's a 20-minute walk from Changchunjie station.

■ There are dozens of mosques in Beijing that cater to around 10,000 Muslims made up of some 10 different ethnic groups.

■ All visitors must wear long trousers or skirts and keep their shoulders covered. Women are not permitted to enter some areas.

More than 1,000 years old, Beijing's oldest and largest mosque sits at the center of the Muslim quarter and mimics a Chinese temple from the outside, with its hexagonal wooden structure. Inside, arches and posts are inscribed with Koranic verse, and a special moon tower helps with determining the lunar calendar. At the rear of the complex is a minaret from which a muezzin calls the faithful to prayer. Because Muslims must pray in the direction of Mecca, which, in Beijing, is toward the west, the main prayer hall opens onto the east. There are also several religious halls, classrooms, and a bathhouse. The mosque has been refurbished in a bid to re-create how it looked back in 1696. The main prayer hall is open only to Muslims and can fit up to 1,000 worshippers.

A MOSQUE IS BORN
Niujie was originally built during the Northern Song Dynasty in 996.

HIGHLIGHTS
The Spirit Wall. Standing opposite the main entrance, and serving to prevent ghosts from entering the mosque, this wall, covered with carved murals, works on the premise that ghosts can't turn sharp corners.

A Tower for Viewing the Moon. From this very tower, imams (the prayer leaders of a mosque) measure the beginning and end of Ramadan, Islam's month of fasting and prayer. Ramadan beings when the imam sights the new moon, which appears as a slight crescent.

The Tombs. Two dark tombs with Chinese and Arabic inscriptions are kept in one of the small courtyards. They belong to two Persian imams who came to preach at the mosque in the 13th and 14th centuries.

LAMA TEMPLE (YONGHE TEMPLE)

✉ 12 Yonghegong Dajie, Beixingqiao, Dongcheng District

☎ 010/6404-3769 or 010/6404-4499

💳 Y25

🕐 Daily 9-5

Ⓜ Yonghegong

TIPS & TRIVIA

■ English-speaking guides offer their services around the entrance. English audio guides can be rented for Y20.

■ Photography inside the temples is prohibited.

■ Unlike most "feudal" sites in Beijing, the Lama Temple survived the 1966-1976 Cultural Revolution unscathed by the orders of Zhou Enlai.

■ Combine a visit to the Lama Temple with the Confucius Temple and the Imperial Academy, which are a 5-minute walk away, within the hutong neighborhood opposite the main entrance.

■ The thick, spicy smoke of incense is one of the first smells you'll receive upon entering. The Wanfu Pavilion has an enormous Maitreya, which is said to have been carved from a single piece of fragrant sandalwood.

★ **Fodor's Choice** Beijing's most visited religious site and one of the most important functioning Buddhist temples in Beijing, this Tibetan Buddhist masterpiece has five main halls and numerous galleries hung with finely detailed *thangkhas* (painted cloth scrolls). The entire temple is decorated with Buddha images—all guarded by somber lamas (monks) dressed in brown robes. Originally a palace for Prince Yongzheng, it was transformed into a temple once he became the Qing's third emperor in 1723. The temple flourished under Emperor Qianlong, housing some 500 resident monks.

While the souvenir shops add some kitsch, the monks temper this with their own brand of serenity. And although indoor photography is prohibited, the exterior of the temple is quite photogenic: the walls are richly painted, and the monks peep through misty incense smoke.

HIGHLIGHTS

The Hall of Heavenly Kings. With statues of Maitreya, the future Buddha, and Weitou, China's guardian of Buddhism, this hall is worth a slow stroll. In the courtyard beyond, a pond with a bronze mandala represents paradise.

Buddhas of the Past, Present, and Future. These Buddhas hold court in the Hall of Harmony. Look on the west wall where an exquisite silk thangkha of White Tara—the embodiment of compassion—hangs.

The Hall of Eternal Blessing. Images of the Medicine and Longevity Buddhas line this hall.

Resident monks. As many as two dozen monks live in this complex today.

Pavilion of Ten Thousand Fortunes. Gaze up at the breathtaking 26-meter (85-foot) Maitreya Buddha carved from a single sandalwood block.

CONFUCIUS TEMPLE (WITH THE IMPERIAL ACADEMY)

✉ Guozijian Lu off
   Yunghegong Lu near
   Lama Temple,
   Dongcheng District

☎ 010/8401-1977

🎟 Y20 (tickets are reduced
   if renovations cause
   restricted access)

🕐 Daily 9–5

Ⓜ Yonghegong

TIPS

■ We recommend combining a tour of the Confucius Temple with the nearby Lama Temple. Access to both is convenient from Yonghegong subway stop.

■ The surrounding hutongs are packed with teahouses, vegetarian restaurants, and quaint shops selling Tibetan and Buddhist artifacts.

★ **Fodor's Choice** This tranquil temple to China's great sage has endured close to eight centuries of additions and restorations. In 2006 it was once again under scaffolding and is now combined with the Imperial Academy (next door), once the highest educational institution in the country. The Great Accomplishment Hall in the temple houses Confucius's funeral tablet and shrine, flanked by copper-color statues depicting China's wisest Confucian scholars. Like in Buddhist and Taoist temples, worshippers can offer sacrifices (in this case, to a mortal, not a deity).

KEEP AN EYE OUT

Two carved stone drums, dating to the Qianlong period (1735–96) flank the Great Accomplishment Gate. In the Hall of Great Perfection you'll find the central shrine to Confucius. Check out the huge collection of ancient musical instruments.

HIGHLIGHTS

A cemetery of stone tablets. These tablets, or stelae, stand like rows of creepy crypts in the front and main courtyards of the temple. On the front stelae you can barely make out the names of thousands of scholars who passed imperial exams. Another batch of stelae, carved in the mid-1700s to record the *Thirteen Classics,* philosophical works attributed to Confucius, line the west side of the grounds.

The Imperial Academy. Established in 1306 as a rigorous training ground for high-level government officials, the academy was notorious, especially during the early Ming Dynasty era, for the harsh discipline imposed on scholars perfecting their knowledge of the Confucian classics.

Wander the Hall. The Riyong Emperors Lecture Hall is surrounded by a circular moat (although the building is rectangular in shape). Emperors would come here to lecture on the classics. This ancient campus would be a glorious place to study today with its washed red walls, gold-tiled roofs, and towering cypresses (some as old as 700 years).

ANCIENT OBSERVATORY

✉ 2 Dongbiaobei Hutong, Jianguomenwai Dajie, Chaoyang District

☎ 010/6524-2202

💴 Y10

🕐 Daily 9-4

Ⓜ Jianguomen

TIPS

■ The observatory sits on top of Jianguomen subway station.

■ The juxtaposition of these ancient devices with the sky-scrapers and elevated high-ways in the background make for curious, thought-provoking photos—the very essence of Beijing, indeed!

This squat tower of primitive stargazing equipment peeks out next to the elevated highways of the Second Ring Road. It dates to the time of Genghis Khan, who believed that his fortunes could be read in the stars. The instruments in this ancient observatory were among the emperor's most valuable possessions. Many of the bronze devices on display were gifts from Jesuit missionaries who arrived in Beijing and shortly thereafter ensconced themselves as the Ming court's resident stargazers. They offered this technology in a bid to persuade the Chinese of the superiority of the Christian tradition that had produced it. The main astronomical devices are arranged on the roof; inside, the dusty exhibition rooms shelter ancient star maps with information dating back to the Tang Dynasty.

HEAVEN-GAZING

To China's imperial rulers, interpreting the heavens was key to holding onto power; a ruler knew when, say, an eclipse would occur, or he could predict the best time to plant crops. Celestial phenomena like eclipses and comets were believed to portend change; if left unheeded they might cost an emperor his legitimacy—or Mandate of Heaven.

HIGHLIGHTS

Writhing bronze dragons. These sculptures adorn some of the astronomy pieces on the black-brick roof of Jianguo Tower, the main building that houses the observatory. Among the sculptures are an armillary sphere to pinpoint the position of heavenly bodies and a sextant to measure angular distances between stars and a celestial globe.

Star map. A Ming Dynasty star map and ancient charts are on display inside.

BIG BELL TEMPLE

✉ 1A Beisanhuanxi Lu,
   Haidian District

☎ 010/6255-0843

💳 Y10

🕐 Daily 8:30–4:30

Ⓜ Dazhong Si

TIPS

■ You can ride the subway to the temple: take overland Line 13 to Dazhong Si station.

■ The temple sometimes plays host to bell concerts and sells CDs of bell music.

This 18th-century temple shields China's biggest bell and hundreds of smaller bells from the Ming, Song, and Yuan dynasties. The Buddhist temple—originally used for rain prayers—has been restored after major damage inflicted during the Cultural Revolution. The bells here range from 7-meters (23-feet) wide to hand-sized chimes, many of them corroded a pale green by time.

FOOD FOR THOUGHT

Before it opened as a museum in 1985, the buildings were used as Beijing No. 2 Food Factory.

HIGHLIGHTS

Ding-dong. The two-story bell, cast with the texts of more than 100 Buddhist scriptures, is also said to be China's loudest. Believed to date from Emperor Yongle's reign, the 46-ton relic is considered a national treasure. People used to throw coins into a hole in the top of the bell for luck. The money was then swept up by the monks and used to buy food. Enough money was collected in a year to buy provisions that would last a month.

Play with handbells. Pretty much everything you'll ever need to know about bells you can find at the Ancient Bell Museum—from displays on how bells are cast to their long history. There are also more than 400 bells and gongs to see here.

MORE HISTORICAL SIGHTS

DONGCHENG DISTRICT

★

Drum Tower. Until the late 1920s, the 24 drums once housed in this tower were Beijing's timepiece. Sadly, all but one of these huge drums have been destroyed, and the survivor is in serious need of renovation. Kublai Khan built the first drum tower on this site in 1272. You can climb to the top of the present tower, which dates from the Ming Dynasty. Old photos of hutong neighborhoods line the walls beyond the drum; there's also a scale model of a traditional courtyard house. The nearby **Bell Tower,** renovated after a fire in 1747, offers fabulous views from the top of a long, narrow staircase. The huge 63-ton bronze bell, supported by lacquered wood stanchions, is also worth seeing. ✉ *North end of Dianmen Dajie, Dongcheng District* ☎ *010/6404–1710* 🚇 *Y20 for Drum Tower, Y15 for Bell Tower* 🕑 *Daily 9–4:30* Ⓜ *Gulou.*

XICHENG DISTRICT

Prince Gong's Palace. This grand compound sits in a neighborhood once reserved for imperial relatives. Built during the Ming Dynasty, it fell to Prince Gong, brother of Qing emperor Xianfeng and later an adviser to Empress Dowager Cixi. With nine courtyards joined by covered walkways, it was once one of Beijing's most lavish residences. The largest hall offers summertime Beijing opera and afternoon tea to guests on guided hutong tours. Some literary scholars believe this was the setting of the *Dream of the Red Chamber,* China's best-known classic novel. ✉ *17 Qianhai Xijie, Xicheng District* ☎ *010/6618–0573* 🚇 *Y20* 🕑 *Daily 8–4.*

Soong Ching-ling's Former Residence. Soong Ching-ling (1893–1981) was the youngest daughter of the wealthy, American-educated bible publisher Charles Soong. At the age of 18, disregarding her family's strong opposition, she eloped to marry the much older Sun Yat-sen. When her husband founded the Republic of China in 1911, Soong Ching-ling became a significant political figure. In 1924 she headed the Women's Department of the Nationalist Party. Then in 1949 she became the vice president of the People's Republic of China. Throughout her career she campaigned tirelessly for the emancipation of women. Indeed, the rights of modern-day Chinese women owe a great deal to her. This former palace was her residence and work place and now houses a small museum, which documents her life and work. ✉ *46 Houhai Beiyan, Xicheng District* ☎ *010/6403–5997* 🚇 *Y20* 🕑 *Daily 9–5.*

Temple of the White Pagoda. This 13th-century Tibetan stupa, the largest of its kind in China, dates from Kublai Khan's reign and owes its beauty to an unnamed Nepalese architect who built it to honor Sakyamuni Buddha. It stands bright and white against the Beijing skyline. Once hidden within the structure were Buddha statues, sacred texts, and other holy relics. Many of the statues are now on display in glass cases in the **Miaoying** temple, at the foot of the stupa. There is a great English-language display on the temple's history and renovation. ✉ *Fuchenmennei Dajie near Zhaodengyu Lu; turn right at first alley east of stupa, Xicheng District* ☎ *010/6616–6099* 🚇 *Y20* 🕑 *Daily 9–5.*

TIPS FOR TOURING WITH KIDS

Although incense-filled temples and ancient buildings do not, at first glance, seem child friendly, Beijing's historical sites do offer some unique and special activities for under-agers. The Summer Palace is a great place for kids to run around and go splashing in paddle boats; the old Summer Palace has a fun maze; Tiananmen Square is a popular spot to fly kites; the Drum Tower holds percussion performances; and the Temple of Heaven's Echo Wall offers up some unusual acoustical fun. Budding astronomers might also be intrigued by the Ancient Observatory with its Ming Dynasty star map and early heaven-gazing devices.

SOUTHERN DISTRICT: XUANWU

Front Gate (Qianmen). From its top looking south, you can see that Front Gate is actually two gates: Sun-Facing Gate (Zhengyangmen) and Arrow Tower (Jian Lou), which was, until 1915, connected to Zhengyangmen by a defensive half-moon wall. The central gates of both structures opened only for the emperor's biannual ceremonial trips to the Temple of Heaven to the south. ⊠ *Xuanwumen Jie, Xuanwu District* Ⓜ *Qianmen.*

Source of Law Temple. This temple is also a school for monks—the Chinese Buddhist Theoretical Institute houses and trains them here. Of course, the temple functions within the boundaries of current regime policy. You can observe both elderly practitioners chanting mantras in the main prayer halls, as well as robed students kicking soccer balls in a side courtyard. Before lunch the smells of vegetarian stir-fry tease the nose. The dining hall has simple wooden tables set with cloth-wrapped bowls and chopsticks. Dating from the 7th century but last rebuilt in 1442, the temple holds a fine collection of Ming and Qing statues, including a sleeping Buddha and an unusual grouping of copper-cast Buddhas seated on a 1,000-petal lotus. ⊠ *7 Fayuan Si Qianjie, Xuanwu District* ☎ *010/ 6353–4171* ᨎ *Y5* ☉ *Daily 8:30–3:30.*

White Clouds Taoist Temple. This lively Taoist temple serves as a center for China's only indigenous religion. Monks wearing blue-cotton coats and black-satin hats roam the grounds in silence. Thirty of them now live at the monastery, which also houses the official All-China Taoist Association. Visitors bow and burn incense to their favorite deities, wander the back gardens in search of a master of *qigong* (a series of exercises that involve slow movements and meditative breathing techniques, which are part of Chinese medicine), and rub the bellies of the temple's three monkey statues for good fortune.

In the first courtyard, under the span of an arched bridge, hang two large brass bells. Ringing them with a well-tossed coin is said to bring wealth. In the main courtyards, the **Shrine Hall for Seven Perfect Beings** is lined with meditation cushions and low desks. Nearby is a museum of Taoist history (explanations in Chinese). In the western courtyard, the temple's oldest structure is a shrine housing the **60-Year Protector.** Here the faithful locate the deity that corresponds to their birth year, bow to it, light incense, then scribble their names, or even a poem, on the wooden statue's red-cloth cloak as a reminder of their dedication. A trinket stall in the front courtyard sells pictures of each protector deity. Also in the west courtyard is a shrine to Taoist sage Wen Ceng, depicted in a 3-meter- (10-foot-) tall bronze statue just outside the shrine's main entrance. Students flock here to rub Wen Ceng's belly for good fortune on their college entrance exams. The area around the temple is packed with fortune-tellers. ⊠ *Lianhuachidong Lu near Xibianmen Bridge, Xuanwu District* ⌑ *Y10* ⊙ *Daily 8:30–4.*

HAIDIAN **Five-Pagoda Temple.** Hidden among trees just behind the zoo and set amid
DISTRICT carved stones, the temple's five pagodas reveal obvious Indian influences. It was built during the Yongle Years of the Ming Dynasty (1403–1424), in honor of an Indian Buddhist who came to China and presented a temple blueprint to the emperor. Elaborate carvings of curvaceous figures, floral patterns, birds, and hundreds of Buddhas decorate the pagodas. Also on the grounds is the **Beijing Art Museum of Stone Carvings,** with its collection of some 1,000 stelae and stone figures. ⊠ *24 Wuta Si, Baishiqiao, Haidian District* ☎ *010/6217–3836* ⌑ *Y20 for both; Y5 only for the temple* ⊙ *Tues.–Sun. 9–4.*

Temple of Azure Clouds. Once the home of a Yuan Dynasty official, the site was converted into a Buddhist temple in 1366 and enlarged during the 16th and 17th centuries by imperial eunuchs who hoped to be buried here. The temple's five main courtyards ascend a slope in **Fragrant Hills Park.** Although severely damaged during the Cultural Revolution, the complex has been beautifully restored.

The main attraction is the Indian-influenced Vajra Throne Pagoda. Lining its walls and five pagodas are gracefully carved stone-relief Buddhas and bodhisattvas. The pagoda once housed the remains of Nationalist China's founding father, Dr. Sun Yat-sen, who lay in state here between March and May 1925, while his mausoleum was being constructed in Nanjing. A hall in one of the temple's western courtyards houses about 500 life-size wood and gilt arhats (Buddhists who have reached Enlightenment)—each displayed in a glass case. ⊠ *Xiangshan Park, Haidian District* ☎ *010/6259–1155* ⌑ *Park Y10; temple Y10* ⊙ *Daily 6–6:30.*

MAO ZEDONG (1893–1976)

Some three decades after his passing, Mao Zedong continues to evoke radically different feelings. Was he the romantic poet-hero who helped the Chinese stand up? Or was he a monster whose policies caused the deaths of millions of people? Born into a relatively affluent farming family in Hunan, Mao became active in politics at a young age; he was one of the founding members of the Chinese Communist Party in 1921. When the People's Republic of China was established in 1949, Mao served as chairman. After a good start in improving the economy, he launched radical programs in the mid-1950s. The party's official assessment is that Mao was 70% correct and 30% incorrect. His critics reverse this ratio.

Continued on page 96

THE AGE OF EMPIRES

When asked his opinion on the historical impact of the French Revolution, Chairman Mao quipped, "it's too early to tell." Though a bit tongue in cheek, China does measure its history in millennia, and in its grand timeline, interactions with the West have been mere blips.

According to historical records, Chinese civilization stretches back to the 15th century BC—markings found on turtle shells carbon dated to around 1500 BC bear some similarity to modern Chinese script. China then resembled city-states rather than a unified nation. Iconic figures such as Lao Tzu (the father of Taoism), Sun Tzu (author of the *Art of War*), and Confucius lived during this period. Generally, 221 BC is accepted as the beginning of Imperial China, when the city-states united under various banners.

Over the next 2,200 years (give or take a few), China alternated between periods of harmony and political upheaval. Its armies conquered new territory and were in turn conquered by external invaders (most of whom wound up themselves being assimilated).

By the early 18th century, the long, slow decline of the Qing—the last of China's Imperial dynasties—was already in progress, making the ancient nation ripe for exploitation by rising European powers. The Imperial era ended with the forced abdication of child Emperor Puyi (whose life is chronicled in Bernardo Bertolucci's *The Last Emperor*), and it's here that the history of modern China, first with the founding of the republic under Sun Yat-sen and then with the establishment of the People's Republic under Mao Zedong, truly begins.

Writing Appears

1500 BC   1200 BC   900 BC

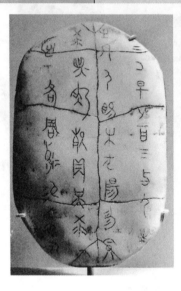

(left) Oracle shell with early Chinese characters. (top, right) The Great Wall stretches 4,163 miles from east to west. (bottom, right) Confucius was born in Qufu, Shandong.

circa 1500 BC

Writing Appears

The earliest accounts of Chinese history are still shrouded in myth and legend, and it wasn't until 1959 that stories were verified by archaeological findings. For millennia, people formed communities in the fertile lands of what is now central China. The first recorded Chinese characters are said to have been developed 3,500 years ago. Though sometimes referred to as the Shang Dynasty, this period was more of a precursor to modern Chinese dynasties than a truly unified kingdom.

722–475 BC

The Warring States Period

China was so far from unified that these centuries are collectively remembered as the Warring States Period. As befitting such a contentious time, military science progressed, iron replaced bronze, and weapons material improved. Some of China's greatest luminaries lived during this period, including the father of Taoism, Lao-tzu, Confucius, and Sun-Tzu, one of the greatest military tacticians and the author of infamous *Art of War*, which is still studied in military academies around the world.

221–207 BC

The First Dynasty

The Qin Dynasty eventually defeated all of the other warring factions thanks to their cutting-edge military technology, namely the cavalry. The Qin were also called Ch'in, which may be where the word China first originated. The first Emperor, Qin Shi-huang, unified much of the lands and established a legal code and vast bureaucracy to hold it together. The Qin dynasty also standardized the written and spoken language and introduced a common currency.

(left) Terracotta warriors in Xian, on the Silk Road. (top right) Buddha statue, Maijishan Cave in Tianshui, Gansa. (bottom left) Sun Tzu, author of The Art of War.

In order to protect his newly unified country, Qin Shihuang ordered the creation of the massive Great Wall of China, which was built and rebuilt over the next 1,000 years. He was also a sculpture enthusiast and commissioned a massive army of stone soldiers to follow him into the afterlife. Buried with him, these terracotta warriors would remain hidden from the eyes of the world for two thousand years, until they were found by a farmer digging in a field just outside of Xian. These warriors are among the most important archaeological finds of the 20th century.

220-265 BC

Buddhism Arrives

Emperor Qin's dreams of a unified China fell apart, and eventually the kingdom split into three warring factions. But what was bad for stability turned out to be a good for literature. The Three Kingdoms Period is still remembered in song and story. *The Romance of the Three Kingdoms* is as popular among Asian bookworms as the *Legend of King Arthur* is among Western readers. It's still widely read and has been translated into almost every language. Variations of the story have been adapted for manga,

television series, and video games.

The Three Kingdoms period was filled with court intrigue, murder, and massive battles that, while exciting to read about centuries later, weren't much fun at the time. Armies ravaged the countryside, and most people lived and died in misery. Perhaps it was the carnage and disunity of the time that turned the country into a magnet for forces of harmony; it was during this period that Buddhism was first introduced into China, traveling over the Himalayas from India, via the Silk Road.

(left) Genghis Khan conquered much of China. (top, right) Islamic lecture at madrassa classroom inside Dongguan mosque, Xinning. (bottom, right) Kublai Khan was the first Mongol Emperor of China.

618–845 Religion Diversifies

Chinese spiritual life continued to diversify. Nestorian Monks from Asia Minor arrived bearing news of Christianity, and Saad ibn Abi Waqqas (a companion of the Prophet Muhammad) supposedly visited the Middle Kingdom to spread the word of Islam. During this era, Wu Zetian, one-time concubine, seized power from the Tang Dynasty and became the first (and only) woman to assume the title of emperor. She ruled for 25 years through puppet emperors and finally, for 15 years as Emperor Shengshen.

1271–1368 Ghengis Invades

In Xanadu did Kublai Khan a stately pleasure dome decree...
Or so goes the famed Coleridge poem. But Kublai's grandfather Temujin (better known as Ghengis Khan) had bigger things in mind. One of the greatest war tacticians in history, he united the restive nomads of Mongolia's grassy plains and eventually sacked, looted, and pillaged much of the known west and most of the Chinese landmass. By the time Ghengis died in 1227, his grandson was well-tutored and ready to take on the rest of China.

By 1271, Kublai had established a capital in a landlocked city that would only much later become known as Beijing. This marks the beginning of the first (but not last) non-Han dynasty. Kublai Khan kept fighting southward and by 1279, Guangzhou fell to the Mongols, and Khan became the ultimate monarch of China. Though barbarians at heart, the Mongols must be credited for encouraging the arts and a number of early public works projects, including extending the highways and grand canals.

(left) Statue of admiral Zheng He. (top right) Forbidden City in Beijing (bottom right) Child emperor Puyi.

1368–1644

Ming Dynasty

Many scholars believe that the Mongols' inability to relate with the Han is what ultimately pushed the Han to rise up and overthrow them. The reign of the Ming Dynasty was the last ethnically Han Dynasty to rule over a unified China. At its apex, the Bright Empire encompassed a landmass easily recognized as China, even by today's mapmakers. The Ming Emperors built a huge army and navy, refurbished the agricultural system, and printed many books using movable type long before Gutenberg. In the 13th century, Emperor Yongle began construction of the famous Forbidden City in Beijing, a veritable icon of China.

Also during the Ming Dynasty, China's best known explorer, Zheng He, plied the seven seas in massive treasure fleets that dwarfed in size and range the ships of Christopher Columbus. A giant both in stature and persona, Admiral Zheng (who was also a eunuch) spent two decades expanding China's knowledge of the world outside of its already impressive borders. He traveled as far as India, Africa, and (some say) even the coast of the New World.

1644–1911

Qing Dynasty

The final dynasty represented a serious case of minority rule. They were Manchus from the northeast. The early Qing dynasty was a brutal period as forces loyal to the new emperor crushed those loyal to the old. The Qing Dynasty peaked in the mid-to-late 18th century but soon after, its military powers began to wane. In the 19th century, Qing control weakened and prosperity diminished. By 1910 China was fractured, a baby sat on the Imperial throne, and the Qing Dynasty was on its deathbed.

(left) Portrait of Marshal Chiang Kai Shek with his wife. (top, right) Mao Zedong on December 6, 1944. (bottom, right) Sun Yat-Sen.

The Opium Wars

1834–1860

European powers were hungry to open new territories up for trade, but the Qing weren't buying. The British East India Company, strapped for cash, realized they could sell opium in China at huge profits. The Chinese government quickly banned the nefarious trade and in response, a technologically superior Britain declared war. After a humiliating defeat in the first Opium War, China was forced to cede Hong Kong. Other foreign powers followed with territorial demands of their own.

Republican Era

1912–1949

China's Republican period was chaotic and unstable. The revolutionary Dr. Sun Yat-sen —revered by most Chinese as the father of modern China— was unable to build a cohesive government without the aid of regional warlords and urban gangsters. When he died of cancer in 1925, power passed to Chiang Kai-shek, who set about unifying China under the Kuomintang. What began as a unified group of both left-and-right wingers quickly deteriorated, and by the mid-1920s, civil war between the Communists and Nationalists was brewing.

The '30s and '40s were bleak decades for the Chinese people, caught between a vicious war with Japan and periodic clashes between Kuomintang and Communist forces. After Japan's defeat in 1945, China's civil war kicked into high gear. Though the Kuomintang were armed with superior weapons and backed by American money, the majority of Chinese people rallied behind the Communists. Within four years, the Kuomintang were driven off the mainland to Taiwan, where the Republic of China exists to the present day.

3

THE AGE OF EMPIRES

(top left) Illiterate soldiers are taught about Mao's *Little Red Book* in Beijing December 1966. (top right) Central Shenzhen, Guangdong (bottom left) Poster of Mao's slogans.

1949 – Present

The People's Republic

On October 1, 1949, Mao Zedong declared from atop Beijing's Gate of Heavenly Peace that "The Chinese People have stood up." And so the People's Republic of China was born. The communist party set out to overhaul China's ancient feudal system, emphasizing class struggle, redistribution of wealth, and elimination of foreign dominance. The next three decades would see a massive, often painful transformation of Chinese society from feudalism into the modern age.

The Great Leap Forward was a disaster—Chinese peasants were encouraged to cram 100 years of industrial development into as many weeks. Untenable decisions led to industrial and agricultural ruin, widespread famine, and an estimated 30 million deaths. The trauma of this period, however, pales in comparison to The Great Proletarian Cultural Revolution. From 1966–1976, fear and zealotry gripped the nation as young revolutionaries heeded Chairman Mao's call to root out class enemies. During this decade, millions died, millions were imprisoned, and much of China's accumulated religious, historical, and cultural heritage literally went up in smoke.

Like a phoenix rising from its own ashes, China rose from its own self-inflicted destruction. In the early 1980s, Deng Xiao-ping took the first steps in reforming China's stagnant economy. With the maxim "To Get Rich is Glorious," Deng loosened central control on the economy and declared Special Economic Zones, where the seeds of capitalism could be incubated. Two decades later, the nation is one of the world's most vibrant economic engines. Though China's history is measured in millennia, her brightest years may well have only just begun.

Temple of Longevity. A Ming empress built this temple to honor her son in 1578. Qing emperor Qianlong later restored it as a birthday present to his mother. From then until the fall of the Qing, it served as a rest stop for imperial processions traveling by boat to the Summer Palace and Western Hills. Today the temple is managed by the Beijing Art Museum and houses a small but exquisite collection of Buddha images. The Buddhas in the main halls include Sakyamuni sitting on a 1,000-petal, 1,000-Buddha bronze throne and dusty Ming-period Buddhas. ⊠ *Xisanhuan Lu, on the north side of Zizhu Bridge, Haidian District* ☎ *010/6841–3380* ⊡ *Y20* ⊙ *Daily 8:30–4:30.*

Temple of the Reclining Buddha. Although the temple was damaged during the Cultural Revolution and poorly renovated afterward, the Sleeping Buddha remains. Built in 627–629, during the Tang Dynasty, the temple was later named after the reclining Buddha that was brought in during the Yuan Dynasty (1271–1368). An English-language description explains that the casting of the beautiful bronze, in 1321, enslaved 7,000 people. The temple is inside the **Beijing Botanical Garden** (www.beijingbg.com/en_index.htm); stroll north from the entrance through the neatly manicured grounds. ⊠ *Xiangshan Lu, 2 km (1 mi) northeast of Xiangshan Park, Haidian District* ⊡ *Temple Y5; gardens Y5* ⊙ *Daily 8:30–4.*

> **WORD OF MOUTH**
>
> We took a fantastic trip to Beijing. We did a lot but were able to keep a reasonable pace:
> - Stayed at Peninsula–excellent!
> - Hutong tour by pedicab (a highlight!)
> - Forbidden City (used audio tour)
> - Summer Palace
> - Great Wall at Mutianyu (with an English-speaking driver)
> - Jingshan Park (climbed to the top of the hill for great view)
> - Temple of Heaven
> - Hongqiao Market
> - Silk Alley Market
> - Tiananmen Square
> - Red Capital Club (funky, Maoist kitsch, good food)
>
> –Lindsey

A woman in traditional dress at the Nine Dragons Screen in Beihai Park.

(top) The dramatic makeup and opulent costumes of Beijing Opera. (bottom) The Temple of Heaven.

(top) A Jackie Chan wax figure strikes a pose at the National Museum of China. (bottom) The view of the Forbidden City from Meridian Gate.

(top left) A street vendor in Dazhalan. (top right) National treasures at the Big Bell Temple.
(bottom) Tiananmen, or the Gate of Heavenly Peace.

(top) Checking out the goods in a Beijing mall. (bottom) A faint smile from Mao Zedong on the 100-Yuan note.

(top) A view across the rooftops of an ancient hutong. (bottom left) Beijing will host the 2008 Olympic Games. (bottom right) The Spring Lantern Festival lights up a Beijing park.

(top) A colorful Chinese New Year celebration. (bottom) Fascinating ruins at the Old Summer Palace.

Stunning views of the Great Wall at Badaling.

At a Glance

ENGLISH	PINYIN	CHINESE CHARACTERS
POINTS OF INTEREST		
Ancient Observatory	Gǔguānxiàngtái	古观象台
Bell Tower	Zhōnglóu	钟楼
Big Bell Temple	Dàzhōng Sì	大钟寺
Confucius Temple	Kǒngzǐ Miào	孔子庙
Danbi Bridge	Dānbì Qiáo	丹陛桥
Drum Tower	Gǔlóu	鼓楼
Five-Pagoda Temple	Wǔtǎ Sì	五塔寺
Forbidden City	zǐ jìn chéng	紫禁城
Fuhai Lake	Fúhǎi Hú	福海湖
Hall of Prayer for Good Harvests	Qíniándiàn	祈年殿
Imperial Academy	Guózǐjiàn	国子监
Kunming Lake	Kūnmíng Hú	昆明湖
Lama Temple	Yōnghé Gōng	雍和宫
Monument to the People's Heroes	Rénmín Yīngxióng Jìniànbēi	人民英雄纪念碑
Niujie (Ox Street) Mosque	Niújiē Qīngzhēnsì	牛街清真寺
Old Summer Palace	Yuánmíngyuán	圆明园
Prince Gong's Palace	Gōng Wángfǔ	恭王府
Qianmen ("front gate")	Qiánmén	前门
Soong Qing-ling's Former Residence	Sòng Qìng Líng Gùjū	宋庆铃故居
Source of Law Temple	Fǎyuán Sì	法源寺
Summer Palace	Yíhéyuán	颐和园
Temple of Azure Clouds	Bìyúnsì	碧云寺
Temple of Heaven	Tiāntán	天坛
Temple of Longevity	Wànshòu Sì	万寿寺
Temple of the Reclining Buddha	Wòfó Sì	卧佛寺
Temple of the White Pagoda	Báitǎ Sì	白塔寺
Tiananmen Square	Tiān'ānmén Guǎngchǎng	天安门广场
White Clouds Taoist Temple	Bái yún guàn	白云观

Shopping

Whether you're searching for the next family heirloom or a fabulous fake, rest assured there's plenty of jewelry in Beijing.

WORD OF MOUTH

"Beijing has lots of markets, and all are about 5 to 6 stories high, selling everything you could possibly imagine. You need to bargain, as opening prices can be very high." —Mole

"Watch out on sizing: everything runs small! Even my sister, who is a size 6–8 in the U.S., is an XL there!" —quimbymoy

"For shopping at the markets, I recommend women wear a tank top, so you can try on clothing over it." —nagiffag

SHOPPING PLANNER

Great Souvenirs

- A pearl necklace with matching earrings from Hongqiao Market
- A pair of Chinese slippers from Nei Lian Sheng Xie Dian
- A hand-embroidered silk qipao, tailored to the perfect fit
- Knockoff designer handbags, shoes, or sunglasses
- Canisters of oolong and jasmine tea
- Beijing 2008 Olympic memorabilia
- Traditional Chinese scrolls
- Calligraphy brushes
- Reproduction Communist propaganda posters
- A vacuum-sealed package of Peking Duck
- A jade pendant representing your Chinese zodiac
- Decorative name chop carved with your Chinese or English name
- Porcelain tea sets from Tea Street

Sample Costs in Beijing

DVD on street	Y6
DVD in store	Y12
Name chop, with inscription	Y50
Genuine Pashmina scarf	Y150
Fake Pashmina scarf	Y30
Knockoff sunglasses	Y40
Mid-quality strand of freshwater pearls	Y115

Top Places to Shop

Dazhalan. This centuries-old shopping street, in the southern part of the city, is packed with old-world charm. The Tongrentang Chinese medicine store and the Nei Lian Sheng shoe shop hawk their time-tested quality goods alongside faddish chain stores and ambulatory vendors whispering "watch, bag, DVD." Three silk shops offer wide selections of real and fake silk, with on-site tailors.

China World Trade Center. High-end clothing shops float above an ice-skating rink in the two towers of the China World Mall. Silk Alley hustles and bustles down the street, and the weekend Panjiayuan Market is just a short cab ride away.

Liulichang. A shopping street in Xuanwu District, just south of the Peace (Hepingmen) Gate, Liulichang exudes a more authentic, old-school feel than Dazhalan. It has clusters of antiques and calligraphy shops. Less crowded than Dazhalan, Liulichang is the place to peruse curio shops, ink-and-brush stalls, and artisan studios.

Sanlitun. Known among foreigners as "bar street," this has developed into a shopping hot spot. Situated between the Workers' Stadium and the Embassy District, Sanlitun offers a wide range of shopping experiences—from the busy Yaxiu Market to glamorous boutiques.

Wangfujing Dajie. Beijing's premier shopping street simply glistens with new malls. This pedestrian-only lane overflows with spending opportunities from Adidas to Tiffany's to snack shops and souvenir stalls.

Ultimate Shopping Tour

Day 1 (weekend): Can't sleep from jet lag? No worries. Rise before dawn and join the hordes at **Panjiayuan,** also known as Dirt Market, for a Beijing Shopping 101. Spend at least two hours on a reconnaissance tour of this vast market before making any purchases. Bags in tow, head directly across the street to **Zhaojia Chaowai** for a more manageable experience of shopping for furniture and goodies. Next direct a pedicab driver to **Beijing Curio City.** From here, take a cab to examine the quality, style, and exorbitant prices of the high-end shops at **China World Shopping Center** and eat lunch in one of the restaurants. You can then ice-skate before marching on toward **Silk Alley.** Haggle hard here and load up on knockoff designer clothes, bags, and accessories.

Day 2: Head south out of Qianmen Metro (Exit C) and grab a fried dough stick and cup of sweetened soy milk from a street-side vendor. Fortified, enter the wonderland of **Dazhalan** (pronounced "Dashilanr" by locals) for an ancient-meets-modern kaleidoscope of sights, smells, and sounds. Travel its length by foot; when the shops taper off, catch a pedicab to **Liulichang.** Linger in this old-time shopping street before re-entering the modern world at **Wangfujing.** This pedestrian-only shopping arcade is just east of the Forbidden City. If this mix of malls, snack shops, and souvenir stalls doesn't wipe you out, take a cab to **Hongqiao Market** for a pearl shopping spree.

Day 3: Kick off the day by sampling teas in the seemingly infinite number of tea vendors pedaling their goods on **Tea Street.** Buy clay or porcelain service sets and tea galore. From here, cab east toward Chaoyangmen and storm the shoe markets on **Alien Street.** Properly outfitted, hit Sanlitun for a visit to **Yaxiu Market,** and the designer boutiques and minimalls that are sprouting all over this bar district. Shop, shop, shop, and then drop—wherever you land, a waiter will appear to offer you an ice-cold cola or Tsingtao beer.

Avoid Scams

Fakes abound—everything from jade, cashmere, Pashminas, silk, and leather to handbags, antiques, and Calvin Klein underwear. Fake is great, if that's what you're after, but do reserve your big purchases for accredited shops or merchants who can prove the quality of their product. Some countries limit the number of knockoffs you can bring back into the country, so don't go overboard on the handbags. If you're buying authentic antiques, you'll need to show customs agents your receipts, embossed with an official red seal.

Chinese medicine is wonderful, but not when practiced by lab-coated "doctors" sitting behind a card table on the street corner. If you're seeking Chinese medical treatment, visit a local hospital, Tongrentang medicine shop, or ask your hotel concierge for a legitimate recommendation.

⚠ Deception is the only real "art" practiced by the charming "art students" who will invite you to their college's art show. The art works are, in fact, usually painted by hand, but they are mass-produced copies. If you want to support Beijing's burgeoning art scene, explore the galleries of Dashanzi, visit an artists' village, or drop by one of the galleries listed in Chapter 5.

Bargaining is acceptable, and expected, in markets and mom-and-pop shops, though not in malls. The bottom line of bargaining is to pay what you think is fair. No matter how much you haggle, foreigners will almost always be charged more than the local price.

By Katharine Mitchell

Large markets and malls in Beijing are generally open from 9 AM to 9 PM, though some shops close at 7 PM. It's always best to call ahead if you hope to shop in the early morning or late evening. Weekdays are always less crowded, and shops tend to be quieter just after lunch, when many Chinese people (including some merchants) take a rest. During rush hour, avoid taking taxis. If a shop looks closed (the lights are out or the owner is resting), don't give up. Many merchants conserve electricity or take catnaps if the store is free of customers. Just knock or offer the greeting "ni hao." More likely than not, the lights will flip on and you'll be invited to come in and take a look.

Major credit cards are accepted in select venues. Cash is the driving currency and ATMs abound. Before accepting those pink, Mao-faced Y100 notes, most vendors will hold them up to the light, tug at the corners, and feel the surface. Counterfeiting is becoming increasingly more difficult, but no one, including you, wants to be cheated. In some department stores, you must settle your bill at a central payment counter.

Almost every shop has at least one employee who speaks English. But money remains the international language. Whether or not the clerk speaks English—or you speak Chinese—he or she will still whip out a calculator, look at you thoughtfully, then type in a starting price. You're expected to counteroffer. Punch in your dream price. The clerk will come down Y10 or Y20 and so on and so on. Remember that the terms "yuan," "kuai," and "RMB" are often used interchangeably. ■ TIP→ **Some folks sheath their calculators, cell phones, and remote controls in plastic in the name of hygiene. If handed a calculator in a plastic bag, go with it.**

FODOR'S FIRST PERSON

Katharine Mitchell
Among the Beijing Teens

In a bright shop stocked with Mickey Mouse T-Shirts and Hello Kitty paraphernalia, I met a 16-year-old spiky-haired student. Dressed in a baggy pair of Fox Racing jeans and a red "EZ Sport," he smiled with the shy-coy demeanor of a boy-band pop star. He pointed at the basket of gummy bracelets I was examining and said, "The girls at my school wear these up to here." He drew an imaginary line across his forearm then grabbed a cluster of all-black gummies. He took a deep whiff. "Ah," he said, "They smell very, very good."

Just outside, we met up with his classmates, who were eager to practice their English. They showed off their cell phones, pencil boxes, and MP3 players, all plastered with stickers of Hong Kong and Taiwanese pop stars.

A slender girl with pigtails served as spokeswoman. She wore aqua-green jeans and a pink jumper that epitomized branding: DESIGN GRAPHICS STORE T-SHIRT. On behalf of the clan, she quizzed me: "Do you like Chinese food? Can you use chopsticks? Do you know Yao Ming? Do you think Leonardo DiCaprio is handsome boy?"

The co-eds sang their ABC's, followed by Lionel Richie's "Say You, Say Me." The boys interrupted with falsetto impressions of Britney Spears and the Backstreet Boys. They agreed, unanimously, that Michael Jackson is a very, very good dancer.

Dongcheng District

With its tiny, crumbling shops perched along old city streets and other-end-of-the-spectrum glitzy shopping malls, Dongcheng is one of the most popular shopping areas for visitors to Beijing. Whether searching for souvenirs, silks, or foreign-language magazines, Dongcheng has everything. Its centralized location makes it simple to combine sightseeing with shopping trips.

Books

Foreign Languages Bookstore. Head directly to the third floor, which is reserved for imported publications. Classics perpetually roost on the shelves of this state-owned shop, but bestsellers, biographies, and decent books about China also make the cut (though don't expect to read anything on the Tiananmen Square incidents). Find maps, Chinese-language learning materials, and children's books here, too, as well as a Starbucks on the ground floor. ⊠ *235 Wangfujing Dajie, Dongcheng District* ☎ *010/6512–6903* Ⓜ *Wangfujing.*

Malls & Department Stores

Beijing Department Store. Wangfujing's grand dame continues to attract large crowds with stores selling everything from jewelry to clothing to sports equipment. ⊠ *255 Wangfujing Dajie, Dongcheng District* ☎ *010/ 6512–6677* Ⓜ *Wangfujing.*

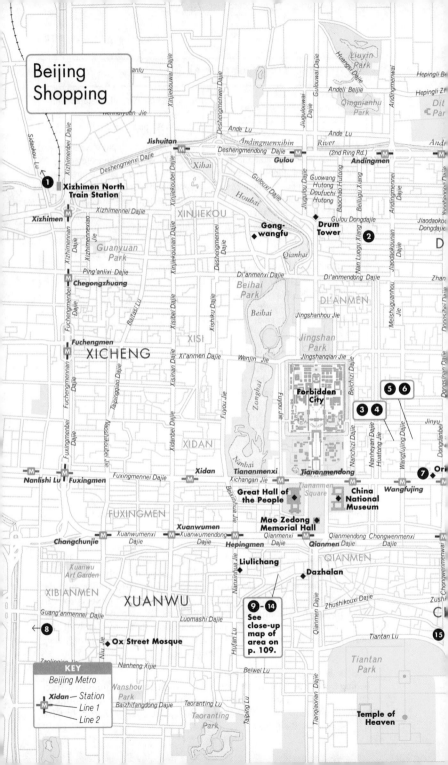

★ **Malls at Oriental Plaza.** This enormous shopping complex originates at the southern end of Wangfujing, where it meets Chang'an Jie, and stretches a city block east to Dongan Dajie. A true city within a city, it's conveniently organized by "street" names, such as Gourmet Street (aka the Food Court) and Sky Avenue. Upscale shops include **Max Mara** and **Sisley.** ✉ *1 Dongchang'an Jie, Dongcheng District* ☎ *010/ 8518–6363* Ⓜ *Wangfujing.*

> ### THE MALLS ARE HOPPIN'
>
> Malls are gradually replacing markets as the main places to shop and socialize in Beijing. Most malls here were built starting in the late 1990s, so they are generally new and shiny, with international chains and independent boutiques as well as food courts, restrooms, and ATMs (which often include English options).

Sun Dongan Plaza. A massive shopping center with dozens of designer shops also makes a concession to Old Peking with a traditional-style shopping street on the second floor. On the third floor, the **Mu Zhen Liao Chinese Fashion Boutique** sells high-quality, ready-made *qipaos* (Chinese-style dresses) as well as tailor-made ones. The store is especially popular with brides-to-be. ✉ *138 Wangfujing Dajie, Dongcheng District* ☎ *010/6528–1788* Ⓜ *Wangfujing.*

Silk & Fabrics

China Star Silk Store. In the Wangfujing area, this is a great place to consider buying a qipao, the traditional Chinese silk dress. ✉ *133 Wangfujing Dajie, Dongcheng District* ☎ *010/6525–7945* Ⓜ *Wangfujing.*

T-Shirt Boutique

Plastered T-Shirts. The recent gentrification of Nanluoguxiang Hutong is due in part to the planned razing of older developments, and in part to the entrepreneurial spirit of bar and restaurant owners, who advertise free Wi-Fi and cheap Tsingtao beer. Directly across from the Downtown Backpackers Hostel, two British lads have raised the ante for T-shirt shopping. Shop here for T-shirts with Chinese slogans, pictures of Gong Bao Ji Ding—the foreign-friendly dish of chicken, peppers, and peanuts—or opt for one that captures those nostalgic days of Old Peking. It's on the expensive side, but fun for the kitsch. ✉ *Nanluoguxiang Hutong off Gulou Dong Da Jie, Dongcheng District* ☎ *134/ 8884–8855* ⊕ *www.plastered.com.cn.*

Xicheng District

Less than 2 km (1 mi) west of the Forbidden City, the massive shopping area of **Xidan,** within the Xicheng district, swarms with local shoppers intent on bargaining for socks, sundresses, men's trousers, and the latest pop-star trends. To get here, take the red subway line to the Xidan stop (exit A). By taxi, simply show the driver the Chinese characters for "Xidan" (*see* the language glossary at the end of this chapter). Quality is equated with price here, and many foreign shoppers prefer to stick with the Silk and Pearl markets for smaller crowds and higher quality goods. But if you're up for this potentially overwhelming jaunt into the crush of young Chinese crowds, you can elbow your way through the labyrinth

EXPLORING TEA STREET

Tea Street. Maliandao hosts the ultimate tea party every day of the week. Literally hundreds of tea shops perfume the air of this prime tea-shopping district, west of the city center. Midway down this near-mile-long strip looms the **Teajoy Market,** the Silk Alley of teas. Unless you're an absolute fanatic, it's best to visit a handful of individual shops, crashing tea parties wherever you go. Vendors will invite you to sit down in heavy wooden chairs to nibble on pumpkin seeds and sample their large selections of black, white, oolong, jasmine, and chrysanthemum teas. Prices range from a few kuai for a decorative container of loose green tea to thousands of yuan for an elaborate gift set. Tea Street is also the place to stock up on clay and porcelain teapots and service sets. Green and flower teas are sold loose; black teas are sold pressed into disks and wrapped in natural-colored paper. Despite the huge selection of drinking vessels available, you'll find that most locals prefer to drink their tea from a recycled glass jar.
✉ *Located near Guanganmen Wai Dajie, Xuanwu District.*

of malls, markets, and chain stores to find some cheap souvenirs clustered along **Xidan Beidajie,** just north of the Xidan subway stop.

Here you'll also find China's crowning **Beijing Book Building** (✉ 17 Changan Jie, Xicheng District ☎ 010/6607–8498 Ⓜ Xidan), a multi-level fortress stocked with hundreds of thousands of books, magazines, maps, and learning materials. The English-language selection is slim, yet travelers still love browsing here.

Southern Districts: Chongwen & Xuanwu

Chinese Medicine

★ **Tongrentang.** A first-time consultation with a Chinese doctor can feel a bit like a reading with a fortune-teller. With one test of the pulse, many traditional Chinese doctors can describe the patient's medical history and diagnose current maladies. China's most famous traditional Chinese medicine shop, Tongrentang, is the jewel of Dazhalan, the charming pedestrian street just south of Qianmen. Palatial, hushed, and dimly lit, this 300-year-old old shop even smells healthy. Browse the glassed displays of deer antlers and pickled snakes, dried seahorse and frog, and delicate tangles of roots with precious price tags of Y48,000.
■ TIP→ **If you don't speak Chinese and wish to have a consultation with a doctor, bring along a translator.** ✉ *24 Dazhalan, Qianmen, Exit C, Chongwen District* Ⓜ *Qianmen.*

Markets

Pearls, pearls, pearls! Few shoppers visit Beijing without a trip to the Hongqiao Market (aka Pearl Market), where mid-quality pearls are cheap and plentiful. An afternoon of shopping in Chongwen and Xuanwu can be balanced with a morning tour of the nearby Temple of Heaven.

You *Can* Judge a Pearl by Its Luster

ALL THE BAUBLES OF BEIJING could be strung together and wrapped around the earth 10-times over—or so it seems with Beijing's abundance of pearl vendors. It's mind-boggling to imagine how many oysters it would take to produce all those natural pearls. But, of course, not all are real: some are cultured and others fake.

The attentive clerks in most shops are eager to prove their product quality. Be wary of salespeople who don't demonstrate, with an eager and detailed pitch, why one strand is superior to another. Keep in mind the following tips as you judge whether that gorgeous strand is destined to be mere costume jewelry or the next family heirloom.

■ **Color:** Natural pearls have an even hue, whereas dyed pearls vary in coloration.

■ **Good Luster:** Pick only the shiniest apples in the bunch. Pearls should have a healthy glow.

■ **Shape:** The strand should be able to roll smoothly across a flat surface without wobbling.

■ **Blemishes:** We hate them on our faces and we hate them on our pearls.

■ **Size:** Smaller pearls are obviously less expensive than larger ones, but don't get trapped into paying more for larger poor-quality pearls just because they're heftier.

The cost of pearls varies widely. A quality strand will generally run around US$50 to $200, but it's possible to buy good-looking but lower-quality pearls much more cheaply. As with any purchase, choose those pearls you adore most, and only pay as much as you think they warrant. After all, we could all use an extra strand of good-looking fakes. Also, if you plan on making multiple purchases and you have time to return to the same shop, go ahead and establish a "friendship" with one key clerk. Each time you return, or bring a friend, the price will miraculously drop.

★ ۞ **Hongqiao Market** (Pearl Market). Hongqiao is full of tourist goods, knock-off handbags, and cheap watches, but it's best known for its three stories of pearls, hence its knick-name: the Pearl Market. Freshwater, seawater, black, pink, white: the quantity is overwhelming and quality varies by stall. Prices range wildly. Fanghua Pearls (No. 4318), on the fourth floor, displays quality necklaces and earrings, with photos of Barbara Bush and Margaret Thatcher shopping there to prove it. Fanghua has a second store devoted to fine jade and precious stones. As a bonus, hold your nose and dive into the fish and meat market in the basement, a veritable aquarium of sea cucumbers, crab, dragon shrimp, squid, and eel. ✉ *Tiantan Lu, between Chongemenwai Lu and Tiyuguan Dajie, Chongwen District, east of the northern entrance to Temple of Heaven* ☎ *010/6711–7630.*

Shoes

Nei Lian Sheng Xie Dian. A few paces down from Tongrentang, Nei Lian Sheng sells traditional Chinese slippers and shoes in all sizes—even for Western feet. Photographs display Mao Zedong and Deng Xiaoping happily wearing the very shoes sold here. ✉ *34 Dazhalan, Qianmen, Exit C, Chongwen District* Ⓜ *Qianmen.*

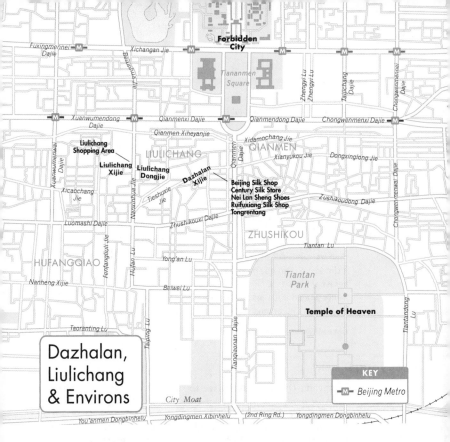

KEY
—Ⓜ— Beijing Metro

Silk & Fabrics

Beijing Silk Shop. Since 1830, the Beijing Silk Shop has been supplying the city with quality silks and fabrics. This formerly musty store is being renovated; expect a supreme shopping experience in the new space by the 2008 Olympic games. Until then, focus on the silk, not the decor. To reach the shop, walk all the way down Dazhalan, then head directly onto Dazhalan West Street. ■ TIP→ **Two other, much larger stores on Dazhalan major in silk. Ruifuxiang, at No. 5, is housed in a beautiful two-story building, as is Century Silk Store at No. 33.** ⊠ *50 Dazhalan Xi Jie, Xuanwu District* ☎ *010/6301–6658* Ⓜ *Qianmen.*

Beijing Yuanlong Silk Corporation. Jars of silkworm pupa and baskets of cocoons greet you on the second floor of Yuanlong. A tour guide will walk you through the silk quilt-making process while women in white lab coats demonstrate how to clean, soak, and stretch the silk of cocoons. It's touristy but fun if you've never seen the process. Silk quilts and duvets are for sale, as well as an on-site tailor for making qipaos. Quilts are craftily compacted into tiny rectangles—especially handy for international travelers. ■ TIP→ **You should avoid this spot entirely if tour buses are lined-up in the parking lot.** ⊠ *55 Tiantan Lu, Chongwen District, between the north gate of Temple of Heaven Park and Hongqiao* ☎ *010/6701–2859.*

DVLs in Beijing

DIGITAL-VIDEO DISCS of current blockbuster movies often hit the streets of Beijing the same week as they open in U.S. theaters—and sometimes even before. Although the sales of these pirated DVDs are illegal (they blatantly disregard international copyright laws), DVD sales take place so openly in Beijing that it doesn't give the impression of being wrong. The government will occasionally crack down on stores or shoo away vendors, but that's all, so, if you're so inclined, you can buy or at least peruse the goods. Unlike in countries where pirated DVDs are sold down back alleys and behind closed doors, in China they are sold in permanent shops that will even exchange your DVD if the quality isn't good. Prices range from Y6 on the street to Y12 in the shops. The latter claim to have better-quality copies than the street vendors.

Most countries, however, including the United States, forbid the importation of pirated DVDs. Those caught carrying DVDs out of China or into another country will likely be requested to surrender their spoils. For more information about U.S. Customs rules visit ⊕ www.customs.gov.

Chaoyang District

Chaoyang District is *the* place to shop in Beijing, with giant markets, well-stocked malls, and endless boutiques. Highlights include Panjiayuan Antique Market, Silk Alley, and Yaxiu Market.

Books

★ **The Bookworm.** Book lovers, hipsters, and aspiring poets take note: this lending library and bookstore offers a spacious second-story reading room with a full café and bar. All are welcome to browse: the magazine and new-books section are a stupendous sight for English-starved travelers. The store frequently hosts poetry readings and lectures; check their Web site for schedule. ⊠ *4 Sanlitun Nan Lu, set back slightly in a parking lot, Chaoyang District* ☎ *010/6586–9507* ⊕ *www.beijingbookworm.com.*

Computers & Electronics

Bainaohui Computer Shopping Mall. Next door to the Wonderful Electronic Shopping Mall is Bainao, literally "one hundred computers." Home to

> **PACK AN EXTRA BOOK**
>
> In general, China has a limited selection of English-language books and magazines, thanks to strict censorship authorities. Some hotel kiosks, such as the Kempinski and China World, sell a small selection of international newspapers and magazines, but they rarely stock novels. If you've got room in your luggage, you're best off bringing enough reading material to last your entire trip.

hundreds of laptops and PCs, this retail mall is crammed with individual vendors. The Chinese word for computer translates literally as "electric brain." ⊠ *10 Chaoyangmenwai Da Jie, Chaoyang District* ☎ *010/
6599–5912* Ⓜ *Chaoyangmen.*

Wonderful Electronic Shopping Mall. Cameras, tripods, flash disks, MP3s
(called MP-San in Chinese) abound. If you forgot the USB cable for your
digital recorder or need extra camera batteries, this is the place to shop.
⊠ *12 Chaoyangmenwai Da Jie, Chaoyang District* ☎ *010/8561–4335*
Ⓜ *Chaoyangmen.*

Fashion Designers & Boutiques

Heyan'er. He Yan's design philosophy is stated in her label: BU YAN BU
YU, or NO TALKING. Her linen and cotton tunics and collarless jackets
speak for themselves. From earth tones to aubergine hues and peacock
patterns, He Yan's designs echo traditional Tibetan styles. ⊠ *15–2
Gongti Bei Lu* ☎ *010/6415–9442* ⊠ *Holiday Inn Lido, 6 Fangyuan
Xi Lu* ☎ *010/6437–6854.*

The Red Phoenix. In this cramped-but-charming Sanlitun studio/show-
room, fashion diva Gu Lin designs embroidered satin qipaos, cropped
jackets, and men's clothing for stylish foreigners and China's *xin xin
ren lei* (literally the "new, new human being," referring to the country's
latest flock of successful young professionals). ⊠ *30 Sanlitun Bei Jie*
☎ *010/6416–4423.*

Tongli Studio. Though Tongli Studio is overhyped, this cluster of inter-
nationally-owned boutiques, cafés, and rooftop bars is worth a gander
if you're already cruising Sanlitun. **Feng Ling Fashion** displays sexy thigh-
high embroidered silk boots and punky qipaos. At **Things of the Jing,**
Londoner Gabrielle Harris alchemizes silver with images of feudal-era
Chinese women to create funky-elegant earrings and pendants. **Radi-
ance** carries pagoda-shaped ceramic birdfeeders. ⊠ *43 Sanlitun Hou Jie,
Chaoyang District* ☎ *010/6417–7715* ⊕ *www.tonglistudio.com.*

Home Decor

Cottage. The cozy Cottage shop at the northeast corner of Ritan Park
only displays a fraction of the antique furniture, modern light fixtures,
and home accessories held within the company's showroom near the Fifth
Ring Road. Like Ikea, Cottage inspires customers by decorating mock
rooms; however, owners Rebecca and David Hsu actually take a unique
approach to fusing Chinese antiques with modern designs in ceramic
and glass. ⊠ *4 Ritan Bei Lu at the northeast corner of Ritan Park,
Chaoyang District* ☎ *Shop: 001/8561–1517, Showroom: 001/8730–1126.*

Torana Handmade Carpets/Gangchen Carpet of Tibet. Rest assured that the
handsome Tibetan carpets sold in this first-floor shop of the Kempinski
Hotel are the handiwork of traditional craftsmen from the Tibetan Autonomous Region. Hand-spun, hand-dyed, and hand-knotted, Torana's
collection of Gangchen Carpets of Tibet aren't cheap. ⊠ *Kempinski
Hotel, 50 Liang Ma Qiao Lu, Chaoyang District* ☎ *010/6465–3388
Ext. 5542.*

Jewelry

Shard Box Store. The signature collection here includes small- to mid-size jewelry boxes fashioned from the broken shards of antique porcelain. Supposedly the shards were collected during the Cultural Revolution, when scores of antique porcelain were smashed in accordance with the law. Birds, trees, pining lovers, and dragons decorate these affordable ceramic-and-metal containers, which range from Y20 to Y200. ⊠ *1 Ritan Bei Lu, near the Fangcaodi Primary School, Chaoyang District* ☎ *010/8561–3712* ⊠ *2 Jiangtai Lu, near the Holiday Inn Lido* ☎ *010/5135–7638.*

> ### EARLY-BIRD CATCHES
>
> A common superstition in Chinese markets is that if you don't make a sale with your very first customer of the day, the rest of the day will go badly. So set out early, and if you know you're the first customer of the day, bargain relentlessly.

Treasure House. Embedded in the Embassy District, a few stores down from foreign-goods meccas April Gourmand and Jenny Lou's, Treasure House has a modest but slick collection, including silver cuff links and charms inscribed with the Chinese symbols for happiness and longevity. ⊠ *5 Sanlitun Xiwujie* ☎ *001/8451–6096.*

Malls & Department Stores

Beijing Friendship Store. The Beijing Friendship Store is like a date you invite to family gatherings: it's reliable, well-groomed, and respectable, yet utterly boring. Years ago, this was the only place sanctioned to sell foreign goods, but with so many cheaper and more glamorous options now, this old mainstay has lost its allure. However, if the thought of bargaining in a loud, crowded market makes your head hurt, or if you're on a single-sweep shopping spree for goods of guaranteed quality, then the Friendship Store will be your haven. There's plenty of traditional Chinese goods and handicrafts, including tablecloths, silk and cashmere, porcelain, watercolor paintings, traditional Chinese medicine, teas, jade and gold jewelry, rugs (both silk and wool), and foreign groceries. And don't miss the bookstore, which stocks the *International Herald Tribune* and books on politics and contemporary literature. ⊠ *17 Jianguomenwai Dajie, Chaoyang District* ☎ *010/6500–3311* Ⓜ *Jianguomen.*

★ **China World Shopping Mall.** Rising up alongside the China World Trade Center, the two towers of Guomao rule the roost with tiers of top-flight designers, such as **Prada, Marc Jacobs, Hermès,** and **Dior.** For quality souvenirs, check out **Tian Fu,** a branch of the famous Chinese tea sellers, or **Emperor,** which sells silk bedding and table linens. ⊠ *1 Jianguomenwai Dajie, Chaoyang District* ☎ *010/6505–2288* Ⓜ *Guomao.*

The Kerry Centre Mall. Located inside a Shangri-La–owned hotel and business center, the Kerry Centre Mall comprises a group of small but top-notch clothing shops, in addition to two golf stores, a post office, and an international food court. Lush piles of silk and wool carpets from Xinjiang & Henan provinces line the walls of **Aladdin Jia Ju Carpets (# B28).**

On the mall's entrance level, **Dave's Custom Tailoring** (☎ 010/8529–9433) turns out quality men's suits in about 10 days. A few doors down, **Mystery Garments** embellishes linens and silks with Chinese embroidery from Guizhou. The designers at Hong Kong–owned **Blanc de Chine** cite Ming and Qing dynasty furniture as inspiration. Additional branches are in the Holiday Inn Lido and the Oriental Plaza. ⊠ *1 Guanghua Rd., Chaoyang District* ☎ *010/8529–9450* Ⓜ *Guomao.*

Lufthansa Youyi Shopping Center. A high-end shopping mall attached to the ritzy Kempinski Hotel, this center is well visited by expat parents, who rave about the selection of children's clothing and baby goods on the sixth floor. International dealers in crystal and glass applaud the jewels and vases sold at **Liuligongfang** on the first floor. ⊠ *52 Liangmaoqiao Lu, Chaoyang District* ☎ *010/6465–1188* ⊕ *www.kempinski-beijing.com.*

3D3, the Fashion Center at Sanlitun. Across the street from Tongli, the Fashion Center at Sanlitun is a tidy, five-story mall stocked with princess punk fashions. Men head to the fourth floor for shops with names such as **Manly. Mughal's Beijing,** a rooftop Pakistani/Xinjiang restaurant, offers an yummy alternative to the Western bars crowding Sanlitun below. Look for a red "3D3" sign as you approach. ⊠ *33 Sanlitun Jie, Chaoyang District* ☎ *001/6417–3333* ⊕ *www.3d3.cn.*

Markets

Alien Street. Big-footed women rejoice: you'll find size 9+ shoes on Alien Street. A more apt name for this short-but-crammed market strip is Russian Street. All shop signs are in Chinese and Cyrillic; swarms of Russian shoppers and traders trawl the aisles and alleyways; advertisements picture blond models wearing bikinis and minks. Several Russian restaurants and more shoe stores are located behind Yabao Lu on Ritan Bei Lu, and a giant new shopping center is in construction directly across from the Beijing Auterlima Shoes Market. ⊠ *Yabao Lu, Chaoyang District* Ⓜ *Chaoyangmen.*

Beijing Curio City. This complex has four stories of kitsch and curio shops and a few furniture vendors, some selling authentic antiques. Prices are high (driven by tour groups), so don't be afraid to low-ball. If you are looking for antiques, try **Dong Fang Yuan** (# 111). ⊠ *Dongsanhuan Nan Lu, Chaoyang District, Exit Third Ring Rd. at Panjiayuan Bridge* ☎ *010/6774–7711 or 010/6773–6021 Ext. 63.*

Fodor'sChoice **Panjiayuan Antique Market.** Every weekend, the sun rises over thousands
★ of pilgrims rummaging through Panjiayuan in search of antiques and the
most curious of curios. With over 3,000 vendors crowding an area of
48,500 square meters, not every jade bracelet, oracle bone, porcelain vase,
and ancient silk screen is authentic, but most people are here for the reproductions anyway. Behold the bounty: watercolors, scrolls, calligraphy, Buddhist statues, opera costumes, old Russian SLR cameras, curio
cabinets, Tibetan jewelry, tiny satin lotus-flower shoes, rotary telephones,
jade dragons, antique mirrors, infinite displays of "Maomorabilia." If
you're buying jade, first observe the Chinese customers, how they hold
a flashlight to the milky-green stone to test its authenticity. As with all
Chinese markets, *bargain, bargain, bargain,* as many vendors inflate
their prices astronomically for *waiguoren* ("outside country people"). A
strip of enclosed stores form a perimeter around the surprisingly orderly
rows of open-air stalls. The friendly owner of the eponymous **Li Shu Lan**
decorates her shop (# 24-D) with antiques from her *laojia,* or countryside hometown. Stop by the **Bei Zhong Bao Pearl Shop** (# 7-A) for
medium-quality freshwater pearls cultivated by the Hu family. Also here
are a sculpture zoo, book bazaar, reproduction-furniture shops, and a
two-story minimarket stashing propaganda posters and Communist literature. ■ TIP➔ **A weekend-only market, it opens at sunrise and empties by
4 PM.** Show the taxi driver the Chinese characters for Panjiayuan Shichang.
✉ *Third Ring Rd. at Panjiayuan Bridge, Chaoyang District.*

Ritan Office Building Market. Don't let the gray-brick and red-trim exterior fool you: the offices inside the Ritan Building are strung with racks
of brand-name dresses and funky-fab accessories. Unlike the tacky variations made on knockoff labels sold in less-expensive markets, the col-
lections here, for the most part, retain their integrity—perhaps because
many of these dresses are actually designer labels. ■ TIP➔ **They're also
more expensive, and bargaining is discouraged.** Of note, the owner Liu Xing-
xing tailors and sells Hunan silk qipaos (# 1019). The **Ruby Cashmere
Shop** (# 1009) sells genuine cashmere sweaters and scarves at reduced
prices. Upstairs, the burning incense and bright red walls of You Gi (#
2006) provide a welcome atmosphere for perusing an overpriced but
eccentric collection of Nepalese and Indian clothing and jewelry. ✉ *15A
Guanghua Lu, just east of the south entrance to Ritan Park, opposite
the Vietnam Embassy, Chaoyang District* ☎ *010/8561–9556.*

Fodor'sChoice **Silk Alley Market.** Once a delightfully chaotic sprawl of hundreds of out-
★ door stalls, the Silk Alley Market is now corralled inside a huge shopping center. The government has cracked down on certain copycat
items, so if you don't see that knockoff Louis Vuitton purse or Chanel
jacket, just ask; it might magically appear from a stack of plastic storage bins. You will face no dearth, however, of knockoff Pumas and Nikes
or North Face jackets. Chinese handicrafts and children's clothes are
on the top floors. Bargain relentlessly, and guard your wallet against pickpockets. Seek the second floor cashmere shop (# B2-0088) for quality
sweaters. ✉ *8 Xiushui Dong Jie, Chaoyang District* ☎ *139/0113–6086
or 010/5169–9003* ⊕ *www.xiushui.com.cn* Ⓜ *Yonganli.*

Continued on page 120

MARKETS
A GUIDE TO BUYING SILK, PEARLS & POTTERY

Chinese markets are hectic and crowded, but great fun for the savvy shopper. The intensity of the bargaining and the sheer number of goods available are pretty much unsurpassed anywhere else in the world.

Nowadays wealthier Chinese may prefer to flash their cash in department stores and designer boutiques, but generally, markets are still the best places to shop. Teens spend their pocket money at cheap clothing markets. Grandparents, often toting their grandchildren, go to their local neighborhood food market almost daily to pick up fresh items such as tofu, fish, meat, fruit, and vegetables. Markets are also great places to mix with the locals, see the drama of bargaining take place, and watch as the Chinese banter, play with their children, challenge each other to cards, debate, or just lounge.

Some markets have a mish-mash of items, whereas others are more specialized, dealing in one particular ware. Markets play an essential part in the everyday life of the Chinese and prices paid are always a great topic of conversation. A compliment on a choice article will often elicit the price paid in reply and a discussion may ensue on where to get the same thing at an even lower cost.

GREAT FINDS

The prices we list below are meant to give you an idea of what you can pay for certain items. Actual post-bargaining prices will of course depend on how well you haggle, while pre-bargaining prices are often based on how much the vendor thinks he or she can get out of you.

PEARLS
Many freshwater pearls are grown in Taihu; seawater pearls come from Japan or the South Seas. Some have been dyed and others mixed with semi-precious stones. Designs can be pretty wild and the clasps are not of very high quality, but necklaces and bracelets are cheap. Post-bargaining, a plain, short strand of pearls should cost around Y40.

ETHNIC-MINORITY HANDICRAFTS
Brightly colored skirts from the Miao minority and embroidered jackets from the Yunnan area are great boho souvenirs. The heavy, elaborate jewelry could decorate a sidetable or hang on a wall. Colorful children's shoes are embellished with animal faces and bells. After bargaining, a skirt in the markets should go for between Y220 to Y300, and a pair of children's shoes for Y40 to Y60.

RETRO
Odd items from the hedonistic '20s to the revolutionary '60s and '70s include treasures like old light fixtures and tin advertising signs. A rare sign such as one banning foreigners from entry may cost as much as Y10,000, but small items such as teapots can be bought for around Y250. Retro items are harder to bargain down for than mass-produced items.

"MAOMORABILIA"
The Chairman's image is readily available on badges, bags, lighters, watches, ad infinitum. Pop-art–like figurines of Mao and his Red Guards clutching red books are kitschy but iconic. For soundbites and quotes from the Great Helmsman, buy the Little Red Book itself. Prebargaining, a badge costs Y25, a bag Y50, and a ceramic figurine Y380. Just keep in mind that many posters are fakes.

CERAMICS
Most ceramics you'll find in markets are factory-made, so you probably won't stumble upon a bargain Ming dynasty vase, but ceramics in a variety of colors can be picked up at reasonable prices. Opt for pretty pieces decorated with butterflies, or for the more risqué, copulating couples. A bowl-and-plate set goes for around Y25, a larger serving plate Y50.

BIRD CAGES

Wooden bird cages with domed roofs make charming decorations, with or without occupants. They are often seen being carried by old men as they promenade their feathered friends. A pre-bargaining price for a medium-sized wooden cage is around Y180.

PROPAGANDA AND COMIC BOOKS

Follow the actions of Chinese revolutionary hero, Lei Feng, or look for scenes from Chinese history and lots of *gongfu* (Chinese martial arts) stories. Most titles are in Chinese and often in black and white, but look out for titles like *Tintin and the Blue Lotus*, set in Shanghai and translated into Chinese. You can bargain down to around Y15 for less popular titles.

SILK

Bolts and bolts of silk brocade with blossoms, butterflies, bamboo, and other patterns dazzle the eye. An enormous range of items made from silk, from purses to slippers to traditional dresses, are available at most markets. Silk brocade costs around Y35 per meter, a price that is generally only negotiable if you buy large quantities.

JADE

A symbol of purity and beauty for the Chinese, jade comes in a range of colors. Subtle and simple bangles vie for attention with large sculptures on market stalls. A lavender jade Guanyin (Goddess of Mercy) pendant runs at Y260 and a green jade bangle about Y280 before bargaining.

MAH-JONGG SETS

The clack-clack of mah-jongg tiles can be heard late into the night on the streets of most cities in summer. Cheap plastic sets go for about Y50. Far more aesthetically pleasing are ceramic sets in slender drawers of painted cases. These run about Y250 after bargaining, from a starting price of Y450. Some sets come with instructions, but if not, instructions for the "game of four winds" can be downloaded in English at www.mahjongg.com.

4

MARKETS: A GUIDE TO BUYING SILK, PEARLS & POTTERY

SHOPPING KNOW-HOW

When to Go

Avoid weekends if you can and try to go early in the morning, from 8 AM to 10 AM, or at the end of the day just before 6 PM. Rainy days are also good bets for avoiding the crowds and getting better prices.

Bringin' Home the Goods

Although that faux-Gucci handbag is tempting, remember that some countries have heavy penalties for the import of counterfeit goods. Likewise, that animal fur may be cheap, but you may get fined a lot more at your home airport than what you paid for it. Counterfeit goods are generally prohibited in the United States, but there's some gray area regarding goods with a "confusingly similar" trademark. Each person is allowed to bring in one such item, as long as it's for personal use and not for resale. For more details, go to the travel section of www.cbp.gov. The HM and Revenue Customs Web site, www.hmrc.gov.uk, has a list of banned and prohibited goods for the United Kingdom.

⚠The Chinese government has regular and very public crackdowns on fake goods, so that store you went to today may have different items tomorrow. In Shanghai, for example, pressure from the Chinese government and other countries to protect intellectual property rights that led to the demise of one of the city's largest and most popular markets, Xiangyang.

BEFORE YOU GO

■ Be prepared to be grabbed, pushed, followed, stared at, and even to have people whispering offers of items to buy in your ear. In China, personal space and privacy are not valued in the same way as in the West, so the invasion of it is common. Move away but remain calm and polite. No one will understand if you get upset anyway.

■ Many Chinese love to touch foreign children, so if you have kids, make sure they're aware of and prepared for this.

■ Keep money and valuables in a safe place. Pickpockets and bag-slashers are becoming common.

■ Pick up a cheap infrared laser pointer to detect counterfeit bills. The light illuminates the hidden anti-counterfeit ultraviolet mark in the real notes.

■ Check for fake items, e.g. silk and pearls.

■ Learn some basic greetings and numbers in Chinese. The local people will really appreciate it.

HOW TO BARGAIN

Successful bargaining requires the dramatic skills of a Hollywood actor. Here's a step-by-step guide to getting the price you want and having fun at the same time.

DO'S	DONT'S

Browsing in a silk shop

Chinese slippers at a ladies' market

- Start by deciding what you're willing to pay for an item.

- Look at the vendor and point to the item to indicate your interest.

- The vendor will quote you a price, usually by punching numbers into a calculator and showing it to you.

- Here, expressions of shock are required from you, which will never be as great as those of the vendor, who will put in an Oscar-worthy performance at your prices.

- Next it's up to you to punch in a number that's around 75% of the original price—or lower if you feel daring.

- Pass the calculator back and forth until you meet somewhere in the middle, probably at up to (and sometimes less than) 50% of the original quote.

- Don't enter into negotiations if you aren't seriously considering the purchase.

- Don't haggle over small sums of money.

- If the vendor isn't budging, walk away; he'll likely call you back.

- It's better to bargain if the vendor is alone. He's unlikely to come down on the price if there's an audience.

- Saving face is everything in China. Don't belittle or make the vendor angry, and don't get angry yourself.

- Remain pleasant and smile often.

- Buying more than one of something gets you a better deal.

- Dress down and leave your jewelry and watches in the hotel safe on the day you go marketing. You'll get a lower starting price if you don't flash your wealth.

★ **Yaxiu Market** (Yashow Market). Especially popular among younger Western shoppers, Yaxiu is yet another indoor arena stuffed to the gills with knockoff brand-name clothing and shoes. Prices are slightly cheaper than Silk Alley, but the haggling no less cruel. Don't be alarmed if you see women sniffing sneakers or suede jackets: they're simply testing if the leather is real. The giant sign outside this bustling clothes market near Sanlitun reads Yashow, but it's written YAXIU in pinyin. ⊠ *58 Gongti Bei Lu, Chaoyang District* ☎ *010/6416–8699.*

Zhaojia Chaowai Market. Beijing's best-known venue for affordable antique and reproduction furniture houses scores of independent vendors who sell everything from authentic Qing Dynasty–era chests to traditional baskets, ceramics, carpets, and curios. Be sure to bargain; vendors routinely sell items for less than half their starting price. ⊠ *43 Huawei Bei Li, Chaoyang District.*

Shoes

Beijing Auterlima Shoes Market. The individual doorways inside this two-story behemoth are draped with curtains identifying the stall's number and name. They also, however, add a sense of mystery and suspense to your shoe-shopping experience: you never know what fabulous black-and-gold stiletto boots will be lurking behind door No. 4. ⊠ *6 Ritan Bei Lu, Chaoyang District* ☎ *010/6506–8003.*

Dragon Shoes. Stop here to refresh your footwear before a night out in Sanlitun with Reef, Puma, Mae Mae, and Nine West sold at discount prices. To find it, head north on Sanlitun Jie, turn right onto a small alley just past Jazz-Ya, then follow signs to Na-Li Market at the rear. ⊠ *Sanlitun Bei Jie, between No. 44 and No. 46, Chaoyang District* ☎ *001/ 6413–2663.*

Haidian District

Travelers usually frequent the northwestern quadrant of Beijing to visit the Summer Palace or the Beijing Zoo. However, collectors of antiques can spend hours perusing the quiet halls of **Ai Jia Gu Dong Market** (⊠ Chengshousi Lu, Beisanhuan Xi Lu, Haidian District ☎ 010/ 6765–7187), a large antiques and jade market, hidden just under the South Fourth Ring Road beside the Big Bell Museum. It's open daily, but shops close early on weekdays.

At a Glance

ENGLISH	PINYIN	CHINESE CHARACTERS
POINTS OF INTEREST		
Ai Jia Gu Dong Market	Aì jiā gǔ dǒng shì chǎng	爱家古董市场
Alien Street	Yǎ Baǒ Lù	雅宝路
Bainaohui Computer Shopping Mall	Bǎi Nǎo Huì Diàn Nǎo Guǎng Chǎng	百脑汇电脑广场
Beijing Auterlima Shoes Market	Běi jīng hǔ jiā lóu xié shì chǎng	北京呼家楼鞋市场
Beijing Curio City	Beǐ Jīng Gǔ Wán Chéng	北京古玩城
Beijing Department Store	Běi jīng shì bǎi huò dà lóu	北京市百货大楼
Beijing Friendship Store	Běi jīng yǒu yì shāng diàn	北京友谊商店
Beijing Silk Shop	Běi jīng sī chóu diàn	北京丝绸店
Beijing Yuanlong Silk Corporation	Yuán lóng sī chóu	元隆丝绸
The Bookworm	Shū Chóng	书虫
Chaowai MEN Market	Cháo wài shì chǎng jiē	朝外市场街
China Star Silk Store	Míng xīng zhōng shì fú zhuāng diàn	明星中式服装店
China World Shopping Mall	guó mào shāng chéng	国贸商城
Cottage	Dōng lí cǎo shè	东篱草舍
The Courtyard Gallery	Sì hé yuàn huà láng	四合院画廊
Dazhalan	Dà zhà lán	大栅栏
Dragon Shoes	Lóng xié	龙鞋
Fashion Center at San Li Tun	Sān lǐ tún sān diǎn sān fú shì dà xià	三里屯3.3服饰大厦
Fengtai	Fēng tái qū	丰台区
Foreign Languages Bookstore	Wài wén shū diàn	外文书店
Jian Guo Men Wai Da Jie	Jiàn guó mén wài dà jiē	建国门外大街
Heyan'er	Hé Yán Fú Zhuāng Diàn	何燕服装店
Hongqiao Market	Hóng qiáo shì chǎng	红桥市场
The Kerry Centre Mall	Jiā lǐ zhōng xīn	嘉里中心
Liulichang Jie	Liú Li Chǎng Jiē	琉璃厂街
Lufthansa Youyi Shopping Center	Yàn shā yǒu yì shāng chéng	燕莎友谊商城
Malls at Oriental Plaza	Dōng fāng guǎng chǎng gòu wù zhōng xīn	东方广场购物中心

Nei Lian Sheng Xie Dian	Nèi lián shēng xié diàn	内联升鞋店
Pacific Century Place	Tài píng yáng bǎi huò	太平洋百货
Panjiayuan Antique Market	Pān Jiā Yuán Shì Chǎng	潘家园市场
Red Gate Gallery at the Watch Tower	Hóng Mén Huà Láng	红门画廊
The Red Phoenix	Hóng Fèng Huáng Fú Zhuāng	红凤凰服装工作室
Ritan Office Building Market	Rì tán shāng wù lóu	日坛商务楼
Sanlitun	Sān lǐ tún	三里屯
Shard Box Store	Shèn Dé Gé	慎德阁
Silk Alley Market	Xiù Shuǐ Shì Chǎng	秀水市场
Sun Dongan Plaza	Xīn Dōng ān Shì Chǎng	新东安市场
Tea Street	Mǎ Lián Daǒ Chá Yè Chéng	马连道茶叶批发市场
Tongli Studio	Tóng Lǐ	同里
Tongrentang	Tóng rén táng	同仁堂
Torana Handmade Carpets	Tú lán nà shǒu gōng dì tǎn	图兰纳手工地毯
Treasure House	Bǎo yuè zhāi	宝月斋
Wangfujing Da Jie	Wāng Fú Jǐng Dà Jiē	王府井大街
Wonderful Electronic Shopping Mall	Lán dǎo dà xià	蓝岛大厦
Yaxiu Market	Yǎ Xiù shì chǎng	雅秀市场
Xidan	Xī dān	西单
Zhaojia Chaowai Market	zhào jiā cáo wà gǔ diǎn jiā jù shì chǎng	赵家朝外古典家具市场

Arts & Nightlife

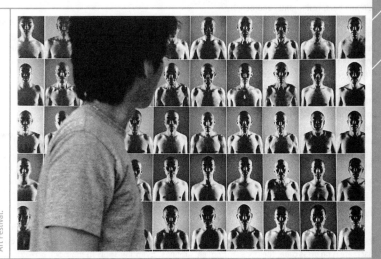

Work by Wang Jinsong on display at the Dashanzi International Art Festival.

WORD OF MOUTH

"Check out the Sanlitun Bar Street, the Houhai bar scene, and the Niu Ren Jie (meaning Lady's Street—but don't let the name mislead you) for emerging bars. Try Suzie Wong's for some good dancing."
—Bchen

"Our daughters recently returned to Beijing for a friend's wedding. They were blown away by how much it had changed in just a short time, at least in terms of their favorite pursuit: nightlife."
—Neil_Oz

www.fodors.com/forums

ARTS & NIGHTLIFE PLANNER

What's Happening Now

The best way to find out what's on or where to party is to pick up one of the free-listing magazines found at many bars, restaurants, and occasionally at hotels around the city. The best ones are the monthly *That's Beijing*, *Time Out Beijing*, and *Beijing Talk*, as well as the biweekly *City Weekend*. *That's Beijing* (⊕ www.thatsbj.com) has the most extensive listings, and *City Weekend* and *Beijing Talk* have maps of central Beijing with restaurants and bars. All give bilingual addresses in their listings, which is very handy since most taxi drivers are unlikely to speak or read English.

What to Wear

The only dress code for Beijing is that there is no dress code. The city's nightlife is such a melting pot that you can find flip-flop-wearing customers in snug jeans sipping extra dirty Grey Goose martinis in the classiest cocktail lounges, and girls done up in their finest finery in piña colada-and-peanut joints. That said, as a general rule people underdress rather than overdress. Remember that Beijing is seriously chilly in the winter (December to March) and you'll need to bundle up. A heavy coat, thick sweater, long pants, hat, scarf, and gloves should keep you nice and toasty.

Top Nightlife Spots

Centro. There's no arguing with the city's darling, which has won a string of local awards for best bar, best barman, and best wine cellar. Centro is a slice of Beijing-style *Sex and the City* with a plush, lush lounge and hotty clientele.

No Name Bar. Its rattan, fans, and ferns in the summer, and wood-stove warmth in the winter make this long-standing bar popular with just about everyone. Houhai's most charming bar offers window perches with views of the lake and *lethal* Long Island Ice Teas.

Top Arts Venues

Chaoyang Theater. The acrobatic shows here are jaw-dropping and beyond memorable.

Forbidden City Concert Hall. The hall is charming for its magical location in the middle of Zhongshan Park next to the Forbidden City. More important, the acoustics in the hall are crisp and gorgeous—a Beijing rarity.

Liyuan Theater. This is the slickest venue for watching Beijing Opera; the pot is sweetened with tea, snacks, and English subtitles. Even the seats in the back have great views.

Word of Mouth

"My husband and I have just returned from a two week trip to China (Beijing, Shanghai, Hangzhou, and Zhuhai) and found the dress code to be very casual. Hope you enjoy China as much as we did—the experience absolutely blew us away."   —chchkiwi

Yo Ho Ho & a Bottle of Rum

China is the world's top producer of pirated goods. It's not just handbags and DVDs: the counterfeiting extends to the alcohol in bars and supermarkets. Fake-booze joints are easy to spot: any bar that charges Y10 for a mixer or Y50 for all-you-can-drink specials is likely using either a mix of *bai jiu* (local rice wine) or really cheap spirits, then passing it off as Jameson's or Absolut. Usually your drink will taste bitter and you'll have a head-banging hangover the next day. Sometimes even more expensive bars, knowingly or unknowingly, serve knockoff alcohol. Booze counterfeiters are clever, and will slip in a few bottles of phony liquor with a genuine crate.

Media reports in 2006 stated that up to 60% of liquor sold in China's four biggest cities—including Beijing—was counterfeit that year. Counterfeit alcohol may contain methanol or formaldehyde so it can, in extreme cases, be quite dangerous. The safest things to do: stick to bottled beers in cheaper bars and return your drink in the more expensive venues if you suspect it is phony fare.

Getting Around Safely

Most of the bars and clubs are clumped together in districts, so you can amble from pub to wine bar to cocktail lounge by foot.

Your best bet is to rely on taxis to get back to your hotel. Most of the taxis you see on the roads are licensed; only take cabs that have meters and their drivers' IDs on the dashboard. Unless it's raining cats and dogs, you should have no problem hailing a cab, even in the early hours of the morning. After 10:30 PM there's no public transport, so you will have to hail a taxi.

Beijing is generally safe after dark; alcohol-fueled street brawls are rare. The worst you will probably witness is heavy-handed security guards getting tough with obnoxious expat youths in the North Sanlitun or Workers' Stadium (Gongti) areas. Stick to well-lit areas, and don't walk by yourself at night.

5

No longer Shanghai's staid sister, Beijing is reinventing herself as a party town, but without the pretensions of her southern sibling. A frenzy of building and refurbishing in recent years means there's now a venue for every breed of boozer, from beer-stained pub to crepuscular cocktail lounge. There are also more dance clubs than you can count—although these mostly rely more on flash than on class. An emerging middle class means that you'll find most bars have a mixed crowd and aren't just swamps of expatriates, but there will be spots where one or the other set will dominate.

Bars aside, Beijing has an active, if not international-standard, stage scene. Besides musicals, though, there's not much to see in English. Music and dance transcend language boundaries, and Beijing attracts some fine international composers and ballet troupes for the crowds. For a fun night on the town that you can enjoy no other place in the world, Beijing Opera, acrobatics, and kung-fu performances remain the best bets.

THE ARTS

The arts in China took a long time to recover from the Cultural Revolution (1966–76), and political works are still generally avoided. Film and theater reflect an interesting mix of modern and avant-garde Chinese and Western influences. On any given night in Beijing, you can see a drama by the famous Chinese playwright Lao She, a satire by a contemporary Taiwanese playwright, or a Chinese stage version of *Animal Farm*.

All of the free-listings magazines will have reviews of plays as well as concerts and dance performances; *Time Out Beijing* and *That's Beijing* carry the most critical and comprehensive coverage. The cheapest seats start at around Y50 and can go up to over Y1,000 for world-class international ballets and musicals.

As most of the stage is inaccessible to non-Chinese speakers, visitors to Beijing are more likely to hunt out the big visual spectacles, such as Beijing Opera or kung-fu displays. These long-running shows are tailored for travelers: your hotel will be able to recommend performances and venues, and will likely be able to help you book tickets.

> **FOR MUSEUMS & MORE**
>
> Check out "Museums & Monuments" in Chapter 1. Our favorite? The National Museum of China, where you can *ooh* and *aah* over sublime jade pieces before checking out the waxworks exhibition.

Acrobatics & Kung Fu

Fodor'sChoice ★ **Chaoyang Theater.** This is the queen bee of acrobatics venues, especially designed to cultivate tourist awe. Spectacular individual and team acrobatic displays involving bicycles, seesaws, catapults, swings, and barrels are performed here nightly. ✉ *36 Dongsanhuan Bei Lu, Chaoyang District* ☎ *010/6507–2421* ⊕ *www.acrobatics.com.cn.*

★ **The Red Theatre.** If it's Vegas-style stage antics you're after, the Legend of Kung Fu show is what you want. Extravagant martial arts are complemented by neon, fog, and heavy-handed sound effects. Shows are garish but also sometimes glorious. ✉ *44 Xingfu Da Jie, Chongwen District* ☎ *101/6710–3671.*

Universal Theater (Heaven & Earth). The China Acrobatic Troupe—made up of extremely bendy preteens—puts on a nightly repertoire of breathtaking, and usually flawless, stunts here. Stunning! ✉ *10 Dongzhimen Nan Da Jie, Chaoyang District* ☎ *010/6416–9893.*

Wan Sheng Theater (Tianqiao Acrobatic Theater). The Beijing Acrobatics Troupe of China is famous for weird, fun shows. Content includes a flashy show of offbeat contortions and tricks, with a lot of high-wire action. ✉ *95 Tianqiao Market, Xuanwu District* ☎ *010/6303–7449.*

Music

Beijing Concert Hall. Beijing's main venue for Chinese and Western classical-music concerts also hosts folk dancing and singing, and many celebratory events throughout the year. The venue is the home of the China National Symphony Orchestra. ✉ *1 Bei Xinhua Jie, Xicheng District* ☎ *010/6605–5812.*

Fodor'sChoice ★ **Forbidden City Concert Hall.** With a seating capacity of 1,400, this is one of Beijing's largest concert halls. It is also one of the most well-appointed, with plush seating and top-notch acoustics. Despite the modern building, you'll walk through ancient courtyards to get to the hall—highly romantic. ✉ *In Zhongshan Park, Xichangan Jie, Xicheng District, on the west side of Tiananmen Square* ☎ *010/6559–8285* Ⓜ *Tiananmen West.*

Poly Plaza International Theater. This is a modern shopping-center-like complex on top of Dongsi Shitiao subway station. One of Beijing's better-known theaters, the Poly hosts Chinese and international concerts,

CLOSE UP

Fringe Art: The Dashanzi 798 Art District

IF YOU ARE KEEN TO SEE what the city's art scene has to offer beyond calligraphy, the Dashanzi 798 Art District boasts a thriving contemporary art community. Just as the city comes of age in the international, political, and economic arena, so too are Chinese artists. Exploration of social taboos, use of digital media, and clever installations are juxtaposed among more orthodox forms of canvas paintings and photography. Some efforts may seem like trite knockoffs of American pop art, and Mao references run rampant, but keep in mind this level of expression is still evolving for the public arena. Complete freedom of expression is not tolerated and governmental closings are not unheard of (though they're increasingly rare).

Built in the 1950s, the factory was a major industrial project designed by East German architects backed by Soviet aid. The factory's decline started in the 1980s, just as Beijing's contemporary art scene began to emerge. The massive relocation of pollutant factories outside the city in preparation for the 2008 Summer Olympic Games has further accelerated the decline of the area's manufacturing roots and allowed for the incubation of modern art. The recent government declaration of Dashanzi as a protected arts district has paved the way for a resurgence of inventive local galleries, as well as design studios, restaurants, cafés, and bars. The annual Dashanzi International Arts Festival—held each May—continues to draw international attention to the 798 area.

The Dashanzi compound is immensely walkable; keep in mind this is solely a pedestrian affair unless you arrive by private car. Cabs are not allowed to enter the compound and you will be required to disembark at any of the entrance gates. Though it's open on weekdays (except Monday), most people visit on weekends, when throngs of locals and foreigners congregate to see what's on display.

Directions to Dashanzi: Traveling from the city by car, take the Dashanzi (#2) exit off the Airport Expressway. Just as you come to the end of the exit ramp, ask the driver to stop at the intersection. Cross the road and walk against oncoming traffic until you see 797 Microphone. Enter through the main gate, onto Jiuxianqiao Road. ■ TIP→ **It may be helpful to ask your hotel staff to instruct the taxi driver before you set off.**

✉ *4 Jiuxianqiao Rd., Dashanzi, Chaoyang District* ☎ *010/6438–4862 or 010/6437–6248* ⊕ *www.798space.com.*

To get a feel for what sells abroad, drop by internationally owned galleries such as White Space Beijing or Art Seasons. These established galleries house perennially hot artists such as Liu Fei, Zhao Bo, and Chen Ke. Time-Zone 8 Book Shop is an avant-garde bookshop in the heart of Dashanzi.

Art Seasons Gallery (☎ 010/6431–1900 ⊕ www.artseasons.com.sg/index.cfm).

Time-Zone 8 Book Shop. (☎ 010/8456–0336 ⊕ www.timezone8.com).

White Space Beijing (☎ 010/8456–2054 ⊕www.alexanderochs-galleries.de/whitespace).

—by Katharine Mitchell

TOP ART GALLERIES

Artist Village Gallery. If you'd like a real change of pace from the city art scene, hire a driver or join a tour to visit the Artists' Village in the eastern suburbs of Beijing. Over 500 artists live and work in studio spaces, peasant homes, and old buildings in and around the central village of Song Zhuang. Though a trip out to the Artist Village can take a chunk out of your day, the trip is worth it. The countryside is a stark contrast to the city, and the art is of excellent quality. The gallery itself displays local works in a modern, well-appointed building. Visits are by appointment only, so talk with your hotel concierge before booking a car. ⊠ *1 Chunbei, Ren Zhuang, Tongxian Songzhuang* ☎ *139/ 0124-4283 or 010/6959-8343* ⊕ *www.artistvillagegallery.com.*

The Courtyard Gallery. Although the space here is minuscule—it's in the basement of the Courtyard Restaurant—this gallery still manages to attract some of the most sought-after names in contemporary Chinese art, such as Wang Qingsong, Zhang Dali, and the Gao Brothers. ⊠ *95 Donghuamen Dajie, Dongcheng District* ☎ *010/6526-8882* ⊕ *www.courtyard-gallery.com.*

Long March Studio. The Long March Project organizes teams of artists, curators, and scholars to travel to various regions in China, where they create projects with the local community. ⊠ *4 Jiuxianqiao Rd., Dashanzi, Chaoyang District* ☎ *010/6438-7107* ⊕ *www. longmarchspace.com.*

Red Gate Gallery at the Watch Tower. This gallery, one of the first to open in Beijing, displays and sells modern Chinese paintings and sculpture in the extraordinary space of the old Dongbianmen Watchtower, a centuries-old landmark. ⊠ *Dongbianmen Watchtower, Second Ring Rd. at Jianguomen, Chongwen District* ☎ *010/6525-1005* ⊕ *www. redgategallery.com* Ⓜ *Jianguomen.*

ballets, and musicals. ■ TIP➔ **If you're seeking a performance in English, this is your best bet.** ⊠ *1/F Poly Plaza, 14 Dongzhimen Nandajie, Dongcheng District* ☎ *010/6506-5343* Ⓜ *Dongsi Shitiao.*

Workers' Stadium. The Workers' Stadium is a Beijing landmark for expatriates—it's surrounded by a network of bar streets. It's usually host to soccer matches, but pop concerts are also sometimes held here (Britney Spears, anyone?). ⊠ *Gongti Bei Lu, Chaoyang District* ☎ *010/6501-6655.*

Theater

Beijing Exhibition Theater. Chinese plays, Western and Chinese operas, and ballet performances are staged in this Soviet-style building that's part of the Exhibition Center complex. Talk about a wide range of shows: in 2006, the musical *West Side Story* was staged and the Black Eyed Peas played, as well. ⊠ *135 Xizhimenwai Dajie, Xicheng District* ☎ *010/ 6835-4455.*

Continued on page 138

BEIJING OPERA

"OPULENT" MAY BE AN UNDERSTATEMENT

For hundreds of years, Beijing opera troupes have delighted audiences—from members of the royal court to marketplace crowds at makeshift stages—with rich costumes, elaborate makeup, jaw-dropping acrobatics, and tales of betrayal and intrigue.

Nowadays, the weird and wonderful operas staged in Beijing's customized theaters are more than likely of the Jing Ju style, which emerged during the Qing Dynasty. There are more than 350 other kinds of Chinese opera, each distinguished by different dialects, music, costumes, and stories.

Why go? For the same amount of time as a movie (and about $20 per person), a night at the opera guarantees you a glimpse at China's past—not to mention a fascinating mix of drama, color, movement, and sound.

INTRODUCING BEIJING OPERA

A RICH & CURIOUS HISTORY

To master the art of Beijing opera's leaping acrobatics, stylized movements, sword dances, and dramatic makeup techniques, actors begin their grueling training as young children. The work pays off: nowhere else in the world can you see a performer in heavy, opulent costume, so artfully singing, miming, turning flips, and brandishing swords.

Opera instrumentation consists of the percussive Wuchang, that is, the gongs, drums, cymbals, and wooden clappers that accompany exaggerated body movements and acrobatics, and the melodic Wenchang, including the Chinese fiddle (*erhu*), the lutelike *pipa*, horns, and flutes.

Neophytes may find two hours of the staccato clanging and nasal singing of Beijing opera hard to take (and most young Chinese fed on a diet of western-style pop agree). But this dramatic, colorful experience might be one of the most memorable of your trip.

FALSETTOS & BACK FLIPS & GONGS, OH MY!

Beijing opera was born out of a wedding between two provincial opera styles from Anhui and Hubei in the 19th century—during China's last dynasty, the Qing Dynasty. It also borrowed from other regional operas and Kunqu, a 500-year-old Chinese musical-theater style. Even though Beijing opera is relatively young, many of its stories are extracted from epics written as far back as the 12th century.

After Mao Zedong took the helm in 1949, opera was molded to reflect the ideals of Chinese communism. The biggest changes occurred under Mao's wife, Jiang Qing, during the Cultural Revolution (1966–1976). Traditional operas were banned; only the so-called eight model plays could be staged. These starred people in plain work clothes singing about the glories of Communism. Traditional opera was reinstated gradually following Mao's death in 1976.

■TIP➔ If you're especially keen to follow the opera closely, choose a theater that displays English subtitles above the stage. Don't mind if things get lost in translation? Sit back and enjoy—the stage antics will be entertainment enough.

MEI LANFANG: GAY ICON & OPERA HERO(INE)

Born in Beijing into a family of performers, Mei Lanfang (1894–1961) perfected the art of female impersonation during his five decades on stage. He is credited with popularizing Beijing opera overseas and was so hip in his day that there was a brand of cigarettes named after him. *The Worlds of Mei Lanfang* (2000) is an American-made documentary about the star, with footage of his performances. You can visit his house at 9 Huguosi, Xicheng District. ⬚Y10 ◷ Tues.–Sun. 9–4 ☎ 010/6618-0351 ⊕ www.meilanfang.com.cn.

Mei Lanfang's gender-bending chops earned him a special place in the hearts of gay activists.

ALL GUSSIED UP

All smiles: elaborate swirls and designs make for quite a done-up countenance.

Towering headdresses and flowing, cotton-candy-soft beards are all part of Beijing opera culture.

The richly embroidered silks in Beijing opera—called *xing tou*—are largely based on Ming Dynasty fashions. These nearly fetishistic costumes are key to identifying each character. The emperor is draped in a yellow robe with a colorful dragon on the back; scholars usually dress in blue and wear a cap with wings; generals don padded armor with bold embroidery; and bandits are often adorned in black capes and trousers.

Painstakingly detailed costumes and towering, bejeweled headdresses enhance the movements of the actors. For example, soldiers wear helmets with pheasant plumes that are waggled and brushed through the air. Cascading sleeves—called water sleeves—are waved and swept to express sorrow or respect.

PAINTED FACES

There are more than 1,000 different kinds of makeup patterns used in Beijing opera. Colors symbolize character traits. For example, red conveys bravery or loyalty, white signifies treachery, yellow suggests brutality, black stands for integrity or fierceness, and purple expresses wisdom. Bandits often have blue faces; gods and spirits are marked with gold and silver.

FACE CHANGING (*BIAN LIAN*)

A specialty of Sichuan opera (Chuan Ju) is the art of face changing, where actors swap masks with lightning speed. One method is to blow into a tiny box of colored powder to camouflage the switch. More spectacular is the mask-pulling routine, in which several masks are painted on thin fabric and attached to the face. Flicking a cloak or sleeve allows the performer to pull the masks off as needed. Masters whisk through as many as 10 masks in 20 seconds.

NOW YOU KNOW

The two most famous Beijing operas are *Peony Pavilion* and *Farewell My Concubine*.

In contrast to the ostentatious costumes, Beijing opera sets are quite sparse: the traditional stage is a simple platform with a silk backdrop.

THE FOUR MAJOR PLAYERS

There are four archetypal characters in Beijing opera: Sheng, Dan, Jing, and Chou. Each one can have variations. The Dan roles, for example, include Qingyi, a shy maiden, and the more promiscuous Huadan. A performer typically devotes a lifetime to perfecting one role.

During the Qing Dynasty, women were banned from performing, so men played the Dan role. These female impersonators were often the most popular actors. Women began performing again in the 1930s; nowadays most female roles are played by women.

SHENG Male characters: Scholars, statesmen

CHOU Clowns: Not always good-natured, wears white patches around eyes/nose

JING Warriors: The roles with the most elaborately painted faces

DAN Female characters: Coquettes, old ladies, warriors, maidens

WHERE TO WATCH

Embellished eyebrows, perfect tendrils of hair, and striking lips—a performer prepares for the show.

Shorter shows put on at venues such as Liyuan Theater are full of acrobatics and fantastic costumes. You can catch an opera performance any night of the week in Beijing, but there will be more options on weekends. Shows usually start around 7 PM and cost between 50 and 200 Yuan. All the free-listing magazines have information, and staff at your hotel can recommend performances and help book tickets. You can also buy tickets online through ⊕ www. piao.com.cn; register online and pay by credit card or phone ☎ 010/6417-7845. Piao.com will send the tickets to your hotel. ■TIP→ **You can also get a taste of Chinese opera for free before you spring for tickets if you have access to a television: nonstop opera is broadcasted on CCTV channel 11.**

★ CHANG'AN GRAND THEATER At this contemporary theater, like at a cabaret, you sit at tables and can eat and drink while watching lively, colorful performances of Beijing opera. ■TIP→ **A great perk? English subtitles appear above the stage.** ⊠ 7 Jianguomennei Dajie, Dongcheng District ☎ 010/6510-1310

HUGUANG GUILDHALL The city's oldest Beijing opera theater, the Guildhall has staged performances since 1807. The hall has been restored to display its original architecture. Although it's the most atmospheric place to take in an opera, it's not the liveliest. The last we heard, the Huguang monkey king was looking washed out. ⊠ 3 Hufangqiao, Xuanwu District ☎ 010/6351-8284 ⊕ www. beijinghuguang.com

LAO SHE TEAHOUSE Performances vary, but usually include Beijing opera and such arts as acrobatics, magic, or comedy. The teahouse is named after Lao She, a playwright and novelist who died in 1966. ⊠ 3 Qianmenxi Dajie, 3rd floor, Xuanwu District ☎ 010/6303-6830 ⊕ www.laosheteahouse.com

★ Fodor's Choice LIYUAN THEATER Though it's unashamedly touristy, it's our top pick. You can watch performers put on makeup before the show (come early) and then graze on snacks and sip tea while watching English-subtitled shows. Glossy brochures complement the crooning. ⊠ Qianmen Hotel, 175 Yongan Lu, Xuanwu District ☎ 010/6301-6688 Ext. 8860 or 010/6303-2301

TIANQIAO HAPPY TEAHOUSE In an old, traditional theater, the teahouse hosts Beijing operas as well as acrobatics, jugglers, and contortionists. ⊠ 113 Tianqiao Shichang, Xuanwu District ☎ 010/6303-9013

RENT IT: *FAREWELL MY CONCUBINE*

Before your trip, rent Chen Kaige's *Farewell My Concubine*, a 1993 film that follows the life, loves, and careers of two male opera performers against a background of political turmoil. It also depicts the brutality of opera schools, where children were forced to practice grueling routines (think splits, balancing water jugs, and head stands).

Capital Theater. This is a busy, modern theater near the Wangfujing shopping street. It often has performances by the respected Beijing People's Art Theatre and various international acts. ✉ *22 Wangfujing Dajie, Dongcheng District* ☎ *010/6524–9847* Ⓜ *Wangfujing.*

🕒 **China National Puppet Theater.** Shadow and hand-puppet shows convey traditional stories—it's lively entertainment for children and adults alike. This venue also attracts overseas performers, including the Moscow Puppet Theater. ✉ *1 Anhuaxili, Chaoyang District* ☎ *010/6425–4849.*

NIGHTLIFE

Beijing has spent the last decade shaking off its grim Communist image and putting the neon into its nightlife. There are a plethora of cocktail lounges, sports pubs, dance spots, beer halls, and girly bars. The city is modernizing at a fever pitch, which means that many bars and even bar streets are short-lived, as construction companies aggressively bulldoze to make way for swanky new developments. Many establishments are knocked together, seemingly overnight, and are of dubious quality.

Sanlitun—the heart of Beijing's nightlife—has spread its party presence around Gongti and Houhai. Sanlitun Jiuba Jie, or "Bar Street," offers mainly crass live-music pubs; it's quite popular with locals. Snuck away in the alleyway behind the giant 3.3 shopping center on Bar Street is an eclectic bunch of bars that range from grungy dance club to rooftop lounge bars serving swanky cocktails and Belgian beer. South Sanlitun Street plays to a more refined crowd of drinkers. On the opposite side of the stadium, on Gongti West Gate, a stream of pumping dance clubs have attracted some big-name DJs—Tiesto, Felix Da Housecat, and Paul Oakenfold, among others. The city's main gay club, Destination, is also here.

Houhai, once a quiet lakeside neighborhood home to Beijing's *laobaixing* (ordinary folk), has exploded into a bumping bar scene. This is a great place to come for a drink at dusk: park yourself on an outdoor seat and enjoy. There are a few hidden gems here, but most of the bars are copycat-bland and expensive, with disappointingly weak drinks. Stick to the bottled beer to get your money's worth. The *hutong,* or mazelike neighborhoods, around the lake also hide some cute bars.

OFF THE BEATEN PATH There are a couple of smaller pockets with notable watering holes, such as Chaoyang West Gate, which has a predominately expat feel; Dashanzi 798, an artsy warehouse area with wine bars; and Wudaokou, a student district in Haidian with cheap drinks aplenty.

Bars

Dongcheng & Xicheng Districts (including Houhai)

Bed. Bed earned its place as a trendy bar through its clever name, and built-in pickup line, "Do you want to go to Bed with me?" Although

7 Nights in Beijing: The Best in Culture, Cocktails & Clubs

CLOSE UP

BEIJING'S BLOSSOMING NIGHTLIFE means there's something new to do every night of the week. Here are some ideas for the best ways to top-off the day with a stiff drink or shot of culture:

■ **Monday**

An acrobatics show mixed with kung-fu magic is a great way to start the week. The yellow-silk-clad Shaolin monks at **The Red Theatre** mix dance, acrobatics, and martial arts every night at 7:30 PM for full house after full house.

■ **Tuesday**

It's not easy to borrow or buy English-language books in Beijing. **The Bookworm** (✉ Building 4, Sanlitun Nan Lu, Chaoyang District ☎ 010/6586-9507 ⊕ www. beijingbookworm.com), a restaurant/bar/bookshop/library, is one of the city's few places that offers a literary outlet for English-reading folk. The Bookworm usually hosts a speaker on Tuesday. Other nights you can enjoy live piano music.

■ **Wednesday**

The middle of the week is usually a good night for the ladies. To celebrate the so-called "little weekend," several bars offer free drinks for women, and although this is in the hope to attract guys on the prowl, it still boils down to . . . free drinks for women. **Brown's** offers one of the least meat-market style Ladies' Nights—plus their range of free drinks includes some tasty cocktails.

■ **Thursday**

If only to check out what all the fuss is about, you should reserve one night for cocktails at **Centro.** Come early (before 8 PM) for happy hour. Nicely soused, you can then hop in a cab to one of the theaters that play host to **Beijing Opera**—try the beautifully restored **Liyuan Theater** for some monkey magic with your classical Chinese music. (*See* "Beijing Opera" on p. 132)

■ **Friday**

This would be the night to go clubbing. Check out **Cargo, Babyface,** or **Tango.** Tickets for famous DJs can go for anything between Y50 and Y200.

■ **Saturday**

This is the ideal night for a romantic evening on **Houhai**—the bar-packed lake north of the Forbidden City. If you are into jazz and blues, head to the excellent **East Shore Live Jazz Café.** Come before 9 PM to get a seat and enjoy the music and some of the best views of the lake, which churns with boats in the summer and ice-skaters in the winter.

■ **Sunday**

Grabbing a drink in one of **Beijing's hutongs**—before they all disappear—is a lovely way to enjoy a city caught between past and future. Try the **Drum & Bell** or **Pass By** (✉ 108 Nanluoguxiang, Dongcheng District ☎ 10/8403-8004). If you want to rub shoulders with the local chic, try the hideaway **Candy Floss Café.**

5

this courtyard bar has cute nooks and crannies and a relaxed feel, it's a bit cold. The beds are all sharp concrete and the shadows are chilly. We'll admit it's worth a one-night stand if you're new to the city. ✉ *17 Zhangwang Hutong, Xicheng District* ☎ *010/8400–1554.*

Candy Floss Café. Beijing's funky young set are falling over themselves to get into this little courtyard bar. Although the service can be sloppy and the drinks are pricey and pretty average, the place is adorable. The central courtyard has been planted with a fairy-tale garden, complete with ponds, stepping stones, gnomes, thick foliage, and a romantic weeping willow. The interior is like stepping into a friend's living room. Each original courtyard house has been converted into a drinking room, packed with sofas, bookshelves, and intimate lamps and mirrors. It is hard to find, though: walk behind the Central Academy of Drama on Nanluogu Xiang, and take your first left down an alleyway that is only wide enough for two people. ✉ *35 Dongmianhua Hutong, Dongcheng District* ☎ *010/ 6405–5775.*

★ **Drum & Bell.** This bar has a perfect location—right between the Drum and Bell towers. The terrace is a comfy perch for a summer afternoon drink, where you scan the surrounding hutong rooftops. Don't get too plastered, though, because the staircase down is very steep. On the ground floor there are jumbles of sofas tossed with Cultural Revolution memorabilia. ✉ *41 Zhonglouwan Hutong, Dongcheng District* ☎ *010/8403–3600* Ⓜ *Gulou.*

★ **East Shore Live Jazz Café.** The closest thing Beijing has to New Orleans is this bar. Expect cigar smoke, velvet, sepia photographs of jazz greats, and plenty of vintage instruments on display. Owner, local jazz legend Liu Yuan, says he wants to use the bar to promote homegrown jazz talents. On top of the live swing and jazz, the bar boasts the best views of Houhai, either through the floor-to-ceiling windows (complete with telescope) in the bar or from the small, sparsely furnished rooftop. ⚠ **There are no guardrails on the roof, so drink and step with extreme care.** ✉ *Qianhai Nanyan Lu, 2nd fl., next to the Post Office, Xicheng District* ☎ *010/8403–2131.*

Fodor'sChoice ★ **No Name Bar.** The first bar to open in Houhai is still around—even though rumors abound that it's on the demolition list. It's also the best by far: many expats still list No Name as their favorite bar in the city. The service is refreshingly low key—a nice change from the sycophantic staff at neighboring venues—and it's all tumbledown elegance with rattan and potted plants. Locals refer to it by the owner's name: Bai Feng. Anyone from tourists to the old-China hands can be found here. ✉ *3 Qianhai East Bank, Xicheng District* ☎ *010/6401–8541.*

Elsewhere in Xicheng

Sanwei Bookstore. Here you'll find the traditional Chinese arrangement of a bookstore with an adjacent café. Traditionally, these bookstore–cafés attract writers who sip tea while listening to live Beijing opera. There's a popular bar upstairs. Saturday brings Chinese classical musicians playing such traditional instruments such as the *pipa* and the *guzheng*. ✉ *60 Fuxingmennei Dajie, Xicheng District* ☎ *010/6601–3204* Ⓜ *Xidan.*

GAY & LESBIAN NIGHTLIFE

Although Beijing is no San Francisco, there are several bars and clubs that woo gays and lesbians. *Time Out Beijing* has a regular gay and lesbian column that includes events and news. Since the scene is quite subject to change—bars frequently open, close, and reopen at new locations—you should also check online resources. Try ⊕ www.fridae.com or www.utopia-asia.com for updates. Here are some popular venues:

Destination (Mudedi). The city's best gay club has a bouncy dance floor, cute DJs, and a small lounge area. It gets super-packed on weekends and attracts a varied crowd of expats and locals. ⊠ *7 Gongti Xi Lu, Chaoyang District* ☎ *010/6551-5138.*

West Wing (Xixiangfang). This is a quirky teahouse/bar, aimed at women and tucked into the Deshengmen Tower. There's karaoke in the courtyard in summer, plus sofas, stools, and board games inside for all year-round. ⊠ *Deshengmen Tower, Xicheng District* ☎ *010/8208-2836.*

Pipe Café (Paipu Jiuba). Lesbian nights are only on Saturday. The bar attracts a crowd of young women dancing to hip-hop. ⊠ *Gongti Nan Lu, Chaoyang District* ☎ *010/6593-7756.*

Chaoyang District

Beer Mania. To enjoy this bar, you must forgive the owners for their *mandopop,* or Mandarin pop music, and rather characterless decor. It's small and the seats are hard. The attraction here is the 60 types of specialty beers—80% of them from Belgium—including Chimay Rouge and the fierce Delirium Tremens. ⊠ *Taiyue Fang, 1st fl., Sanlitun Nanlu, Chaoyang District* ☎ *010/6417–8318.*

Brown's. Set inside a massive, multileveled space, Brown's could be called a wannabe Hard Rock Cafe. Still, it's a fun party pub where you can dance on the bar and dodge pyrotechnic cocktails. It's heavy on the big-screen sports, drink choices (including 500 different shooters), and cheesy 1980s music. Weekend nights are wild, but for the rest of the time you'll be drinking with a well-behaved crowd of relaxed locals and expats. ⊠ *Sanlitun Nan Lu, above the Loft, Chaoyang District* ☎ *010/6591–2717.*

Fodor's Choice ★ Centro. We don't always vote for hotel bars, but this one is decidedly different. It's huge and luxurious, with cavernous wine cellars—and it also has Bruce Lee, the city's favorite cocktail master. Drinks are expensive. Come for the early-evening happy hour, when the prices are more polite, and feast your eyes on the nouveau riche showing off their labels. ⊠ *1/F Kerry Center Hotel, 1 Guanghua Lu, Chaoyang District* ☎ *010/6561–8833 Ext. 42* Ⓜ *Guomao.*

The Den. Sour staff and crumbling elegance are indeed this bar's attraction. The owner runs the city's amateur rugby club, and you'll find players and their supporters drinking rowdily here. Open 24-hours a day, it's guaranteed to be buzzing every night. There's a disco upstairs. ⊠ *4 Gongti Donglu, next to the City Hotel, Chaoyang District* ☎ *010/6592–6290.*

BARROOM WITH A VIEW

Although some people go to bars to be seen, you'll be richly rewarded if you check out those venues that actually have a *scene*. Beijing is glorious observed from above—with a drink in hand, it's even better. Here are three of our favorite spots:

Drum & Bell. A relaxed rooftop that tempts you to peer through the trees at the Drum Tower in front, the Bell Tower behind, and the rolling tops of hutong 'hoods to the side. ⊠ *41 Zhonglouwan Hutong, Dongcheng District* ☎ *010/8403-3600.*

East Shore Live Jazz Café. There's no competition: this place has the most fabulous views of Houhai lake, hands-down. ⊠ *Qianhai Nanyan Lu, 2nd fl., next to the Post Office, Xicheng District* ☎ *010/8403-2131.*

Top Club & Lounge. This rooftop lounge has chilled-out summer music and sneaky views of construction craters and bar alleyways from above. ⊠ *Tongli Studios, 4th fl., Sanlitun Beilu, Chaoyang District* ☎ *010/6413-1019.*

Kai. A sometimes-rowdy club with cheap, cheap drinks, a pole, and sardine-tin dance floor, Kai attracts hordes of college students and young locals on the weekends. On weeknights, however, you can hold a comfortable conversation on the sofas upstairs and admire the surreal art. ⊠ *Sanlitun Beijie, Chaoyang District* ☎ *010/6416-6254.*

Maggie's Bar. Though more of a tourist attraction than a bar to chill out in, this long-running joint is enjoying a new location (complete with what one fan called "deep hooker-handbag red" decor). The scrumptious hotdogs from the stand outside are another reason to come. ⊠ *South Gate of Ritan Park, Chaoyang District* ☎ *010/8562-8142* Ⓜ *Jianguomen.*

★ **Press Club Bar.** This haunt offers soft leather chairs, tinkling piano serenades, brass rails, and a whiff of history. Stuffy and pompous say some; tip-top cocktails worth the trip say others. Rumor has it you can taste Beijing's best Bloody Mary here. ⊠ *1/F St Regis Hotel, 21 Jianguomenwai Da Jie, Chaoyang District* ☎ *010/6460-6688 Ext. 2360* Ⓜ *Jianguomen.*

★ **Stone Boat.** This watering hole is a pavilion-style hut on the edge of a pretty lake in Ritan Park. There are ducks, feisty fishermen, and park joggers to observe while you sip chilled white wine. This is one of Beijing's nicest outdoor bars, as long as you don't mind having to use the public toilets opposite the building. The delicious peace is shattered by often amateurish DJs on weekend nights. ⊠ *Lakeside, southwest corner of Ritan Park, Chaoyang District* ☎ *010/6501-9986* Ⓜ *Jianguomen.*

Top Club & Lounge. This top-floor club, decked out in deep red, looks like a Ming Dynasty disco. Sofas are squishy, the bar staff quirky, and the rooftop gives wide-open views of the crane-pocked construction valleys in the area. There are DJs every night, and Thursday is especially gay friendly. Top Club attracts a more mellow crowd than its neighbor, zippy Bar Blu. ⊠ *Tongli Studios, 4th fl., Sanlitun Beilu, Chaoyang District* ☎ *010/ 6413-1019.*

The Tree. Expats crowd this bar for its Belgian beer, wood-fired pizza, and quiet murmurs of conversation. ✉ *43 Sanlitun Beijie, Chaoyang District* ☎ *010/6415–1954.*

Fodor'sChoice
★ **Q Bar.** George and Echo's cocktails—strong, authentic, and not super expensive—are a small legend here in Beijing. This tucked-away orange lounge bar adds an unpretentious note to an evening out. Don't be put off by the fact it's in a bland motel stuck in the 1980s: the drinks are worth it (especially the whiskey sours!). ✉ *Top floor of Eastern Inn Hotel, Sanlitun Nan Lu, Chaoyang District* ☎ *010/6595–9239.*

★ **Yugong Yishan.** This Beijing institution is a chilled-out live-music club at the back of the parking lot opposite the Workers' Stadium. It plays host to a range of live bands from blues to jazz to Afro-Caribbean beats and attracts an equally diverse crowd. It occasionally charges an entrance fee, depending on the band. ✉ *1 Gongti Beilu, Chaoyang District* ☎ *010/6415–0687.*

Chaoyang West Gate

Souk. Although the Middle Eastern food here is nothing to write home about, the Moroccan interior is splendid. Recline on a sultry bed, sip a cocktail, and puff on a hookah. This venue is one of the few places in Beijing to try absinthe. ✉ *Chaoyang West Gate, behind Annie's, Chaoyang District* ☎ *010/6506–7309.*

The World of Suzie Wong. It's no coincidence this bar is named after a 1957 novel about a Hong Kong prostitute. Come here late at night and you'll find a healthy supply of modern Suzie Wongs and a crowd of expat clients. The sleaze factor is enhanced by its 1930s opium-den design, with China-chic beds overrun with cushions. Suzie Wong's, however, has a good reputation for mixing a more-than-decent cocktail. ✉ *1A South Nongzhanguan Lu, Chaoyang West Gate, Chaoyang District* ☎ *010/6593–6049 or 010/6500–3377* ⊕ *www.suziewong.com.cn.*

Haidian District

Zub. A cozy little basement bar and club, Zub is a touch more sophisticated than the student haunts in the area. Local DJ talent often gets the place rocking—we think it's a much funkier place to shake your stuff than the flashy spots on Gongti Xi Lu. ✉ *Huaqing Jiayuan, Chengfu Lu, Wudaokou, Haidian District* ☎ *010/8286–6240* Ⓜ *Wudaokou.*

Dance Clubs

Dongcheng District

Tango. A huge warehouse-style top-floor club makes this the odd one out in the China Clubland, and that's a good thing. Without the usual gaudiness, Tango is a solid club, roomy enough to take the crowds, and often playing some good tunes. ✉ *79 Hepingli Xijie, South Gate of Ditan Park, Dongcheng District* ☎ *010/6428–2288.*

Chaoyang District

Babyface East. Now a nationwide brand of clubs spread across China, Babyface East is often full of young-money types rattling dice and drinking Chivas-and-green-tea cocktails. It attracts some good dance DJs, including the occasional international name. The interior is best described as quintessential Chinese club, with bling-bling gaudiness and scantily clad dancers. Prepare to be crushed while you shake your groove thing on the weekend. ✉ 6 Gongti Xi Lu, Chaoyang District ☎ 010/6551–9091 ⊕ www.faceclub.com.cn/.

Cargo Club. Fierce promotions have won this club some top-name international DJs. Many expats consider Cargo the best of the clubs along Gongti Xi Lu, especially for its 1980s kitsch. Renovations (in the works) may change all this. ✉ 6 Gongti Xi Lu, Chaoyang District ☎ 010/6551–6898.

At a Glance

ENGLISH	PINYIN	CHINESE CHARACTERS
POINTS OF INTEREST		
Bed	Zài Chuángshàng Jiǔbā	在床上酒吧
Beer Mania	Màiní Píjiǔ Ba	麦霓啤酒吧
Beijing Concert Hall	Běijīng Yīnyuètīng	北京音乐厅
Beijing Exhibition Theater	Běijīng Zhǎnlǎnguǎn Jùchǎng	北京展览馆剧场
Candy Floss Café	Miánhuātáng Kāfēiguǎn	棉花糖咖啡馆
Capital Theater	Shǒudū Jùchǎng	首都剧场
Centro	Xuàn Kù	炫酷
Chang'an Grand Theater	Cháng'ān Dàxìyuàn	长安大戏院
Chaoyang Theater	Cháoyáng Jùchǎng	朝阳剧场
China National Puppet Theater	Zhōngguó Guójiā Mù'ǒujù Yuàn	中国国家木偶剧院
Dashanzi	Dà shàn zi	大山子
The Den	Dūnhuáng	敦煌
Destination	Mùdìdì	目的地
Drum & Bell	Gǔzhōng Kāfēiguǎn	鼓钟咖啡馆
East Shore Live Jazz Café	Dōng'àn Kāfēi	东岸咖啡
Forbidden City Concert Hall	Zhōngshān Gōngyuán Yīnyuè Táng	中山公园音乐堂
Huguang Guildhall	Húguǎng Huìguǎn	湖广会馆
Kai	Kāi Ba	开吧
Lao She Teahouse	Lǎo Shě Cháguǎn	老舍茶馆
Liyuan Theater	Lí yuán jù chǎng	梨园剧场
Maggie's Bar	Měiqí Jiǔbā	美琪酒吧
No Name Bar (Bai Feng's)	Wúmíng Jiǔbā	无名酒吧
Pipe Café	Pàipǔ Jiǔbā	派普酒吧
Poly Plaza International Theater	Bǎolì Jùyuàn	保利剧院
Press Club Bar	Jìzhě Ba	记者吧
The Red Theatre	Hóng Jùchǎng	红剧场
Sanwei Bookstore	Sānwèi Shūwū	三味书屋
Souk	Sū Kè Huìguǎn	苏克会馆
Stone Boat	Shífǎng	石舫
Tango	Tàn gē	探戈

Tianqiao Happy Teahouse	Tiānqiáo Lè Cháguǎn	天桥乐茶馆
The Tree	Yǐnbì De Shù	隐蔽的树
Universal Theater	Tiāndì Jùchǎng	天地剧场
Wan Sheng Theater (Tianqiao Acrobatic Theater)	Tiānqiáo Zájì Jùchǎng	天桥杂技剧场
West Wing	Xīxiāng Fáng	西厢房
Workers' Stadium	Gōngréntǐ Yùchǎng	工人体育场
The World of Suzie Wong	Sūxīhuáng Jùlèbù	苏西黄俱乐部
Yugong Yishan	Yúgōng Yíshān	愚公移山

Where to Eat

The culinary delights of the capital can keep you happy—and full—for your entire stay.

WORD OF MOUTH

"We just got back from our two-month stay in Beijing. We ate like kings there and, most of the time, spent very little money."

—mochao

"There is a great place in Beijing for food stalls, Wangfujing Snack Street, which sells any type of food you could imagine (even scorpions and seahorse kebabs). We also liked the food court at the bottom of the Silk Market."

—Catherine

DINING PLANNER

Dining Hours

People tend to eat around 6 PM. Although the last order is usually taken around 9 PM, some places remain open until the wee morning hours.

Reservations

Reservations are always a good idea. Book as far ahead as you can, and reconfirm as soon as you arrive.

Paying & Tipping

Tipping is not required, although some of the larger, fancier restaurants will add a 15% service charge to the bill. Small and medium venues only take cash payment, but more established restaurants usually accept credit cards.

Top 5 Restaurants

■ **Alameda.** Every dish on this Brazilian restaurant's selective menu is made with the utmost care. From the dining area you can watch the chef at work.

■ **Din Tai Fung.** Come here for renowned *xiaolong bao* (steamed pork buns) and *cairou zhengjiao* (steamed dumplings).

■ **Huang Ting.** Munch on exquisite dim sum and refined Cantonese food in a tastefully re-created traditional courtyard house.

■ **The Red Capital Club.** Many of the dishes served in this painstakingly restored Qing Dynasty courtyard house are the favorites of previous top Chinese Communist leaders.

■ **Yotsuba.** The fresh seafood is flown in daily from Tokyo's Tsukiji fish market, making this spot a sushi mecca.

Prices

Dining out is one of the great bargains in Beijing, where it's still possible to have a three-course meal with drinks for less than $10. As in other cities, drinks can push up the price of a meal, so study the drink options and costs carefully. Although one tea may cost Y40 a pot, another may just be Y10. A soda could be Y25 a glass, and a bottle of beer is just Y10.

What It Costs In Yuan

	$$$$	$$$	$$	$	¢
AT DINNER	over Y180	Y121–Y180	Y81–Y120	Y40–Y80	under Y40

Prices are for a main course. Note: the term "main course" may not be appropriate for some restaurants, as Chinese dishes are normally shared.

On the Menu

Peking duck is the capital's most well-known dish, but there's much more to the city's cuisine than just the famous fowl. Despite rising competition, traditional Beijing dining is making a comeback. Waiters whisk dishes through crowded, lively rooms furnished with wooden menu boards and lacquered square tables, while doormen, dressed in traditional cotton jackets, loudly announce each arrival and departure. Beijing-style eateries offer many little-known but excellent specialties, such as *dalian huoshao* (meat and vegetable-filled dumplings) and *zha-jiangmian* (thick noodles with meat sauce). If you're adventurous, sample a bowl of intestines brewed in an aromatic broth mixed with bean curd, baked bread, and chopped cilantro.

Beijingers complement their meals with locally brewed beer, such as Yanjing or Beijing beer, or the fiery *erguoto*, an alcoholic beverage distilled from wheat and fermented sorghum (a cereal with a 100-year history). Or try *Suan-meitang*, a delightful nonalcoholic drink made from dried plums—it's perfect in summer. Imperial-style banquets, serving Manchu and Han dishes, offer an alternatively lavish dining experience.

SO YOU THINK YOU'RE TOUGH?

Are you itching to try some of Beijing's more daring cuisine? These menu items fit the bill:

■ Intestines and lungs cooked in a bubbly cauldron

■ The Feng family's flash-boiled tripe

■ Paper-thin sliced meat from a boiled lamb's head

■ Braised pig's ear and tongue

■ An organ banquet, starring the most private parts of cow, lamb, deer, and donkey. Each organ is paired with herbs to create the most potent aphrodisiac.

■ Deep-fried scorpions

■ Salted seahorse

■ "Fish" and "Duck" made entirely of tofu

■ Braised ox tongue

6

By Eileen Wen Mooney

China's economic boom has revolutionized dining culture in Beijing, with the city today boasting a wide variety of regional cuisines, including unusual, tasty specialties from Yunnan, earthy Hakka cooking from southern China, Tibetan yak and *tsampa* (barley flour), Sichuan's spicy and numbing flavors, and chewy noodles from Shaanxi. The capital also offers plenty of international cuisine, including French, German, Thai, Japanese, Brazilian, Malaysian, and Italian, among others.

You can spend as little as $2 per person for a decent meal to $100-and-up on a lavish banquet. The venues are part of the fun, ranging from swanky restaurants to holes-in-the-wall and refurbished courtyard houses. Beer is available everywhere in Beijing, and although wine was once only available in Western-style restaurants, many Chinese restaurants now have extensive wine menus.

DONGCHENG DISTRICT

Dongcheng runs from the eastern flank of the Forbidden City to the Second Ring Road. There are plenty of good restaurants here, along with an impressive wealth of historical sights. Try one of Beijing's growing number of traditional courtyard eateries, where you can dine alfresco in the warmer months, including the Red Capital Club, Gui Gongfu, and the Source. Or walk down Nan Luogu Xiang, an old alleyway, where you pick from more than a dozen Western and Chinese restaurants, coffeehouses, and hip bars located in traditional Chinese structures. Good places here are Café de la Poste for inexpensive French cuisine, the Pass By Restaurant for Western food, Fish Nation for fish-and-chips, and Thule for home-style Chinese cooking.

Chinese

$$$$
Fodor'sChoice
★
✕ **Huang Ting.** Beijing's traditional courtyard houses, which are fast facing extinction as entire neighborhoods are demolished to make way for new high-rises, provide the theme here. This is arguably Beijing's best Cantonese restaurant, serving southern favorites such as braised shark fin with crab meat, seared abalone with seafood, and steamed scallop and bean curd in black-bean sauce. The dim sum is delicately refined, and the deep-fried taro spring rolls and steamed pork buns are not to be missed. The walls are constructed from original *hutong* bricks taken from centuries-old courtyard houses that have been destroyed. ☒ *The Peninsula, 8 Jinyu Hutong, Wangfujing, Dongcheng District* ☎ *010/ 6512–8899 Ext. 6707* ▤ *AE, MC, V* Ⓜ *Dongdan.*

$$$–$$$$
Fodor'sChoice
★
✕ **Red Capital Club.** Occupying a meticulously restored courtyard home in one of Beijing's few remaining traditional Chinese neighborhoods, the Red Capital Club oozes nostalgia. Cultural Revolution memorabilia and books dating from the Great Leap Forward era (1958–60) adorn every nook of the small bar, while the theme of the dining room is imperial. The fancifully written menu reads like a fairy tale, with dreamily named dishes. "South of Clouds" is a Yunnan dish of fish baked over bamboo—it's said to be a favorite of a former Communist marshal. "Dream of the Red Chamber" is a fantastic eggplant dish cooked according to a recipe in the classic novel by the same name. ☒ *66 Dongsi Jiutiao, Dongcheng District* ☎ *010/6402–7150* ⌂ *Reservations essential* ▤ *AE, DC, MC, V* ☉ *No lunch.*

$$$–$$$$
Fodor'sChoice
★
✕ **The Source.** The Source serves a set menu of Sichuan specialties, changing it every two weeks. The menu includes several appetizers, both hot and mild dishes, and a few surprise concoctions from the chef. On request, the kitchen will tone down the spiciness of your food. The Source's location was once the backyard of a Qing Dynasty general regarded by the Qing court as "The Great Wall of China" for his military exploits. The grounds have been painstakingly renovated; an upper level overlooks a small garden filled with pomegranate and date trees. The central yard's dining is serene and acoustically protected from the hustle and bustle outside. ☒ *14 Banchang Hutong, Kuanjie, Dongcheng District* ☎ *010/6400–3736* ⌂ *Reservations essential* ▤ *AE, DC, MC, V.*

$$–$$$$
Fodor'sChoice
★
✕ **Din Tai Fung.** The arrival of Din Tai Fung—one of Taipei's most famous restaurants—was warmly welcomed by Beijing's food fanatics. The restaurant's specialty is *xiaolong bao* (juicy buns wrapped in a light unleavened-dough skin and cooked in a bamboo steamer), which are served with slivers of tender ginger in a light black vinegar. *Xiaolong bao* have three different fillings: ground pork, seafood, or crabmeat. If you can, leave some room for the scrumptious tiny dumplings packed with red-bean paste. This restaurant is frequented by both Beijing's up-and-coming middle class and old Taiwan hands, who are fervently loyal to its delicate morsels. ☒*22 Hujiayuan, Yibei Building* ☎*010/6462–4502* ▤ *AE, MC, V.*

$–$$$$
✕ **Sifang Jie.** Serving the cuisine of southwestern China's Yunnan province, this eatery is located in Nanxincang, a restored imperial granary complex. The menu features a wide range of wild mushrooms, Yunnan vegetables, and varieties of chicken soup, such as *qiguo ji* (soup cooked

6

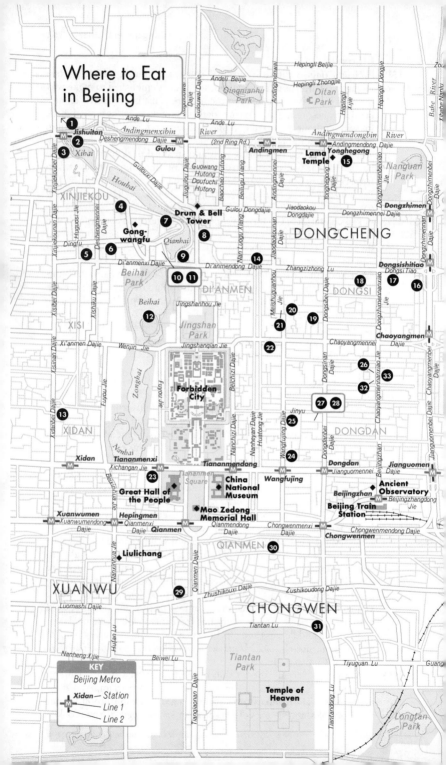

in a special red-clay pot). Natural bean curd from Shiping is one delicious stir-fry ingredient. Sifang Jie is popular among a younger generation of Beijingers infatuated with China's minority cultures. ⊠ *A16 Nanxincang Warehouse Complex, Dongcheng District* ☎ *010/6409–6403* 🖃 *No credit cards* Ⓜ *Dongsi Shitiao.*

$$–$$$ ✕ **Lai Jin Yu Xuan.** A gem tucked inside Zhongshan Park on the west side of the Forbidden City, Lai Jin is known for its Red Mansion banquet, based on dishes from Cao Xueqin's classic novel, *The Dream of the Red Chamber,* written circa 1760. The two-story restaurant sits beside a small pond amid willow and peach trees. The two daily dishes are *qie xiang* (eggplant with nuts) and *jisi haozigan* (shredded chicken with crown-daisy chrysanthemum). To sample more than 40 dishes made famous in this novel, you must order a banquet meal (from Y300–Y440) three days in advance. After your meal, take a lazy stroll across the park to the nearby teahouse with the same name, where you can enjoy a cup of tea in the courtyard surrounded by ancient cypress and scholar trees. ⊠ *Inside Zhongshan Park, on the west side of the Forbidden City, Dongcheng District* ☎ *010/6605–6676* 🖃 *No credit cards.*

$$ ✕ **Dong Lai Shun.** Dating to 1903, this is one of Beijing's oldest Hui (Chinese Muslim) restaurants. Its specialty is a mutton dish famous for three attributes: paper-thin slices, high-quality meat, and an excellent dipping sauce. The hotpot dishes are amazingly flavorful: the best part is near the end, when the broth reaches a tongue-tingling climax. If you like, drop some cilantro into the bowl. *Zhima shaobing* (small baked sesame bread) is the perfect accompaniment. ⊠ *5/F Xin Dongan Plaza, Wangfujing Dajie, Dongcheng District* ☎ *010/6528–0932* 🖃 *No credit cards* Ⓜ *Wangfujing.*

$$ ✕ **Gui Gongfu.** Known as the "Lair of Queens" because two former Qing empresses once lived here, this space was also home to the infamous Empress Dowager Cixi and her niece Logyu. A large courtyard house with wisteria and crab-apple trees in the garden make this ideal for dining alfresco in the summer. Some of the dishes are flavored with tea leaves, and are accordingly named. *Lu Yu zhucha,* or "Lu Yu cooking tea," is the restaurant's signature dish: Lu Yu is the author of the ancient *Book of Tea* and the dish is stir-fried beef with chilies and tea leaves. Green-tea flavored noodles and oolong spareribs are also excellent choices. This quiet restaurant attracts people keen to experience a bit of Old Beijing. ⊠ *11 Fang Jia Yuan Hutong, Dongcheng District* ☎ *010/6512–7667* 🖃 *AE, V.*

$$ ✕ **Jinyang Shuanglai Fanzhuang.** This spot is known for its hearty Shaanxi cuisine, famous for its heavy use of dark vinegar. *Kao laolao* is a favorite noodle cooked in a honeycomb-like shape, which is dipped into sauces of tomato and egg, minced-meat, or vinegar. *Guoyou ro* (tender pork sautéed with chives) is the signature dish of this province. ⊠ *36 Dengshikou Xijie, Dongcheng District* ☎ *010/8511–1115* 🖃 *No credit cards.*

$–$$ ✕ **Baodu Feng Jinshenglong.** *There are 13 different kinds of tripe, which one haven't you tried?* the restaurant's single-page menu asks at this centuries-old eatery. *Yangsiyang* ("lamb, four types") consists of four "tough" types of tripe, accompanied by a homemade ground-sesame sauce. You may want to take the advice in Yang Miren's famous poem, which advises: "Just swallow the whole bit" when it's impossible to

Continued on page 161

A CULINARY TOUR OF CHINA

For centuries, the collective culinary fragrances of China have drifted far beyond its borders and tantalized the entire world. In the decades following the revolution, most Westerners couldn't get anything close to genuine Chinese cuisine. But with China's arms now open to the world, a vast variety of Chinese flavors are more widely accessible than ever.

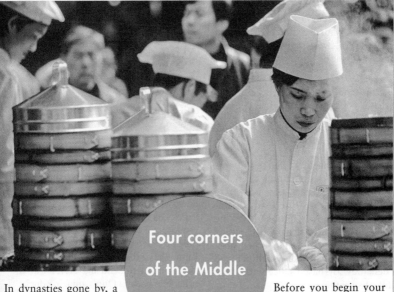

Four corners of the Middle Kingdom

In dynasties gone by, a visitor to China might have to undertake a journey of a thousand li just to feel the burn of an authentic Sichuanese hotpot, and another to savor the crispy skin and juicy flesh of a genuine Beijing roast duck. Luckily for us, the vast majority of regional Chinese cuisines have made successful internal migrations. As a result, Sichuanese cuisine can be found in Guangzhou, Cantonese dim sum in Urumuqi, and the cumin spiced lamb-on-a-stick, for which the Uigher people of Xinjiang are famous, is now grilled all over China.

Before you begin your journey, remember, a true scholar of Middle Kingdom cuisine should first eliminate the very term "Chinese food" from their vocabulary. It hardly encompasses the variety of provincial cuisines and regional dishes that China has to offer, from succulent shanghainese dumplings to fiery Sichuanese hotpots.

To guide you on your gastronomic journey, we've divided the country's gourmet map along the points of the compass—North, South, East, and West. Bon voyage and *bon appétit!*

NORTH

THE BASICS

Cuisine from China's Northeast is called *dongbei cai,* and it's more wheat than rice based. Vegetables like kale, cabbage, and potatoes are combined with robust, thick soy sauces, garlic (often raw), and scallions.

Even though many Han Chinese from southern climates find mutton too gamey, up north it's a regular staple. In many northern cities, you can't walk more than a block without coming across a small sidewalk grills with *yang rou chua'r,* or lamb-on-a-stick.

NOT TO BE MISSED

The most famous of all the northern dishes is Peking duck, and if you've ever had it well prepared, you'll know why Beijingers are proud of the dish named for their city.

The fowl is cleaned, stuffed with burning millet stalks and other aromatic combustibles, and then slow-cooked in an oven heated by a fire made of fragrant wood. Properly cooked, Peking duck should have crispy skin, juicy meat, and none of the grease. Peking duck is served with pancakes, scallions and a delicious soy-based sauce with just a hint of sweetness.

The ultimate window dressing.

LEGEND HAS IT

Looking for the best roast duck in Beijing? You won't find it in a luxury hotel. But if you happen to find yourself wandering through the Qianmendong hutong just south of Tiananmen Square, you may stumble upon a little courtyard home with a sign in English reading Li Qun Roast Duck. This small and unassuming restaurant is widely considered as having the best Peking roast duck in the capital. Rumor has it that the late leader Deng Xiaoping used to send his driver out to bring him back Li Qun's amazing ducks.

THE CAPITAL CITY'S NAMESAKE DISH

Soy-based hoisin sauce

A perfectly prepared duck

Pancakes

Scallions

SOUTH

(left) Preparing for the feast. (top right) Dim sum as art. (bottom right) Meat-filled Beijing dumplings.

THE BASICS

The dish most associated with Southern Chinese Cuisine is dim sum, which is found in great variety and abundance in Guangdong province, as well as Hong Kong and Macau. Bite sized dim sum is usually eaten early in the day. Any good dim sum place should have dozens of varieties. Some of the most popular dishes are *har gao*, a shrimp dumpling with a rice flour skin, *siu maai*, a pork dumpling with a wrapping made of wheat flour, and *chaahabao*, a steamed or baked bun filled with sweetened pork and onions. Adventerous eaters should order the chicken claws. Trust us, they taste better than they look.

> The Cantonese saying *"fei qin zou shou"* roughly translates to "if it flies, swims or runs, it's food."

For our money, the best southern food comes from Chaozhou (Chiuchow), a coastal city only a few hours drive north of its larger neighbors. Unlike dim sum, Chaozuo cuisine is extremely light and under-stated. Deep-fried bean curd is also a remarkably fresh Chaozuo dish.

NOT TO BE MISSED

One Chaozuo dish that appeals equally to the eye and the palate is the plain-sounding mashed vegetable with minced chicken soup. The dish is served in a large bowl, and resembles a green-and-white yin-yang. As befitting a dish resembling a Buddhist symbol, a vegetarian version substituting rice gruel for chicken broth is usually offered.

SOUTHWEST AND FAR WEST

Southwest

THE BASICS

When a person from the Southwest asks you if you like spicy food, consider your answer well. Natives of Sichuan and Hunan take the use of chilies, wild pepper, and garlic to blistering new heights. These two areas have been competing for the "spiciest province in China" title for centuries. The penchant for fiery food is likely due to the weather—hot and humid in the summer and harshly cold in the winter. But no matter what the temperature, if you're eating Sichuan or Hunan dishes, be prepared to sweat.

Southwest China shares some culinary traits with both Southeast Asia and India. This is likely due to the influences of travelers from both regions in centuries past. Traditional Chinese medicine also makes itself felt in the regional cuisine. Theory has it that sweating expels toxins and equalizes body temperature.

As Chairman Mao's hometown province, Hunan has a number of dishes with revolutionary names. The most popular are red-cooked Hunan fish *(hongshao wuchangyu)* and red-cooked pork *(hongshao rou),* which was said to have been a personal favorite of the Great Helmsman.

The hotter the better.

NOT TO BE MISSED

One dish you won't want to miss out on in Sichuan is *mala zigi,* or "peppery and hot chicken." It's one part chicken meat and three parts fried chilies and a Sichuanese wild pepper called *huajiao* that's so spicy it effectively numbs the tongue. At first it feels like eating Tiger Balm, but the hot-cool-numb sensation produced by crunching on the pepper is oddly addictive.

KUNG PAO CHICKEN

One of the most famous Chinese dishes, Kung Pao chicken (or *gongbao jiding,*) enjoys a legend of its own.

Though shrouded in myth, its origin exemplifies the improvisational skills found in any good Chinese chef. The story of Kung Pao chicken has to do with a certain Qing dynasty era (1644-1911) provincial governor named Ding Baozhen, who arrived home unexpectedly one day with a group of friends in tow. His cook, caught in between shopping

trips, had only the chicken breast and a few vegetables he was planning to cook for his own dinner. The crafty chef diced the chicken into tiny bits and fried it up with everything he could find in the cupboard—some peanuts, sugar, onion, garlic, bits of ginger, and a few handfuls of dried red peppers—and hoped for the best.

(top left) Chowing down at Kashgar's Sunday Market. (center left) Eat, drink, and be merry! (bottom left) Monk stirring tsampa barley. (right) Juggling hot noodles in the Xinjiang province.

Far West

THE BASICS

Religion is the primary shaper of culinary tradition in China's far west. Being a primarily Muslim province, chefs in Xinjiang don't use pork products of any kind. Instead, meals are likely to be heavy on spiced lamb. Baked flat breads coated in sesame seeds are a specialty. Whole lamb roasted on a spit, fine spicy tomato salads, and lightly spiced mutton and vegetable soups are also favorites.

NOT TO BE MISSED

In Tibet, climate is the major factor dictating cuisine. High and dry, the Tibetan plateau is hardly suited for rice cultivation. Whereas a Han meal might include rice, Tibetan cuisine tends to include tsampa, a ground barley usually cooked into a porridge. Another staple that's definitely an acquired taste is yak butter tea. Dumplings, known as *momo,* are wholesome and filling. Of course, if you want to go all out, order the yak penis with caterpillar fungus.

EAST

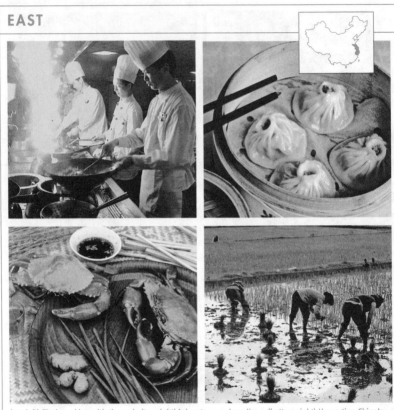

(top left) Flash cooking with the wok. (top right) Juicy steamer dumplings. (bottom right) Harvesting China's staple. (bottom left) Shanghai's sublime hairy crab.

THE BASICS

The rice, seafood, and fresh vegetable-based cooking of the southern coastal provinces of Zhejiang and Jiangsu are known collectively as *huiyang cai*. As the areas biggest city, Shanghai has become a major center of the culinary arts. Some popular dishes in Shanghai are stir-fried fresh-water eels and finely ground white pepper, and red-stewed fish—a boiled carp in sweet and sour sauce. Another Shanghai favorite are *xiaolong bao*, or little steamer dumplings. Similar to Cantonese dim sum, xiaolong bao tend to be more moist. The perfect steamed dumpling is meant to explode in your mouth in a juicy burst of meat.

NOT TO BE MISSED

Drunken anything! Shanghai chefs are known for their love of cooking with wine. Dishes like drunken chicken, drunken pigeon, and drunken crab are all delectable meals cooked with prodigious amounts of Shaoxing wine. People with an aversion to alcohol should definitely avoid these. Another meal not to be missed is hairy freshwater crabs, which only come into season in October. One enthusiast of the dish was 15th-century poet and essayist Li Yu, who wrote of the dish in near-erotic terms. "Meat as white as jade, golden roe. . .to use seasoning to improve its taste is like holding up a torch to brighten the sunshine."

chew it. *Shandan,* or accordionlike tripe, is the most popular, although *duren* is amazing: tender but crispy. In addition to their tripe, they serve mutton prepared in a traditional coal-heated brass pot. ⊠ *Qinglan Daxia, 24 Dongsi Shitiao, Dongcheng District* ☎ *010/6527–9051* ▭ *No credit cards.*

★ $ ✕ **Jingsi Su Shifang.** Soft Buddhist chants hum in this clean, cheerful restaurant, which serves no meat dishes. Carnivores may still be happy here, though, as much of the food is prepared to look and taste like meat. Try the crispy Peking "duck," or a "fish" (made of tofu skin) that even has scales carved into it. *Zaisu jinshen,* another favorite, has a filling that looks and tastes like pork. It is wrapped in tofu skin, deep-fried, and coated with a light sauce. ⊠ *18A Dafosi Dongjie, Dongcheng District* ☎ *010/6400–8941* ▭ *No credit cards.*

★ $ ✕ **Jun Qin Hua.** A hole-in-the-wall in an ancient neighborhood, this small eatery serves specialties of the Miao minority of Guizhou province. Many Guizhou natives adore the sour fish soup. Other dishes prepared with *zaola* (fermented ground chilies) stimulate your appetite, so you can later enjoy *Xiaomizha,* Guizhou's special millet made with dates and lotus seeds in a small bamboo steamer: it's a sticky, sweet indulgence. ⊠ *88 Meishuguan Houjie, Dongcheng District* ☎ *010/6404–7600* ▭ *No credit cards.*

¢–$ ✕ **Paomo Guan.** The bright red and blue bamboo shading the front porch of this adorable spot will immediately catch your eye. Paomo Guan focuses on *paomo*—a Shaanxi trademark dish. Guests break a large piece of unleavened flat bread into little pieces and then put them in their bowl. After adding condiments, the waiter takes your bowl to the kitchen where broth—simmered with spices, including star anise, cloves, cardamom, cinnamon sticks, and bay leaves—is poured over the bread bits. ⊠ *59 Chaoyangmennei Nanxiaojie, Dongcheng District* ☎ *010/ 6559–8135* ▭ *No credit cards.*

¢–$ ✕ **Qin Tangfu.** Authentic Shaanxi fare, including *roujia mo* (bread stuffed with meat), noodles, and dumplings are served up next to the traditional stove, which produces hot, fresh breads. The low tables and chairs here reflect the lifestyle of Shaanxi people. Lending a bit of charm are framed paper cuts (a form of Chinese folk art in which red paper is cut into animal, flower, or human shapes), traditional handicrafts, and big baskets (where you can store your purse or bags while you eat). ⊠ *69 Chaoyangmennei Nanxiaojie, Dongcheng District* ☎ *010/ 6559–8135* ▭ *No credit cards.*

6

A BOOKWORM'S FOOD TOUR

Throughout China's history, there has been a love affair between the literati and food. So grab a copy of these books and try the following plates:

Qiexiang: a simple eggplant dish depicted in the classic *The Dream of Red Chamber,* a novel about 1700s scholar-gentry life.

Huixiang dou: a bean boiled with star anise, made famous through Lu Xun's short story "Kong Yi Ji," which takes place in a traditional wine house.

Lu Yu zhucha: beef cooked in tea leaves, inspired by Lu Yu, the author of the *Book of Tea.*

Contemporary

★ **$$$–$$$$** ✕ **Jing.** Rated "One of the 75 Hottest Tables in the World" by *Condé Nast Traveler* in 2003, Jing serves up East–West fusion cuisine in an ultramodern setting replete with polished red wooden floors, cream-colored chairs, and gauzy curtain dividers. Signature appetizers include outstanding duck rolls, tiger prawns, and fragrant coconut soup. The fillet of barramundi and risotto with seared langoustines are standout main courses. For dessert, don't miss the warm chocolate cake with almond ice cream. There's also an excellent selection of international wines. ⊠ *The Peninsula Beijing, 8 Jinyu Hutong, Wangfujing, Dongcheng District* ☎ *010/6523–0175 Ext. 6714* ▤ *AE, DC, MC, V* Ⓜ *Dongdan.*

$$$–$$$$ ✕ **My Humble House.** From its decor to dinnerware, there's nothing humble about this fusion restaurant. The main dining area is designed around a pool covered with rose petals; gingko leaves scatter the hallway. We found this to be one of the few restaurants that successfully creates fusion dishes, tapping Western ingredients while retaining a distinct Chinese flavor. The lightly fried crispy prawn glazed with wasabi-mayonnaise sauce is unforgettable. For dessert try cool lemongrass jelly served with red wolfberries. ⊠ *W307 Oriental Plaza, 1 Dong Changan Jie, Dongcheng District* ☎ *010/8518–8811* ▤ *AE, DC, MC, V* Ⓜ *Wangfujing.*

French

$$$–$$$$ ✕ **Flo Justine's.** Classic French cuisine and wine, including foie gras, snails, and Château Haut-Brion, are served with the utmost attention at Beijing's oldest French restaurant. Justine's is well known for its delicious desserts. ⊠ *Jianguo Hotel, 5 Jianguomenwai Dajie* ☎ *010/6500–2233 Ext. 8039* ▤ *AE, MC, V.*

¢–$$$ ✕ **Caribou Café.** You'll find Caribou tucked in the middle of Qianliang Hutong. Cartoons drawn by customers cover the walls at this homey spot. Choose from a variety of pastas, risotto, poultry, steaks, and salmon. For a delicious end to the meal, try the crème brûlée, chocolate flan, red-wine-poached pear served with rice pudding, or Vietnamese coffee with sweet condensed milk. The apple tea is delightful, too. ⊠ *32 Qianliang Hutong, Dongcheng District* ☎ *010/8402–1529* ▤ *No credit cards.*

$$ ✕ **Café de la Poste.** In almost every French village, town, or city there is a Café de la Poste, where people go for a cup of coffee, a beer, or a simple family meal. This haunt lives up to its name: It's a steak-lover's paradise, with such favorites as finely sliced marinated beefsteak served with lemon-herb vinaigrette and steak tartare. If the next table orders banana flambé, we promise the warm scent of its rum will soon have you smitten enough to order it yourself. ⊠ *58 Yonghegong Dajie, Dongcheng District* ☎ *010/6402–7047* ▤ *No credit cards* Ⓜ *Yonghegong.*

TOP OF THE CARTS: BEST STREET-VENDOR SNACKS

Part of the fun of exploring Beijing's lively hutongs is the chance to munch on the city's traditional snacks, served up by itinerant food sellers. Sweet-potato sellers turn their pedicabs into restaurants on wheels. An oil drum, balanced between the two rear wheels, becomes a makeshift baking unit, with small cakes of coal at the bottom roasting sweet potatoes strung around the top. In fall and winter, sugar-coated

delicacies are a popular treat. Hawthorne berries, crabapples, water chestnuts, grapes, and yams are placed on skewers, about a half-dozen to a stick; the fruit is then bathed in rock-sugar syrup that hardens into a shiny candy coating, providing a healthy sugar rush for those all-day walks. Not in the mood for sweets? Look for roasted chestnuts, egg crepes, and lamb kebabs.

XICHENG DISTRICT

Xicheng extends north and west of the Forbidden City, and includes Beihai Park and Houhai. Dive into the hutongs here and try one of the excellent local restaurants, such as **Jiumen Xiaochi,** which serves Old Beijing favorites, or Zhang Qun Jia, for its homemade Suzhou cooking. Or try pizza in a refurbished courtyard house at popular Hutong Pizza (⇨ See p. 47), a few minutes' walk from the Silver Ingot Bridge.

Chinese

$$$$ ✕ **Lijiacai.** Owner Li Li established this restaurant in 1985 after winning a cooking contest, using recipes handed down from her great-grandfather, once a Manchu guard and imperial cook in the Qing court. The Li family restaurant serves several set meals, beginning at Y200 per person and going up to Y500. The menus include a combination of imperial and Old Beijing favorites. ⊠ *11 Yangfang Hutong, Denei Dajie, Xicheng District* ☎ *010/6618–0107* ⌚ *Reservations essential* ▤ *No credit cards.*

$$$$ ✕ **Mei Fu.** In a plush, restored courtyard on Houhai's south bank, Mei
Fodor'sChoice Fu oozes intimate elegance. The interior is filled with antique furniture
★ and velvet curtains punctuated by pebbled hallways and waterfalls. Black-and-white photos of Mei Lanfang, China's most famous opera star, who performed female roles, hang on the walls. Diners choose from set menus, starting from Y300 per person, which feature typical Jiangsu and Zhejiang cuisine, such as fried shrimp, pineapple salad, and tender leafy vegetables. A Y200 (per person) lunch is also available. ⊠ *24 Daxiangfeng Hutong, south bank of Houhai Lake, Xicheng District* ☎ *010/ 6612–6845* ⌚ *Reservations essential* ▤ *MC, V.*

$$$$ ✕ **Zhang Qun Jia.** You may never guess that behind the old fading wooden door with the number 5 written on it, set on "Bending Pipe

CLOSE UP

Legendary Eats in the Xiaoyou Hutong

A DOZEN WELL-KNOWN RESTAURANTS, some dating back more than a century and threatened by the urban renewal of the old Qianmen business district, have found refuge in a large traditional courtyard house in Xiaoyou Hutong. Some of Beijing's oldest and most famous eateries have regrouped here under one roof. Our favorites are:

Baodu Feng. This vendor specializes in tripe. The excellent accompanying dipping sauce is a long-guarded family secret. You'll see upon entering that this stall has the longest line.

Chatang Li. On offer here is *miancha*, a flour paste with either sweet or salty toppings. Miancha was created by an imperial chef who ground the millet, poured boiling water into it, mixed it into a paste, and added brown sugar and syrup. The imperial family loved it, and it soon became a breakfast staple.

Niangao Qian. This stall makes sticky rice layered with red-bean paste. It's the most popular sticky rice snack made by the Hui, or Chinese Muslims.

Yangtou Ma. Known for thin-sliced meat from boiled lamb's head, this shop was once located on Ox Street, in the old Muslim quarter.

Doufunao Bai. These folks sell soft bean curd, recognized for its delicate texture. It's best topped with braised lamb and mushrooms.

En Yuan Ju. Sample the *chaogeda*, which are small, stir-fried noodles with vegetables and meat.

Yue Sheng Zhai. Line up for excellent *jiang niurou* (braised beef), *shao yangrou* (braised lamb), and *zasui tang* (mutton soup).

Xiaochang Chen. The main ingredient of this vendor's dish is intestines, complemented with pork, bean curd, and *huoshao* (unleavened baked bread). The contents are simmered slowly in an aromatic broth.

Dalian Huoshao. This stall serves pot stickers in the shape of old-fashioned over-the-shoulder satchels that the Chinese once wore. These pot stickers were the creation of the Yao family of Shunyi, who set up their small restaurant in the old Dong'an Market in 1876.

The Jiumen Xiaochi (Nine Gates Snacks). The archway by the lake in front of Xiaoyou Hutong refers to the former nine gates in the inner city of the Forbidden City. The private dining rooms in the courtyard are named after these gates.

✉ *1 Xiaoyou Hutong, Xicheng District* ☎ *010/6402-5858* 🗪 *Reservations not accepted* 💳 *No credit cards.*

Street," lies a gourmet restaurant. "Zhang Qun's Home" was opened in 2003 by a Beijing artist as a place where she and her creative friends could relax. Soon it turned into a small restaurant, serving the home-style specialties of her native Suzhou. Light shining through a small skylight, scattered books, and fresh-cut flowers create the welcoming feeling of a friend's home. The aroma and taste of the spring onion in the yangchun noodles is captivating. The set meal costs Y200 to Y500 a person, and includes a large number of appetizers, hot dishes, and a dessert, all selected by Ms. Zhang. ⊠ *5 Yandai Xiejie, Houhai, Xicheng District* ☎ *010/8404–6662* ⚜ *Reservations not accepted* ▤ *No credit cards.*

★ **\$\$\$–\$\$\$\$** ╳ **Fangshan.** In a traditional courtyard villa on the shore of Beihai, you can get a taste of China's imperial cuisine. Established in 1925 by three royal chefs, Fangshan serves dishes once prepared for the imperial family, based on recipes gathered across China. Fangshan is best known for its filled pastries and steamed breads—traditional snack foods developed to satisfy Empress Dowager Cixi's sweet tooth. To experience Fangshan's exquisite imperial fare, order one of the banquet-style set meals at Y500 per person. Be sure to make reservations two or three days in advance. ⊠ *Beihai Park, northwest of the Forbidden City, Xicheng District, enter through east gate, cross stone bridge, and bear right* ☎ *010/6401–1879* ⚜ *Reservations essential* ▤ *AE, DC, MC, V* Ⓜ *Tiananmen West.*

\$\$\$–\$\$\$\$ ╳ **Gu Zhenhuang.** A Cantonese eatery located in hutong-enclosed courtyard house, Gu Zhenhuang is just a short walk from Houhai. You can dine in one of the four rooms that look out on the courtyard. Several set menus are available with prices running from Y150 to Y1,400 per person. Specialties include Cantonese dishes like turtle shell, fish maw, and braised ox tongue. Owner Albert Wong, a Hong Kong gourmet and food writer whose pen name is Gu Zhenhuang, has selected a good wine list—with some wines breaking the bank at over $1,000 per bottle. ⊠ *3 Qianhai Xijie, Xicheng District* ☎ *010/6613–9641* ⚜ *Reservations essential* ▤ *No credit cards.*

\$–\$\$\$ ╳ **South Silk Road.** China is an immense country populated with 56 ethnic minority groups that have little in common with the Han majority. If you're curious about cuisine from a minority group, consider a meal at this trendy restaurant, which serves food from Yunnan province, China's southernmost province bordering Thailand, Vietnam, and Laos. Yunnan is home to a distinctive type of cuisine that you'd be hard pressed to find outside of the country. Typical—and delicious—Yunnan specialties include smoked ham, wild mushrooms, and goat cheese. A tasty homemade rice wine is the perfect accompaniment. The two-story glass venue, owned by artist Fang Lijun, has plenty of outdoor seating and excellent lake views. ⊠ *19A Lotus La., Shichahai, Xicheng District* ☎ *010/6615–5515* ▤ *No credit cards.*

\$\$ ╳ **Xi Xiangzi.** "Spring from Hunan" is a small venue specializing in Hunan cuisine with a French touch—Aymeric, the owner, is French. The seven-table restaurant has an extensive menu; smoked bean curd (*xianggan*), and cured meat (*larou*) are prepared splendidly here. In addition to classic Hunan dishes, you can also sample fondue Bouguignone and banana flambé. ⊠ *36 Ding Fu Jie, Xicheng District* ☎ *137/0108–0959* ⚜ *Reservations accepted* ▤ *No credit cards.*

FodorŚChoice
★

\$ ╳ **Han Cang.** In the mood for something other than the ubiquitous home-style Beijing or Sichuan fare? Try Hakka cuisine. Specialties like *sanbei ya* (three-cup duck), *yanju* (salt-baked) shrimp, and *zhi bao luyu* fish (baked in aluminum foil) are served at this casual restaurant, flanked by the many watering holes around Houhai. If you're in a group, be sure to book one of the tables on the second floor so you enjoy views of the

FodorŚChoice
★

lake. ⊠ *Shichahai Dongan, Houhai, Xicheng District, across the street from the north gate of Beihai Park* ☎ *010/6404–2259* ⌖ *Reservations essential* ⊟ *No credit cards.*

$ ✕ **Jing Wei Lo.** Always crowded with locals, this "House of Beijing Flavors" focuses on traditional Beijing food. Dishes include *madoufu* (sautéed mung-bean pulp), *zhagezha* (French fries made with mung-bean flour), and a variety of mutton dishes. The two-story building has red pillars; the entrance is guarded by a statue of a man traditionally dressed and holding a bird cage—check out his Manchu queue (the hair braid men were forced to wear during the Qing Dynasty). A semi-open kitchen around the inner dining room give the restaurant the flavor of an Old Beijing courtyard house. ⊠ *181 A Dianmen Xidajie, Xicheng District* ☎ *010/6617–6514* ⊟ *No credit cards.*

¢–$ ✕ **Kong Yi Ji.** Named for the down-and-out protagonist of a short story by Lu Xun (China's most famous modern writer), this restaurant is set behind a small bamboo forest. Upon entering, the first thing you'll see is a bust of Lu Xun. The old-fashioned menu, which is traditionally bound with thread, features some of the dishes made famous in the story, such as *huixiang dou,* or aniseed-flavored broad beans. A wide selection of *huangjiu,* sweet rice wine, is served in heated silver pots; it's sipped from a special ceramic cup. ⊠ *South shore of Shichahai, Deshengmennei Dajie, Xicheng District* ☎ *010/6618–4915* ⌖ *Reservations not accepted* ⊟ *No credit cards.*

¢–$ ✕ **Shaguo Ju.** Established in 1741, Shaguo Ju serves a simple Manchu favorite—*bairou,* or white meat (pork), which first became popular 300 years ago. The first menu pages list all the dishes cooked in the *shaguo* (the Chinese term for a casserole pot). The classic *shaguo bairou* consists of strips of pork neatly lined up, concealing bok choy and glass noodles below. Shaguo Ju emerged as a result of ceremonies held by imperial officials and wealthy Manchus in the Qing Dynasty, which included sacrificial offerings of whole pigs. The meat offerings were later given away to the nightwatch guards, who shared the "gifts" with friends and relatives. Such gatherings gradually turned into a small business, and white meat became very popular. ⊠ *60 Xisi Nan Dajie, Xicheng District* ☎ *010/6602–1126* ⊟ *No credit cards* Ⓜ *Xidan.*

SOUTHERN DISTRICTS: CHONGWEN & XUANWU

These two districts stretch south of the Forbidden City and Tiananmen Square. Once a bustling center of commerce and street life, with opera theaters, street performers, and many of Beijing's *laozihao,* or famous old restaurants, both Chongwen and Xuanwu are undergoing major renovations nowadays. Venture here to sample some of the city's most famous eateries, such as Li Qun Roast Duck Restaurant and Jinyang Fangzhuang, which serves Shanxi specialties.

Chinese

$$ ✕ **Li Qun Roast Duck Restaurant.** Juicy, whole ducks roasting in a tradi-
Fodor'sChoice tional oven greet you upon entering this simple courtyard house. It's a
★ small, casual, family-run restaurant far from the crowds and commercialism of Quanjude, Beijing's most famous Peking duck eatery. Li Qun is a choice option for those who enjoy a good treasure hunt: the restaurant is hidden deep in a hutong neighborhood. It should take about 10 minutes to walk there from Chongwenmen Xi Dajie, though you may have to stop several times and ask for directions. It's so well known by locals, however, that when they see foreigners coming down the street, they automatically point in the restaurant's direction. Sure, the restrooms and dining room are a bit shabby, but the restaurant is charming. Ask for an English menu and feast to your heart's content! ✉ *11 Beixiangfeng, Zhengyi Lu, Chongwen District* ☎ *010/6705–5578* 🚗 *Reservations essential* 🖃 No credit cards Ⓜ *Chongwen.*

$–$$ ✕ **Jinyang Fangzhuang.** Reliable, standard Shanxi fare is the order of the day here, alongside famous crispy duck and small niblets of pasta shaped like "cat ears" stir-fried with meat and vegetables. End your meal with a "sweet happiness" pastry. Jinyang Fangzhuang is attached to the ancient courtyard home of Ji Xiaolan, a Qing Dynasty scholar, the chief compiler of the *Complete Library of the Four Branches of Literature.* You can visit the old residence without admission fee and see Ji Xiaolan's study, where he wrote his famous essays. The crabapple trees and wisteria planted during his lifetime still bloom in the courtyard. ✉ *241 Zhushikou Xi Dajie, Xuanwu District* ☎ *010/6354–1107* 🖃 No credit cards ☉ No lunch.

¢ ✕ **Old Beijing Noodle King.** Close to the Temple of Heaven and Hongqiao market, this noodle house serves hand-pulled noodles and traditional Beijing dishes in a lively old-time atmosphere. Waiters shout across the room to announce customers arriving. Try the tasty *zhajiang* noodle accompanied by meat sauce and celery, bean sprout, green beans, soy beans, sliver of cucumber, and red radish. ✉ *29 Chongwenmen Dajie, Hongqiao Market, Chongwen District* ☎*010/ 6705–6705* 🚗 *Reservations not accepted* 🖃 No credit cards.

CHAOYANG DISTRICT

The huge Chaoyang district extends east from Dongcheng, encompassing Beijing's Jianguomen diplomatic neighborhood, the Sanlitun bar area, the Central Business District, and several outdoor markets and upscale shopping malls. The large foreign population living and working here has attracted a bevy of international restaurants, making this a fine place to sample dishes from around the world. If you're in Sanlitun, try Brazilian fare at Alameda, Vietnamese food at Nam Nam, or Italian dishes at Assaggi. In Jianguomenwai, head to the Jianwai Soho complex for Taiwanese dishes at Anping Gujie, or fiery Guizhou dishes at Three Guizhou Men.

American

$$ ✕ **One East on Third.** Though it's not the swankiest spot in the district, the modern Cajun cuisine is excellent. The blackened king prawns on crispy grits served with roasted tomatoes and spinach puree is one-of-a-kind. Other dishes to sample include barbecued pork shoulder with garlic greens and double-baked beans. You'll find one of Beijing's best wine lists here, being sampled by a crowd that is a mix of wealthy Chinese, expats, and hotel guests drifting down from their rooms. ⊠ *2/F, Beijing Hilton Hotel, Dong Sanhuan Beilu, 1 Dongfang Lu, Chaoyang District* ☏ *010/5865–5000 Ext. 5030* ▭ *AE, MC, V.*

Brazilian

$–$$$$ ✕ **Alameda.** Voted "Restaurant of the Year" in 2005 by *That's Beijing*
FodorsChoice magazine, Alameda has a simple but reliably delicious menu. The week-
★ day Y60 lunch specials are one of the best deals in town. On Saturday, try the *feijoada*—Brazil's national dish—a hearty black-bean stew with pork and vegetables, served with rice. The glass walls and ceiling make it a bright, pleasant place to dine. ⊠ *Sanlitun Beijie, by the Nali shopping complex, Chaoyang District* ☏ *010/6417–8084* ▭ *AE, MC, V.*

Café

★ **$–$$$** ✕ **The Bookworm.** We love this Beijing hotspot when we're craving a double-dose of intellectual stimulation and good food. Thousands of English-language books fill the shelves and may be borrowed for a fee or read inside. New books and magazines are also for sale. This is a popular venue for guest speakers, poetry readings, and live-music performances. The French chef offers a three-course set lunch and dinner. For a nibble, rather than a full meal, sandwiches, salads, and a cheese platter are also available. ⊠ *Building 4, Nan Sanlitun Lu, Chaoyang District* ☏ *010/6586–9507* ▭ *No credit cards.*

Chinese

$–$$$ ✕ **Shin Yeh.** The long line that persists since the restaurant opened proves
FodorsChoice that Shin Yeh diners are hooked. The focus here is on Taiwanese flavors
★ and freshness. *Caipudan* is a scrumptious turnip omelet. *Fotiaoqiang* ("Buddha jumping over the wall") is a delicate soup with medicinal herbs and seafood. Last but definitely not least, try the *mashu*, a glutinous rice cake rolled in ground peanut. Service is friendly and very attentive. ⊠ *6 Gongti Xilu, Chaoyang District* ☏ *010/6552–5066* ▭ *AE, MC, V.*

\$-\$\$\$ ╳ **Xiheyaju.** Nestled in one of Beijing's embassy neighborhoods, Xiheyaju is a favorite of diplomats and journalists, many of whom live and work nearby. The outdoor courtyard is perfect on a sunny spring day. Not many places can do as well as Xiheyaju in four regional cuisines: Sichuan, Shandong, Cantonese, and Huaiyang. *Ganbian sijidou* (stir-fried green beans), *mapou doufu* (spicy bean curd), and *gongbao jiding* (chicken with peanuts) are all great choices. ⊠ *Northeast corner of Ritan Park, Chaoyang District* ☎ *010/8561–7643* ▤ *AE, MC, V.*

¢-\$\$\$ ╳ **La Galerie.** Choose between two outdoor dining areas: one a wooden platform facing the bustling Guanghua Road; the other well hidden in the back, overlooking the greenery of Ritan Park. Inspired Cantonese food and dim sum fill the menu: *Changfen* (steamed rice noodles) are rolled and cut into small pieces then stir-fried with crunchy shrimp, strips of lotus root, and baby bok choy, accompanied by sweet soybean, peanut, and sesame pastes. The *xiajiao* (steamed shrimp dumplings) envelop juicy shrimp and water chestnuts. ⊠ *South gate of Ritan Park, Guanghua Rd., Chaoyang District* ☎ *010/8563–8698* ▤ *AE, MC, V* Ⓜ *Jianguomen.*

\$-\$\$ ╳ **Anping Gujie.** The two-story Anping, with a bar on the first floor and dining upstairs, is located in the sprawling Jianwai Soho complex. Dine amidst dark wood, marble tables, velour armchairs, gauzy burgundy drapes, and traditional lamps hung from the ceiling. Hakka and Taiwanese dishes dominate the menu; our top picks are *caipudan,* a Hakka turnip omelet, and *o a jian,* a popular Taiwanese oyster omelet. *Zha xia juan,* or deep-fried shrimp, and *suzha kezai,* deep-fried oysters, are other toothsome specialties. Conclude your meal with a refreshing dessert of shaved ice with red bean, pineapple, or taro drizzled with sweet condensed milk. ⊠ *Tower A, 106 Jianwai Soho, 39 Dong Sanhuan Zhonglu, Chaoyang District* ☎ *010/5869–2083* ▤ *AE, MC, V* Ⓜ *Guomao.*

\$-\$\$ ╳ **Jinshancheng Chongqing.** Join the crowds at one of Beijing's largest and most popular Sichuan restaurants, and come prepared to wait in line unless you arrive by 6 PM. When you are finally seated, order the *laziji* (chicken buried under a mound of hot peppers), *ganbian sijidou* (stir-fried green beans), and *mapou doufu* (spicy tofu). All three are superb, and even people unaccustomed to spicy food love them. The cuisine is definitely the focus here—don't expect much by way of decor. ⊠ *Zhongfu Mansion, second floor, 99 Jianguo Lu, Chaoyang District, across from the China World Trade Center* ☎ *010/6581–1598* ⌂ *Reservations not accepted* ▤ *AE, MC, V* Ⓜ *Guomao.*

\$-\$\$ ╳ **Jun Wangfu.** Tucked inside Chaoyang Park, Jun Wangfu excels in classical Cantonese fare; it's frequented by Hong Kong expats. The comprehensive menu includes steamed tofu with scallops, spinach with taro and egg, crispy goose, roast chicken, and steamed fish with ginger and scallion. The fresh baked pastry filled with *durian* (a spiny tropical fruit with a smell so notoriously strong it is often banned from being brought on airplanes) is actually a mouthwatering rarity—don't be scared off by its overpowering odor. ⊠ *19 Chaoyang Gongyuan Nanlu, east of Chaoyang Park south gate, Chaoyang District* ☎ *010/6507–7888.*

\$-\$\$ ╳ **Noodle Loft.** A first-floor noodle bar is surrounded by stools, where several dough masters are working in a flurry, snipping, shaving, and pulling dough into noodles. The stainless-steel stairway leads to a second dining space, this one spacious, with high ceilings. The black-and-white color scheme plays backdrop to a trendy, preclubbing crowd. Do as they do and order yummy fried "cat ears," which are actually small nips of dough, boiled and then topped with meat, scrambled eggs, and shredded cabbage. ⊠ *18 Baiziwan, Chaoyang District* ☎ *010/6774–9950* ⊟ *AE, MC, V.*

$–$$ ✕ **South Silk Road.** Serving the specialties of southwest China's Yunnan province in a minimalist setting, South Silk Road is a joy. Waitresses in the colorful outfits of the Bai minority guide you to a sprawling dining room resembling a factory loft. The paintings of Fang Lijun, its artist-owner, are displayed on the walls. Treebark salad, sliced sausages with Sichuan peppercorn, and *qiguoji* (a clay-pot soup with tonic herbs) are all tasty. One of the house specialties is *guoqiao mixian* ("crossing the bridge" noodles): a scorching bowl of broth, kept boiling by a thin layer of hot oil on top. The fun lies in adding small slivers of raw fish, chicken, ham, and rice noodles, which cook instantly in the pot. Female diners take note: the floor of the restaurant's upper level is made of glass, so don't wear a skirt when you dine here! ⊠ *Building D, Soho New Town, 88 Jianguo Lu, Chaoyang District* ☎ *010/8580–4286* ⊟ *AE, MC, V* Ⓜ *Dawang Lu.*

$–$$ ✕ **Three Guizhou Men.** The popularity of this ethnic cuisine prompted three Guizhou friends to set up shop in Beijing. There are many dishes here to recommend, but among the best are "beef on fire" (pieces of beef placed on a bed of chives over burning charcoal) accompanied by ground chilies, spicy lamb with mint leaves, and *mi doufu,* a rice-flour cake in spicy sauce. ⊠ *Jianwai SOHO, Bldg. 7, 39 Dong Sanhuan Zhonglu, Chaoyang District* ☎ *010/5869–0598* ⊟ *AE, MC, V* Ⓜ *Guomao.*

$–$$ ✕ **Xiao Wangfu.** Beijing residents—locals and expats—enjoy Xiao Wangfu's home-style cooking. Thanks to rampant reconstruction, it has moved from location to location as neighborhoods have been torn down. But fans can now happily find the newest site inside Ritan Park, located in a small, two-story building, with a rooftop area overlooking the park's greenery. The Peking duck is delicious, and the *laziji* (deep-fried chicken smothered in dried red chilies) is just spicy enough. The second-floor dining area overlooks the main floor, with plenty of natural sunlight pouring through the surrounding windows. ⊠ *Ritan Park North Gate, Chaoyang District* ☎ *010/8561–5985* ⊟ *AE, MC, V* Ⓜ *Jianguomen.*

$–$$ ✕ **Yuxiang Renjia.** There are many Sichuan restaurants in Beijing, but if Fodor'sChoice you ask native Sichuanese, Yuxiang Renjia is their top choice. Huge ★ earthen vats filled with pickled vegetables, hanging bunches of dried peppers and garlic, and simply dressed waitresses evoke the Sichuan countryside. The restaurant does an excellent job of preparing provincial classics such as *gongbao jiding* (diced chicken stir-fried with peanuts and dried peppers) and *ganbian sijidou* (green beans stir-fried with olive leaves and minced pork). Thirty different Sichuanese snacks are served for lunch on weekends, all at very reasonable prices. ⊠ *5/F, Lianhe Daxia, 101 Chaowai Dajie, Chaoyang District* ☏ *010/6588–3841* ⊟ *AE, MC, V* Ⓜ *Chaoyangmen.*

★ ¢–$ **Bellagio.** Chic Bellagio is a bright, trendy-but-comfortable restaurant serving up typical Sichuan dishes with a Taiwanese twist. A delicious choice is their *migao* (glutinous rice with dried mushrooms and dried shrimp, stir-fried rice noodles, and meatball soup). You can finish your meal with a Taiwan-style crushed ice and toppings of red bean, green bean, mango, strawberry, or peanut. Bellagio is open until 4 AM, making it a favorite with Beijing's chic clubbing set. The smartly dressed all-female staff—clad in black and white—have identical short haircuts. ⊠ *6 Gongti Xilu, Chaoyang District* ☏ *010/6551–3533* ⌖ *Reservations essential* ⊟ *AE, MC, V.*

¢ ✕ **Hai Wan Ju.** Haiwan means "a bowl as deep as the sea," fitting for this eatery that specializes in large bowls of hand-pulled noodles. The interior is simple, with traditional wooden tables and benches. A *xiao er* (a "young brother" in a white mandarin-collar shirt and black pants) greets you with a shout, which is then echoed in a thundering chorus by the rest of the staff. The clanking dishes and constant greetings re-create the busy atmosphere of an old teahouse. There are two types of noodles here: *guoshui,* noodles that have been rinsed and cooled; and *guotiao,* meaning "straight out of the pot," which is ideal for winter days. Vegetables, including diced celery, radish, green beans, bean sprouts, cucumber, and scallion, are placed on individual small dishes. Unless you specify otherwise, everything will be flipped into your bowl of noodles in one deft motion. Nothing tastes as good as a hand-pulled noodle: it's doughy and chewy, a texture that can only be achieved by strong hands repeatedly stretching the dough. ⊠ *36 Songyu Dongli, Chaoyang District* ☏ *010/8731–3518* ⊟ *AE, MC, V.*

Continental

★ $–$$$$ ✕ **Aria.** Aria's outdoor dining is secluded within neatly manicured bushes and roses, providing a perfectly quiet lunch spot amid Beijing's frenetic downtown. Sample the fish fillet topped with crispy pork skin. The best deal at this elegant restaurant is the weekday business lunch: for just Y128 you can enjoy a soup or salad, main course, dessert, and coffee or tea. Renaissance-style paintings decorate the walls. There is a posh dining area and bar on the first floor, and more intimate dining at the top of the spiral staircase. Live jazz plays in the evenings. ⊠ *2/F China World Hotel, 1 Jianguomenwai Dajie, Chaoyang District* ☏ *010/ 6505–2266 Ext. 38* ⊟ *AE, MC, V* Ⓜ *Guomao.*

French & Belgian

$ ✕ **Comptoirs de France Bakery.** This contemporary French-managed café serves a variety of sandwiches, excellent desserts, coffees, and hot chocolates. Besides the standard Americano, cappuccino, and latte, Comptoirs has a choice of unusual hot-chocolates flavors, including banana and

Rhum Vieux and orange Cointreau. In the Sichuan peppercorn–infused hot chocolate, the peppercorns float in the brew, giving it a pleasant peppery aroma. ⊠ *China Central Place, Building 15, N 102, 89 Jianguo Rd. (just northeast of Xiandai Soho), Chaoyang District* ☎ *010/6530–5480* ▭ *No credit cards.*

$ ✕ **Le Palais.** For mousse lovers, Le Palais is the place. The theme colors here are purple and white; the swirly wall behind the counter resembles meringue—an apt choice, as many desserts here are frothy, magnificent meringue-, mousse-, and chocolate-based concoctions. Le Palais also has wonderful plain, chocolate, and apple-filled croissants. Stop by for an afternoon tea, weekdays from 3 PM to 5 PM, when every dessert is served with a free coffee or tea. ⊠ *Zhuzong Plaza, 25 Dongsanhuan Zhonglu, Chaoyang District* ☎ *010/6508–4209* ▭ *No credit cards* Ⓜ *Guomao.*

German

$–$$$ ✕ **Café Constance.** The opening of Café Constance, a German bakery, has brought excellent rye, pumpernickel, and whole-wheat breads to Beijing. The hearty "small" breakfast begins with coffee, fresh fruit, muesli, unsweetened yogurt, eggs and bacon; the big breakfast adds several cold cuts and breads and rolls. This is a true winner if you're looking for a good breakfast, simple meal, or a good cup of java and dessert. ⊠ *Lucky St. B5&C5, 29 Zaoying Lu, Chaoyang District* ☎ *010/5867–0201* ▭ *No credit cards.*

$$ ✕ **Paulaner Brauhaus.** Traditional German food is dished up in heaping portions at this spacious, bright restaurant in the Kempinski Hotel. Wash it all down with delicious Bavarian beer made right in the restaurant: try the Maibock served in genuine German steins. In summer, you can enjoy your meal outdoors in the beer garden. ⊠ *Kempinski Hotel, 50 Liangmaqiao Lu, Chaoyang District* ☎ *010/6465–3388* ▭ *AE, MC, V.*

Indian

$–$$$ ✕ **Taj Pavilion.** Beijing's best Indian restaurant, Taj Pavilion serves up all the classics, including chicken tikka masala, *palak panir* (creamy spinach with cheese), and *rogan josht* (tender lamb in curry sauce). Consistently good service and an informal atmosphere make this a well-loved neighborhood haunt. ⊠ *China World Trade Center, L-1 28 West Wing, 1 Jianguomenwai Dajie, Chaoyang District* ☎ *010/6505–5866* ▭ *AE, MC, V* Ⓜ *Guomao.*

Italian

$–$$$$ ✕ **Assaggi.** Your mood brightens the minute you walk up the sun-lightened spiral staircase to the rooftop patio, which includes glassed-in and open-air sections. The flowerbox-lined side of the roof overlooks the tree-lined street below. There is a comprehensive four-course Italian menu, including fish, chicken, pork, ham, and pastas in pesto and tomato sauces. The spaghetti with fresh clams and extra-virgin olive oil, ravioli, and tortellini are all superb. Check out the reasonable prix fixe business lunches. ⊠ *1 Sanlitun Bei Xiaojie, Chaoyang District* ☎ *010/8454–4508* ▭ *AE, MC, V.*

★ $–$$$$ ✕ **La Dolce Vita.** The food lives up to the name here: a basket of warm bread is served immediately, a nice treat in a city where good bread is hard to come by. The tough decision is between ravioli, tortellini, and oven-fired pizza. The rice-ball appetizer, with cheese and bits of ham inside, is fantastic. ⊠ *8 Xindong Lu North, Chaoyang District* ☎ *010/6468–2894* ⊟ *AE, MC, V.*

$$$ ╳ **Metro Café.** A good assortment of fresh Italian pastas, soups, bruschettas, and meat dishes round out the menu at this informal eatery. Although service is inconsistent, the food is usually very good, and the outdoor tables are wonderful (if you can get one) on spring and summer evenings. ⊠ *6 Gongrentiyuguan Xi Lu, Chaoyang District* ☎ *010/6501–3377 Ext. 7706* ⊟ *AE, V* ☉ *Closed Mon.*

Japanese

$$–$$$$ ╳ **Hatsune.** Owned by a Chinese-American with impeccable taste, this is one of the best Japanese restaurants in Beijing. Ultramodern interiors and friendly service make for busy lunches and dinners—make a reservation. Try the fresh sashimi, tempura, grilled fish, or one of the many innovative sushi rolls. There's also an extensive sake menu. ⊠ *8 Guanghua Dong Lu, Heqiao Daxia, Building C, second floor, Chaoyang District* ☎ *010/6581–3939* ⌀ *Reservations essential* ⊟ *AE, MC, V.*

$$–$$$$
Fodor's Choice
★
╳ **Yotsuba.** This tiny, unassuming restaurant is arguably the best Japanese restaurant in town. It consists of a sushi counter—manned by a Japanese master working continuously and silently—and two small tatami-style dining areas, evoking an old-time Tokyo restaurant. The seafood is flown in daily from Tokyo's Tsukiji fish market. Reservations are a must for this dinner-only Chaoyang gem. ⊠ *2 Xinyuan Xili Zhongjie, Chaoyang District* ☎ *010/6467–1837* ⌀ *Reservations essential* ⊟ *AE, MC, V* ☉ *No lunch.*

Korean

$–$$$ ╳ **Gaon.** A quirky mixture of classic and contemporary decor backdrop traditional Korean food with a modern twist. Korean savory "pancakes" are normally too heavy to have with a big meal, but at Gaon they are small and served as appetizers. The *bulgogi* (beef mixed with mushrooms and scallion and served on a hot plate) is subtle yet tasty. We promise you won't leave the restaurant hungry. ⊠ *5/F, East Tower, Twin Towers, B-12 Jianguomenwai Dajie, Chaoyang District* ☎ *010/5120–8899* ⊟ *No credit cards* Ⓜ *Yonganli.*

Mediterranean

$$ ╳ **Souk.** Enjoy Mediterranean and Middle Eastern specialties, and maybe a long toke on a pipe, while looking out over the green fields of Chaoyang Park from the outdoor dining area at this eatery beside the park's west gate. In Arabic *souk* means market or bazaar—a place where people gather—and the laid-back ambience here, with lights and music both dimmed, champions the concept. The lamb kebabs, humus, pita bread, couscous, and falafel are surprisingly delicious. And if it gets too hot or cold outdoors, retreat inside to one of the comfortable daybeds. ⊠ *Chaoyang Park west gate, Chaoyang District, Behind Annie's* ☎ *010/6506–7309* ⌀ *Reservations not accepted* ⊟ *No credit cards.*

Thai

$–$$ ╳ **Serve the People.** This eatery—a favorite of Thais living in Beijing—serves all the traditional Thai dishes. Try the duck salad, pomelo salad, green curry, or one of the plentiful hot-and-spicy soups. ☒ *1 Xiwujie, Sanlitun, Chaoyang District, across the street from the Spanish embassy* ☎ *010/8454–4580* ☰ *AE, MC, V.*

Tibetan

$ ✕ **Makye Ame.** Prayer flags lead you to the second floor entrance of this Tibetan restaurant, where a pile of mani stones and a large prayer wheel greet you. Long Tibetan Buddhist trumpets, lanterns, and Tibetan handicrafts decorate the walls, and the kitchen serves a range of hearty dishes that run well beyond the Tibetan staples of yak-butter tea and *tsampa* (roasted barley flour). Try the vegetable *pakoda* (a deep-fried dough pocket filled with vegetables), curry potatoes, or roasted lamb spareribs. Heavy wooden tables with brass corners, soft lighting, and Tibetan textiles make this an especially soothing choice. ☒ *11 Xiushui Nan Jie, 2nd floor, Chaoyang District* ☎ *010/6506–9616* ☰ *No credit cards* Ⓜ *Jianguomen.*

Vietnamese

$–$$ ✕ **Nam Nam.** A sweeping staircase to the second floor, a tiny indoor fish pond, wooden floors, and posters from old Vietnam set the scene in this atmospheric restaurant. The light, delicious cuisine is paired with speedy service. Try the chicken salad, beef noodle soup, or the raw or deep-fried vegetable or meat spring rolls. The portions are on the small side, though, so order plenty. Finish off your meal with a real Vietnamese coffee prepared with a slow-dripping filter and accompanied by condensed milk. ☒ *7 Sanlitun Jie, Sanlitun, Chaoyang District* ☎ *010/6468–6053* ☰ *AE, MC, V.*

HAIDIAN DISTRICT

Whether you're visiting the Summer Palace, Beijing's university area, or the electronics mecca of Zhongguancun, make a stop at Baijia Dazhaimen, a sprawling courtyard mansion with a beautiful lantern-lit garden. You'll be greeted by hosts in colorful, elaborate Manchu costumes serving imperial cuisine. You can also walk around the university campuses and pick one of the many Western-style restaurants catering to the local and international student population.

Chinese

$–$$$$ ✕ **Baijia Dazhaimen.** Staff dressed in rich-hued, traditional outfits welcome you at this grand courtyard house. Bowing slightly, they'll say *"Nin jixiang"* ("May you have good fortune"). The mansion's spectacular setting was once the garden of Prince Li, son of the first Qing emperor. Cao Xueqin, the author of the Chinese classic *Dream of the Red Chamber,* is said to have lived here as a boy. Featured delicacies include bird's nest soup, braised sea cucumber, abalone, and authentic imperial snacks. On weekends, diners are treated to short, live performances of Beijing opera. ☒ *15 Suzhou St., Haidian District* ☎ *010/6265–4186* ⌾ *Reservations essential* ☰ *No credit cards.*

At a Glance

ENGLISH	PINYIN	CHINESE CHARACTERS
POINTS OF INTEREST		
Anping Gujie	Ānpíng gǔ jiē	安平古街
Aria	ā lì yǎ	阿郦雅
Assaggi	chángshì	尝试
Baodu Feng Jinshenglong	bàodù jīn shēng lóng	爆肚金生隆
Baijia Dazhaimen	bái jiā dà zháimén	白家大宅门
Bellagio	lùgǎng xiǎo zhèn	鹿港小镇
Café de la Poste	yúnyóu yì	云游驿
Caribou Café	xùnlù	驯鹿
Comptoirs de France Bakery	fǎ pài	法派
Din Tai Fung	dǐng tài fēng	鼎泰丰
La Dolce Vita	tiánmì shēnghuó	甜蜜生活
Dong Lai Shun	dōng lái shùn	东来顺
Fangshan	fǎng shàn	仿膳
Flo Justines's	fú lóu jié sī tīng	福楼杰斯汀
La Galerie	Zhōngguó yìyuàn	中国艺苑
Gaon	gāo ēn	高恩
Gui Gongfu	guì gōngfǔ	桂公府
Gu Zhenhuang	gǔ zhèn huáng	古镇皇
Hai Wan Ju	hǎiwǎn jū	海碗居
Han Cang	hàn cāng	汉仓
Hatsune	yǐn quán rìběn liàolǐ	隐泉日本料理
Huang Ting	huáng tíng	凰庭
Jing	jīng	京
Jing Wei Lo	jīng wèi lóu	京味楼
Jingsi Su Shifang	jìngsī sùshí fāng	静思素食坊
Jinshancheng Chongqing	jīnshān chéng chóngqìng	金山城重庆
Jinyang Shuanglai Fanzhuang	jìn yáng shuāng lái fànzhuāng	晋阳双来饭庄
Jun Qin Hua	jūn qín huā	君琴花
Jun Wangfu	jūnwáng fǔ	君王府
Kong Yi Ji	kǒng yǐ jǐ	孔乙己
Lai Jin Yu Xuan	láijīn yǔ xuān	来今雨轩
LijiaCai	lì jiācài	历家菜

Li Qun Roast Duck Restaurant	lì qún kǎoyādiàn	利群烤鸭店
Makye Ame	mǎ jí ā mǐ	玛吉阿米
Mei Fu	méi fǔ	梅府
Metro Café	měi tè róu	美特柔
My Humble House	hánshè	寒舍
Noodle Loft	miàn kù	面酷
Old Beijing Noodle King	lǎo Běijīng zhájiàngmiàn dàwáng	老北京炸酱面大王
One East on Third	dōngfāng lù yīhào	东方路一号
Le Palais	pǐn yàn	品雁
Paomo Guan	pào mó guǎn	泡馍馆
Paulaner Brauhaus	pǔ lā nà píjiǔ fāng cāntīng	普拉那啤酒坊餐厅
Qin Tangfu	qín táng fǔ	秦唐府
RBL	kù bīng	库冰
Red Capital Club	xīn hóng zī jùlèbù	新红资俱乐部
Serve the People	wèi rénmín fúwù	为人民服务
Shaguo Ju	shāguō jū	沙锅居
Shin Yeh	xīn yè	欣叶
Sifang Jie	sìfāng jiē	四方街
Souk	sū kè	苏克
The Source	dōu jiāng yuán	都江源
South Silk Road	chá mǎ gǔdào	茶马古道
Taj Pavilion	tài jī lóu	泰姬楼
Three Guizhou Men	sānge guìzhōu rén	三个贵州人
Xiao Wangfu	xiǎo wángfǔ	小王府
Xiheyaju	xì hé yǎ jū	义和雅居
Xi Xiangzi	Xī xiāng zi	西厢子
Yotsuba	sì yè	四叶
Yuxiang Renjia	yú xiāngrén jiā	渝乡人家
Zhang Qun Jia	zhāng qún jiā	张群家

Where to Stay

WORD OF MOUTH

"Beijing is a big, busy city but not too difficult to get the hang of. You can take a taxi (or walk, if your hotel is very central) to the Forbidden City; from there you can walk south to Tiananmen Square, or north to Jingshan Park. Likewise, cab it to historic sites like the Summer Palace (allow half a day), Temple of Heaven, Lama Temple, and the Drum and Bell Towers. Cabs are efficient and very cheap: just make sure you have the name of your destination written in Chinese to show the driver." —Neil Oz

LODGING PLANNER

Which Neighborhood Is Right for Me?

Hotels in Beijing are clustered in neighborhoods with different advantages.

Wangfujing is one of Beijing's oldest streets and still a popular shopping area; it's within walking distance to Tiananmen Square, the Forbidden City, and other historical sites.

Jianguomenwai is in the business hub and close to the Friendship Store, the Silk Alley Market, Ritan Park, foreign embassies, and many large office complexes, such as the China World Trade Center.

The **Sanlitun** area is known for its shopping venues, bustling bar and restaurant scene, and proximity to one of the city's embassy areas.

Haidian is the university area; nearby Zhongguancun has countless shops selling inexpensive no-frills electronics. This northwestern district is home to the zoo and the Summer Palace.

Top 5 Hotels

■ **St. Regis.** Although the St. Regis is not as grandiose as other international hotels in Beijing, it's centrally located, and is one of the city's most elegant places to stay. It also has one of the best health clubs in Beijing, with excellent exercise equipment, an atrium-style swimming pool, and hot pools fed by a real hot spring located deep beneath the hotel.

■ **China World Hotel.** Set in a convenient location for both business travelers and tourists, the China World is known as one of the best business hotels in town, with a wide range of facilities and services, including conference venues, good shopping, and a top-notch fitness center with indoor tennis courts.

■ **Peninsula Beijing.** One of Beijing's oldest foreign-managed hotels, the Peninsula has lost none of its luster. It boasts excellent restaurants and a convenient location—within walking distance to the Forbidden City!

■ **Grand Hyatt.** This is one of Beijing's most popular hotels because of its stylish decor, proximity to key attractions, and location on top of the Oriental Plaza Shopping Mall, Beijing's premier shopping center.

■ **Kempinski Hotel.** Located in the new embassy area, in the Lufthansa Complex, the Kempinski Hotel is a good budget choice: it comes complete with shopping center, airline offices, and superb restaurants, including the Paulaner Brauhaus, Beijing's best German restaurant and microbrewery.

Prices & Tipping

Rates are generally quoted for the room alone; breakfast, whether continental or full, is usually extra. We've noted at the end of each review if breakfast is included in the rate ("CP" for continental breakfast daily and "BP" for full breakfast daily). All hotel prices listed here are based on high-season rates. There may be significant discounts on weekends and in the off-season. All hotels add a 15% service charge to the bill. It's usually not difficult finding a hotel in Beijing, so booking two weeks in advance should suffice.

Discounts on room rates can reach 40% during quieter times of the year, which come in winter and summer. In general, five-star hotels will be as expensive as those in other major Western cities, but small three- and four-star hotels can be a bargain in Beijing. You can sometimes get good deals by booking online through agents such as Ctrip ⊕ www.ctrip.com, which has both English and Chinese Web sites. Individual hotel Web sites are also a good bet.

China is one of the few remaining places in the world where tipping is not the norm. The exception: bell boys will expect a tip for carrying your bags to your room— give about Y10 per bag.

Facilities

■ The lodgings we list are the cream of the crop in each price category. We always list the facilities that are available, but we don't specify whether they cost extra.

■ When pricing accommodations, always ask what's included and what costs extra. Generally, you'll find the room size comparable to American hotels, and most of the better hotels have double-, queen-, and king-sized beds, although this is not the case in the smaller Chinese-run hotels.

■ All hotels should have air-conditioning.

■ Additionally, all hotels listed have private baths unless otherwise noted.

7

What It Costs In Yuan

	$$$$	$$$	$$	$	¢
FOR 2 PEOPLE	over Y1,800	Y1,401–Y1,800	Y1,101–Y1,400	Y700–Y1,100	under Y700

Prices are for two people in a standard double room in high season, excluding 15% service charge.

By Eileen Wen Mooney

China's 1949 Communist victory closed the doors on the opulent accommodations once available to visiting foreigners in Beijing and elsewhere. Functional concrete boxes served the needs of the few "fellow travelers" admitted into the People's Republic of China in the 1950s and '60s. By the late 1970s, China's lack of high-quality hotels had become a distinct embarrassment; the only answer seemed to be opening the market to foreign investment. Many new hotels, built to handle the 2008 Olympic crowds, are emerging; they are bound to change the landscape further in the coming years.

A multitude of polished palaces await you, with attentive service, improved amenities—such as conference centers, health clubs, spas, and nightclubs—and, of course, rising prices. Glitz and "Western-style" comfort, rather than history and character, are the main selling points for Beijing's hotels. Some traditional courtyard houses have been converted into small hotels—they offer a quiet alternative to the fancier establishments.

BOOKING IT

Booking hotel rooms in advance is always recommended, but the current glut of accommodations means room availability is rarely a problem, whatever the season. Most hotels can help you book restaurants, day tours, taxis, drivers, and opera tickets.

Courtyard hotels usually have a more distinct Chinese character, but those in older buildings may be lacking in facilities. They are often managed by entrepreneurs who bought the courtyard houses from previous residents. Given that fewer and fewer ancient courtyards exist in China, these hotels are often favored by travelers who visit China for its history. Because of the smaller number of rooms in courtyard hotels, reservations are important for these select accommodations. If you're looking to stay in a more traditional Chinese-style accommodation, consider the LüSongyuan, Haoyuan, Bamboo Garden, and the Red Capital Residence guesthouses.

WHICH
LOCALE?

As traffic conditions worsen, more travelers are choosing hotels closer to their interests. However, the more distant hotels—such as the Lido, the Friendship Hotel, and Shangri-La—do offer shuttle-bus service into the city center.

DONGCHENG DISTRICT

Dongcheng District lies north and east of the Forbidden City and incorporates the city's most important historical sites and temples. The hotels off Dongchang'an Jie and Wangfujing Dajie are within walking distance of Tiananmen Square.

★ **$$$$** ▦ **Grand Hotel Beijing.** This lovely hotel on the north side of Chang'an Avenue blends the traditions of China's past with modern comforts and technology. It's worth it to book the room with the Forbidden City view. The Red Wall Café, Ming Yuan dining room, Rong Yuan Restaurant, and Old Peking Grill provide a range of cuisines, from Chinese to European. The Grand is convenient to the Forbidden City, Tiananmen Square, and the Imperial Wall Ruins Park, but its service and Western food aren't as up-to-snuff as some other überfancy foreign-managed hotels. Even if you don't stay here, visit the rooftop terrace and toast the yellow roofs of the Forbidden City with your sunset drink. The terrace is open only from May through October, from 5 PM to 9:30 PM. ⊠ *35 Dongchang'an Jie, Dongcheng District, 100006* ☎ *010/ 6513–7788* 🖷 *010/6513–0048* ⊕ *www.grandhotelbeijing.com* ➘ *217 rooms, 50 suites* ↻ *6 restaurants, bar, in-room fax, in-room safes, cable TV, in-room data ports, pool, health club, sauna, spa, bicycles, shops, Internet, business services, meeting rooms, car rental* ▤ *AE, DC, MC, V* Ⓜ *Wangfujing.*

$$$$ ▦ **Grand Hyatt Beijing.** The impressive Grand Hyatt Beijing, with its
Fodor'sChoice bustling lobby, is the centerpiece of Oriental Plaza, a mammoth com-
★ plex that includes a fancy mall, a cinema screening films in English, and a wide range of inexpensive eateries. Rooms and suites, many with floor-to-ceiling windows, are decorated with beige carpets and curtains, cherry-color wood furnishings, and black-and-white photos. The hotel's Olympic-size swimming pool is surrounded by lush vegetation, waterfalls, statues, and comfortable teak chairs and tables. Over the pool, a "virtual sky" ceiling imitates different weather patterns. The gym is equipped with state-of-the-art exercise equipment. The Red Moon on the lobby level is one of the city's chicest bars, with live music every night. The lobby bakery has excellent pastries and coffee, with seating away from the busy main lobby. Shanghai Tang, in the lower level, offers well-crafted and innovative Chinese clothing, accessories, and home items. The hotel is within walking distance to Tiananmen Square and the Forbidden City. ⊠ *1 Dongchang'an Jie, Dongcheng District, 100738, corner of Wangfujing* ☎ *010/8518–1234* 🖷 *010/8518–0000* ⊕ *www.*

7

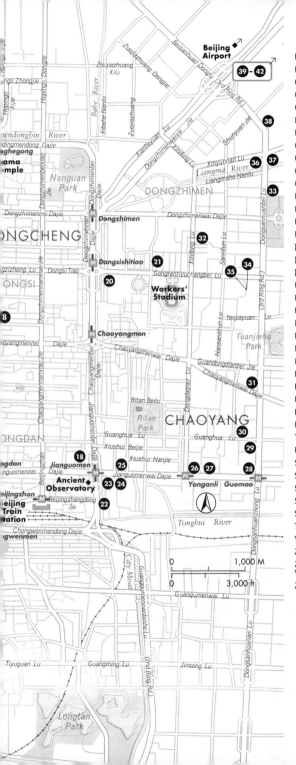

beijing.grand.hyatt.com ⇨ *825 rooms, 155 suites* ⇨ *5 restaurants, cable TV, in-room data ports, indoor pool, health club, sauna, spa, steam room, bar, shops, Internet, business services, meeting rooms, airport shuttle, no-smoking floors* ▭ *AE, DC, MC, V* Ⓜ *Wangfujing.*

$$$$ **Raffles Beijing Hotel.** Singaporean designer Grace Soh and her team have transformed this hotel into a vivid, charming space, while retaining its history, as highlighted by the black-and-white photographs of dignitaries in the lounge. Think fancy: crystal chandeliers illuminate the lobby, and the grand white staircase is enveloped in a royal-blue carpet. The atrium is adorned with 13 large cloth lanterns in olive green, plum, purple, and yellow—a welcome change to the ubiquitous red. The Presidential Suite is one of the largest, most luxurious suites in Beijing. For dining, choose between French and Italian. The Writer's Bar is replete with large leather armchairs and dark, polished floors. This is a great location for visitors who plan to do some sightseeing: Tiananmen Square, the Forbidden City, and Wangfujing are all nearby. ✉ *33 Dongchang'an Jie, off Wangfujing Dajie, Dongcheng District, 100004* ☎ *010/6526–3388* 🖷 *010/6527–3838* 🌐 *www.beijing.raffles.com* ⇨ *171 rooms, 24 suites* ⇨ *2 restaurants, lounge, 2 bars, room service, minibars, cable TV, in-room data ports, indoor pool, bar, Internet, business services* ▭ *AE, DC, MC, V* Ⓜ *Wangfujing.*

$$$–$$$$ Fodor's Choice ★ **Peninsula Beijing.** Guests at the Peninsula Beijing enjoy an impressive combination of ultramodern facilities and traditional luxury. A waterfall cascades through the spacious lobby, which is decorated with Chinese antiques. Rooms have teak-and-rosewood flooring, area rugs, high-quality wood and upholstered furnishings, and flat-screen TVs. A custom bedside control panel lets you adjust lights, temperature, television, and radio. Food fanatics, take note: one on-site restaurant, Jing, serves yummy East-meets-West fusion food. Huang Ting, a second restaurant, provides a rustic setting for some of Beijing's tastiest dim sum. Work off the meals in the fully equipped gym or swimming pool—or take the 10-minute walk to the Forbidden City. If you're less ambitious, relax in the hotel's steam rooms and saunas. The Peninsula's arcade has designer stores, including Chanel, Jean Paul Gaultier, and Tiffany & Co. ✉ *8 Jinyu Hutong (Goldfish La.), Wangfujing, Dongcheng District, 100006* ☎ *010/8516–2888* 🖷 *010/6510–6311* 🌐 *www.peninsula.com* ⇨ *525 rooms, 59 suites* ⇨ *2 restaurants, snack bar, room service, some in-room faxes, in-room safes, minibars, cable TV, in-room data ports, tennis court, indoor pool, health club, hair salon, massage, sauna, steam room, bar, lobby lounge, shops, laundry service, business services, meeting rooms, travel services* ▭ *AE, DC, MC, V* 🍽 *EP* Ⓜ *Dongdan.*

WORD OF MOUTH

"The five nights spent at the Peninsula didn't disappoint. We were upgraded to an "executive" floor, which entitled us to perks such as happy hour, computers, and breakfast. There is an excellent detailed map of the surrounding area in the Peninsula stationery folder in the room desk. We ate at the Peninsula's Hutong restaurant Huang Ting, which was good." –Marija

$$–$$$$ ⊞ **Beijing Hotel.** One of the capital's oldest hotels, this property was born in 1900 as the Hotel de Pekin. Within sight of Tiananmen Square, it has housed countless foreign delegations, missions, and friends of China, such as Field Marshal Montgomery from Britain and the American writer Edgar Snow. China's longtime premier Zhou Enlai stayed and worked in room #1735. The rooms retain an old-fashioned splendor with French-classic touches. The west wing—now the Grand Hotel—was added in 1955 and the east wing debuted in 1974. This is the place for people in search of some history or proximity to nearby tourist sites, such as Tiananmen Square and the Forbidden City. ⊠ *33 Dongchang'an Jie, off Wangfujing Dajie, Dongcheng District, 100004* ☎ *010/6513–7766* 🖷 *010/6523–2395* ⊕ *www.chinabeijinghotel.com.cn* 🛏 *800 rooms, 51 suites* ⟨ *5 restaurants, room service, minibars, cable TV, in-room data ports, indoor pool, gym, bowling, billiards, tennis court, squash court, chess and card rooms, café, Internet, business services, meeting rooms* ⊟ *AE, DC, MC, V* Ⓜ *Wangfujing.*

$$–$$$ ⊞ **Beijing International.** This white monolith, built in the mid-1980s, symbolized a true take-off for China's tourism industry. Nowadays, the rooms and reliable service here attract many tour groups. Opposite the Beijing train station (westbound), the hotel is only a few minutes' ride from Tiananmen Square. Many great restaurants—including Qin Tangfu, Paomo Guan, and Gui Gongfu—are close by. ⊠ *9 Jianguomennei Dajie, off Wangfujing Dajie, Dongcheng District, 100005* ☎ *010/6512–6688* 🖷 *010/6512–9961* ⊕ *www.bih.com.cn* 🛏 *916 rooms, 60 suites* ⟨ *8 restaurants, snack bar, cable TV, pool, gym, massage, sauna, steam room, bowling, bar, shops, Internet, business services* ⊟ *AE, DC, MC, V* Ⓜ *Dongdan.*

★ ¢–$$$ ⊞ **Zhuyuan Hotel** (Bamboo Garden Hotel). The Bamboo Garden is a charming hotel that was once the residence of Sheng Xuanhuai, a high-ranking Qing official, and, later, of Mao's henchman Kang Sheng. A powerful and sinister character, responsible for "public security" during the Cultural Revolution, Kang nevertheless had fine taste in art and antiques. The Bamboo Garden cannot compete with the high-rise crowd when it comes to comfort and facilities, but its lovely bamboo-filled courtyards and gardens make it a genuine treasure for those looking for a true Chinese experience. It's within walking distance to the colorful Houhai, or Rear Lakes, area, and the Drum and Bell Towers; the neighborhood is perfect if you want to experience the lifestyles of ordinary Beijingers. ⊠ *24 Xiaoshiqiao Hutong, Jiugulou Dajie, Dongcheng District, 100009* ☎ *010/5852–0088* 🖷 *010/5852–0066* 🛏 *40 rooms, 4 suites* ⟨ *Restaurant, hair salon, sauna, bicycles, bar* ⊟ *AE, DC, MC, V* Ⓜ *Gulou.*

$$ ⊞ **Red Capital Residence.** Beijing's first boutique courtyard hotel is located in a carefully restored, traditional Chinese courtyard house in historically preserved Dongsi Hutong. Each of the five rooms is decorated with antiques and according to a different theme, including the "Chairman's Suite," the two "Concubines' Private Courtyards," and the two "Author's Suites" (one inspired by Edgar Snow, an American journalist who lived in Beijing in the 1930s and 1940s, and the other

Fodor'sChoice
★

by Han Suyin, a famous novelist). The bathrooms are modern, and all rooms have satellite television. There is also a cigar lounge where you can sit on original furnishings used by China's early revolutionary leaders, as well as a wine bar in a Cultural Revolution–era bomb shelter. Special arrangements can also be made for guests to tour Beijing at night in Madame Mao's Red Flag limousine. The Red Capital Residence offers a continental breakfast; for other meals take the hotel pedicab to the nearby Red Capital Club, a sister establishment also set in a restored courtyard home. ⊠ *9 Dongsi Liutiao, Dongcheng District, 100007* ☎ *010/6402–7150* 🖷 *010/6402–7153* ⊕ *www. redcapitalclub.com.cn* 🛏 *5 rooms* ⚘ *Cable TV, bar, laundry service* 🖃 *AE, DC, MC, V* ❍ *CP.*

$–$$ 🏨 **Crowne Plaza Beijing.** The Crowne Plaza is located on Wangfujing, in the center of Beijing's tourist, shopping, and business districts, and is a great place for walking and window shopping. The hotel underwent a major renovation in 2005, and now has a more modern ambience. The lobby's champagne bar serves light Japanese and Vietnamese food. Huang Yue, a stylish Cantonese restaurant, is on the second floor. The standard rooms are small, but have top-rate amenities, such as flat-screen TVs and comfortable bathrooms. Craving more space? Try the executive floor, where rooms have extra work space and sprawling bathrooms with showers and separate baths. Take a look at the photographs of Beijing covering many of the hotel's warm-hued walls. This is one of the better deals in town, providing a great location and luxury for your dollar. ⊠ *48 Wangfujing Dajie, Dongcheng District, 100006* ☎ *010/6513–3388* 🖷 *010/6513–2513* ⊕ *www. ichotelsgroup.com* 🛏 *360 rooms, 27 suites* ⚘ *2 restaurants, room service, minibars, cable TV, in-room data ports, indoor pool, gym, hair salon, sauna, bicycles, bar, shops, babysitting, laundry service, business services, travel services, free parking, no-smoking rooms* 🖃 *AE, DC, MC, V* Ⓜ *Wangfujing.*

> **WORD OF MOUTH**
>
> "We stayed at the Crowne Plaza on Wangfujing in June and loved it. We got a great rate via their official website (they guarantee to be cheapest on the net). We stayed on the Club floor which entitled us to free breakfast (in either the executive lounge or restaurant), evening cocktails & nibbles in executive lounge, and free Internet. The location is great and service was very good." —Mole

¢–$$ 🏨 **Haoyuan Hotel.** Tucked away in a hutong, the tiny Haoyuan has rooms surrounding two courtyards. Try to book one of the larger, more expensive rooms in the tranquil back courtyard, where you can sit under the date trees and listen to the evening chorus of cicadas in the summer. The hotel's small restaurant serves good Sichuan, Guangdong, and Shandong dishes. Nearby Nan Luogu Xiang, with its many Western and Chinese restaurants, coffee shops, bars, boutiques, and local Beijing color, is reason enough to stay here if luxury is not your top priority. ⊠ *53 Shijia Hutong, Dongsi Nan Dajie, Dongcheng Dis-*

trict, 100010 ☎ 010/6512–5557 ⊠ 010/6525–3179 ⊕ www. haoyuanhotel.com ⤳ 19 rooms ⚐ Restaurant, laundry facilities, Internet ⊟ AE, MC.

¢–$$ 🏨 **LüSongyuan.** In 1980, the China
Fodor's Choice Youth Travel Service set up this
★ delightful courtyard hotel on the site of an old Qing Mandarin's residence. The traditional wooden entrance is guarded by two *menshi* (stone lions). Inside are five courtyards decorated with pavilions, rockeries, and greenery. Rooms are basic, with large windows. Though it calls itself an International Youth Hostel, the hotel has no self-service cooking facilities, but it has

a reasonable Chinese restaurant. It's all about location here: you're in the middle of an ancient neighborhood, within walking distance to Houhai, and just a block away from many restaurants and delightful coffee shops on Nan Luogu Xiang. ⊠ 22 Banchang Hutong, Kuanjie, Dongcheng District, 100009 ☎ 010/6401–1116 ⊠ 010/6403–0418 ⤳ 55 rooms ⚐ Restaurant, bar, Internet room ⊟ AE, DC, MC, V.

¢–$ 🏨 **Novotel Peace Hotel.** Twenty-two stories of tinted-glass windows play home to a bevy of rooms with floor-to-ceiling windows and accompanying stellar city views. The hotel is a stroll away from plenty of shops and restaurants, as well as Tiananmen Square. Although service is fairly basic, and the ambience low-key, the hotel offers good value for the location. For dinner, you might try one of the three Chinese restaurants, or Le Cabernet, a French-style brasserie. Our vote? Head out onto the street and try one of the many restaurants in the bustling neighborhood. ⊠ 3 Jinyu Hutong, Wangfujing Dajie, Dongcheng District, 100004 ☎ 010/6512–8833 ⊠ 010/6512–6863 ⊕ www.accorhotels-asia.com ⤳ 337 rooms, 33 suites ⚐ 4 restaurants, room service, minibars, cable TV, indoor pool, gym, hair salon, sauna, bicycles, 2 bars, dance club, laundry service, concierge, Internet, business services, car rental, parking (fee), no-smoking rooms ⊟ AE, DC, MC, V Ⓜ Wangfujing.

¢ 🏨 **Dongtang Inn.** This small, privately owned inn has two types of rooms: with and without windows. The crowd here is quite young—mainly international backpackers and university students. It's an inexpensive place to stay located in Nan Luogu Xiang, a 700-year old hutong. This area is fast becoming one of the latest up-and-coming night spots in Beijing, with small coffee shops and good restaurants, including Fish Nation (which serves fish-and-chips). Dongtang Inn's coffee shop has built-in bookshelves stacked with English-language guidebooks, a television, and Internet service. Bikes are available for rental. ⊠ 85 Nan Luogu Xiang, Dongcheng District, 100009 ☎ 010/8400–2429 ⊠ 010/6404–9677 ✉ downtown@backpackingchina.com ⤳ 20 rooms ⚐ Lounge, laundry service; no room TVs ⊟ No credit cards.

XICHENG DISTRICT

Xicheng District, north and west of the Forbidden City, lies opposite Dongcheng. This is the place to lose yourself among Beijing's old hutong alleyways and take long walks by Qianhai and Houhai.

$$$$ ⬚ **Ritz-Carlton Beijing.** A 253-room hotel designed with ample amounts of glass and chrome, the Ritz fits in with many of the city's sleek financial buildings. The interior is stylish and contemporary. There are two restaurants and a café; a lobby lounge also serves afternoon tea and evening cocktails. The enormous health club has an indoor swimming pool and a spa with six treatment rooms. The Ritz-Carlton is located in the western part of the city on the up-and-coming Financial Street, which is being touted as Beijing's Wall Street; it's a smart choice for business visitors with offices or clients on that side of the city. ⊠ *18 Beijing Financial St., Xicheng District, 100032* ☎ *010/6601–6666* 🖷 *010/6601–6029* ⊕ *www.ritzcarlton.com* ⇌ *253 rooms, 33 suites* ♿ *3 restaurants, bar, spa, indoor pool, whirlpool, room service, business services, meeting rooms* 🖃 *AE, DC, MC, V* Ⓜ *Fuchengmen.*

$ ⬚ **Minzu Hotel.** When it opened in 1959, the Minzu (Nationalities) Hotel was labeled one of the 10 great buildings in Beijing. This paean to the unity of China's different people has welcomed many prominent foreign visitors over the years. It's been renovated into yet another shiny pleasure dome but maintains its original local appeal. The hotel lies on western Chang'an Jie, 10 minutes from Tiananmen Square and next to the Nationalities' Cultural Palace. With the rise in the number of luxury hotels around Beijing, the hotel no longer attracts prominent visitors and the only reason to stay here—other than price—

WORD OF MOUTH

"If you want to see the Great Wall, I suggest you join a tour through your hotel (don't accept an invitation from a tour on the street). I enjoyed exploring the hutong and the Forbidden City on my own."

–Lincoln

is if you have business in the immediate area. ⊠ *51 Fuxingmennei Dajie, Xicheng District, 100031* ☎ *010/6601–4466* 🖷 *010/6601–4849* ⊕ *www.minzuhotel.cn* ⇌ *509 rooms, 40 suites* ♿ *4 restaurants, cable TV, hair salon, massage, sauna, bar, shops, business services, meeting rooms, car rental* 🖃 *AE, DC, MC, V* Ⓜ *Xidan.*

SOUTHERN DISTRICT: CHONGWEN

The Chongwen District, just south of the Forbidden City, is one of Beijing's oldest neighborhoods, with beautiful Chinese and Western architecture. It was once a bustling center of business activity and home to many of the city's time-honored name-brand shops. It's now undergoing a major renovation in the run-up to the 2008 Olympics: no one knows yet what the new Chongwen will look like.

★ **$-$$** ⊡ **Courtyard Beijing.** Merging Eastern and Western culture and style, the Courtyard is situated at the heart of the nation's capital. Guests have easy access to many of Beijing's historical sites, and it's connected to the huge New World Shopping Center, one of the busiest in the city, selling a wide variety of international and domestic products. One problem is that this is a super-congested part of the city. However, there's a subway station just one block away, making quick escapes to quieter areas quite easy. ✉ *3C Chongwenmenwai Dajie, Chongwen District, 100062* ☎ *010/ 6708–1188* 🖷 *010/6708–1808* ⊕ *www.courtyard.com/bjscy* ⇌ *283 rooms, 16 suites △ Restaurant, babysitting, satellite TV, children's pool, sauna, fitness room, laundry service, Internet* ☰ *AE, DC, MC, V* Ⓜ *Chongwenmen.*

¢ ⊡ **Hademen Hotel.** A short taxi ride to Tiananmen Square, the Temple of Heaven, and the famous Hongqiao Market, the state-run Hademen is also right next door to the oldest Peking duck restaurant in the city, Bianyi Fang, which dates back to the early 1900s. It's all about location here; the rooms are quite simple and the service basic. ✉ *2A Chongwenmenwai Dajie, Chongwen District, 100062* ☎ *010/6711–2244* 🖷 *010/6711–6865* ⊕ *www.hademenhotel.com* ⇌ *215 rooms, 30 suites △ 2 restaurants, coffee shop, hair salon, sauna, massage, karaoke, business center* ☰ *AE, DC, MC, V* Ⓜ *Chongwenmen.*

> [!NOTE] WORD OF MOUTH
>
> "Go to Beijing! I took my 8-year-old son one October a couple of years ago and we did it all on our own. I asked the hotel concierge to write out directions in Chinese. We hired a guide through the hotel for a day at the Great Wall. The guide was superb and the whole day was quite economical (probably $100). You can also join half-day tours. I hope you have a joyous time."
>
> –EllenLM

CHAOYANG DISTRICT

Chaoyang District extends east of Dongcheng and includes Sanlitun, Beijing's main nightlife area, plus some of the city's best shopping malls and markets. The hotels in this urban district are nearly all modern high-rises and mid-rises.

$$$$ ⊡ **China World Hotel.** One of the finest hotels in Beijing, the China
Fodor'sChoice World is part of the prestigious China World Trade Center, which is home
★ to offices, luxury apartments, and premium retail outlets. The lobby, conference center, ballroom, and all guest rooms were given a $30-million renovation in 2003. Marble floors and gold accents in the lobby lead to comfortable, contemporary rooms with marble baths. The dining choices are diverse and enticing: Scene a Café is a casual eatery featuring eight different cuisines, Aria serves a wonderful and inexpensive business lunch, Summer Palace serves dim sum, and Nadaman has superb seafood teppanyaki. The subway station is a one-minute walk away. The hotel is quite popular with business travelers, who crowd here during conferences and exhibitions. ✉ *1 Jianguomenwai Dajie, Chaoyang District, 100004* ☎ *010/6505–2266* 🖷 *010/6505–3167 or 010/*

6505–0828 ⊕ *www.shangri-la.com* 📨 *716 rooms, 26 suites* 🛆 *4 restaurants, snack bar, in-room safes, minibars, cable TV, in-room data ports, health club, hair salon, massage, 2 bars, dance club, shops, laundry service, Internet, business services, meeting rooms, airport shuttle, car rental, travel services, parking (fee), no-smoking rooms* ▤ *AE, DC, MC, V* Ⓜ *Guomao.*

$$$$ 🏨 **New Otani Changfugong.** Managed by the New Otani Group from Japan, this hotel combines that country's signature hospitality and attentive service, and enjoys a premium location in downtown Beijing (near the Friendship Store and the Ancient Observatory). Overlooking a lovely garden, where guests can participate in morning exercises, the lobby's coffee shop serves Chinese meals as well as Western dishes. Or you can try the excellent Japanese restaurant. The hotel is popular with businesspeople and large groups from Japan. ■ TIP→ **It's also accessible for people with disabilities–sadly, not always the norm for Beijing.** ✉ *26 Jianguomenwai Dajie, Chaoyang District, 100022* ☎ *010/6512–5555* 🖳 *010/6513–9810* ⊕ *www.cfgbj.com* 📨 *500 rooms, 18 suites* 🛆 *2 restaurants, in-room safes, cable TV, tennis court, pool, gym, hair salon, massage, sauna, bicycles, bar, shop, laundry service, concierge, Internet, car rental* ▤ *AE, DC, MC, V* ⍩ *BP* Ⓜ *Jianguomen.*

$$$$
FodorśChoice
★
🏨 **St. Regis.** Considered by many to be the best hotel in Beijing, the St. Regis is a favorite of foreign businesspeople and visiting dignitaries. This is where President Bush stayed during his visit to China, and where Uma Thurman and Quentin Tarantino stayed during the filming of *Kill Bill.* You won't be disappointed: the luxurious interiors combine classical Chinese elegance and fine, modern furnishings. The Press Club Bar, with its grand piano, dark wood, and stocked bookcases, feels like a private club. And the on-site Japanese restaurant has good, moderately priced lunch specials. The Astor Grill is known for its steak and seafood dishes, and Danielli's serves authentic Italian food. We went back for seconds of waffles with fresh blueberries at the Coffee Garden's incredible breakfast buffet. The St. Regis health club is arguably the most unique in Beijing: the equipment is state-of-the-art; the Jacuzzi is supplied with natural hot spring water pumped up from deep beneath the hotel; and the glass-atrium swimming pool, with plenty of natural light, is a lovely place for a relaxing swim. An added plus is that it's just a 10-minute taxi ride to the Forbidden City. If you can afford it, this is the place to stay. ✉ *21 Jianguomenwai Dajie, Chaoyang District, 100020* ☎ *010/6460–6688* 🖳 *010/6460–3299* ⊕ *www.stregis.com* 📨 *273 rooms, executive suites* 🛆 *5 restaurants, in-room safes, some kitchenettes, cable TV, in-room data ports, golf privileges, tennis court, 2 indoor pools, health club, hair salon, hot tub, massage, sauna, spa, steam room, bicycles, badminton, billiards, racquetball, squash, 4 bars, 3 lounges, recreation room, shops, babysitting, playground, laundry service, Internet, business services, convention center, airport shuttle, car rental, travel services, parking (fee), no-smoking rooms* ▤ *AE, DC, MC, V* Ⓜ *Jianguomen.*

★ **$$$–$$$$** 🏨 **Kerry Centre Hotel.** The Shangri-La hotel chain opened this palatial, upscale hotel to much fanfare in 1999. Its ultramodern interiors and convenient location close to Beijing's embassy and business district make it an excellent choice for business travelers and anyone who wants to be near shopping. The Forbidden City is a 10- to 15-minute drive away. What really distinguishes it from other glitzy hotels in Beijing is the amazing health club. With a full-service fitness center and spa, a jogging track, squash and tennis courts, and, of course, a pool, it's *the* health club of choice for expats living in Beijing. Centro, the lobby bar, is arguably the most popular hotel bar in the city. The free wireless Internet throughout the lobby, including in the bar and restaurants, is an added plus. ✉ *1 Guang Hua Lu, Chaoyang District, 100020* ☏ *010/6561–8833* 🖷 *010/6561–2626* ⊕ *www.shangri-la.com* 📞 *487 rooms, 23 suites* ⚘ *2 restaurants, in-room safes, minibars, cable TV, in-room data ports, 2 tennis courts, pool, health club, hot tub, massage, sauna, spa, steam room, basketball, billiards, Ping-Pong, squash, bar, shops, playground, Wi-Fi* ▭ *AE, DC, MC, V* Ⓜ *Guomao.*

$$$–$$$$ ◫ **Kunlun Hotel.** Kunlun's 2006 renovations unveiled a fresh, new gold-accented look, albeit somewhat overdone. Topped by a revolving restaurant, this 28-story property's impressive presentation and a full range of facilities make up for occasional service lapses. The hotel was named for the Kunlun Mountains, a range between northwestern China and northern Tibet that features prominently in Chinese mythology. The lovely rooms are spacious, with armchairs, entertainment cabinets, slippers, and robes. The business and superior suites, with hardwood floors, marble baths, and new furnishings, are the most attractive. The hotel restaurant serves great Shanghai-style food as well as reliable Thai and Japanese fare in very nicely designed venues. The Kunlun, close to Beijing's rising new diplomatic area, is popular with Chinese business travelers. This shouldn't be your top choice if sightseeing is your priority. ✉ *2 Xinyuan Nan Lu, Sanlitun, Chaoyang District, 100004* ☏ *010/6590–3388* 🖷 *010/6590–3214* ⊕ *www.hotelkunlun.com* 📞 *701 rooms, 50 suites* ⚘ *6 restaurants, teashop, some kitchens, cable TV, indoor pool, health club, hair salon, hot tub, massage, sauna, steam room, bicycles, billiards, bar, lounge, Internet, business services, meeting rooms* ▭ *AE, DC, MC, V* ⦿ *EP.*

$$$–$$$$ ◫ **Radisson SAS.** A boxy mid-rise near the international exhibition center in northeast Beijing, this high-end hotel receives business travelers from around the world. The good rates reflect the slightly out-of-the-way location. You can choose between rooms decorated in Chinese style, in navy and beige with gold accents, or Italian style, in bright green and yellow. The restaurants—one open-air—offer good food, including a Western-style Sunday brunch with music. Located beside the China Exhibition Center, in a congested area far from most attractions, the Radisson only makes sense if your attending one of the nearby conventions. ✉ *6A Beisanhuan Dong Lu, Chaoyang District, 100028* ☏ *010/ 5922–3388* 🖷 *010/5922–3399* ⊕ *www.radisson.com* 📞 *362 rooms, 16 suites* ⚘ *3 restaurants, in-room safes, minibars, cable TV, tennis court, indoor pool, gym, massage, sauna, bicycles, squash, bar, dance club, shop, babysitting, broadband, business services, meeting rooms, airport shuttle, car rental* ▭ *AE, DC, MC, V.*

$$–$$$$ ◫ **Great Wall Sheraton.** The oldest luxury hotel in Beijing, the Great Wall Sheraton is still going strong as a favorite of tour groups. Rooms are comfortable, though no different from rooms in any other Sheraton. The top-floor restaurant has pleasing city views and serves Sichuan and Cantonese food. The hotel also has two restaurants serving French and Italian cuisine. Although the Sheraton is an old standby, the service is uneven and the room rates a bit hard to swallow. ⊠ *10 Dongsanhuan Bei Lu, Chaoyang District, 100026* ☎ *010/6590–5566* 🖷 *010/6590–5504* ⊕ *www.sheraton.com/beijingcn* 🛏 *827 rooms, 83 suites* ♨ *Restaurants, in-room safes, minibars, cable TV, in-room data ports, indoor pool, health club, sauna, bar, lounge, Internet, business services, meeting rooms, no-smoking floors* ⊟ *AE, DC, MC, V.*

$$–$$$$ 🏨 **Holiday Inn Lido.** This enormous Holiday Inn is part of Lido Place, a commercial and residential complex northeast of the city center. With a high concentration of international businesses, including retail stores, a deli, and a Starbucks, Lido Place is home to a number of expats, and the Holiday Inn, too, is a haven for visitors. The hotel has an Italian restaurant called Pinocchio, a steak restaurant called the Texan Bar & Grill, and a British-style pub called the Pig and Thistle. Key cards let you into your hotel room, and you also need them to turn on the room lights. Located in the northeast of the city, this isn't our top choice for sightseers, as it's far from all the major attractions. However, it's a good location if you want to get to and from the airport quickly, or if you have friends or business associates in the northeast suburbs of Beijing. ⊠ *Jichang Lu at Jiangtai Lu, Chaoyang District, 100004* ☎ *010/ 6437–6688, 800/810–0019 in China* 🖷 *010/6437–6237* ⊕ *www.beijing-lido.holiday-inn.com* 🛏 *433 rooms, 89 suites* ♨ *4 restaurants, ice-cream parlor, room service, cable TV, indoor pool, health club, hair salon, hot tub, massage, sauna, steam room, bar, lounge, shops, babysitting, laundry service, concierge, Internet, business services, meeting rooms, airport shuttle, car rental, travel services, free parking, no-smoking rooms* ⊟ *AE, DC, MC, V.*

$$–$$$$ 🏨 **Swissôtel.** In the large, impressive marble lobby you can enjoy jazz every Friday and Saturday evening. Rooms have high-quality, European-style furnishings in cream and light grey, plus temperature controls and coffeemakers. The hotel health club has an atrium-style swimming pool and an outdoor tennis court. The Western coffee shop has one of the best hotel buffets in Beijing. It's a short walk to the bustling Sanlitun bar area and the Nanxincang complex of restaurants, which are housed in a former Ming dynasty granary. A subway entrance is just outside the hotel's front door. ⊠ *2 Chaoyang Mennei Dajie, Dongsishiqiao Fly-over Junction (Second Ring Rd.), Chaoyang District, 100027* ☎ *010/ 6553–2288* 🖷 *010/6501–2501* ⊕ *www.swissotel-beijing.com* 🛏 *362 rooms, 50 suites* ♨ *2 restaurants, room service, some in-room faxes, in-room safes, minibars, cable TV, in-room data ports, indoor pool, gym, hair salon, sauna, bar, shops, babysitting, laundry service, concierge, Internet, business services, meeting rooms, car rental, travel services, no-smoking rooms* ⊟ *AE, DC, MC, V* Ⓜ *Dongsi Shitiao.*

$$ 🏨 **Hilton Beijing.** Considered to be one of the city's oldest and most comfortable hotels, the Hilton lies at Beijing's northeast corner; it's a good choice for those wanting easy access to Beijing's airport, which is about a 20-minute drive away. Rooms are simply furnished, and most have two large picture windows and balconies. The hotel underwent a major

Kid-Friendly Hotels in Beijing

Many Beijing hotels have special programs and facilities that appeal to children. **Holiday Inn Lido,** in the Chaoyang District, has an ice-cream parlor, a 20-lane bowling alley, video games, a sprawling swimming pool, and a park next door. **Kerry Centre Hotel,** also in the Chaoyang District, has two indoor tennis courts, a large pool, a special splash pool, a play area for kids, and a rooftop outdoor track for in-line skating. **Sino-Swiss Hotel Beijing,** near the Capital Airport, has children's programs in summer; among its outdoor facilities are a playground, tennis courts, a volleyball court, an indoor–outdoor swimming pool, and horse stables nearby.

renovation in 2006, giving the lobby and restaurants a posh new look. One East on Third is designed like a Louisiana mansion, with dark wood and louvered windows, and offers light American cuisine with an extensive wine list. The very cool Zeta Bar has a retro-Beijing ambience with Bauhaus chairs and Chinese-inspired bird cages hanging above the crescent-shaped bar. A resident DJ spins here every night. ✉ *1 Dongfang Lu, Dongsanhuan Bei Lu, Chaoyang District, 100027* ☎ *010/5865–5000* 🖶 *010/5865–5800* ⊕ *www.beijing.hilton.com* 🛏 *375 rooms, 12 suites* ♿ *2 restaurants, in-room safes, minibars, refrigerators, cable TV, indoor pool, hot tub, sauna, bicycles, bar, babysitting, business services, meeting rooms, car rental, no-smoking rooms* ⊟ *AE, DC, MC, V.*

$$ 🏨 **Zhaolong Hotel.** This property was a gift to the nation as a sign of friendship from Hong Kong shipping magnate Y. K. Pao, who named it for his father. Located at the intersection of Gongti Beilu and the Third Ring Road, the Zhaolong is next door to the Pacific Century building, which houses a great Cantonese restaurant, De Luxe, and L'Isola, an Italian restaurant. The Bookworm, a popular expat coffee shop and restaurant, is a few blocks away. Its location within Sanlitun puts you close to the capital's nightlife. The back of the hotel now houses a youth hostel. ✉ *2 Gongren Tiyuchang Bei Lu, Sanlitun, Chaoyang District, 100027* ☎ *010/6597–2299* 🖶 *010/6597–2288* ⊕ *www.zhaolonghotel.com.cn* 🛏 *260 rooms, 16 suites* ♿ *3 restaurants, cable TV, in-room data ports, pool, gym, hair salon, massage, sauna, bicycles, bar, Internet, business services* ⊟ *AE, DC, MC, V* ⊙ *EP.*

$–$$$ 🏨 **Traders Hotel.** Inside the China World Trade Center complex, this hotel is connected to its sister property, the China World Hotel, and a shopping mall. The hotel is a favorite of international business travelers, who appreciate its central location, good service, top-notch amenities, and excellent value. Rooms are done up in muted colors, such as beige and light green, with queen- or king-size beds. Guests have access to the excellent health club at the China World Hotel. ✉ *1 Jianguomenwai Dajie, Chaoyang District, 100004* ☎ *010/6505–2277* 🖶 *010/6505–0828* ⊕ *www.shangri-la.com* 🛏 *570 rooms, 27 suites* ♿ *2 restaurants, in-room safes, minibars, cable TV, in-room data ports, massage, bar, shop,* *babysitting, business services, meeting rooms, airport shuttle, car rental, travel services, no-smoking rooms* ▭ *AE, DC, MC, V* Ⓜ *Guomao.*

$–$$ 🏨 **Gloria Plaza Hotel.** Built in the late 1990s, this hotel is situated in the Jianguomenwai commercial area of Beijing, not far from the embassy district. From the hotel, it's just a 10-minute walk to the Ancient Observatory, Silk Market, Friendship Store, and to the Red Gate Gallery, which exhibits contemporary Chinese art in one of the few remaining towers of the old city wall. ■ TIP➡ **A restored section of the city wall begins at the Red Gate Gallery, making for a pleasant stroll.** The simple rooms have good city views. The Sports City Café broadcasts sports events from around the world and serves up American food along with beer, wine, and cocktails. Sampan (in the lobby) serves decent dim sum and other Cantonese dishes. ✉ *2 Jiangguomen Nan Dajie, Chaoyang District, 100022* ☎ *010/6515–8855* 🖷 *010/6515–8533* ⊕ *www.gphbeijing.com* 🛏 *432 rooms, 50 suites* ♿ *2 restaurants, room service, cable TV, in-room data ports, indoor pool, health club, hot tub, massage, sauna, bar, lobby lounge, laundry service, business services, meeting rooms, airport shuttle, travel services, parking (fee)* ▭ *AE, DC, MC, V* Ⓜ *Jianguomen.*

$–$$ 🏨 **Jianguo Hotel.** Despite its 1950s-style name ("build the country"), Jianguo Hotel was the very first U.S.–China joint venture hotel in the city. Wonderfully central, it is close to the diplomatic compounds, southern embassy area, and the Silk Market. It's also a reasonable alternative for people taking part in conferences at the more expensive China World Hotel, just one block away. Nearly half the rooms have balconies overlooking busy Jianguomenwai Dajie. The Jianguo has maintained its friendly and cozy feel and continues to attract many diplomats, journalists, and businesspeople. The popular, renovated atrium lobby is bright and furnished with comfortable cushioned rattan sofas and arm chairs. Charlie's Bar, an old favorite, has a good lunch buffet, and Flo Justine's is one of the best French restaurants in the city. The gym and pool facilities, however, are very basic. ✉ *5 Jianguomenwai Dajie, Chaoyang District, 100020* ☎ *010/6500–2233* 🖷 *010/6501–0539* ⊕ *www.hoteljianguo.com* 🛏 *462 rooms, 68 suites* ♿ *4 restaurants, in-room safes, cable TV, indoor pool, hair salon, massage, bar, shop, laundry service, concierge, Internet, business services, meeting rooms, no-smoking rooms* ▭ *AE, DC, MC, V* Ⓜ *Yonganli.*

$–$$ 🏨 **Jinglun Hotel.** The rooms of the elegantly refurbished Jinglun Hotel are decorated in a minimalist style. Just a 10-minute drive to Tiananmen Square, and a few minutes from the China World Trade Center, the Jinglun is a well-appointed business and leisure hotel with competitive prices. The tiny, crowded lobby gives way to simple rooms with white-linen beds accented by dark purple, olive-green, and yellow cushions. ✉ *3 Jianguomenwai Dajie, Chaoyang District, 100020* ☎ *010/6500–2266* 🖷 *010/6500–2022* ⊕ *www.jinglunhotel.com* 🛏 *642 rooms, 126 suites* ♿ *Restaurant, in-room safes, minibars, refrigerators, cable TV, indoor pool, gym, hair salon, hot tub, massage, sauna, bicycles, bar, shops, babysitting, Internet, business services, car rental, travel services* ▭ *AE, DC, MC, V* Ⓜ *Yonganli.*

★ **$–$$** 🏨 **Kempinski Hotel.** This fashionable hotel forms part of the Lufthansa Center, together with a department store, offices, and apartments. It's within walking distance of the Sanlitun bar area, with its dozens of bars and restaurants, popular Ladies' Street, and Lucky Street, home to more than a dozen moderately priced Western and Asian restaurants. ■ **TIP→ There is an excellent German restaurant here, the Paulaner Brauhaus, which has its own microbrewery.** A deli, with an outstanding bakery frequented by expats, is also on-site. We love the newly designed Kranzler's Coffee Shop, which has an excellent Sunday brunch. A gym and swimming pool are on the 18th floor. ⊠ *50 Liangmaqiao Lu, Chaoyang District, 100016* ☎ *010/6465–3388* ⊕ *www.kempinski-beijing.com* 🖷 *010/6465–3366* ⥥ *526 rooms, 114 suites* ⚐ *6 restaurants, room service, in-room safes, some minibars, cable TV, in-room data ports, indoor pool, gym, bicycles, 2 bars, shops, laundry service, concierge, business services, meeting rooms, car rental, travel services* ▤ *AE, DC, MC, V.*

$ 🏨 **Jingguang New World.** Modern China's obsession with dark glass finds its most monstrous expression in this 53-story building. We will admit, though: the rooms have some of the most spectacular and unobstructed city views in Beijing. The Jingguang Center houses the hotel plus offices, shops, and luxury apartments. It's hard to miss on the eastern Third Ring Road, not far from Jianguomenwai Dajie. The restaurants serve Cantonese, Korean, and Western food. ⊠ *Jingguang Center, Hujialou, Chaoyang District, 100020* ☎ *010/6597–8888* 🖷 *010/6597–3333* ⊕ *www.jingguangcentre.com* ⥥ *446 rooms, 47 suites* ⚐ *3 restaurants, cable TV, pool, gym, hair salon, massage, sauna, 2 bars, shops, Internet, business services, meeting rooms* ▤ *AE, DC, MC, V.*

¢–$ 🏨 **The Red House.** A budget hotel conveniently located in the Sanlitun embassy district, the Red House is just a few blocks from the Dongzhimen subway station. Close to booming nightlife and numerous good restaurants, it's a clean, comfortable place for people traveling on a budget. ⊠ *10 Taiping Zhuang, Chun Xiu Lu, Dongzhimenwai, Chaoyang District, 100027* ☎ *010/6416–7810 or 010/6416–7828* 🖷 *010/6416–7600* ⊕ *www.redhouse.com.cn* ⥥ *40 rooms* ⚐ *Coffee shop, Internet, bar, travel services, laundry facilities* ▤ *AE, DC, MC, V* Ⓜ *Dongzhimen.*

¢–$ 🏨 **Scitech Hotel.** This hotel is part of the Scitech complex, comprised of an office tower, hotel, and shopping center. The hotel enjoys a good location on busy Jianguomenwai Dajie, opposite the Friendship Store. You are greeted by a small fountain in the lobby, which also has a small teahouse off to one side. The rooms are nondescript and the service is nothing to write home about, but the room rates are quite reasonable for this area. ⊠ *22 Jianguomenwai Dajie, Chaoyang District, 100004* ☎ *010/6512–3388* 🖷 *010/6512–3542* ⊕ *www.scitechgroup.com* ⥥ *294 rooms, 32 suites* ⚐ *3 restaurants, room service, in-room safes, minibars, cable TV, tennis court, indoor pool, gym, hair salon, hot tub, sauna, bar, dance club, shops, babysitting, laundry service, business services, meeting rooms, car rental, parking (fee), no-smoking rooms* ▤ *AE, DC, MC, V* ⍾ *EP* Ⓜ *Yonganli.*

¢ 🏨 **You Yi Youth Hostel.** Backpackers who don't mind that this youth hostel is attached to one of Beijing's most popular bars (Poachers) should stay here. Rooms sleep two to four people and are well-kept, with clean white walls and dark-wood trim. Best of all, the hostel is located smack in the middle of Beijing's bar-street area. ✉ *43 Beisanlitun Nan, Sanlitun, Chaoyang District, 100027* ☎ *010/6417–2632* 🖷 *010/ 6415–6866* ⊕ *www.poachers.com.cn* 🖘 *35 rooms with shared bath* ☖ *Restaurant, bar, laundry service; no TV in some rooms* ▤ *No credit cards* ¶◯¶ *BP.*

¢ 🖭 **Zhaolong International Youth Hostel.** If partaking in Beijing's lively nightlife scene is on your itinerary, consider this comfortable youth hostel in Sanlitun for your stay. The hostel offers clean rooms with two to six beds each, a reading room, a kitchen, and bicycle rentals. ✉ *2 Gongti Bei Lu, Sanlitun, Chaoyang District, 100027* ☎ *010/6597–2299 Ext. 6111* 🖷 *010/6597–2288* ⊕ *www.zhaolonghotel.com.cn* 🖘 *30 rooms* ☖ *Bar, laundry facilities; no room phones, no room TVs* ▤ *AE, MC, V* ¶◯¶ *CP.*

HAIDIAN DISTRICT

The Haidian District, in the far northwestern corner of Beijing, is where you'll find the university district, the city zoo, and numerous parks. The main attractions here for visitors are the Summer Palace and Old Summer Palace.

$$$ 🖭 **Shangri-La Hotel.** Set in delightful landscaped gardens in the western part of the city, 30 minutes from downtown, this Shangri-La is a wonderful retreat for business travelers and those visitors who don't mind being far from the city center. The lobby and restaurants underwent a major renovation in early 2004, and a new wing, the Horizon Tower, was completed in 2006. ✉ *29 Zizhuyuan Lu, Haidian District, 100084* ☎ *010/6841–2211* 🖷 *010/6841–8002* ⊕ *www.shangri-la.com* 🖘 *616 rooms, 19 suites, 15 1- to 3-bedroom apartments* ☖ *3 restaurants, room service, in-room safes, some kitchenettes, minibars, cable TV, in-room data ports, indoor pool, gym, health club, hair salon, massage, sauna, bar, lobby lounge, shops, babysitting, laundry service, Internet, business services, meeting rooms, car rental, travel services, parking (fee)* ▤ *AE, DC, MC, V.*

$–$$ 🖭 **Friendship Hotel.** The Friendship's name is telling: it was built in 1954 to house foreigners, mostly Soviet, who had come to help build New China. Beijing Friendship Hotel is one of the largest "garden-style" hotels in Asia. The architecture is Chinese traditional and the public spaces are classic and elegant. Rooms are large with somewhat outdated furnishings. With 14 restaurants, an Olympic-size pool, and a driving range, the hotel aims to be a one-stop destination. Its location far from the main tourist stops means that it's better situated for people who need to be close to the university area or to Zhongguancun, in the northwest of Beijing. ✉ *3 Baishiqiao Lu, Haidian District, 100873* ☎ *010/ 6849–8888* 🖷 *010/6849–8866* ⊕ *www.cbw.com/hotel/friendship* 🖘 *1,700 rooms, 200 suites* ☖ *14 restaurants, minibars, cable TV, driving range, tennis courts, 2 pools (1 indoor), gym, massage, sauna, billiards, bowling, bar, dance club, theater, business services, meeting rooms, car rental* ▤ *AE, DC, MC, V.*

BEDDING DOWN OUTSIDE THE CITY

★ **Red Capital Ranch.** Only a 90-minute drive from Beijing, the Red Capital Ranch ($$$) sits at a scenic foothill of the Ming-era Great Wall—and has private access to a wild section of that wall. There are 10 traditional houses, some Shaanxi-style cavelike dwellings with a roof. A terrace is nestled in a forest of walnut and apricot trees, and each room has views of the wall. This is an ideal spot to escape the crowds and souvenir hawkers that often spoil the fun at the Great Wall's other more popular sections. The restaurant features Manchurian cuisine in an open-air pavilion, with roast lamb and wild vegetables. The Tiger Bar is packed with colorful Tibetan furniture and rugs; sip a cognac next to the stone fireplace and enjoy the view of a flowing stream. Transportation from the Red Capital Club Residence downtown is included. ✉ *28 Xiaguandi Village, Yanxi Township, Huairou District, 101407, northeast of Beijing* ☎ *010/8401–8886* ⊕ *www. redcapitalclub.com.cn* ☞ *10 courtyard houses* ⚫ *1 restaurant, bar, room service* ▭ *AE, DC, MC, V.*

BEIJING AIRPORT AREA

7

★ **$$** 🏨 **Sino-Swiss Hotel.** This nine-story contemporary hotel near the airport overlooks a gorgeous outdoor pool surrounded by trees, shrubs, and colorful umbrellas. All the rooms and public areas are completely up-to-date. You'll find large standard rooms with deep-blue carpeting and white bedcovers. The restaurant Mongolian Gher offers barbecue and live entertainment inside a traditional-style felt yurt (a tentlike structure), whereas Swiss Chalet serves familiar continental food to tables on the outdoor terrace. The hotel caters to business travelers with a full-service conference center and duplex business suites. Just five minutes from the airport, the Sino-Swiss Hotel is convenient if you have an early-morning flight or get stuck at the airport. ✉ *9 Xiao Tianzhu Nan Lu (Box 6913), Beijing Capital Airport, Shunyi County, 100621* ☎ *010/ 6456–5588* 🖨 *010/6456–1588* ⊕ *www.sino-swisshotel.com* ☞ *408 rooms, 35 suites* ⚫ *4 restaurants, in-room safes, minibars, cable TV, 2 tennis courts, 2 pools (1 indoor), gym, hot tub, massage, sauna, bicycles, billiards, Ping-Pong, squash, 2 bars, shop, laundry service, business services, meeting rooms* ▭ *AE, DC, MC, V* ⦿*l BP.*

At a Glance

ENGLISH	PINYIN	CHINESE CHARACTERS
POINTS OF INTEREST		
Beijing Hotel	Běijīng fàndiàn	北京饭店
Beijing International	Běijīng guójì fàndiàn	北京国际饭店
China World Hotel	zhōngguó dàfàndiàn	中国大饭店
Courtyard Beijing	Běijīng wàn yí jiǔdiàn	北京万怡酒店
Crowne Plaza Beijing	Běijīng guójì yìyuàn huángguān jiàrì jiǔdiàn	北京国际艺苑皇冠假日酒店
Dongtang Inn	dōng tángkè zhàn	东堂客栈
Friendship Hotel	yǒuyì Bīnguǎn	友谊宾馆
Gloria Plaza Hotel	Běijīng kǎi lái dà jiǔdiàn	北京凯莱大酒店
Grand Hotel Beijing	Běijīng guìbīn lóu fàndiàn	北京贵宾楼饭店
Grand Hyatt Beijing	Běijīng dōngfāng jūn yuè jiǔdiàn	北京东方君悦酒店
Great Wall Sheraton	Běijīng chángchéng fàndiàn	北京长城饭店
Hademen Hotel	Hādémén fàndiàn	哈德门饭店
Haoyuan Hotel	hǎo yuán bīnguǎn	好园宾馆
Hilton Beijing	Běijīng xī ěr dùn jiǔdiàn	北京稀尔顿酒店
Holiday Inn Lido	lìdū jiàrì fàndiàn	丽都假日饭店
Jianguo Hotel	jiànguó fàndiàn	建国饭店
Jingguang New World	jīng guǎng xīn shìjiè jiǔdiàn	京广新世界酒店
Jinglun Hotel	jīng lún fàndiàn	京伦饭店
Kempinski Hotel	kǎi bīn sī jī fàndiàn	凯宾斯基饭店
Kerry Centre Hotel	Běijīng jiā lǐ zhōngxīn fàndiàn	北京嘉里中心饭店
Kunlun Hotel	Běijīng Kūnlún fàndiàn	北京昆仑饭店
LüSongyuan	lǚ sōng yuán bīnguǎn	侣松园宾馆
Minzu Hotel	mínzú fàndiàn	民族饭店
New Otani Changfugong	Běijīng cháng fù gōng fàndiàn	北京长富宫饭店
Novotel Peace Hotel	hépíng bīnguǎn	和平宾馆
Peninsula Beijing	wángfǔ bàndǎo jiǔdiàn	王府半岛酒店
Radisson SAS	Běijīng huángjiā dàfàndiàn	北京皇家大饭店
Raffles Beijing Hotel	Běijīng fàndiàn lái fó shì	北京饭店莱佛士

Red Capital Ranch	xīn hóng zī Bìshǔ shānzhuāng	新红资避暑山庄
Red Capital Residence	xīn hóng zī kèzhàn	新红资客栈
Ritz-Carlton Beijing	Běijīng jīnróng jiē lì sī kǎ'ěrdùn jiǔdiàn	北京金融街丽思卡尔顿酒店
The Red House	ruì xiù bīnguǎn	瑞秀宾馆
St. Regis	Běijīng guójì jùlèbù fàndiàn	北京国际俱乐部饭店
Scitech Hotel	Sài tè fàn diàn	塞特饭店
Shangri-La Hotel	Běijīng xiānggélǐlā fàndiàn	北京香格里拉饭店
Sino-Swiss Hotel	Běijīng guódū dàfàndiàn	北京国都大饭店
Swissôtel	gǎng Ào zhōngxīn ruìshì jiǔdiàn	港澳中心瑞士酒店
Traders Hotel	guó mào fàndiàn	国贸饭店
You Yi Youth Hostel	Běijīng yǒuyì qīngnián jiǔdiàn	北京友谊青年酒店
Zhaolong International Youth Hostel	Zhào lóng qīng nián lǚshè	兆龙青年旅舍
Zhaolong Hotel	zhào lóng fàndiàn	兆龙饭店
Zhuyuan Hotel	zhú yuán bīnguǎn	竹园宾馆

7

Best Side Trips

INCLUDING THE GREAT WALL
& THIRTEEN MING TOMBS

The Great Palace Gate of the Thirteen Ming Tombs.

WORD OF MOUTH

"Start really, really early to get to the Eastern Qing Tombs. The area is vast and there's lots of walking involved." —rkkwan

"Bring layers, such as a warm fleece and a windbreaker. Hiking boots may not be necessary (they take up room and are heavy) but a pair of walking shoes are a must." —lye

BEST SIDE TRIPS PLANNER

What to Wear

The weather in Beijing and neighboring areas is notoriously fickle, so make sure you dress appropriately. In the summer it's hot; travel with sunglasses, sunscreen, and a wide-brimmed hat. It gets terribly cold in the winter, so dress in layers and pack gloves, a hat, and a scarf. And if you plan to do any hiking, make sure to bring sturdy, comfortable shoes.

Also, checking the weather forecast before an excursion is always a good idea for last-minute wardrobe changes. ■ TIP→ **Don't carry too much cash or expensive jewelry.** Other things to bring along? A camera, a change of clothes if you're staying overnight, and your common sense.

Tours

Every major hotel can arrange guided tours to sites outside Beijing. Among the hotel-based travel agencies are **Beijing Panda Tour** and **China Swan International Tours. China International Travel Service (CITS),** the official government agency, can also arrange tours.

Beijing Hikers (⊠ Jingsong Xikou 9, Qu Building 904, Suite 407 Chaoyang District ☎ 139/1002–5516 or 010/6779–9365 ⊕ www.beijinghikers.com) leads hiking tours to assorted locations every weekend.

Beijing Panda Tour (⊠ Holiday Inn Crowne Plaza, 48 Wangfujing Dajie, Dongcheng District, Beijing ☎ 010/6513–3388 Ext. 1212)

China International Travel Service (⊠ 28 Jianguomenwai Dajie, Chaoyang District, Beijing ☎ 010/6515–8565 🖷 010/6515–8603)

China Swan International Tours (⊠ Rm. 718, Beijing Capital Times Square, 88 Changan Jie, Xicheng District, Beijing ☎ 010/8391–3058 ⊕ www.china-swan.com/english.htm)

Chinese Culture Club/The Beijing Amblers (⊠ Kent Center, 29 Lingmaqia Lu, Dongcheng District, Beijing ☎ 010/6432–9341 ⊕ www.chinesecultureclub.com)

Compass Tourist Information. This is a cheap tour service that caters to backpackers. Tours are generally ½ to ⅓ the price of CITS. (⊠ 5 Youanmen Dongjie, Xuanwu District ☎ 010/8353–6028)

Cycle China (☎ 1391/188–6524 ⊕ www.cyclechina.com)

Wild China. This group tours destinations all over China, and Great Wall, with tours run by Great Wall historian David Spindler. (⊠ Dongfang International Building 9 Dongfang Dong Lu suite 801, Chaoyang District ☎ 010/6465–6602 ⊕ www.wildchina.com)

Getting There

Taxis, which in Beijing are both plentiful and reasonably priced, are a good way to get to sights outside the city. If you do decide to take a taxi, be sure to set a price beforehand, as the metered fare can add up quickly (generally, rides start at Y10 with an additional Y2 per kilometer and another Y2 per every five minutes of waiting time). As Beijing traffic is getting more congested, the potential for some time stuck in traffic (and the associated cost jump) is high.

Private-car services are available in Beijing, but they aren't always cheap, though they are in most cases worth the investment. **Beijing Limo** (☎ 010/6546–1688 or 010/6546–1688 ⊕ www.beijinglimo.com) has English-speaking drivers, and a variety of cars and buses.

Trains are also a good way to get to your side trips. Some sites, such as Yesanpo, Tianjin, Beidaihe, and Shanhaiguan, are accessible by train. Some trains leave from Beijing Station, in the middle of the city, and others leave from Beijing West Station. Plan to get to the train station at least 30 minutes before your train leaves, as the stations can be confusing for visitors. It's easy to buy train tickets at the station, but if you're on a tight schedule and can't afford a delay, buy a ticket beforehand, especially if you're traveling on peak dates. Most hotels will help you purchase tickets up to four days in advance for a fee (typically Y5 to Y15 per ticket).

Timing

It'll take you several days to see all the sights outside of Beijing. If you only have time for one, go to the **Great Wall.** If you have two days, head to **Fahai Temple,** about an hour's drive from the center, on the second day. Afterward you can see **Jietai** and **Tanzhe** before returning to the city in the afternoon. If you have more time to see the sights outside the city, check out the **Eastern Qing Tombs** on your third day. Wear walking shoes and bring a lunch.

If you have three days or more, and you're looking for a little summertime relaxation, take a day and a night (or, for real relaxation, two days) at **Beidaihe,** to bask on the beach, chow down on seafood, and crash at one of the ubiquitous hotels along the coast.

If you have another day in Beijing for a side trip, and you're a history buff, check out the **Marco Polo Bridge** or the **Peking Man** site at **Zhoukoudian.**

8

By Alex Miller

Not only is Beijing a fascinating city to visit, but its outskirts are packed with history- and culture-laden sites for the admirer of early empires and their antiquities. First and foremost, a trip to the Great Wall is a must—you simply can't miss it! After the Great Wall, there are a variety of wonderful things to do and see: you can go horseback riding at Yesanpo, take a dip at the beach and gorge yourself with fresh seafood in Beidaihe, or travel to Laolongtou (the Old Dragon's Head), and see another section of the Great Wall in all its majesty as it collides with the ocean.

Buddhist temples and ancient tombs, as well as historical bridges and anthropological digs, are all located within a few hours of Beijing. For all these sites, getting there is half the fun—traveling through rural China, even for a day trip, is always something of adventure.

THIRTEEN MING TOMBS

48 km (30 mi) north of Beijing.

A narrow valley just north of Changping is the final resting place for 13 of the Ming Dynasty's 16 emperors (the first Ming emperor was buried in Nanjing; the burial site of the second one is unknown; and the seventh Ming emperor was dethroned and buried in an ordinary tomb in western Beijing). Ming monarchs once journeyed here each year to kowtow before their clan forefathers and make offerings to their memory. The area's vast scale and imperial grandeur convey the importance attached to ancestral worship in ancient China.

The road to the Thirteen Ming Tombs begins beneath an imposing stone portico that stands at the valley entrance. Beyond the entrance, the

TO MING OR NOT TO MING?

Most visitors to the Ming Tombs visit them as part of a longer excursion, usually to the Great Wall. A leisurely walk down spirit way, inspecting the series of charming statues, which represent the subjects and possessions of the emperors buried here, is probably the best way to spend an hour or two. Only three of the Ming Tombs are open to visitors (Changling, Dingling, and Zhaoling), and none of them are much more than a deep concrete bunker with a huge nondescript concrete coffin at the bottom, which you have to buy a ticket to visit. If you're blessed with a little more time, you can pay a more private homage to the spirit of Emperor Zhu Zhaigou at his tomb at Zhaoling, which is at the far end of the valley. It's quainter and much less frequently visited.

Shenlu (☎ Y16 ☉ Daily 9–5:30), or Spirit Way, once reserved for imperial travel, passes through an outer pavilion and between rows of stone sculptures—imperial advisers and huge elephants, lions, and horses—on its 7-km (4½-mi) journey to the burial sites.

The spirit way leads to **Changling** (☎ 010/6076–1886 ☎ Y30), the head tomb built for Emperor Yongle in 1427. The designs of Yongle's great masterpiece, the Forbidden City, are echoed in this structure. The tomb is open daily from 8:30 to 4:30.

Changling and a second tomb, **Dingling** (☎ 010/6076–1424 ☎ Y60 Mar.–June and Sept.–Nov.; Y40 July and Aug. and Dec.–Feb.), were rebuilt in the 1980s and opened to the public. Both complexes suffer from over-restoration and overcrowding, but they're worth visiting if only for the tomb relics on display in the small museums at each site. Dingling is particularly worth seeing because this tomb of Emperor Wanli is the only Ming Dynasty tomb that has been excavated. Unfortunately, this was done in 1956 when China's archaeological skills were sadly lacking, resulting in irrecoverable losses. Nonetheless, it is interesting to compare this underground vault with the tomb of Emperor Qianlong at Qingdongling. Dingling is open daily from 8:30 to 5:30. Allow ample time for a hike or drive northwest from Changling to the six fenced-off **unrestored tombs,** a short distance farther up the valley. Here, crumbling walls conceal vast courtyards shaded by pine trees. At each tomb, a stone altar rests beneath a stela tower and burial mound. In some cases the wall that circles the burial chamber is accessible on steep stone stairways that ascend from either side of the altar. At the valley's terminus (about 5 km [3 mi] northwest of Changling), the **Zhaoling tomb** (☎ Y30) rests beside a traditional walled village. This thriving hamlet is well worth exploring.

Picnics amid the ruins have been a favorite weekend activity among Beijingers for nearly a century; if you do picnic here, be sure to carry out all trash. ⊠ *Changping County.*

8

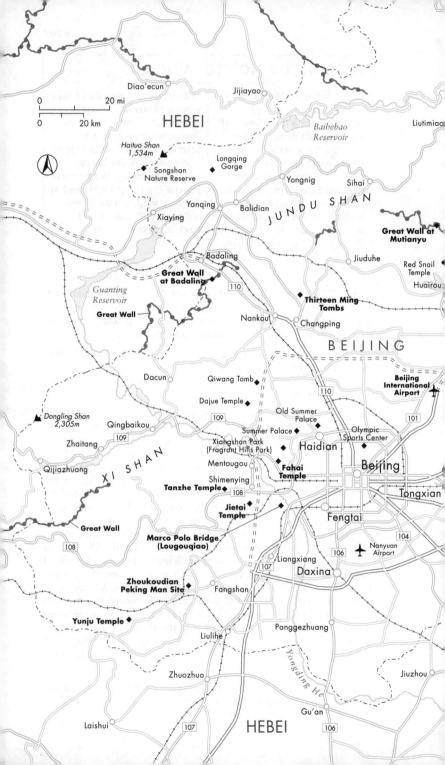

Side Trips
from Beijing

101

Gubeikou **Great Wall at
Jinshanling**

Beidianzi

**Great Wall at
Simatai**

▲ *Wuling Shan
2,116m*

112

Taishitun

Great Wall

*Miyun
Reservoir*

*Under
Construction*

111

Xinglong 112

Dayingpan

Miyun

101

Great Wall

Ninshan

**Eastern Qing
Tombs**

Shunyi

Pinggu

Luozhuangzi

Shimen

Ji Xian

*Yuqiao
Reservoir*

HEBEI

Sanhe

102

Xiadian

102 Yutian

Huoxian Xianghe

103

Baodi

HEBEI

Shijiuwo

105

TANJIN

Dakoutun

Da Yunhe

Langfang

Cuihuangkou

103

Huangzhuang

104 112

YESANPO & BEIDAIHE

Yesanpo (150 km [90 mi] northeast of Beijing) is a sleepy village between Beijing and neighboring Hebei province. Go here if you're craving a slower-paced scene and some outdoor fun. The accommodations aren't first class, but there are plenty of great things to do. Leave Beijing from Beijing West Station for the 2-hour ride. Traditionally, locals have houses with extra rooms for guests, and owners will strive to make your stay as comfortable as possible. A clean room with two beds and an air conditioner should run you no more than Y150. There are also a few hotels on the main street by the train station with rooms running approximately Y200. This scenic town is nestled in a valley. The area is best toured on horseback, and horses are available for rent for Y300 per day (with a guide), or Y100 for an hour or so. Yesanpo is also known for its whole barbecued lamb. At the time of this writing, trains leave Beijing West station at 6:38 AM and 2:40 PM. They come back twice daily.

Chairman Mao and the party's favorite spot for sand, sun, and seafood, **Beidaihe** (250 km [170 mi] northeast of Beijing) is one of China's premier beach resorts (though it's definitely no Bali). This crowded spot is just a 2½ hour train ride from Beijing Station. Nearly every building in town has been converted to a hotel, and every restaurant has tanks of pick-your-own seafood lining the street.

FAHAI TEMPLE

20 km (12 mi) west of Beijing.

The stunning works of Buddhist mural art at Fahai Temple are among the most underappreciated sights in Beijing. Li Tong, a favored eunuch in the court of Emperor Zhengtong (1436–49), donated funds to construct Fahai Temple in 1443. The project was highly ambitious: Li Tong invited only celebrated imperial and court painters to decorate the temple. As a result, the murals in the only surviving chamber of that period, Daxiongbaodian (the Mahavira Hall), are considered the finest examples of Buddhist mural art from the Ming Dynasty. Sadly, statues of various Buddhas and one of Li Tong himself were destroyed during China's Cultural Revolution.

The most famous of the nine murals in Mahavira Hall is a large-scale triptych featuring Guanyin (the Bodhisattva of Compassion) and Wenshu (the Bodhisattva of Marvelous Virtue and Gentle Majesty) in the center, and Poxian (the Buddha of Universal Virtue) on either side. The

Continued on page 218

THE GREAT WALL

■ One misconception is that the Great Wall is the only man-made structure visible from space. We say there's no better way to see it than up close.

■ Sections of this magnificent, ancient wall were built from the 5th century BC until the 17th century AD.

■ The Great Wall is the longest man-made structure on Earth. It was designated a UNESCO World Heritage Site in 1987.

For some people, the Great Wall is the main reason for a trip to China; for any visitor to Beijing, it's a must-see. Originally intended to keep foreigners out, the world's most famous wall has become the icon of an increasingly open nation. One of the country's most accessible attractions, the Great Wall promises both breathtaking scenery and cultural illumination. As you explore this snaking structure, often compared to a dragon, try to imagine the monumental task of building such a behemoth, and how imposing it must have appeared from horseback, to a nomadic invader trying to penetrate its near-perfect strategic location. Even for those who have conquered it, the Great Wall still has a way of defying imagination.

HISTORY & MYSTERY

Built by successive dynasties over two millennia, the Great Wall isn't one structure built at one time, but a series of defensive installations that shrank and grew. Especially vulnerable spots were more heavily fortified, while some mountainous regions were left un-walled altogether. The actual length of the wall remains a topic of considerable debate: at its longest, some estimates say the protective cordon spans 6,437 km (4,000 mi)—a distance wider than the United States. Although attacks, age, and pillaging (not to mention today's tourist invasion) have caused the crumbling of up to two-thirds of its length, new sections are being uncovered even today.

As kingdoms scrambled to protect themselves from marauding nomads, portions of wall cropped up, leading to a motley collection of northern borders. It was the first emperor of a unified China, Qin Shi-huang (circa 259–210 BC), founder of the Qin Dynasty, who linked these fortifications into a single network. By some accounts, Qin mustered nearly a million people, or one-fifth of China's workforce, to build this massive barricade, a mobilization that claimed countless lives and gave rise to many tragic folktales.

The Ming Dynasty fortified the wall like never before: for an estimated 5,000 km (3,107 mi), it stood 26 feet tall and 30 feet wide at its base. However, the wall failed to prevent the Manchu invasion that toppled the Ming in 1644. That historical failure hasn't tarnished the Great Wall's image, however. Although China once viewed it as a model of feudal oppression, the Great Wall is now touted as the national symbol. "Love China, Restore the Great Wall," declared Deng Xiaoping in 1984. Since then large sections have been repaired and opened to visitors, turning it also into a symbol of the tension between preservation and restoration in China.

AN ETERNAL WAIT

One legend concerns Lady Meng, whose husband was kidnapped on their wedding night and forced to work on the Great Wall. She traveled to the work site to await his return, believing her determination would bring him back. She waited so long that, in the end, she turned into a rock, which to this day stands at the head of the Great Wall in the beautiful seaside town of Qinhuangdao.

MATERIALS & TECHNIQUES

During the 2nd century BC, the wall was largely composed of packed earth and piled stone.

Some sections, like those in the Taklimakan Desert, were fortified with twigs, sand, and even rice (the jury's still out on whether workers' remains were used, as well).

The more substantial brick-and-mortar ruins that wind across the mountains north of Beijing date from the Ming Dynasty (14th–17th centuries). Some Ming mortar kilns still exist in valleys around Beijing.

YOUR GUIDE TO THE GREAT WALL

As a visitor to Beijing, you simply must set aside a day to visit one of the glorious Great Wall sites just outside the capital. The closest, Badaling, is just an hour from the city's center—in general, the farther you go, the more rugged the terrain. So choose your adventure wisely!

BADALING, the most accessible section of the Great Wall, is where most tours go. This location is rife with Disneylike commercialism, though: from the cable car you'll see both the heavily reconstructed portions of wall and crowds of souvenir stalls.

If you seek the wall less traveled, book a trip to fantastic **MUTIANYU**, which is about the same distance as Badaling from Beijing. You can enjoy much more solitude here, as well as amazing views from the towers and walls.

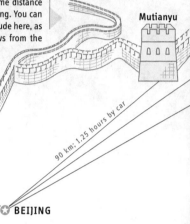

Mutianyu

Badaling

90 km; 1.25 hours by car

70 km; 1 hour by car

⭐ BEIJING

TRANSPORTATION

CARS: The easiest and most comfortable way to visit the wall is by private car. Though taxis are occasionally willing to make the trip to more accessible sections like Badaling and Mutianyu, most hotels can arrange a four-passenger car and an English-speaking driver for Y400–Y600 (about 8 hours). Settle details in advance, and remember that it's polite to invite your driver to eat meals with you. To ensure your driver doesn't return to Beijing without you, pay after the trip is over.

TOURS: In addition to the tour buses that gather around Tiananmen Square, most hotels and tour companies offer trips (in comfortable, air-conditioned buses or vans) to Badaling, Mutianyu, Simatai, and Jinshanling.

■ TIP→ **Smaller, private tours are generally more rewarding than large bus trips.** Trips will run between Y100 and Y500 per person, but costs vary depending on the group size, and can sometimes be negotiated. Wherever you're headed, book in advance.

TOUR OPERATORS

OUR TOP PICKS

■ **CITS (China International Tour Service)** runs bus tours to the Great Wall at Badaling (with Ming Tombs), and private tours to Badaling, Mutianyu, and Simatai. (Y370–Y640 per person) ✉ 28 Jianguomen Wai Dajie, Chaoyang District ☎ 010/6522–2991 ⊕ www.cits.net

■ **Beijing Service** leads private guided tours by car to Badaling, Mutianyu, and Simatai (Y260–Y680). ☎ 010/5166–7026 ✎ travel@beijingservice.com ⊕ www.beijingservice.com

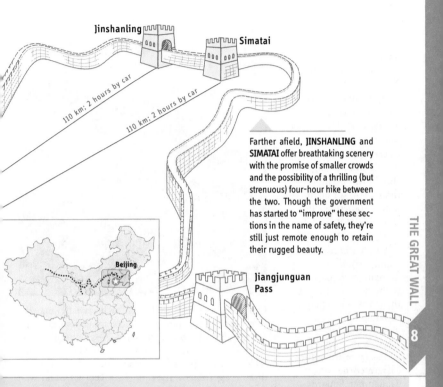

Jinshanling

Simatai

110 km; 2 hours by car

110 km; 2 hours by car

Beijing

Farther afield, **JINSHANLING** and **SIMATAI** offer breathtaking scenery with the promise of smaller crowds and the possibility of a thrilling (but strenuous) four-hour hike between the two. Though the government has started to "improve" these sections in the name of safety, they're still just remote enough to retain their rugged beauty.

Jiangjunguan Pass

THE GREAT WALL

8

■ **Great Wall Adventure Tour** organizes private bus and car trips to Jinshanling-Simatai (Y380-Y650) and Mutianyu (Y160-Y350). ☎ 138/1108-9985 ✉ greatwall@greatwalladventure.com ⊕ www.greatwalladventure.com

ADDITIONAL TOURS

■ **Abercrombie & Kent** also offers pricey personalized group tours to the wall. Call for prices. ☎ 010/6507-7125 ⊕ www.abercrombiekent.com

■ **Cycle China** runs good guided hiking tours of the unrestored Wall at Jiankou,

as well as personalized tours to Simatai and Mutianyu. (Y300-Y600). ☎ 010/6402-5653, ⊕ www.cyclechina.com

■ **David Spindler**, a Great Wall expert, runs private tours to various sites. Contact him for prices, schedules, and details through Wild China ☎ 010/6465-6602 Ext. 314 ✉ info@wildchina.com ⊕ www.wildchina.com

■ **Dragon Bus Tours**, which picks up at major hotels, has tours to Badaling (with Ming Tombs), Mutianyu, and a bus

to Simatai—with an occasional stop at a souvenir factory. (Y280-350; Y140 for Simatai) ☎ 010/6515-8565 ✉ service@beijinghighlights.com

■ **Gray Line/Panda Tours**, with branches in a dozen high-end hotels in Beijing, runs bus tours to Badaling (and Ming Tombs), Mutianyu, and Simatai—but beware of stops at souvenir factories. (Y280-Y590 per person) ✉ 5/F, Grand Rock Plaza, No. 13 Xinzhongxili ☎ 010/6525-8372 ⊕ www.pandatourchina.cn

GREAT WALL AT BADALING

GETTING THERE

Distance: 70 km (43 mi) northwest of Beijing, in Yanqing County

Tours: Beijing Service, CITS, Dragon Bus Tours, Gray Line/Panda Tours

By Car: A car for four people to Badaling should run no more than Y600 for eight hours, sometimes including a stop at the Thirteen Ming Tombs.

By Bus: It's hard to wander south of Tiananmen Square without encountering the many buses going to Badaling. Choose wisely: look for the 1 or 5 bus at Qianmen, across from the southeastern corner of Tiananmen Square (departs 6:30 AM–11:30 AM for Y12–Y18 per person).

FAST FACTS

Phone: 010/6912–1383

Hours: Daily 6:30 AM– 7 PM

Admission: Y40 Nov.–Mar.; Y45 Apr.–Nov.; cable car is an additional Y40 one-way, Y60 round-trip

Web Site: www.badaling. gov.cn

Only one hour by car from downtown Beijing, the Great Wall at Badaling is where visiting dignitaries go for a quick photo-op. Postcard views abound here, with large sections of the restored Ming Dynasty brick wall rising majestically to either side of the fort. In the distance, portions of the early-16th-century Great Wall disintegrate into more romantic but inaccessible ruins.

Badaling is convenient to the Thirteen Ming Tombs and outfitted with tourist-friendly facilities, so it's popular with tour groups and is thus often crowded, especially on weekends. ■ TIP➔ **People with disabilities find access to the wall at Badaling better than elsewhere in the Beijing area.** You can either take the cable car to the top, or you can walk up the gently sloping steps, relying on handrails if necessary. On a clear day you can see for miles across leafy, undulating terrain from atop the battlements. The admission price also includes access to the China Great Wall Museum and the Great Wall Circle Vision Theater.

■ TIP➔ **Most tours to Badaling will take you to the Thirteen Ming Tombs, as well. If you don't want a stop at the tombs—or at a tourist-trapping jade factory or herbal medicine center along the way—be sure to confirm the itinerary before booking.**

GREAT WALL AT MUTIANYU

GETTING THERE

Distance: 90 km (56 mi) northeast of Beijing, in Huairou County

Tours: CITS, Gray Line/ Panda Tours, Great Wall Adventure Tour

By Car: A car to Mutianyu should cost no more than Y500 for the day—it takes about an hour to get there.

By Bus: Take Bus 916/ 936 from Dongzhimen to Huairou (Y5). From there take a minibus to Mutianyu (Y25–Y30) or hire a taxi to take you there and back to the bus station (about Y50 each way, Y100–Y150 round-trip after bargaining). On weekends and national holidays, the tourist Bus 6 from outside the South Cathedral at Xuanwumen goes directly to Mutianyu (Y50, leaves 6:30–8:30 AM).

FAST FACTS

Phone: 010/6162–6873 or 010/6162–6022

Hours: Daily 7 AM– 6:30 PM

Admission: Y35 (students half-price); chairlift, Y35; cable car, Y50 one-way, Y55 with toboggan descent

★ Fodor's Choice Slightly farther from downtown Beijing than Badaling, the Great Wall at Mutianyu is more spectacular and, despite the occasional annoyances of souvenir stands, significantly less crowded. This long section of wall, first built during the Northern Qi Dynasty (6th century) and restored and rebuilt throughout history, can offer a solitary Great Wall experience, with unforgettable views of towers winding across mountains and woodlands. On a clear day, you'll swear you can see the deserts of Mongolia in the distance.

The lowest point on the wall is a strenuous one-hour climb above the parking lot. As an alternative, you can take a cable car on a breathtaking ride to the highest restored section (this is how President Bill Clinton ascended in 1998), from which several hiking trails descend. Take a gorgeous 1.5-hour walk east to reach another cable car that returns to the same parking lot. Mutianyu is also known for its toboggan run.

■ TIP➔ For those taking a car, the road from Huairou, a suburb of Beijing, to Mutianyu follows a river upstream and is lined with restaurants selling fresh trout. In addition, Hongluo Temple is a short drive from the bottom of the mountain.

THE GREAT WALL

8

GREAT WALL AT SIMATAI

GETTING THERE

Distance: At around 110 km (68 mi) northeast of Beijing, Simatai is farther than Badaling and Mutianyu, but is well worth the trip—the road runs through lovely farmland, and few visitors make the trek.

Tours: Most hotels offer tours here, as do CITS, Gray Line/Panda Tours, and Great Wall Adventure Tour.

By Car: A car to Simatai should be no more than Y700 for the day. If you plan to hike from Jinshanling to Simatai, or vice versa, have your car drop you off at one and pick you up at the other.

By Bus: Take the early-morning Bus 916 from the bus station at Dongzhimen (Y20), starting at 6 AM. On weekends and holidays, a luxury bus leaves Qianmen at 8:30 AM (Y85 round-trip) and leaves Simatai at 3 PM.

FAST FACTS

Phone: 010/6903–5025 or 010/6903–1051

Hours: Daily 8 AM–5 PM

Admission: Y20; cable car, Y40 one-way, Y60 round-trip. If you hike to Jinshanling, you will have to buy another Y5 ticket at the border.

★ Remote and largely unrestored, the Great Wall at Simatai is ideal if you're seeking adventure. Near the frontier garrison at Gubeikou, the wall traverses towering peaks and hangs precariously above cliffs. Be prepared for no-handrails hiking, tough climbs, and unparalleled vistas. Several trails lead to the wall from the parking lot.

In summer, a cable car takes you two-thirds of the way up; from there it's a steep 40-minute climb to the summit. Heading east from the Miyun reservoir at a moderate pace will take you to Wangjing Ta, the 12th watchtower, after about 3 hours. For a longer hike, head west over the bridge toward the restored Jinshanling section.

The hike to Jinshanling is a strenuous 9 km (5.6 mi), usually taking around 4 hours up and down sublime sections of the wall. Be aware that crossing to Jinshanling costs Y5. People who wish to hike from one to the other often ask their driver to wait for them at their destination. (Note that hikers usually go from Jinshanling to Simatai, where buses back to Beijing are easier to find.)

GREAT WALL AT JINSHANLING

GETTING THERE

Distance: 110 km (68 mi) northeast from Beijing

Tours: CITS, Cycle China, Gray Line/Panda Tours, Great Wall Adventure Tour

By Car: A car should be no more than Y700; the ride is about two hours. If you plan to hike from Jinshanling to Simatai, as many do, it makes sense to be dropped off at Jinshanling and have your car pick you up at Simatai.

By Train: Take train L671, which departs at 7:25 AM from Beijing North Railway Station, to Gubeikou; there switch to a local minibus or taxi to Jinshanling.

By Bus: Take a minibus from Dongzhimen long-distance bus station to Miyun (Y8) and then change to a local bus or taxi. Or take a Chengde-bound bus from Dongzhimen and get off at Jinshanling; a cab can bring you to the entrance for Y10.

★ Though it lacks the rugged adventure of Simatai, Jinshanling is perhaps the least restored of the major Great Wall sections near Beijing, as well as the least visited. Besides being the starting point for a fantastic four-hour hike to Simatai, Jinshanling also serves as one of the few sections of the Great Wall on which you can camp overnight.

A starry night here is gorgeous and unforgettable—go with a tour group such as Cycle China. Don't forget to pack a piece of charcoal and paper to make rubbings of bricks that still bear the stamp of the date they were made.

FAST FACTS

Phone: 031/4883–0222 or 0138/3144–8986

Hours: Daily 8 AM–5 PM

Admission: Y30; Y50 for overnight stays. If you hike to Simatai, you will have to buy another Y5 ticket at the border.

GREAT WALL MARATHON

Not for the faint of heart, the Great Wall Marathon (and half marathon) takes place each May. The marathon covers approximately 6.5 km (4 mi) of the Great Wall, with the rest of the course running through lovely valleys in rural Tianjin.
⊕ www.great-wall-marathon.com

A Swanky Night at the Wall

Call it boutique Great Wall: **The Red Capital Ranch** (✉ 28 Yanxi Township, Huairou District ☎ 010/8401-8866 ⊕ www.redcapitalclub.com.cn), an outpost of Beijing's swanky Red Capital Club, lets Great Wall visitors feel more like Ming emperors than mere foot soldiers. Located snugly alongside a secluded and unrestored section of the Wall near Miyun, the Ranch offers a tranquil and extravagant experience, complete with spa and Zen-friendly decor (rooms run Y1,900–Y2,000 per night). Trips leave daily from Beijing's Red Capital Club at 10 AM.

Near Badaling, the **Commune By the Great Wall** (✉ Yanqing County

☎ 010/8118-1888 ⊕ www.commune.com.cn) is one of China's most distinctive and stunning architectural projects (it won the "Special Prize" at the 2002 Venice Biennial) and the Great Wall's most expensive camp site (J. Lo stayed here on a recent visit). Eleven villas each showcase the work of a different Asian architect; an overnight in one of the sophisticated homes, constructed out of a range of wood, glass, steel, bamboo, and Great Wall-style stone, will set you back a whopping Y9,000–Y14,000. Never fear: butlers, saunas, a restaurant, a gallery, theater, swimming pool, and children's facility are included.

depiction of Guanyin follows the theme of "moon in water," which compares the Buddhist belief in the illusoriness of the material world to the reflection of the moon in the water. Typically painted with Guanyin are her legendary mount Jin Sun and her assistant Shancai Tongzi. Wenshu is often presented with a lion, symbolic of the bodhisattva's wisdom and strength of will, while Poxian is shown near a six-tusked elephant, each tusk representing one of the qualities that leads to enlightenment. On the opposite wall is the *Sovereign Sakra and Brahma* mural, with a panoply of characters from the Buddhist canon.

The murals were painted during the time of the European Renaissance, and though the subject matter is traditional, there are comparable experiments in perspective taking place in the depiction of the figures, as compared with examples from earlier dynasties. Also of note is a highly unusual decorative technique; many contours in the hall's murals, particularly on jewelry, armor, and weapons, have been set in bold relief by the application of fine gold threads.

The temple grounds are also beautiful, but of overriding interest are the murals themselves. Plans are in the works to limit access to the poorly lit original murals by one day creating a visitor center with well-illuminated reproductions. For now, visitors stumble through the dark temple with rented flashlights (free with your ticket). Viewing the murals in this way, it's easy to imagine oneself as a sort of modern day Indiana Jones unraveling a story of the Buddha as depicted in ancient murals of unrivaled beauty. Fahai Temple is only a short taxi ride from Beijing's Pingguoyuan subway station. ☒ *Moshikou Lu, Shijingshan District, Beijing, take an approximate Y10-taxi ride from Pinguoyuan subway station directly to the temple* ☎ 010/8871–5776 ☒ Y20 ☉ *Daily 9–4:30.*

Eunuchs have played an important role throughout Chinese history, often holding great influence over affairs of state, yet surprisingly little is known about them. The **Beijing Eunuch Culture Exhibition Hall,** near the magnificent **Tian Yi Mu,** begins to redress this lack of information. Tian Yi (1534–1605) was only nine when he was castrated and sent into the service of the Ming emperor Jiajing. He spent the next 63 years of his life serving three emperors and rose to one of the highest ranks in the land, the Director of Ceremonies. His tomb, though not as magnificent as the Thirteen Ming Tombs, nonetheless befits a man of such high social status. Particularly noteworthy in the tomb complex are the stone carvings around the base of the central mound depicting ancient anecdotes. The four smaller tombs on either side belong to other eunuchs who wished to pay tribute to Tian Yi by being buried in the same compound with him.

The small exhibition hall at the front of the tomb complex contains limited background information, most of it in Chinese, about famous eunuchs. Keep an eye out for the ancient Chinese character meaning "to castrate," which resembles two knives, one inverted, side by side. Also here is a list of all the temples in Beijing that were founded by eunuchs. The hall and tomb are a five-minute walk from Fahai Temple; just ask people the way to Tian Yi Mu. ☒ *80 Moshikou Lu, Shijingshan District, Beijing* ☎ 010/8872–4148 ☒ Y8 ☉ *Daily 9–5.*

JIETAI TEMPLE

★ *35 km (22 mi) west of Beijing.*

On a wooded hill west of Beijing, Jietai Temple is one of China's most famous ancient Buddhist sites. Its four main halls occupy terraces on a gentle slope up to Ma'an Shan (Saddle Hill). Originally built in AD 622, the temple complex expanded over the centuries and grew to its current scale in a major renovation conducted by devotees during the Qing Dynasty (1644–1912). The temple buildings, plus three magnificent bronze Buddhas in the Mahavira Hall, date from this period. There is also a huge, potbellied Maitreya Buddha carved from the roots of what must have been a truly enormous tree. To the right of this hall, just above twin pagodas, is the Ordination Terrace, a platform built of white marble and topped with a massive bronze Sakyamuni (Buddha) seated on a lotus flower. Tranquil courtyards, where ornate stelae and well-kept gardens bask beneath the Scholar Tree and other ancient pines, add to the temple's beauty. Many modern devotees from Beijing visit the temple on weekends. ⊠ *Mentougou County* ☎ *010/6980–6611* 🖃 *Y35* ⊗ *Daily 8–5.*

> ### GETTING THERE
>
> Getting to Jietai and Tanzhe temples is easy using public transportation. Simply take Beijing's Line 1 subway to its westernmost station, Pingguoyuan. From Pingguoyuan, take the #931 public bus to either temple. Or you can opt for a quicker taxi ride to and from the station. A taxi from Pingguoyuan to Jietai Temple should be Y30 to Y50; the bus fare is Y6.

NEARBY

Farther along the road past Jietai Temple, **Tanzhe Temple** is a Buddhist complex nestled in a grove of *zhe* (cudrania) trees. Established around AD 400 and once home to more than 500 monks, Tanzhe was heavily damaged during the Cultural Revolution; it has since been restored, but if you look closely at some of the huge stone tablets, or *bei,* littered around the site you'll see that many of the inscriptions have been destroyed. The complex makes an ideal side trip from Jietai Temple or Marco Polo Bridge. ⊠ *Mentougou County* ☎ *010/6086–2500* ✛ *10 km (6 mi) northeast of Jietai Temple, 45 km (28 mi) west of Beijing* 🖃 *Y35* ⊗ *Daily 8–5.*

MARCO POLO BRIDGE

16 km (10 mi) southwest of Beijing's Guanganmen Gate.

Built in 1192 and reconstructed after severe flooding during the Qing Dynasty, this impressive span—known as Marco Polo Bridge because it was praised by the Italian wayfarer—is Beijing's oldest bridge. Its 11 segmented stone arches cross the Yongding River on what was once the imperial highway that linked Beijing with central China. The bridge's marble balustrades support nearly 485 carved stone lions that decorate elaborate handrails. Note the giant stone slabs that comprise the bridge's original roadbed. Carved imperial stelae at either end of the span commemorate the bridge and surrounding scenery.

The Marco Polo Bridge is best remembered in modern times as the spot where invading Japanese armies clashed with Chinese soldiers on June 7, 1937. The assault began Japan's brutal eight-year occupation of eastern China, which ended with Tokyo's surrender at the end of World War II. The bridge has become a popular field-trip destination for Beijing students. On the Beijing side of the span is the **Memorial Hall of the War of Resistance Against Japan.** Below the bridge on the opposite shore, local entrepreneurs rent horses (the asking price is Y120 per hour, but you should bargain) and lead tours of the often-dry grassy riverbed.

✉ *Near Xidaokou, Fengtai District, Beijing* ☎ *010/8389–3919* 💳 *Y10*
🕐 *Daily 8:30–6.*

ZHOUKOUDIAN PEKING MAN SITE

48 km (30 mi) southwest of Beijing.

This area of lime mines and craggy foothills ranks among the world's great paleontological sites (and served as the setting for Amy Tan's *The Bonesetter's Daughter*). In 1929 anthropologists, drawn to Zhoukoudian by apparently human "dragon bones" found in a Beijing apothecary, unearthed a complete cranium and other fossils dubbed homo erectus pekinensis, or Peking Man. These early remains, believed to be nearly 700,000 years old, suggest (as do similar homo-erectus discoveries in Indonesia) that humankind's most recent ancestor originated in Asia, not Europe (though today some scientists posit that humans evolved in Africa first and migrated to Asia). A large-scale excavation in the early 1930s further unearthed six skullcaps and other hominid remains, stone tools, evidence of fire, plus a multitude of animal bones, many at the bottom of a large sinkhole believed to be a trap for woolly rhinos and other large game. Sadly, the Peking Man fossils disappeared under mysterious circumstances during World War II, leaving researchers only plaster casts to contemplate. Subsequent digs at Zhoukoudian have yielded nothing equivalent to Peking Man, although archaeologists haven't yet abandoned the search. Trails lead to several hillside excavation sites. A small museum showcases a few (dusty) Peking Man statues, a collection of Paleolithic artifacts, two mummies, and some fine animal fossils, including a bear skeleton and a saber-toothed tiger skull. Because of the importance of Peking Man and the potential for other finds in the area, Zhoukoudian is a UNESCO World Heritage Site, but it may not be of much interest to those without a particular inclination for the subject. If you should find yourself here with little to do after your museum visit and the few dig locations, consider a little hike into the surrounding hills, which are named the Dragon Bone Mountains. ✉ *Zhoukoudian* ☎ *010/6930–1272* 💳 *Y30* 🕐 *Daily 9:30–5.*

INTERACTING WITH THE LOCALS

A foreigner traveling in rural China is something of a sensation. The attention visitors receive may seem overwhelming, but it is usually good-natured and best responded to with politeness. Chinese locals can be extremely kind, inviting you to their homes for tea, a meal, or even to stay the night. If you wish to turn them down, do so politely. However, if you have time, taking them up on their hospitality can be extremely rewarding. Mostly, those who invite you to their homes are doing it out of kindness (Confucius said, "To have friends come from afar, isn't that happiness?"). A gift of a small quantity of fruit or a bottle of *Baijiu* (a Chinese liquor) is always appreciated.

8

OLD DRAGON'S HEAD

GETTING THERE

Distance: Approximately 300 km (186 mi) northeast of Beijing

Tours: Contact Cycle China, Beijing Service, Wild China, or Abercrombie & Kent

By Car: A car to Shanhaiguan is expensive (around Y2,500 for two days)

FAST FACTS

Hours: 7:30 AM to 5 PM

Admission: Y40

Laolongtou ("Old Dragon's Head") is where the Great Wall, likened to a dragon slithering over mountains, sticks its head into the Bohai Sea. The wall's easternmost surviving section, which was destroyed by invading British forces in 1900, is now renovated and flat with an old brick jetty and temple at its terminus, where the emperor once prayed to the sea god. If you stay overnight, as many do, choose either to stay in courtyard-style homes hidden around the backstreets or the lovely **Haisheng Garden Hotel** (✉ 118 Nanhai Xi Lu ☎ 033/5517–2999 ⊕ www.hshy.com).

The train ride is long from Beijing (3 hours), so set out early. If you want to see more wall, the First Pass Under Heaven (Tianxiadiyiguan; thought to be the first major guard house on the Great Wall) is just a short walk or cheap taxi ride from the train station. The very steep and scenic Jiaoshan Great Wall is another short ride from there.

■ TIP➔ Note that, though a popular site for Chinese tourists, this area is far from Beijing and not well set up for foreign tourists.

YUNJU TEMPLE

75 km (47 mi) southwest of Beijing.

Yunju Temple is best known for its mind-boggling collection of 14,278 minutely carved Buddhist tablets. To protect the Buddhist canon from destruction by Taoist emperors, the devout Tang-era monk Jing Wan carved Buddhist scriptures into stone slabs that he hid in sealed caves in the cliffs of a mountain. Jing Wan spent 30 years creating these tablets until his death in AD 637; his disciples continued his work for the next millennium into the 17th century, thereby compiling one of the most extensive Buddhist libraries in the world. A small pagoda at the center of the temple complex commemorates the remarkable monk. Although the tablets were originally stored inside Shijing Mountain behind the temple, they are now housed in rooms built along the temple's southern perimeter.

Four central prayer halls, arranged along the hillside above the main gate, contain impressive Ming-era bronze Buddhas. The last in this row, the Dabei Hall, displays the spectacular *Thousand-Arm Avalokiteshvara*. This 13-foot-tall bronze sculpture—which actually has 24 arms and 5 heads and stands in a giant lotus flower—is believed to embody boundless compassion. A group of pagodas, led by the 98-foot-tall Northern Pagoda, is all that remains of the original Tang complex. These pagodas are remarkable for their Buddhist reliefs and ornamental patterns. Heavily damaged during the Japanese occupation and again by Maoist radicals in the 1960s, the temple complex remains under renovation. ⊠ *Off Fangshan Lu, Nanshangle Xiang, Fangshan County* ☎ *010/ 6138–9612* ✑ *Y40* ☉ *Daily 8:30–5:30.*

EASTERN QING TOMBS

125 km (78 mi) east of Beijing.

Modeled on the Thirteen Ming Tombs, the Eastern Qing Tombs replicate the Ming spirit ways, walled tomb complexes, and subterranean burial chambers. But they're even more extravagant in their scale and grandeur, and far less touristy. The ruins contain the remains of 5 emperors, 14 empresses, and 136 imperial concubines, all laid to rest in a broad valley chosen by Emperor Shunzhi (1638–61) while on a hunting expedition. By the Qing's collapse in 1911, the tomb complex covered some 18 square mi (46 square km) of farmland and forested hillside, making it the most expansive burial ground in all China.

The Eastern Qing Tombs are in much better repair than their older Ming counterparts. Although several of the tomb complexes have undergone extensive renovation, none is overdone. Peeling paint, grassy courtyards, and numerous stone bridges and pathways convey a sense of the area's original grandeur. Often, visitors are so few that you may feel as if you've stumbled upon an ancient ruin unknown beyond the valley's farming villages.

Of the nine tombs open to the public, two are not to be missed. The first is **Yuling,** the resting place of the Qing Dynasty's most powerful sovereign, Emperor Qianlong (1711–99), who ruled China for 59 years. Beyond the outer courtyards, Qianlong's burial chamber is accessible from inside Stela Hall, where an entry tunnel descends some 65 feet (20 m) into the ground and ends at the first of three elaborately carved marble gates. Beyond, exquisite carvings of Buddhist images and sutras rendered in Tibetan adorn the tomb's walls and ceiling. Qianlong was laid to rest, along with his empress and two concubines, in the third and final marble vault, amid priceless offerings looted by warlords early in the 20th century.

Dingdongling was built for the infamous Empress Dowager Cixi (1835–1908). Known for her failure to halt Western-imperialist encroachment, Cixi once spent funds allotted to strengthen China's navy on a traditional stone boat for the lake at the Summer Palace. Her burial compound, reputed to have cost 72 tons of silver, is the most elaborate (if not the largest) at the Eastern Qing Tombs. Many of its stone carvings are considered significant because the phoenix, which symbolized the female, is level with, or even above, the imperial (male) dragon— a feature, ordered, no doubt, by the empress herself. A peripheral hall paneled in gold leaf displays some of the luxuries amassed by Cixi and

TIANJIN

Tianjin (96 km [60 mi] east of Beijing) is a huge port city of 10 million people known to Beijingers for its *baozi* (steamed buns), wonderful antiques market, and international architecture, including British, French, American, German, Japanese, Russian, Italian, Austrian-Hungarian, and Belgian examples. For the best antiques shopping in China, head to Tianjin on a Wednesday evening train, check into your hotel, have dinner, and go to bed so you can wake up early for the **Shenyangdao Antiques Market,** which opens at 4 AM every Thursday and is well picked over by mid-morning. When buying at Shenyangdao, be wary of items dubbed genuine antiques. They do exist, but are very rare; even the prettiest, oldest looking pieces can be fake. Some are made with antique wood that has been recently recycled into "antiques" by skilled artisans. The casual collector should remember: buy things because you like them, not because you think they are inherently valuable. Feel free to haggle relentlessly. Trains (Y30) to Tianjin leave Beijing Station every hour from 6 AM until 5:30 PM, and buses (Y25) leave around the clock.

her entourage, including embroidered gowns, jewelry, imported cigarettes, and even a coat for one of her dogs. In a bow to tourist kitsch, the compound's main hall contains a wax statue of Cixi sitting Buddha-like on a lotus petal flanked by a chambermaid and a eunuch.

The Eastern Qing Tombs are a two- to three-hour drive from the capital. The rural scenery is dramatic, and the trip is one of the best full-day excursions outside Beijing. Consider bringing a bed sheet, a bottle of wine, and boxed lunches, as the grounds are ideal for a picnic. ⊠ *Near Malanguan, Hebei province, Zunhua County* ☎ *0315/694–5348* 🖃 *Y80* ⊗ *Daily 8:30–5.*

At a Glance

ENGLISH	PINYIN	CHINESE CHARACTERS
POINTS OF INTEREST		
Beidaihe	Běidàihé	北戴河
Beijing Eunuch Culture Exhibition Hall	Běijīng huànguān wénhuà chénlièguǎn	北京宦官文化陈列馆
Changling	cháng líng	长陵
Dingling	dìng líng	定陵
Eastern Qing Tombs	qīng dōnglíng	清东陵
Fahai Temple	fǎhǎi sì	法海寺
The Great Wall	Cháng chéng	长城
Jietai Temple	jiè tái sì	界台寺
Marco Polo Bridge	lú gōu qiáo	卢沟桥
The Spirit Way	shén lù	神路
Tanzhe Temple	tán zhè sì	潭柘寺
Thirteen Ming Tombs	míng Shísānlíng	明十三陵
Tianjin	Tiānjīn	天津
Tomb of Tian Yi	Tián yì mù	田义墓
Yesanpo	yě sān pō	野三坡
Yunju Temple	yún jū sì	云居寺
Zhaoling tomb	zhāo líng	昭陵
Zhoukoudian Peking Man Site	Zhōu kǒu diàn běi jīng rén yí zhǐ	周口店北京人遗址

8

VOCABULARY
GUIDE

**PRONUNCIATION
& VOCABULARY**

PRONUNCIATION & VOCABULARY

	Chinese	English Equivalent	Chinese	English Equivalent
Consonants				
	b	boat	p	pass
	m	mouse	f	flag
	d	dock	t	tongue
	n	nest	l	life
	g	goat	k	keep
	h	house	j	and yet
	q	chicken	x	short
	zh	judge	ch	church
	sh	sheep	r*	read
	z	seeds	c	dots
	s	seed		
Vowels				
	ü	you	ia	yard
	üe	you + e	ian	yen
	a	father	iang	young
	ai	kite	ie	yet
	ao	now	o	all
	e	earn	ou	go
	ei	day	u	wood
	er	curve	ua	waft
	i	yield	uo	wall
	i (after z, c, s, zh, ch, sh)	thunder		

Word Order
The basic Chinese sentence structure is the same as in English, following the pattern of subject-verb-object:

He took my pen.	Tā ná le wǒ de bǐ.
s v o	s v o

Nouns
There are no articles in Chinese, although there are many "counters," which are used when a certain number of a given noun is specified. Various attributes of a noun—such as size, shape, or use—determine which

counter is used with that noun. Chinese does not distinguish between singular and plural.

a pen	yìzhī bǐ
a book	yìběn shū

Verbs

Chinese verbs are not conjugated, and they do not have tenses. Instead, a system of word order, word repetition, and the addition of a number of adverbs serves to indicate the tense of a verb, whether the verb is a suggestion or an order, or even whether the verb is part of a question. *Tāzài ná wǒ de bǐ.* (He is taking my pen.) *Tā ná le wǒ de bǐ.* (He took my pen.) *Tā you méi you ná wǒ de bǐ?* (Did he take my pen?) *Tā yào ná wǒ de bǐ.* (He will take my pen.)

Tones

In English, intonation patterns can indicate whether a sentence is a statement (He's hungry.), a question (He's hungry?), or an exclamation (He's hungry!). In Chinese, words have a particular tone value, and these tones are important in determining the meaning of a word. Observe the meanings of the following examples, each said with one of the four tones found in standard Chinese: *mā* (high, steady tone): mother; *má* (rising tone, like a question): fiber; *mǎ* (dipping tone): horse; and *mà* (dropping tone): swear.

Phrases

You don't need to master the entire Chinese language to spend a week in China, but taking charge of a few key phrases in the language can aid you in just getting by.

Common Greetings

Hello/Good morning.	Nǐ hǎo/Zǎoshàng hǎo.
Good evening.	Wǎnshàng hǎo.
Good-bye.	Zàijiàn.
Title for a married woman or an older unmarried woman	Tàitai/Fūrén
Title for a young and unmarried woman	Xiǎojiě
Title for a man	Xiānshēng
How are you?	Nǐ hǎo ma?
Fine, thanks. And you?	Hěn hǎo. Xièxie. Nǐ ne?
What is your name?	Nǐ jiào shénme míngzi?
My name is . . .	Wǒ jiào . . .

Beijing
Essentials

PLANNING TOOLS, EXPERT INSIGHT,
GREAT CONTACTS

There are planners, and there are those who fly by the seat of their pants. We happily place ourselves among the planners. Our writers and editors try to anticipate all the issues you may face before and during any journey, and then they do their research. This section is the product of their efforts. Use it to get excited about your trip to Beijing, to inform your travel planning, or to guide you on the road should the seat of your pants start to feel threadbare.

GETTING STARTED

We're proud of our Web site: Fodors.com is a great place to begin any journey. Scan "Travel Wire" for suggested itineraries, travel deals, and restaurant and hotel openings. Check out "Booking" to re-search prices and book plane tickets, hotel rooms, rental cars, and vacation pack-ages. Head to "Talk" for on-the-ground pointers from travelers who frequent our message boards. You can also link to loads of other travel-related resources.

▌RESOURCES

ONLINE TRAVEL TOOLS

For a general overview of traveling in China, try the China National Tourism Office's Web site. The state-run travel agency, China Travel Services, is another helpful starting place.

All About Beijing **Beijing Expat** ⊕ beijing. asiaxpat.com has pages and pages of advice and listings from foreigners living in Beijing.

Beijing Guide ⊕ www.thebeijingguide.com is a quirky, interactive guide bursting with local information; it's maintained by a local expat.

Beijing International ⊕ www.ebeijing.gov. cn, if slightly dry, is the comprehensive gov-ernment guide to the city.

Beijing Tourism Administration ⊕ english. bjta.gov.cn offers well-organized information on sights and activities in Beijing, as well as hotel and restaurant information.

China Digital Times ⊕ www. chinadigitaltimes.net is an excellent Berkeley-run site tracking China-related news and culture.

Chinese Government Portal ⊕ english.gov.cn.

China National Tourism Office ⊕ www.cnto. org.

China Travel Services ⊕ www. chinatravelservice.com.

Business **China Business Weekly** ⊕ www. chinadaily.com.cn is a weekly magazine from *China Daily* newspaper. **Chinese Government Business Site** ⊕ english.gov.cn/business.htm offers news, links, and information on busi-ness-related legal issues from the Chinese government.

Culture & Entertainment **Beijing Scene** ⊕ www.beijingscene.com is an online version of a quirky local English-language weekly, packed with cultural insight and listings. **Beijing This Month** ⊕ www.btmbeijing.com is the online version of a free monthly magazine with useful information for tourists. **Beijing Weekend** ⊕ www.chinadaily.com.cn is a weekly supplement from *China Daily* news-paper, with shopping, dining, and entertain-ment reviews. **Chinese Culture** ⊕ www. chinaculture.org has a detailed, searchable database with information on Chinese art, lit-erature, film, and history. **China Vista** ⊕ www.chinavista.com/experience presents incredibly detailed information on all aspects of Chinese arts and culture. **That's Beijing** ⊕ www.thatsbj.com has a weekly e-mail newsletter about what's going on in the city. Their classifieds are excellent, too.

Newspapers *China Daily* ⊕ www.chinadaily. com.cn is a leading English-language daily. *People's Daily* ⊕ english.peopledaily.com.cn is the English edition of China's most popu-lar—and most propagandistic—local daily.

Safety **Transportation Security Administra-tion** (TSA) ⊕ www.tsa.gov.

Time Zones **Timeanddate.com** ⊕ www. timeanddate.com/worldclock can help you figure out the correct time anywhere in the world.

VISITOR INFORMATION

For general information, including advice on tours, insurance, and safety, call or visit China National Tourist Office's Web site, as well as that run by the Beijing Tourism Administration (BTA). ▌TIP→ **The BTA maintains a 24-hour hotline for tourist in-quiries and complaints, with operators fluent** in English. BTA also runs Beijing Tourist Information Centers, whose staff can help you with free maps and directions in Beijing.

The two best-known Chinese travel agencies are China International Travel Service (CITS) and China Travel Service (CTS), both under the same government ministry. Although they have some tourist information, they are businesses, so don't expect endless resources if you're not booking through them.

China National Tourist Offices United States ☎ 888/760-8218 New York, 800/670-2228 Los Angeles ⊕ www.cnto.org.

Beijing Tourist Information Beijing Tourism Administration BTA ☎ 010/6513-0828 ⊕ english.bjta.gov.cn. **China International Travel Service** CITS ☎ 010/6522-2991 Beijing ⊕ www.cits.com.cn ☎ 626/568-8993 U.S. ⊕ www.citsusa.com. **China Travel Service** CTS ☎ 010/6462-2288 Beijing Head Office ⊕ www.ctsho.com ✉ New York ☎ 800/899-8618 ⊕ www.chinatravelservice.com.

■ THINGS TO CONSIDER

GOVERNMENT ADVISORIES

As different countries have different world views, look at travel advisories from a range of governments to get more of a sense of what's going on. And be sure to parse the language carefully. For example, a warning to "avoid all travel" carries more weight than one urging you to "avoid nonessential travel," and both are much stronger than a plea to "exercise caution." A U.S. government travel warning is more permanent (though not necessarily more serious) than a so-called public announcement, which carries an expiration date. The U.S. Department of State's Web site has more than just travel warnings and advisories. The consular information sheets issued for every country have general safety tips, entry requirements (though be sure to verify these with the country's embassy), and other useful details.

GET INSPIRED

GOOD READS

Award-Winning Fiction: Exiled Nobel Prize-winner Gao Xinjiang's novel *Soul Mountain* is part-travelogue, part-reflection on recent Chinese history. Ha Jin's *Waiting*, a Communist-era love story, won the 1999 National Book Award.

China 101: China's big issues of the last 25 years form *The China Reader: The Reform Era*, edited by Orville Schell and David Shambaugh. *The Search for Modern China* by Jonathan Spence, is a hefty but accessible introduction to the last 400 years of Chinese history.

How About Mao: Dr. Li Zhisui's *The Private Life of Chairman Mao* gives readable insight into the red-book-toting leader.

CINEMA PLEASE

Our Favorites: Chen Kaige's *Together* chronicles a father and his violin-prodigy son coming to Beijing. Sex, drugs, and rock and roll play a big role in indie director Zhang Yuan's *Beijing Bastards*. A country boy becomes an urban bicycle messenger in newcomer Wang Xiaoshuai's coming-of-age drama *Beijing Bicycle*.

Censored!: Lou Ye's *Summer Palace* is a love story hinging on the Tiananmen Square demonstrations—it's banned in China.

Wuxia Wonders: Graceful martial arts and classic stories come together in Ang Lee's *Crouching Tiger, Hidden Dragon* and Zhang Yimou's *Hero*.

Beijing Opera: Chen Kaige's *Farewell, My Concubine* reveals the turbulent world of Beijing opera.

General Information & Warnings **U.S. Department of State** ⊕ www.travel.state.gov.

GEAR

Most Chinese people dress for comfort, and you can do the same. There's little risk of offending people with your dress; Westerners tend to attract attention regardless of attire. Although miniskirts are best left at home, pretty much anything else goes. Sturdy, comfortable, closed-toe walking shoes are a must. Summers are dusty and hot, so lightweight slacks, shorts, and shirts are great options. A light raincoat is useful in spring and fall. Come winter, thermal long underwear is a lifesaver. A long overcoat, scarf, hat, and gloves will help keep icy winds at bay. That said, in Beijing you can arrive unprepared: the city is a shopper's paradise. If you can't fit a bulky jacket in your suitcase, buy a cheap one upon arrival. Scarves, gloves, and hats are also cheap and easy to find.

Carry packets of tissues and anti-bacterial hand wipes with you—toilet paper isn't common in Chinese restrooms. A small flashlight with extra batteries is also useful. Chinese pharmacies can be limited, so take adequate stocks if you're picky about lotions and potions. Beijing is quite dry, so cream is a must. Choice is also limited for feminine-hygiene products, so bring along extra.

If you're planning a longer trip or will be using local guides, bring a few items from your home country as gifts, such as candy, T-shirts, and small cosmetic items such as lipstick and nail polish. Be wary of giving American magazines and books, though, as these can be considered propaganda.

■ TIP➔ **If you're a U.S. citizen traveling abroad, consider registering online with the State Department (⊕ https://travelregistration.state.gov/ibrs/), so the government will know to look for you should a crisis occur in the country you're visiting.**

PASSPORTS & VISAS

All U.S. citizens, even infants, need a valid passport with a tourist visa stamped in it to enter China (except for Hong Kong, where you only need a valid passport). Getting a tourist visa (known as an "L" visa) in the United States is straightforward. Standard visas are for single-entry stays of up to 30 days and are valid for 90 days from the day of issue (NOT the day of entry), so don't get your visa too far in advance. Costs range from $50 for a tourist visa issued within 2 to 3 working days to $80 for a same-day service.

Travel agents in Hong Kong can also issue visas to visit mainland China. ■ TIP➔ **The visa application will ask your occupation. The Chinese don't look favorably upon those who work in publishing or the media. People in these professions routinely state "teacher" under "occupation."**

Under no circumstances should you overstay your visa. To extend your visa, go to the Division of the Entry and Exit of Aliens of the Beijing Municipal Public Security Bureau a week before your visa expires. The office is also known as the Foreigner's Police; it's open weekdays 8 AM to noon, 1:30 PM to 4 PM. It's usually no problem to get a month's extension on a tourist visa. Bring your passport and a registration of temporary residency from your hotel. Keep in mind that you'll need to leave your passport there for 5 to 7 days. If you are trying to extend a business visa, you'll

---

WORD OF MOUTH

"Unless you'll be attending a formal business or social meeting you will not need dressy clothing in China. The Chinese themselves tend to dress quite casually. I would just take one 'smart casual' outfit for eating out, theatre performances and the like." —Neil Oz

need the above items as well as a letter from the business that originally invited you to China.

Info **Visa to Asia** ⊕ www.visatoasia.com/china.html has up-to-date information on visa application to China.

In the U.S. Chinese Consulate, New York ☎ 212/244-9456 ⊕ www.nyconsulate.prchina.org. **Visa Office of Chinese Embassy, Washington** ☎ 202/338-6688 ⊕ www.china-embassy.org.

Visa Extensions **Division of the Entry and Exit of Aliens, Beijing Municipal Public Security Bureau** ✉ 2 Andingmen Dong Dajie, Beijing ☎ 010/8401-5292 ⊕ http://www.ebeijing.gov.cn/Government/Organizations/t1528.htm.

PASSPORTS

We're always surprised at how few Americans have passports—only 25% at this writing. This number is expected to grow in coming years, when it becomes impossible to re-enter the United States from trips to neighboring Canada or Mexico without one. Remember this: a passport verifies both your identity and nationality—a great reason to have one.

U.S. passports are valid for 10 years. You must apply in person if you're getting a passport for the first time; if your previous passport was lost, stolen, or damaged; or if your previous passport has expired and was issued more than 15 years ago or when you were under 16. All children under 18 must appear in person to apply for or renew a passport. Both parents must accompany any child under 14 (or send a notarized statement with their permission) and provide proof of their relationship to the child.

There are 13 regional passport offices, as well as 7,000 passport-acceptance facilities in post offices, public libraries, and other governmental offices. If you're renewing a passport, you can do so by mail. Forms are available at passport-acceptance facilities and online.

The cost to apply for a new passport is $97 for adults, $82 for children under 16; renewals are $67. Allow six weeks for processing, both for first-time passports and renewals. For an expediting fee of $60 you can reduce this time to about two weeks. If your trip is less than two weeks away, you can get a passport even more rapidly by going to a passport office with the necessary documentation. Private expediters can get things done in as little as 48 hours, but charge hefty fees for their services.

■ TIP➔ Before your trip, make two copies of your passport's data page (one for someone at home and another for you to carry separately). Or scan the page and e-mail it to someone at home and/or yourself.

VISAS

A visa is essentially formal permission to enter a country. Visas allow countries to keep track of you and other visitors—and generate revenue (from application fees). You *always* need a visa to enter a foreign country; however, many countries routinely issue tourist visas on arrival, particularly to U.S. citizens. When your passport is stamped or scanned in the immigration line, you're actually being issued a visa. Sometimes you have to stand in a separate line and pay a small fee to get your stamp before going through immigration, but you can still do this at the airport on arrival. Getting a visa isn't always that easy. Some countries require that you arrange for one in advance of your trip. There's usually—but not always—a fee involved, and said fee may be nominal ($10 or less) or substantial ($100 or more).

If you must apply for a visa in advance, you can usually do it in person or by mail. When you apply by mail, you send your passport to a designated consulate, where your passport will be examined and the visa issued. Expediters—usually the same ones who handle expedited passport applications—can do all the work of obtaining your visa for you; however, there's always an additional cost (often more than $50 per visa).

Trip Insurance Resources

INSURANCE COMPARISON SITES		
Insure My Trip.com		www.insuremytrip.com.
Square Mouth.com		www.quotetravelinsurance.com.
COMPREHENSIVE TRAVEL INSURERS		
Access America	866/807-3982	www.accessamerica.com.
CSA Travel Protection	800/873-9855	www.csatravelprotection.com.
HTH Worldwide	610/254-8700 or 888/243-2358	www.hthworldwide.com.
Travelex Insurance	888/457-4602	www.travelex-insurance.com.
Travel Guard International	715/345-0505 or 800/826-4919	www.travelguard.com.
Travel Insured International	800/243-3174	www.travelinsured.com.
MEDICAL-ONLY INSURERS		
International Medical Group	800/628-4664	www.imglobal.com.
International SOS	215/942-8000 or 713/521-7611	www.internationalsos.com.
Wallach & Company	800/237-6615 or 504/687-3166	www.wallach.com.

Most visas limit you to a single trip—basically during the actual dates of your planned vacation. Other visas allow you to visit as many times as you wish for a specific period of time. Remember that requirements change, sometimes at the drop of a hat, and the burden is on you to make sure that you have the appropriate visas. Otherwise, you'll be turned away at the airport or, worse, deported after you arrive in the country. No company or travel insurer gives refunds if your travel plans are disrupted because you didn't have the correct visa.

U.S. Passport Information U.S. Department of State ☎ 877/487-2778 ⊕ http://travel. state.gov/passport.

U.S. Passport & Visa Expediters A. Briggs Passport & Visa Expeditors ☎ 800/806-0581 or 202/464-3000 ⊕ www.abriggs.com. **American Passport Express** ☎ 800/455-5166 or 603/559-9888 ⊕ www. americanpassport.com. **Passport Express** ☎ 800/362-8196 or 401/272-4612 ⊕ www. passportexpress.com. **Travel Document Systems** ☎ 800/874-5100 or 202/638-3800 ⊕ www.traveldocs.com. **Travel the World Visas** ☎ 866/886-8472 or 301/495-7700 ⊕ www.world-visa.com.

SHOTS & MEDICATIONS

No immunizations are required for entry into China, but it's a good idea to be immunized against typhoid and Hepatitis A and B before traveling to Beijing; also a good idea is to get routine shots for tetanus-diphtheria and measles. In winter, a flu vaccination is also smart.

Health Warnings National Centers for Disease Control & Prevention (CDC) ☎ 877/394-8747 international travelers' health line ⊕ www.cdc.gov/travel. **World Health Organization** (WHO) ⊕ www.who.int.

TRIP INSURANCE

Comprehensive trip insurance is valuable if you're booking a very expensive or complicated trip, or if you're booking far in advance. Comprehensive travel policies typically cover trip cancellation and interruption due to personal emergency, illness, or, in some cases, acts of terrorism. Such policies also cover evacuation and medical care. Another type of coverage is financial default—that is, when your trip is disrupted because a tour, airline, or cruise line goes out of business.

BOOKING YOUR TRIP

Unless your cousin is a travel agent, you're probably among the millions of people who make most of their travel arrangements online. But have you ever wondered just what the differences are between an online travel agent (a Web site through which you make reservations instead of going directly to the airline, hotel, or car-rental company), a discounter (a firm that does a high volume of business with a hotel chain or airline and accordingly gets good prices), a wholesaler (one that makes cheap reservations in bulk and then resells them to people like you), and an aggregator (one that compares all the offerings so you don't have to)? Is it truly better to book directly on an airline or hotel Web site? And when does a real live travel agent come in handy?

ONLINE

You really have to shop around. A travel wholesaler such as Hotels.com or Hotel-Club.net can be a source of good rates, as can discounters such as Hotwire or Price-line, particularly if you can bid for your hotel room or airfare. Indeed, such sites sometimes have deals that are unavailable elsewhere. They do, however, tend to work only with hotel chains (which makes them just plain useless for getting hotel reservations outside of major cities) or big airlines (so that often leaves out upstarts like jetBlue and some foreign carriers like Air India). Also, with discounters and wholesalers you must generally pre-pay, and everything is nonrefundable. And before you fork over the dough, be sure to check the terms and conditions, so you know what a given company will do for you if there's a problem and what you'll have to deal with on your own.

■ TIP → To be absolutely sure everything was processed correctly, confirm reservations made through online travel agents, discounters, and wholesalers directly with your hotel before leaving home.

Booking engines like Expedia, Travelocity, and Orbitz are actually travel agents, albeit high-volume online ones. And airline travel packagers like American Airlines Vacations and Virgin Vacations—well, they're travel agents, too. But they may still not work with all the world's hotels.

An aggregator site will search many sites and pull the best prices for airfares, hotels, and rental cars from them. Most aggregators compare the major travel-booking sites such as Expedia, Travelocity, and Orbitz; some also look at airline Web sites, though rarely the sites of smaller budget airlines. Some aggregators also compare other travel products, including complex packages—a good thing, as you can sometimes get the best overall deal by booking an air-and-hotel package.

WITH A TRAVEL AGENT

If you use an agent—brick-and-mortar or virtual—you'll pay a fee for the service. And know that the service you get from some online agents isn't comprehensive. For example Expedia and Travelocity don't search for prices on budget airlines like jetBlue, Southwest, or small foreign carriers. That said, some agents (online or not) do have access to fares that are difficult to find otherwise, and the savings can more than make up for any surcharge.

A knowledgeable brick-and-mortar travel agent can be a godsend if you're booking a cruise, a package trip that's not available to you directly, an air pass, or a complicated itinerary including several overseas flights. What's more, travel agents that specialize in a destination may have exclusive access to certain deals and insider information on things such as charter flights. Agents who specialize in types of travelers (senior citizens, gays and lesbians, naturists) or types of trips (cruises, luxury travel, safaris) can also be invaluable.

Online Booking Resources

AGGREGATORS		
Kayak	www.kayak.com	looks at cruises and vacation packages.
Mobissimo	www.mobissimo.com.	
Qixo	www.qixo.com	compares cruises, vacation packages, and even travel insurance.
Sidestep	www.sidestep.com	compares vacation packages and lists travel deals.
Travelgrove	www.travelgrove.com	compares cruises and vacation packages.
BOOKING ENGINES		
Cheap Tickets	www.cheaptickets.com	discounter.
Expedia	www.expedia.com	large online agency that charges a booking fee for airline tickets.
Hotwire	www.hotwire.com	discounter.
lastminute.com	www.lastminute.com	specializes in last-minute travel; the main site is for the U.K., but it has a link to a U.S. site.
Luxury Link	www.luxurylink.com	has auctions (surprisingly good deals) as well as offers on the high-end side of travel.
Onetravel.com	www.onetravel.com	discounter for hotels, car rentals, airfares, and packages.
Orbitz	www.orbitz.com	charges a booking fee for airline tickets, but gives a clear breakdown of fees and taxes before you book.
Priceline.com	www.priceline.com	discounter that also allows bidding.
Travel.com	www.travel.com	allows you to compare its rates with those of other booking engines.
Travelocity	www.travelocity.com	charges a booking fee for airline tickets, but promises good problem resolution.
ONLINE ACCOMMODATIONS		
Asia Hotels	www.asiahotels.com	good selection of hotels.
Asia Travel	www.asiatravel.com	popular place to get hotel deals.
CTrip	www.ctrip.com	China-based site with great information on hotels.
Hotelbook.com	www.hotelbook.com	focuses on independent hotels worldwide.
Hotel Club	www.hotelclub.net	good for major cities worldwide.
Hotels.com	www.hotels.com	big Expedia-owned wholesaler that offers rooms in hotels all over the world.
Quikbook	www.quikbook.com	offers "pay when you stay" reservations that allow you to settle your bill when you check out, not when you book.
Sino Hotel	www.sinohotel.com	has a good range of pricier hotels in Beijing.
OTHER RESOURCES		
Bidding For Travel	www.biddingfortravel.com	good place to figure out what you can get and for how much before you start bidding on, say, Priceline.

A top-notch agent planning your trip will make sure you get the correct visa application and complete it on time; the one booking your cruise may get you a cabin upgrade or arrange to have a bottle of champagne chilling in your cabin when you embark. And complain about the surcharges all you like, but when things don't work out the way you'd hoped, it's nice to have an agent to put things right.

■ TIP→ Remember that Expedia, Travelocity, and Orbitz are travel agents, not just booking engines. To resolve any problems with a reservation made through these companies, contact them first.

Booking hotels and flights for Beijing is easy to do without a travel agent, though you may get preferable rates (or room upgrades) if you use one. If you're planning to visit other places in China, a travel agent can save time and hassle, especially with internal flights, as schedules can change without warning. Be careful booking with Internet-based Chinese agencies from abroad, as not all are legal travel agencies.

Agent Resources **American Society of Travel Agents** ☎ 703/739-2782 ⊕ www.travelsense. org.

Beijing Travel Agents China Highlights ☎ 773/283-1999 China, 800/268-2918 U.S. ⊕ www.chinahighlights.com. **Wings Across Continents Travel Services** ☎ 010/5129-6371 Beijing, 708/409-1244 U.S ⊕ www.wacts.com.

ACCOMMODATIONS

Opening a hotel seems quite the thing to do in Beijing these days. That said, it's not always easy to choose a hotel: the Chinese star system is a little unpredictable, and Web sites are often misleading. For lesser establishments, try to get recent personal recommendations: the forums on Fodors. com are a great place to start.

Location, location, location" should be your mantra when booking a Beijing hotel, especially if you're only in town for a few days. It's a big city: there's no point schlepping halfway across it for one particular

hotel when a similar option is available in a more convenient area. Consider where you'll be going (Summer Palace? Forbidden City? Great Wall?), then pick your bed.

For dining and lodging price charts, *see* the opening pages of Chapters 6 and 7. Most hotels and other lodgings require you to give your credit-card details before they will confirm your reservation. If you don't feel comfortable e-mailing this information, ask if you can fax it (some places even prefer faxes). However you book, get confirmation in writing and have a copy of it handy when you check-in.

Be sure you understand the hotel's cancellation policy. Some places allow you to cancel without any kind of penalty—even if you prepaid to secure a discounted rate—if you cancel at least 24 hours in advance. Others require you to cancel a week in advance or penalize you the cost of one night. Small inns and B&Bs are most likely to require you to cancel far in advance. Most hotels allow children under a certain age to stay in their parents' room at no extra charge, but others charge for them as extra adults; find out the cutoff age for discounts.

■ TIP→ Assume that hotels operate on the European Plan (EP, no meals) unless we specify that they use the Breakfast Plan (BP, with full breakfast), Continental Plan (CP, continental

10 WAYS TO SAVE

1. Join "frequent guest" programs. You may get preferential treatment in room choice and/or upgrades in your favorite chains.

2. Call direct. You can sometimes get a better price if you call a hotel's local toll-free number (if available) rather than a central reservations number.

3. Check online. Check hotel Web sites, as not all chains are represented on all travel sites.

4. Look for specials. Always inquire about packages and corporate rates.

5. Look for price guarantees. For overseas trips, look for guaranteed rates. With your rate locked in you won't pay more, even if the price goes up in the local currency.

6. Look for weekend deals at business hotels. High-end chains catering to business travelers are often busy only on weekdays; to fill rooms they often drop rates dramatically on weekends.

7. Ask about taxes. Verify whether local hotel taxes are included in quoted rates. In some places taxes can add 20% or more to your bill.

8. Read the fine print. Watch for add-ons, including resort fees, energy surcharges, and "convenience" fees for such things as unlimited local phone service you won't use or a free newspaper in a language you can't read.

9. Know when to go. If your destination's high season is December through April and you're trying to book, say, in late April, you might save money by changing your dates by a week or two. Ask when rates go down, though: if your dates straddle peak and non-peak seasons, a property may still charge peak-season rates for the entire stay.

10. Weigh your options (we can't say this enough). Weigh transportation times and costs against the savings of staying in a hotel that's cheaper because it's out of the way.

breakfast), Full American Plan (**FAP**, all meals), Modified American Plan (**MAP**, breakfast and dinner) or are **all-inclusive** (**AI**, all meals and most activities).

APARTMENT & HOUSE RENTALS

There's an abundance of furnished short- and long-term rental properties in Beijing. Prices vary wildly. The priciest are luxury apartments and villas, usually far from the city center and best accessible by (chauffeur-driven) car. Usually described as "serviced apartments," these often include gyms and pools; rents can be over $2,000 a month. There are a lot of well-located mid-range properties in the city. They're usually clean, with new furnishings; rents start at $500 a month. Finally, for longer, budget-friendly stays, there are normal local apartments. These are firmly off the tourist circuit and often cost only a third of the price of the mid-range properties. Expect mismatched furniture, fewer amenities, and—we won't lie—varying insect populations.

Property sites like Wuwoo, Move and Stay, Sublet, and Pacific Properties have hundreds of apartments all over town. The online classifieds pages in local English-language magazines such as *That's Beijing* or *Beijing Scene* are good places to start.

HOMESTAYS

Single travelers can arrange homestays (often in combination with language courses) through China Homestay Club. Generally these are in upper-middle class homes that are about as expensive as a cheap hotel—prices range from $150 to $180 a week. Nine times out of 10, the family has a small child in need of daily English conversation classes. ChinaHomestay.org is a different organization that charges a single placement fee of $300 for a stay of three months or less.

Organizations China Homestay Club ⊕ www.homestay.com.cn. **ChinaHomestay. org** ⊕ www.chinahomestay.org.

HOSTELS

Hostels offer bare-bones lodging at low, low prices—often in shared dorm rooms with shared baths—to people of all ages, though the primary market is young travelers. Most hostels serve breakfast; dinner and/or shared cooking facilities may also be available. In some hostels you aren't allowed to be in your room during the day, and there may be a curfew at night. Nevertheless, hostels provide a sense of community, with public rooms where travelers often gather to share stories. Many hostels are affiliated with Hostelling International (HI), an umbrella group of hostel associations with some 4,500 member properties in more than 70 countries. Other hostels are completely independent and may be nothing more than a really cheap hotel.

Membership in any HI association, open to travelers of all ages, allows you to stay in HI-affiliated hostels at member rates. One-year membership is about $28 for adults; hostels charge about $10 to $30 per night. Members have priority if the hostel is full; they're also eligible for discounts around the world, even on rail and bus travel in some countries.

Budget accommodation options are improving in Beijing. However, the term "hostel" is still used vaguely—the only thing guaranteed is shared dorm rooms; other facilities vary. There are several clean youth hostels downtown, including three HI affiliates properties, but flea-ridden dumps are also common, so always ask to

see your room before paying. Try to pick a hostel close to a subway, and avoid properties beyond the Third Ring Road. A private room in a low-end hotel is often just as cheap as these so-called hostels; some guesthouses and hotels also have cheaper dorm beds in addition to regular rooms. **Hostelling International–USA** ☎ 301/495-1240 ⊕ www.hiusa.org.

Youth Hostel Association of China ☎ 020/8734-5080 ⊕ www.yhachina.com.

▌AIRLINE TICKETS

Most domestic airline tickets are electronic; international tickets may be either electronic or paper. With an e-ticket the only thing you receive is an e-mailed receipt citing your itinerary and reservation and ticket numbers. The greatest advantage of an e-ticket is that if you lose your receipt, you can simply print out another copy or ask the airline to do it for you at check-in. You usually pay a surcharge (up to $50) to get a paper ticket, if you can get one at all. The sole advantage of a paper ticket is that it may be easier to endorse over to another airline if your flight is canceled and the airline with which you booked can't accommodate you on another flight.

▌ TIP→ Discount air passes that let you travel economically in a country or region must often be purchased before you leave home. In some cases you can only get them through a travel agent.

Online Booking Resources

CONTACTS		
Beijing Scene		www.beijingscene.com.
Pacific Properties	010/6581-3728	www.worthenpacific.com.
Move and Stay		www.moveandstay.com/beijing.
Sublet.com		www.sublet.com.
That's Beijing		www.thatsbj.com.
Wuwoo	010/5166-7126	www.wuwoo.com.

Beijing, Xiamen, and Hong Kong are three of the cities included in the One World Alliance Visit Asia Pass. Cities are grouped into zones, and there's a flat rate for each zone. It doesn't include flights from the United States, however. Inquire through American Airlines, Cathay Pacific, or any other One World member. It won't be the cheapest way to get around, but you'll be flying on some of the world's best airlines.

If you are flying into Asia on a SkyTeam airline (Delta or Continental, for example) you're eligible to purchase their Asia Pass. It includes over 10 Chinese cities (including Beijing, Shanghai, Xian, and Hong Kong) as well as destinations in 20 other Asian and Australasian countries. The pass works on a coupon basis; the minimum three coupons cost $750, whereas six come to $1,410.

China Southern Airlines's China Air Pass offers excellent value if you're planning to fly to several destinations within the country: the minimum 3-coupon pass comes to $329, whereas 10 cost $909. The catch? You have to be flying in from abroad on one of their flights. Hong Kong isn't included in the pass, but Shenzhen, just over the border, gets you close enough. Bear in mind that Chinese domestic flight schedules can be changed or cancelled at a moment's notice.

Air Pass Info **Asia Pass** SkyTeam ☎ Continental: 800/523-3273, Delta: 800/221-1212 ⊕ www.skyteam.com. **China Air Pass** China Southern Airlines ☎ 888/338-8988 ⊕ www.cs-air.com. **Visit Asia Pass** OneWorld Alliance ☎ Cathay Pacific: 800/233-2742 ⊕ www.oneworld.com.

▌ RENTAL CARS

In a nutshell, renting a car is not a possibility when vacationing in Beijing: Neither U.S. licenses nor IDPs are recognized in China. However, this restriction should be cause for relief, as the city traffic is terrible and its drivers manic. A far better idea, if you want to get around by car, is to put yourself in the experienced hands of a local driver and sit back and relax. All the same, consider your itinerary carefully before doing so—the subway can be far quicker for central areas. Save the cars for excursions outside the city.

The quickest way to hire a car and driver is to flag down a taxi and hire it for the day. After some negotiating, expect to pay between Y350 and Y600, depending on the type of car. Most hotels can make arrangements for you, though they often charge you double that rate—you can probably guess whose pocket the difference goes into. Most drivers do not speak English, so it's a good idea to have your destination and hotel names written down in Chinese.

Another alternative is American car-rental agency Avis, which includes mandatory chauffeurs as part of all rental packages. A car and driver usually cost Y740 to Y850 per day for an economy vehicle. **Avis** ☎ 800/331-1084 ⊕ www.avis.com.

▌ VACATION PACKAGES

Packages *are not* guided excursions. Packages combine airfare, accommodations, and perhaps a rental car or other extras (theater tickets, guided excursions, boat trips, reserved entry to popular museums, transit passes), but they let you do your own thing. During busy periods packages may be your only option, as flights and rooms may be sold out otherwise. Packages will definitely save you time. They can also save you money, particularly in peak seasons, but—and this is a really big "but"—you should price each part of the package separately to be sure. And be aware that prices advertised on Web sites and in newspapers rarely include service charges or taxes, which can up your costs by hundreds of dollars.

▌ TIP→ Some packages and cruises are sold only through travel agents. Don't always assume that you can get the best deal by booking everything yourself. Each year consumers are stranded or lose their money when packagers—even large ones with excellent reputations—go out of business. How can you protect yourself? First, always pay with a credit card; if you have a problem, your credit-card company may help you resolve it. Second, buy trip insurance that covers default. Third, choose a company that belongs to the United States Tour Operators Association, whose members must set aside funds to cover defaults. Finally, choose a company that also participates in the Tour Operator Program of the American Society of Travel Agents (ASTA), which will act as mediator in any disputes. You can also check on the tour operator's reputation among travelers by posting an inquiry on one of the Fodors.com forums.

A vacation package to Beijing is unlikely to save you much money over booking things yourself, though it will make things quicker and easier. One of the services the company will provide is arranging your Chinese visa. If you're only staying in Beijing, it's probably just as easy to book your hotel online, though. You don't need a package for other activities—in fact it's cheaper to book excursions through one of Beijing's many local tour companies. It's smart to do this before your trip.

Organizations American Society of Travel Agents (ASTA) ☎ 703/739-2782 or 800/965-2782 ⊕ www.astanet.com. **United States Tour Operators Association** (USTOA) ☎ 212/599-6599 ⊕ www.ustoa.com.

▌ GUIDED TOURS

Guided tours are a good option when you don't want to do it all yourself. You travel along with a group (sometimes large, sometimes small), stay in prebooked hotels, eat with your fellow travelers (the cost of meals sometimes included in the price of your tour, sometimes not), and follow a schedule. But not all guided tours are an if-it's-Tuesday-this-must-be-Belgium experience. A knowledgeable guide can take you places that you might never discover on your own, and you may be pushed to see more than you would have otherwise. Tours aren't for everyone, but

they can be just the thing for trips to places where making travel arrangements is difficult or time-consuming (particularly when you don't speak the language). Whenever you book a guided tour, find out what's included and what isn't. A "land-only" tour includes all your travel (by bus, in most cases) in the destination, but not necessarily your flights to and from or even within it. Also, in most cases prices in tour brochures don't include fees and taxes. And remember that you'll be expected to tip your guide (in cash) at the end of the tour.

Few companies organize package trips only to Beijing. It's usually part of a bigger China or Asia multidestination package. You usually get a day or two in Beijing, with the same sights featured in most tours. If you want to explore the city in any kind of depth, you're better doing it by yourself or getting a private guide.

Shopping stops plague China tours, so inquire before booking as to when, where, and how many to expect. Although you're never obliged to buy anything, they can take up big chunks of your valuable travel time, and the products offered are always overpriced.

Overseas Adventure Travel takes pride in small groups and excellent guides. Their three China tours all have stops in Beijing. The Adventure Center has a huge variety of China packages, including trekking, cycling, and family tours. China Focus Travel has 10 different China tours—they squeeze in a lot for your money. R. Crusoe & Sons is an offbeat company that organizes small group or tailor-made private tours. For something more mainstream, try Pacific Delight; for luxury, check out Artisans of Leisure.

Recommended Companies Adventure Center ☎ 800/228-8747 ⊕ www.adventurecenter.com. **Artisans of Leisure** ☎ 800/214-8144 ⊕ www.artisansofleisure.com. **China Focus Travel** ☎ 800/868-7244 ⊕ www.chinafocustravel.com. **Overseas Adventure Travel** ☎ 800/493-6824 ⊕ www.oattravel.com. **Pacific Delight** ☎ 800/221-7179

⊕ www.pacificdelighttours.com. **R. Crusoe & Sons** ☎ 800/585-8555 ⊕ www.rcrusoe.com.

SPECIAL-INTEREST TOURS

BIKING

The Adventure Center has two cycling packages to China, one of which follows the route of the Great Wall. You can hire bikes from them, or take your own. Bike China Adventures organize trips of varying length and difficulty all over China. **Adventure Center** ☎ 800/228-8747 ⊕ www.adventurecenter.com. **Bike China Adventures** ☎ 800/818-1778 ⊕ www.bikechina.com.

CULTURE

Local guides are often creative when it comes to showing you the history and culture, so having an expert with you can make a big difference. Learning is the focus of Smithsonian Journeys' small-group tours, which are led by university professors. China experts also lead National Geographic's trips, but all that knowledge doesn't come cheap. Wild China is a local company with unusual trips: one of their cultural trips explores China's little-known Jewish history. **Smithsonian Journeys** ☎ 877/338-8687 ⊕ www.smithsonianjourneys.org. **National Geographic Expeditions** ☎ 888/966-8687

⊕ www.nationalgeographicexpeditions.com. **Wild China** ☎ 010/6465-6602 ⊕ www.wildchina.com.

CULINARY

Intrepid Travel is an Australian company offering a China Gourmet Traveler tour with market visits, cooking demonstrations, and plenty of good eats. Imperial Tours Culinary Tour combines sightseeing with cooking lectures and demonstrations, and lots of five-star dining. **Imperial Tours** ☎ 888/888-1970 ⊕ www.imperialtours.net. **Intrepid Travel** ☎ 61/3/9473-2626 ⊕ www.intrepidtravel.com.

HIKING

The Adventure Centre's Walking the Great Wall is an eight-day hiking tour along the wall itself. **The Adventure Center** ☎ 800/228-8747 ⊕ www.adventurecenter.com.

▌CRUISES

Crystal and Princess Cruises both have East Asia cruises.

Cruise Lines **Crystal Cruises** ☎ 310/785-9300 or 800/446-6620 ⊕ www.crystalcruises.com. **Princess Cruises** ☎ 661/753-0000 or 800/774-6237 ⊕ www.princess.com.

TRANSPORTATION

With the Olympics on China's mind, it's a feverish time for urban planners. The sound of pile-drivers fills the air as expressways, subways, buildings, and whole neighborhoods are being built or renovated. Maps go out of date almost overnight—try to get the latest one and hope not too much has changed.

On a map, the city's five concentric ring roads look like a target. At the heart is the Forbidden City. The Second Ring Road follows the line of the old city walls, and circular subway Line 2 runs below it. Note that, oddly, there is no First Ring Road. The Third Ring Road passes through part of Beijing's Central Business District (CBD) and links up with the Airport Expressway. Both of these ring roads are useful for cutting journey time between areas of central Beijing—they bypass the traffic-clogged downtown streets. However, even on the ring roads gridlock is common at rush hour.

The city's wide main streets are laid out on a grid system. Roads run north–south or east–west. These compass points often make up part of the street name, so *bei* (north), *dong* (east), *nan* (south), *xi* (west), and *zhong* (middle) are useful words to know. Networks of ancient lanes and alleys known as *hutong* run between these main streets—be sure to explore them as they're fast falling prey to developers.

Beijing's most important thoroughfare runs east–west along the top of Tiananmen Square. Generally known as Chang'an Jie, it actually changes names several times along its length (as do many other major streets).

The three remaining ring roads have equally unimaginative names (Fourth, Fifth, Sixth). They are too far out (5, 6½, and 10 mi, respectively) to be much use for getting around central Beijing, though fare-hungry taxi drivers would love you to believe otherwise.

▌ BY AIR

Beijing is one of China's three major international hubs, along with Shanghai and Hong Kong. You can catch a nonstop flight here from New York (13¾ hours), Chicago (13½ hours), Sydney (11½ hours), Los Angeles (13 hours), and London (11 hours). Note that Air China is the only operator that runs nonstop Los Angeles and London flights. Otherwise flights from Los Angeles generally stop in Tokyo, Seoul, Hong Kong, or Vancouver, taking between 17 and 25 hours.

Though most airlines say that reconfirming your return flight is unnecessary, some local airlines cancel your seat if you don't reconfirm. Play it safe: check with your airline beforehand.

Airlines & Airports Airline and Airport Links.com ⊕ www.airlineandairportlinks.com has links to many of the world's airlines and airports.

Airline Security Issues Transportation Security Administration ⊕ www.tsa.gov has answers for almost every question that might come up.

AIRPORTS

The efficient Beijing Capital International Airport (PEK) is 27 km (17 mi) northeast of the city center. There are two terminals, connected by a walkway. China Southern's domestic flights operate out of Terminal 1; all other airlines out of Terminal 2. If you can't find your flight on the departure board when you arrive, check that you're in the correct terminal.

Beijing's airport tax (enigmatically known as the "airport construction fee") is Y90 for international flights and Y50 for domestic. You pay before check-in by purchasing a coupon from the booths inside the terminal, which is then collected at the entrance to the main departure hall.

Clearing customs and immigration can take a while, especially in the morning, so make sure you arrive at least two hours before your scheduled flight time.

Both Chinese and Western-style fast-food outlets abound—Starbucks and KFC are just two names you'll recognize. Most are open from around 7 AM to 11 PM. Be warned that prices for even a soft drink vary wildly from place to place.

The airport is open all day and there is an uninspiring transit lounge in which to while away the hours. If you've got a long stopover and need a rest, consider buying a package from the Plaza Premium Traveler's Lounge, near Gate 11. It has comfortable armchairs, Internet access, newspapers, and a buffet. Unfortunately, it's closed between midnight and 6 AM. There's another rest area in the basement, with private rooms, which is open 24 hours. The third-floor recreation center has traditional massage facilities and a hairdresser.

While wandering the airport, someone may approach you offering to carry your luggage, or even just to give you directions. Be aware that this "helpful" stranger will almost certainly expect payment.

Airport Information Beijing Capital International Airport (PEK) ☎ 010/6456-3604 ⊕ www.bcia.com.cn.

GROUND TRANSPORTATION

The easiest way to get from the airport to Beijing is by taxi. In addition, most major hotels have representatives at the airport able to arrange a car or minivan. When departing from Beijing by plane, prebook airport transport through your hotel.

When you arrive, head for the clearly labeled taxi line just outside the terminal, beyond a small covered parking area. The (usually long) line moves quickly. Ignore offers from touts trying to coax you away from the line—they're privateers looking to rip you off. At the head of the line, a dispatcher will give you your taxi's number, useful in case of complaints or forgotten luggage. Prices per kilometer are displayed on the side of the cab. Insist that drivers use their meters, and do not

negotiate a fare. If the driver is unwilling to comply, feel free to change taxis.

Most of the taxis serving the airport are large-model cars, with a flagfall of Y12 (good for 3½ km) plus Y2 per additional kilometer. The trip to the center of Beijing costs around Y100, including the Y10 toll for the airport expressway. If you're caught in rush-hour traffic, expect standing surcharges. In light traffic it takes about 40 minutes to reach the city center, during rushhour expect a one-hour cab ride. After 11 PM, taxis impose a 20% late-night surcharge.

Air-conditioned airport shuttle buses are a cheaper way of getting into town. There are six numbered routes, all of which leave from outside the arrivals area. Tickets cost Y16—buy them from the ticket booth just inside the arrivals hall. Most services run every 15 to 30 minutes. There's a detailed route map on the airport Web site.

FLIGHTS

Air China is the country's flagship carrier. It operates nonstop flights from Beijing to various North American and European cities. Its safety record has improved dramatically, and it is now part of Star Alliance. China Southern is the major carrier for domestic routes. Like all Chinese carriers, it's a regional subsidiary of the Civil Aviation Administration of China (CAAC).

You can make reservations and buy tickets in the United States directly through airline Web sites or with travel agencies. It's worth contacting a Chinese travel agency like China International Travel Service (CITS) (⇨ Visitor Information) to compare prices, as these can vary substantially.

The service on most Chinese airlines is more on-par with low-cost American airlines than with big international carriers—be prepared for limited legroom, iffy food, and possibly no personal TV. More important, always arrive at least two hours before departure, as chronic overbooking means latecomers lose their seats.

Airline Contacts Continental Airlines
☎ 800/523-3273 for U.S. and Mexico reser-

vations, 800/231-0856 for international reservations ⊕ www.continental.com. **Delta Airlines** ☎ 800/221-1212 for U.S. reservations, 800/241-4141 for international reservations ⊕ www.delta.com. **Northwest Airlines** ☎ 800/225-2525 ⊕ www.nwa.com. **United Airlines** ☎ 800/864-8331 for U.S. reservations, 800/538-2929 for international reservations ⊕ www.united.com.

Air Canada ☎ 010/6468-2001 ⊕ www.aircanada.com. **Air China** ☎ 010/6601-7755 ⊕ www.airchina.com. **Air France** ☎ 010/6588-1388 ⊕ www.airfrance.com. **All Nippon** ☎ 010/6590-9191 ⊕ www.fly-ana.com. **Asiana** ☎ 010/6468-4000 ⊕ www.us.flyasiana.com. **Austrian Airlines** ☎ 010/6462-2161 ⊕ www.austrianair.com. **British Airways** ☎ 010/6512-4070 ⊕ www.ba.com. **Cathay Pacific** ☎ 010/8486-8532 ⊕ www.cathaypacific.com. **China Eastern** ☎ 010/6468-1166 ⊕ www.ce-air.com. **China Southern** ☎ 010/6459-0539 or 010/6459-6490 ⊕ www.cs-air.com/en. **Emirates** ☎ 021/3222-9999 Shanghai ⊕ www.emirates.com. **Japan Airlines** ☎ 010/6513-0888 ⊕ www.jal.com. **KLM** ☎ 010/6505-3505 ⊕ www.klm.com. **Lufthansa** ☎ 010/6468-8838 ⊕ www.lufthansa.com. **Korean Air** ☎ 010/6505-0088 ⊕ www.koreanair.com. **Northwest** ☎ 010/6505-3505 ⊕ www.nwa.com. **Singapore Airlines** ☎ 010/6505-2233 ⊕ www.singaporeair.com. **Thai Airways** ☎ 010/8515-0088 ⊕ www.thaiair.com. **United** ☎ 010/6463-1111, 800/810-8282 in China ⊕ www.ual.com.

For information about exploring Beijing by bike, *see* Chapter 1.

▌ BY BUS

TO BEIJING

China has fabulous luxury long-distance buses with air-conditioning and movies. However, buying tickets on them can be complicated if you don't speak Chinese and you may end up on a cramped school bus. Taking a train or an internal flight is often much easier. Buses depart from the city's several long-distance bus stations. The main ones are: Dongzhimen (Northeast);

LUCKY NUMBER

Sichuan Airlines bought the number 28/8888-8888 for 2.33 million yuan ($280,723) during an auction of more than 100 telephone numbers in 2003, making it the most expensive telephone number in the world. The number eight (*ba* in Chinese) is considered lucky in China, as it sounds similar to the character for "rich."

Muxiyuan (at Haihutun in the South); Beijiao, also called Deshengmen (North); and Majuan or Guangqumen (East).

Bus Information Note that information is not usually available in English at any of these phone numbers.

Beijiao ⊠ Deshengmenwai Dajie, Xicheng District ☎ 010/6204-7096. **Dongzhimen** ⊠ Dongzhimenwaixie Jie, Chaoyang District ☎ 010/6467-4995 or 010/6460-8131. **Muxiyuan** ⊠ Yongwai Chezan Lu, Fengtai District ☎ 010/6726-7149 or 010/6722-4641. **Majuan** ⊠ Guangqumenwai Dajie, Chaoyang District ☎ 010/6771-7620 or 010/6771-7622. **Xizhimen** ⊠ 2 Haidian Tou Duicun ☎ 010/6217-6075.

WITHIN BEIJING

Unless you know Beijing well, public buses aren't the best choice for getting around. There are hundreds of routes, which are hot and crowded in summer and cold and crowded in winter. Just getting on and off can be, quite literally, a fight. Pickpocketing is rife so watch your belongings very carefully.

The Beijing Public Transportation Corporation is the city's largest bus service provider. Routes 1 to 199 are regular city buses, and cost a flat fare of Y1. Routes 201 through 212 only run at night, costing Y2. Routes numbered 300 or higher are suburban, and fares depend on how far you're going—have your destination written in Chinese, as you have to tell the conductor so they can calculate your fare. Newer, air-conditioned buses have an 800 route number; prices vary, but start at Y3. They also run more expensive tourist buses going to sights in and around the city—to the Summer Palace and Great Wall, for example. Prices start at Y40.

Beijing Public Transportation Corporation
🌐 www.bjbus.com.

For information about exploring Beijing by pedicab, *see* Chapter 1.

▌ BY SUBWAY

With street-level traffic getting more crazed by the minute, Beijing's quick and efficient subway system is an excellent way to get about town. After operating for years with only two lines, the network is growing exponentially—seven new lines are under construction, and a couple more are being planned.

At this writing, there are four lines open. Line 1 (red) runs east–west under Chang'an Jie, crossing through the heart of the city. The circle line, or Line 2 (blue), runs roughly under the Second Ring Road. There are interchange stations between lines 1 and 2 at Fuxingmen and Jianguomen. The two remaining lines are mainly used by commuters and are less useful for sightseeing. The Batong Line extends Line 1 eastward, whereas Line 13 loops north off Line 2. The first north–south line, Line 5, is due to open in mid-2007, and two other lines are scheduled to open in time for the 2008 Olympics.

Subway stations are marked by blue signs

with a "D" (for *di tie,* or subway) in a circle. Signs are not always obvious, so be prepared to hunt around for entrances or ask directions; *Di tie zhan zai nar?* (Where's the subway station?) is a useful phrase to remember.

Stations are usually clean and safe, as are trains. Navigating the subway is very straightforward: station names are clearly displayed in Chinese and pinyin, and there are maps in each station. Once on board, each stop is clearly announced on a loud-speaker.

TICKET/PASS PRICE	
Single fare anywhere on Lines 1 and 2	Y3
Single fare on Line 13	Y3
Single fare on Batong line	Y2
Single transfer ticket Lines 1, 2, and 13	Y5
Single transfer ticket Lines 1, 2, and Batong	Y4

▌ BY TAXI

Taxis are plentiful, easy to spot, and by far the most comfortable way to get around Beijing, though increasing traffic means they're not always the fastest. There's a flagfall of Y10 for the first 4 km (2½ mi), then Y2 per kilometer thereafter. After 11 PM flagfall goes up to Y11, and there's a 20% surcharge per kilometer. Drivers usually know the terrain well, but most don't speak English; having your destination written in Chinese is a good idea. (Keep a card with the name of your hotel on it for the return trip.) Hotel doormen can also help you tell the driver where you're going. It's a good idea to study a map and have some idea where you are, as some drivers will take you for a ride—a much longer one—if they think they can get away with it.

■ BY TRAIN

China's enormous rail network is one of the world's busiest. Trains are usually safe and run strictly to schedule. Although there are certain intricacies to buying tickets, once you've got one, trips are generally hassle-free. Beijing is a major rail hub. Services to all over China leave from its four huge stations. The Trans-Siberian Railway and services to Shanghai, among others, leave from Beijing Zhan, the main station. Trains to Hong Kong and to areas in the west and south of China leave from Beijing Xi Zhan (West). Most of the Z-series trains (nonstop luxury services) come into these two stations. Lesser lines to the north and east of the country leave from Beijing Bei Zhan (North) and Beijing Dong Zhan (East).

You can buy most tickets 10 days in advance; 2 to 3 days ahead is usually enough time, except during the three national holidays—Chinese New Year (2 days in mid-January to February), Labor Day (May 1), and National Day (October 1). If you can, avoid traveling then—tickets sell out weeks in advance.

The cheapest rates are at the train station itself; there are special ticket offices for foreigners at both the Beijing Zhan (first floor) and Beijing Xi Zhan (second floor). You can only pay using cash. Most travel agents, including CITS, can book tickets for a small surcharge (Y20 to Y50), saving you the hassle of going to the station. You can also buy tickets through online retailers like China Train Ticket. They'll deliver the tickets to your hotel (keep in mind you often end up paying double the station rate).

Overpriced dining cars serve meals that are often inedible, so you'd do better to make use of the massive thermoses of boiled water in each compartment and take along your own noodles or instant soup, as the locals do.

Trains are always crowded, but you are guaranteed your designated seat, though not always the overhead luggage rack. Note that theft on trains is increasing; on overnight trains, sleep with your valuables or else keep them on the inside of the bunk.

You can find out just about everything about Chinese train travel at Seat 61's fabulous Web site. China Highlights has a searchable online timetable for major train routes. The tour operator Travel China Guide has an English-language Web site that can help you figure out train schedules and fares.

Beijing Bei Zhan ✉ North Station, 1 Xizhimenwai Beibinhelu, Xicheng District ☎ 010/6223-1003. **Beijing Nan Zhan** ✉ South Station, Yongdingmen, Chongwen District ☎ 010/6303-0031. **Beijing Xi Zhan** ✉ West Station, Lianhuachi Dong Lu, Haidian District ☎ 010/5182-6253. **Beijing Zhan** ✉ Main Station, Beijing Zhan Jie, Dongcheng District ☎ 010/6563-3262. **China Highlights** ⊕ www.chinahighlights.com/china-trains/index.htm. **Seat 61** ⊕ www.seat61.com/China.htm. **Travel China Guide** ⊕ www.travelchinaguide.com/china-trains/index.htm.

SERIOUS TRAINING

The most dramatic Chinese train experience is the 6-day trip between Beijing and Moscow, often referred to as the Trans-Siberian railway, though that's actually the service that runs between Moscow and Vladivostok. Two weekly services cover the 5,000 mi between Moscow and Beijing. The Trans-Manchurian is a Russian train that goes through northeast China, whereas the Trans-Mongolian is a Chinese train that goes through the Great Wall and crosses the Gobi Desert. Both have first-class compartments with 4 berths (Y2,500), or luxury 2-berth compartments (Y3,000). Trains leave from Beijing Station, which is the cheapest place to buy tickets, though it's easier to get them through CITS. Many Western travel agents specialize in selling Trans-Siberian tickets, but their prices are often much higher.

ON THE GROUND

■ COMMUNICATIONS

INTERNET

Beijing is a very Internet-friendly place for travelers with laptop computers. Most mid- to high-end hotels have in-room Internet access—if the hotel doesn't have a server you can usually access a government-provided ISP, which only charges you for the phone call. Wi-Fi is growing exponentially. Café chains like Starbucks are good places to try.

Most hotels usually have a computer with Internet access that you can use. Internet cafés are ubiquitous; it's an unstable business and new ones open and close all the time—ask your hotel for a recommendation. Prices vary considerably. Near the northern university districts you could pay as little as Y2 to Y3 per hour; slicker downtown places could cost 10 times that.

■ TIP➜ Remember that there is strict government control of the Internet in China. There's usually no problem with Web-based mail, but you may be unable to access news and even blogging sites.

Cybercafes ⊕ www.cybercafes.com lists over 4,000 Internet cafés worldwide.

PHONES

The good news is that you can now make a direct-dial telephone call from virtually any point on earth. The bad news? You can't always do so cheaply. Calling from a hotel is almost always the most expensive option; hotels usually add huge surcharges to all calls, particularly international ones. In some countries you can phone from call centers or even the post office. Calling cards usually keep costs to a minimum, but only if you purchase them locally. And then there are cell phones (See ⇨ p. 250), which are sometimes more prevalent—particularly in the developing world—than landlines; as expensive as cell-phone calls can be, they are still usually a much cheaper option than calling from your hotel.

The country code for China is 86; the city code for Beijing is 10 (omit the first "0"), and the city code for Shanghai is 21. To call China from the United States or Canada, dial the international access code (011), followed by the country code (86), the area or city code, and the eight-digit phone number.

Numbers beginning with 800 within China are toll-free. Note that a call from China to a toll-free number in the United States or Hong Kong is a full-tariff international call.

CALLING WITHIN CHINA

The Chinese phone system is cheap and efficient. You can make local and long-distance calls from your hotel or any public phone on the street. Some pay phones accept coins, but it's easier to buy an IC calling card, available at convenience stores and newsstands (See ⇨ Calling Cards, below). Local calls are generally free from landlines, though your hotel might charge a nominal rate. Long-distance rates in China are very low. Calling from your hotel room is a viable option, as hotels can only add a 15% service charge.

Beijing's city code is 010, and Beijing phone numbers have eight digits. When calling within the city, you don't need to use "010." In general, city codes appear written with a 0 in front of them; if not, you need to add this when calling another city within China.

For directory assistance, dial 114, or 2689–0114 for help in English (though you may not get through). If you want information for other cities, dial the city code followed by 114 (note that this is considered a long-distance call). For example, if you're in Beijing and need directory assistance for a Shanghai number, dial 021–114. The operators do not speak English, so if you don't speak Chinese you're best off asking your hotel for help.

LOCAL DO'S & TABOOS

GREETINGS

■ Chinese people aren't very touchy-feely with one another, even less so with strangers. Keep bear-hugs and cheek-kissing for your next European trip and stick to handshakes.

■ Always use a person's title and surname until they invite you to do otherwise.

RULES & RULE-BREAKING

■ By and large, the Chinese are a rule-abiding bunch. Follow their lead and avoid doing anything signs advise against.

■ Beijing is a crowded city, and pushing, nudging, and line-jumping are commonplace. It may be hard to accept, but it's not considered rude, so avoid reacting (even verbally) if you're accidentally shoved.

OUT ON THE TOWN

■ It's a great honor to be invited to someone's house, so explain at length if you can't go. Arrive punctually with a small gift for the hosts; remove your shoes outside if you see other guests doing so.

■ Tea, served free in all Chinese restaurants, is a common drink at mealtimes, though many locals only accompany their food with soup.

■ Smoking is one of China's greatest vices. No-smoking sections in restaurants are nonexistent, and people light up anywhere they think they can get away with it.

■ Holding hands in public is fine, but keep passionate embraces for the hotel room.

DOING BUSINESS

■ Time is of the essence when doing business in Beijing. Make appointments well in advance and be extremely punctual.

■ Chinese people have a keen sense of hierarchy in the office: the senior member should lead proceedings.

■ Suits are the norm in China, regardless of the outside temperature. Women should avoid plunging necklines, overly short skirts, or very high heels.

■ Respect silences in conversation and don't hurry things or interrupt.

■ When entertaining, local businesspeople may insist on paying: after a protest, accept.

■ Business cards are a big deal: not having one is a bad move. If possible, have yours printed in English on one side and Chinese on the other (your hotel can often arrange this). Proffer your card with both hands and receive the other person's in the same way.

■ Many gifts, including clocks and cutting implements, are considered unlucky in China. Food—especially presented in a showy basket—is always a good gift choice, as are imported spirits.

LANGUAGE

■ Learn a little of the local language. You need not strive for fluency; even just mastering a few basic words and terms is bound to make chatting with the locals more rewarding.

■ Everyone in Beijing speaks Putonghua (*pǔtōnghuà*, the "common language") as the national language of China is known. It's written using ideograms, or characters; in 1949 the government also introduced a phonetic writing system that uses the Roman alphabet. Known as pinyin, it's widely used to label public buildings and station names. Even if you don't speak or read Chinese, you can easily compare pinyin names with a map.

To make long-distance calls from a public phone you need an IC card (⇨ Calling Cards). To place a long-distance call, dial 0, the city code, and the eight-digit phone number.

Contacts Local directory assistance ☎ 114 in Chinese, 2689-0114 in English. **International Directory Assistance** ☎ 100. **Time** ☎ 117. **Weather** ☎ 121.

CALLING OUTSIDE CHINA

To make an international call from within China, dial 00 (the international access code within China) and then the country code, area code, and phone number. The country code for the United States is 1.

IDD (international direct dialing) service is available at all hotels, post offices, major shopping centers, and airports. By international standards prices aren't unreasonable, but it's vastly cheaper to use a long-distance calling card, known as an IP card (⇨ Calling Cards, *below*), whose rates also beat AT&T, MCI, and Sprint hands-down.

CALLING CARDS

Calling cards are a key part of the Chinese phone system. There are two kinds: the IC card (integrated circuit; *àicei ka*), for local and domestic long-distance calls on pay phones; and the IP card (Internet protocol; *aipi ka*) for international calls from any phone. You can buy both at post offices, convenience stores, and street vendors.

IC cards come in values of Y20, Y50, and Y100 and can be used in any pay phone with a card slot—most Beijing pay phones have them. Local calls using them cost around Y0.30 a minute, and less on weekends and after 6 PM.

To use IP cards, you first dial a local access number. This is often free from hotels, however at public phones you need an IC card to dial the access number. You then enter a card number and PIN, and finally the phone number complete with international dial codes. When calling from a pay phone both cards' minutes are deducted at the same time, one for local access (IC card) and one for the long-distance call you placed (IP card). There are countless different card brands; China Unicom is one that's usually reliable. IP cards come with values of Y20, Y30, Y50, and Y100. However, the going rate for them is up to half that, so bargain vendors down.

CELL PHONES

If you have a multiband phone (some countries use different frequencies than what's used in the United States) and your service provider uses the world-standard GSM network (as do T-Mobile, Cingular, and Verizon), you can probably use your phone abroad. Roaming fees can be steep, however: 99¢ a minute is considered reasonable. And overseas you normally pay the toll charges for incoming calls. It's almost always cheaper to send a text message than to make a call, since text messages have a very low set fee (often less than 5¢).

If you just want to make local calls, consider buying a new SIM card (note that your provider may have to unlock your phone for you to use a different SIM card) and a prepaid service plan in the destination. You'll then have a local number and can make local calls at local rates. If your trip is extensive, you could also simply buy a new cell phone in your destination, as the initial cost will be offset over time.

■ TIP→ If you travel internationally frequently, save one of your old cell phones or buy a cheap one on the Internet; ask your cell-phone company to unlock it for you, and take it with you as a travel phone, buying a new SIM card with pay-as-you-go service in each destination.

If you have a GSM phone, pick up a local SIM card (*sim ka*) from any branch of China Mobile or China Unicom. You'll be presented with a list of possible phone numbers, with varying prices—an "unlucky" phone number (one with lots of 4s) could be as cheap as Y50, whereas an auspicious one (full of 8s) could fetch Y300 or more. You then buy prepaid cards to charge minutes onto your SIM—do this straight away as you need credit to receive calls. Local calls to landlines cost Y0.25 a minute, and to cell phones Y0.60. International calls from cell phones are very expensive. Remember to bring an adapter for your phone charger. You can also buy cheap handsets from China Mobile. If you're planning to stay even a couple of days this is probably cheaper than renting a phone.

Beijing Limo rents cell phones, which they can deliver to your hotel or at the airport. Renting a handset starts at $5 a day, and you buy a prepaid package with a certain amount of call time; prices start at $50. Beijing Impression travel agency rents handsets at similar rates, and you buy a regular prepaid card for calls.

Contacts Beijing Impression ☎ 010/8446–7137 ⊕ www.beijingimpression.com **Beijing Limo** ☎ 010/6546–1588 ⊕ www.beijinglimo.com **Cellular Abroad** ☎ 800/287–5072 ⊕ www.cellularabroad.com rents and sells GMS phones and sells SIM cards that work in many countries. **China Mobile** ☎ English-language assistance 1860 ⊕ www.chinamobile.com is China's main mobile-service provider. **China Unicom** ☎ English-language assistance 1001 is China's second-largest main mobile-phone company. **Mobal** ☎ 888/888–9162 ⊕ www.mobalrental.com rents mobiles and sells GSM phones (starting at $49) that will operate in 140 countries. Per-call rates vary throughout the world. **Planet Fone** ☎ 888/988–4777 ⊕ www.planetfone.com rents cell phones, but the per-minute rates are expensive.

▌CUSTOMS & DUTIES

You're always allowed to bring goods of a certain value back home without having to pay any duty or import tax. But there's a limit on the amount of tobacco and liquor you can bring back duty-free, and some countries have separate limits for perfumes; for exact figures, check with your customs department. The values of so-called "duty-free" goods are included in these amounts. When you shop abroad,

save all your receipts, as customs inspectors may ask to see them as well as the items you purchased. If the total value of your goods is more than the duty-free limit, you'll have to pay a tax (most often a flat percentage) on the value of everything beyond that limit.

Except for the usual prohibitions against narcotics, explosives, plant and animal material, firearms, and ammunition, you can bring anything into China that you plan to take away with you. Cameras, video recorders, GPS equipment, laptops, and the like should pose no problems. However, China is very sensitive about printed matter deemed seditious, such as religious, pornographic, and political items, especially articles, books, and pictures on Tibet. All the same, small amounts of English-language reading matter aren't generally a problem. Customs officials are for the most part easygoing, and visitors are rarely searched. It's not necessary to fill in customs declaration forms, but if you carry in a large amount of cash, say several thousand dollars, you should declare it upon arrival.

On leaving, you're not allowed to take out any antiquities dating to before 1795. Antiques from between 1795 and 1949 must have an official red seal attached.

U.S. Information U.S. Customs and Border Protection ⊕ www.cbp.gov.

For information about sightseeing tours in Beijing, *see* Chapter 1.

▌EATING OUT

In China, meals are a communal event, so food in a Chinese home or restaurant is always shared. Although cutlery is available in many restaurants, it won't hurt to brush up on your use of chopsticks, the utensil of choice. The standard eating procedure is to hold the bowl close to your mouth and eat the food. Noisily slurping up soup and noodles is also the norm, as is belching when you're done. It's considered bad manners to point or play with your chopsticks, or to place them on top of your rice bowl when you're finished eating (place the chopsticks horizontally on the table or plate). Avoid, too, leaving your chopsticks standing up in a bowl of rice—they look like the two incense sticks burned at funerals.

If you're invited to a formal Chinese meal, be prepared for great ceremony, endless toasts and speeches, and a grand variety of elaborate dishes. Your host will be seated at the "head" of the round table, which is the seat that faces the door. Wait to be instructed where to sit. Don't start eating until the host takes the first bite, and then simply help yourself as the food comes around, but don't take the last piece on a platter. Always let the food touch your plate before bringing it up to your mouth; eating directly from the serving dish is bad form.

Beijing's most famous dish is Peking Duck. The roast duck is served with thin pancakes, in which you wrap pieces of the meat, together with spring onions, vegetables, and plum sauce. Hotpot is another local trademark: you order different meats and vegetables, which you cook in a pot of stock boiling on a charcoal burner. *Baozi* (small steamed buns filled with meat or vegetables) are particularly good in Beijing—sold at stalls and in small restaurants everywhere, they make a great snack or breakfast food.

MEALS & MEALTIMES

Food is a central part of Chinese culture, and so eating should be a major activity on any trip to Beijing. Breakfast is not a big deal in China—congee, or rice porridge (*zhou*), is the standard dish. Most mid- and upper-end hotels do big buffet spreads, whereas Beijing's blooming café chains provide lattes and croissants all over town.

Snacks are a food group in themselves. There's no shortage of steaming street stalls selling kebabs, grilled meat or chicken, bowls of noodle soup, and the ubiquitous *baozi* (stuffed dumplings). Pick a place where lots of locals are eating to be on the safe side.

The food in hotel restaurants is usually acceptable but overpriced. Restaurants frequented by locals always serve tastier fare at better prices. Don't shy from trying establishments without an English menu—a good phrasebook and lots of pointing can usually get you what you want.

Lunch and dinner dishes are more or less interchangeable. Meat (especially pork) or poultry tends to form the base of most Beijing dishes, together with wheat products like buns, pancakes, and noodles. Beijing food is often quite oily, with liberal amounts of vinegar; its strong flavors come from garlic, soy sauce, and bean pastes. Vegetables—especially winter cabbage and onions—and tofu play a big role in meals. As in all Chinese food, dairy products are scarce. Chinese meals usually involve a variety of dishes, which are always ordered communally in restaurants. Eat alone or order your own dishes and you're seriously limiting your food experience.

If you're craving Western food, rest assured that Beijing has plenty of American fast-food chains. Most higher-end restaurants have a Western menu, but you're usually safer sticking to the Chinese food.

Meals in China are served early: breakfast until 9 AM, lunch between 11 and 2, and dinner from 5 to 9. Unless otherwise noted, the restaurants listed in this guide are open daily for lunch and dinner. Restaurants and bars catering to foreigners may stay open longer hours.

WORD OF MOUTH

"If you're familiar with eating Chinese-style (shared dishes, chopsticks) you can seek out local restaurants with English-translation menus or illustrations of dishes—a good meal for two will cost no more than 100 yuan (US$12). Hotel restaurants may be convenient but are very poor value for money."   –Neil_Oz

PAYING

At most restaurants you ask for the bill at the end of the meal. At cheap noodle bars and street stands you pay upfront. Only very upmarket restaurants accept payment by credit card.For guidelines on tipping *see* Tipping *below*.

For dining and lodging price charts, *see* the opening pages of chapters 6 and 7.

RESERVATIONS & DRESS

Regardless of where you are, it's a good idea to make a reservation if you can. In some places (Hong Kong, for example), it's expected. We only mention them specifically when reservations are essential (there's no other way you'll ever get a table) or when they are not accepted. For popular restaurants, book as far ahead as you can (often 30 days), and reconfirm as soon as you arrive. (Large parties should always call ahead to check the reservations policy.) We mention dress only when men are required to wear a jacket or a jacket and tie.

▌ELECTRICITY

The electrical current in China is 220 volts, 50 cycles alternating current (AC) so most American appliances can't be used without a transformer. A universal adapter is especially useful in China as wall outlets come in a bewildering variety of configurations: two- and three-pronged round plugs, as well as two-pronged flat sockets.

Consider making a small investment in a universal adapter, which has several types of plugs in one lightweight, compact unit. Most laptops and cell-phone chargers are dual voltage (i.e., they operate equally well on 110 and 220 volts), so require only an adapter. These days the same is true of small appliances such as hair dryers. Always check labels and manufacturer instructions to be sure. Don't use 110-volt outlets marked FOR SHAVERS ONLY for high-wattage appliances such as hair dryers. **Steve Kropla's Help for World Traveler's** ⊕ www.kropla.com has information on elec-

trical and telephone plugs around the world. **Walkabout Travel Gear** ⊕ www. walkabouttravelgear.com has a good coverage of electricity under "adapters."

▌EMERGENCIES

The best place to head in a medical emergency is the Beijing United Family Health Center, which has 24-hour emergency services. Asia Emergency Assistance Center (AEA) has 24-hour emergency and pharmacy assistance. SOS is another international clinic with a good reputation; they also arrange Medivac.

Beijing has different numbers for each emergency service, though staff often don't speak English. If in doubt, call the U.S. embassy first: staff members are available 24 hours a day to help handle emergencies and facilitate communication with local agencies.

Doctors & Dentists Asia Emergency Assistance Center ✉ 2-1-1 Tayuan Diplomatic Office Bldg., 14 Liangmahe Nan Lu, Chaoyang District ☎ 010/6462-9112 during office hrs, 010/6462-9100 after hrs. **Beijing United Family Health Center** ✉ 2 Jiangtai Lu, near Lido Hotel, Chaoyang District ☎ 010/6433-3960, 010/6433-2345 for emergencies ⊕ www. unitedfamilyhospitals.com. **SOS International** ✉ Building C, BITIC Leasing Center, 1 North Road, Xing Fu San Cun, Chaoyang District ☎ 010/6462-9112 ⊕ www.internationalsos. com.

U.S. Embassy ⊠ 3 Xiushui Bei Jie, Chaoyang District ☎ 010/6532-3431 Ext. 229 or 010/6532-3831 Ext. 264 🖷 010/6532-2483 ⊕ beijing.usembassy-china.org.cn.

General Emergency Contacts **Fire** ☎ 119. **Police** ☎ 110. **Medical Emergency** ☎ 120. **Traffic Accident** ☎ 122.

Hospitals & Clinics **Asia Emergency Assistance Center** (private) ⊠ 2-1-1 Tayuan Diplomatic Office Bldg., 14 Liangmahe Nan Lu, Chaoyang District ☎ 010/6462-9112 during office hrs, 010/6462-9100 after hrs. **Beijing United Family Health Center** (private) ⊠ 2 Jiangtai Lu, near Lido Hotel, Chaoyang District ☎ 010/6433-3960, 010/6433-2345 for emergencies ⊕ www.unitedfamilyhospitals.com. **China Academy of Medical Science (Peking Union Hospital)** (public) ⊠ 1 Shui Fu Yuan, Dongcheng District ☎ 010/6529-5120. **Hong Kong International Medical Clinic** (private) ⊠ Office Tower, 9th fl., Hong Kong Macau Center-Swissotel, 2 Chaoyangmen Bei Da Jie, Chaoyang District ☎ 010/6553-2288 ⊕ www.hkclinic.com. **Sino-Japanese Friendship Hospital** (public) ⊠ Ying Hua Dong Lu, He Ping Li ☎ 010/6422-2965. **SOS International** (private) ⊠ Building C, BITIC Leasing Center, 1 North Road, Xing Fu San Cun, Chaoyang District ☎ 010/6462-9112 ⊕ www.internationalsos.com.

Pharmacies **Beijing United Family Health Center** (private) ⊠ 2 Jiangtai Lu, near Lido Hotel, Chaoyang District ☎ 010/6433-3960, 010/6433-2345 for emergencies ⊕ www.unitedfamilyhospitals.com. **International Medical Center (IMC)** (private) ⊠ Beijing Lufthansa Center, Room 106, 50 Liangmaqiao Lu, Chaoyang District ☎ 010/6465-1561. **Watsons** ⊠ Holiday Inn Lido Hotel, Jichang Lu, Chaoyang District ⊠ Full Link Plaza, 18 Chaoyangmenwai Dajie, Chaoyang District.

▌ HEALTH

The most common types of illnesses are caused by contaminated food and water. Especially in developing countries, drink only bottled, boiled, or purified water and drinks; don't drink from public fountains or use ice. You should even consider using bottled water to brush your teeth. Make sure food has been thoroughly cooked and is served to you fresh and hot; avoid vegetables and fruits that you haven't washed (in bottled or purified water) or peeled yourself. If you have problems, mild cases of traveler's diarrhea may respond to Imodium (known generically as loperamide) or Pepto-Bismol. Be sure to drink plenty of fluids; if you can't keep fluids down, seek medical help immediately. Tap water in Beijing is safe for brushing teeth, but you're better off buying bottled water to drink.

Infectious diseases can be airborne or passed via mosquitoes and ticks and through direct or indirect physical contact with animals or people. Some, including Norwalk-like viruses that affect your digestive tract, can be passed along through contaminated food. If you are traveling in an area where malaria is prevalent, use a repellent containing DEET and take malaria-prevention medication before, during, and after your trip as directed by your physician. Condoms can help prevent most sexually transmitted diseases, but they aren't absolutely reliable and their quality varies from country to country. Speak with your physician and/or check the CDC or World Health Organization Web sites for health alerts, particularly if you're pregnant, traveling with children, or have a chronic illness.

SPECIFIC ISSUES IN BEIJING

Pneumonia and influenza are common among travelers returning from China—talk to your doctor about inoculations before you leave. If you need to buy prescription drugs, try to go to the pharmacies of reputable private hospitals like the Beijing United Family Health Medical Center. Do *not* buy them in streetside pharmacies as the quality control is unreliable.

OVER-THE-COUNTER REMEDIES

Most pharmacies carry over-the-counter Western medicines and traditional Chinese medicines. By and large, you need to ask for the generic name of the drug you're looking for, not a brand name.

▌ HOURS OF OPERATION

Most offices are open between 9 and 6 on weekdays; most museums keep roughly the same hours six or seven days a week. Everything in China grinds to a halt for the first two or three days of Chinese New Year (sometime in mid-January to February), and opening hours are often reduced for the rest of that season.

Banks and government offices are open weekdays 9 to 5, although some close for lunch (sometime between noon and 2). Bank branches and CTS tour desks in hotels often keep longer hours and are usually open Saturday (and occasionally even Sunday) mornings. Many hotel currency-exchange desks stay open 24 hours.

Pharmacies are open daily from 8:30 or 9 AM to 6 or 7 PM. Some large pharmacies stay open until 9 PM or even later.

Shops and department stores are generally open daily 8 to 8; some stores stay open even later in summer, in popular tourist areas, or during peak tourist season.

HOLIDAYS

National holidays include New Year's Day (January 1); Spring Festival aka Chinese New Year (late January/early February); Qingming Jie (a spring festival when families sweep ancestors' graves; April 5); International Labor Day (May 1); Dragon Boat Festival (late May/early June); anniversary of the founding of the Communist Party of China (July 1); anniversary of the founding of the Chinese People's Liberation Army (August 1); and National Day—founding of the Peoples Republic of China in 1949 (October 1); Chongyang Jie or Double Ninth Festival (ninth day of ninth lunar month).

▌ MAIL

Sending international mail from China is reliable. Airmail letters to any place in the world should take 5 to 14 days. Express Mail Service (EMS) is available to many international destinations. Letters within Beijing arrive the next day, and mail to the rest of China takes a day or two longer. Domestic mail can be subject to search so don't send sensitive materials, such as religious or political literature, as you might cause the recipient trouble.

Service is more reliable if you mail letters from post offices rather than mailboxes. Buy envelopes here, too, as there are standardized sizes in China. You need to glue stamps onto envelopes as they're not self-adhesive. Most post offices are open daily between 8 and 7. Your hotel can usually send letters for you, too.

You can use the Roman alphabet to write an address. Do not use red ink, which has a negative connotation. You must also include a six-digit zip code for mail within China. The Beijing municipality is assigned the zip code 100000, and each neighboring county starts with 10. For example, the code for Fangshan, to the immediate southwest of Beijing proper, is 102400.

Sending airmail postcards costs Y4.20 and letters Y5.40 to Y6.50.

Main Branches **International Post and Telecommunications Office** ✉ Jianguomen Bei Dajie, Chaoyang District ☎ 010/6512-8114.

SHIPPING PACKAGES

It's easy to ship packages home from China. Take what you want to send *unpacked* to the post office—everything will be sewn up officially into satisfying linen-bound packages, a service that costs a few yuan. You have to fill in lengthy forms, and enclosing a photocopy of receipts for the goods inside isn't a bad idea, as they may be opened by customs along the line. Large antiques stores often offer reliable shipping services that take care of customs in China. Large international couriers operating in Beijing include DHL, Federal Express, and UPS.

Express Services **DHL** ☎ 010/6466-5566 ⊕ www.cn.dhl.com. **FedEx** ☎ 010/6462-3183 ⊕ www.fedex.com. **UPS** ☎ 010/6505-5005 ⊕ www.ups.com.

▮ MONEY

The best places to convert your dollars into Yuan are at your hotel's front desk or a branch of a major bank, such as Bank of China, CITIC, or HSBC. All these operate with standardized government rates—anything cheaper is illegal, and thus risky. You need to present your passport to change money.

Although credit cards are gaining ground in China, for day-to-day transactions cash is definitely king. Getting change for big notes can be a problem, so try to stock up on 10s and 20s when you change money. ATMs are widespread, but not always reliable. Hunt around enough, though, and you're sure to find one that accepts your card.

Prices throughout this guide are given for adults. Substantially reduced fees are almost always available for children, students, and senior citizens.

ITEM AVERAGE COST	
Cup of coffee at Starbucks	Y20
Glass of local beer	Y10
Set lunch in a cheap restaurant	Y20
2-km (1-mi) taxi ride in Capital City	Y10
Hour-long foot massage	Y50

▮ TIP→ Banks never have every foreign currency on hand, and it may take as long as a week to order. If you're planning to exchange funds before leaving home, don't wait until the last minute.

ATMS & BANKS

Your own bank will probably charge a fee for using ATMs abroad; the foreign bank you use may also charge a fee. Nevertheless, you'll usually get a better rate of exchange at an ATM than you will at a currency-exchange office or even when changing money in a bank. And extracting funds as you need them is a safer option than carrying around a large amount of cash.

▮ TIP→ PIN numbers with more than four digits are not recognized at ATMs in many countries. If yours has five or more, remember to change it before you leave.

Out of the Chinese banks, your best bet for ATMs is the Bank of China, which accepts most foreign cards. That said, machines frequently refuse to give cash for mysterious reasons. Move on and try another. Citibank and HSBC have lots of branches in Beijing, and accept all major cards. On-screen instructions appear automatically in English.

CREDIT CARDS

Throughout this guide, the following abbreviations are used: **AE**, American Express; **DC**, Diners Club; **MC**, MasterCard; and **V**, Visa.

It's a good idea to inform your credit-card company before you travel, especially if you're going abroad and don't travel internationally very often. Otherwise, the credit-card company might put a hold on your card owing to unusual activity—not a good thing halfway through your trip. Record all your credit-card numbers—as well as the phone numbers to call if your cards are lost or stolen—in a safe place, so you're prepared should something go wrong. Both MasterCard and Visa have general numbers you can call (collect if you're abroad) if your card is lost, but you're better off calling the number of your issuing bank, since MasterCard and Visa usually just transfer you to your bank; your bank's number is usually printed on your card.

If you plan to use your credit card for cash advances, you'll need to apply for a PIN at least two weeks before your trip. Although it's usually cheaper (and safer) to use a credit card abroad for large purchases (so you can cancel payments or be reimbursed if there's a problem), note that some credit-card companies *and* the banks that issue them add substantial percentages to all foreign transactions, whether they're in a foreign currency or not. Check on these fees before leaving home, so there won't be any surprises when you get the bill.

■ TIP→ Before you charge something, ask the merchant whether or not he or she plans to do a dynamic currency conversion (DCC). In such a transaction the credit-card *processor* (shop, restaurant, or hotel, not Visa or MasterCard) converts the currency and charges you in dollars. In most cases you'll pay the merchant a 3% fee for this service in addition to any credit-card company and issuing-bank foreign-transaction surcharges.

Dynamic currency conversion programs are becoming increasingly widespread. Merchants who participate in them are supposed to ask whether you want to be charged in dollars or the local currency, but they don't always do so. And even if they do offer you a choice, they may well avoid mentioning the additional surcharges. The good news is that you *do* have a choice. And if this practice really gets your goat, you can avoid it entirely thanks to American Express; with its cards, DCC simply isn't an option.

In Beijing, American Express, MasterCard, and Visa are accepted at most major hotels and a growing number of upmarket stores and restaurants. JCB and Diners Club are accepted at many hotels and some restaurants.

Reporting Lost Cards **American Express** ☏ 800/992-3404 in the U.S., 336/393-1111 collect from abroad ⊕ www.americanexpress.

com. **Diners Club** ☏ 800/234-6377 in the U.S., 303/799-1504 collect from abroad ⊕ www.dinersclub.com. **MasterCard** ☏ 800/622-7747 in the U.S., 636/722-7111 collect from abroad, or 010/800-110-7309 in China ⊕ www.mastercard.com. **Visa** ☏ 800/847-2911 in the U.S., 410/581-9994 collect from abroad, or 010/800-711-2911 in China ⊕ www.visa.com.

CURRENCY & EXCHANGE

The Chinese currency is officially called the yuan (Y), and is also known as *renminbi* (RMB), or "People's Money." You may also hear it called *kuai,* and informal expression like "buck." It's pegged to the dollar at around Y8.

Both old and new styles of bills circulate simultaneously in China, and many denominations have both coins and bills. The Bank of China issues bills in denominations of 1 (burgundy), 2 (green), 5 (brown or purple), 10 (turquoise), 20 (brown), 50 (blue or occasionally yellow), and 100 (red). There are Y1 coins, too. The yuan subdivides into 10-cent units called *jiao* or *mao*; these come in bills and coins of 1, 2, and 5. The smallest denomination is the *fen*, which comes in coins (and occasionally tiny notes) of 1, 2, and 5. Counterfeiting is rife in China, and even small stores inspect notes with ultraviolet lamps. Change can be a problem—don't expect much success paying for a Y13 purchase with a Y100 note, for example.

Exchange rates in China are fixed by the government daily, so it's equally good at branches of the Bank of China, at big department stores, or at your hotel's exchange desk, which has the added advantage of often being open 24 hours a day. Any lower rates are illegal, so you're exposing yourself to scams. A passport is required. Hold on to your exchange receipt, which you need to convert your extra yuan back into dollars.

TRAVELER'S CHECKS & CARDS

Some consider this the currency of the cave man, and it's true that fewer establishments accept traveler's checks these days. Nevertheless, they're a cheap and secure way to carry extra money, particularly on trips to urban areas. Both Citibank (under the Visa brand) and American Express issue traveler's checks in the United States, but AmEx is better known and more widely accepted; you can also avoid hefty surcharges by cashing AmEx checks at AmEx offices. Whatever you do, keep track of all the serial numbers in case the checks are lost or stolen.

■ TIP→ **Most hotels don't accept traveler's checks as payment, and only some branches of the Bank of China exchange them, usually at a worse rate than cash.**

American Express now offers a stored-value card called a Travelers Cheque Card, which you can use wherever American Express credit cards are accepted, including ATMs. The card can carry a minimum of $300 and a maximum of $2,700, and it's a very safe way to carry your funds. Although you can get replacement funds in 24 hours if your card is lost or stolen, it doesn't really strike us as a very good deal. In addition to a high initial cost ($14.95 to set up the card, plus $5 each time you "reload"), you still have to pay a 2% fee for each purchase in a foreign currency (similar to that of any credit card). Further, each time you use the card in an ATM you pay a transaction fee of $2.50 on top of the 2% transaction fee for the conversion—add it all up and it can be considerably more than you would pay when simply using your own ATM card. Regular traveler's checks are just as secure and cost less.

Contacts **American Express** ☎ 888/412-6945 in the U.S., 801/945-9450 collect outside of the U.S. to add value or speak to customer service ⊕ www.americanexpress.com.

▌RESTROOMS

Public restrooms abound in Beijing—the street, parks, restaurants, department stores, and major tourist attractions are all likely locations. Most charge a small fee (usually less than Y1), and seldom provide Western-style facilities or private booths. Instead, expect squat toilets, open troughs, and rusty spigots; WC signs at intersections point the way to these facilities. Toilet paper or tissues and antibacterial hand wipes are good things to have in your day pack. The restrooms in the newest shopping plazas, fast-food outlets, and deluxe restaurants catering to foreigners are generally on a par with American restrooms.

Find a Loo **The Bathroom Diaries** ⊕ www. thebathroomdiaries.com is flush with unsanitized info on restrooms the world over—each one located, reviewed, and rated.

▌SAFETY

There is little violent crime against tourists in China, partly because the penalties are severe for those who are caught—China's yearly death-sentence tolls run into the thousands. Single women can move about Beijing without too much hassle. Handbag-snatching and pickpocketing do occur in markets and on crowded buses or trains—keep an eye open and your money safe and you should have no problems. Use the lockbox in your hotel room to store any valuables, but always carry your passport with you for identification purposes.

Beijing is full of people looking to make a quick buck. The most common scam involves people persuading you to go with them for a tea ceremony, which is often so pleasant that you don't smell a rat 'til several hundred dollars appear on your credit-card bill. "Art students" who pressure you into buying work is another common scam. The same rules that apply to hostess bars worldwide are also true in Beijing. Avoiding such scams is as easy as refusing *all* unsolicited services—be it from taxi or pedicab drivers, tour guides, or potential "friends."

Beijing traffic is as manic as it looks, and survival of the fittest (or the biggest) is the main rule. Crossing streets can be an extreme sport. Drivers rarely give pedestrins the right-of-way and don't even look for pedestrians when making a right turn on a red light. Cyclists have less power but are just as aggressive.

Beijing's severely polluted air can bring on, or aggravate, respiratory problems. If you're a sufferer, take the cue from locals, who wear surgical masks, or a scarf or bandana as protection.

TIP→ Distribute your cash, credit cards, IDs, and other valuables between a deep front pocket, an inside jacket or vest pocket, and a hidden money pouch. Don't reach for the money pouch once you're in public.

TAXES

There is no sales tax in China. Hotels charge a 5% tax; bigger, joint-venture hotels also add a 10% to 15% service fee. Some restaurants charge a 10% service fee.

A departure tax of Y50 (about $6) for domestic flights and Y90 (about $11) for international flights (including flights to Hong Kong and Macau) must be paid in cash in dollars or yuan at the airport. People holding diplomatic passports, passengers in transit who stop over for less than 24 hours, and children under 12 are exempt from the departure tax.

TIME

Beijing is 8 hours ahead of London, 13 hours ahead of New York, 14 hours ahead of Chicago, and 16 hours ahead of Los Angeles. There's no daylight saving time, so subtract an hour in summer.

TIPPING

Tipping is a tricky issue in China. It's officially forbidden by the government, and locals simply don't do it. In general, follow their lead without qualms. Nevertheless, the practice is beginning to catch on, especially among tour guides, who often expect Y10 a day. You don't need to tip in restaurants or in taxis—many drivers insist on handing over your change, however small.

INDEX

PHOTO CREDITS

Cover Photo (Chinese New Year, Beijing): *Keren Su/danitadelimont.com*. 5, *Dennis Cox/age fotostock*. **Chapter 1: Experience Beijing:** 9, *Richard T. Nowitz/age fotostock*. 10, *Tim Graham/Alamy*. 12 (left), *ImagineChina*. 12 (top right), *Wendy Connett/Alamy*. 12 (bottom center), *Jon Arnold/age fotostock*. 12 (bottom right), *Toño Labra/age fotostock*. 13 (top left), *Antonio D'Albore/Marka/age fotostock*. 13 (bottom left), *China National Tourist Office*. 13 (right), *ImagineChina*. 14, *Wendy Connett/Alamy*. 15 (left), *A. Parada/Alamy*. 15 (right), *Tina Manley/Alamy*. 16, *BL Images Ltd/Alamy*. 17-18, *ImagineChina*. 19 (left), *ImagineChina*. 19 (right), *Dennis Cox/Alamy*. 20, *ImagineChina*. 21, *Renaud Visage/age fotostock*. 22, *Robert Fried/Alamy*. 23, *Kevin Foy/Alamy*. 24, *Keren Su/China Span/Alamy*. 25, *Beijing Municipal Commission of Urban Planning*. 26, *ImagineChina*. 27, *Keren Su/China Span/Alamy*. 28-29, *SuperStock/age fotostock*. 30-31, *ImagineChina*. 32 (left and top right), *ImagineChina*. 32 (bottom right), *Bruno Perousse/age fotostock*. **Chapter 2: Neighborhoods:** 35, *Kevin Foy/Alamy*. 40-51, *ImagineChina*. 52, *Lou Linwei/Alamy*. 55, *Dennis Cox/Alamy*. 56-59, *ImagineChina*. **Chapter 3: Historical Sights:** 63, *John Henshall/Alamy*. 68, *Luis Castañeda/age fotostock*. 69, *SuperStock/age fotostock*. 70-71, *ImagineChina*. 71 (bottom), *Juan Carlos Muñoz/age fotostock*. 72, *Luis Castañeda/age fotostock*. 73 (top), *Dennis Cox/age fotostock*. 73 (2nd from top), *Richard T. Nowitz/age fotostock*. 73 (3rd from top), *ImagineChina*. 73 (bottom left), *Wendy Connett/Alamy*. 73 (bottom right), *Jon Arnold Images/Alamy*. 74 (top), *Robert Harding Picture Library Ltd/Alamy*. 75 (top), *Scott Kemper/Alamy*. 76, *Toño Labra/age fotostock*. 78, *Dbimages/Alamy*. 80, *Toño Labra/age fotostock*. 81, *ImagineChina*. 82, *Jon Arnold/age fotostock*. 83, *Lou Linwei/Alamy*. 84, *Dennis Cox/Alamy*. 85, *Luis Castañeda/age fotostock*. 88, *Martin Norris/Alamy*. 89, *SuperStock/age fotostock*. 90 (top right), *José Fuste Raga/age fotostock*. 90 (bottom right), *Mary Evans Picture Library/Alamy*. 91 (top left), *China National Tourist Office*. 91 (bottom left), *Visual Arts Library (London)/Alamy*. 91 (right), *Panorama Media (Beijing) Ltd./Alamy*. 92 (left), *Popperfoto/Alamy*. 92 (top right), *Eddie Gerald/Alamy*. 92 (bottom right), *North Wind Picture Archives/Alamy*. 93 (left), *Beaconstox/Alamy*. 93 (top right), *Bruno Perousse/age fotostock*. 94 (left), *Kevin O'Hara/age fotostock*. 94 (bottom right), *A.H.C./age fotostock*. 95 (top left), *Tramonto/age fotostock*. 95 (bottom left), *ImagineChina*. 95 (right), *Iain Masterton/Alamy*. **Chapter 4: Shopping:** 99, *ImagineChina*. 100, *Kevin Foy/Alamy*. 102, *Bill Bachmann/Alamy*. 115, *ImagineChina*. 116 (top and center), *Elyse Singleton*. 116 (bottom), *Pat Behnke/Alamy*. 117 (top left), *Elyse Singleton*. 117 (top right), *ImagineChina*. 117 (bottom left), *ImagineChina*. 117 (bottom right), *Elyse Singleton*. 118 (top), *Kevin O'Hara/age fotostock*. 118 (bottom), *Pixonnet.com/Alamy*. 119 (left), *ImagineChina*. 119 (right), *Ulana Switucha/Alamy*. **Chapter 5: Arts & Nightlife:** 123-25, *ImagineChina*. 128, *Peter Adams/age fotostock*. 132-33, *Dennis Cox/age fotostock*. 134 (bottom), *ImagineChina*. 135 (left), *SuperStock/age fotostock*. 135 (right), *Sun Liansheng/age fotostock*. 136 (all), *ImagineChina*. 137, *SuperStock/age fotostock*. **Chapter 6: Where to Eat:** 147, *Tina Manley/Alamy*. 149, *Per Karlsson-BKWine.com/Alamy*. 150, *Bruno Perousse/age fotostock*. 155, *Peter Adams/age fotostock*. 156 (both), *ImagineChina*. 157 (left), *ImagineChina*. 157 (top right), *JTB Photo/Alamy*. 157 (bottom right), *Iain Masterton/Alamy*. 158 (top), *ImagineChina*. 158 (bottom), *Profimedia.CZ S.r.o./Alamy*. 159 (top left), *Iain Masterton/Alamy*. 159 (center left), *Tim Graham/Alamy*. 159 (bottom left), *Craig Lovell/Eagle Visions Photography/Alamy*. 159 (right), *Cephas Picture Library/Alamy*. 160 (top and bottom left), *ImagineChina*. 160 (top right), *Doug Scott/age fotostock*. 160 (bottom right), *ImagineChina*. **Chapter 7: Where to Stay:** 177-80, *Shangri-La Hotels and Resorts*. **Chapter 8: Best Side Trips:** 201, *Richard T. Nowitz/age fotostock*. 202, *ImagineChina*. 203, *China National Tourist Office*. 204, *ImagineChina*. 209, *Lucid Images/age fotostock*. 210 (left), *Mary Evans Picture Library/Alamy*. 210-11, *Liu Jianmin/age fotostock*. 214, *Peter Bowater/Alamy*. 215, *ImagineChina*. 216, *Nic Cleave Photography/Alamy*. 217, *ImagineChina*. **Color Section:** Nine Dragons Screen in Beihai Park: *Luis Castañeda/age fotostock*. Beijing Opera: *Sylvain Grandadam/age fotostock*. Temple of Heaven: *SuperStock/age fotostock*. National Museum of China: *ImagineChina*. Forbidden City: *Dennis Cox/age fotostock*. Street vendor in Dazhalan: *P. Narayan/age fotostock*. Big Bell Temple: *Luis Castañeda/age fotostock*. Tiananmen: *John Henshall/Alamy*. Beijing mall: *Kevin Foy/Alamy*. 100-Yuan note: *ImagineChina*. Hutong rooftops: *Dbimages/Alamy*. 2008 Olympic Games: *ImagineChina*. Spring Lantern Festival: *ImagineChina*. Chinese New Year: *Keren Su/China Span/Alamy*. Old Summer Palace: *ImagineChina*. Great Wall at Badaling: *ImagineChina*.

NOTES

NOTES

NOTES

NOTES

NOTES

NOTES

NOTES

ABOUT OUR WRITERS

Dinah Gardner is a freelance writer living in Beijing. She's written more than a dozen guidebooks on Asia. After more than a decade on the continent, Dinah still refuses to wear a conical bamboo hat. She updated the Historical Sights and Arts & Nightlife chapters for this book.

A native New Yorker and longtime Beijing resident, **Alex Miller** wrote about Beijing's vibrant neighborhoods and side trips for this edition. Fluent in Mandarin, Alex studied economics at Beijing University and graduated from Oberlin College. He has a fascination with jerry-rigged motor vehicles and can be found riding motorcycles around Beijing and greater East Asia.

Katharine Mitchell writes for various publications in China and abroad. Currently she covers the international school beat as a reporter for the Western Academy of Beijing. Her travels have carried her to Shakespeare's England, Dostoevsky's Russia, Kipling's India, and the China of Pearl S. Buck, Li Bai, and Kunqu opera. She holds an MA in Literature from the University of Mississippi and an MFA in Fiction Writing from the University of Montana. She updated the Shopping chapter this year.

Eileen Wen Mooney, a native of Bali, Indonesia, has lived in Taiwan, Hong Kong, and China for more than 20 years—the last 12 have been in Beijing. Her articles have appeared in *Silk Road, That's Beijing, CAAC Magazine,* and *City Weekend.* She is the Food & Drink editor for *TimeOut,* and combs the city each week searching for interesting new and old restaurants.

Eileen lent her incredible know-how and insider secrets to the Where to Eat and Where to Stay chapters for this edition.

Paul Mooney, a New York native, is a freelance writer who has studied and worked in Asia for more than 25 years. His articles have appeared in publications such as *Newsweek,* the *Asian Wall Street Journal, Asiaweek,* the *Far Eastern Economic Review,* and the *International Herald Tribune.* A graduate of the School of International and Public Affairs of Columbia University, Paul is the author of several travel books on China and Taiwan. He updated the Experience chapter and contributed his expertise to the Neighborhoods chapter for this book.

After adventures in Siberia and Hong Kong, **Alex Pasternack** could no longer ignore the elephant on the continent and skipped New York for Beijing. When he's not teaching or exploring the hutong by bicycle, he writes about the environment, art, and architecture for *That's Beijing.* He also contributes to national magazines, Web sites, and guidebooks. For this edition, he wrote about the Great Wall and Beijing's architecture.

Victoria Patience grew up in Hong Kong, and she's never stopped calling it home. Her first solo trip was through China at the age of 16; she's been fascinated with the country ever since. She studied Spanish and Latin American literature in London. She now lives in Buenos Aires and returns to China regularly. Victoria updated the Beijing Essentials chapter.